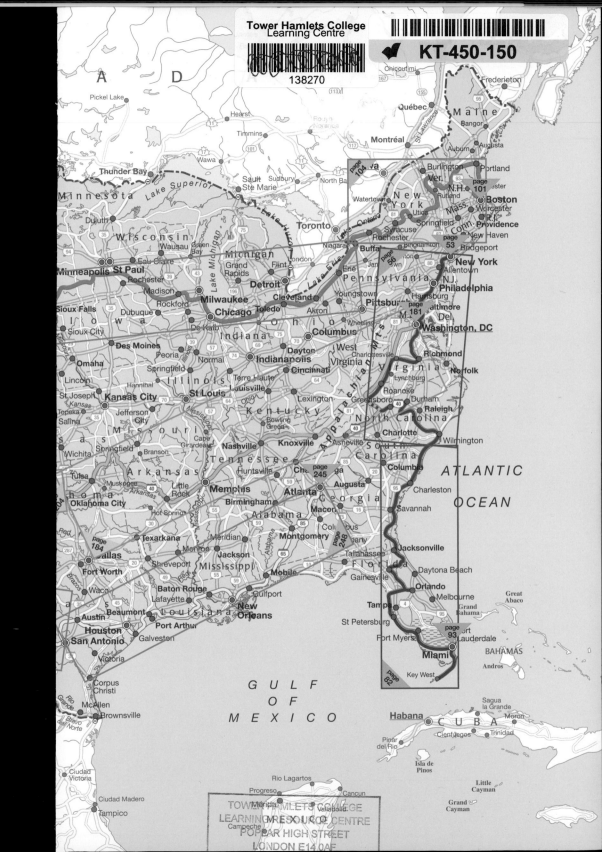

INSIGHT GUIDES

UNITED STATES
ON THE ROAD

APA PUBLICATIONS L
Part of the Langenscheidt Publishing Group

About this Book

The first Insight Guide pioneered the use of creative full-color photography in travel guides in 1970. Since then, we have expanded our range to cater for our readers' need not only for reliable information about their chosen destination but also for a real understanding of the culture and workings of that destination.

Now, when the internet can supply inexhaustible (but not always reliable) facts, our books marry text and pictures to provide those much more elusive qualities: knowledge and discernment. To achieve this, they rely heavily on the authority of locally based writers and photographers. This book is structured to convey an understanding of the United States and its unique on-the-road culture, as well as to guide readers through the country's variety of sights and activities:

The **Best of USA On the Road** section, with a yellow bar at the top of each page, highlights all the very best sights and attractions on the routes, so you can prioritise what you want to see and do.

The **Features** section, indicated by a pink bar at the top of each page, covers the history and travel culture of the United States in a series of informative essays.

The main **Routes** section, indicated by a blue bar, is a complete guide to all the sights and areas worth visiting along five east-west and north-south routes. Places of special interest are coordinated by number with the maps. The route guides begin, and some end, with photo features illustrating our recommendations for short stays in major "hub" cities.

The **Travel Tips** listings section, with a yellow bar, provides full information on transportation, hotels, activities from sports to shopping, and an A–Z section of essential practical information. A contents list for Travel Tips is printed on the back flap, which also serves as a bookmark.

The contributors

This new edition was commissioned by **Rachel Lawrence** at Insight Guides' London office, and builds on the experience of **Alyse Dar**. She enlisted a team of experienced travel writers who covered many thousands of miles to research places of interest and to find the best places to eat, sleep and shop along each route.

One of four writers responsible for updating this book was veteran Insight Guide contributor **Nicky Leach**, who is based

in Santa Fe, New Mexico. Nicky was inspired by the discoveries she made on the backroads along the Southern Route, like the Cajun music at Breaux Bridge; and modern-art-meets-cowboy culture in Marfa, Texas.

Kristan Schiller is a travel journalist whose writing has appeared in *The New York Times*, *National Geographic Traveler*, *Town & Country*, *Conde Nast Traveler*, Salon.com, and *Forbes*, among other publications.

Fran Severn has written for publications as varied as *Delta Sky* and *Western Horseman*, and is a contributing writer to the on-line travel publication *Striped Pot*, and blogs for *Chesapeake Life Magazine*.

Bill Scheller has worked with Insight guides since 1999. Among the books he's updated are Insight Guides to New England and Florida, and City Guide Boston.

Previous contributors include **Donna Dailey** and **Mike Gerrard**, who drove the Pacific Route as well as parts of the Southern, Central and Northern Routes. Dailey's work appears in magazines, newspapers and websites worldwide. Both have won prestigious travel writing awards. Thanks also go to **Martha Ellen Zenfell**, who was the original force behind Insight Guide USA On the Road.

Map Legend

▬▬ ▬ ▪	International Boundary
▬ ▬ ▬ ▬	State Boundary
⊖	Border Crossing
▬ ▪ ▬ ▪	National Park/Reserve
▬▬▬▬▬	Highway
▭▭▭▭▭	Other Multi-lane Highway
▬▬▬▬	Principal Highway
▭▭▭▭	Through Highway
▬▬▬	Other Road
⑤	Interstate Highway
⟮1⟯ ⟮29⟯	US Highway
⟮50⟯ ⟮239⟯	Other Highway
↖	On the Road Routes
✈ ✈	Airport: International/Regional
★	Place of Interest

The main places of interest in the Places section are coordinated by number with a full-colour map (eg ❶), and a symbol at the top of every right-hand page tells you where to find the map.

Contents

THE BEST OF THE UNITED STATES: TOP ATTRACTIONS

From soaring skyscrapers to plunging canyons, and Native American pueblos to gracious Southern mansions, here are some of the most spectacular places in the United States.

▽ **Savannah.** Dripping with Spanish moss and Southern charm, this town is the jewel of the Old South. Take a carriage round its cobbled squares and visit its gracious antebellum mansions. See page 78.

△ **The Grand Canyon.** The Colorado River carved out the colorful bluffs, mesas, and rock formations, creating one of the great natural wonders of the world. See page 226.

◁ **Saguaro cactus.** This symbol of the American Southwest is a stunning sight against the backdrop of an Arizona sunset. These prickly giants grow only in the Sonoran Desert. See page 303.

▽ **San Francisco.** Fisherman's Wharf, Golden Gate Park, hill-climbing historic cable cars, and an incomparable peninsular setting make this city the jewel of America's Pacific coast. See page 350.

△ **The Everglades.** This unique environment forms the largest subtropical wilderness in the country. It protects rare and endangered plant and animal species, some found nowhere else in the world. See page 88.

▷ **Big Sur.** California's rugged cliffs and pounding surf fringe one of the most dramatic stretches of the Pacific coast, a road trip you'll never forget. See page 344.

▷ **Yellowstone National Park.** Spewing geysers, bubbling mudpots, sizzling hot springs, and other geothermal features are scattered amid the spectacular beauty of the Rocky Mountains. See page 157.

◁ **New York City.** This is the nation's capital of art, commerce, fashion, and culture, with world-class museums, restaurants, and shopping. From its skyscraper skyline to the lights of Times Square, it never fails to impress. See page 52.

▽ **Olympic Peninsula.** Walk among towering ancient trees, lush ferns, and dripping mosses, which form one of the largest areas of temperate rainforest in the country. See page 168.

△ **Niagara Falls.** The thundering cascades mark the border between the United States and Canada. The boat ride into the mist at the base of the falls is an unforgettable thrill. See page 120.

THE BEST OF THE UNITED STATES: EDITOR'S CHOICE

With its magnificent sweeping landscapes, ethnic and regional cultures and cuisines, and an endless capacity for fun, there's always something new to explore on the road in the United States. Here are some of the editor's American favorites:

Monument Valley in Arizona and Utah.

BEST FOR FAMILIES

Orlando. Nonstop entertainment at Walt Disney World's four theme parks, Universal Studios, the Kennedy Space Center, and a host of family attractions See page 86.

San Diego. From SeaWorld and the San Diego Zoo to whale-watching cruises and trolley tours, there's plenty to delight all ages. See page 322.

Williamsburg. Step back in time and see how people lived in the early days of the country. See page 66.

Monterey Bay Aquarium. One of the best in the world, with mesmerizing exhibits and touch tanks that bring you up close to the undersea world. See page 348.

Tombstone. The Wild West lives on in this historic town of boardwalks, Boot Hill, and shoot-outs at the OK Corral. See page 301.

Arizona-Sonora Desert Museum. Watch raptors in flight and observe javelinas, coyote, mountain lions, and other desert creatures in their natural setting. See page 304.

Seaworld in San Diego.

BEST SCENIC DRIVES

The Pacific Coast Highway. Highways 1 and 101 take you from California's rugged shores to Oregon's idyllic beaches. See pages 339 and 353.

Blue Ridge Mountains. Enjoy the stunning vistas of this romantic mountain chain along Skyline Drive and the Blue Ridge Parkway. See page 187.

Going to the Sun Road. Traversing Glacier National Park, this is one of the most dramatic drives in the Rocky Mountains.

See page 163.

Atchafalaya Swamp Freeway. Watch out for alligators as you drive across the largest swamp in the country. See page 267.

Monument Valley. These awesome buttes and mesas rising up from the desert floor formed the backdrop for many Hollywood Westerns. See page 223.

Outer Banks. Pristine dunes, beaches, islands, and lighthouses along the Atlantic coast are preserved in two national seashores. See page 71.

The Badlands. A starkly beautiful landscape of rolling grasslands and twisted rocky canyons stretches right across the windswept plains of South Dakota. See page 139.

BEST HISTORICAL SITES

Independence National Historical Park. The United States was founded in these Philadelphia buildings. See page 58.

Charleston. The first shots of the Civil War were fired in the harbor of this city of elegant 18th-century houses. See page 75.

Freedom Trail. A walker's route through Boston links the most hallowed sites of the Revolution's birthplace. See page 100.

Washington, DC. The capital's center takes in the White House, Capitol, and memorials to Washington, Lincoln, FDR, King, WWII, and Vietnam casualties. See page 181.

St Augustine, Florida. The oldest city in the US preserves its Spanish colonial past in a stone fortress and old-world downtown. See page 83.

Little Bighorn Battlefield. The tragic clash of cultures that defined the Old West came to a head at "Custer's Last Stand" on the high prairie. See page 153.

BEST MUSEUMS AND GALLERIES

Getty Villa at Malibu. The re-created 1st-century Roman villa is an impressive home for this collection of Greek and Roman antiquities. See page 339.

Smithsonian Institution. A group of museums highlighting the nation's best achievements in art, history, and science line the Mall in Washington, DC. See page 180.

National Civil Rights Museum. The moving story of the Civil Rights movement, set around the Memphis motel where Martin Luther King, Jr was assassinated. See page 196.

Heard Museum. This beautiful collection of Native American arts and crafts in Phoenix, Arizona is among the finest in the country. See page 314.

New Mexico Museum of Space History. Fly a space shuttle simulator and follow the story of early pioneers in the space race. See page 292.

The Chrysler Building, New York.

BEST ARCHITECTURE AND BUILDINGS

Miami's Art Deco District. Pastel-painted hotels and shops with striking nautical motifs line Miami's South Beach. See page 93.

Hearst Castle. Filled with exquisite art and furnishings, this opulent hilltop residence was a playground for Hollywood's elite. See page 343.

Midtown Manhattan. New York's skyward climb reached its pinnacle in the Empire State Building, Rockefeller Center, and the Art Deco exuberance of the Chrysler Building. See page 52.

Las Vegas. Kitsch is king in Sin City's neon-lit, mind-blowing casinos designed after such world landmarks as the Egyptian pyramids. See page 230.

Golden Gate Bridge. Graceful and romantic, this San Francisco landmark is said to be the most photographed bridge in the world. See page 350.

French Quarter. Beautiful wrought-iron galleries line the historic buildings in the heart of old New Orleans. See page 262.

Find Greek and Roman sculpture at the Getty Villa, Malibu.

The open road in Monument Valley.

Skyscrapers and Highway I-280 as seen from Potrero hill, San Francisco.

An armed guard accompanies a
stagecoach in John Marchand's
depiction of an Old West journey,
The Narrow Pass.

WE'RE ON THE ROAD TO SOMEWHERE

Americans are always on the move. A French observer in the 1800s identified this unique trait and called it "restlessness amidst prosperity".

Route 66 winding through the desert near Williams, Arizona.

The most basic images of American life – the heavy wagon train rumbling across the prairie, a railroad car speeding through the night, the arrival of immigrants at Ellis Island – are powerful symbols of the United States' timeless obsession with movement. In fact, in a nation where change is the only constant, movement and travel have established the ever-quickening tempo of American history, from Lewis and Clark's exploration of the territories west of the Mississippi River, to Neil Armstrong's historic walk on the moon.

If the exploration and colonization of America is an example of travel, is there any real connection with the day trip into the countryside? Is it possible seriously to suggest that the 17th-century Puritan seeking refuge in Boston has anything in common with the 22-year-old computer whiz who moves from Lexington, Massachusetts to Seattle, Washington, in search of a higher-paying job? Do Lewis and Clark have any common bond with vacationers of the 1950s rolling down Route 66?

The Immigrants, by Ellen Bernard Thompson, 1899.

Every one of these travelers believed that movement might bring prosperity, discovery, and renewal. The difference lies in the purpose of the journey. Travel in pre-modern America was a very serious affair: an essential part of discovering and populating the continent. While a few wealthy Americans embarked on European *wanderjahrs*, and some even traveled for pleasure to Newport and Saratoga Springs, we do not associate such ease and comfort with the days of old. Rather, we recall Daniel Boone leading pioneers through the Cumberland Gap; young men heeding Horace Greeley's advice and going West to grow up with the country; the Mormons' perilous flight across the Great Plains; or the stagecoach company that warned its riders not to "point out where murders have been committed, especially if there are women passengers." Given the harsh landscape, we think of travel in early America as a dangerous and epic adventure.

In the early 21st century, when we take a trip there is little heroic about it. Yet, Americans still migrate for economic reasons, particularly to the Sunbelt states in the South, or to the Pacific Northwest. But this isolated movement of people lacks the drama of the pioneers, or the great "Dust

Bowl" migration of the 1930s, immortalized in the ballads of Woody Guthrie and in John Steinbeck's novel *The Grapes of Wrath*. Still, it is very likely that future historians will judge this movement to be as significant a force as it was in past times.

The number of automobiles in America today suggests that the experience of travel is now available to almost everyone. Travel has been democratized, and plays no small role in contributing to the American tendency to view cars, boats, and planes as symbols of equality. For better or worse, to be an American is to believe that personal liberty and the freedom to travel are inseparable.

Rush-hour congestion on a Los Angeles freeway.

Is there any truth in this belief? Is there a vital link between the uniquely democratic culture of the United States and the transportation revolution of the past two centuries? Michael Chevalier thought so. Chevalier, a French aristocrat sent to the United States in the 1830s to study its public works, believed that improved means of travel would hasten the collapse of the old order and play an important role in the emergence of "modern society." During his tour, he was amazed by the readiness with which Americans embraced new means of travel: first (after initial disinterest), roads had been constructed with passionate intensity, then canal building had become a national mania. And Chevalier bore witness to the birth of the age of the railroad, for which he rightly forecast a glorious future.

As avenues of economic exchange opened to increasing numbers of people, both ideas and populations were transmitted hither and yon along with pelts, peppers, and teas. Travel became, in Chevalier's words, a catalyst "to equality and liberty."

Restless spirits

Chevalier wrote at the beginning of the Industrial Revolution in America, and believed deeply in the 19th-century maxim of progress through science. Today, faced with global warming, oil shortages, and soaring gas prices, people look to the promise of hybrid cars and alternative sources of energy to keep them on the road. For even though the pursuit of freedom and adventure at the end of the road is now much costlier, the allure of crossing America has lost little of its appeal to restless spirits.

For, as Alexis de Tocqueville – author of the quote about "restlessness amidst prosperity" – observed two centuries ago: "An American will build a house in which to pass his old age and sell it before the roof is on; he will plant a garden and rent it just as the trees are coming into bearing; he will clear a field and leave others to reap the harvest; he will take up a profession and leave it, settle in one place and soon go off elsewhere with his changing desires. If his private business allows him a moment's relaxation, he will plunge at once into the whirlpool of politics. Then, if at the end of a year crammed with work he has a little spare leisure, his restless curiosity goes with him traveling up and down the vast territories of the United States. Thus he will travel 500 miles in a few days as a distraction from his happiness."

DECISIVE DATES

1492
Explorer Christopher Columbus reaches America, landing at San Salvador.

1607
Jamestown, Virginia settled by the British.

1620
Sixty-six Puritans found Plymouth Colony, Cape Cod Bay.

1773
In the "Boston Tea Party," men dump tea crates into the harbor to protest against taxes.

Paul Revere's midnight ride.

1775
Paul Revere rides from Boston warning of the arrival of British troops. The American Revolution begins.

1776
On July 4, the Continental Congress adopts the Declaration of Independence, penned by Thomas Jefferson.

1789
George Washington takes the first presidential oath at New York's Federal Hall.

1804
Lewis and Clark set out on their 8,000-mile (13,000km) expedition to the Pacific Coast.

1848
Gold is discovered at Sutter's Fort, California, bringing over 200,000 prospectors within the next three years.

1860
South Carolina secedes from the Union, and the Confederate states are born.

1861
Confederates open fire on Fort Sumter, in the first shots of the Civil War.

1863
Abraham Lincoln frees slaves in rebelling states by issuing the Emancipation Proclamation.

1864
The transcontinental telegraph connects Seattle, Washington, with the rest of the US.

1865
The Civil War ends. President Abraham Lincoln is assassinated in Washington, DC. The 13th Amendment to the Constitution ends slavery throughout the US.

1869
The Central Pacific and Union Pacific railroads meet in Ogden, Utah, completing the first transcontinental railroad.

1876
Lieutenant Colonel George A. Custer and his men are wiped out by Sioux and Cheyenne warriors at Little Bighorn Creek.

1890
A US Army regiment attacks a camp near Wounded Knee Creek in South Dakota's Pine Ridge Reservation, killing 300 Indians.

1906
A massive earthquake measuring 8.2 on the Richter Scale, followed by a devastating fire, flattens San Francisco.

1908
Henry Ford begins mass production of the Model T car.

Henry Ford, American automobile manufacturer.

1920
Nineteenth Amendment to the Constitution guarantees women's right to vote. Thirteen-year experiment with prohibition of alcohol begins; law widely flouted.

Abandoned Dust Bowl farm.

2005

Hurricane Katrina causes major flooding and destruction in New Orleans and along the Gulf Coast, killing more than a thousand residents.

2008

The collapse of the housing bubble and the failure of banking house Lehman Brothers. trigger the "Great Recession".

2009

Barack Obama is sworn in as the 44th President of the United States, becoming the first African-American to hold the nation's highest office.

1929

Wall Street crashes, heralding the Great Depression. US unemployment reaches 25 percent.

1930s

The Dust Bowl forces thousands from farmlands around Oklahoma on a migrant trek west to California in search of work.

1932

Franklin D. Roosevelt elected president in a landslide; commences New Deal programs in response to Depression; FDR re-elected a record three times.

1941

Japan attacks Pearl Harbor, and the United States enters World War II.

1945

First atomic bomb detonates in New Mexico; bombs dropped on Hiroshima and Nagasaki. United Nations charter drafted in San Francisco.

1955

Rev. Martin Luther King, Jr. leads the Montgomery (Alabama) Bus Boycott.

1963

President John F. Kennedy is assassinated while touring Dallas, Texas.

1968

Martin Luther King, Jr. and Senator Robert Kennedy are assassinated.

1969

Apollo 11 lands on the moon.

1974

Richard M. Nixon, 37th president, resigns after facing impeachment over Watergate.

2000

Incompletely punched ballot cards cause rage in Florida as George W. Bush becomes president.

2001

Passenger jets hijacked by suicide bombers destroy New York City's World Trade Center. The US invades Afghanistan to pursue al Qaeda.

2003

President George W. Bush orders the invasion of Iraq to overthrow Sadaam Hussein.

2010

Congress passes President Obama's controversial health care reform. Deeply conservative Tea Party movement pushes Republican Party to the right as Democrats lose control of House of Representatives.

2011

American combat forces leave Iraq.

2012

Barack Obama is re-elected for a second term as President, beating the Republican candidate Mitt Romney.

Barack Obama.

THE TRANSPORTATION REVOLUTION

From wagon trains to the iron horse to today's superhighways, travel is at the heart of America's history.

During the 17th and 18th centuries, white settlers in early America followed the network of paths that Native Americans had carved out for themselves, and travel conditions were notoriously wretched. During the time of colonization with Great Britain, it cost less to transport goods across the Atlantic Ocean from London to Philadelphia than to carry those same goods 100 miles (160km) to Lancaster, Pennsylvania. In 1776, news of the Declaration of Independence took 29 days to reach the people of Charleston, South Carolina. No wonder New England delegates at the Constitutional Convention in 1787 had more things in common with their brethren in Britain than with their fellow countrymen down South in the Carolinas and Georgia.

Fifty years later, when Alexis de Tocqueville, Michael Chevalier, and a host of European travelers examined the American experiment of self-government, conditions on dry land were little improved. Whereas the Roman Empire made the construction of great roads an important function of its central government, in 19th-century America laissez-faire attitudes predominated, leaving the construction of highways a state and local responsibility. Often, farmers and laborers who were unable to meet their tax obligations ended up doing the little road work that was done.

Tolerance of mud

As a direct consequence of the American belief in "the less government the better," roads suffered from neglect and disrepair. Pioneers, such as Abraham Lincoln's father, Thomas, had to possess courage, physical strength, and an incredible tolerance of mud. William Herndon, Lincoln's law partner and biographer, described

Bygone mode of transportation recalled in song.

the Lincoln family's move from Indiana to Illinois in March of 1830 as one which "suited the roving and migratory spirit of Thomas Lincoln." With the "obscure and penniless" 21-year-old Abe commanding a wagon drawn by two oxen, "the journey was a long and tedious one." Basing his literary account of the trip on Lincoln's recollections, Herndon memorably evokes the experience of thousands of similar travelers. "The rude, heavy wagon," he wrote, "with its primitive wheels, creaked and groaned as it crawled through the woods and now and then stalled in the mud. Many were the delays."

In antebellum America, geography created a formidable barrier to migration. Even as

> Thomas Jefferson thought it would take close to a thousand years to settle the lands west of the Mississippi River; he was mistaken by more than 900 years.

late as the 1830s, approximately 80 percent of the American population still lived east of the Allegheny Mountains.

Thomas Jefferson's decision to send Captain Meriwether Lewis and Lieutenant William Clark, to explore the territories west of the

tribes, flora and fauna, and topography along their route. Their wide range of learning, courage displayed in the face of physical deprivation, and eloquence are inspiring. Lewis and Clark prepared the way for the invasion of the West that is still in progress today.

In the 1840s, the journalist John O'Sullivan popularized the phrase "manifest destiny" to describe a widespread expansionist ideology.

Western politicians such as Stephen Douglas based their political fortunes on promoting the future greatness of the West as the ultimate destination and demanded the construction of a

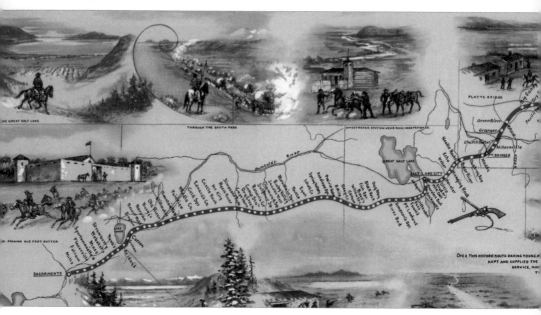

Mississippi River charted the way for settlement of the vast region. The president dispatched Lewis and Clark shortly after the Louisiana Purchase in 1803. His motives for asking for a $2,500 appropriation from Congress to finance the expedition were mixed. Even at this late date, it appears Jefferson had not abandoned all hope that a passage to Asia might be found. He was also confident that the explorers would discover trade routes to benefit fur traders. Jefferson wanted to expand his "Empire of Liberty" – but as a child of the Enlightenment, he was equally interested in the advancement of knowledge of the physical world. Lewis and Clark did not disappoint Jefferson. Their voluminous journals provided detailed descriptions of Native American

transcontinental railroad in order to link the nation's rapidly expanding economy. But even before the tracks were laid, settlers were heading west along wagon routes such as the fabled Oregon Trail.

Age of the iron horse

Before the Union could be linked by rail, the United States was plunged into the Civil War. It took four weeks for the news of the opening volley at Fort Sumter to reach San Francisco, but, by the end of the war, the nation was forging the bonds of union. The age of the turnpike, steamboat, and canal had been overtaken by the iron horse; it is widely conceded that the North's superior transportation system played a crucial role in crushing the Southern rebels. In 1863, the North was able to transport 25,000 troops by rail from Washington, DC, to Chattanooga, Tennessee, to turn the tide in a major battle.

Mark Twain and Charles Dudley Warner dubbed the final third of the 19th century "the Gilded Age," an era of conspicuous consumption and corruption. Perhaps the age might better be thought of as being the age of the railroad. The railroad barons – the Goulds, Huntingtons, and Vanderbilts – all understood that the railroad was the lubricant of both a booming economy and sleazy politics.

The railroads, with their new sleeping and dining accommodations, also made long-distance travel for pleasure a realistic possibility for middle-class Americans. Although a period of rest and relaxation did not sit well with those devoted to work, publicists for the new leisure ethic stressed that Americans were growing unhealthy – both physically and spiritually – as a result of their obsession with success. Regeneration through contact with the great outdoors and the vigorous life was a stock promise from popularizers of the West.

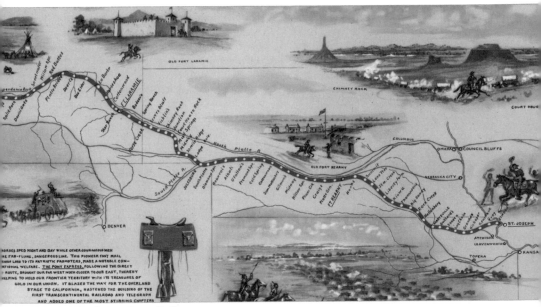

Map depicting the Pony Express Trail.

THE PONY EXPRESS

One of the 19th century's most romantic enterprises, the Pony Express, galloped across the western landscape and into the history books in just over 18 months. From April 1860 to October 1861, Express horsemen formed a record-setting, trans-Mississippi relay team that won over the hearts of Americans, if not the pocketbooks of the US Congress. The daring young mail carriers braved rain, snow, sleet, dead of night, and Native American attacks between St Joseph, Missouri, and Sacramento, California, to deliver over 35,000 letters, telegrams, and newspapers. The riders tallied up 650,000 miles (1 million km) on the 1,966-mile (3,164km) -long Pony Express Trail. And they lost only one mailbag.

Newspaper ads for Express riders did not mince words: "WANTED – Young, skinny, wiry fellows not over 18. Must be expert riders willing to risk death daily. Orphans preferred." Eighty riders, almost all weighing less than 125lbs (57kg), were hired initially, including a fatherless 15-year-old named William F. Cody, later known as Buffalo Bill. The pay was attractive, at least $50 a month, plus free lodging and food. Each rider took an oath, agreeing not to use profane language, not to get drunk, and not to fight with other employees. Each horseman also received a copy of the Bible, plus two Colt revolvers, a knife, and a carbine. The journey took 10 days each way.

In 1893, the year of the Chicago World's Fair, two bicycle mechanics, Charles and J. Frank Duryea, successfully tested what became the first commercially successful American automobile on the streets of Springfield, Massachusetts, and a new age began.

Car crazy

Public roads were among the initial benefits of the age of the automobile. The movement to upgrade the quality of highways had begun during the 1880s when bicycling organizations led the call for improved roads. When automobiles

Gridlock on a New Jersey highway – with paved roads and cheaper cars came traffic jams.

began to appear in the streets in greater numbers after 1900, the drive for surfaced roads attracted increasing support. In 1916, President Woodrow Wilson signed a Federal Aid Road Act which was the first of a series of occasions when Federal intrusion into the nation's transportation system met with widespread public approval.

The constituency for such governmental action grew larger with each passing decade. And the person who probably deserves the greatest share of credit for democratizing the automobile and travel is Henry Ford, who introduced to the industry the assembly line, which revolutionized the production and sale of cars; by 1922, he was selling an astonishing

1.3 million Model Ts. The Tin Lizzie had made the automobile a badge of social distinction as well as a necessity.

The impact of the widespread ownership of cars upon travel cannot be overstated. It was probably the single most important factor in the opening of American life not only to travelers seeking remote scenes, but also to 20th-century movers and migrants.

What would the 1930s have been like, after all, if John Steinbeck's literary Tom Joad and his fellow wandering poor could not have climbed into a car and headed for California where, as a Jimmie Rodgers song promised, the "water tastes like cherry wine"? The increased mobility the automobile offered underscores the judgment of George F. Pierson, who in his book *The Moving American* describes this freedom as "the great American permit to be both more free and more equal than our contemporaries could manage to become in the more static societies of Europe."

But the early years of the new millennium brought a challenge to this American dream. Concern over air pollution had already led to government-imposed emission standards; now, the realities of global warming forced people to look harder at the environmental cost of their cherished mobility. As gas prices rose to $4 and beyond, Americans realized that they could no longer take for granted the cheap transportation that they had enjoyed from birth. At the same time, a world economic recession, brought on by severe problems in the financial and housing sectors, brought further pressures on mobility as the nation faced unemployment, plunging house values, and the near collapse of its automotive industry.

As in the past, Americans are rising to the challenge with the production of ethanol blends that mix grain fuels with gasoline, and the exchange of gas-guzzling SUVs for a new breed of cars that can run partly on electricity. Hybrids are now produced by US as well as foreign manufacturers, and one American company, Tesla, is set to market a fully electric sedan in 2013. Conventional engines have gotten significantly smaller: figures released in mid-2012 show that for the first time, more than half of new cars purchased in the US were powered by four-cylinder motors. A new transportation revolution is under way – in hearts and minds, as well as on the road.

AMERICAN ARTISTS AND THE ROAD

America's creative spirit is forever energized by the allure of the open road. Novelists, poets, songwriters, filmmakers – all are seduced by the romance of going places.

American artists are perpetually on the run. Their work epitomizes the wanderlust of the American people: the belief in movement for movement's sake. "The sound of a jet," John Steinbeck wrote in 1961, "an engine warming up, even the clopping of shod hooves on pavement brings an ancient shudder, the dry mouth and vacant eye, the hot palms and the churn of stomach high up under the rib cage."

A century before Steinbeck, Herman Melville depicted travel as a balm to a depressed soul. "Whenever I find myself growing grim about the mouth," he mused in the famous first paragraph of *Moby Dick*, "whenever it is a damp, drizzly November in my soul; ...whenever my hypos get such an upper hand of me, that it requires a strong moral principle to prevent me from deliberately stepping into the street, and methodically knocking people's hats off – then, I account it high time to get to sea as soon as I can." In the classic American fiction of Melville, Edgar Allan Poe, James Fenimore Cooper, and Mark Twain, we encounter characters fleeing the inertia of polite society for a jaunt into the wild.

A stay against confusion

The great writers of 19th-century America celebrated the movement away from complex modern life. They viewed travel as a "stay against confusion" in a society committed to material gain. Melville, Nathaniel Hawthorne, and Cooper felt alienated from the climate of the times and sought refuge in foreign travel.

Their despair with the democratic masses stands in marked contrast to one of the greatest American poets of the open road, Walt

Tom Hanks as Forrest Gump, who runs across America and participates in much of its recent history.

Whitman. A journey along the open highway suited his desire to comprehend the whole of life: the casual meeting, the encounter between the eye of the seer and the landscape, and the timelessness of nature. Whitman saw the open road as the passage to wisdom and fraternity.

The very act of traveling is a democratic gesture to the poet, a source of inspiration, and a symbol of his personal liberty. Not only were the "American people the greatest poem," but the American environment itself was an incubator of freedom and unity. As he wrote in his acclaimed "Song of the Open Road:"
I think all heroic deeds were all conceiv'd

> I wish for a change of place, The hour is come at last, that I must fly from my home and abandon my farm! J. Hector St John de Crevecoeur, Letters from an American Farmer

in the open air, and all free poems also,
I think I could stop here myself and do miracles,
I think whatever I shall meet
on the road I shall like, and
whoever beholds me shall like me.
I think whoever I see must be happy.

characteristic of American literature: loneliness, and the traveler as a solitary figure.

Since World War II, the accelerated pace of travel has produced a literature equally frenetic. The most famous road book has been Jack Kerouac's *On the Road*, the definitive statement of his "Beat Generation" and an incalculable influence on the counterculture of the 1960s and 1970s. Kerouac's prose may impress less now, but his celebration of finding spiritual truths while racing across the continent makes the work transcend conventional literary canons.

Jack Kerouac.

Woody Guthrie.

Mark Twain used the voyage as a metaphor for change. In his novel *The Adventures of Huckleberry Finn*, he made it clear that the voyage was a learning experience and a rebellion against conventional morality. Some of the book's most moving passages are Huck's accounts of life on the river. Each time Huck and the escaped slave Jim encounter people on shore, trouble, trickery, and cruelty predominate. The book ends with Huck's famous vow to flee civilization and its hypocrisy. But, of course, the old-fashioned frontier was disappearing when Twain was writing in the 1880s, so Huck's dream of flight belonged to a vanishing world. Still, Huck's words at the close of *Huckleberry Finn* bring to mind another

Kerouac's work continued the tradition of writer as pathfinder and spiritual voyager, as did Native American writer William Least Heat-Moon's *Blue Highways*. Heat-Moon traversed the nation in his van "ghost dancing." His report is both a rumination on travel literature and a revealing study of the state of the nation. Richard Grant, a British journalist, fell in love with the American nomadic lifestyle. His *Ghost Riders* tells the story of nomads present (in their own words from boxcar slang to cowboy drawl) and past.

Whereas Kerouac filtered experience through his a historical frame of mind, Heat-Moon and Grant, by letting people speak for themselves, capture the diversity of the landscape that often overwhelms the trans-American traveler.

Travel continues to be a method by which writers question where we have come and where we are going, whether collectively as a society, as in Dave Gorman's *American Unchained*, or personally, as in Dan Jackson's *Old Bug: The Spiritual Quest of a Skeptical Guy on a Road Trip Across America with a Long Lost Friend in a Beat-Up Beetle*. Both are comic and touching odysseys of self-discovery.

Today, television, which has replaced literature as the medium for the masses, has picked up the tradition and writers have adapted to a visual role. In *Stephen Fry in America*, the writer

*I'm going down that long, lonesome road
And I ain't gonna be treated this a-way.
Lonesome Road Blues, Bill Monroe*

to fight off despair and keep cattle from stampeding, often reworked old Irish and English ballads about murder and betrayal. Much of the music produced under such circumstances was often grim and filled with resignation. In the

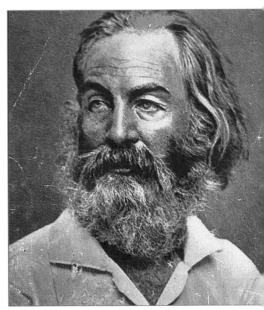

John Steinbeck.

Walt Whitman.

and comedian traveled across all 50 states to find the heart and psyche of the nation, while historian Simon Schama took to the road to understand the contemporary political situation in *The American Future*. BBC environmental journalist Justin Rowlatt spent six weeks traveling 6,500 miles (10,400km) across the US on public transportation while reporting on climate change.

Music to their ears

It is not just literary artists who have sung of the loneliness and vagaries of the open road. Country music in particular often focuses on that "lonesome guy" Hank Williams sang about on "the lost highway." Cowboys, singing at night

1940s and 1950s, cowboy singers such as Roy Rogers and Gene Autry evoked the nostalgia of the open range for a populace increasingly constrained by urban and suburban conventions.

Not all country music is downbeat, however. A whole genre of music has arisen devoted to the lives of the modern riders of the open range: truck drivers. These contemporary folk figures form a loyal audience for country music, and songs like the admired and much-recorded "Six Days on the Road" are pure Walt Whitmanesque whoops of triumph over the law, the cops, and anything that might get in the way.

The theme of the open road extends to rock music and blues as well. Is it any wonder that one of the rock anthems of the 1970s was Bruce

Springsteen's "Born to Run"? Ace bluesman Robert Johnson evoked the road as a haunting meeting place. In his highly influential song "Cross Road Blues", the narrator's fear and anguish are clear as he prays at the crossroad for mercy for (so the legend goes) having sold his soul to the devil in exchange for mastery of the guitar.

Surely Woody Guthrie is the "bard of the open road." Even a simple listing of some of his songs – "Dust Bowl Refugees," "I Ain't Got No Home," "Walkin' Down the Railroad Line" – suggests the prominence he assigned to "walkin' down the

encounter solitary figures in an uncomfortable relationship with polite society. Ready to right wrong wherever he finds it, the cowboy must move along in the last reel.

George Stevens' 1953 classic Shane set the pattern for all the films about righteous, wandering loners to follow. Clint Eastwood's *Pale Rider* attempted to revive this formula in the 1980s, but, since the 1960s, motor-driven outlaws have replaced the cowboy as the stars of road films. From Marlon Brando in the *The Wild One* to Mel Gibson in *The Road Warrior*, films set on the road have focused on wander-

Dennis Hopper and Peter Fonda hit the open road in Easy Rider.

line." Like Whitman, he attempted to capture the whole of America in the verses of "This Land is Your Land." Guthrie lived the life he wrote about after his family was wrecked by tragedy and disease. His best work is timeless – not surprisingly, many of his tunes borrow heavily from hymns and ballads – and will live as long as there are roads to walk and people to sing.

Sagas of the silver screen

The great road films of Hollywood are the best visual sagas of the open plains. People all over the world think of the United States as a land of wide-open spaces, thanks to the images they receive from the films of directors such as John Ford and other Western moviemakers. Again we

ing antisocial anti-heroes alienated from society.

Bonnie and Clyde (Arthur Penn, 1967) is an example of the perfect tragi-comic road picture. Viewed through the countercultural lens of the 1960s, the story of Clyde Barrow and Bonnie Parker seems like a folk tale of the Depression-era 1930s. Bonnie and Clyde rob banks that rob the poor of their dreams and make their getaway to the sound of rebellious country music.

Few films of the recent past inspired more real-life voyages than *Easy Rider* (Dennis Hopper, 1969). Those who see the film as a period piece and high camp have no idea how its original viewers saw it. *Rider* was probably the most powerful advertisement for the counterculture to appear in movie houses throughout the heartland of the nation. To this day, there are middle-aged workers who dream of throwing away their cellphones, mounting a Harley motorcycle, and setting off for Mardi Gras in New Orleans.

Thelma and Louise (Ridley Scott, 1991) updated this story, using cars and women to illustrate the hi-jinks and low life of on-the-road escapism. The final scene, when the women end it all, is in the tradition of the best Westerns of the 1950s.

But the public has an appetite for softer films too, which portray the road as an antidote to modern angst. Witness the hit sleeper *Little Miss Sunshine*, which has a dysfunctional family hobbling across the miles in a broken-down VW bus to help a little girl pursue her dream of entering a beauty pageant. Or a man shaking off a midlife crisis in California's wine country in *Sideways*.

The swoop of history follows us down every highway, and the traveler has many teachers to choose from before embarking on an adventure. For William Least Heat-Moon, Walt Whitman served as the model. For Ridley Scott, John Ford was the inspiration. As you head out on the highway, listen to these voices, but be aware that there is no experience like an original one.

Pursuing a family dream in Little Miss Sunshine.

ON THE ROAD MOVIES

About Schmidt (Alexander Payne, 2002)
Badlands (Terrence Malick, 1973)
Bonnie and Clyde (Arthur Penn, 1967)
Breakdown (Jonathan Mostow, 1997)
Due Date (Todd Phillips, 2010)
Duel (Steven Spielberg, 1971)
Easy Rider (Dennis Hopper, 1969)
The Grapes of Wrath (John Ford, 1939)
Joy Ride (John Dahl, 2001)
Little Miss Sunshine (J. Dayton and V. Faris, 2006)
Natural Born Killers (Oliver Stone, 1994)
The Outlaw Josey Wales (Clint Eastwood, 1976)
O Brother, Where Art Thou? (Joel Coen, 2000)

Paris, Texas (Wim Wenders, 1984)
Planes, Trains, and Automobiles (John Hughes, 1987)
Rain Man (Barry Levinson, 1988)
Sideways (Alexander Payne, 2004)
The Sugarland Express (Steven Spielberg, 1974)
Smoke Signals (Chris Eyre, 1998)
Stranger Than Paradise (Jim Jarmusch, 1984)
The Searchers (John Ford, 1956)
The Wild One (Laslo Benedek, 1953)
Thelma and Louise (Ridley Scott, 1991)
Transamerica (Duncan Tucker, 2005)
Two Lane Blacktop (Monte Hellman, 1971)
Wild at Heart (David Lynch, 1990)

Family outings along Route 66 were common in the 1940s and '50s.

ROUTE 66: AMERICA'S MAIN STREET

Quirky motels, mom 'n' pop diners, drive-in movie
theaters: in its heyday, many thought this was the
most magical road in the world.

In 1926, a road with its eastern terminus at the corner of Michigan Avenue and Jackson Boulevard in Chicago, Illinois received its official designation as Route 66. With its catchy double-six road markers, this ribbon of asphalt and concrete stretched westward for 2,448 miles (3,940km) through three time zones and across eight states – Illinois, Missouri, Kansas, Oklahoma, Texas, New Mexico, Arizona, and California – to the shores of the Pacific Ocean at Santa Monica. Route 66 was one of the country's first continuous spans of paved highway, linking the eastern part of America with the vast spaces and burgeoning new cities of the West.

No other road like it

US Highway 66 reigns as the most storied highway in the annals of American travel. A recurring theme in American literature, Route 66 has been the star of more stories, books, songs, movies, and television shows than any other

Happy Lou Phillips made headlines by roller-skating from Washington, DC to San Francisco.

> If you ever plan to motor west;
> travel my way, take the highway
> that's the best.
> Get your kicks on Route Sixty-Six!

road. From the mid-1920s to the mid-1970s, it was more heavily traveled than scenic Highway 101 on the Pacific Coast, better known than the Pennsylvania Turnpike or the Alcan Highway, and surely better loved than busy US 1 between Maine and Key West, with its maddening traffic snarls around metropolitan New York. And before the advent of the interstate systems, US 66 came closer than any other highway to

becoming the National Road. Route 66 was soon known as "the most magical road in all the world." A legend was in the making.

And what a legend it would be. Nobody could possibly know how many Americans – from Oklahoma's Dust Bowl refugees, to starry-eyed aspirants to Hollywood fame, to 1960s counterculture types "splitting for the Coast" – followed Route 66 on their way from their old lives to new ones in the California sun.

The nation first became aware of US Highway 66 when the 1928 International Transcontinental Foot Marathon (affectionately known as the Bunion Derby) tramped along the road from Los Angeles to Chicago, then on to Madison Square Garden in New York, a distance of 3,448 miles (5,548km). The winner was handed $25,000. Andy Payne, a part-Cherokee Indian from Oklahoma, won the purse.

Three decades later, for a fee of $1,500, Peter McDonald walked on stilts from New York City to Los Angeles, a distance of 3,200 miles (5,150km). From Chicago to Los Angeles, his way out west was Route 66. Pete was neither the first nor the last to place the road in the public eye – wild, weird, and wondrous celebrants were to follow. Two such celebrities were Happy

Joggers and baton twirlers

In 1972, John Ball, a 45-year-old South African, jogged from California to Chicago on Route 66, and then became a hero on the East Coast. The journey took 54 days.

The Mother Road has also seen its share of high school baton twirlers, who have marched along Old 66 setting dubious records.

Route 66 was a highway of flat tires, overheated radiators, motor courts, cars with no air-conditioning, tourist traps, treacherous curves, narrow lanes, and detour signs.

In the Roaring Twenties, desperadoes and

Whimsical establishments like the Iceberg Café in Albuquerque, New Mexico, have been demolished.

Lou Phillips and his friend Lucky Jimmy Parker. The pair of intrepid travelers strapped on skates and rolled their way along America's Main Street, as it was called, during their cross-country journey from Washington, DC, to San Francisco. Through the state of Arizona, a newspaper reported, "They walked a great deal, since at that time (1929) Route 66 was only paved through towns."

Another student of perambulating the old highway was "Shopping Cart" Doughtery, who, sporting a white beard and turban, traveled 9 to 16 miles (14 to 26km) a day on Route 66 with all his worldly possessions in a shopping cart. History doesn't tell us the final destination of Doughtery.

bootleggers – the likes of John Dillinger, Al Capone, Bugs Moran, Bonnie and Clyde, and Ma Barker and her god-fearing boys – lurched down Old 66, using it as an escape route. Occasionally, the Associated Press warned travelers of the dangers of "the criminally few who mix with the tourist throng."

Route 66 was Burma Shave signs, neon signs, full-service gas stations, mom 'n' pop diners, blue-plate specials, homemade pies, and waitresses who called everybody "honey," winked at the kids, and yelled at the cook. Hitchhiking was safe, and billboards along the highway were legal. People guzzled Grape Nehi, and summer lasted longer because of drive-in movies, miniature golf, and slow-pitch softball under the lights. Motels didn't take reservations. And doctors didn't mind making house calls.

Through good times and hard times, the highway became a symbol of faith for the future. Novelist John Steinbeck set the tone of the highway in his Pulitzer Prize-winning book *The Grapes of Wrath*, when he found a nurturing quality in Route 66 and called her "the mother road." It was the "Road of Second Chance." To some, like the immigrants of the Dust Bowl, it was the "Glory Road." To architect Frank Lloyd Wright, it was the chute of a tilting continent, on which everything loose seemed to be sliding

It winds from Chicago to L.A.
More than two thousand miles all the way.
Get your kicks on Route Sixty-Six!

sprinkled with a little local folklore – is told of the town's baseball team. They wanted to play the team in a nearby community but there was no connecting road. So the ambitious folks in this small Texas town built one. Today, that former deep-rutted path is said to be part of Route 66.

DJ Wolfman Jack was the voice on the radio accompanying most long-distance drives.

into Southern California. And to travel agencies it was the chosen thoroughfare of the growing numbers of discriminating American tourists.

Route 66 was to carry a sundry of names at different locations throughout her history – names like the Pontiac Trail, Osage Indian Trail, Wire Road, Postal Highway, Grand Canyon Route, National Old Trails Highway, Ozark Trail, Will Rogers Highway, and, because it went through the center of so many towns, the Main Street of America.

All-night radio

Route 66 was hundreds of locally improved and maintained lanes going from one town to the next. In Vega, Texas, a story – probably

Route 66 was all-night radio out of Del Rio, Texas, Continental Trailways, and Greyhound buses, lemonade stands, family reunions, 25 cents haircuts, and a 5 cents cup of coffee. Kids counted telephone poles on the road, waved at engineers on trains, slept in a wigwam in Holbrook, Arizona, and signs in New Mexico promised "Tucumcari Tonight."

"Route 66," Bobby Troup's hit song of 1946, became a highway national anthem. Originally crooned by Nat "King" Cole, the simple tune went on to be immortalized by Bing Crosby, Chuck Berry, The Rolling Stones, and a host of other recording artists – at last count over 100 of them. Nothing captured America's love affair with the road more than this song.

Burma Shave

Exploiting the potential of a captive audience, the verses along the Mother Road entertained the road-weary and accelerated sales.

The Burma Shave company was founded by an imaginative insurance salesman to provide a speedy, brushless shave for the businessman on the go. Clinton Odell, father of the company's former CEO, collaborated with pharmacist Carl Noren

Burma Shave signs were once a familiar sight along US highways.

to produce an item that became one of the most famous in America by virtue of being seen along every highway.

"By the start of the year we were getting the first repeat orders in the history of the company – all from druggists serving people who traveled these roads," Odell told Frank Rowsome, Jr, who wrote the history of the company.

Does Your Husband/Misbehave/Grunt and Grumble/Rant and Rave/Shoot the Brute Some/ Burma Shave was one of the earliest signs, its lines spaced 100 paces apart – like most of the thousands that followed. In his book, *The Verse by the Side of the Road*, Rowsome explained that,

traveling at 35mph, the sequence took 18 seconds to read – "far more time and attention than a newspaper or magazine advertiser could reasonably expect from the casual viewer." Alexander Woollcott maintained that it was as difficult to read a single sign as it was to eat one salted peanut.

In those early days, rival advertisers soon became jealous. Many of them had been spending thousands on marketing their product, only to see a perky upstart impress its name on the consumer in a way that was remembered long after the signs ceased to exist. Sensing their annoyance, the signs cheekily responded by rubbing it in: *Let's Give the/ Clerk a Hand/Who Never/Palms Off/Another Brand*. Burma Shave also knew how to needle the latest electric competition: *A Silky Cheek/Shaved Smooth/ And Clean/Is Not Obtained/With a Mowing Machine*.

There were once 35,000 Burma Shave signs, but by 1963 they were removed. By this time, they were costing the company almost a quarter of a million dollars a year and clearly were having a diminishing effect on sales.

"The commercial fortunes of the Burma-Vita Company can be read like tea leaves in the jingles themselves," wrote Rowsome. There were many reasons for the downturn in sales: people were driving too fast, superhighway rights of way frequently banned commercial signs, and possibly people were becoming too sophisticated to regard them as anything more than corny relics.

Most people were sad to see the Burma Shave signs disappear, as their growing insignificance proved to be just one more nail in the coffin of the vibrant Mother Road. As early as 1930, the company had been spending $65,000 a year (prompting $3 million in annual sales), but it was not only passing drivers that enjoyed them: friendly relations had been established with hundreds of farmers on whose land the red-and-white signs appeared. Although rentals rarely topped $25 per year, many farmers were so proud of the signs that they made their own repairs when necessary. Incidentally, horses found them to be perfect backscratchers – until the company got wise and raised the height of the signs.

There was never a chance that Burma Shave would run out of slogans. An annual contest offering $100 for each jingle used drew more than 50,000 entries. These would be whittled down to the best 1,000 stanzas. Of course, there were thousands of entries that were not considered "appropriate" and hence never used: *Listen, Birds/These Signs Cost Money/So Roost a While/But Don't Get Funny*.

It celebrated the end of World War II, and the end of gas and food rationing. The lyrics invited Americans to get their kicks on Route 66, and millions of motoring adventurers, addicted to the smell of gasoline and the drone of rubber on the pavement, took Bobby's suggestion to heart.

Itchy feet

Americans with itchy feet were ready to hit the road. They removed the musty canvas that had covered and protected the Plymouth ragtop and the Oldsmobile Woody since the outbreak of the outskirts of St Louis, Missouri advertised "the Greatest Show under the Earth" at the nearby Merimac Caverns.

The 1950s saw Route 66 reach genuine celebrity status. Families could leave their homes in the East and Midwest and drive to the Painted Desert or Grand Canyon. They could drive all the way to the Pacific Ocean on a highway that passed through towns where the young outlaw Jesse James robbed banks, where Abraham Lincoln practiced law, and cross the great river Mark Twain wrote about. Tourists could see snake pits and caged wild critters and

Route 66, the 1960s weekly TV series, sold more Corvette sports cars than any TV commercial.

the war. And although the cars had been stored on blocks, folks replaced the prewar tires with a set of six-ply Allstate clinchers at a total cost of $43.80. Vacationers shined up their new postwar sedans and thumbed through state maps and plotted a course on the road to adventure – Route 66.

Mom wrote "Wish you were here" messages on picture postcards. The kids bought rich, gooey Pecan *Log Rolls* at Stuckey's *Candy Shoppe* while Dad filled the gas tank at 17 cents a gallon and bought the entire family sticky, orange-flavored Popsicles out of the freezer.

The toll fare at the Chain of Rocks Bridge over the mighty Mississippi River was 35 cents per automobile, and brightly colored signs on

mysterious caverns and real-life cowboys and Indians, and visit Mickey's Magic Kingdom in Disneyland, California.

Route 66 reached even greater popularity when a nomadic potboiler of a book by the same name as the highway became a hit TV show from 1960 to 1964. *route 66* (yes, the "r" was not capitalized in the show title) was the

Because Route 66 is no longer marked on most roadmaps, many sections are often hard to find. But the website www.historic66.com gives a turn-by-turn route description of old Route 66 through every state.

"Hobo" Dick Zimmerman routinely walked Route 66 from California to Michigan, pushing a wheelbarrow, to visit his 101-year-old mother. Dick was 78.

story of two young adventurers, Buz (George Maharis) and Tod (Martin Milner), getting their kicks on Route 66 in a Corvette. Among its 116 episodes, few were actually filmed on Route 66. Sponsored in part by Chevrolet, the show itself inspired more Corvette sales than

Vintage Wurlitzer jukeboxes keep the romance of the open road alive in diners along the Mother Road.

any TV commercial, and established the Vette as an American icon.

When the Federal Highway Act of 1956 called for the construction of interstate systems throughout the United States, it looked as if the bright lights of fame and fortune that had shone on Route 66 for so many years were beginning to dim.

Little by little, here and there, pieces of Route 66 were replaced by the interstate. Bypassing of the towns that the fabled highway served was a task that took five different superhighways to achieve – Interstate 55 from Chicago to St Louis, Interstate 44 from St Louis to Oklahoma City, Interstate 40 from Oklahoma

City to Barstow, Interstate 15 from Barstow to San Bernardino, and Interstate 10 from San Bernardino to Santa Monica.

The last stretch of Route 66 was bypassed in 1984 at Williams, Arizona, when the old highway was replaced by Interstate 40. There was a ceremony, almost a wake. Bobby Troup, since deceased, was there to give a speech. As tears streamed from his eyes, he called the occasion "a very sad day."

Wurlitzer jukeboxes

In 1985, US Highway 66 was decertified, giving way to superhighways of diesel fumes and fast-food chains. Because the road is no longer classified as a federal highway, some folks will tell you the road is no longer there. For a while, the route that symbolized America's love affair with the open road seemed destined to live on only in memories and museums.

But progress does not necessarily conquer all. Beyond the endless blandness of the interstates, there is a powerful rhythm in an old two-lane highway that still rises and twists and turns across rolling hills, the mountains, and the deserts. Slowing through quiet towns, then rushing on and up again to the next ridge, you'll find the road waiting to be discovered in each of the eight Route 66 states.

In rural areas you may come across abandoned and decaying remnants that pay an evocative tribute to the heyday of Route 66. Elsewhere, however, cafés and roadside attractions have been revived, restored, and reopened. Vintage Wurlitzer jukeboxes blare out old road songs. Folks in classic cars cruise into a drive-in for a hamburger and shake. Service station attendants offer to check under the hood and wash the windshield. Family-owned restaurants serve homemade pie, and a waitress in a starched pink uniform still calls you "Hon!" and yells at the cook. The old road still beckons pilgrims not only from across the US, but from nearly every compass point of the world.

With the car open to the wind, and an AM station riddled with static from a thunderstorm on the horizon, memories flicker in the sweetness of the moment. The miles themselves dissolve every question except the one that matters. What lies waiting, there, just over the next rise of Route 66?

ORIGINAL

OLD ROUTE
66

CLUB CAFE
SINCE 1935

Route 66 passing through Amboy, California.

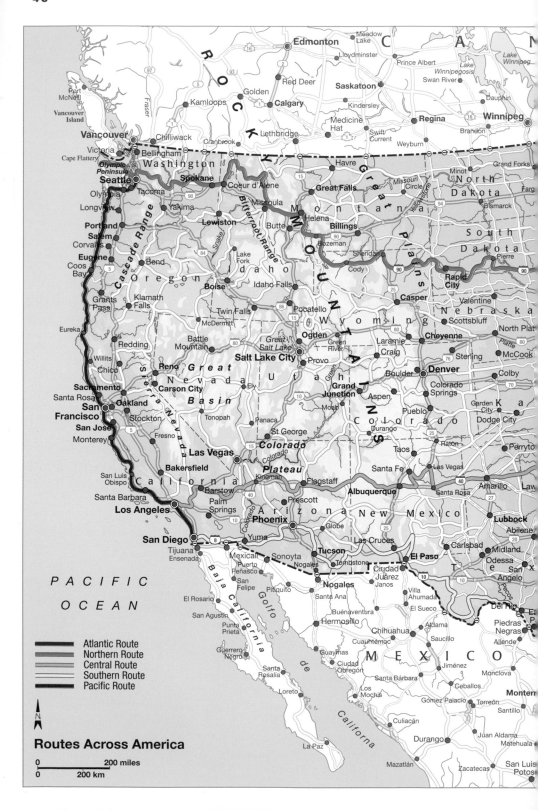

Routes Across America

Atlantic Route
Northern Route
Central Route
Southern Route
Pacific Route

N

0   200 miles

0   200 km

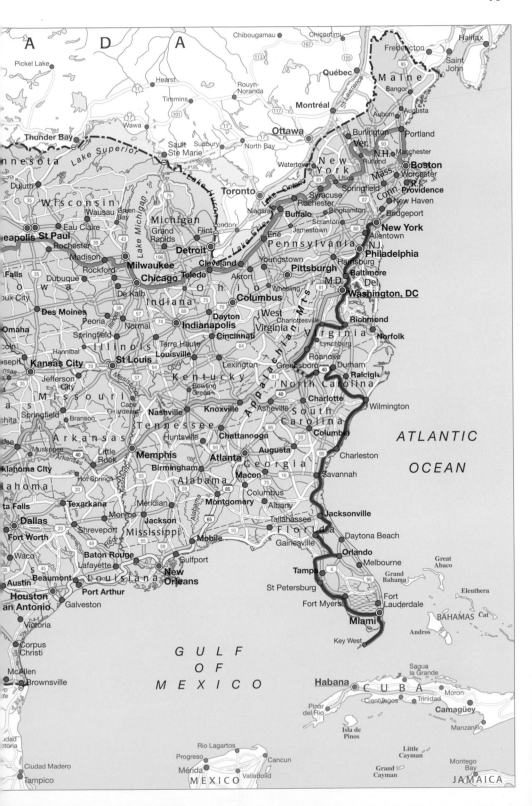

THE ATLANTIC ROUTE

A detailed guide to the attractions of the eastern seaboard, with principal sites cross-referenced by number to the maps.

Right at the start on US 1 in Key West, Florida.

The systematic colonization by the British of America's East Coast was only accomplished once settlers had learned to use its waterways: the Atlantic coastline's bays, the long rivers running out of the Appalachian Mountains and the languid tidal inlets so vital to inland transport in the flat but densely foliated southern states. It was at the mouths of rivers and ports that virtually every important Eastern city sprang up.

Appropriately, then, our route south will rarely stray very far from water. Beginning in New York City, undisputed king of America's cities, we will then pass through a close succession of two more important cities, each with its own distinct personality: Philadelphia, cradle of American independence, and Baltimore, originally a fishing town and one still largely dependent on port activities.

Row houses in Baltimore.

From there, we will move inland to make two exceptionally scenic drives in Virginia, passing at last into North Carolina and examining one of the South's most pleasantly diverse states. We will cut east through tobacco fields to the coastline and ride along water once again through South Carolina and Georgia, each time stopping to linger over a beautiful old city or a small, half-forgotten town.

Once in Florida, the weather – and the temperature of the water – will turn steadily warmer as we zigzag south from the nation's oldest settlement, St Augustine on the Atlantic Ocean, to Orlando's lakes, Tampa's mild Gulf of Mexico waters, and past the edge of south Florida to the vast (and moist) natural area known as the Everglades. At long last, we will emerge at the Atlantic coast once more, skimming past Miami and its attached beaches – in order to come back later – to continue on to the Florida Keys, a place where water is more influential and obvious than it is anywhere else, probably, in North America.

A SHORT STAY IN NEW YORK CITY

New York is the city that never sleeps; it has energy and confusion, culture, and great charm. Here's a list of the not-to-be-missed attractions.

Central Park, stretching from 59th to 110th streets, hosts ice skating in winter and outdoor concerts in summer. You can hire a boat on its lake.

9/11 Memorial. Passes are required to tour the site, which you can get online (www.911memorial.org).

The **Ellis Island Immigration Museum** provides a visual history of the port that 40 percent of all Americans can trace their roots to, and documents the migration from the world to the United States.

The **Museum of Modern Art** (**MoMA**), on West 53rd Street, is considered by many to be the most influential modern art museum in the world. Founded in 1929, the museum's building was beautifully redesigned in the early 21st century.

Famous for the Rockettes, **Radio City Music Hall** hosts spectacular music and theater shows. Tours are available during the day.

Lincoln Center, on the Upper West Side, is home to the **New York City Opera**, the **New York City Ballet**, the **American Ballet Theater**, and the **Metropolitan Opera**.

The hub of much of New York City's nightlife, **Greenwich Village** is still a center for musicians, artists, shoppers, and the eccentric.

SoHo and **Tribeca**, with their art galleries and restaurants, are perfect for Saturday strolling. **Chinatown** is close by if you're hungry.

Although its financiers are no longer lords of the universe, **Wall Street** in historic downtown New York is lined with some notable architecture.

Statue of Liberty. Boats from South Ferry take visitors to Liberty Island to view the icon that has greeted immigrants since 1886.

The famous skyline viewed from Brooklyn Bridge.

Zoom up to the 102nd-floor observation deck of the Empire State Building for a different perspective. The 360° views over Manhattan and beyond are stunning.

Chinatown is one of the city's most vibrant areas.

THE BIG APPLE

There is a mix of fantasy and foreignness in New York that is unsurpassed anywhere. You want to have a cocktail on a level with the clouds? Go dancing when the moon is high and the mood overtakes you? Want to go in-line skating, ice skating, or take in that Broadway show? You've come to the right town. New York's skyline is instantly recognizable; its attractions the best in the world. Its cultural life is matched only by its culinary awareness; there are over 15,000 eating places. If there are more ways of making it here, there are also more ways of spending it, so bring a fat wallet and lots of stamina.

Times Square. The bright lights of the renovated square, gateway to Broadway, have made it a tourist magnet once again.

USEFUL INFORMATION

Population: 8.3 million
Dialing codes: 212, 347, 646, 718, 917
Website: www.nycgo.com
Tourist information: 810 Seventh Avenue, NY 10019; tel: 212-484-1200

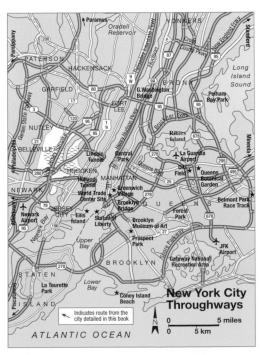

NEW YORK TO VIRGINIA

Just beyond the frenzy of New York City lie national historic sites and cities of colonial and Civil War importance, as well as the green, green hills of Virginia.

Map on page 56

This first leg of the Atlantic route takes in some of the most historic sites in the United States – places where the Revolutionary and Civil Wars were fought, and where the brash, new nation was conceived. But in order to take this cruise through history, a bit of contemporary, behind-the-wheel negotiation is required first. There are three ways to leave **New York City ❶** (see page 52) and cross the Hudson River into the neighboring state of New Jersey. From downtown Manhattan, your escape routes are the **Holland** or **Lincoln tunnels**, both of which are in the southern end of Manhattan. Your ultimate objective is I-280W toward the **Oranges**. From the Holland Tunnel, take US 1/9 to I-95N to I-280. From the Lincoln, take I-495 to I-95S to I-280. Your other option is the **George Washington Bridge** at the north end of Manhattan. From the bridge, take I-95S to I-280. The drive is more hair-raising than a thrill ride at a theme park; New Jersey and New York drivers have a reputation for almost pathologically aggressive driving.

Edison's lab and home

Sometimes described as "the cradle of American industry," the **Edison National Historic Site** (tel: 973-736-0550; www.nps.gov/edis; Wed–Sun) is a fascinating visit through the complex that was the Silicon Valley and Research Triangle of its time. To reach the site, take I-280W to Exit 10 (West Orange) and follow the brown signs. Most of the buildings are as they were the day the company closed in 1931, with the original lathes, tool shop, drafting tables, and equipment waiting patiently for the inventive workers, chemists, and engineers to return. Edison's desk is covered with papers and notepads; his office is part of a fabulous library that workers used daily, lined with thousands of

Main Attractions

New York City
Independence National Historical Park
Baltimore
Brandywine Valley
Fredericksburg
Williamsburg
Richmond
Monticello
Blue Ridge Parkway

George Washington Bridge spans the Hudson.

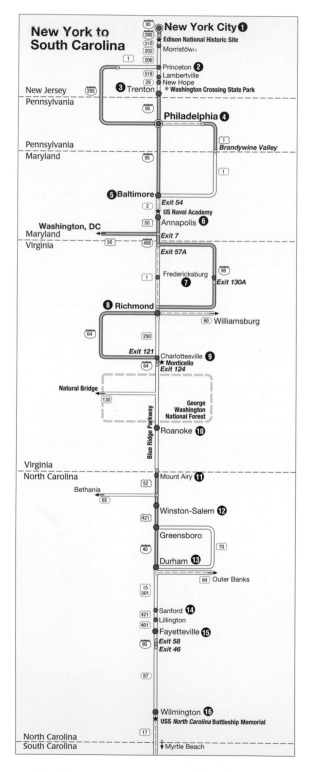

New York to South Carolina

New York City ❶
Edison National Historic Site
Morristown
Princeton ❷
Lambertville
New Hope
❸ Trenton ● Washington Crossing State Park
New Jersey
Pennsylvania
Philadelphia ❹
Pennsylvania
Maryland
Brandywine Valley
❺ Baltimore
Exit 54
US Naval Academy
Washington, DC
Maryland
Annapolis ❻
Virginia
Exit 7
Exit 57A
Fredericksburg
❼
Exit 130A
❽ Richmond
Williamsburg
Exit 121
Charlottesville ❾
★ Monticello
Exit 124
Natural Bridge
George
Washington
National Forest
Blue Ridge Parkway
Roanoke ❿
Virginia
North Carolina
Mount Airy ⓫
Bethania
Winston-Salem ⓬
Greensboro
Durham ⓭
Outer Banks
Sanford ⓮
Lillington
Fayetteville ⓯
Exit 58
Exit 46
Wilmington ⓰
USS North Carolina Battleship Memorial
North Carolina
South Carolina
Myrtle Beach

leather-bound volumes. Rangers give a walking tour of the chemistry lab. At the Visitor Center, there's a film about Edison's work and a showing of *The Great Train Robbery*, the 1903 film that was made by Edison's film company. The Black Maria, the first film studio, is also at the site.

A few minutes away is **Glenmont** (tel: 973-736-0550; July–Aug Wed–Sun, Sept–June Fri–Sun, tours noon–4pm. Ticketed admission only; tickets available at the Edison Lab site), Edison's grand estate, which he purchased for his second wife, Mina. (His first wife, Mary, died at the age of 29). Mina was well aware of her husband's reputation and legacy and protected both the house and the factory for posterity.

Morristown

There are two ways to reach **Morristown**: you can return to I-280, and traverse it and I-80 for about 15 miles (24km) before joining the I-287, or you can follow Route 510 (South Orange Avenue). The benefit of the country road is that it goes through some pleasant, tree-lined areas and toney neighborhoods rather than less-than-scenic highways.

A lovely village that dates back to colonial times, Morristown is home to several Revolutionary War sites. Six universities and colleges are nearby, and it is home to the **Seeing Eye** (tel: 973-539-4425, ext. 1762; www.seeingeye.org; telephone for tour information) the organization which trains guide dogs for the blind. You will see dogs in training all over town. During the Revolution, the **Jacob Ford Mansion** at 230 Morris Street (tel: 973-539-2016; daily) was the elegant home George Washington used as his headquarters during the bitter winters of 1777 and 1780. Behind it, the **Washington Headquarters Museum** (tel: 973-543-4030; www.nps.gov/morr; daily) has a wealth of original documents, china, maps, and period weapons. The **Morris Museum** (tel: 973-971-3737; www.morrismuseum.org;

Wed–Sun) features a delightful collection of working mechanical instruments and toys, while the **Museum of Early Trades and Crafts** (tel: 973-377-2982; www.metc.org; Tue–Sun) is housed in a building which is itself an attraction with stained glass windows, stenciled walls, and mosaics. In nearby **Parsippany**, the **Stickely Museum at Craftsman Farms** (tel: 973-540-0311; www.stickleymuseum.org; Apr–Nov: Wed–Fri; Dec–Mar Sat–Sun,) is the 1911 home of Gustav Stickely, one of the partiarchs of the American Arts & Crafts Movement.

Head south on US 202 and find yourself surrounded by deep forests and more small towns. **Jockey Hollow**, the Revolutionary War encampment is 6 miles (10km) from Morristown. The driving or walking tour goes past recreated cabins where reenactors sometimes demonstrate life in the Continental Army.

Princeton

At Bridgewater, take the sharp left onto US 206 and you will soon arrive at **Princeton ❷**, home to **Princeton**

University. The epitome of the Ivy League campus, the air exudes intellectual aspirations, youthful idealism, and more than a touch of privilege. Two American presidents, James Madison and Woodrow Wilson, graduated from Princeton, as did First Lady Michelle Obama.

Nassau Hall, the oldest building on campus, played host to the Continental Congress in 1783 when mutinous soldiers forced Congress to leave Philadelphia. One-hour campus tours are run year-round, departing from Clio Hall on weekdays and from Frist Campus Center at weekends (www.princeton.edu/main/visiting/tours).

Backtrack north up US 206 to State 518, then head west for a detour through the lovely **Delaware River Valley**. Look sharp for the right-hand turn to Lambertville on Broad Street in the village of Hopewell, itself worth a stop. At the river, quiet **Lambertville** has old inns, antique shops, and a narrow bridge connecting it to **New Hope**, Pennsylvania. The Pennsylvania side has several riverside dining establishments. Follow the river on the

A Princeton University graduate.

Fall foliage mirrored in a lake in Morristown, New Jersey.

Signpost marking an intersection named after two great cities on the Atlantic Route.

New Jersey side along Route 29. There are excellent displays at **Washington Crossing State Park** (tel: 609-737-9304; daily), where General George Washington landed on Christmas Eve in 1776, and at the **Old Barracks Museum** (tel: 609-396-1776; www.barracks.org; Mon–Sat) in **Trenton ❸**, where Washington's army captured Hessian soldiers in battle that night. The **New Jersey State Museum** (tel: 609-292-6464; www.statemuseumnj.gov; Tue–Sun;) in Trenton is a one-stop exploration of the archeology, fine arts, culture, and natural history of The Garden State. The **State House** is the second-oldest in the country (Maryland's is number one); across the street is the **New Jersey World War II Memorial.**

From Trenton, take US 1 to I-95 into Philadelphia.

Philadelphia

Philadelphia's South Street attracts big crowds on weekend nights.

At the time of the American Revolution, **Philadelphia ❹** was the economic and political center of the fledgling United States. During the early years of the Republic, however, the nation's economic heart was transplanted north to New York City while governmental power traveled south to the new city of Washington, DC. This left the city with a bit of an identity crisis. An interesting ethnic mix has sustained the place ever since, however, making it today one of America's most vibrant large cities.

The nation's fifth most populous city, this is, for tourists and historians – along with Boston – an American city *par excellence.* Situated at the conjunction of the Schuylkill (pronounced "skoo-kill") and Delaware rivers, the city was founded in 1682 by the English Quaker William Penn. Penn envisioned a colony in which the right to freedom of religious expression would not be quashed. That open-minded attitude pervaded the colony and the city, so it's not surprising that when representatives of the 13 colonies convened to debate independence, they did so here. The result was, of course, signing the Declaration of Independence on July 4, 1776 – thereby giving birth to the United States of America.

Revolutionary sites

The best place to start a tour is at the **Independence National Historical Park Visitor Center** at Sixth and Market streets (tel: 800-537-7676; www.nps.gov.inde and www.independencevisitorcenter.com; daily). It has free films about the city's history, computer kiosks with tourist information, costumed interpreters, and a reservation service for many tours and attractions.

It also issues the free tickets necessary between March and December for entry to **Independence Hall** at Chestnut Street between Fifth and Sixth streets (tel: 877-444-6777 for ticket reservations; daily), where the Declaration of Independence and the Constitution were signed. Tickets are issued for times, and the earlier in the day you can tour, the better your chances of getting tickets. The

Assembly Room contains the inkstand used by the signers of the Declaration as well as the chair on which George Washington sat during the drafting of the Constitution. To the west of Independence Hall is **Congress Hall**, where the US Congress convened between 1790 and 1800 when Philadelphia was briefly the nation's capital. On Sixth Street, between Market and Chestnut streets, stands the **Liberty Bell Center**, with exhibits about its origins and role as an international icon of freedom. Reservations are not necessary, but expect lines at peak times.

On Independence Mall, between Race and Arch streets, is the **National Constitution Center** (tel: 215-409-6600; www.constitutioncenter.org; daily). Using interactive exhibits and live actors, the museum tells the story of the constitution – its creation in early America, its application in history, and its continuing impact on the lives of Americans today.

On Market Street, toward the Delaware River, is **Franklin Court**, site of Ben Franklin's residence. His home no longer exists but is commemorated by an evocative outline of painted white steel beams. The underground museum about Franklin is currently closed for major renovations. It is expected to reopen in late 2013. **Christ Church**, at Second Street just above Market Street, was built in 1695 and was the preferred house of worship for the men of the Continental Congress. Plaques mark pews once occupied by George Washington, Ben Franklin, and Betsy Ross. Tours are given daily. **Betsy Ross House** at 239 Arch Street (tel: 215-629-4026; www.historicphiladelphia.org/betsy-ross-house; Mar–Nov daily, Dec–Feb Tue–Sat) was the place where Ross stitched the new nation's first flag.

Reading Terminal Market

After the Liberty Bell and Independence Hall, the most popular tourist attraction is **Reading Terminal Market** at 12th and Arch streets (tel: 215-922-2317; www.readingterminal market.org; daily). First opened in 1893, the market is a gastronomic bazaar of 80 stalls tended by farmers, bakers,

TIP

Parking is available in central Philadelphia in an underground lot beneath Independence Mall. Entrances are at Fifth and Sixth streets between Market and Arch. Parking is also available at the National Constitution Center at Fifth and Arch streets.

Philadelphia's Independence Hall.

Baltimore: Charm City

Baltimore is a big city with a small-town feel – the home of good food, great baseball, and "The Star Spangled Banner".

The National Aquarium overlooks Inner Harbor.

Start with an overview of the city from the **Top of the World** observation deck (tel: 410-837-VIEW; www.lviewbaltimore.org; daily), located on the 27th floor of the pentagonal World Trade Center. The Inner Harbor is the focus of the city's attractions and the Water Taxi (www.baltimorewatertaxi.com) is a good way to visit the sights. Here waterfront pavilions house restaurants and specialty shops and an outdoor amphitheater hosts street performers and planned performances. On the water, you can tour the historic **USS Constellation** (tel: 410-539-1797; www.historicships.org; daily),a 22-gun, three-masted sloop-of-war launched in 1854.

A short stroll along the brick waterfront boulevard leads to the fine **National Aquarium** (tel: 410-576-3800; www.aqua.org; daily), one of the nation's best, with a simulated Australian Outback, Amazon rainforest, coral reef display, and 220,000-gallon

Washington Monument in Mount Vernon Place.

(830,000-liter) open ocean tank. Across the harbor on Light Street, the Maryland Science Center (tel: 410-685-5225; www.mdsci.org; Tue–Sun) has hands-on exhibits on topics such as dinosaurs and space travel. Nearby, the Visionary Art Museum (tel: 410-244-1900; www.avam.org; Tue–Sun) features fantastic visions of self-taught and experimental artists. Take a picnic to **Federal Hill** and enjoy a wonderful view of the harbor. Baseball fans will relish the memorabilia-filled **Babe Ruth Museum** (tel: 410-727-1539; www.baberuthmuseum.com; daily) at 216 Emory Street. Babe Ruth, often hailed as the game's greatest ever player, was born in this modest house in 1895. **Oriole Park at Camden Yards** stadium started the trend of ballparks reflecting the classic era of baseball, and the behind-the-scenes tour is fascinating. The **Geppi's Entertainment Museum** (tel: 4210-625-7060; www.geppismuseum.com; Tue–Sun) next to the stadium celebrates comics and pop culture from the 1940s onward.

Fell's Point, Baltimore's first ship-building and maritime center, still has the charm of an old port town. Among the cobbled streets stand more than 350 original Colonial townhouses. Interspersed are old pubs, antique shops, and great places to eat. Further east, renovated once working-class neighborhood of Canton boasts upscale shopping and dining venues along a yacht-filled marina.

The waterfront's best-known attraction is **Fort McHenry** (tel: 410-962-4290; www.nps.gov/fomc; daily). During the War of 1812, this fort withstood a 25-hour bombardment from the British fleet, prompting Francis Scott Key in 1814 to pen the lyrics that in 1931 became America's national anthem, "The Star Spangled Banner."

Head up Charles Street to visit Walters Art Gallery (tel: 410-547-9000; www.thewalters.org; Wed–Sun) with its renowned collection of Oriental art, and the **Baltimore Museum of Art** (tel: 443-573-1700; www.artbma.org; Wed–Sun), which contains works by Picasso and Matisse, art from Africa, and a beautiful modern sculpture garden.

butchers, and greengrocers. It's a good place to pick up lunch. Try a Philly cheese steak, the regional favorite, and look for Tasty Cakes – butterscotch krimpets are sweet decadence.

Historic and lively neighborhoods

From Independence Hall, wend your way toward South Street via the cobblestone streets and garden paths of **Society Hill**, Philly's original residential district and a place of elegant 300-year-old Federal-style homes. Its boundaries are roughly Walnut, Lombard, Front, and Eighth streets.

During the late 1970s, Philadelphia's waterfront underwent considerable rehabilitation. **Penn's Landing**, between Market and Lombard streets along the Delaware River, is where William Penn came ashore in 1682. Today, the area features the **Independence Seaport Museum** (tel: 215-413-8615; daily) – several historic ships moored in the harbor – and views of **Camden**, New Jersey (home to the American poet Walt Whitman), across the river. One block below Lombard at **South Street**, you will find a stimulating array of punk haberdashers as well as chic boutiques. It's easily the most interesting shopping district.

City Hall, at Broad and Market streets, is the largest municipal building in the US. It was patterned after the Louvre. The 37ft (11-meter) -high rooftop statue of William Penn is the tallest atop any building in the world. Until recently, the Philadelphia skyline was capped by an ordinance declaring no structure could exceed the height of Penn's hat.

The **Benjamin Franklin Parkway**, built in the 1920s, was modeled after the Champs-Elysées in Paris. This broad road cuts diagonally through Philly's square grid from City Hall to Fairmount Park. On the parkway at 20th Street, visit the **Franklin Institute** (tel: 215-448-1200; daily), a science museum that is also a

memorial to Franklin containing many of his personal possessions. Four floors of science exhibits and a planetarium amuse and educate all ages.

Art in the city

Two blocks away is the **Rodin Museum** (tel: 215-763-8100; www.rodin museum.org; Wed–Sun), with an excellent collection of casts and originals by the great French sculptor. Among them is *The Thinker*, one of the world's most beloved statues, along with extensive interpretive materials.

At the end of the parkway stands the **Philadelphia Museum of Art** (tel: 215-763-8100; www.philamuseum. org; Tue–Sun), one of the great American art museums. Among the works in its collection are Breughel's *Village Wedding* and Picasso's *Three Musicians*, as well as an extraordinary collection of art and artifacts from the Middle Ages.

After hours spent walking the streets of Philly's historic districts and visiting its museums, the greenery of **Fairmount Park** rejuvenates even the most exhausted traveler. The country's

Sign depicting the past action on Spotsylvania, a Civil War battlefield.

Rodin Museum.

TIP

In Baltimore, the Old City Art Association sponsors First Friday. On the first Friday evening of every month, galleries host open houses. The event is followed by First Saturday, when artists, curators, and gallery owners offer workshops, lectures, and other informal get-togethers.

Civil War cannon at Chatham Manor.

largest municipal park, it's a system of 63 parks and green spaces throughout the city. In addition to grassy meadows and acres of woodland, it features a horticultural center, zoo, Japanese house, tea garden, and several historic homes along the banks of the Schuylkill. Once you have rested, take to the highway again toward **Baltimore ❺** (see page 60). From Philadelphia, it's about two hours down I-95. Far lovelier is the ride down US 1 through the **Brandywine Valley**. Between **Chadd's Ford** and **Kennett Square**, you'll pass the **Brandywine Battlefield**, (tel: 610-388-2700; www.brandywinebattlefield.org) site of an early Revolutionary battle the Colonials lost; **Brandywine River Museum** (www.brandywinemuseum.org; daily) which presents the works of Andrew, N.C., and Jamie Wyeth; **Longwood Gardens** (tel: 610-388-1000; www.longwoodgardens.org; Tue–Sun) with a 4-acre (1.6-hectare) indoor conservatory and 1000 acres (405 hectares) of outdoor gardens; and **Winterthur Museum** (tel: 302-888-4600; www.winterthur.org; Tue–Sun),

Henry DuPont's one-time home and the premier museum of American Decorative Arts. You'll go through the northern Maryland landscape, cross the Conowingo Dam over the Susquehanna River, and go through some Baltimore suburbs before connecting with I-695, the Baltimore Beltway and I-95.

ON TOWARD VIRGINIA

Leaving Baltimore, take I-695 (the Baltimore Beltway) to I-97, the direct road to Annapolis. Connect with US 50 East and take the Rowe Boulevard exit to reach downtown **Annapolis ❻**. The city sparkles in a way particular to towns built on and sustained by the sea – at dusk, its elegant Georgian houses and winding narrow streets shimmer in the dying light of day. Walking is an easy way to see the town, starting at the top where the **Maryland State House** sits. It was here that the Continental Congress ratified the Treaty of Paris, which officially ended the War of Independence and where Washington resigned his commission.

Wind your way toward the beautifully preserved 18th-century waterfront to the **US Naval Academy** and its museum at **Preble Hall** (tel: 410-293-2108; www.usna.edu; daily), with exhibits on maritime life and the history of this venerable institution. There are hourly walking tours of the Academy, which leave from the Visitor Center. You'll be feeling suitably red, white, and blue by the time you climb back into your car and drive the short 30 miles (48km) west along US 50 toward America's capital, **Washington, DC** (see page 180). For our purposes on this route, we'll bypass the city using the I-495 loop; take Exit 57A to I-95. While Maryland is below the Mason-Dixon Line, which traditionally separates the "North" and "South," it's not until you enter Virginia that the accent softens and the "real" south begins.

Confederate South

Midway between Washington, DC and Richmond, the capital of the Confederacy, it is not surprising that **Fredericksburg** ❼ was a major battleground during the Civil War. In fact, with 110,000 casualties occurring during the four major battles fought in the vicinity of the city, it has been said that it is the "bloodiest ground" on the North American continent.

Fredericksburg and Spotsylvania County Battlefields Memorial National Military Park (tel: 540-373-6122; www.nps.gov.frsp; daily), is the second-largest military park in the world. It incorporates the battlefields of Fredericksburg, Chancellorsville, the Wilderness, and Spotsylvania Court House. Both the Fredericksburg battlefield near the town's historic district and Chancellorsville west of town on Route 3 have visitor centers that are open daily with brochures, knowledgeable staff, and touring options.

On a bluff above the Rappahannock River overlooking Fredericksburg just north of Route 3, imposing brick **Chatham Manor** (tel: 540-373-6122; www.nps.gov/frsp/chatham; daily), built in 1771, welcomed Washington and Jefferson in Colonial times. It served as Union headquarters and hospital during the battle of Fredericksburg.

FACT

The Maggie L. Walker House (600 North Second Street, Richmond) memorializes the woman who, in 1903, founded the nation's oldest, continuously operated, black-owned bank. Nearby, a statue commemorates Bill "Bojangles" Robinson (1878–1949), the fast-as-lightning local boy who found fame as a tap dancer.

The Rotunda, University of Virginia.

Linn Cove Viaduct on the Blue Ridge Parkway.

Clara Barton and Walt Whitman joined in the efforts to treat hundreds of wounded soldiers there.

Fredericksburg was also the childhood home of George Washington. **Ferry Farm** (tel: 540-370-0732; daily), where he grew up, is also on Route 3. You will need to look sharp for the small sign by a gravel driveway. Archeologists recently found the site of the original house, which burned when Washington was still a child; visitors can watch, and sometimes participate, in the ongoing excavations.

The nation's fifth president, James Monroe, also hailed from here; the **James Monroe Museum and Memorial Library** (tel: 540-654-1043; www.jamesmonroemuseum.umw.edu; daily) on Charles Street contains a collection of the personal possessions, furnishings, and papers of Monroe and his wife, Elizabeth.

Today's Fredericksburg still retains its historic ambiance. The 40-block downtown is a National Historic District with antiques shops and restaurants sharing space with museums like the **Hugh Mercer Apothecary Shop** (tel: 540-373-3362; www.apva.org; daily) – where visitors can hear about how to treat a lady's hysteria – and the **Rising Sun Tavern** (tel: 540-371-1494; www.apva.org, daily), which provides an interpretation of 18th-century tavern life. George Washington's brother-in-law owned the elegant **Kenmore Plantation and Gardens** (tel: 540-373-3381; www.kenmore.org; Mar–Dec daily). Including that in a visit gives a thoroughly rounded idea of life in that era.

Richmond

Head back down for the 55-mile (88km) trip to **Richmond ❽**. Exit 92 leads to Scotchtown, home of Patrick Henry. The day after he buried his young wife on its grounds, Henry rode to Richmond to deliver his "Give Me Liberty, or Give Me Death" speech.

Take Exit 75 to the Richmond Visitor Center. There is free off-street parking in front of the building. Inside there are brochures, maps, and a staff well versed in the region's attractions and history. They can also make hotel reservations and suggest restaurants and shopping. The gift

shop features Virginia-made products. Important in both Revolutionary and Civil War history, the city merits some time. At pretty **St John's Church** on Broad Street, the Second Virginia Convention met in 1775. The debate that culminated in Patrick Henry's cry is reenacted every Sunday in the summer, with visitors sitting alongside the delegates. Laid out on the fall line of the James River, its location made Richmond a natural center for commerce. By 1779, the city had replaced Williamsburg as the capital of Virginia.

Thomas Jefferson designed the striking neoclassical **State Capitol** (www.virginiacapitol.gov; daily), which is home to Jean-Antoine Houdon's full-size statue of George Washington, one of America's most valuable pieces of sculpture. During the Civil War, Richmond was the capital of the Confederacy. Much of it was destroyed when Union troops set fire to the city. Perhaps the best museum about the Civil War anywhere is The American Civil War Center (tel: 804-780-1865; www.tredegar.org; daily) west of the State Capitol at 500 Tredegar Street. The thought-provoking exhibits require visitors to examine the political, ethical, military, moral, and practical aspects of the war from the point of view of the Union, the Confederates, African-Americans, and themselves. At 12th and Clay streets, the **Museum of the Confederacy** (tel: 804-649-1861; www.moc.org; daily) has the largest collection of Confederate memorabilia in the world. The Confederate White House, adjacent to the museum, has been restored as a shrine to the Lost Cause.

Confederate President Jefferson Davis and 18,000 Confederate dead are buried at the **Hollywood Cemetery** (www.hollywoodcemetery.org) on Cherry Street. The expansive, park-like grounds are also the final resting place of US presidents James Monroe and John Tyler. Downtown Richmond is a pleasant business and government center. Modern office buildings are designed around plazas and fountains; historic buildings are restored as shops and restaurants; the 1.25-mile (2 km) Canal Walk opens the James River waterfront for recreation. The city is renowned for its symphony, opera, and ballet, as well as for the **Virginia Museum of Fine Arts** (tel: 804-340-1400; www.vfma.state.va.us; Wed–Sun) on Grove Avenue.

Jefferson and Monticello

From Richmond, take I-64W for 74 miles (119km) toward Charlottesville, site of the University of Virginia and the home of Thomas Jefferson. For a more scenic route, take Exit 167 to US 250 West. The two-lane road rolls through the hills and past the horse farms, rolls of baled hay, ponds, and old timers sitting in their front yards. The curvy roads were the ones Jefferson knew. As you near the town, signs on Route 729 direct you to Monticello; if you took I-64, take Exit 121.

Americans arriving at **Monticello** (tel: 434-977-7757; www.monticello.org; daily), the "little mountain" estate of Thomas Jefferson, will be familiar with

Every aspect of Thomas Jefferson's home, Monticello, was designed by the inventive president.

Virginia's limestone Natural Bridge.

FACT

The Blue Ridge Parkway, "America's Favorite Drive," was conceived in the 1930s as a Depression-era public works project, and driving it through mountainous terrain was an engineering challenge that involved digging 26 tunnels. The last stretch of parkway was completed in 1987.

Shoemaker in Colonial Williamsburg.

its shape; its image adorns the tail side of the US nickel. This elegant, dome shape is particularly Jeffersonian, for not only does it appear on the Rotunda at the University of Virginia, but also as the roof of the Jefferson Memorial building in Washington, DC. Jefferson designed every aspect of Monticello, and the imprint of his active mind is everywhere apparent.

Try to arrive early, as the wait for the mandatory tour is known to extend up to two hours at midday. The tour takes you through the ground floor of the residence, with guides pointing out Jefferson's inventions and innovations, like a double-writing machine and dumbwaiter system. Equal attention is spent on the family's personal lives. The self-guided exploration of the work areas underneath the mansion is fascinating, as it shows how slaves, servants, and hired hands kept the estate operating. Shuttle buses from the visitor center to the mansion stop at the family plot where Jefferson and about 200 of his family are buried.

Jefferson's good friend James Monroe, fifth president of the United States, lived about 3 miles (4.8km) away at **Ash Lawn-Highland** (tel: 434-293-8000; www.ashlawnhighland.org; daily). Turn left out of Monticello on Route 53, then right on Route 795. The unpretentious retreat reflects Monroe's introverted, thoughtful nature, with its ash tree-lined lane bordered by post and rail fencing leading to a simple country home. It's Monroe's peaceful contrast to Jefferson's frenetic energy.

As you backtrack past Monticello toward I-64 to continue to Charlottesville, you pass by **Michie Tavern**, (tel: 434-977-1234; www.michietavern. com; lunch and tours daily) once a pre-Revolutionary watering hole but now a museum filled with colonial furniture and artifacts. It also serves a period-inspired lunch menu.

Charlottesville

It is barely 6 miles (9km) from Monticello to **Charlottesville** ❾ and the **University of Virginia**. Continue on Route 53; turn right onto Route 20, and then take I-64W to the Fifth Street exit which leads directly into the heart of the town and

DETOUR TO WILLIAMSBURG

A 54-mile (87km) drive from Richmond along SR 60 ends at Colonial Williamsburg, which recreates the everyday life of the nation's infancy. Established in 1633, Williamsburg grew into a center of culture, fashion, and festive living. After the state government moved to Richmond in 1780, the city languished until Dr William R. Goodwin approached John D. Rockefeller, Jr in 1926 for funds to save those historic buildings still standing and to rebuild others. Using original blueprints and materials, Goodwin resurrected the entire town, from the Congress – where George Mason's Declaration of Rights to the House of Burgesses laid the foundation for the Constitution – to the Raleigh Tavern, where George Washington plotted military strategy in the revolt against Great Britain. Nearly 2,000 "residents" recreate the original Williamsburg community. The blacksmith pounds away at glowing iron; a maid in a bonnet weaves linen; horse-drawn carriages trundle through the streets; militiamen drill on the town green. The baker, the printer, and the glassblower are represented, too. For the full Early American heritage experience, the Jamestown settlement (both the original site with archeological digs and an authentic recreation) and Yorktown, where the British surrendered to the Americans, are less than an hour's drive away. For information, tel: 757-220-7645, 800-HISTORY or 757-229-1000; www.colonialwilliamsburg.com.

the university area. Jefferson designed the original buildings and campus in the 1820s and claimed that it was of this achievement that he was most proud. His architecture is based on European classical style, adapted to local materials such as red brick and painted wood. Looking out from the elevated walkway of the **Rotunda**, you see the splendid swath of grass known as "**The Lawn**," bordered by columned pavilions. Originally, these were the residences of all the students and professors of Jefferson's "academic villages"; now they are inhabited by school officials and top students. **West Range** on McCormack Road is where Edgar Allan Poe (1809-49) lived during his unsuccessful tenure here. His former room is open to visitors.

Continue down University Avenue to "**The Corner**," a collection of restaurants and shops catering to students, tourists, and local residents.

The Blue Ridge Parkway

Take I-64W to Rockfish Gap, where the breathtaking 459-mile (739km) **Blue Ridge Parkway** (www.blueridge parkway.org) begins. Cutting through the **George Washington National Forest**, the Parkway – like its nearby counterpart, the Skyline Drive – rides atop the Blue Ridge Mountains. However, as this is not a national park, you will note one big difference: this drive is filled not only with forest and flowers but also with working farms. Trees carpet the surrounding mountains, which seem bluer and bluer as they recede into the distance. This is caused by chemicals emitted by the trees, a prosaic explanation which in no way diminishes the beautiful result. If you're traveling alone, don't allow the superb views to lure your eyes too far from the road or you will end up driving into a tree.

At Mile Marker 61, Route 130 West leads to **Natural Bridge** (tel: 540-291-2121; www.naturalbridgeva.com; daily). The 215ft (66-meter) -high natural rock formation was cherished as "The Bridge to God" by the Monocan tribe. To view this wonder, however, you have to buy tickets and go through an unapologetic array of tacky tourist stuff: a wax museum, butterfly house, and enormous gift shop.

Roanoke

Back on the Parkway, continue south. Route 220 leads to the pretty town of **Roanoke** ❿ (see page 187). Mabry Mill at Milepost 176 is a restored 1900-era gristmill, smithy, and moonshine still. The gem of this trip is at Milepost 210. The Blue Ridge Music Center (tel: 276-236-5309; www.blueridgemusiccenter. org) chronicles the distinctive mountain music played on fiddle, mandolin, guitar, and banjo via excellent displays and videos. Musicians jam in the covered courtyard every afternoon.

Depart the Parkway at Route 89 and head southeast into North Carolina where the pace of life is as relaxed as a sigh and the conversation is laced with the slow Southern drawl that's sometimes difficult for outsiders to understand. You have now entered the Deep South.

Star-gazing in Roanoke.

Entrance to Bethesda, the former orphanage near Savannah.

NORTH CAROLINA TO SAVANNAH

This diverse region offers university towns and sandy beaches, antebellum plantations and Civil Rights landmarks, pastoral farmland and history-filled cities, plus the unique culture and cuisine of the Lowcountry.

A ll that remains of the first-known settlement in present-day North Carolina is one word. That word – Croatan – has kept etymologists and philologists busy for centuries, ever since it was found scraped into a tree in the vanished colony of Fort Raleigh on Roanoke Island. Nothing else was left of the "lost colony," which was founded in 1587.

Today, the state is experiencing rapid transformation from a country backwater to a manufacturing and educational power. Jobs and suburbs are sprouting up all along the I-85 corridor, particularly in light industrial trades. Charlotte has become the banking power of the South. And the Raleigh-Durham area contains a very high concentration of quality universities. It's a measure of this success that you can now watch ice hockey in a state where it rarely snows, and professional football, too; both have recently arrived along with the new jobs. Strains of folk and bluegrass music are still the anthem heard in the mountainous Appalachian west.

Moravian history

US 52 takes you over the border from Virginia's Blue Ridge Parkway through trim **Mount Airy** ⑪ – birthplace of Carolina hero, the late actor and producer Andy

Griffith, and the model town for his wildly popular classic TV program *Mayberry RFD* – then on down to Winston-Salem.

US 52 leads on to **Winston-Salem** ⑫ (see page 188), home of the R.J. Reynolds tobacco factory, which produces more than 450 million cigarettes daily. Despite the negative image of the product, tobacco remains the second-largest industry in North Carolina (textiles are first). Winston Cigarettes have long sponsored NASCAR's Winston Cup; many

Main Attractions

Greensboro
Durham
Chapel Hill
Fayetteville
Outer Banks
Wilmington
Georgetown
Charleston
Savannah

Vintage diner table jukebox and 1932 Ford Model B in Winston-Salem.

Winston-Salem man in Moravian costume working with tobacco.

Downtown Winston-Salem.

NASCAR greats were reared and still live in the area.

The Salem half of Winston-Salem was founded by Moravians in 1766. The name is derived from the Hebrew word "shalom," meaning peace. In 1913, it was incorporated with its neighbor Winston, and when its old buildings fell into disrepair, a restoration project during the 1930s saved them. The success of this effort can be seen in **Salem Old Town**, which is entered from the Old Salem Road near the center of town. Particularly interesting are the **Mikisch Tobacco Shop**, thought to be the oldest tobacco shop still standing in America; the **Winkler Bakery**, a restored Moravian bakery that produces lovely bread and unique wafer-thin cookies Monday through Saturday; and the **Salem Tavern** with its **Barn and Farm Museum**. **God's Acre**, a Moravian graveyard nearby, possesses 4,000 graves, many graced with flat marble markers symbolizing the equality of the deceased.

Busy four-lane US 421 leads to **Greensboro**, the site of a pivotal moment in the Civil Rights movement – the first sit-in by blacks demanding an end to segregation. The Woolworth store where the sit-in occurred is now the **International Civil Rights Center and Museum** (tel: 336-274-9199; www.sitinmovement. org; Tue–Sun). The hour-long guided tour takes visitors on an uneasy journey through the historical and moral elements of America's legacy of slavery and segregation. The lunch counter where four black college freshmen sat has remained untouched since those days in 1960. Other exhibits revisit "Jim Crow" laws, the role of churches in the non-violent movement, and a Wall of Remembrance of those who died during the Civil Rights struggle.

Durham

Continue along either US 70 or I-40E to **Durham ⑬**. On the way, look for the **Piedmont Farmers' Market** at Exit 210 off I-40. This is a massive covered market occupying three buildings where area farmers sell produce, meats, cheese, and greenery (tel: 336-606-9157; daily).

Durham is home of **Duke University**. Along with **Chapel Hill** and **Raleigh**, it is part of the Research Triangle, a liberal oasis in the middle of North Carolina, which claims to have more PhDs per capita than any other area in the nation. This is also the place to come for top-quality college basketball. North Carolina is a hoops-crazy state, and its Duke Blue Devils, North Carolina Tar Heels, and North Carolina State Wolfpack – all playing in the Triangle – do the state proud. Duke's campus is among the most beautiful in the South, with Gothic and Georgian buildings filling neat quadrangles. **Duke Garden** (tel: 919-684-3698; www.hr.duke.edu/dukegardens; daily) is 55 acres (22 hectares) of incredibly manicured formal gardens, fountains, picnic areas, and ponds. Find a legal place to park, then head for the Duke University Chapel to see the **Benjamin N. Duke Memorial Flentrop Organ**, a 5,000-pipe extravaganza. Walking tours of the university are coordinated through the Admissions Office.

Durham's culture

The city is a lively mixture of abandoned tobacco warehouses and factories transformed into businesses, artists' galleries, and chic restaurants. Working-class mill hands and college professors, old Southerners and new Yankee upstarts share their love of the city to create an involved community. **Ninth Street** is the place to go, with plenty of good record shops, bookstores, coffee shops, and eateries.

Also make a point of finding the Durham Bulls' minor-league ballpark, one of the nation's finest and the perfect spot to spend a warm summer evening. Note the outfield bull, which snorts steam when a home run is hit. The Bulls' former ballpark, El Toro Field, was even more authentic – one side consisted of tobacco warehouses, and the steam-snorting bull made its debut here during the filming of the baseball film *Bull Durham*. It is easily walkable from Downtown.

Durham is also a culinary magnet. Several chefs with national reputations cook here. There are over 300 locally owned restaurants, a high

---

FACT

Why is North Carolina known as the Tar Heel state? The prosaic explanation is that workers making tar by burning longleaf pine trees still had the sticky substance on their heels after leaving the woods. The poetic explanation is that, during the Civil War, North Carolina soldiers told a group of retreating troops that they'd put tar on their heels to make them stick in the next battle.

Bodie Island lighthouse, Cape Hatteras National Seashore, Outer Banks.

DETOUR TO OUTER BANKS

A leisurely 193-mile (311km) drive along SR 64 from Raleigh leads to the Outer Banks, which emerge like the head of a whale breaching into the Atlantic. Two national seashores, Cape Hatteras and Cape Lookout, preserve 120 miles (190km) of these beaches on Bodie, Hatteras, and Ocracoke islands, and Core and Shackleford banks. While most coastal islands lie within 10 miles (16km) of shore, the Outer Banks belong to the realm of the sea; in places, 30 miles (48km) of water separate Hatteras Island from the mainland. The National Seashores of the Outer Banks have personalities unique to the rest of North Carolina. The islands have wide, water-thrashed beaches, while scattered patches of sea oats and beach grasses bind low dunes behind them. Clumps of shrubby marsh elder and bayberry dot the swales. The mainland side of each island hosts extensive tidal marshes of swaying cordgrass. Distinctly patterned lighthouses mark the shores for passing ships, in particular the spiral-painted Cape Hatteras lighthouse. Beach erosion threatened to topple the lighthouse into the sea, so in 1999 the 4,400 ton lighthouse was carefully rolled along steel tracks to a new location 1,600ft (487 meters) inland. For more information, telephone the Outer Banks Chamber of Commerce on 252-441-8144 or visit the Outer Banks Visitors Bureau website at www.outerbanks.org.

*A rural mailbox in
North Carolina.*

*1950s stock car, South
Carolina.*

in the lot adjacent to the Planetarium.
Franklin Street is the center for shopping, eating, and socializing with students. The 80 acres (32 hectares) of the
North Carolina Botanical Garden
(919-962-0522; www.ncbg.umnc.edu;
daily) show the indigenous plants of
the state's different regions in natural
settings. The education building and
information center is a Leadership in
Energy and Environmental Design
platinum-certified building, and worth
a visit on its own.

Toward the coast

From Durham, take the US 15-501
(also known as the Jefferson Davis
Highway) south toward **Sanford** ,
where pottery has become a popular
cottage industry. At Sanford, change
onto US 421. Roadside fields are again
densely covered with tobacco plants
and the occasional weeping willow or
algae-covered pond does little to dispel summer's oppressive heat.

This road runs through farm country, through corn and tobacco fields
extending for acres back from the
highway. There are innumerable small
churches along the road, the majority
of which are Baptist with marquees
exhorting passersby to reconsider their
sin-filled lives. At **Lillington**, turn
south on US 401 toward **Fayetteville**
which is home to the Army's Ft.
Bragg. The military is highly respected
and honoured here. The **Airborne
and Special Operations Museum**
(tel: 910-643-2766; www.asomf.org; Tue–
Sun) tracks the development of paratroopers from World War II through
their missions today. Life-sized, walk-
through dioramas give a unique sense
of being part of the action, be it in a
French village in 1944 or an Afghan
camp in 2012. A separate exhibit of the
ordeal of POWs in Vietnam is chilling.

Adjacent, the very moving **North
Carolina Veterans Park** (tel: 910-
433-1547; www.ncveteranspark.org;
daily) honors those Tar Heels who
have served since Revolutionary
times. Casts of hands from veterans

number for a relatively small city.
Durham Performing Arts Center is
the fourth-busiest in the country, after
Radio City Music Hall and Caesar's
Palace in Las Vegas.

Just to the southwest of Durham,
smaller **Chapel Hill** is the home of the
pleasant **University of North Carolina**
campus. UNC was the first state university chartered in the US. Fans of
astronomy will enjoy the **Morehead
Planetarium and Science Center** at
250 East Franklin Street (tel: 919-962-
1236; www.moreheadplanetarium.org; Tue–
Sun) Visitors to the campus can park

as though raised while being sworn in cover 100 obelisks – one for each county in the state. Inside, rows of dog tags of each North Carolinian who died in the wars are on one wall. One empty row is labelled "Future."

Cape Fear Botanical Garden (tel: 910-486-0221; www.capefearbg.org; daily) at 536 North Eastern Boulevard is a tonic after contemplating the impact of war. However, it is a little disconcerting that the police firing range is nearby; the sound of cicadas and bird songs are sometimes drowned out by the popping of small arms fire. The garden encompasses 77 acres (31 hectares) of pine and hardwood forest. Cultivated garden areas showcase more than 2,000 varieties of ornamental plants, and include beautiful Daylily, Camellia, and Hosta gardens. There are plenty of viewing areas, including rope hammock-style stools overlooking a pond.

Wilmington

If you have an audio book, the two-hour drive from Fayetteville to Wilmington along State Route 87 is the time to listen to it. The road is flat; the scenery is unexciting, and the towns little more than gas stations.

Your reward is the coastal town of **Wilmington** ⑯. On the Cape Fear River near the Atlantic Ocean, it's been a deep water port since colonial times. After the long, hot drive, treat yourself to one of the many sightseeing cruises along the river or sign on for a kayak or nature trip to the surrounding coastal islands. The breeze almost always blows along the 2-mile (3km) -long boardwalk which stretches past former warehouses and chandlers' stores, now a collection of shops, restaurants, and hotels with water views. Many fine old houses line the cobblestone streets near the waterfront, including the **Zebulon Latimer House** (126 South Third Street) and the **Burgwin-Wright House** (Third and Market streets).

On the other side of the river, visit the *USS North Carolina* **Battleship Memorial** (tel: 910-251-5787; www. battleshipnc.com; daily). Commissioned in 1941, she was considered the greatest fighting vessel in the United States

TIP

Southerners are great storytellers. In Wilmington, North Carolina, ask about the unsolved murder of 1760, which involved a man, a snake ring, and a riderless horse on a rainy night.

Myrtle Beach State Park Pier.

Pineapple-shaped fountain in Waterfront Park, Charleston.

Mature trees and elegant porches provide welcome shade in Charleston.

of her time. The self-guided tour allows visitors to envision the daily life and fierce combat her crew experienced in the Pacific.

SOUTH CAROLINA

Of all the southern states, South Carolina was the most virulent in its defence of slavery and its right to leave the Union. On December 20, 1860, it became the first state to secede from the Union. Six other states quickly followed suit. When Confederate forces opened fire on Union troops stationed at Ft. Sumter in Charleston harbour in April 1861, it plunged the nation into a war with itself.

Holding South Carolina responsible for the war, General William Tecumseh Sherman was particularly harsh in the region during his march to the sea, devastating its agricultural base and torching its ports. Between that and the end of slavery, South Carolina's economic base was destroyed. It wasn't until after World War II, when the state's economy began to switch from agriculture to textiles, furniture, and chemical industries that the state's fortunes began to flourish. (Agriculture remains strong, however: this is America's top peach producer and its only producer of tea.) Tourism is another economic mainstay along the Carolina coast from beach resorts to historic cities.

As you leave the USS North Carolina, turn left onto US 17 south into South Carolina. You enter the 55-mile (88km) stretch of beach resort known as the **Grand Strand.** Several towns dot the sandy shore, each one with its own personality. Atlantic Beach retains much of its fishing village atmosphere. Pawley's Island is an enclave of summer cottages. Seaside attracts families, and Muretta Inlet attracts surfers. The largest and busiest town is **Myrtle Beach ⑰**, the third most popular tourist resort on the East Coast, after Disney World and Atlantic City. The extraordinary commercialization of the area may well overwhelm you, as the grandly named King's Highway (US 17) consists of mile after mile

of miniature golf courses, shopping centers, theatres, and shops dispensing the accessories that go with beach culture. But the town's hotels and resorts are removed from the highway and share a broad, clean, sandy beach that rarely feels crowded, even at the height of the summer tourist season. South of Myrtle Beach on US 17, on the Sampit River, lies the quieter and more genteel **Georgetown** ⑱. A thriving port during the lumber era, it is still the state's second busiest seaport. You wouldn't know it from the slow pace of life and its lovely downtown with grand old houses and a boardwalk along the river. The **Rice Museum** (tel: 843-546-7423; Mon–Sat) gives a look at the crop that sustained this area for much of its early history. Just a few steps away, the **South Carolina Maritime Museum** (tel: 843-520-0111; www. scmaritimemuseum.org; Mon–Sat) chronicles 300 years of maritime commerce. **Kaminski House** (1769) and **Parker House** (1740) are side-by-side on Front Street; the tours are friendly and informal. (tel: 843-546-7706; daily).

Historic Charleston

South again along US 17, you'll notice small frame structures on the side of the road from Awendaw to Mount Pleasant. This is the **Sweetgrass Basketweavers Highway**, the heart of the Gullah region. Gullah culture developed among the slaves from West Africa who worked the vast rice plantations along the coast. They adapted their traditional lifestyle, crafts, language, and cuisine to create a unique folkway. About 300,000 people who claim Gullah roots live along the coast from South Carolina to northern Florida. The women in the roadside stands practice the craft of weaving that was brought from Africa by their enslaved ancestors and passed down through the generations as part of the Gullah culture. Pull off the road to watch, browse, and buy.

In 1670, English colonists founded Charles Towne, named after Charles II, on the Ashley River, 5 miles (8km) from the present location of **Charleston** ⑲. This was the first permanent settlement in the Carolinas. After 10 years of battling malaria, heat, flooding, and the Kiawah tribe, they packed up and headed to the peninsula where modern Charleston was built. The prosperity of the city's early days is reflected in elegant 18th-century homes that fill the residential area south of Broad Street. In fact, this is one of America's top walking cities.

Museum Mile

The Visitor Center at Meeting and Anne streets is at the north end of Charleston's **Museum Mile.** From there to Charleston Harbor, Meeting Street and the adjacent side streets have over 30 museums, historic houses, churches, and other notable sites. These include the **Charleston Museum** (tel: 843-722-2996; www. charlestonmuseum.org; daily) across the street from the Visitor Center. The first museum in America (1773), it

Interior of a slave cabin.

The wedding cake steeple of St Michael's Episcopal Church, Charleston.

Luxurious houses on the waterfront in Charleston.

showcases artifacts of the natural and cultural history of the Lowcountry – South Carolina's coastal region including its sea islands. The area is so called because the land is at or near sea level. At one time, agriculture – particularly rice plantations – was the main Lowcountry activity. Now, tourism – focused on seaside resorts, historic sites, cuisine, and culture – drives the economy. The **Gibbes Museum** (tel: 843-722-2706; www.gibbesmuseum.org; daily) tells Charleston's story through art. The **Joseph Manigault House** (350 Meeting Street) and **Nathaniel Russell House** (51 Meeting Street) are two examples of the luxury the upper classes enjoyed. The enclosed and outdoor **City Market** occupying two blocks of the appropriately names Market Street houses 140 merchant stalls. This is the district for galleries, boutiques, specialty shops, and restaurants.

Meeting Street ends at the palmetto-lined **Battery** and **White Point Gardens**. Looking across the water, the almost nondescript island

at the entrance to the harbour is **Fort Sumter** (tel: 843-883-3123; www.nps.gov.fosu; daily). The Confederate bombardment of the Union fortifications was the action that touched off the Civil War. The interpretive center on Concord Street is the departure point for cruises to the fort. The cruise and tour take 2.5 hours.

At the **Old Slave Mart Museum** (tel: 843-958-6467 www.oldslavemart.org; Mon–Sat) on Chalmers Street, you can see, among other items, facsimiles of bills of sale used in the slave trade. "A prime gang of 25 negroes accustomed to the culture of Sea Island Cotton and Rice," reads one placard advertising the upcoming sale of 25 human beings into bondage. It is a startling and sobering museum, especially so when one realizes this heinous practice was still in full swing just a century and a half ago. The self-contented opulence south of Broad suddenly appears quite different after a long, thoughtful visit to the slave market.

Charleston is chock-full of historic churches, as well as all its other cultural and social attractions. Two of the more interesting are the **Huguenot Church**, a Gothic structure built by French Protestants, and **St Michael's Episcopal Church** with its 186ft (57-meter) -high steeple.

Plantations and tea

Three plantations in the vicinity of Charleston are also worth a visit. **Magnolia Plantation and Gardens** (tel: 843-571-1266; www.magnoliaplantation.com; daily) at 3550 Ashley River Road (State Route 61). In addition to the 19th-century plantation house, Magnolia also has beautiful gardens first planted in 1870, a nature center, and offers a boat tour of the old rice fields (look for alligators). Several slave cabins are being restored, which date from the 1850s and are a focal point for an award-winning program on the area's African-American history and culture.

Middleton Place (tel: 843-556-6020; www.middletonplace.org; daily), has the oldest landscaped gardens in the country, 65 acres (26 hectares) and a rejuvenated stableyard with livestock from the antebellum period and interpreters demonstrating the skills slaves used to keep the place running. **Boone Hall Plantation** (tel: 843-884-4371; www.boonehallplantation. com; daily) has the achingly beautiful avenue of live oak trees featured in *Gone With the Wind*. The mansion is most people's idea of the perfect antebellum residence. In fact, the house was rebuilt only in 1935. The plantation has a unique presentation about the unique Gullah culture adapted by African slaves.

Were tea plants faster-growing, the history of the US may have been a little different. The climate of the Lowcountry is perfect for tea propagation, but it takes about four years before tea leaves can be harvested, so the colonists concentrated on the faster growing rice and cotton. The **Charleston Tea Plantation** (tel: 843-559-0383; www.charlestonteaplantation. com; daily), about 30 minutes south of Charleston, cultivates plants imported for another tea experiment a century ago on 127 acres (51 hectare) on the only tea plantation in America.

After Charleston, follow US 17 south through the Lowcountry toward the Georgia border. Turning east onto US 21 from US 17, is **Beaufort** (pronounced "bew-ford"), the second-oldest town in South Carolina and one that's still quite compact and attractive. Hollywood movie producers use the gorgeous antebellum waterfront homes as set pieces. Indigo and rice cultivation brought wealth during the 18th century, when the majority of these houses (some are inns) were constructed. The best way to experience this town is to wander about, enjoying the friendly talk of residents at any one of the seafood restaurants before moving on south again into Georgia. Take Route 170 south across the Broad River, pick up US 17 again, and cross the bridge to that beautiful "Southern belle" of a city, **Savannah** ⓴ (see page 78).

Azaleas and moss-draped live oaks in Magnolia Plantation and Gardens, Charleston.

Savannah: First City of Georgia

The port of Savannah is an enticing, seductive place – equal parts history, gentility, revelry, and eccentricity.

Tombstone in Bonaventure Cemetery.

Best known for its gorgeous, moss-draped live oaks, cobblestone streets, and light, pastel-colored buildings, an air of mystique still hovers over Savannah, Georgia's original settlement.

The saucy, best-selling book *Midnight in the Garden of Good and Evil* made this city a household name, with a corresponding increase in the city's tourism. Today, a visit is likely to consist of a horse-drawn carriage ride through stately squares, lunch in an outdoor café – and an evening seeking ghosts in the shadowy passageways. In 1733, James Edward Oglethorpe received a royal charter to establish "the colony of Georgia in America" – and protect the coast from Spanish Florida while producing wine and silk for the Crown. Oglethorpe laid out a grid of broad thoroughfares, punctuated at regular intervals with two dozen spacious public

The grand Forsyth Park fountain.

squares. The 20 that remain have been refurbished, forming the nucleus of **Savannah's Historic District** – one of the largest urban national historic landmark districts in the United States, and probably the most beautiful. The district is bounded by the Savannah River to the north and Forsyth Park to the south, covering a 2.5-mile (4km) radius.

Bull Street, running the length of the district north to south, links some of the most beautiful squares. These squares excel in Savannah's most characteristic details: fancy ironwork and atmospheric Spanish moss. They are also enlivened with daily activity – art vendors, hot dog stands, and street performers. Summer brings free jazz concerts to John Square near the river, but early spring is the best time to visit, when the city's azaleas are in full blossom.

Walking is the best way to see the city, unless the heat is oppressive, in which case a horse-drawn carriage ride or a trolley tour are better options. **Old Town Trolleys** (www.trolleytours.com) and **Oglethorpe Tolleys** (www.oglethorpetours.com) both offer on-off tours. You'll see horse carriages near several squares.

One of the most entertaining ways to tour the historic squares is with **Savannah Dan** (912-398-3777). Dressed in a seersucker suit, broad-brimmed hat, and bow tie, and exuding pure Southern charm, he is a native with an encyclopaedic knowledge of the town and a gift for tale-telling. The two-hour walking tours leave you feeling that you know the town like an insider.

Most of the houses surrounding the squares have great history, and several are open for tours. If you see no other, tour the **Owens-Thomas House** (124 Abercorn Street; www.telfair.org). Built with an obsessive attention to symmetry, some doors open to blank walls in order to maintain the gracious balance and design. Marquis de Lafayette stayed there during his visit to the US in 1825. The **Cathedral of St John the Baptist**, by Lafayette Square, is another worthy stop. **Juliette Gordon Low's birthplace** (www.julietgordonlowborthplace. org) at 142 Bull Street is the handsome childhood home of the founder of the Girl Scouts of America.

Lucas Theater for the Arts (www.lucastheatre. com) at 32 Abercom Street first opened in 1921 with what was then the largest screen in Savannah. Eventually, TV and suburbia stole its customers, and it closed in 1976. Slated for demolition, local citizens rescued and restored it as a theatrical venue. It's open Tuesday through Friday for self-guided tours (tel: 912-525-5040). Around the corner, Broughton Street is the main shopping thoroughfare with a mix of mostly locally owned stores and a few major retailers. **Leopold's Ice Cream** (www.leopoldsicecream.com) has been making their own cold treats for 93 years.

Horticulturists should seek out **Trustees' Garden** (www.trusteesgarden.com) on East Broad Street. Planted in the 1700s as Georgia's first experimental garden, it is filled with exotic plants from around the world.

In colonial and antebellum times, cobblestoned River Street along Savannah's harborside was the hub of the city's shipping. Now this strip at the foot of a very steep hill is the hub of the tourist trade. The old brick warehouses, cotton exchange, and shipping offices are now inns, pubs, restaurants, and gift shops. Parking is a challenge; the lots along the river fill quickly. Better to use the public lots along Bay Street and reach River Street via steep stairways. **Savannah History Museum** (tel: 912-238-1779;

www.visit-historic-savannah.com; daily) at 303 Martin Luther King Jr. Blvd. is a one-stop blitz of the city's fascinating past, with lots of artifacts, from Forrest Gump's bench to Revolutionary War weapons. It is in the same building as the **Visitor Center.** A block away at MLK Blvd. and Turner Blvd., the **Savannah College of Art and Design (SCAD) Gallery** (tel: 912-525-7191; www.scadmoa.org; Tue–Sun) features ever-changing exhibits by contemporary and avant-guard artists. All of the guides are students at the school. Further up MLK Blvd., the **Ships of the Sea Museum** (tel: 912-232-1511; www.shipsofthesea. org; Tue–Sun) is an often-overlooked gem. It is filled with intricately detailed scale models of dozens of ships. Many of them are cutaways with the cargo and crew, fittings and machinery all looking as though ready to sail to Lilliput.

Leave Downtown by heading east on Victory Drive in the direction of the coastal islands to visit **Bonaventure Cemetery** (www.bonaventurehistorical. org), a luxurious final resting place for Savannah's most distinguished citizens. A former plantation, Bonaventure is wistfully beautiful, dripping with moss and overflowing with azaleas, jasmine, magnolias, and live oak trees. The images on several of the gravestones have become synonymous with both the *Midnight* book and the city itself.

Brightly painted gingerbread row houses.

GEORGIA TO THE FLORIDA KEYS

Small-town ambiance, a tropical paradise, alligators in the Everglades, and the southernmost point in the US highlight the end of the Atlantic Route.

The Georgia coast is one of the Southeast's most interesting natural regions, a string of marshes, largely undeveloped islands, and good beaches rarely sought out by the traveler focused solely on getting through the state via I-95 as quickly as possible. No wonder this region is known locally as the Golden Isles. The inattentive traveler's loss, however, has been others' gain: a number of unusual birds live secreted along this coast, and there are also vestiges of African culture from the dark days when slaves were shipped across the Atlantic to work the plantations of the South.

From Savannah, take Victory Drive (US 17) west out of town, where it shortly becomes Ogeechee Road – and also becomes more rural in character. About 25 miles (40km) along, stop in **Midway** ㉑ for a look at the small, whitewashed village church, built in 1792 to replace the 1752 original, erected by displaced New Englanders and destroyed during the Revolutionary War. Note the section that was designated specifically for slaves and a gracefully kept cemetery outside. The church and grounds are managed by the adjacent small **Midway Museum** (tel: 912-884-5837; www.themidwaymuseum.org; Tue–Sun), which houses a collection of period items.

Ripe Georgia peaches at a roadside stand.

Harris Neck NWR to Brunswick

Past Riceboro, home to an agricultural research station, the highway passes beneath I-95 again and crosses a bridge over a tidal inlet into McIntosh County. To learn more about the politics, poverty, and small-town intrigue of the county, look for the biting nonfiction book *Praying for Sheetrock*, which won awards for its clear-eyed portrait of local life.

If you make a left just after the bridge onto unnumbered Harris Neck Road,

Main Attractions
Midway
Cumberland Island
St Augustine
Castillo de San Marcos
Orlando
Clearwater Beach
Alligator Alley
The Everglades
Key West

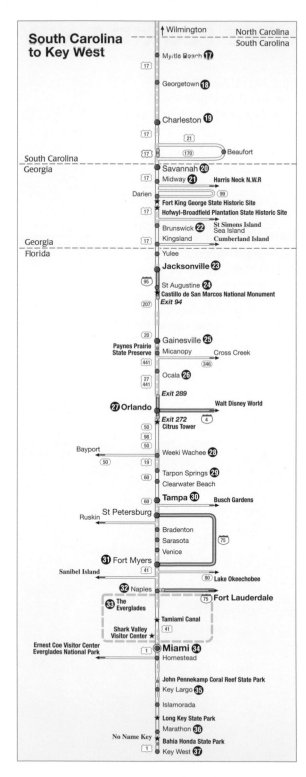

South Carolina to Key West

↑ Wilmington

North Carolina
South Carolina

Myrtle Beach **17**
17

Georgetown **18**

Charleston **19**
17
21
17 170 ● Beaufort

South Carolina
Georgia

Savannah **20**
17 Midway **21** **Harris Neck N.W.R**
Darien 99
★ **Fort King George State Historic Site**
17 ■ **Hofwyl-Broadfield Plantation State Historic Site**
Brunswick **22** **St Simons Island**
Sea Island
17 Kingsland **Cumberland Island**

Georgia
Florida

Yulee
Jacksonville 23
95 St Augustine **24**
■ **Castillo de San Marcos National Monument**
207 *Exit 94*

20 Gainesville **25**
Paynes Prairie Micanopy **Cross Creek**
State Preserve 441 346
27 Ocala **26**
441
Exit 289
Walt Disney World
27 Orlando
50 *Exit 272* 4
98 **Citrus Tower**
Bayport 50
Weeki Wachee **28**
50 19
60 Tarpon Springs **29**
Clearwater Beach
60 **Tampa 30** **Busch Gardens**
St Petersburg
Ruskin
Bradenton
Sarasota 75
Venice
31 Fort Myers
Sanibel Island 41
80 Lake Okeechobee
32 Naples
33 The 75 **Fort Lauderdale**
Everglades
★ **Tamiami Canal**
Shark Valley 41
Visitor Center ★
Ernest Coe Visitor Center 1 ● **Miami 34**
Everglades National Park
Homestead

★ **John Pennekamp Coral Reef State Park**
Key Largo **35**
Islamorada
★ **Long Key State Park**
Marathon **36**
No Name Key ★ **Bahia Honda State Park**
1 ● Key West **37**

you can find **Harris Neck National Wildlife Refuge**, a pocket of wilderness that was saved from development because a former military airstrip occupied the land. Fishing is the most popular activity here, but you can also drive a one-way dirt loop road for a look at the waterfowl in their natural environs. Just offshore sits St Catherines Island, an off-limits island used by the Bronx Zoo as a breeding ground for rare birds and animals.

South again on US 17, make a brief detour onto Georgia 99, which reveals some truly old-fashioned towns and dwellings – shacks, mostly, many of them occupied by the modern-day descendants of freed slaves. These small communities – Crescent, Valona, Meridian, Carnigan, and Ridgeville – are fishing and shellfishing communities now.

At **Darien**, rustic Georgia 99 rejoins US 17 again. The **Fort King George State Historic Site** (tel: 912-437-4770; www.gastateparks.org/FortKingGeorge; Tue–Sun) here re-creates a Colonial-era blockhouse; this is where the British first settled Georgia and for a brief period administered to the area.

Five miles (8km) south, at the mouth of the Altamaha River, sits the **Hofwyl-Broadfield Plantation** (tel: 912-264-7333; www.gastateparks.org/HofwylBroadfield; Tue–Sun) – prettifying the story of slavery somewhat as it demonstrates how the know-how of slaves imported from Africa was crucial to the successful cultivation of rice on these islands.

Hold your nose as you enter industrial **Brunswick 22**, a major center for paper and chemical production. Despite its industrial character, Brunswick's Downtown is surprisingly slow-paced and old-Southern, with an attractive grid of streets, homes, and moss-draped live oak trees. One such oak tree, the so-called Lover's Oak, is believed to have stood for hundreds – possibly even close to one thousand – years.

The city is also set on a wide, beautiful (if not exactly pure) marsh immortalized by poet Sidney Lanier as the **"Marshes of Glynn"** (for Glynn County). A turnout facing the marshes has information explaining their formation, which provides an opportunity to stretch your legs, take some snapshots, and pick up lots of tourist information.

Lush islands

From the marshes, turn east and cross the toll bridge for a look at lush, though somewhat exclusive, **St Simons Island**. Palm fronds, live oak trees, and flowers cover both sides of the road in perpetual green as you drive through the road to the single attractive harborfront, and you might consider staying the night in these restful environs. A museum in the former lighthouse tells the history of coastal Georgia, and there's a good beach out beyond the main settlement. **Sea Island**, an even more exclusive resort reached via another series of roads on the island, possesses beautiful beaches and a world-class golf course.

South again on US 17, you cross more bridges and then pivot inland through tiny towns. At Kingsland, you can make a turnoff to catch the ferry for unspoiled **Cumberland Island**, one of the most attractive islands in the Georgia chain. Once the exclusive domain of wealthy families, it is now mostly owned by the US government as a "national seashore," meaning there are a small number of rudimentary campsites available to the public (www.nps.gov/cuis). Spirited jockeying for these few camping spots begins well in advance, however, so don't expect to just waltz in and secure one at the last moment.

FLORIDA

Crossing the St Marys River, a broad watershed that reaches the Okefenokee, you're greeted with a double row of palm trees and, possibly, the presence of police cars: you have arrived in Florida. The first town you reach is **Yulee**, named for legislator and entrepreneur David Yulee. Mr Yulee built a railroad from coast to Florida coast, and it thrived for a short time, but politics and the Civil War soon did it in and the town is of little consequence today. It isn't very long afterward that the rural roads give way to sprawl, announcing the outskirts of **Jacksonville ㉓**.

Jacksonville is trying hard to remake itself as a new urban destination, and corporate headquarters are relocating here to take advantage of the excellent weather and pristine beaches. There are cultural attractions, too – the town is justly proud of its north and south bank **Riverwalks** and the associated **Museum of Science and History** (tel: 904-396-6674; www.themosh.org; daily), for example, while the **Cummer Museum of Art and Gardens** (tel: 904-356-6857; www.cummer.org; Tue–Sun except holidays) stands amid lush gardens right on the St Johns River.

Head south on I-95 to the indisputable jewel of northern Florida: **St Augustine ㉔**. Founded by Spanish

Taking it easy on a Georgia beach.

Salt marshes edging St Simons Island.

Shady porch on a rural Georgia log house.

Castillo de San Marcos, St Augustine, Florida.

explorers in 1565 and later occupied by the British, it is America's oldest continuously occupied city. Most of Downtown's buildings aren't nearly so ancient, but a pleasantly Mediterranean atmosphere has been preserved with narrow alleys, flowers, shops, and Spanish architecture. A number of museums and attractions compete for the traveler's attention – some boasting rather dubious "oldest this" or "oldest that" claims – and there are several excellent beaches and state parks just across the Lions Bridge, accessed from the city center.

The city's major attraction is the star-shaped 17th-century **Castillo de San Marcos** fort (tel: 904-829-6506; daily), right on the water, which defended the Spanish town from invaders. Nearby, **The Spanish Quarter** interprets 18th-century Spanish life with blacksmiths, woodworkers, and the like. A series of buildings constructed by oil and railroad magnate Henry Flagler is notable, particularly the **Memorial Presbyterian Church** that Flagler built in memory of his daughter. Finally, note the huge

round **zero milestone** across the road from the visitors' center: this stone marks the endpoint in a string of Spanish missions that once stretched all the way to San Diego. Old Town Trolley (tel: 888-910-8687) offers a fine tour of the city.

Gainesville

From St Augustine, head southwest out of town on Florida 207, passing beneath the interstate and then through fields of sweet potatoes, cabbages, and greens – you are back in deep-Southern farm country – across the broad St Johns River the highway becomes Florida 20. The route passes Newnans Lake, a beautiful spot to stop for a picnic, and comes directly into **Gainesville ㉕**, home to the University of Florida. Highlights include the Florida Museum of Natural History's Butterfly Rainforest (tel. 352-846-2000; www.flmnh.ufl.edu; daily).

US 441 exits the city south, shortly cutting right through the middle of **Paynes Prairie State Preserve** (tel: 352-466-3397; daily), a huge expanse of marsh and grassland bridged by the four-lane highway. Though located here in Florida, it aims to preserve some of the Great Plains species that once thrived in the wild, untamed west. Home to rare bison and cranes, among other creatures, the park offers glimpses of this lost world either through the viewing tower or from regular park-sponsored tours. Just south is tiny **Micanopy**, a town of dirt roads and simple buildings – an anomaly, something like how the old Florida must have looked.

For an even closer look at the state's recent past, take State Route 346 a few miles east, then follow signs south along Route 325 to **Cross Creek** – a tiny town, not even a town, really, but rather a place strongly identified with Florida author Marjorie Kinnan Rawlings. You can tour her former home, now part of Marjorie Kinnan Rawlings Historic State Park (tel: 352-466-3672; tours Oct–July Thur–Sun;

grounds open daily), where she penned her most famous work, *The Yearling*, and endured a tough life of farming and ranching. Highway 441 continues south through horse country to **Ocala** ㉖, a small Southern market town with a pretty square and several old-fashioned eateries. From Ocala, US 441 gets busy and inches through quiet lake towns, lush citrus groves, and sharp-smelling juice-processing plants. Soon enough, you enter the extensive suburbs announcing the most improbable Florida success story of all, **Orlando** ㉗ (see page 86).

SOUTH FLORIDA
Along the Gulf of Mexico

The vast majority of those travelers heading out from Orlando use the interstates and toll roads, but for more of the real Florida take the state highways a bit longer. Get off the beaten path (in this case the paved four-lane highway) and you'll see small-town life that hasn't changed for decades. Florida 50 (also called West Colonial Drive) leaves Orlando's city center and cuts due west, shedding the suburbs. In about 15 miles (24km), you come to Clermont, singular for its **Citrus Tower** (tel: 352-394-4061; Mon–Sat), where you can pay to ride an elevator 22 stories to the top for a view of the surrounding lakes and hills. Though eclipsed now by far more famous theme parks, the tower, built in 1956, was one of Florida's first tourist attractions.

Florida 50 now passes through the limestone spine of central Florida – a land of scrubby trees and prickly plants, sand dunes, citrus groves heavy with fruit in mid-winter, golf courses, even cowboys working cattle herds. Backroad stands sell everything from bovine medicine to boiled peanuts, and you'll also see plenty of churches in all the various denominations.

The route continues west, brushing the edge of Withlacoochee State Forest (tel: 352-754-6896; daily, visitor center Mon–Fri except holidays)

before arriving at whimsically named **Weeki Wachee** ㉘, famous with generations of tourists for its natural warmwater springs and "mermaid" shows. Today, the tradition lives on at Weeki Wachee State Park (tel: 352-592-5656; daily), where visitors can catch a water show, take a riverboat cruise, swim, boat, and see live animal shows.

If you're in a hurry to get a glimpse of the **Gulf of Mexico**, press west a few additional miles to tiny **Bayport** with its picnic area overlooking the water. Otherwise, turn south down US 19 and prepare for a spell of thick four-lane traffic and plenty of stoplights. Bring your baseball cap – during early spring, the area from Dunedin to Fort Myers (www.floridagrapefruitleague.com) is home to the training grounds for a number of major league baseball teams.

It's 30 miles (48km) down US 19 to the junction with Alt-19. Take Alt 19 to **Tarpon Springs** ㉙, a harbor community that is fascinating not for its physical appearance but its population: the town is largely Greek. Greeks originally settled this area to dive for the sponges that live abundantly in

Marmalade from local oranges makes a great gift.

Disney World's Epcot Center.

Orlando: The World's Best Playground

Not long ago, Orlando was just another agricultural town. Now it's Florida's best success story, a transformation made possible by a cartoon mouse.

Orlando's best known, best loved, and best reviled attraction is just southwest of the city. Walt Disney World (tel: 407-934-7639; www.disneyworld.disney.go.com; daily), with its four enormous complexes of entertainments, is thronged year-round by American and international tourists alike, and similar parks have sprung up around the globe.

The **Magic Kingdom** is Mickey Mouse's domain, and the original facility. It still remains the most popular with visitors of all ages, and is divided into four distinctive theme areas – Tomorrowland, Adventureland, Fantasyland, and Frontierland.

Cinderella Castle in Fantasyland at the Magic Kingdom.

Introduced by a glittering "geospherical" dome, the Future World exhibits at **Epcot Center** (the second part of the Disney complex) provide an invigorating look at science past, present, and future. The other half of Epcot is its World Showcase, where you can "travel the world" in less than a day through a variety of cultural (and culinary) attractions.

Rides and tours in the **Disney-MGM Studios** portion of the Disney World experience give a closer look at "show business," with perspectives as seen from both sides of the cameras. Disney's **Animal Kingdom**, the most recent addition to the Mickey Mouse empire is the largest of the parks, with over 1,700 animals representing 250 species. The park invites visitors to explore the world of animals on a safari, in a prehistoric world, and at special stage shows held throughout the day.

Not far from Disney World – but a completely separate entity – is **Universal Orlando Resort** (tel: 407-363-8000; www.universalorlando.com; daily). Opened the same year as Disney-MGM's facility, the resort offers a similar experience in its two theme parks, Universal's Islands of Adventure and Universal Studios Florida, where you will have the chance to learn more about live television and film production, with a number of exciting movie-themed rides thrown in as well. Look for the spotlights just west of I-4.

There are dozens of similar amusements scattered about the greater Orlando area. Water slides, weird museums, and amusement park rides are especially prevalent, and kids will go crazy with joy as parents just go crazy.

The most intriguing non-Disney non-movie-related non-theme-park attraction nearby isn't within the city limits at all, but is worth traveling the few extra miles to see. Approximately 40 miles (64km) to the east, on a sandy stretch known as Cape Canaveral, the **Kennedy Space Center** (tel: 321-452-2121; www.kennedyspace-center.com; daily) provides a fascinating up-close look at the workings of America's space program, and the Astronauts' Hall of Fame. If you're lucky, your visit will coincide with a space shuttle or rocket launch. When it doesn't, you can still tour the same runways, training areas, assembly buildings, and launch pads that NASA uses to prepare the crafts – and their crews – for flight. The center's popular "Lunch With an Astronaut" allows members of the public to spend an hour with one of NASA's Astronaut Corps (tel: 866-737-5235).

the warm surrounding seas, and today local shops and restaurants continue to reflect this heritage.

Past Dunedin, take Florida 60 west across the causeway to **Clearwater Beach**, a touristy town of seafood restaurants, motels, hotels, and resorts, and beach homes. It's a fine place to swim in warm water and lie on the beautiful – and public – white sand beaches.

Turn south down the beach road (which eventually becomes Florida 699). You will pass through more waterfront towns, most with excellent sand but some too overdeveloped for their own good. The finest beach on the entire string is probably the southernmost one, **Passe-a-Grille Beach**, some 20 miles (32km) of slow driving onward from Clearwater. Gawk at the huge pink **Don Ce Sar Hotel** an Art Deco masterpiece right beside the blue Gulf waters, then pass through the low-key village and hit the sand. For yet another magical beach experience, head over the toll bridge on Route 682 and turn right onto Route 679 to Fort De Soto Park (tel: 727-552-1862; daily); this 1,136-acre (459-hectare) swath of beach, wetlands and forest on Tampa Bay is a paradise for both nature and sun lovers (and there's even a historic fort to explore).

Tampa

In central downtown St Petersburg on Third Street the **Salvador Dalí Museum** (tel: 727-823-3767; www.the dali.org; daily) displays the country's largest collection of the artist's works and is without question the central cultural attraction of the city. East across Tampa Bay via either I-275 or US 92, and set right on the water facing St Pete, is **Tampa ㉚**. This city's Cuban influence is nowhere clearer than in **Ybor City**, with its concentration of Cuban restaurants and atmospheric cigar manufacturers. Ybor City was built on empty scrub by a local cigar maker in the late 1800s; now it still retains the Spanish influence, but

also sports posh pubs and some hot nightlife, and often hosts movie festivals and other cultural events.

Be a little bit careful here if you come after dark, but that doesn't mean you shouldn't venture out for a taste of what this city has to offer. Other city attractions include a full February slate of events, kicked off by a wild Mardi Gras-like parade, and Tampa Bay itself – best viewed during a stroll along the sidewalk arcing around upscale Bayshore Boulevard, or by zipping over the stunning Sunshine Skyway, a long suspension bridge that spans this beautiful body of water.

South from Tampa

Most visitors to Tampa also make a visit to **Busch Gardens** (tel: 888-800-5447; www.buschgardens.com/busch gardens/fla; daily), the area's "other" famous theme park, which will appeal to anyone who likes those sorts of things. The park features heart-dropping roller coasters, water slides, and simulated rapids, not to mention world-famous performances of water ballet, waterskiing skills, and the like.

TIP

Florida Gulf Coast's network of shallow coves and lagoons is great for sport fishing. Yet this is also a prime area for manatees, so boaters should be ever-vigilant and observe the signs and warnings to avoid collisions.

Locally caught sponges for sale, Tarpon Springs.

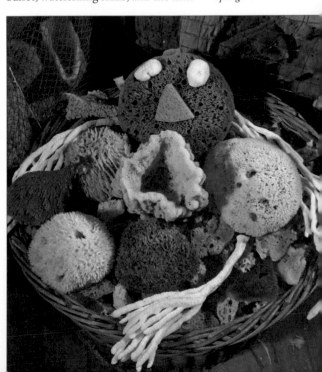

Take US 41 south out of Tampa, stopping a moment outside **Ruskin** where the Little Manatee River empties into the bay. As you'd expect from the name, you can sometimes find manatees frolicking at this inlet in winter, when they swim here to enjoy the warm water. In winter it's not uncommon to see dozens of them clustering around the outflow.

US 41 plunges due south through strings of heavily built-up towns and cities, many catering to retirees. A much faster route would take the parallel I-75.

Bradenton and **Sarasota** are next, twin cities on the Gulf of Mexico offering very favorable weather, spring baseball and more good sandy beaches with warm ocean water. Circus master John Ringling built his mansion, Ca' d'Zan on the Sarasota shore, and visitors to the Ringling Museum of Art (tel: 941-359-5700; daily) can tour the estate, which encompasses his mansion, art collection, and a circus exhibit.

The beaches continue through Siesta Key and Casey Key to **Venice** and beyond. The highway circles

SheiKra dive rollercoaster at Busch Gardens, Tampa.

around Charlotte Harbor and crosses the Caloosahatchee River into well-known **Fort Myers** ③. The mild climate has made this a popular winter resort town for a very long time; Northerners Thomas Edison and Henry Ford were neighbors on the riverfront, for example, and you can tour both the Edison & Ford Winter Estates (tel: 239-334-7419; www.edison fordwinterestates.org; daily) on one combined ticket. Highlights include the magnificently landscaped grounds and the Edison Ford Museum.

If you're in a mood to do some seashell collecting (known here as "shelling"), follow signs over the toll bridge to **Sanibel Island**. Sanibel may offer the finest shell collecting in all of America. Devotees come out here so frequently that someone coined a phrase to describe the parade of hunched-over collectors inspecting the backwash of each wave for new finds: they call this posture the "Sanibel stoop." It's possible to find a number of brightly colored shells here as well as the occasional fossilized shark's tooth.

The route continues south to exclusive **Naples** ㉜, haunt of the rich and the beautiful. Downtown is lined with elegant shops, restaurants, and outdoor cafés perfect for people watching. Most seem to be heading up Fifth Avenue to **Adelheidi's Organic Sweets** (tel: 239-304-9870; daily) for a homemade gelato. The 1888 Naples Pier is a historic landmark.

Into the Everglades

Now, you have a choice of routes to head east: either **Alligator Alley**, as the high-speed toll route of I-75 is known, or older US 41 (Tamiami Trail) farther south, which passes alongside the **Tamiami Canal** that connects the Atlantic Ocean with the Gulf of Mexico. Those wanting close-up views of North America's largest reptile will not be disappointed if they take the former route. The animals sun themselves in large numbers all along

the swampy canal. Pictures are easy to take, but watch for traffic as you too-dle along, and don't get too close to the water either – alligators can move surprisingly fast, and you do not want your last picture to be the one of you getting eaten.

US 41 cuts through the quiet and unspoiled heart of Florida. There are no towns because you are slowly penetrating the **Everglades** ㉝, a vast pocket of swampland partially pro-tected by law and difficult, in any case, to build on.

This strange landscape is home to alligators, venomous snakes, sinu-ous blackwater creeks overhung by lush vegetation, and probably a few desperado-like characters too; it also supplies the bulk of the drinking water to greater Miami. Authors, includ-ing Marjory Stoneman Douglas and Peter Matthiessen, have written about the unique people and creatures here in books like *River of Grass* and *Killer Mister Watson*, but the place to this day remains somewhat inscrutable. Susan Orlean's bestseller *The Orchid Thief* touches on this unique landscape

and its colorful characters in wonderful detail. You will see "Jaguar Crossing" road signs, and – if you are really lucky – perhaps even a real-life jaguar. And like all natural parks, the Everglades is a unique and fas-cinating area with a multitude of outdoor activities, although at certain times of year, the entire plain floods, sometimes by inches, sometimes by feet. It then grad-ually drains off into the Gulf of Mexico.

Nearby, at the **Miccosukee Indian Village/Resort** (tel: 305-552-8365), you can get supplies, stay overnight, gamble (it's legal within the reserva-tion), watch alligator wrestling, or take an airboat ride through the Everglades. But there is little mention of the tribe's history: heroic Seminole warriors like Osceola outfoxed Federal troops in these endless swamps for more than a year rather than surrender. Just a few miles east is one of the two main entrances to Everglades National Park (the other is in Homestead). At the Shark Valley Visitor Center (tel: 305-221-8776; daily), visitors can rent a

A hawksbill turtle just off Florida Keys.

Seminole children operating an airboat in the Everglades.

DETOUR TO LAKE OKEECHOBEE

A 58-mile (93km) drive along Florida 80 from Fort Myers brings you to Lake Okeechobee and its 750 sq miles (1,940 sq km) of crystal waters. Florida's largest lake is as beautiful as it is sad; the lake reflects the damage being done to the sensitive Everglades' environ-ment by the inexorably burgeoning population of Florida.

The water from Lake Okeechobee once fed the wide shallow river of the Everglades, but dikes, pumping stations, and canals were con-structed to tame this dramatic lake and its flooding waters. While this has made the surrounding area an agricultural paradise (the area produces enough sugar to supply the sweet tooth of 15 million Americans for an entire year), the projects have brought ecological hardships to the surrounding environment, and, to some degree, to the residents as well. Both the Everglades and South Florida's cities have been threatened with drought by the dwindling water level of the lake. Excessive pumping of the Everglades' mother waters for the booming population along the Gold Coast is also sucking it dry. Still a popular destination for anglers, fish camps punctuate the lake's perimeter. Okeechobee, the largest town on the north shore of the lake, is the best base if you want to explore the area. Boat trips can be easily arranged. For more information visit www.visitflorida.com/Okeechobee/Lake_Okeechobee.

Florida wildlife is not for feeding.

bicycle or board a tram for the 15-mile park loop.

FLORIDA KEYS

This string of tiny islands holds some of the world's most unique plant and animal life, and is where noted literati and glitterati have visited, put roots down, and decided to stay. The most famous is perhaps Ernest Hemingway, but numerous others have passed through, by, or lived here in the "Conch Republic." Recent decades have made it quite a hit with gay and lesbian travelers, perhaps in part because of the laid-back, carefree attitude that pervades (often referred to as "Keys Disease").

Don't come here expecting to fret and stress during your vacation. Find a beach chair and a spot in the sun, get a beverage of choice, and leave your worries at the doorstep... or better yet, leave your worries back home. Even the light is different here, a mysterious, turquoise shade of blue that reflects off everything it touches. It is a wonder, really, that these disparate islands are connected to each other

The Overseas Highway, Florida Keys.

or the mainland at all. Yet a series of 42 highway bridges does indeed bridge the many gaps between land and water.

From **Miami** ❸ (see page 92) US 1 proceeds south through the quiet community of **Homestead**. A branch road here, Florida 9336, leads through **Everglades National Park** (Ernest Coe Visitor Center; tel: 305-242-7700; www.nps/ever; daily) and offers glimpses of cypress swamp, grassland, mangroves, and more. Be sure to watch out for 'gators, and resist the temptation to put the pedal to the metal – the rangers are polite but zealous about tickets. Those with a sweet tooth will enjoy sampling Key Lime ice cream at the roadside stands.

Key Largo

Be sure to allow plenty of time if you're aiming to reach Key West. Much of the drive will be at or around 30mph (48kph). US 1 enters the Keys as the Overseas Highway at **Key Largo** ❸, immortalized in the Humphrey Bogart/Lauren Bacall film of the same name (which wasn't actually filmed here), and right away you get an opportunity to view the sea up-close. At **John Pennekamp Coral Reef State Park** (tel: 305-451-6300; www.pennekamppark.com; daily), one of the most popular parks in Florida, you can gaze through glass-bottomed boats at the most incredible formations of coral reef under the sea. Equally compelling are the fish and shellfish swimming and living throughout this delicate ecosystem. Snorkeling and diving are a must, and there are canoe and kayak rentals.

If this reef is the best place to see the nature of the Keys, the next park, **Long Key State Park** (tel: 305-664-4815; daily), some 30-odd miles (48km) farther along US 1, is your best bet for a swim or reclining in the sun before proceeding west. There is also a canoe and kayak rental.

For a lesson on what made the Keys into such a unique place, journey 20

more miles (32km) beyond Long Key to the best museum in the region, the **Crane Point Museum and Nature Center** (tel: 305-743-9100; www.cranepoint.net; daily) in the resort town of **Marathon** ㊱. Be sure to visit the museum's wild bird center. Marathon itself is more like a big town than an island paradise, and is best used for stocking up on supplies. As you leave Marathon, watch on the left for the Pigeon Key Visitor Center (tel: 305-743-5999; daily departures at 10am, 11.30am, 1pm, and 2.30pm) on Knight Key. Motorboats ferry visitors out to the Key which housed more than 400 workers for Flagler's railroad (it is also possible to walk here).

The mangrove forests thicken beyond here as nature begins reclaiming the westernmost islands. You will get plenty of water views on both sides of the car now as you cross **Seven Mile Bridge**, landing briefly on beautiful **No Name Key** and its **Bahia Honda State Park** (tel: 305-872-3210; www. floridastateparks.org/bahiahonda; daily) – yet another wonderful state-run park that offers snorkeling tours, kayaking, and an excellent beach. The Key Deer are an endangered species well worth stopping for and relatively easy to see, especially on No Name Key.

Key West

You cross more bridges still, landing on **Big Pine Key**, **Sugarloaf Key**, and **Looe Key**, each with its own personality and laid-back eateries. Eventually, the highway comes to rest upon balmy **Key West** ㊲, last island in the chain – and also the name of the town that has been drawing interesting characters for a very long time. Today, it's a mixture of fishermen, retirees, Cubans, and tourists, and a large gay and lesbian population.

The writer Ernest Hemingway lived here, and purveying "Papa's" image has become one of the town's hottest cottage industries. To get a taste of how he lived, visit the **Ernest Hemingway Home and Museum** (tel: 305-295-1575; www.hemingwayhome.com; daily), where the colourful writer lived for a decade; notable are the gardens he personally tended and the cats that overrun the place. Most are descended from the writer's own cats; others were strays who happened to know a good thing when they saw it. Duval Street – the hub of the town – is lined with tacky tourist shops, restaurants, and extremely noisy bars (several which were patronized by Hemingway himself). The writer's look-alike contest held every year is a highlight of the social season.

The two most popular sights in town, however, are both free. The first is **Mallory Square Dock**, where residents and tourists alike have been turning out every night for decades to cheer the beautiful sunsets over the water. The other is the brightly colored buoy that marks the **southernmost point** in the continental 48 states. Locals claim that on a very clear night you can even faintly make out the lights of Cuba, lying less than 100 miles (160km) away.

WHERE

No Name Key is one of the best places to see the rare, endangered Key Deer. A subspecies of the larger, mainland White Tail, the diminutive Key Deer's size is an adaptation to life on the Keys. These animals are often struck by cars and speed limits are strictly enforced; even if you are driving slowly however, keep a careful eye out to avoid hitting these rare animals. Other wildlife will also thank you.

Ernest Hemingway Home.

A SHORT STAY IN MIAMI

Sensual and warm, spicy and seductive, Miami appeals to the visitor who is longing for escape. Here's a list of the not-to-be-missed attractions.

Coral Gables is an enchanting Mediterranean-style neighborhood, home to the glorious **Biltmore Hotel** (1926) and the **Venetian Pool**, sometimes called "the most beautiful swimming hole in the world."

The Kampong, the house where David Fairchild lived, is a lush, tropical garden with numerous botanical wonders and Indonesian-inspired architecture and pools.

Coconut Grove is a vibrant, eclectic neighborhood of funky houses, dense natural greenery, and good shopping at **Coco Walk**.

I.M. Pei designed the futuristic **International Place**, a 47-story building in downtown Miami that changes color at the flick of a switch.

The **Wolfsonian** features an eclectic collection of art and miscellany that Mitchell Wolfson Jr collected during his lifetime.

Lummus Park combines the oldest structures in Miami (the **William English Slave Plantation House** and the **William Wagner House**) with a white-sand beach stretching along the coastline.

Vizcaya Museum and Gardens, the Italian Renaissance-style villa built in 1916 by industrialist James Deering, remains one of Miami's top tourist destinations.

Key Biscayne, an island paradise connected by bridge, offers many water-related recreations, like jet-skiing, windsurfing, and, of course, lying on your back under the sun.

Bill Baggs Cape Florida State Park, on the very tip of **Key Biscayne** and with a view of **Cape Florida Lighthouse**, has few facilities and little shade – just peace and solitude.

Art Deco District. Pastel-colored fantasies line Ocean Drive in South Beach.

Lifeguard hut on Miami Beach.

Mile after mile of golden sand, upscale communities, and the eye-catching architecture of Miami Modernism, known locally as MiMo, mean that Miami Beach is back on the scene.

CITY OF FANTASY

Miami is everything other cities are not – pastel colors, swaying palms, and Art Deco balconies are not only easy on the eye, but also kind to the disposition: it's impossible to fret when there's a fizzy cocktail on the table, a pink plastic flamingo on the counter, and a three-piece band playing loud and sassy salsa in your eardrums. If you're staying in South Beach, you can also leave your car behind and stretch those weary legs before getting them tanned on the sandy beach across the street. Or give yourself a workout surfing some of this area's best waves. Miami has a lot of things worth discovering. Just don't forget the sunscreen.

Beach volleyball on South Beach, the new American Riviera, where the buff, bronzed, and beautiful come to play.

IMPORTANT INFORMATION

Population: 400,000
Dialing codes: 305, 786
Website: www.gmcvb.com
Tourist information: Convention & Visitors Bureau, 701 Brickell Avenue, Suite 2700, FL 33131; tel: 305-539-3000

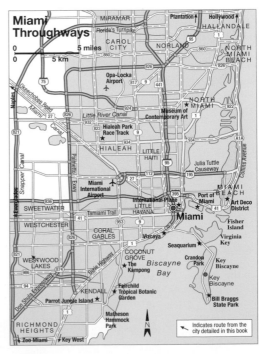

Skyscrapers of Chicago, Illinois.

The majesty of Wyoming's Grand
Teton National Park.

THE NORTHERN ROUTE

A detailed guide from east to west, with principal
sites clearly cross-referenced by number to the maps.

A Montana cowboy.

On our northern route between Boston and Washington state's Olympic Peninsula, you will encounter a collage of farmlands, ranches, wilderness, port towns, declining industrial cities, reborn urban centers, and constant reminders of the nation's history.

The first half of the journey is largely marked and guided by water. From Boston, you follow the Atlantic coast through New England up to Maine; later, from the Albany area, your route will swing west alongside the once-busy, now-dormant Erie Canal.

The Great Lakes dominate the next portion of the trip, including Chicago, the great Midwestern crossroads at the southern tip of Lake Michigan. From here to the thriving twin cities of Minneapolis and St Paul, the tour is never far from water, most significantly when it runs right beside the mighty Mississippi. Once you reach western Minnesota, however, the character of the land begins to change. As you cut across South Dakota, the geography overwhelms: rising out of the prairie are the otherworldly Badlands, the Black Hills, and Wounded Knee – a reminder of the nation's brutal treatment of Native Americans. Along a legendary stagecoach route come towns of the notorious Wild West. The sky here is huge and the land seems vast, characterized by small buttes and sagebrush. The route through Wyoming and Montana passes the site of Lieutenant Colonel Custer's last stand against Native American forces.

Brass sidewalk marker on the Freedom Trail.

From here, the tour passes into the northern Rocky Mountains with its gorgeous national parks. Crossing the Continental Divide on paths previously traveled by mountain tribes, gold prospectors, and homesteaders, the route cuts through the forests, lakes, and buffalo reserves of Montana, the Idaho panhandle and into the state of Washington, where the land modulates between deserts, canyons, and irrigated farmland.

The final portion of the route runs westward toward the Pacific Ocean through Seattle and the Olympic Peninsula. Suddenly, water is abundant again as you enter America's only rainforest. This wildly beautiful spot is an ideal place to reflect upon your just-completed trans-American journey.

A SHORT STAY IN BOSTON

The many colleges in this historic and attractive city ensure it retains a youthful, vibrant outlook. Here's a list of the not-to-be-missed attractions.

Full-scale replicas of three 18th-century ships – *Beaver II*, *Dartmouth*, and *Eleanor* – sit in the harbor at the **Boston Tea Party Ships and Museum**. They commemorate the 1773 dunking of taxed tea from Britain, an incident that fueled the flames of the American Revolution.

Built in 1676, the **Paul Revere House** is the oldest residence in downtown Boston; Revere lived here from 1770 to 1800. Exhibits include the saddlebags the patriot used on his famous midnight ride to warn of a British attack. One of 17 historic sites along Boston's Freedom Trail, the 1676 Paul Revere House is the city's oldest downtown residence. Exhibits include the saddlebags the patriot used on his 1775 midnight ride to warn of a British attack.

Since 1877 **swan-shaped boats** have been plying the **Public Garden lagoon**. Inspired by *Lohengrin*, the boats, which make lazy figure eights in the water, have been operated by the same family for three generations.

The oldest botanical garden in America, the **Public Garden** is Boston's prettiest green space. The focus is the lagoon, surrounded by willow trees and crossed by a mock suspension bridge.

Trinity Church, H. H. Richardson's 1877 masterpiece in **Copley Square**, is one of America's finest ecclesiastical buildings. Its wealth of murals, mosaics, carvings, and stained glass makes it Boston's most sumptuous interior space.

Opened in 1895, the **Boston Public Library** is a Renaissance Revival, masterpiece by Charles McKim, with a 1972 addition by Philip Johnson. The interior includes murals by John Singer Sargent and Puvis de Chavannes; the courtyard is reminiscent of 16th-century Italy.

The 1903 **Isabella Stewart Gardner Museum** has many architectural elements, from Venetian window frames to Roman mosaic floor tiles. The galleries hold paintings by Titian, Raphael, Degas, and Rembrandt.

Massachusetts State House. On July 4, 1795, Massachusetts Governor Samuel Adams and Paul Revere laid the cornerstone for the "new" State House. The building overlooks Boston Common and can be explored on a free guided tour.

Nichols House Museum. Housed in a splendid 1804 Federal-style townhouse attributed to Bulfinch, Nichols House is a true Beacon Hill period piece.

USS Constitution. Known as "Old Ironsides," the 1797 frigate won all 40 of the battles she fought. Still seaworthy, she is berthed in Charlestown.

THE BACK BAY CITY

"I have learned never to argue with a Bostonian," said poet Rudyard Kipling in the early 1900s, and that is still true now. By American standards, Boston is old. Cobbled streets lit by gas-lamps; National Historic Landmarks; individual buildings of great stature and charm. Fifty years ago, Boston was in danger of becoming a museum of living history, forever trapped in its 1700s and 1800s heyday. Then a change took place: the basin was cleaned, the buildings washed and, due to the high-tech industries of nearby Cambridge, businesses began to flock back. Boston is now modern-minded, so go check it out. And no arguing.

...owntown. To walk the streets of downtown Boston today is to ...alk with the ghosts of colonial settlers upon ground now ...adowed by modern skyscrapers. Street names have changed ...t the design is much the same as it was in the 1600s.

IMPORTANT INFORMATION

Population: 635,000
Dialing codes: 617, 857
Website: www.bostonusa.com
Tourist information: Greater Boston C&VB, 2 Copley Place, Suite 105, MA 02116; tel: 888-SEE-BOSTON

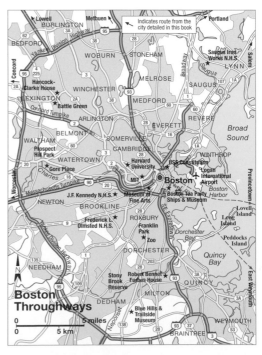

John Hancock building and Trinity church on Boston's Copley Square.

BOSTON TO BUFFALO

Take a drive through the prettiest parts of New England before beginning a coast-to-coast trek to the West, starting with the old route of the Erie Canal.

Beginning in downtown **Boston** ❶ (see page 100), the Northern route across the United States starts out by visiting "suburban Boston." This is accomplished by crossing the Charles River into busy **Cambridge** ❷ Cambridge's combination of old-fashioned leafy streets, active squares, and buzzing student life makes it one of Greater Boston's most interesting areas. The activity focuses around triangular **Harvard Square** and more rough-and-tumble but no less vibrant **Central Square**. While here, explore the brick buildings and carefully manicured greens of **Harvard University**, the second-oldest educational institution in the land; it was chartered back in 1636 and remains one of the finest universities in America, with museums such as Peabody Museum of Archaeology and Ethnology (tel: 617-496-1027; www.peabody.harvard.edu; daily) and Harvard Museum of Natural History (tel: 617-495-3045; www.hmnh.harvard.edu; daily).

The city's beautifully kept **Mount Auburn Cemetery** is worth seeing as well; its peaceful grounds harbor the remains of such artistic luminaries as Henry Longfellow, Oliver Wendell Holmes, and Winslow Homer.

Keep following signs for 2A, a scenic route that leads out from Massachusetts Avenue into quieter towns. You soon come to **Arlington**,

now suburban and high-tech but once a textile community where retreating British soldiers skirmished with local residents known as "Minutemen" (they were said to have been ready at a minute's notice to fight) in April of 1775 as the British backtracked along this road.

Paul Revere's ride

At **Lexington**, about 10 miles (16km) outside Boston proper, turn off State Route 2A into the downtown area for a look at the town green, the main stage of the Battle of Lexington on

Main Attractions

Boston
Salem
York
Nubble Light
Appalachian Trail
Norman Rockwell Exhibit
National Baseball Hall of Fame
National Women's Hall of Fame
Niagara Falls

Paul Revere statue, Boston.

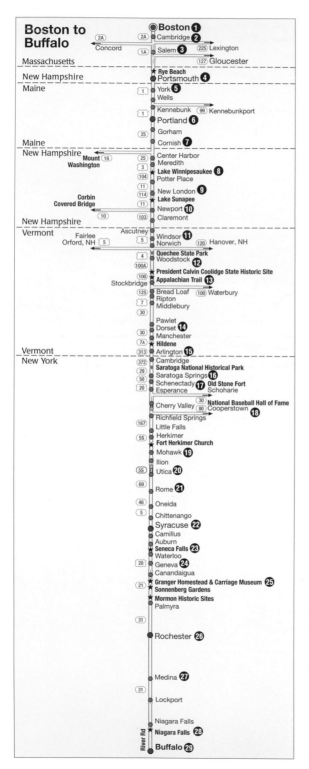

Boston to Buffalo

Massachusetts

New Hampshire

Maine

Maine

New Hampshire

New Hampshire

Vermont

Vermont

New York

◉ Boston **1**
Cambridge **2**
2A — Concord
2A
1A — Salem **3** — 225 Lexington
127 Gloucester

★ Rye Beach
Portsmouth **4**
1 — York **5**
Wells
1 — Kennebunk — 99 Kennebunkport
Portland **6**
25 — Gorham
Cornish **7**
Mount 16 — 25 Center Harbor
Washington — Meredith
3 — ★ Lake Winnipesaukee **8**
104 — Potter Place
11
Corbin — 114 — New London **9**
Covered Bridge — 11 — ★ Lake Sunapee
10 — 103 — Newport **10**
Claremont
Fairlee — Ascutney
Orford, NH 5 — 5 — Windsor **11**
Norwich — 120 Hanover, NH
4 — ◼ Quechee State Park
100A — Woodstock **12**
100 — ◼ President Calvin Coolidge State Historic Site
Stockbridge — ● Appalachian Trail **13**
125 — Bread Loaf — 100 Waterbury
7 — Ripton
30 — Middlebury
Pawlet
30 — Dorset **14**
Manchester
7A — ★ Hildene
313 — Arlington **15**
372 — Cambridge
◼ Saratoga National Historical Park
29 — Saratoga Springs **16**
50 — Schenectady **17** Old Stone Fort
20 — Esperance — Schoharie
30 — ◼ National Baseball Hall of Fame
Cherry Valley — 80 Cooperstown **18**
Richfield Springs
167 — Little Falls
5S — Herkimer
★ Fort Herkimer Church
Mohawk **19**
Ilion
5S — Utica **20**
69 — Rome **21**
46 — Oneida
5 — Chittenango
Syracuse **22**
Camillus
Auburn
★ Seneca Falls **23**
Waterloo
20 — Geneva **24**
Canandaigua
21 — ★ Granger Homestead & Carriage Museum **25**
★ Sonnenberg Gardens
★ Mormon Historic Sites
Palmyra
31
Rochester **26**
Medina **27**
31
Lockport
Niagara Falls
★ Niagara Falls **28**
Buffalo **29**
River Rd

that fateful morning of April 19, 1775. A number of statues and monuments commemorate this spirited American defense of their town, considered the opening battle of the American Revolution; silversmith Paul Revere had ridden his horse here from Boston under cover of night to warn the residents of a British attack. There are also several old taverns in the area, one of which – Munroe Tavern – served as the makeshift British hospital and command center during the battle.

Continue west along State Route 2A, where American Revolution events are further cataloged in the now-peaceful **Minute Man National Historical Park** (tel: 978-369-6993; www.nps.gov/mima; daily), which occupies both sides of the highway in a green patch just northwest of the village green.

Concord, the next town, was the scene of the second battle on that April morning. The site of the skirmish, at a bridge (now reconstructed) across the Concord River, is preserved as part of the Historical Park. Concord was a center of literature and philosophy during the 19th century, as evidenced by such prominent residents as Ralph Waldo Emerson, Henry David Thoreau, and Louisa May Alcott, among others. Alcott's former home, **Orchard House** (tel: 978-369-4118; daily), where she wrote *Little Women*, is first as you approach town, on the right. **Emerson House** (tel: 978-369-2236; mid-Apr–Oct Thur–Sun) comes next, less than half a mile beyond, with items from the life and work of the influential Transcendentalist thinker.

From the center of town, take Walden Street south a short distance to visit **Walden Pond State Reservation** (tel: 978-369-3254), a testament to Henry Thoreau's life, work and unique viewpoint. Thoreau built a simple cabin beside this pond in 1845 and lived there for a time, later writing *Walden* about the experience. "I went to the woods because I wished to live deliberately," he proclaimed, emerging with a view of nature as teacher – rather than slave – of man, and though the book sold poorly in his time, it has since become one of the enduring classics of American literature. The pond isn't nearly as peaceful as it was in his time, but you can still get a sense of what Thoreau must have felt.

HEART OF NEW ENGLAND

Before leaving Boston bound for the wild West, it's worth a short detour north first through the splendors of back-road New England, where America began and a delightful small-town neighborliness can still be felt today.

Begin, then, by heading north from downtown Boston on Route 1A (North Street from Downtown) toward **Salem ❸**. This sea town was one of the earliest capitals of the Massachusetts Bay Colony, and is filled with period captains' homes, several of which can be visited (Peabody Essex Museum; tel: 978-744-3390). It's more famous, though, for the **Salem Witch Trials** that began in 1692, an attempt to root out suspected witchcraft among local women and children; nearly two dozen were killed during the height of the frenzy – a symbol, ever after, for misplaced persecution. (The term "witch hunt," broadly applied to political activities, remains in the American lexicon today.) The **Salem Witch Museum** (tel: 978-744-1692; www.salemwitchmuseum.com; daily), beside the city's large central green, offers an explanation of the trials. Writer Nathaniel Hawthorne was born in one of the houses on the **House of the Seven Gables Historic Site** (tel: 978-744-0991; www/7gables.org; daily), on the city waterfront nearby; the famed gabled house about which he later penned the well-known novel is also there; its "official" name is the Turner-Ingersoll Mansion.

State Route 1A heads due north from Salem and continues on a scenic track through salt marshes, small drawbridges, farmland, and little fishing and commuter towns such as Ipswich, Rowley, and Newbury. Along the way, you may wish to detour east to **Gloucester**, the entrance to lovely Cape Ann and home port to large numbers of fishing and whale-watching boats.

New Hampshire and Maine

After entering **New Hampshire**, State Route 1A frees itself from ticky-tacky beach development to reveal the Atlantic itself at **Rye Beach** – your first true glimpse of the open ocean on this tour. Continue a few miles to **Portsmouth ❹**, New Hampshire's most attractive city and one with a salty taste.

Originally known as Strawbery Banke for the wild fruits covering the ground, Portsmouth was ideally situated at the meeting place of a river mouth and the ocean; founded in 1631, it has been a fishing and shipping center ever since. Fine old seamen's homes still crowd the downtown area, and while designer coffee shops and microbreweries are rapidly crowding out the old salts (this is only an hour's commute from Boston, remember) you can still find good clam chowder in the local diners.

The uniform of a Civil War sergeant of the 13th Massachusetts Volunteers.

Salem Witch Museum.

FACT

One-mile-high
(5,271ft/1,606-meter) Mt
Katahdin in Maine
signals the northern end
of the Appalachian Trail.

North across the Piscataqua River and its bridges lies **Maine**, the "Pine Tree State." Pull off busy US 1 after 6 miles (10km) to visit **York ❺**, Maine's first settlement, which possesses a clutch of old buildings (including an old jail) by the waterfront, all connected by the Cliff Walk coastal track. Most visitors come, however, for the stretch of good beach known as **Long Sands**, framed at one end by a much-photographed lighthouse, the Cape Neddick Light Station, known locally as **Nubble Light**. Buy exceptional locally made ice cream in the summer months from Brown's Old Fashioned Ice Cream, just uphill of the famous beacon; choose between blueberry, checkerberry (a New England berry tasting of wintergreen) or cinnamon flavors if they're in stock.

North again on US 1, **Wells** is a fairly forgettable beach town, but just north lies the **Wells National Estuarine Reserve** – a protected section of marshland on the sea. It incorporates the National Wildlife Refuge which commemorates scientist Rachel Carson, whose books about the ocean,

Portland Head Light, built on Cape Elizabeth in 1794.

songbirds, and ecology changed the way Americans thought about the natural world.

Portland and Cornish

Farther north, you hit the Kennebunks, two towns physically joined at the hip by a bridge but quite different in character. **Kennebunk** is more workaday, with an exclusive beach several miles east, while **Kennebunkport** is a slice of quaint, upper-crust New England – all gift shops, designer beers, and fish houses, and a bit rich for the blood. Former president George Bush Sr's family compound stands among dramatic shore rocks and crashing waves east of Downtown.

It's 20 more slow miles (32km) north along US 1 (or you can pay to take I-95) to **Portland ❻**, the state's largest city and cultural center. **Eastern Promenade Park** makes a good first stop, with its panoramic view of islands in the bay and part of the city's working waterfront. The **Old Port** district, once a maze of rough streets frequented by sailors, has been tidied up over the past few

decades and is now a lively quarter of boutiques and restaurants. The **Arts District**, where the **Victoria Mansion** (also known as the Morse-Libby House; tel: 207-772-4841; May–Oct) on Danforth Street stands as an excellent example of Victorian architecture. Or take a ferry to tranquil little **Peaks Island** for a closer look at the sea. Back in the center of town, the **Portland Museum of Art** (tel: 207-775-6148; www.portlandmuseum.org; June–Sept Tue–Sun, Oct–May Mon–Sun) sometimes hangs good exhibits and has a permanent collection of Winslow Homer's work. Just watch the time on your parking meter: ticketers around town are needlessly ruthless.

From Portland, quieter Route 25 cuts swiftly west through suburbs and then rolling farmland. The town of **Gorham** is little more than a four-way intersection and the rural main campus of the University of Southern Maine; stay on Route 25, proceeding through more small towns. At East Limington, the bridge crosses the Saco River, a superb canoeing river that winds from deep in western Maine to the sea. A free park on the left-hand side of the road here provides a scenic picnic spot; rocks make for good sunning, and a pathway leads downriver to a small swimming beach, out of the sometimes-swift current.

Farther west, the route passes through more countryside to **Cornish** ❼, one of western Maine's very handsome towns. The activity here is focused around a small triangular green space lined with small shops and a hardware store, most in typical whitewashed New England fashion. Each September, an annual apple festival showcases local pies, cider, and other apple products on the town common – with the apple pie contest held on the porch of the venerable Cornish Inn that stands beside the green. The best part comes after the judging, when all pies – winners and losers – are auctioned off to lingering spectators.

Lake country

Keep to Route 25 as it jogs west into New Hampshire, the "Granite State," then briefly north; if you kept going north on Route 16, you would soon pass **Mount Washington**, at 6,288ft (1,917 meters) the tallest peak east of the Mississippi – and home to the highest recorded winds on the planet.

At West Ossipee, however, make a turn inland again and follow Route 25 through Moultonborough, **Center Harbor** – whose little general store features New Hampshire's Squamscot soda – and finally **Meredith**, a resort town with the Annalee Doll Museum, set on big, pretty **Lake Winnipesaukee** ❽, New Hampshire's largest body of water.

Head south a short while on US 3 as the road passes right beside the lake. Going uphill as you leave the town, bear right to take state Route 104 through small, typically New Hampshire towns. At Danbury, cut south on US 4 a short distance to Route 11, and then turn west again just after **Potter Place**.

It's only 10 miles (16km) more to the prim town of **New London** ❾

The lobster fishing industry contributes greatly to Maine's economy. The majority are caught between late June and late December.

Lobster boats in Maine.

A typical New England covered bridge, Vermont.

(turn right onto Route 114 just past Elkins), which has a fine central green and good views of the surrounding hills and mountains. This is known locally as a college town, with attractive Colby-Sawyer College located right next to the village green. This former women's college was long one of America's few remaining single-sex institutions of higher education, and became co-educational only in 1990. Connecting with Route 11 from Route 114, the road passes through the hamlets of Georges Mills (a general store, coves on either side of the road and little more) and the lake town of Sunapee, with a pretty harbor on **Lake Sunapee** – reputedly one of the cleanest lakes in America, and one circled by hills of hardwoods.

Six more miles (10km) east on Route 11, **Newport** ❿ spreads out in the Sugar River Valley, a small textile and arms manufacturing town with an old opera house, wooden covered bridge, and the handsome rectangular "town common" so typical of older New England towns. These green pastures once served as common grazing spaces for local livestock, but today serve mostly as the settings for soccer matches, carnivals, and farmers' markets.

Newport is perhaps best known for Sarah Josepha Buell Hale (1788–1879). Despite early tragedies including the loss of her mother, sister, and husband, Hale rose to prominence in Boston and Philadelphia as one of America's early feminists and female editors. She advocated education and equal opportunity for women, convinced President Abraham Lincoln to create Thanksgiving Day and penned the popular children's nursery rhyme "Mary Had a Little Lamb." Her birth home is on Route 11 a few miles before you enter town, across the street from a once-famous woolen mill.

Connecticut Valley towns

For a look at the **Corbin Covered Bridge**, drive through Newport's main street and continue north on Route 10 for a mile or so, then turn left, passing the town airport and driving through a corridor of pine trees. The bridge at the edge was constructed as a copy to replace the original jewel, which was burned by a thoughtless arsonist in 1993. Such bridges are sprinkled throughout New England, their distinctive design a way to delay the wood rotting as creosote wasn't around. They were also, some say, a method of keeping horses drawing carriages from being spooked by rushing rivers below.

The craftsman who built this particular bridge was such a perfectionist for detail that he copied the original design and then hauled the bridge to its Sugar River home with an oxen team – both to transport it undamaged and to preserve a sense of history.

From central Newport, Route 103 proceeds west through **Claremont**, previously a fading mill city that is redeveloping its old decaying riverside mill buildings. The historic Opera House located on Opera House Square has

year-round performances from opera and theater to comedy and music. Just west of the city, the highway crosses the broad and picturesque Connecticut River dividing New Hampshire from its similar-sized (but very different-thinking) cousin, Vermont.

At **Ascutney**, on the far side of the river, the antenna-topped peak of Mount Ascutney fills the eye; Vermont 5 keeps it to one side and the broad Connecticut River to the other as it heads due north. Shortly thereafter, the road arrives in **Windsor ⑪** – a town that rightly claims itself the "Birthplace of Vermont." In Elijah West's tavern on Main Street, now known as **Old Constitution House** (tel: 802-672-3773; late May–mid-Oct Sat–Sun), Vermont's Constitution was drafted and signed in 1777, making it for a time an independent republic that was neither British nor American. This independent streak still marks Vermonters today – in the 1990s, they elected and re-elected a socialist, Bernie Sanders, to sit in the US House of Representatives. And in 2005, Sanders became the first socialist Senator.

The **Simon Pearce** glassblowing shop, also in Windsor, may be one of the nation's finest such shops. The establishment also operates a restaurant on Main Street in **Quechee**, serving meals on glassware from the shop.

Still heading north on Vermont 5, you dip and curve riverside and soon enough come to **Norwich**, a tiny, typical Vermont town with its classic general store – the first of many you'll see on this drive. Near the interstate, the local **King Arthur Flour Baker's Store** sells the company's superior stone-milled flour, plus some top-grade cooking supplies and cookbooks, at a picturesque store on Vermont 5. Outside town, the **Montshire Museum of Science** (tel: 802-649-2200; www.montshire.org; daily) provides children with a terrific hands-on look at ecology and nature amid riverside fields.

Ivy-clad Dartmouth

Cross the Connecticut River into New Hampshire once more on Route 120 to **Hanover**, an attractive town largely thanks to the elegant, ivy-clad presence of **Dartmouth College**. Dartmouth was founded in 1769 by the Reverend Eleazer Wheelock to educate (and, of course, convert) local Native American children. Now, it is one of America's finest private colleges, with especially strong programs in the sciences, humanities, and Native American studies. The pleasing Dartmouth Green is a center of town life, surrounded on all sides by college buildings, including the **Hopkins Center** performing arts space – designed by Wallace K. Harrison, lead architect of New York's Lincoln Center and UN Headquarters.

The downtown district also features the excellent Dartmouth Bookstore, as well as one of New England's most-beloved natural food cooperatives. It is not unusual to see haggard, unshaven hikers lugging huge backpacks tramping through town, either, as the bridge from Norwich and downtown Hanover form one of the

Famous Dartmouth College alumni include Daniel Webster, Robert Frost, Theodore "Dr" Seuss, and Nelson Rockefeller.

Kids will love the tour of Ben & Jerry's ice-cream factory in Waterbury, Vermont.

It is estimated that walking the entire length of the Appalachian trail requires 5 million steps.

Killington Resort has reliably good snowfall and a long season.

most civilized stretches of the entire Appalachian Trail.

For a little more of New England character before moving west, continue farther north on Vermont 5, which snuggles between the interstate and the river, mostly passing through dairy pastures and cornfields. Several of the small towns have interesting gathering spots, such as the Fairlee Diner (see page 434) in **Fairlee**, Vermont. Across a small bridge from Fairlee, in **Orford**, New Hampshire, beautiful white wooden and red brick homes from the early 1800s – not to mention the Orford Social Library and a general store full of local characters – line the town's main street. It was from here that local car salesman Mel Thomson rose to become a multi-term governor of the state, never straying from his extremely Republican view of things. On summer weekends, the **Mount Cube Sugar House**, in the hills east of Orford down Route 25A, serves huge breakfasts with their own maple syrup: a delicious taste of the region that should not be missed if you are in the area. Locals swear by them.

From Hanover, cross back to Vermont and proceed a short distance south before turning west on US 4 at White River Junction. You soon come to little Quechee, nondescript but for deep **Quechee Gorge**. This 165ft (50-meter) cut in the rock, made by the Ottauquechee River, is accessible from several viewpoints; you can't hike down the steep, narrow walls, but you can hike the woods and camp in a state park across the street.

Woodstock

Ten miles (16km) beyond, compact **Woodstock** ⑫ sits prettily among trees, ridges, and river. On an autumn afternoon, the town is jammed tightly with leaf-peepers touring the area to view the fall foliage, but early October is the time to come – an annual chili cook-off and apple festival, and other autumn events compete with the stunning foliage. From Downtown, it is just a few paces to the handsome **Middle Bridge** covered bridge, which is located beside a row of exceptionally fine homes surrounding the village green.

The Woodstock Historical Society leads tours of some of these homes that encircle the central common, and two outstanding museums nearby – the **Billings Farm & Museum** providing a look at 19th-century dairy farming (tel: 802-457-2355; www.billingsfarm.org; May–Oct daily, Nov–Feb Sat–Sun) and the **Vermont Institute of Natural Science** (tel: 802-359-5000; May–Oct, Nov–Apr Wed–Sun), with its good record of nursing birds of prey back to health – provide additional diversion. The Marsh-Billings-Rockefeller National Historical Park (tel: 802-457-3368; grounds: daily, tours: June–Oct) is a 500-acre (202-hectare) preserve crowned by the sumptuous home of the late Laurance Rockefeller, the park's benefactor. Just 2 miles (3km) west of town via US 4, the community of **West Woodstock** already has a slightly less manicured feel. The seasonal White Cottage

Snack Bar serves up fried clams, ice cream, and similar summertime snacks, while the Woodstock Farmers' Market purveys gourmet foods next door. Drive several more miles to **Bridgewater Corners**, home of the Long Trail Brewing Company and its locally popular Long Trail Ale.

Turn left onto Route 100A for a beautiful little detour through some of the state's nicest scenery – past hay bales and syrup signs, red barns, spotted cows, and grazing horses: pure Vermont. The stretch is particularly beautiful when leaves are changing color. About 6 miles (10km) along, take a right onto the dirt drive for a look at the **President Calvin Coolidge State Historic Site** (tel: 802-672-3773; www.historicsitesvermont.gov/coolidge; end May–mid-Oct daily), the farm homestead where "silent Cal" was raised and to which he periodically returned.

When President Warren G. Harding died in office in 1923, Coolidge was sworn into office on the spot here by his father, a notary public. He remains to this day a hero to Vermonters, symbol of a kind of taciturn, humanistic work ethic that still drives Vermont farmers and politicians alike.

Green mountains and southern Vermont

Continue on Route 100A until it ends at Route 100, making a right and driving north. You pass numerous bed-and-breakfasts in the agreeable small towns; if you're in a hurry to get west, turn left where Routes 100 and Route 4 diverge at **Killington** and cut through the scenic mountains to Rutland. Near this junction is where two of America's famous hiking trails – the **Appalachian Trail** ⑬ (see page 111) and Vermont's **Long Trail** – diverge. If you continue north on Route 100 for a short distance, you can park and take a short stroll on the trail to the left (through Gifford Woods State Park) or the right, around the shore of Kent Pond.

Heading north on Route 100, continue through little **Stockbridge** until Route 100 connects with Route 125, then make a choice: food or nature? If you have a sweet tooth, continue north

Bright fall foliage heralds the "leaf-peeper" season.

APPALACHIAN TRAIL

A pleasant 19-mile (31km) drive along Route 100A, then Route 100, from the town of Bridgewater Corners, Vermont, leads to one of the longest marked footpaths in the world, winding a total of 2,178 miles (3,505km) from Maine to Georgia. Benton MacKaye, who proposed the trail in 1921, wrote about his great project: "The ultimate purpose? There are three things: 1) to walk; 2) to see; 3) to see what you see... Some people like to record how speedily they can traverse the length of the trail, but I would give a prize for the ones who took the longest time." His idea was for a super-trail running the length of the industrialized East Coast. This would be a trail that was wild, yet within reach of major urban centers and the throngs of workers who were alienated from outdoor life. He felt the trail would grace all who spent time on it with the healing tonic of wilderness.

Winding from north to south, it traverses the many distinct ranges that make up the Appalachian chain, touching the tops of many of the states it enters. Though not the first of its kind, the Appalachian Trail remains a favorite with outdoors people, enjoying celebrity status among the great hikes of the world. For more information, call the Appalachian Trail Conservancy on tel: 304-535-6331 or visit www.appalachiantrail.org.

FACT

The illustrator Norman Rockwell (1894–1978) was known for his realistic and humorous scenes of small-town life. His best work appeared as covers for the magazine *The Saturday Evening Post*.

West Arlington covered bridge.

up Route 100 to **Waterbury** and take a tour of the Ben & Jerry's ice-cream factory. A more scenic route, however, is to turn left onto Route 125 to begin 13 gorgeous miles (21km) of national forest land. You will discover why it's been designated a state scenic route as you wind through **Green Mountain National Forest**. Partway along, just before **Ripton**, pull over for a peek at several Robert Frost-related sites.

Frost, one of America's best-loved poets, moved to this area and wrote his finest poetry in a farmhouse here. **Bread Loaf**, the complex of yellow buildings on the right, is a campus of Middlebury College that becomes an internationally famous school of writing each summer; the yellow Bread Loaf Inn offers lodging on-site. The **Robert Frost Interpretive Trail**, on the left, combines passages from his writing with the typical elements – stone walls, maple trees – that inspired it. There are also a number of impressive hikes off the main road, clearly signposted, although to reach them requires driving some rough gravel and dirt roads. The twisty final miles

of Route 125 snake down the western slope of the Green Mountains beside the Middlebury River and must be driven carefully, but they are rewarded with a stunning view of the misty stacks of the Adirondacks as the route coasts down into the village of East Middlebury. At US 7, turn right and enter **Middlebury**, a college town with its own handsome buildings and microbrewery.

Now, we head south on Route 30, which angles almost due south. It's delightful driving through classic Vermont scenes of grazing spotted cows, rivers, red barns, and the like. You pass several quiet lakes with good camping grounds, then through **Pawlet**, which possesses one of Vermont's best country stores, now called Mach's: among the wooden iceboxes of beer and stacks of rakes and rubber boots, you can actually see the brook running beneath the store through a grate. It was once a hotel, and there's a sepia 1900s photograph of dapper men with mustaches who once stayed at the place.

Next comes East Rupert, and then **Dorset ⓮**, an attractive town with a golf course and summer theatre close beside classic New England homes, many of which are now characteristic bed-and-breakfast establishments.

Shopping, history, and art

Crowds begin appearing again in **Manchester**, a tourist-filled town nestled on the **Battenkill River**, itself one of the world's finest fly-fishing rivers. You can learn more at the **American Museum of Fly Fishing** (tel: 802-362-3300; Tue–Sat), which displays the rods and gear of famous fishermen like Hemingway and Eisenhower, among others. Not surprisingly, this is also home to the outdoor equipment and clothing manufacturer Orvis and loads of other shops – many of them discount outlets for famous fashion brands.

Breeze right through town and continue south down Route 7A, here

known as "Historic 7A," as it passes **Hildene** (tel: 802-362-1788; www. hildene.org; daily), the former home of Abraham Lincoln's son, Robert Todd Lincoln. This beautiful Georgian Revival mansion features a huge pipe organ. The road then takes in the pleasing ridge of **Mount Equinox**, especially stunning in fall. A toll road rises to the top, if you wish to drive it. Apple orchards, meadows, and cows continue to be the prevailing themes along Route 7A.

At **Arlington** ⑮, you can have a look at the famed **Norman Rockwell Exhibit** (tel: 802-375-6423; Feb–Dec daily), a collection of the artist's work. The artist lived in two homes in this area, and locals often served as models for his so-American portraits.

Turn west onto Route 313, and as you leave town and Vermont, there's one final treat: just before the New York border you pass by the covered **West Arlington Bridge**, a small bridge over the Battenkill with a plain, typical New England church behind – a composition Rockwell himself was said to have especially loved. As these are a local specialty, this is the last one you'll see on this cross-country trip. Linger awhile contemplating the river – and the New England – you have seen.

NEW YORK STATE

As you greet the sign welcoming you to **New York** state, you have not only crossed a line on a map separating one state from another. You have also crossed an imaginary, but no less real, boundary where yard sales at once become tag sales, tonic becomes soda, and an "Empire State" mindset takes over from the "think small" Vermont mentality. Entering the Hudson Valley, you'll also discover a history forged by Dutch settlers rather than New England Yankees.

Entering on Route 313, you arrive shortly at a pleasant picnic spot beside the Battenkill River. Then you pass through **Cambridge**, a small town with antiques and an attractive little general store, more form than function these days. You'll also pass the Cambridge Hotel, built in 1885, self-proclaimed home of "pie à la mode."

Fresh spring water from Saratoga Springs.

Race meeting at Saratoga race course.

*Actors by the
encampment tents at a
Revolutionary War
re-enactment in
Mohawk Valley.*

Change to Route 372, join Route 29 and continue driving west. Ten or 12 miles (16 to 19km) on, the road crosses the **Hudson River** at Schuylerville, unimpressive here since it's split up into so many parts; in fact, the great river seems tame indeed – there is no hint yet of the power and beauty that will soon fill a great valley and inspire countless artists.

It was only a few miles downstream from these banks that the two Battles of Saratoga were fought in 1777, resulting in a crushing defeat of British troops – a crucial momentum swing in the Revolution. A turnoff leads to the **Saratoga National Historical Park** (tel: 518-664-9821; www.nps.gov/sara; battlefield: daily, tour road: Apr–Nov daily), commemorating the battles, where you can drive or be guided through the fields.

Continue to **Saratoga Springs** ⑯, long a resort town due to the mineral springs that bubble up from beneath it and more recently a popular weekend town. It is also home to Skidmore College students and faculty, and thus a fair number of coffeehouses, ice-cream shops, and bookstores speckle the downtown district. The Saratoga Performing Arts Center, within a green park on the southern edge of town, frequently hosts big-name concerts. Summertime also brings crowds to the harness track here, where horse racing is king – witness the presence here of the **National Museum of Racing and Hall of Fame** (tel: 518-584-0400; www.racingmuseum.org; Apr–Oct daily, Nov–Dec Tue–Sun, Jan–Mar Wed–Sun). Finally, don't miss **Caffé Lena**, an upstairs joint on a central street, which is said to have been the first American coffeehouse to host regular folk music performances. It still does.

Erie Canal

Route 50 brings you south through Ballston Spa, home of the eccentric **National Bottle Museum** (tel: 518-885-7589; June–Sept daily, Oct–May Mon–Fri), to the Mohawk River and the Erie Canal. Tracing this great inland water route west to Buffalo is not the shortest way to get from here to there, but it is a route that runs rich with American history.

The idea of a canal connecting the port cities of Albany (on the Hudson River) and Buffalo (on Lake Erie) was greeted with skepticism and derision at first. Detractors called it "Clinton's Ditch" after New York Governor DeWitt Clinton, champion of the project. Completed in 1825, and eventually bypassed in the early 20th century, the Erie Canal was responsible for the settling of the Midwest and the rise of the state of New York. The old canal towns, once the sites of boisterous activity, are quiet now, many down on their luck.

Begin tracing the route in **Schenectady** ⑰. A plaque in this town sums up its early history: "Settled by Van Curler 1661. Burned by French and Indians Feb 8, 1690."

Because it was the farthest west of all Dutch settlements in the New World, the town's settlers built a

stockade around the land, which was bounded by the Mohawk River and a branch called the Binne Kill. The stockade is now gone, dismantled during the American Revolution, but the area it protected is still known as the **Stockade** and is now a historic district containing an eclectic array of buildings that spans over three centuries of American life.

Schenectady's strategic riverfront location has historically made it an important center for commerce and transportation. The city supplied Revolutionary troops battling in the Mohawk Valley, and in the 19th century it was a major port. In 1931, it became the terminus of the nation's first passenger steam train, the "DeWitt Clinton," an innovation stimulated by the protracted process of traversing the 23 locks between Albany and Schenectady.

Schenectady has not been exempt from the exodus of industry out of the Northeast. In the 19th century, it progressed from being a center for the manufacture of brooms, to "the city that lights and hauls the world." The Schenectady Locomotive Works (later the American Locomotive Company) opened in 1851, followed by Edison and his Machine Works – which later became General Electric. The Locomotive Company pulled out of town in 1969, but the lights are still switched on at GE.

Leatherstocking trails

New York's heartland is generally considered to begin west of the industrial triangle of Albany, Troy, and Schenectady. This essentially rural area north of the Catskill Mountains and south of the Adirondacks is also known as the **Leatherstocking District**, after the protective garb once worn by trailblazers. Native son James Fenimore Cooper immortalized the region in his *Leatherstocking Tales* and other works. And the numerous Revolutionary War battles that took place throughout the Mohawk River

Valley are the subject of Walter D. Edmonds' historical novel *Drums Along the Mohawk*.

Schenectady's Broadway leaves town in a southwesterly direction (Route 7). It passes through Rotterdam and Duanesburg, where Route 7, US 20 and I-88 converge. From there, US 20 travels to **Esperance** on Schoharie Creek. This pleasant town features old houses, antique shops and the obligatory country store. About 8 miles (13km) south of here along Route 30, which follows the creek, is the town of **Schoharie**, the third-oldest village upstate. Its **Old Stone Fort Museum Complex** (tel: 518-295-7192; July–Aug daily, May–June, Sept–Oct Tue–Sun) started as a church in 1772, became a fort during the Revolution, and has served as museum and library specializing in early Americana since 1889.

An interesting chapter out of Schoharie's past includes the Middleburgh and Schoharie Railroad, built in the late 1860s. This short, 5.7-mile (9.2km) run down the Schoharie Creek Valley transported hops and other local products. The railroad's

Cooperstown village.

president was fond of pointing out that although it wasn't as long as other railroads, it was just as wide. In its last days, the line's single locomotive faltered physically and financially, and operation was finally stopped in 1936.

A shrine to baseball

US 20 west of Sharon and Sharon Springs is one of the loveliest stretches of road in central New York, providing a panoramic view of **Cherry Valley**, the site of an infamous massacre in 1778, now crimson only in autumn.

It would be a mistake not to detour 10 miles (16km) south at Springfield Center down Route 80 to visit **Cooperstown** ⑱, a charming town with several important attractions. The Fenimore Art Museum (tel: 607-547-1400; Apr–mid-May, Oct–Dec Tue–Sun, mid-May–early Oct daily) and Farmers Museum (tel: 607-547-1450; times same as Fenimore Museum) are worthwhile, but the main draw is the **National Baseball Hall of Fame** (tel: 607-547-7200; www.baseballhall. org; daily) – a tremendous experience of the history of the sport, which has

Patriotic Paul Revere mural in Rome, New York state.

inspired countless novels, films, and even poems. Make time for a visit to the monuments, biographies, and collections here.

Past **Richfield Springs**, known for its sulfur springs and fossil-hunting grounds, Route 167 travels north toward **Little Falls**. Not far up this road stands the **Russian Orthodox Holy Trinity Monastery**, startling to the eye in a land of colonial history, 19th-century buildings and rustic farmhouses. Little Falls' **Herkimer Home**, former residence of Revolutionary War hero Brigadier General Nicholas Herkimer, provides a glimpse of colonial life, with maple sugar gathering, sheep shearing, and other exhibitions. This canal town once had the world's highest lock, at 41ft (12.5 meters).

West along Route 5 is Herkimer, named after Nicholas Herkimer, the American Revolutionary War general whose statue still commands attention. The **Herkimer County Courthouse** was the site of the Gillette murder trial, which inspired Theodore Dreiser to write *An American Tragedy*, depicting the dark side of the American dream. George Stevens' film version, *A Place in the Sun*, featured Montgomery Clift, Shelley Winters, and Elizabeth Taylor. Between Herkimer and **Mohawk** ⑲, along Route 5S, stands the **Fort Herkimer Church**, built in 1730.

Ilion, a small industrial pocket, is located just beyond Mohawk. The interesting **Remington Firearms Plant and Museum** (tel: 315-895-3200; museum: Mon–Fri, plant tours: Memorial Day–Labor Day Mon–Fri) here is devoted to the great guns made by Remington Arms Company, past and present. Continuing west, the road terminates in **Utica** ⑳, the only city of any size you will have seen since Schenectady.

Utica, once named Fort Schuyler, is rich in colonial and revolutionary history. But the biggest attraction here is the **Munson-Williams-Proctor Arts Institute** (tel: 315-797-0000; www.

mwpai.org; Tue–Sun), reputed to have one of the finest collections of 18th- through 20th-century American and European art in the northeast, housed in a building designed by Philip Johnson. On a much less cultural note, Utica's **Matt Brewery** (tel: 315-732-0022; tours: June–Aug Mon–Sat, Sept–May Fri–Sat) serves its beer up in a Victorian-era tavern built in 1888. It's all part of a brewery tour that culminates in a trolley ride to the tavern.

Erie Canal Village

Route 69 leaves Utica for **Rome ㉑**, best known for its crucial role in the building of the Erie Canal. Beyond this point, there were no continuous natural water routes westward. This is where excavation began. Commemorating this important chapter in its history is the **Erie Canal Village** (tel: 315-337-3999; www.erie canalvillage.net; Memorial Day–Labor Day Wed–Sat), a reconstructed 1840s village near a refurbished section of the old canal. The biggest tourist attractions here are a ride on a narrow-gauge railroad train; the Hudson Museum of horse-drawn vehicles; the New York State Museum of Cheese; and a museum telling the story of the great canal itself.

The canal brought industry to Rome, some of which remains. Rome has always been serious about America: this, after all, is where native son Francis Bellamy wrote the famous "Pledge of Allegiance" that every American school child learns by heart.

Route 46 takes you from Rome to **Oneida**, still home to the Oneida Indians. The Oneida Community – associated with this town, but actually just southeast in Sherrill – was established in the mid-19th century by John Humphrey Noyes and his followers. Calling themselves perfectionists, they adhered to a strict sexual code as part of a community-determined system of selective breeding. In their spare time, they produced high-quality silver-plated flatware. The community was dissolved in 1881, but the silver-plate business continues to thrive.

From Oneida, **Chittenango** is a short drive along Route 5. Don't be surprised, in town, to see a yellow brick sidewalk, for this is "Oztown, USA." The sidewalk is a tribute to L. Frank Baum, author of the beloved *Wizard of Oz*. Stay on Route 5 and it will lead right into Syracuse, the biggest city for miles around in these parts.

Finger Lakes

Busy **Syracuse ㉒** is the urban gateway to the Finger Lakes. Route 5 becomes Erie Boulevard as it cuts through the heart of the city along a path carved by the Erie Canal. The **Weighlock Building**, built in 1849 in Greek Revival style, once weighed canal boats for the purpose of toll collection. At the turn of the 20th century, it was converted into an office building, while in its most recent reincarnation it serves as the **Erie Canal Museum** (tel: 315-471-0593; www.eriecanalmuseum.corg; daily).

Thanks to the canal, this was once a center for the salt trade, and some

EAT

Try a *pustie* (short for *pasticciotti* – an Italian custard-filled tart), one of Utica, New York's signature dishes.

Clinton Square in Syracuse, New York state.

TIP

In Auburn, New York, be sure to visit the Harriet Tubman home. Tubman was an escaped slave who coordinated a network called the Underground Railroad to spirit other slaves out of the South.

The impressive 16-sided Nott Memorial Building on Schenectady's Union College campus integrates symbols from major world religions.

still refer to it as "Salt City." The town boomed during the 19th and early 20th centuries on the back of salt and other industries, and its well-preserved architecture testifies to former prosperity. The **Landmark Theatre**, an ornate "fantasy palace" built in the 1920s, now functions as a multi-dimensional entertainment center. But the main draw here today is **Syracuse University**, elevated on a hill above the city, which brings crowds of students, sports fans, and other audiences to its huge **Carrier Dome**. Basketball games are especially well-attended, though football games and rock concerts follow a close second. For the more sedate, the campus also offers the **SUArt Galleries**. Those same art lovers also should not miss the **Everson Museum of Art** (tel: 315-474-6064; www.everson.org; Tue–Sun), designed by renowned architect I.M. Pei. Route 5 leaves Syracuse on its way to **Camillus**, where you can canoe and kayak to your heart's content along 7 miles (11km) of navigable canal in the **Camillus-Erie Canal Park**. Farther along, Route 5 merges with US 20, a

route that strings together the northern tips of the largest **Finger Lakes**.

Following close on the heels of the Leatherstocking region, this series of 11 watery depressions was created by scraping glaciers. The region is characterized by vineyards, gracious inns, water pursuits, and hot-air ballooning. The area's vines look especially beautiful when their leaves begin to turn coppery red in late summer, and the colorful balloons are also an attractive sight. The small city of **Auburn**, on US 20/Route 5, isn't quite set on the lakes but does have one site to visit: the **home of Harriet Tubman** (tel: 315-252-2081; www.harriethouse.org; Tue–Sat) on South Street.

Seneca Lake

After Auburn, US 20/Route 5 then passes Cayuga Lake and follows the Seneca River to **Seneca Falls ㉓**, where the first Women's Rights Convention was convened. The site has been developed into a National Historic Site and includes the **National Women's Hall of Fame** (tel: 315-568-8060; www.greatwomen.org; May–Sept daily, Oct–Apr Wed–Sat). **Waterloo**, also in between the lake fingers, prides itself on being the birthplace of Memorial Day. The road through here passes by the old Scythe Tree, upon which local farm boys planted their scythes on their way to wars past.

Seneca Lake follows – the town of **Geneva ㉔** its jewel, replete with elegant inns and mansions. This town is also the gateway to a circuit round the lake known as the Seneca Lake Wine Trail; the drive takes in several dozen vintners, including four specializing in champagne and mead (honey wine). It is very pretty in fall, when the grape and maple leaves are changing color. Seneca Lake may seem small and thin, but it's actually one of the deepest freshwater lakes in the world – going down to a depth of more than 600ft (180 meters). The US Navy used the lake to test depth charges during World War II.

Approximately 20 miles (32km) west of Geneva on US 20/Route 20 is **Canandaigua**, at the northern tip of Canandaigua Lake. Of particular interest here is the Federal-style **Granger Homestead and Carriage Museum** ㉕ (tel: 585-394-1472; late May–late Oct Tue–Fri, June–Sept Tue–Sun), built in 1816, with its collection of nearly 70 horse-drawn vehicles. North of town – take Route 21 – are the **Sonnenberg Gardens** (tel: 585-394-4922; www.sonnenberg.org; mid-May–mid-Oct daily), acres of Victoriana with a mansion incorporating the Wine Center, a collection of gourmet foods and wines from the Finger Lakes region. There is a rotating-inventory tasting bar in the cellar.

Remain on Route 21 and you will pass through Shortsville on the way to **Palmyra**, a pilgrimage site for Mormons. This was the home of Joseph Smith who, according to Mormon belief, received and translated ancient records in the Book of Mormon, buried them here and subsequently founded the Church in the 1820s. Religious sites, the original home built by the Smiths and a replica of Smith's farm homestead are open to the public, as is the **Martin Harris Landmark Cobblestone House**. Built in 1850, the house is typical of the farmers' homes that sprang up along the Erie Canal.

It is approximately 20 miles (32km) from Palmyra to Rochester along Route 31. The names of the towns along the way are perhaps more exotic than the towns: after Palmyra comes Macedon and then Egypt, where the New York State Barge Canal stands in for the Nile.

Rochester

Like other upstate cities, **Rochester** ㉖ thrived during the canal era and suffered economically with the advent of alternative modes of transportation. But it has adjusted to change better than its siblings and is on the upswing as a center for high-tech industries,

while continuing to preserve much of its 19th-century architectural ambiance. Eastman Kodak, struggling since the advent of digital photography, is still a presence here, as is Xerox Corporation.

The former mansion of George Eastman, who founded Kodak, now houses the **International Museum of Photography and Film** (tel: 585-271-3361; www.eastmanhouse.org; Tue–Sun), devoted to the history of this art and science. The **Eastman School of Music** sponsors musical events, from jazz to rock to folk to symphonic works, while the **Eastman Theatre** is the home of the Rochester Philharmonic. For those who still enjoy childish things, the **Strong National Museum of Play** (tel: 585-263-2700; www.museumofplay.org; daily) has one of the most extensive collections of dolls and toys in the world, in addition to a butterfly garden and coral reef aquarium. Winters are severe in Rochester, thanks to its northern location on Lake Ontario, the easternmost Great Lake. But in spring, when **Highland Park** is

Ride a bike along the Seneca Lake Wine Trail that winds around Seneca Lake.

International Museum of Photography and Film.

abloom, Rochester is as colourful as one of Kodak's Kodachrome slides. During May, the park (which bills itself as the "Lilac Capital of the World") is the setting for the Lilac Festival featuring the world's largest display of these blossoms.

On to the falls

Route 31 continues along the path of the Erie Canal from Rochester to Niagara Falls. The names of the towns along this route, including Spencerport, Brockport, Middleport, and Gasport, continue to remind the traveler of the canal's former importance. But there are other reminders as well. **Medina** ㉗ has its cobblestone buildings and Culvert Road, which passes beneath the canal. **Lockport** also has its share of cobblestone houses, though it is best known for its magnificent flight of five locks.

From Lockport, Route 31 (here called Saunders Settlement Road) travels directly to **Niagara Falls** ㉘. Once known as America's "Honeymoon Capital," the town is fond of referring to itself as an international tourist destination. And, indeed, this remains one of the top tourist draws in all the US despite its endless tackiness. Quite simply, the 700,000 gallons (3 million liters) of water plummeting from top to bottom each second here are a wondrous assault on the senses, something that must be experienced while in America. The magnetic draw of these falls has even inspired some visitors to attempt crossing them on a tightrope or riding them in a barrel, with sometimes-tragic results; both activities are now illegal, though daredevils still occasionally try.

The natural beauty of the site might have been irreparably compromised had it not been for the efforts of landscape architect Frederick Law Olmsted, landscape painter Frederic Church and others. Their "Free Niagara" (from commercialism) campaign resulted in the establishment of the Niagara Reservation in 1885. One of the best ways to experience the falls today is by donning the provided foul-weather gear and taking a boat ride on the *Maid of the Mist*. Alternatively, assuming you have your passport with you, you might drive across the river to Canada and enjoy what many consider to be a superior view.

River Road hugs the eastern branch of the Niagara River, past the falls and through industrial landscape to **Buffalo** ㉙. As with other industrial giants past their prime, New York's second-largest city has acquired a somewhat bad reputation. As the 19th-century terminus of the Erie Canal, Buffalo once served as a funnel through which raw materials, cash, pioneers, and immigrant labor flowed into the Midwestern states. Today, it is a bit ragged. Nevertheless, there are reasons to stop for a visit; you can eat well and cheaply here. A local specialty is spicy chicken wings, which anywhere else are called "Buffalo wings," but here are "wings." You might like to go to the source, the Anchor Bar (see page 434), whose owner is said to have invented the dish.

Seneca Lake.

Beach volleyball on Chicago's lakefront.

BUFFALO TO THE BADLANDS

Follow the shores of Lake Erie into New York, Pennsylvania, and Ohio, then continue through the Midwest and the Great Lakes for the bleak, beautiful hills of the Badlands.

Buffalo was an important point of departure for 19th-century settlers heading for the Midwest. From Buffalo, they traveled to major ports of the Great Lakes in order to start their new life. Today, the road from Buffalo to the Midwestern states follows the shore of Lake Erie through New York, Pennsylvania, and Ohio. Although known primarily as an industrial area, there are still some unspoiled stretches of coastline that are remarkable for their beauty. At Toledo, the highway diverges from the shoreline on its way to big, busy, beautiful Chicago.

South of Buffalo along US 62 is the town of **Hamburg**, where the hamburger – perhaps America's greatest contribution to world cuisine – was purportedly invented in 1885. In celebration of the centennial of this event, J. Wellington Wimpy came to town and was honored as the undefeated hamburger-eating champion of the world. Essentially a rural town, Hamburg has been host to America's largest county fair since 1868. It's only about 5 miles (8km) from here to Lake Erie, where you can pick up State 5, a lakeside road that takes you to Ohio.

Antique trail

Lake Erie has suffered more than its sister Great Lakes at the hands of industry, yet miles of its beautiful, sandy,

ocean-like shoreline are still unspoiled. The stretch from Silver Creek, New York, to the Pennsylvania border has been called an "antique trail" for the abundance of antique shops.

State 5 takes you past terrain blanketed with grape vines and other fruit trees. In **Silver Creek**, go straight to the site of the **Skew Arch Railroad Bridge** on Jackson Street. Built on an angle in 1869, it is one of only two such bridges in the world.

Dunkirk and Fredonia follow, in the heart of the Concord Grape Belt (the

Main Attractions

Lake Erie State Park
Chain O'Lakes State Park
Chicago
Taliesin
Walker Art Center
Minnesota State Fair
Corn Palace
Badlands National Park

Chicago Cubs fans.

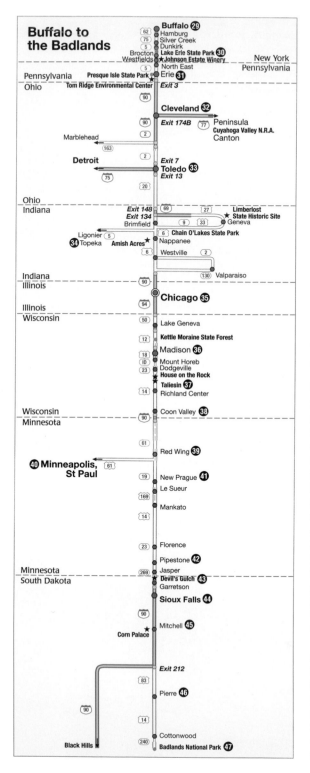

**Buffalo to
the Badlands**

Buffalo ⓐ
62 — Hamburg
75 — Silver Creek
5 — Dunkirk
Brocton — Lake Erie State Park ⓑ
Westfields — ★ Johnson Estate Winery — New York
5 — North East — Pennsylvania
Pennsylvania — Presque Isle State Park — Erie ⓒ
Ohio — Tom Ridge Environmental Center — Exit 3
90
Cleveland ⓓ
90 — Exit 174B — 77 — Peninsula
2 — Cuyahoga Valley N.R.A.
Marblehead — Canton
163
2 — Exit 7
Detroit — Toledo ⓔ
75 — Exit 13
20
Ohio
Indiana — Exit 148 — 69 — 27 — Limberlost
Exit 134 — ★ State Historic Site
Brimfield — 9 — 33 — Geneva
Ligonier 5 — 6 — Chain O'Lakes State Park
ⓕTopeka — Amish Acres ★ — Nappanee
6 — Westville — 2
Indiana — 130 — Valparaiso
Illinois — 90
Illinois — 94 — **Chicago** ⓖ
Wisconsin — 50 — Lake Geneva
12 — Kettle Moraine State Forest
18 — Madison ⓗ
ID — Mount Horeb
23 — Dodgeville
House on the Rock
★ Taliesin ⓘ
14 — Richland Center
Wisconsin — Coon Valley ⓙ
Minnesota — 90
61
Red Wing ⓚ
ⓛ **Minneapolis,** — 61
St Paul — 19 — New Prague ⓜ
169 — Le Sueur
14 — Mankato
23 — Florence
Pipestone ⓝ
Minnesota — 269 — Jasper
South Dakota — ★ Devil's Gulch ⓞ
Garretson
Sioux Falls ⓟ
90
★ Mitchell ⓠ
Corn Palace
Exit 212
83
Pierre ⓡ
90
14
Cottonwood
Black Hills — 240 — Badlands National Park ⓢ

world's largest), which extends into Pennsylvania. **Dunkirk**, with its natural harbor, is also a center for boating and the "Chautauqua (County) wine trail." **Fredonia**, to the south, is home to the Fredonia campus of State University of New York, which was co-designed and modernized in the late 1960s by renowned architects I.M. Pei and Henry N. Cobb.

Continuing along the lake, the road passes pretty **Lake Erie State Park** ⓑ (tel: 716-792-9214; http://nysparks.com/parks/129/details.aspx; May–Oct daily) in **Brocton**, where campers will find a place to pitch their tents. **Westfield** follows, calling itself "The Grape Juice Capital of the World" and dominated by the various production facilities of a popular grape jelly and grape juice. Combined with peanut butter and two pieces of bread, the peanut butter and jelly sandwich vies with Hamburg's hamburgers as *the* American food.

There is no obvious transition between New York and its westerly neighbor, Pennsylvania. The landscape remains the same – a sparkling lake on one side and lush vineyards on the other. In season, roadside stands sell the local grapes in every imaginable form. Only 63 miles (101km) of Lake Erie shoreline prevent Pennsylvania from being a landlocked state (an economic decision to do with lake access), and it knows just what to do with it. Past the state line is the town of **North East**, center of the state's tiny wine industry. Several wineries do fairly good business here and all offer tours and tastings. Johnson Estate Winery In Westfield – New York's oldest estate winery – is one of the best.

About 15 miles (24km) west of wine country on State 5 sits the city of **Erie** ⓒ, off whose shores Commander Oliver Hazard Perry's fleet defeated the British in the Battle of Lake Erie during the War of 1812. Despite his motto – "Don't give up the ship!" – the flagship *Niagara* was left to sink in what later became known as

Misery Bay. That bay is now a quiet fishing cove off Presque Isle, and the ship was rescued a century later. A reconstructed *Niagara* is now docked behind the **Erie Maritime Museum** (tel: 814-452 2744; www.eriemaritime-museum.org; Apr–Oct daily, Nov–Mar Thur–Sat). When docked here, guided tours onboard are included in the museum's admission price, but be aware that the boat has an active sailing schedule in the summer.

On the other side is Erie's finest physical feature, **Presque Isle**, a claw of land – almost an island, really – reaching out into the lake. You can drive its length, pass Presque Isle Lighthouse, and then loop around along the southern end going past Misery Bay. You'll find lovely sand beaches, wooded trails, fishing holes, and lazy lagoons. While in Presque Isle, pay a visit to the Tom Ridge Environmental Center (tel: 814-833-6050; www.trecpi.org; daily), which offers interactive exhibits on the natural history of the region as well as a large-format movie theatre that often shows documentaries on issues of concern to the Great Lakes.

Due south of Erie is Pittsburgh, the quintessential American city so eloquently recalled in Pulitzer Prize-winning writer Annie Dillard's novel *An American Childhood*.

CLEVELAND

Before you can say "knee high by the Fourth of July," you're in Ohio. I-90 cuts through the gently rolling farmland of this part of the state past Ashtabula, Geneva, and Euclid before reaching the **Cleveland** ❸❷ area. Cleveland has its share of high culture – the Cleveland Orchestra and its home, Severance Hall, as well as the **Cleveland Museum of Art** (tel: 216-421-7350; www.clevelandart.org; Tue–Sun) – and pop culture – the **Rock and Roll Hall of Fame** (tel: 216-781-ROCK; www.rockhall.com; daily). The latter covers everyone from Louis Jordan to John Lennon, with exhibits including report cards and Jim Morrison's Cub Scout uniform. And let's not forget the **Museum of Contemporary Art** (tel: 216-42-8671; www.mocacleveland.

Time for lunch: this part of the US has claims to both hamburgers and peanut butter and jelly sandwiches.

Cleveland skyscrapers catching the setting sun.

An Indiana farm.

org; Tue–Sun11am–5pm, Thur until 10pm) which opened in October 2012 in a modern mirrored structure at University Circle designed by renowned London architect Farshid Moussavi. Popular American Chef Michael Symon hails from Cleveland and has three award-winning restaurants here.

It's well worth a short detour south from Cleveland to explore the green **Cuyahoga Valley**. The valley's ridges were settled during the late 18th century by the New Englanders who first surveyed its boundaries, and their influence remains today.

Pro Football Hall of Fame

Sport fans will want to make a brief detour south down I-77, through Akron – tire and rubber capital of America – to the city of **Canton**. Here, the **Pro Football Hall of Fame** (tel: 330-456-8207; www.profootballhof.com; daily) offers a look at the heroes of American football. Things peak in August, when an annual game is played here to kick off each season and to celebrate the new class of inductees.

State 2 leaves Cleveland on its way west, diverging from I-90 and running closer to Lake Erie. At Ceylon, it comes right to the lake, loops around Sandusky, then bridges Sandusky Bay to arrive on the Marblehead Peninsula. State 163 takes you out to land's end and reveals the peninsula as a slightly rundown but refreshingly unpretentious place, full of lively harbors, the African adventure-themed Kalahari Waterpark Resort, orchards, and fruit stands. At its rocky tip is **Marblehead Lighthouse**, which has been in continuous use since 1822, longer than any other beacon on the Great Lakes. The quaint Kelleys Island is a 20-minute ferry ride from Marblehead and offers boating, swimming, wineries, and even the South Shore Historic District which was placed on the National Register of Historic Places in 1975. Looking back south across the bay, you'll see the roller coasters of **Cedar Point** (tel: 419-627-2350; www.cedar.point; mid-May–Aug daily, Sept–Oct Sat–Sun), a popular 364-acre (147-hectare) amusement park in Sandusky. Off the Marblehead Peninsula, State 2 proceeds toward Toledo. This region was once part of the **Black Swamp**, a refuge for wildlife, which extended from Sandusky to Detroit. Small remnants of the swamp have managed to survive along this route.

Toledo

The road emerges from the swamp and continues straight as an arrow to the town of **Toledo** ㉝, past bait shops, drive-through liquor stores and drive-in movie theaters. The "Toledo Strip" was once the subject of a border dispute between Ohio and Michigan. When Ohio got the Strip, Michigan got its Upper Peninsula from Wisconsin Territory as compensation – a swap in which Michigan probably made out like a bandit.

At first glance, Toledo seems like an industrial wasteland. Still, there are signs of rejuvenation and redevelopment in the downtown riverfront area

along the Maumee. If you've got the time, drop into Tony Packo's café (see page 435) – made famous by Corporal Max Klinger in the long-running TV series *M*A*S*H* – a fun restaurant known for its "Hungarian hot dogs" and quirky collection of hot dog buns autographed by celebrities.

Leaving Toledo and Lake Erie behind at last, US 20 heads due west, cutting straight through Ohio farm country to the Indiana border, a distance of about 60 miles (100km). The road here parallels the Michigan border, which is just a few miles to the north.

INDIANA

They call **Indiana** the Hoosier state, and native Indianans Hoosiers. Some say the name comes from a common inquiry from the pioneer days, "who's yer?" Others say the nickname comes from a canal-builder named Samuel Hoosier, who liked to hire Indiana men over other workers; the workers became known as Hoosiers, and the name stuck. (There was even a film called *Hoosiers* – widely considered one of the best sports films ever made

– which told the story of an Indiana high school basketball team that wins the state championship.) Whatever the origin of the name, this state has produced such high-profile celebrity residents as basketball star Larry Bird, singer John Mellencamp, and television talk show host David Letterman.

Historic state parks

Ten miles (16km) inside the state at Angola, leave US 20 for I-69S fifteen miles (24km) later, cut over to US 6, which will carry you westward through northern Indiana to Illinois. Fields of golden grain (mostly corn) and silos announce it: you are solidly in the Midwest now. At Brimfield, detour a few miles north up Indiana 9 to the **Limberlost State Historic Site** (tel: 260-368-7428; Apr–mid-Dec Wed–Sun, mid-Dec–Mar Tue–Sat), a log cabin where Gene Stratton-Porter lived and wrote her well-loved books and essays about Midwestern nature. It's a peaceful spot among trees on a lake, and perfect for a picnic.

On the other side of Brimfield, south on Indiana 9, sits another fine

Marblehead Lighthouse on Lake Erie.

Michigan Avenue's brick road in Detroit.

DETOUR TO DETROIT

A 45-mile (72km) drive beside Lake Erie on I-75 leads from Toledo, Ohio, to Detroit, Michigan – the Motor City. Henry Ford was the single most influential American in motoring history, forming the Ford Motor Company in 1903. Six years later, he had 10,000 orders for his newest car, the Model T, and, by 1919, was selling close to a million cars. His innovations bolstered Detroit's economy, increased the automobile's popularity and gave more people jobs; though the company has been severely shaken by bankruptcies and lay-offs as a result of the global financial crisis. Nevertheless, the 260-acre (105-hectare) Henry Ford Museum (www.thehenryford.org) and Greenfield Village complex in the nearby town of Dearborn is the world's largest indoor/outdoor museum, commemorating Ford's contribution to the city. The Ford Museum holds Henry's collection of early automobiles and historic airplanes, while the Village houses recreations of famous businesses and residences, including Thomas Edison's Menlo Park laboratory. Detroit is also the home of Motown records, created by former Ford assembly line worker Berry Gordy, Jr, in 1958, which produced stars of the Detroit Sound such as Smokey Robinson and Diana Ross. The Motown Historical Museum charts the label's influence from the 1960s to the present. The Detroit Visitors Bureau is at 800-338-7648 or www.visitdetroit.com.

The Amish shun worldliness for small-scale values, with emphasis on the community.

Amish buggy on a country road.

park – **Chain O' Lakes State Park** is a refreshing string of oases in the middle of Noble County.

Indiana's Amish country

Back on US 6, tiny towns punctuate a landscape of corn in this region, known for the productivity of its land and for its considerable Amish population. The Amish have been in this area for more than a century. These inventive, industrious, and deeply religious people go about their business while shunning worldly things such as buttons, zippers, electricity, and motor vehicles. Cut north up Indiana 5 for a look at their farms, homes, and horse-drawn buggies, however, be respectful: most Amish do not like to have their photo taken as they believe it is an act of pride. It's also a good idea to drive slowly while in Amish country as you never know when a horse drawn buggy might round the corner.

As you pass through **Ligonier**, you'll see a small town with an attractive main street and a number of handsome Victorian mansions. The interesting town clock here was erected by John Cavin, son of local pioneer Isaac Cavin, in memory of the father who laid the town out in 1835. Also have a look at the **Indiana Ligonier Visitor's Bureau and Heritage Station Museum**, (tel: 260-894-9000; Tue–Sat) with its exhibits from the now-shuttered Wilkinson Quilt Factory and the original Kidd's Marshmallow Company. In addition, there are approximately a dozen antique radios displayed, on loan from the Indiana Historical Radio Society.

Continue north on Indiana 5 and then turn right at a gas station to reach **Topeka** ㉞, a tiny town whose slogan is "Life in the Past Lane." It's the kind of place where Amish buggies line up in parking lots, and hardware and feed stores outnumber banks three-to-one. Amish ride bicycles around town, work the counter at restaurants, and just generally blend into life in this farming community. For a more intimate experience, inquire locally about the Amish Country Bed and Breakfast network, or just drive one of the many other county roads in this area. White farmhouses with full clotheslines and empty driveways are usually Amish, though you should always check ahead with tourism offices before attempting to visit a private home.

Now, retrace your steps back to US 6 and continue west. **Amish Acres** in **Nappanee** (tel: 800-800-4942; www. amishacres.com; closed Jan–Feb, variable days Mar–Dec), a historic farm homestead that interprets the Amish lifestyle for visitors, is fun though a bit over-commercialized. The round red barn hosts theater performances.

Beyond that, it's more lovely country driving through more fields of corn and occasional stands of maple trees. Drifting along US 6 like the "Windiana winds" through the last of rural Indiana before Chicago's industrial fringe, the route takes you over the Kankakee River (a good fishing stream) and on to **Westville**, home of an annual Pumpkin Festival that brings a carnival – and piles of

orange pumpkins, of course – to town in late September.

Orville Redenbacher's hometown

If you're hungry, make a quick swing down to US 30, on Indiana 2, and the town of **Valparaiso**, where Schoop's Hamburgers serves up old-fashioned atmosphere in the form of "Green River" sodas. The town was also the home of bow-tied popcorn magnate Orville Redenbacher, and you'll still find occasional popcorn stands in these parts of northern Indiana. In fact, this is a region of America that sometimes appears permanently frozen in 1950 – you are likely to encounter classic cars, crew cuts, and friendly folks. Make the most of it before you reach the sensory assault – and very different pace – of **Chicago** ㉟ (see page 140).

WISCONSIN

Leaving Chicago, take Lake Shore Drive straight north out of the city and follow either US 41 or hop onto I-94 for a spell. Soon enough, you're in **Wisconsin**, the unofficial Cheese Capital of America, a friendly place settled by blond Scandinavians still very much in evidence today.

A few miles inside the state, turn west on Wisconsin 50 to make a lovely country drive past orchards, fruit stands, and small lake towns – one of which is called **Lake Geneva**, attractive if not exactly a match for its counterpart in Switzerland. Turn north on US 12, passing plenty of maple trees, small cafés, burger joints, and rustic roads (so marked by state road signs). You'll also come through **Kettle Moraine State Forest**, named for unusual features of the landscape – ridges of rock and silt, and circular ponds – produced here by the last great glaciation of North America. Rent a cycle from LaGrange General Store to explore the area at your leisure.

At Whitewater, a small university town, you'll note a preponderance of custard stands serving burgers and frozen custard – a concoction invented in nearby Milwaukee. By state law, custard must contain a certain percentage

Indiana farmer and his corn crop.

Wisconsin's rural road sign is in the shape of the state.

Wisconsin State Capitol, Madison.

of cream and a certain number of eggs. It's like ice cream, but sinfully richer; a spoon is barely adequate to pry it from the cup.

Madison

US 12 brings you to **Madison** ❸❻, Wisconsin's capital and one of the Midwest's most agreeable cities. The city boasts a splendid downtown grid of streets with a capital building at its center, a university district to match and miles of lake frontage popular with joggers, cyclists, boaters, skiers, and skaters – depending on the season. Snack on "brats" (short for bratwurst, local sausages of German origin) and beer, or enjoy the open-air farmers' market that takes over the city's main square in summer (Saturdays), a market purveying everything from organic produce to goat, bison, and emu meat, all produced in the state. There are also a number of museums here.

From Madison, take US 18 west through green pastures and roadcuts revealing the limestone underlying the countryside. This area is an anomaly in the normally flat Midwest, with numerous ridges popping up between you and the horizon; farms top distant hilltops like ships on sea swells. At the little town of **Mount Horeb**, exit onto County Road ID – in Wisconsin, unusually, minor roads are lettered instead of numbered – for a look at two attractions. The National Natural Landmark, **Cave of the Mounds** (tel: 608-437-3038; www.caveofthemounds.com), provides a scenic look below ground; **Little Norway** (tel: 608-437-8211; May–Oct daily) is a somewhat tacky attraction celebrating the Norwegian immigrants who largely settled this state.

Get back onto US 18 and continue to County Road BB, where a short detour south brings you to the **Folklore Village** (tel: 608-924-4000; Tue–Sun), a small complex of period buildings. It offers folk art workshops ranging from cooking to dancing and spinning wool. Call about the culture and recreation programs when in the area. The highlight is a one-room 1882 church, very simple but nicely restored; it was jacked up and moved from a nearby town.

Dodgeville, home to clothier Land's End, is just a few miles on. Take Wisconsin 23 north past the headquarters. On the way out of town you will pass the **Don Q Inn**, an eccentric lodge. Themed rooms include an igloo built for two, a hot-air balloon gondola, and many other options suitable for all levels of taste.

More dips and rises in the road lead to the **House on the Rock** (tel: 608-935-3639; www.thehouseontherock.com; May–Oct daily), Wisconsin's quirkiest must-see attraction. This unique complex of buildings on top of an odd rock formation was built up over a period of decades by inveterate collector Alex Jordan, Jr. Its many attractions include rooms and rooms of art, antiques and oddities, an "Infinity Point" glass bridge with views down a gorge, a huge assemblage of doll houses, a collection of rare book vintage cars, and the world's larg

carousel. It's well worth the expensive admission price, if only for a look at the fruits of a single man's manic obsession – you could easily spend the better part of a day roaming around this kitschy complex. If you don't have time for a long visit, there's an attractive spot just north of the entrance to park, walk a spell and get a distant glimpse of the house.

Frank Lloyd Wright's Wisconsin

Wisconsin 23 soon comes to the sandy banks of the Wisconsin River, where you'll be surprised to suddenly come upon Frank Lloyd Wright's **Taliesin** ③⑦ (tel: 608-588-7900; www.taliesin preservation.org; May–Oct daily, Nov Mon–Fri.), which means "shining brow" in Welsh. This 600-acre estate includes the Taliesin residence, the Hillside Home School, Midway Barns, and Tan-y-Deri, the house that Wright designed for his sister and brother-in-law, Janc and Andrew Porter; you must be on a guided tour to access this private estate. The setting is peaceful and lovely.

The route continues to the pretty little town of Spring Green, turns west onto US 14 and abruptly flattens before passing through **Richland Center**, where you can view the A.D. German warehouse designed by Wright in 1915. Known today as "The Warehouse," this red brick structure topped by a band of concrete frieze illustrates a distinctive Mayan influence. Then the road begins climbing and wrinkling again, indicating the approach of the Mississippi River. At **Coon Valley** ③⑧, neatly tucked within a surprisingly deep valley, you'll marvel at the surroundings and the town's solid Lutheran church. The **Norskedalen** (tel: 608-452-3424; www.norskedalen.org; May–Oct daily, Nov–Apr Sun–Fri) complex outside town provides a pleasant look at Norwegian heritage in a quiet natural setting. Speed right through industrial La Crosse, hop onto I-90 and take the big bridge across the Mississippi; get off again on the other side at signs for Highway 61, the road Bob Dylan called attention to in the namesake album and song. You have entered

FACT

The Seth Peterson Cottage (www. sethpeterson.org) in Mirror Lakes State Park, just outside Lake Delton, Wisconsin, was designed by Frank Lloyd Wright in 1958. The home was restored by community members in a successful grassroots restoration campaign and is the only Frank Lloyd Wright designed building available for rent by overnight visitors.

A Wisconsin dairy farm.

Minnesota and are now following the **Great River Road** toward the river's source. The route north clings to the bluffs of the Mississippi River, revealing spectacular colors in fall and outstanding river views at any time of the year. Patrons once rode steamboats all the way upriver from St Louis to gaze upon these high, beautiful bluffs.

Highway 61 is mostly grand views and ordinary towns from here to the Twin Cities, but there are a few worthy stops along the way. **Pepin**, back across the great river on the Wisconsin side, is renowned for being the birthplace of author Laura Ingalls Wilder. There's a copy of the cabin "Little House Wayside" just north of town, and a small museum (mid-May–mid-Oct daily) as well.

North again, **Red Wing** ㊴, with an especially good vista of the valley, makes a good place for a picnic and a photograph. There's an Indian reservation close by, as well, and it's good to have a look round before plunging into the suburban ring of towns and highways that have replaced what were once cornfields, but now serve as the suburban bases for legions of commuters into Minneapolis and St Paul.

The Twin Cities

Because of their proximity, **Minneapolis** and **St Paul** ㊵, on opposite sides of the Mississippi, will eternally be known as Minnesota's "Twin Cities." Fraternal rather than identical, they are like sides of the same coin: different, yet inseparable. St Paul, the more conservative, ethnic, and parochial of the two, presents an earthier and more weatherbeaten appearance. There's a more neighborly feel, too, and malt shops, health-food stores, and homes are more common here than the apartments, condos, and skyscrapers across the river.

Minneapolis, more competitive and cosmopolitan, dresses for success while living and breathing the concept of quality time. Local radio humorist Garrison Keillor puts it this way: "The difference between St Paul and Minneapolis is the difference between pumpernickel and Wonder Bread."

Yet together they are responsible for an urban success story, the envy of every overcrowded, and crime-ridden metropolis. Minnesota pioneers were forced by circumstances to cooperate with one another, and a genuine spirit of friendliness toward strangers prevails to this day.

People here put a lot of stock in politics and have developed a rather civic, populist bent: this state nourished the careers of Hubert Humphrey and Walter Mondale, the late Senator Paul Wellstone, and, outrageously, former Governor Jesse "The Body" Ventura, once a professional wrestler, who continued this populist tradition, if in very different ways.

MINNESOTA: LAND OF 10,000 LAKES

It always comes back to the lakes. Without its waters, Minnesota wouldn't even be Minnesota; the name itself comes from the Sioux, meaning "sky-blue water." The shore of

Minneapolis.

Lake Superior marks the border of its northeast corner and the **Mississippi River** courses down its eastern flank. State license plates affirm "Land of 10,000 Lakes," but there are even more than that in the state.

During the 18th century, French explorers stumbled onto this region and named it *L'Etoile du Nord* – the Star of the North. Over the following 150 years, the Sioux and Ojibwa who originally occupied the territory were frequently set upon by hundreds of white settlers, and violent clashes between the two Indian groups escalated.

In order to protect the early settlers and establish a secure trading station, **Fort Snelling** was built in 1819, high on river bluffs at the site of what is now Minneapolis. As rampaging Native Americans crossed the plains, white farmers fled to the fort for refuge; thus was the city born. Today, Fort Snelling has been reconstructed and staffed with actors who give visitors a first-hand glimpse of frontier life, *c.*1825.

An increase in commerce along the river gave birth to the towns of St Paul and Minneapolis. The former sprang up as a local center of navigation and was originally known as Pig's Eye, after "Pig's Eye" Parrent, proprietor of a riverfront saloon. Seeking a better image, its residents renamed it St Paul.

Ever-industrious Minneapolis, "the city of water," evolved upstream around **St Anthony Falls**, source of power for sawmills and gristmills. Both towns were flooded with a wave of immigrants, mostly northern Europeans, on their way to harvest the bounty of the Great North Woods: lumber and iron ore. In the wake of the Homestead Act, more settlers then poured in to help cultivate a sea of wheat.

The Twin Cities' status in the world of agriculture, in fact, is never far from the minds of Minnesotans. Reports from the Minneapolis Grain Exchange, the nation's largest cash market, monopolize the

local airwaves; General Mills and Pillsbury are headquartered here (as is the Target Corporation, the second largest retailer in the United States.) Magnificent grain elevators, standing tall above the Mississippi, vie for attention with the likes of Minneapolis's **Investors Diversified Services** (IDS) building – the tallest one between Chicago and San Francisco – **St Paul's Cathedral** and the handsome **Capitol Building**.

Metrodome and Walker Art Center

Characterized by stable neighborhoods and superbly planned public places and open spaces, the Twin Cities run smoothly even in cold weather. They've given a lot of thought to the weather here, after all, and over the years have refined methods of dealing with a winter that is typically cruel and unrelenting. Glass-enclosed skywalks radiate from the Crystal Court of the IDS building, as they do in downtown St Paul, and the enclosed **Hubert H. Humphrey Metrodome** hosts sports events and

Canoeing on a Minnesota lake in the morning calm.

St Paul's Cathedral.

Gondola Ferris Wheel, one of the many rides at the Minnesota State Fair.

concerts year-round – and was the setting for two World Series titles for baseball's Minnesota Twins and success for the football team, the Vikings.

Yet people here are also perversely proud of their ability to withstand record-cold temperatures, and they celebrate the ice and snow at the St Paul's Winter Carnival, an annual event since 1886.

Culture is well endowed and thriving, particularly in Minneapolis. The **Walker Art Center** (tel: 612-375-7600; www.walkerart.org; daily), along with its sculpture garden, is a forum for contemporary visual and performing arts that *The New York Times* called "one of the best contemporary art exhibition facilities in the world." The **Guthrie Theatre** (www.guthrietheater.org), sited next to the Mississippi River with great views of St Anthony Falls, is indisputably one of the premier repertory theaters. The **Northrop Dance Season** (http://northrop.umn.edu/events/northrop-dance) puts together one of the most impressive dance series. The **American Swedish Institute** archives and the European collections of the **Minneapolis Institute of Arts** (tel: 888-642-2787; www.arsmia.org; Tue–Sun) are within a short distance of each other; both are terrific.

And there's still more to be found – avant-garde films, classical music, art galleries, jazz. The **Dakota Jazz Club** features the best local and international musicians nightly in downtown Minneapolis.

Minnesota State Fair

The annual **Minnesota State Fair** (www.mnstatefair.org) the nation's second-largest (behind New York's), should not be missed if you're coming through in late summer. Held at the State Fairgrounds over a week and a half, it is a stream of fishing and farming demonstrations, folk and country music performances, horse shows, special exhibitions for children, and carnival rides – accompanied by every sort of meat or cheese one can imagine, placed onto a stick and fried. The fair celebrated its centenary in 2009 – it's a huge dose of Midwestern popular culture, a little overwhelming but absolutely authentic.

THE MISSISSIPPI TO THE BADLANDS

The region extending from the Mississippi River in Minnesota to the Missouri River in South Dakota marks the transition from the Midwestern to the Western states – geographically, culturally, and spiritually.

The transition can be subtle. If you listen to the car radio, up-to-the-minute reports from the floor of the Minneapolis Grain Exchange will be heard with progressively less frequency. Western idioms begin to turn up in small farm towns. The changes in geography are more abrupt, as the Missouri River serves as a sharp boundary between the Grain Belt and the true West.

Minnesota Farm Country

The region of Minnesota southwest of "The Cities" is unmistakably farm country. This land was settled by European and Scandinavian immigrants during the latter half of the 19th century. Some called them "sodbusters" as they indiscriminately cleared land and penetrated virgin sod, exposing the rich soil of the Midwestern prairie. Many of their grandchildren and great-grandchildren still farm the land here, an occupation known these days as agribusiness.

The founders of **New Prague** ❹, a town dominated by **St Wenceslaus Church**, clearly had no desire to conceal their Eastern European heritage. West of the town, along State 19, are peculiarly medieval-looking buildings with domed roofs, looking incongruous in the midst of all-American corn country.

Those who believe the Valley of the Jolly Green Giant to be a mythical place created by television advertising executives are mistaken. At **Le Sueur**, renowned for its peas, US 169 intersects the Minnesota River and passes through this lush, green valley, marked by the Green Giant himself sprouting on the top of a billboard.

Branching southwest toward **Mankato**, the road enters Blue Earth country across the **Blue Earth River**. This is some of the most productive farmland in the state, a green expanse interrupted only by lakes. Modern farming is still a family business here, and it isn't unusual to see an entire family out in the fields working various pieces of machinery.

From Mankato, take US 14 west as far as tiny Florence, passing many more farms along the way, and then turn south onto Minnesota 23 for a more scenic stretch. In **Pipestone** ❷, near the South Dakota border, the strong suit is Sioux quartzite rather than agriculture. Buildings constructed from this local, pinkish stone appear up and down historic Main and Hiawatha streets; significant not only because they are lovely to look at, but because they are among the last of their kind. The use of Sioux quartzite is no longer considered cost-effective.

However, for a period of less than 20 years before the turn of the 19th century, Pipestone went to town with it – the **County Courthouse**, the

Harvested hay bales in a Minnesota field.

University of Minnesota marching band at the State Fair.

Prairie sunset.

Public Library, the **National Bank Building**, the **Calumet Historic Inn** (www.calumetinnn.com), and, most impressively, **Moore Block** (1896) are all made of this material. L.H. Moore, a local businessman who owned a Sioux quartzite quarry, embellished the block bearing his name with fanciful images of the sun, angels, gargoyles, a jester, and the devil.

Underlying and veining Sioux quartzite is a material called pipestone, which gave the town its name. Longfellow's *The Song of Hiawatha* tells of "the great Red Pipestone Quarry," and the quarries in Pipestone and the land that surrounds them are still sacred ground of the Sioux and other Native Americans today – a land of legend and tradition, and now also a national monument.

To see more, take the **Circle Trail**, a mile loop through the prairie surrounding the quarries. It goes past **Hiawatha Lake**, **Winnewissa Falls**, quartzite cliffs and wind-carved formations known as **Old Stone Face** and the **Oracle**. A stone inscription along the trail documents the past presence of the Nicollet expedition, members of which traveled through here in 1838 while exploring the lands of the isolated Upper Mississippi region.

Continue south from Pipestone along Minnesota 23, passing through **Jasper** (which also has its share of quartzite buildings). Angle onto Route 269, and in a few miles you will have crossed another state line – and you will be poised exactly halfway between the Atlantic and the Pacific oceans.

THE PINK ROAD TO SOUTH DAKOTA

The South Dakota Department of Highways chose to make use of the locally plentiful quartzite, and so a pink road unfolds at the border of their state. It takes you to **Garretson**, known for its **Devil's Gulch ㊸**. The gulch is a sliver in the quartzite cliffs that loom above **Split Rock Creek**. According to one legend, the rocks were split by the Great Spirit's tomahawk. According to another, outlaw Jesse James jumped across the gap while being pursued by a posse. Fortunately for modern travelers, they

can now cross the gap over a short bridge. Devil's Gulch lends Garretson an Old West image, but it is primarily a small farming community.

The prairies of eastern South Dakota and the pioneers who settled this land have been immortalized both on canvas and in popular literature. The paintings of Harvey Dunn, son of homesteaders and sod-busters, depict the reality and the dignity of these people. These same themes are mirrored in the work of Laura Ingalls Wilder, author of the beloved *Little House on the Prairie* and other books concerning life in the pioneer era before it was changed by modern times. (The books have now become an enormous industry, with over 50 million volumes having been sold. With the aid of some of Ingalls' descendants, ghostwriters have been employed to continue the series.)

To save time through this stretch of the Great Plains, get onto I-90, which cuts through eastern South Dakota in a nearly straight line through terrain that becomes a bit hillier and less green as rainfall becomes scarcer and the cultivation of hay and wheat mingles with that of corn.

These crops will eventually be taken to busy and industrious **Sioux Falls** ㊹, the state's commercial center, a city of little interest apart from the waterfalls themselves in Falls Park.

Farther west, in **Mitchell** ㊺, they have created a monument to – and with – all the amber-colored grains: the **Corn Palace** (tel: 866-273-2676; www.cornpalace.org; Dec–Mar Mon–Sat). It's one good reason to stop in Mitchell – the other being to take a much-needed break from the interstate. The Corn Palace is most certainly the world's only Byzantine structure decorated with murals of corn and other grains; each year, the patterns change according to local whim. It is a slice of quintessential Americana.

As I-90 approaches the Missouri River, which divides South Dakota

into "East River" and "West River," a very different type of terrain lies ahead.

Deadwood Trail and Cottonwood

Western South Dakota is unquestionably where the West begins. Visually, the Badlands and the Black Hills rise out of the prairie and hit you with a one-two punch; they are equally unexpected and stunning. But there is more to these regions than just their bleak beauty. They have been witnesses to some pretty tumultuous history.

If you're hurrying, stay on I-90 through to these twin wonders, but if you've got the time and inclination to explore rural South Dakota, then meander west instead along US 14, which you can pick up at the rather ordinary state capital of **Pierre** ㊻, reached on US 83 North from Vivian. After crossing the banks of the Missouri River, set your watch back an hour and prepare to traverse mound after mound of prairie grass. This route also coincides with a section of the old **Deadwood Trail**, a legendary wagon train and stagecoach route.

TIP

After crossing the Missouri River at Pierre, South Dakota, set your watch back by one hour; Central time gives way to Mountain time here.

The Corn Palace, Mitchell, South Dakota.

*Badlands National
Park – a landscape
etched by wind and
water.*

The wagon-trains and stagecoaches were destined for uncivilized parts of the expanding nation; nevertheless, they had certain rules. "If you must drink, share the bottle," was one. Chewing tobacco was permitted, though it was requested the chewer spit "with the wind, not against it." And specified topics of conversation were forbidden: stagecoach robberies and Indian uprisings, to name but two.

US 14 cuts due south and then west again toward **Cottonwood**, foretold by grove after grove of cottonwood trees – the almost magical tree with the ability to "find" water in an arid landscape, and then reproduce in small communities. This tree was the single most useful tool the prairie settlers had: they could build a fence with it, sit under its shade, even cut into its bark to drink a bit of watery pulp in an emergency. Whenever you see the cottonwood's big-toothed leaves in a valley, you know there is water nearby, whether it be in the form of river, stream or some other hidden source.

Continuing west, motorists are besieged by a growing number of signs imploring them to stop at Wall Drug, located in Wall on the northern edge of the Badlands. Depending on your degree of thirst, hunger, illness, or defiance, you can continue west and arrive at Wall in no time at all, or turn south at Cottonwood directly into the Badlands.

This area is also known as the Dakota by the Sioux Indians, which roughly translates as "land bad." French trappers in the early part of the 19th century described it as "a bad land to cross." Many contemporary travelers bypass the Badlands (rarely visible from the interstate) while rushing to the Black Hills and the stone faces of Mount Rushmore, but it is a unique landscape and one that is certainly worth seeing – even if it can be a brutally hot place in summer.

Badlands National Park

This constantly eroding landscape has often served as a metaphor of youthful malaise and rootlessness: Terence Malick used it as a title for an acclaimed film (*Badlands*, 1973), and Bruce Springsteen later sang about "Badlands"

on his 1978 album "Darkness at the Edge of Town." Despite all the discouraging words, there is a rare and striking beauty to be found here – it's well worth a detour off the interstate and the $15 per vehicle charge that it costs to enter the national park.

The Badlands have been described as "Hell with the fires burned out," but, fire has played no part in it; it has been shaped chiefly by wind and water. Spires, turrets, and ridges form a silent skyline, which changes with each gust of wind and torrential (although infrequent) downpour. **Badlands National Park** ❼ (tel: 605-433-5361; www.nps. gov/badl; daily) is not a single piece of land, but rather several chunks of territory loosely strung together and carved out of **Buffalo Gap National Grassland** and the **Pine Ridge Indian Reservation**.

It is possible to be driving through rolling grasslands and suddenly be confronted without warning with Badlands terrain: huge sand castles and canyon walls. A 40-mile (64km) loop road traverses the park and provides access to points of geological and paleontological interest, including a number of hikes through the strange terrain.

This was once the stomping ground of ancient camels, three-toed horses, and saber-toothed tigers, whose fossilized remains continue to be uncovered by the elements. Many of these fossils, dating back to the Oligocene epoch, 24 to 34 million years ago, have been preserved by the **South Dakota School of Mines and Technology** and are exhibited at their **Museum of Geology** (tel: 605-394-2467; http://museum.sdsmt. edu; May–Aug daily, Sept–Apr Mon–Sat) in Rapid City. The largest of the Oligocene mammals was the titanothere, known in Sioux mythology as the Thunderhorse. It was believed by the Sioux that this creature descended from the heavens during thunderstorms and killed buffalo.

Enthusiasts were well on their way oward cleaning out the Badlands of its ssil treasures before the government and Federal protection intervened, and the abundant wildlife that once roamed here was also largely gone by the 1890s – depleted by the throng of humanity en route to the Black Hills in search of "the devil's metal" – gold.

Wildlife sanctuary

Thanks to reintroduction and protection, however, the park is today a sanctuary for pronghorn antelope and buffalo. Prairie dogs also thrive here in their own metropolis. These peculiar rodents employ an elaborate system of tunnels, entry holes, and sentries; a shrill "barking" rings throughout the prairie if anyone ventures too closely.

Ranchers neither particularly like these creatures – as cattle can be severely injured by stepping into their holes – nor the weather, which here is as severe as it is unpredictable. Old-timers still talk about the blizzard of May 1905, when the weather progressed from balmy to icy. Thousands of head of cattle and horses drifted south with the wind and eventually fell to their death by pitching over the north wall of the Badlands.

Where the buffalo roam – across a road in South Dakota.

Chicago: The Windy City

Broad-shouldered and big-hearted, Chicago has a long list of aliases: Chitown and Second City are just two.

Although a few people might well dispute the authenticity of some of Chicago's various nicknames, one in particular will remain forever true: Crossroads of the Midwest. Chicago's railroad yards are the largest in the world. O'Hare claims to be the world's busiest airport. Even the famed Art Institute of Chicago straddles train tracks. Visitors get around the city by a light railway known as the El, for "elevated," because it usually is.

The site, at the confluence of the Midwestern prairie, the Chicago River, and Lake Michigan, was an obvious place for a town to spring up. With the building of a canal in the 1840s – essentially linking the Great Lakes with the Mississippi River drainage system – followed by the advent of railroading, Chicago spread like the proverbial wildfire as commerce and masses of immigrants descended upon it.

Then, in 1871, wildfire became a reality. As the story goes, a certain Mrs O'Leary's cow knocked over a certain lantern, starting a disastrous blaze known as the "Great Chicago Fire." After the fire,

Willis Tower (formerly called the Sears Tower).

the city became the workshop of architects like William LeBaron Jenny (the father of the skyscraper), Louis H. Sullivan, Frank Lloyd Wright, and later Ludwig Mies van der Rohe.

From the **Chicago Water Tower and Pumping Station**, the only public building to survive the Great Fire, to the **Sears Tower**, tallest building in America, the city's buildings and skyline are built to impress.

A few remnants of the 19th century have managed to survive, particularly in the **Prairie Avenue Historic District**. Once known as the "Avenue of Avenues," the area experienced a mass exodus during the early part of the 20th century. However, the buildings that remain are now being restored and lovingly protected.

Chicago has made the most of its magnificent lakeshore. A huge front yard encompasses 29 miles (47km) of beaches, wonderful parks with distinct personalities and some of the nation's finest cultural institutions: open daily are the **Museum of Science and Industry** (tel: 773-684-1414) on the South Side; the **Field Museum** (tel: 312-922-9410), the excellent **Shedd Aquarium** (tel: 312-939-2438; www.sheddaquarium.org; daily), and the **Art Institute of Chicago** (tel: 312-443-3600; www.artic.edu; daily), all in **Grant Park**. The Art Institute, with its suberb Modern Wing designed by celebrated architect Renzo Piano, is known for its collection of works by the French Impressionists, and is also the home of that famous stoic couple staring out of Grant Wood's painting *American Gothic*.

Chicago is crazy about outdoor sculpture. All the big names are represented – including Oldenburg, Calder, Picasso, Miro, and Dubuffet. Chicago is the ultimate *film noir* set piece. Never has a place been

Live music venue The Back Room.

so closely associated with gangsters and political corruption, the latter almost an institution. Eternally proud of those things that set it apart, the city has made little attempt to dispel these images even if they are quite unrealistic today. The real life of Chicago is a bit different. Politics are one face of it: black activist Jesse Jackson started his political career here and former mayor Richard J. Daley – gone but never forgotten – pulled the town's strings for so long that time is now measured in years AD ("After Daley"). And of course, no one can forget former Governor of Illinois Rod Blagojevich who was impeached by the Illinois Senate in 2009 for attempting to sell President Barack Obama's former Senate seat then later appeared on Donald Trump's reality TV show, *The Celebrity Apprentice*.

This is also a writer's town, as articulate as it is brash. A steady stream of writers have interpreted their hometown for the rest of the world, everyone from James T. Farrell and Richard Wright to Saul Bellow, Studs Terkel, David Mamet, and the columnist Mike Royko. The Second City, an edgy improv comedy group that originated in Chicago, is an incubator for comedians who then go on to star on the nationally broadcast *Saturday Night Live* late-night show based in New York City.

Dark, smoky blues clubs have long been part of the Chicago scene, ever since players and singers from fields in the rural South relocated and invented "electric blues" here. You can hear all about it at **B.L.U.E.S.** on North Halsted or at the relocated **New Checkerboard Lounge** on the city's rougher South Side, where generations of University of Chicago undergraduates have learned about the important things in life from bluesman Muddy Waters.

There's a new brightness to the hip North Side of Chicago; after an impassioned debate, Wrigley Field, the home of the Chicago Cubs, was the last Major League baseball park to get lights, thereby facilitating night games.

The communities flanking Chicago have become part of the silver screen in a number of films poking fun at suburbia. **Glencoe**, to the north, is familiar to many as the home of Joel, the fictional teenager played by Tom Cruise in the movie *Risky Business* who submerges his father's Porsche in Lake Michigan. **Aurora** was the setting for the wacky comedy *Wayne's World*. And Joliet's penitentiary briefly housed John Belushi in *The Blues Brothers*.

Landlocked **Oak Park** is west of Chicago's Loop via I-290, on the other side of the city limits. Ernest Hemingway grew up here, and Frank Lloyd Wright lived and worked in Oak Park during the early part of his career before moving to Wisconsin. He left behind 25 buildings, making this the world's largest repository of his work. Wright's home and studio, built in 1889, is most revealing of his personality and genius: every touch, from the distinctive and renowned streamlined Prairie Style to the Scottish proverb that's carved over a fireplace, bears his characteristic imprint.

Thanksgiving Day parade on State Street.

THE BADLANDS TO YELLOWSTONE

Drive through the land of Buffalo Bill, Wild Bill Hickok,
Calamity Jane, and the Sundance Kid to see Mount
Rushmore and the tragic sites of the Indian Wars.

Seattle

Leaving the Badlands behind and heading west through South Dakota on Route 44, you will come upon tiny Scenic, a ramshackle place named by someone with an extremely wry sense of humor; in exactly the same spirit, a sign along the main road ("Business District") signals your arrival. There's a tiny church here, a few abandoned shacks, several vintage mobile homes, a hole-in-the-wall US Post Office, a heap of junked cars, and, on the edge of town, the place people come here to see: the Longhorn Saloon.

The Longhorn was established in 1906, and the ankle-deep sawdust on the floor has been collecting ever since, as have the bullet holes and cattle brands on the ceiling. In its heyday, it was always the site of a recent shootout, and even now discomfort pervades the atmosphere. Tractor seats mounted on metal barrels serve as bar stools. Its facade features longhorn skulls and a weather-beaten sign that originally read "no Indians allowed," the "no" of which has been removed; the staff are often Oglala Sioux from the nearby Pine Ridge Reservation. Route 44 will take you on to Rapid City.

Wounded Knee

The Pine Ridge Reservation surrounds the southern tier of Badlands National Park and coincides with Shannon County, which has the lowest per capita income in the United States. On this bleak land, Wounded Knee Creek bleeds off from the White River to the site of the infamous massacre of December 29, 1890 – when 250 Sioux, mostly unarmed, were slaughtered by the army. Chief Sitting Bull was a casualty of this skirmish – the last tragic episode of the Indian Wars – and the name "Wounded Knee" has become an enduring symbol of unfathomable loss.

Main Attractions
Black Hills
Mount Rushmore National
  Memorial
Deadwood
Devils Tower
Denver
Sheridan
Little Bighorn Battlefield
Big Horn County Historical
  Museum
Buffalo Bill Historical Center

Rock tunnel on Iron Mountain Road in the Black Hills.

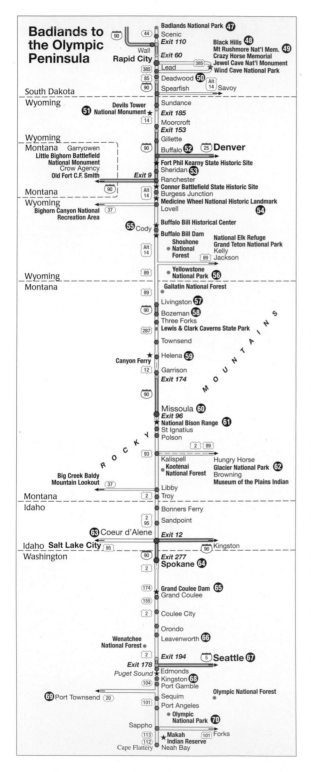

Badlands to
the Olympic
Peninsula

90   44

Wall
Rapid City

South Dakota
Wyoming

Wyoming

Wyoming
Montana   Garryowen
Little Bighorn Battlefield
National Monument
Crow Agency
Old Fort C.F. Smith

Montana
Wyoming
Bighorn Canyon National
Recreation Area

55 Cody

Wyoming
Montana

Canyon Ferry

Big Creek Baldy
Mountain Lookout   37

Montana
Idaho

63 Coeur d'Alene

Idaho Salt Lake City   95
Washington

Wenatchee
National Forest

69 Port Townsend   20

Badlands National Park   47
Scenic
Exit 110   Black Hills   48
385   Mt Rushmore Nat'l Mem. 49
385   Crazy Horse Memorial
Lead   Jewel Cave Nat'l Monument
85 Deadwood   50   Wind Cave National Park
90 Spearfish   Alt 14 Savoy

Sundance
Exit 185
Moorcroft
Exit 153
Gillette
90 Buffalo 52   25 Denver
★ Fort Phil Kearny State Historic Site
Sheridan 53
Ranchester
Alt 14 ★ Connor Battlefield State Historic Site
Burgess Junction
Medicine Wheel National Historic Landmark
Lovell   54
Buffalo Bill Historical Center
Buffalo Bill Dam   National Elk Refuge
Shoshone   Grand Teton National Park
Alt 14 ● National   Kelly
Forest   89 ● Jackson
89 ● Yellowstone
National Park   56
89 ● Gallatin National Forest
● Livingston   57
90 ● Bozeman   58
Three Forks
287 ● Lewis & Clark Caverns State Park
● Townsend
★ Helena 59
12 ● Garrison
Exit 174
90
● Missoula   60
Exit 96
★ National Bison Range   61
● St Ignatius
● Polson
2   89
93 ● Kalispell   Hungry Horse
● Kootenai   Glacier National Park   62
National Forest Browning
Museum of the Plains Indian
● Libby
2 ● Troy
● Bonners Ferry
2
95 ● Sandpoint
Exit 12
90 Kingston
90
Exit 277
2 Spokane   64

174 ● Grand Coulee Dam   65
155 Grand Coulee
2 ● Coulee City
● Orondo
2 ● Leavenworth   66
2 Exit 194   5 Seattle   67
Exit 178
Puget Sound ★ Edmonds
104 ● Kingston 68
● Port Gamble
● Sequim   Olympic National Forest
101 ● Port Angeles
● Olympic
National Park   70
Sappho
113 ★ Makah   101 Forks
112 Indian Reserve
Cape Flattery Neah Bay

51 Devils Tower
National Monument ★
14

ROCKY MOUNTAINS

Wall Drug (tel: 605-279-2175; www. walldrug.com), in the town of Wall (located on I-90 after completing a loop of the park), is a one-of-a-kind roadside stop – though it can't possibly live up to the miles of repeated advertising painted onto abandoned trucks and wooden signs as you come west. Never has there been a more elaborate drugstore: located on the northern wall of the Badlands alongside the interstate, it is difficult to pass through this part of South Dakota without dropping in.

Apothecary Ted Hustead began posting the ubiquitous signs along the highway in the early 1930s, inspired by the old Burma Shave (see page 38) signs. By the time drivers hit the Missouri River, even the most stoic of travelers perceives a need for a glass (or maybe even a jug) of Wall Drug's famous ice water which has been offered free of charge for decades. Hence, what began as the only drugstore in a small, dusty town became famous as the "Ice Water Store" and now takes up most of Main Street.

Wall Drug has, among other things, a chapel for those in need of solace; a clothing and boot shop for those in need of Western duds; a bookstore; jewelry made from Black Hills gold, and a Western art gallery. There is also a staggering assortment of Western "attractions," from a replica of Mount Rushmore (for those tired of driving) to a mythical 6ft (2-meter) "jackalope" (a rabbit with antlers for the uninitiated), a mounted buffalo, and life-sized carvings of Butch Cassidy and the Sundance Kid. Donuts and coffee are free year-round for honeymooners and veterans and during the season for skiers and hunters. Approximately 20,000 folks stop by Wall Drug on a good day. It's the archetypal American success story, and Ted Hustead defines the lesson of his success in this way: "there's absolutely no place on God's earth that's godforsaken."

The ride from Wall to **Rapid City** along I-90 is approximately 50 mile (80km) of rolling, treeless prairie a wheat fields. You'll note black cattle dotting the grasslands, rolling hills slowly increasing in elevation and occasional patches of sunflowers. Rapid City, settled by prospectors in 1876 and slowly be-coming a sophisticated place, is the gateway to the Black Hills.

The Black Hills

"... *as long as rivers run and grass grows and trees bear leaves, Paha Sapa, the Black Hills of South Dakota, will forever be the sacred land of the Sioux Indians.*" excerpt, 1868 Treaty between US Government and Sioux Nation
"*There's gold in them thar hills.*" attribuited to US Army scouts, 1874.
These words, taken together, summarize the course of late 19th-century history in the **Black Hills** ❽ and indeed throughout the West; an era characterized by greed, deception, and bloodshed. The Sioux were "granted" eternal rights to this land that held little interest for the white man until the discovery of gold. After that, of course, it was a different story.

George Armstrong Custer led an army reconnaissance expedition through here in 1874. The presence of gold was barely confirmed before a deluge of humanity swept through the hills, leaving the treaty of 1868 shredded in its wake. Years of bloodshed followed, and the Sioux would never regain exclusive rights to their sacred *Paha Sapa*. However, In 2012, a United Nations Special Rapporteur conducted a 12-day tour of the region and concluded that the Black Hills should be given back to the Sioux tribe. The dispute is still being settled. Meanwhile, a stream of travelers flow through the Black Hills every day – mostly past Mount Rushmore, the "shrine of democracy" that was never completed.

Going on past Rapid City and all the rampant commercialism of US 16, you'll encounter a road of another color, a 17-mile (27km) corkscrew known as the **Iron Mountain Road**. It is one of the spectacular, specially engineered Black Hills highways built in the 1930s and intended for pleasure

You are now in rattlesnake country.

Mount Rushmore National Memorial.

driving. The inspiration of Highway Commissioner Peter Norbeck, the roads are characterized by hairpin turns, switchbacks, granite tunnels (placed to provide remarkable vistas) and pigtail bridges using native pine columns in place of steel.

Mount Rushmore National Memorial

Rather than sashaying around the mountain, Iron Mountain Road heads straight for the top. It passes by **Mount Rushmore National Memorial** ㊾ (tel: 605-574-2523; www.nps.gov.moru; daily), which first appears framed at the end of a tunnel. This sight is akin to watching Hitchcock's *North by Northwest* (1959) on television from across the room. You may find yourself squinting to see if those specks up there are actually Cary Grant and Eva Marie Saint escaping across the six-story, granite faces.

Rushmore, the (uncarved) mountain, was purportedly named for Charles E. Rushmore, a New York attorney who visited here in 1885. When he asked a local about the name of the (then-nameless) peak, the fellow

The head of Crazy Horse Memorial.

is said to have obligingly replied, "It is called Mount Rushmore." In the 1920s, Doane Robinson, the official historian of South Dakota, was considering various projects aimed at attracting visitors to the Black Hills. He decided on the concept of a colossal mountain carving, envisioning statues of legendary mountain men such as Jim Bridger, John Colter, and Kit Carson. But the more universally admired presidential subjects (George Washington, Thomas Jefferson, Abraham Lincoln, and, later, Theodore Roosevelt) were finally chosen.

In 1927, sculptor Gutzon Borglum (then 60 years old) was commissioned to do the work. The enormous endeavor took him the remainder of his life, and work on the mountain came to a permanent halt following Borglum's death and then the Japanese attack on Pearl Harbor. It's interesting to note that Borglum had intended the figures to be carved to the waist, and had he begun from the bottom rather than the top, the US would have been left with a rather peculiar shrine to democracy.

The project was always plagued by controversy and a lack of funding, largely as a result of the Depression and Borglum's artistic temperament and egotism. Some say he pushed for the inclusion of Roosevelt because he considered the president's spectacles to be a particular challenge to his skills, for instance. Also controversial is the fact that the monument sits on a site considered sacred by the Sioux. The granite promontory is part of the United Nations inquiry and it has been suggested by the UN that the site be given back to the Sioux.

Crazy Horse

Mount Rushmore is not the only mountain carving in the Black Hills. There is also the Crazy Horse Memorial (tel: 605-673-4681; daily), a work-in-progress by the late Korczak Ziolkowski. Whereas Mount Rushmore remains incomplete, Crazy Horse, even more ambitious in scale, is still in its infancy. Ziolkowski left detailed plans and instructions behind, and the grounds – the town of Crazy Horse now – are literally abuzz with workers.

Ziolkowski was engaged to carve this depiction of the great Sioux warrior by Chief Henry Standing Bear so that the white man might know that "the red man had great heroes, too." Although some 8 million tons of rock have been blasted off the mountain since 1949, it is still difficult to visualize a figure on horseback without the aid of a 1/34th scale plaster model. Still, the figure is gradually taking shape. Come for a look at the mountain and also to visit the ever-expanding **Indian Museum of North America**, as well as Ziolkowski's studio. Learning about the sculptor, his life and his ambitions for this place is time well spent. Ziolkowski was a fascinating giant of man, as a father, artist, and humanitarian. He liked to think of himself as a "storyteller in stone," and these are words he personally inscribed on the door of his tomb.

South of Mount Rushmore and Crazy Horse is **Wind Cave**, the first cave to be named a National Park. Wind Cave and **Jewel Cave** (its sister to the west) are the fourth- and second-longest caves in the world, respectively. They are characterized by calcite crystals and honeycomb formations known as "boxwork," found more extensively here than anywhere else in the world. The National Parks Service offers scheduled Candlelight Cave Tours of Wind Cave during the summer months, a mystical experience for most visitors.

Driving Needles Highway

North of Wind Cave in the direction of Lead is Needles Highway, another Black Hills driving experience. The road was built to show off the Needles, granite spires which reach for the sky. The highway meanders and climbs several miles up into the firmament, at times through tiny granite tunnels. You must sound your horn before proceeding and don't let your attention stray too far.

Past Needles Highway, continuing north toward **Lead** on US 385, the

Cathedral Spires – Needles Highway was built to show them off.

A drive through Spearfish Canyon, South Dakota.

"Wild Bill" Hickok's grave in Mount Moriah Cemetery.

Dancing and singing at a South Dakota tribal gathering.

aroma of pine pervades the atmosphere as the road passes through thick, dark stands of ponderosa pine. The appearance of these trees from afar gave the Black Hills its name. Lead (pronounced "*leed*"), named for a lode or vein of ore, is the site of **Homestake Gold Mine**, which produced more gold than any other gold mine in the Western Hemisphere during its 125 years of operation. It's still a company town of pickup truck-driving roughnecks, though tourists now mix curiously with them on the patchwork main street. The town's main tourist attraction is the old "**Open Cut**" – a gash in the side of the mountain where gold was originally discovered in 1876. **Deadwood** ⑳, 3 miles (5km) northeast of Lead on US 85, is the other Black Hills town built by gold. In fact, this was the original center of local gold mining activity – called to mind in the Eric Taylor/Nanci Griffith song "Deadwood, South Dakota" – before Lead overtook it. During the 1870s, Deadwood gained a reputation as the quintessential Wild West town thanks to local characters like "Wild Bill" Hickok, Calamity Jane, and

others. Wild Bill and Calamity are buried beside each other in **Mount Moriah Cemetery** high above Deadwood, in accordance with Jane's last wishes, but today the place is rather tame and highly overdeveloped, its every nook devoted either to perpetuating a faux-"Wild West" image or to milking tourists out of their cash at one of the many gambling casinos. *Deadwood* was even the name of a popular, award-winning television series that aired on HBO from 2004 to 2006 which depicted the town in its infancy and used newspaper accounts and diaries from the 19th century in the formation of the story and plot lines.

If you must, visit **Saloon No. 10**, where Wild Bill was fatally shot by Jack McCall – but you have to find it first, as several bars claim the location. The real one is billed as "Home of the Deadman's Hand" and "The Only Museum in the World With a Bar," but the most interesting attractions of this area lie outside the town as you head further west. Descend from the hills via spectacular **Spearfish Canyon**, reached by driving north from Deadwood on

US 85 for a few miles, then west on I-90, then US Alt-14 south. You can turn off onto a still rougher Forest Service road at the town of **Savoy** to glimpse the landscape where part of the movie *Dances With Wolves* was filmed.

Spearfish River country

On US Alt-14, the canyon, threaded by the highway, winds down and down right alongside the cool, shaded Spearfish River. You'll have plenty of motorcycles and recreational vehicles for company, but there are a number of pull-offs where you can park and hike up or down the canyon in some solitude, noting the striking high cliffs of sandy-colored rock topped with aspen and pine trees. As this is the last green oasis before some very long and open stretches of forlorn Western country, you'd be well advised to do so.

WYOMING AND SOUTHERN MONTANA

Quite simply, the West is not like the rest of the country. The professional sport of choice here is not football, nor baseball, but rodeo. The sky seems larger than anywhere else, and you'll see frequent references to "Big Sky" country. This is a land of last stands, last chances, lost dreams; it is also a region of sparsely populated open spaces characterized by a wild natural beauty. The 2005 Academy Award-winning film *Brokeback Mountain*, directed by Ang Lee and starring Heath Ledger and Jake Gyllenhaal as sheepherders, is set in Wyoming and beautifully depicts the state's stark wilderness.

Both Wyoming and Montana are the quintessential Western states. They lead all others in statistical extremity – the most bars, drive-ins, gas stations, cars, and mobile homes per capita. The myths of the West live on here in the hearts and lives of the people who call this vast country home; theirs is not an easy life, they will tell you, but they would not trade it for anything.

Descending from the Black Hills of South Dakota by way of Spearfish Canyon brings you right to I-90, less than 10 miles (16km) from the **Wyoming** border. The "Cowboy State," known locally as simply "Wyo," greets you with a sign proving you are in the West: while neighboring South Dakota has chosen somber presidential faces for its license plates, Wyoming has opted for a silhouette of a cowboy riding a bucking bronco. You'll notice this icon everywhere you go in the state.

Wyoming has a small piece of the **Black Hills National Forest**, located not far from the border outside of plain **Sundance** – the town "Where the Kid Got His Name." Indeed, Harry Longabaugh, better known as the "Sundance Kid," was said to have shot a deputy sheriff near here and subsequently headed for his infamous **"Hole-in-the-Wall"** hideout about 150 miles (240km) southwest. Once little known outside the West, his memory now lives on – and his name has become a household word – thanks to Robert Redford and Paul Newman, stars of the everlastingly popular movie *Butch Cassidy and the Sundance Kid*.

Devils Tower is well known to fans of "Close Encounters of the Third Kind".

A bison (buffalo) calf frolicking in the grasslands.

Denver State Capitol Building.

Past Sundance, US 14 loops up toward the Black Hills and **Devils Tower** ⑤, the object of obsession in a very different but equally popular film, *Close Encounters of the Third Kind*. Visible from almost 100 miles (160km) away, this 867ft (264-meter) fluted, butte-like rock formation is the tallest of its kind in America. It stands on the other side of the Belle Fourche River, where the Black Hills meet the gullies and grasslands of the plains.

The first white men to explore this region, supposedly misinterpreting a benign name ascribed to it by Native Americans, called it Devils Tower. It held a prominent place in the folklore and legends of the Sioux, and it later served as a landmark for those traveling west, just as it does today.

You can hike around the base of the tower, but beware of rattlesnakes. The majority of visitors simply stare at its almost supernatural shape and size – particularly luminous at sunrise or by the light of the moon. The sight of it so impressed Teddy Roosevelt that he designated it the nation's first national monument in 1906.

South of the monument, the road loops back onto I-90 at **Moorcroft**, an old cow town. The old Texas Trail made its way through here in the 19th century, trampled by cowboys driving cattle all the way to Montana. Farther west, through and beyond drab **Gillette**, the plains are vast and beautiful, marked only by cattle and the occasional river bottom of aspen and cottonwood trees. Even before crossing the Powder River and its tributary, Crazy Woman Creek, you can see the improbable pile of the Crazy Mountains looming, and then the snow-streaked peaks of the **Bighorn Mountains** in the distance: a tremendous relief for the traveler weary of the Great Plains.

Buffalo, Wyoming

If you're taking US 14, you'll go through towns with colorful names such as Spotted Horse and Ucross. Take I-90, though, and you must drive

---

DETOUR TO DENVER

A drive of grand vistas along the base of the Rocky Mountains on I-25 from Buffalo, Wyoming, leads after 388 miles (624km) to Denver, the Mile-High City. Celebrating the Gold Rush that built it is the grand Capitol building, covered in 250oz (7kg) of 28-carat gold leaf. In the mid-1800s, weary, unlucky prospectors flocked to Denver for guns, booze, and women; the gambling halls never closed. Throughout the 1880s, money from silver camps bolstered the economy, and the population increased nearly threefold. The Black American West Museum, and Buffalo Bill Museum and Grave (www. buffalobill.org) atop Lookout Mountain hark back to these early days. A metropolitan flair is added by attractions like the Coors Brewery (free samples) and the Denver Art Museum (www.denverartmuseum.org), specializing in Asian, pre-Columbian, and Native American art (with a titanium and glass wing designed by Daniel Libeskind). But for all its culture, the city's natural setting is an easy distraction. Not only do the Rocky Mountains lie less than an hour away, but Denver is in charge of the largest park system in the country. Even its ever-popular concert venue, Red Rocks Amphitheatre (www.redrockson-line.com), is a natural outdoor wonder, hollowed out of red sandstone on a site high above the city. For information telephone The Denver Visitors Bureau on 800-233-6837 or visit www.denver.org.

a sparse (if beautiful) 70-mile (113km) stretch without so much as a town or gas pump to interrupt you, only miles of empty ranch lands. The lone break in this stretch is a forlorn rest area among trees at the crossing of the Powder River.

Traveling westward, the Bighorns gradually become closer. They were named for bighorn sheep, once prevalent here but now infrequently seen. As abrupt as they are majestic, the Bighorns foretell the Rocky Mountain ranges just beyond. These eastern foothills are today traversed by I-90 just as they once were by the Bozeman Trail, a bloody short cut in the 19th-century push westward through Sioux, Crow, and Cheyenne Indian hunting grounds.

Buffalo 52, where the interstate highway bends north for Montana, was actually named after the town in New York and not for the formidable animals that once thundered across the plains. It was one of the earliest settlements in this corner of Wyoming, and its main street was formerly an old trail that negotiated Clear Creek. The road from Buffalo to Sheridan passes near the remains – now a state historic site – of Fort Phil Kearny (tel: 307-684-7629; daily). This was the most hated army outpost of all along the Bozeman Trail, and when it was finally abandoned in 1868, it was immediately burned to the ground by local Native Americans.

Historic Sheridan

About 20 miles (32km) south of the Montana border lies the small historic city of **Sheridan 53**, where I-90 and US 14 meet, and county seat in a region once inhabited by Crow Indians but now a major cattle-producing area. The railroad came to town in 1890 and played a major role in the development of the city. There are a number of historic homes, but the real pleasure is strolling Main Street among real-life saloons, and cowboys. Have a drink at the Mint Bar, whose shingle walls are carved with hundreds of brands – each one different – of the cowboys who drank here. Across the street, through the back of King's Saddlery, is **Don King's Museum** (tel: 307-672-2702; Mon–Sat). You could spend hours perusing this fascinating private

Bison in Yellowstone National Park. A mature bull can weight around 2,000lbs and run up to 40mph.

FACT

The Battle of Little Bighorn, also known as "Custer's Last Stand," took place on June 25, 1876. The battle lasted only one hour, during which time the Seventh Cavalry lost over 200 soldiers, the Sioux and Cheyenne fewer than 100 men.

Bighorn Canyon.

collection of Western items, which includes cowboy and Native American memorabilia, historic photos, leatherwork, and around 600 saddles, many with intricately carved decoration.

Across the street from the old railroad station is the **Sheridan Inn** (now sadly closed, see below), a gracious structure with a long, inviting front porch. It was built in 1893 by the Burlington Railroad and Sheridan Land Company. William F. "Buffalo Bill" Cody once owned part of this inn and made it his second home; it was customary for Cody to sit on the porch and audition acts for his Wild West Show.

Modeled after a Scottish inn, most of the materials used in its construction were shipped from back East by rail. In its day, it was considered to be the finest hotel between Chicago and San Francisco; presidents and such celebrities as Ernest Hemingway, General Pershing, and Will Rogers all stayed the night here, and this was the first building in the area to feature bathtubs and electric lights. The lights were powered by an abandoned threshing machine and illuminated from dusk until midnight, when a whistle was blown to warn of impending darkness. Later came a telephone, first in the county. But the inn's pride and joy was its bar, constructed in England from oak and mahogany and hauled from Gillette by ox team. Still in use today, it's known as the "Buffalo Bill Bar."

Unfortunately, the historic inn is struggling to raise funds and stay afloat, and its future is uncertain; in 2012, the bank began foreclosure proceedings.

Along I-90 north of Sheridan, as you approach the Montana border, sit two of the most infamous sites of the 1860s "Indian Wars." **Ranchester** is the location of **Connor Battlefield**, where General Patrick E. Connor led a division of more than 300 soldiers in an ambush of an Arapaho encampment. The Arapaho lost 64 of their people and their camp was virtually destroyed. Women and children were brutally massacred here, and as a result Connor lost his command.

Just north of Ranchester is the **Montana** line – also the beginning of the massive, empty-seeming **Crow**

Indian Reservation. I-90 passes right through its heart, through the desolate-looking but neatly kept ranch lands of the reserve.

Battle of Little Bighorn

The town of Garryowen, named after an Irish drinking song, leads you into the legendary **Little Bighorn Battlefield** (tel: 406-638-2621; www. nps.gov/libi; daily), now a national monument. The Battle of Little Bighorn, better known as "Custer's Last Stand," took about as long as it takes for a white man to eat his dinner, according to one observer. But the Sioux and Cheyenne who fought that day were to lose the greater struggle. Two-hundred and sixty white marble stones along with the words of Oglala Chief Black Elk, in Lakota and English: "Know the Power that is Peace" now sanctify the field where Custer's men died.

Beyond the battle site is **Crow Agency**, headquarters of this 2.5 million-acre (1 million-hectare) reservation – far less than the lands outlined in the original treaty, which designated 38 million acres (15 million hectares) as Crow land. This area, bisected by the Bighorn River and characterized by rolling hills, was described by Crow Chief Rotten Belly in the 1830s as being "exactly in the right place. Everything good is to be found there. There is no country like the Crow Country." To get a glimpse of what modern Indian life is like out here today, pull off the interstate and drop into the gas station or grocery store.

Back on the highway, you'll begin to notice the first of many signs indicating "chain up" areas – turnouts where truckers wrap heavy chains around their tires in foul weather to obtain better traction through the treacherous mountain passes that await further inside Montana.

Make time at the northern edge of the Crow reservation, just south of Hardin, for a stop at the **Big Horn County Historical Museum** (tel: 406-665-1671; www.bighorncountry museum.org; May–Sept daily, Oct– Apr Mon–Fri). This collection of architectural structures from around the huge, spare county – which is tops in agricultural production for this state – includes a train station, German church, and the original farmhouse and barn that occupied the site. The museum also serves as your first pickup point for Montana information, and its helpful staff can direct you to area attractions such as the superb fishing in **Bighorn Canyon**. Crow guides will take you up the canyon for a price, and if you'd like to stay on the reservation, lodges and motels are thick on the ground in **Fort Smith**.

From Crow Agency to Billings, I-90 skirts the northern boundary of the reservation through towns with names like Big Timber. It doesn't get interesting again until you've reached Livingston and Bozeman. If you wish to see Yellowstone, you can also reach those towns via a scenic – if roundabout – method, by backtracking south a bit to Ranchester, Wyoming.

Graves at Little Big Horn Battlefield, Montana.

Buffalo Bill rose to fame through a series of dime novels based on his character. His Wild West show hit the road in 1883 and by the 1890s was performing in Europe in front of royalty.

William F. Cody's buffalo hide coat (c.1871) in the Buffalo Bill Museum.

Toward Yellowstone

Approaching the Bighorn Mountains via I-90 in clear weather, you can sometimes discern a road switch-backing its way up the snow-streaked slopes. Traveling west from Ranchester to Lovell allows you to experience it first-hand. US 14 out of Ranchester ascends Bighorn National Forest past bullet-ridden signposts to Burgess Junction. The road is treacherous beyond this point: several runaway truck ramps and brake-cooling turnouts help drivers negotiate the steep grades and sharp turns.

About 20 miles (32km) beyond Burgess Junction is a 3-mile (5km) bumpy gravel road, US 14A, leading to the largest ancient **Medicine Wheel** 54 **site in North America**. Although well paved, the road is extremely narrow and winding, at one point crossing a narrow ridge. But the views from these highest reaches of the Bighorns are stupendous, and the immediate countryside is sprinkled with wildflowers. Near its end, the road forks and presents you with a clear choice: the 20th-century radar facility to the left or the medicine wheel to the right. Go right.

This medicine wheel is the most elaborate of a series of stone circles found east of the Rocky Mountains, its 28 spokes forming an almost perfect circle 74ft (23 meters) in diameter. It is thought to be about 600 years old, but its creators and its purpose still remain a mystery. According to Crow legend, the wheel was here when they arrived in the 1770s. Today, it serves a ceremonial function for Native Americans. Perhaps a certain amount of visitors, looking over at the radar station, might wonder how *that* structure will be interpreted centuries from now.

Past the Medicine Wheel, US 14A, also known as Big Horn Scenic Byway, plunges down the mountain into the **Big Horn Basin**. Protected by the mountains, this region enjoys a milder climate than the rest of Wyoming. It is a prime cattle-producing area that saw one of the last great range wars between cattlemen and sheepherders in the early 20th century.

Stay on US 14A to travel from Lovell to Cody through Shoshone River Valley. **Lovell**, a well-groomed town, was founded by ranchers in the 1870s and remains identified with cattle, though it is also known as the "Rose Town of Wyoming." Past Garland, the Rocky Mountains come into view for the first time, with square-topped **Heart Mountain** in the foreground. A short drive from here is Cody, a town named after William F. "Buffalo Bill" Cody.

Cody

You can't pass through **Cody** 55 without confronting the memory of Buffalo Bill, that one-time Pony Express rider, soldier, buffalo hunter, Army Chief of Scouts, rancher, frontiersman, actor, and showman. He has accurately been called a "kaleidoscope of white man's western experience." Through his Wild West Show, his own screen roles and other films that dealt with his character (played by everyone from Roy Rogers to Charlton Heston and Paul Newman), he has, more than any single person, influenced the world view

of the West – for better and worse. And he certainly left his mark on Cody.

The place is unquestionably tourist-crazy. When Yellowstone attained national park status, this town jumped in with both feet, billing itself as gateway to the park. Today, there are enough tour buses, tourist attractions, and hoopla in the town that the inclination is to step on the gas. If you can withstand souvenir shops and the phony facade, however, you will discover a bit of the Old West here.

Best is the **Buffalo Bill Historical Center** (tel: 307-587-4771; www.bbhc. org; Mar–Nov daily, Dec–Feb, Thur–Sun), which is actually five outstanding museums in one. The **Buffalo Bill Museum** is devoted to the man's vast collection of memorabilia. He was known for his flamboyance and excess, and the collection is all the better for it. The **Whitney Gallery of Western Art** spans the period from the 1800s to the present. All the greats are represented – Catlin, Bierstadt, Moran, Remington, Russell; Remington's studio has been re-created here, as well. The **Plains Indian Museum** displays perhaps the world's finest collections of Sioux, Cheyenne, Shoshone, Crow, Arapaho, and Blackfoot artifacts. Extremely interesting is a series of precise pictographs executed by Chief Sitting Bull while imprisoned at Fort Randall in 1882. Drawn on Fort Randall stationery, they depict what he considered to be the important events in his life.

Rodeo capital of the world

Cody is also known for its Night Rodeo, a tradition which, along with the annual Fourth of July Cody Stampede, legitimizes the town's claim to be the "Rodeo Capital of the World." Old Trail Town (tel: 307-587-5302; mid-May–mid-Sept daily), which includes the Museum of the Old West, is located west at the original town site. The beloved obsession of Bob and Terry Edgar, this is an impressive collection of authentic frontier buildings, horse-drawn vehicles and other artifacts from

Wyoming's past. The "Hole-in-the-Wall Cabin," used by Butch Cassidy and the Sundance Kid, is also here, marked by a rock with the oldest inscribed date in northern Wyoming (1811).

A number of legendary frontiersmen have been reburied here at the cemetery, among them John "Jeremiah Liver-eating" Johnson, portrayed by Robert Redford in the film *Jeremiah Johnson*. Johnson died in an old soldiers' home far from the mountains where he lived, and his reburial was marked by a moving ceremony attended by Robert Redford and the Utah Mountain Men, who served as pallbearers. The plaque on his grave simply reads "No More Trails."

US 14 West out of Cody follows the Shoshone River, winding through the formations of **Shoshone Canyon** and past the **Buffalo Bill Dam**, the world's first concrete arch dam. It tunnels through **Rattlesnake Mountain** and continues on through the **Shoshone National Forest** (the nation's first). As you take leave, you will soon find yourself at the entrance to Yellowstone National Park.

Winding highway near Buffalo Bill State Park, Cody.

Geothermal landscape of
Yellowstone National Park.

YELLOWSTONE TO THE OLYMPIC PENINSULA

The Northern Route concludes its coast-to-coast journey by traveling through several of the most glorious national parks in the land to the far northwestern corner of the US.

The national parks of the northern Rockies – Yellowstone, Grand Teton, and Glacier – are regions of breathtaking natural beauty, vignettes from a more primitive North America. These mountain parks all share an abundance of wildlife, but each possesses a distinct personality. Yellowstone has its geysers; Grand Teton encompasses the incomparable Teton Range, rising above cattle country; and Glacier has its spectacular mountain passes.

The route between Yellowstone and Glacier passes through the westernmost **Great Plains**, the traditional hunting grounds of the Plains Indians. First described by Lewis and Clark in the early part of the 19th century, and later depicted by Charles Russell, the landscape is now dominated by cattle ranches and wide-open fields of wheat.

Oldest national park

Yellowstone National Park 56 (tel: 307-344-7381; www.nps.gov/yell; mid-Apr–Nov daily, weather permitting; most roads closed in winter) is both symbol and sanctuary. Located in the northwest corner of Wyoming, it was the world's first national park – and for many people still the most magnificent. This primitive landscape, forged by fire and water, has been called the "greatest concentration of wonders on the face of the earth," its shapes and colors "beyond the reach of human

art." It is a hotbed of geothermal activity, with more than 10,000 thermal features, as well as being one of the last remaining habitats of the grizzly bear in the United States outside of Alaska. All this, and enough canyons, cliffs, and cataracts to please the most jaded eye.

Though Native Americans hunted here for centuries, credit for the region's discovery goes to John Colter, the first white man to set foot in what is now Wyoming. Later in the 19th century, trappers and prospectors passed through, among them Jim

Main Attractions

Yellowstone National Park
Grand Teton National Park
Museum of the Rockies
Montana Historical Society
National Bison Range
Glacier National Park
Museum of the Plains Indian
Lake Pend d'Oreille
Seattle
Olympic National Park

Pike Place Market, Seattle.

Cowboy country around Yellowstone is also bison, elk, and black bear country.

The stunning Grand Tetons.

Bridger, a celebrated mountain man and teller of tall tales. Impressed by the petrified trees of **Specimen Ridge**, he embellished his description a bit, raving of "petrified trees full of petrified birds singing petrified songs." In 1870, Henry Washburn, the Surveyor General of Montana Territory, headed up a more illustrious expedition endeavoring to set the record straight. They returned awestruck and committed to the creation of a "nation's park" – a dream realized in 1872.

Yellowstone encompasses an area of more than 2 million acres (800,000 hectares). Those who prefer being at one with nature can rest assured that 95 percent of this area is backcountry. For the less intrepid, there are nearly 300 miles (480km) of roads. The **Grand Loop Road** provides access to most of the major attractions, from **Yellowstone Lake** and the **Grand Canyon of Yellowstone** to **Mammoth Hot Springs** and **Old Faithful**. They are simply magnificent.

Many visitors view Old Faithful's performance with a sense of obligation. Although not as faithful as it once was, the geyser pleases the crowd regularly – 21 to 23 times daily. This is also a prime location for people-watching; a chance to glimpse a real slice of American life frozen in anticipation.

Yellowstone wildlife

Some come to Yellowstone primarily to view wildlife, and few depart disappointed. Stopped cars along the road generally indicate that some large mammal is grazing nearby. Unfortunately for both man and beast, visitors tend to forget their natural fear of and respect for these truly wild creatures. A park ranger relates that people who would ordinarily be reluctant to pet a neighbor's dog have no qualms about posing for a snapshot with a wild animal twice their size. Bison are best left alone – visitors getting too close are sometimes gored, and the result can be fatal. Of ever-greater concern to park officials are the bears – both black bears and grizzlies, but the latter are more dangerous and more endangered. One way to avoid bears is to visit the park in winter, a time of hibernation and a season that comes early to Yellowstone.

Grand Teton National Park

With the arrival of winter, the Yellowstone elk population leaves the high country and heads for the National Elk Refuge outside of Jackson, Wyoming. Though not exactly following in their hoofprints, US 89 South nevertheless takes you from the southern boundary of Yellowstone Park, through majestic **Grand Teton National Park** (tel: 307-739-3300; www.nps.gov/grte; daily) and Jackson Hole, alongside the refuge, to Jackson, the perennial boomtown.

If the Rockies are the crown, then the **Teton Range** is its jewel. Exquisitely beautiful, amethyst-tinged, jagged, snowcapped, and hypnotic, they loom above the horizon west of the highway. The **Snake River**, running true to its name, intervenes. The Tetons and **Gros Ventre** ranges encircle the **Jackson Hole** valley. Trappers worked this territory in the early 19th century and it was named for David E. Jackson, a prominent member of the trade. Settlers came in the 1880s as outlaws, homesteaders, and ranchers. This is a gorgeous landscape, never more visually stunning than in the classic 1953 western movie *Shane*, filmed on location here.

It is still cattle country, but tourism has become the economic mainstay now. People flock from all over the country to ski here, especially the well-to-do. Nearby is **Rendezvous Mountain** whose claim to fame is its vertical drop – the greatest of any US ski resort, which can be appreciated even in summer by taking a ride on the aerial tram (tel: 307-733-2292; late May–Sept) with a sheer ascent of nearly 1 mile (1.6km). The view from the summit is stupendous – across Grand Teton and far beyond.

Jackson

The Old West and the New West have converged in **Jackson**, land of condos and cowboys. This is a big-name resort with its share of local color; you just have to look for it. Look beyond the boutiques, the ski chalets, the nightly "shootouts" and the stagecoach rides. Bars are generally the best place for this sort of quest, so pull up a saddle (mounted on a bar stool) at the **Million Dollar Cowboy Bar** and hoist a few beers with the locals.

North of Jackson is the **National Elk Refuge** (tel: 307-733-9212; daily), established in 1912 and now the winter habitat of a herd some 5,000 strong. Once victims of starvation and disease, these elk are now protected by law. Regularly scheduled sleigh rides transport visitors briefly into the company of these graceful creatures. In spring, the elk shed their antlers, which are expeditiously retrieved by area Boy Scouts and later auctioned off at a considerable profit.

MONTANA

Gardiner, Montana, sits along US 89 just north of Yellowstone on the southern fringe of **Gallatin National Forest**. Out of Yellowstone, the road passes through barren plains, irrigated farms, and a land of many hot springs – mineral bath resorts are thick on the ground here – before reaching the

TIP

The best way to explore the Yellowstone and Tetons backcountry in winter is on Nordic skis or snowshoes. Snowmobiles and snowcoaches only provide limited access as roads are closed to most vehicles. The thermal areas are good places to spot wildlife warming their hooves and paws.

Around 5,000 elk spend the winter near Jackson, Wyoming.

Sunrise over the Bitterroot Mountains, near Bozeman.

forest, rich in minerals. The road plays hide-and-seek with the Yellowstone River a while longer before intersecting with US 191 at Livingston.

Livingston ❺ was put on the map by both the Northern Pacific Railroad and its proximity to Yellowstone, just 56 miles (90km) to the south. Retaining some of its pure-West authenticity, it has also been the popular haunt of Western authors and painters such as Russell Chatham and Jim Harrison – not to mention modern movie stars and media types such as Andie MacDowell and Ted Turner, among others. The town consists of a small grid of streets with bars and cafés; its proximity to Bozeman has also brought an increasing number of university students and professors.

A little west along I-90 sits **Bozeman** ❺, nestled in the Gallatin Valley beneath 9,000ft (2,700-meter) peaks that seem close enough to touch in the gin-clear air. This was known as the "Valley of Flowers" by the Blackfeet, Crow, Cheyenne, and Snakes who hunted here. William Clark passed through the area with

their blessing in 1806 on the return trip of his path-finding expedition. John Bozeman and Jim Bridger later guided wagon trains through in direct violation of treaty, at considerable risk. The trail became Bonanza Trail, the Bridger Cut-Off, and the Bloody Bozeman – a treacherous short cut for impatient pioneers.

Like so many other Western cities, Bozeman has a historic main street, though several of its century-old buildings were destroyed in a gas explosion in 2009. It also has a state university – which has brought outdoor gear shops, health-food stores, and the like. The Gibson Guitar company manufactures quality guitars at a plant just outside town. You might also care to make a visit to the **Museum of the Rockies** (tel: 406-994-2251; www.museumoftherockies.org; daily), an institution devoted to the physical and cultural heritage of the northern Rockies. Bozeman's own "boot hill" is **Sunset Hills Cemetery**, final resting place of journalist Chet Huntley, pioneer John Bozeman, and Nevada miner Henry T.P. Comstock.

Lewis and Clark

Northwest of Bozeman, along Montana 2, sits Manhattan – which doesn't have much of a skyline at all – followed by the town of **Three Forks** across the Madison River. This town was named for the Missouri Headwaters – the Gallatin, Madison, and Jefferson rivers – all named by Lewis and Clark. Meriwether Lewis and William Clark led their historic expedition through here in July 1805, having accepted the challenge of exploring the recently acquired Louisiana Purchase by tracing the Missouri River and its tributaries to (they hoped) the Northwest Passage. By the time they reached the Three Forks area, however, they realized that the Missouri drainage system did not in fact lead to the Pacific. Nevertheless, the success of their expedition remains undisputed. They opened up the West for a generation and for all time; a deluge of exploration – and exploitation – soon followed.

Gone today is the abundant wildlife Lewis and Clark found at the headwaters, although a state park has been developed to commemorate and interpret its historical significance. Here, you can have a picnic at the very spot where the expedition stopped to have breakfast on July 27, 1805, and then climb up to "**Lewis Rock**," where Lewis sketched a map of the countryside. At the entrance to the park are the remains of a ghost town, **Second Gallatin City**.

The town moved here from across the headwaters so as to sit astride a main stagecoach route, having by that time been abandoned by the steamboat. But its existence was unfortunately short-lived, bypassed by the next wave of transportation – the "iron horse" itself, the mighty railroad.

A few miles west of Three Forks on I-90, the color suddenly changes to the gold of wheat, and US 287 enters, going north toward Helena. Past **Townsend**, **Canyon Ferry Lake** appears to the east of the road like an oasis on the prairie. Behind it stand the **Big Belt Mountains**. US 287 continues north and merges with I-15, skirting **Helena ⑲**, Montana's seat of government.

Across the Divide to Glacier

In Helena, they continue to make Lewis and Clark ale, and you still hear talk of Last Chance Gulch – though now it's a pedestrian mall. Fans of cowboy-artist Charles Russell, for whom acclaim runs high in Montana, will want to stop by the **Montana Historical Society** (tel: 406-444-2694; www.montanahistoricalsociety.org; Mon–Sat), which houses a collection of his work.

From Helena, US 12 runs up and over 6,300ft (1,920-meter) MacDonald pass (don't try this if winter is approaching) and the **Continental Divide**. Watersheds from this point flow into the Pacific instead of the Atlantic. To the west of the Divide, at Garrison, you must get back onto I-90 for another stretch of rugged mountains; you are solidly within the Rockies now, with minor ranges such as the Garnet Range to either side of

Montana State Capitol building in downtown Helena.

the road. A rest area on the interstate provides a good chance for you (and your vehicle) to take a break from all the mountain-climbing while gazing at the surrounding peaks.

Then it's down to **Missoula 60**, the state's most liberal-leaning town thanks to the influence of the University of Montana. You will note a giant "M" carved in the hills outside town, and that marks the university. A trail leading to the "M" runs on campus property and makes for a popular hike. The town boasts the usual rough-and-tumble Western bars, certainly, but also good health-food shops, bookstores, and music – not a bad place to spend the night.

From Missoula, take US 93 due north and begin climbing again, at least for a bit, as you begin to enter the **Flathead Indian Reservation**. Roadside stands and restaurants sell bison burgers and huckleberry shakes, the local twist on fast food. This area was once all Flathead territory by decree of treaty, but the tribal lands were gradually settled by missionaries and sold piecemeal to speculators.

Today, a mixture of residents manage to coexist amid lovely, wild scenery.

At the junction of Montana 200, turn west a short way to tour the **National Bison Range 61** (tel: 406-644-2211; daily, weather permitting), where some 350 to 500 of these magnificent animals – as well as many other species of wildlife – roam over more than 19,000 acres (7,700 hectares) of beautiful grassland and park-like patches of timber. Again, however, remember not to get too close – technically, you are not even supposed to get out of your car while traveling through the range.

A few miles north again on US 93, **St Ignatius** beckons as a turn-off beneath the splendid Mission Mountain range. The town's chief draw today is actually its impressive mission church (tel: 406-745-2768; daily), built in 1854 and possessing some interesting fresco work within. The surrounding mountains are still occupied by Flatheads, and you need tribal permits to fish, hunt or visit. It's a beautiful and rugged country; bears and mountain lions are frequently seen.

Hidden Lake, Glacier National Park.

North again, US 93 becomes ramrod-straight – one of the most accident-prone stretches of highway in the land, so look sharp. It continues north alongside the mountains to the folksy town of **Polson**, where huge **Flathead Lake** drains through a gorge; then the road bends to circle the lake's western shore. A giant Flathead-owned casino has somewhat marred what was once pristine scenery here, but the lake is still marvelous to contemplate as you climb around it to **Kalispell**, population center of the area and a base for excursions into Glacier National Park. Fittingly, its name means "prairie above the lake."

US 2 turns east to pass through Columbia Falls and then **Hungry Horse**. The highway crosses the middle fork of the Flathead and meanders through the pristine, cathedral-like wilderness of **Flathead National Forest** before finally reaching the natural wonders of the park.

Glacier National Park

Glacier National Park ㉒ (tel: 406-888-7800; www.nps.gov/glac; daily) is more remote and less crowded than Rocky Mountain Park or Yellowstone, yet traffic can still be heavy. Traveling here is therefore most satisfying at off-peak times – at sunrise or sunset or during early summer and autumn. It is generally plowed and fit for driving from mid-June to mid-October, when the Park Service closes it down for the winter.

Near the park's western edge is **McDonald Creek**, a final resting place for kokanee salmon which travel here in late autumn from Flathead Lake to spawn. This event attracts hundreds of bald eagles, which in turn attracts an increasing number of birdwatchers.

The Continental Divide forms Glacier's backbone, crossed by spectacular **Going-to-the-Sun Road** at Logan Pass. Opened in 1933, this is the only road that crosses the park, bisecting it into two nearly equivalent sections. It has been called "the most beautiful stretch of road in the world," its twisting 50 miles (80km) of two-lane pavement climbing from the settlement of West Glacier to the shore of Lake McDonald, to Garden Wall, and finally crossing Logan Pass and descending to St Mary. The entire road is open mid-June to mid-September, but portions may be closed for roadwork outside this season through 2015.

Along the road, stop for spectacular vistas of the **Hanging Garden Trail**, which leads to vast alpine meadows. Columbian ground squirrels greet hikers at the trailhead, which proceeds past wind-deformed trees known as *Krummholz* (the German word for "elfin timber" or "crooked wood") and across the meadow. There is an ever-changing repertoire of glacier lilies, Indian paintbrush, red monkey flowers, and mountain heath. Mountain goats can sometimes be sighted from here, as well as grizzly bears, which feed on the meadow's plentiful bulbs and roots. **the Highline Trail**, across the road from the Hanging Garden, is a more challenging and potentially dangerous trail – not recommended for the faint-hearted. Opportunities

Glacier National Park.

for backcountry hiking abound inside the park. Its approximately 50 glaciers, 200 lakes, alpine meadows, and forests are a haven for fishermen, hikers, and wildlife alike. And two rustic stone chalets (called **Granite Park** and **Sperry**), reached only by foot or horseback, offer overnight accommodations; both were built around 1914 by the Great Northern Railroad. The glaciers which created this magnificent park are rapidly disappearing, owing to global warming, and the only way to see many of them is on foot.

At the eastern edge of the park – and Going-to-the-Sun Road – sits the small, friendly town of **St Mary**, which separates Lower St Mary Lake from St Mary Lake proper. Even the drive out of the park along US 89 is dramatically beautiful, descending rapidly from St Mary to Kiowa and winding sharply as it goes, then turning due east out of the mountains. From there, the enticing road goes to **Browning**, headquarters of the **Blackfeet Reservation** and home of the truly interesting **Museum of the Plains Indian** (tel: 406-338-2230; www.browningmontana.

Continental Divide sign.

com/museum; June–Sept daily, Oct–May Mon–Fri), which houses the most comprehensive collection of Blackfeet artifacts in existence.

Of particular note are the Assiniboine drums, some of which have been painted with wonderful visionary designs suggesting hallucinatory images; it is thought the hallucinations were caused by prolonged fasting.

BEYOND THE GREAT DIVIDE

As waters flow west of the **Continental Divide** toward the Pacific, so too do paths of civilization. The Nez Percé, the Kootenai, the Pend d'Oreille, the Flathead and other mountain tribes once lived and hunted here in peace. Later, the Blackfeet came from the plains across the Divide on horse-stealing raids, a journey many have since followed for different reasons.

The first white people to arrive were trappers and traders in the early part of the 19th century, followed by prospectors in search of gold and silver. Homesteaders heading west conquered the Rockies and moved on, some settling in eastern Washington.

Continental Divide
Milner Pass   elev. 10,759 ft.

The "Great Divide" separates drainage to the Atlantic from drainage to the Pacific. It traverses America from Alaska almost to Cape Horn.

Atlantic Ocean drainage ←   Pacific Ocean drainage →

Cache La Poudre Creek drains into the Platte River which flows to the Missouri, then to the Mississippi, thus reaching the Gulf of Mexico. (part of the Atlantic Ocean)

Beaver Creek drains into the Colorado River, which then flows through Grand Canyon National Park and on to the Gulf of California. (A part of the Pacific Ocean)

With the coming of the railroad, the lumber industry found a permanent home in the forests west of the Divide.

Vast timberlands

From Browning, take US 2 west over **Marias Pass** and skirt the southern edge of Glacier Park, passing through Hungry Horse and Kalispell once more. West of Kalispell, the **Kootenai National Forest** takes over where the Flathead leaves off. Along the highway toward **Libby**, the lumber industry's presence in this area becomes progressively more apparent. Lumber has been big business here since 1892, when the Great Northern Railroad arrived. But as with all national forests, the Kootenai is a mixed-use area and within its boundaries (an area nearly three times the size of Rhode Island) lie many acres of wilderness: the habitat of elk, moose, deer, and Rocky Mountain bighorn sheep. A system of observation towers, manned around the clock, was once the primary method of forest fire surveillance. As fire detection methods became more sophisticated, these structures were gradually vacated. The **Canoe Gulch Ranger Station** (tel: 406-293-8861; Mon–Fri) has opened its lookout atop **Big Creek Baldy Mountain** to the public, on a reserve-ahead and pay-ahead basis (tel: 877-444-6777; mid-June–Sept). You will be given the combination to the lock and directions, or call the Canoe Gulch Ranger Station for further details. State Highway 37 out of Libby leads to forestry service access roads, the last of which winds its way up to the foot of Big Creek Baldy Lookout. The last mile or so is extremely rough and steeply graded. However, the thrill of making it to the top, mingled with awe upon viewing the panorama that awaits, will take anyone's breath away. And it gets even better after climbing the steps of the 41ft (12-meter) tower.

The 225-sq-ft (21-sq-meter) space with unobstructed windows and an observation deck on all sides contains items essential to survival and comfort and nothing more – save a fire-sighting device smack in the middle of the floor. Below, the tranquil beauty of the forest stretches for many miles in all directions; the wind becomes much more

Mormon Temple, Salt Lake City.

DETOUR TO SALT LAKE CITY

A long but beautiful 793-mile (1,276km) journey from Coeur d'Alene, Idaho, on US 95 goes through five national forests on the way to the capital of the Mormon church. Salt Lake City, Utah, was founded in 1847 by Brigham Young, who led Mormons from the persecution in the East to the promised lands of the Utah basin. About 70 percent of Salt Lake's current population belong to the church. The Mormon temple (one of over 100 in the world) is the town's focal point, and is a sacred place for members; the faith reserves the temple for its most special occasions, so it is not open to visitors. However, the immaculate grounds and visitors' center do allow a glimpse into this close and well-ordered religion. The Mormons live by a strict code shunning alcohol, tobacco, and even hot drinks like tea and coffee. There are a number of historic sites to visit, including the Mormon Tabernacle and the Beehive House, home of Brigham Young; and, a few miles west, the phenomenal Great Salt Lake itself. Like many cities in the Southwest, Salt Lake is blessed with a breathtaking setting: mountains in the background offset the desert in the foreground and the strikingly distinctive architecture of this rare religious capital. The Salt Lake Convention and Visitors Bureau can be reached on 801-534-4900 or visit www.visitsaltlake.com.

TIP

On the way to Coeur d'Alene, Idaho, plan for a close-up encounter with wolves. Wolf People manage a 21-strong pack of these fascinating and elusive animals in a natural habitat compound. Telephone 208-263-1100 for details.

than a whistle, no longer muffled by the trees. This is a solitary, spiritual, romantic place to spend the night.

From Libby, where the **Cabinet Mountains** can be seen from downtown, it is a short drive west along US 2 to the Idaho border along the Kootenai River, passing near lovely and dramatic **Kootenai Falls** and through **Troy**, home of the largest silver mine in the United States. You are leaving a land of cowboy hats and rejoining a land of loggers and miners.

INTO IDAHO

The road enters Boundary County – aptly named, as it borders not just Montana but also British Columbia in Canada and Washington – joining US 95 just north of **Bonners Ferry**. Backed by the Selkirk Mountain Range, **Sandpoint** lies on the shores of the huge **Lake Pend d'Oreille**.

Here, US 2 splits off to the west, while US 95 crosses the lake on the two-mile Long Bridge on its way southwest toward Coeur d'Alene. From 1890 to 1910, three transcontinental railroad lines forged their way

through this part of Idaho, creating a string of towns that dot the highway.

Before reaching **Coeur d'Alene** ⬦, US 95 greets the interstate. It is worth back-tracking east along I-90 a little here, not only because the road hugs the banks of **Coeur d'Alene Lake** for some 11 miles (18km), but primarily because it leads to two vestiges of 19th-century Idaho, both unique in their way.

The **Coeur d'Alene Mission of the Sacred Heart** (also known as the Old Mission; tel: 208-682-3814; daily) stands atop a hill overlooking the main road (I-90). It is the oldest standing building in Idaho, constructed of timber, mud, and wooden pegs in 1853 by Father Anthony Ravalli and the Coeur d'Alene Indians.

The Jesuits came to this part of Idaho knowing they would be welcomed by the Coeur d'Alene Indians, who had been told by neighboring tribes of the great powers of the "Black Robes." Truly a Renaissance man, Ravalli designed the mission in European style, perhaps best described as Native American-Italianate. The spacious, cathedral-like interior is decorated with chandeliers made from tin cans, whitewashed newspaper painted with floral motifs, carved pine crosses, a wooden altar painted to resemble marble, and many other precious artifacts.

In 1877, the Coeur d'Alene were forced to abandon their beloved mission for a reservation to the south, but they still consider it their mission today and return each August 15 to celebrate the Feast of the Assumption. Due to its location, the mission also became a rendezvous point for mountain men, fur traders and "all sorts of riff-raff," in the words of the cavalrymen who were often called in to maintain peace and order. The annual Historic Skills Fair in July recalls those days with traditional crafts, music, and food.

The Old Mission had no confessional until the late 1800s when one was established, presumably to serve white settlers, some of whom may have sinned at an establishment now called

Horseback ride in Washington State.

the **Enaville Resort** (tel: 208-682-3453; daily) located in **Kingston**, east of the mission along I-90 and then north on Coeur d'Alene River Road. It was built in 1880 as an overnight stop en route to gold and silver country, gaining several nicknames over the years – locals still call it the SnakePit. Located across from a lumberyard, a rail crossroads, and a fork of the Coeur d'Alene River, it has served in its time as boomtown bar, hotel, and house of ill repute.

Today, the Enaville is merely a relaxing place to stop for a drink and a bite to eat. Furnishings have piled up over the years and include many pieces handwrought by a mysterious man from Finland known only as Mr Egil. His materials were pine burls, antlers, horns, and animal hides; his only recompense was a room, board, and free beer.

WASHINGTON STATE

A short drive west on I-90 takes you out of Idaho and into eastern **Washington**, a land of deserts, canyons, coulees, wheat fields, and irrigated farmland – a sharp contrast to the densely forested terrain of northern Idaho.

Historically, this region was home to numerous Native American peoples, most of whom lived along the banks of the Columbia River. Their descendants, members of the Colville Confederated Tribes, live today on a reservation bordered on two sides by the Columbia River. This was uninviting territory for early white explorers. The Grand Coulee itself presented a major obstacle, with few openings through which to pass. In the 1880s, the first white settlers in the region faced enormous hardships. Their numbers remained relatively few until the completion of the Grand Coulee Dam. Built during the height of the Great Depression, the dam and the Columbia Basin irrigation and electrification project changed the face of this region for all time.

Outside **Spokane** ⑥, US 2 travels through golden wheat fields toward the dam. Road signs become a little confusing as the road approaches not only the Grand Coulee Dam, but the towns of Electric City, Grand Coulee,

The Washington State Ferry system, the largest in the US, runs ferries to the Olympic Peninsula from Seattle.

Grand Coulee Hydroelectric Dam

Grand Coulee Dam, and Coulee City. At Wilbur, State 174 goes north to the town of Grand Coulee, where State 155 continues on to the dam. As they say, "You can't miss it." The impact of the **Grand Coulee Dam** ⑥⑤ cannot be overestimated – economically or visually. Its aims, achievements, and sheer size are all on a grand scale, and the design of the dam is of such stylistic integrity that it still looks modern today.

The drive along State 155, from the dam to **Coulee City** and US 2, is surprisingly scenic. The road skirts the lake on one side and the algae-clad coulee walls on the other. West of Coulee City, along US 2, gently sloping fields of wheat, dotted with the occasional farmhouse, give the appearance of a vast desert. Layers of blue mountains appear in the distance like a mirage – the first of the coastal chains.

At **Orondo**, the highway meets, follows, and crosses the **Columbia River** and then branches off, tracing its tributary, the Wenatchee, into foothills of the **Cascade Range**. This is orchard country: green patches of fertile land jut into the river and contrast with the golden hills; some of the local stands put out ripe apricots for sale.

Now US 2 climbs and enters a realm of tall timber, passing through the town of **Leavenworth** ⑥⑥ – a self-styled, pseudo-Bavarian ski resort and gateway to the **Wenatchee National Forest**. Over the rushing south fork of the Skykomish River, and through the **Snoqualmie National Forest**, past several small towns with no-nonsense names like Gold Bar and Startup, US 2 continues west, bringing you just to the northeast of **Seattle** ⑥⑦ (see page 172), where you catch the expressway and (hopefully) breeze into one of America's most interesting and attractive cities.

THE OLYMPIC PENINSULA

Before you dig in your heels in Seattle, however, another nearby destination beckons. Washington's **Olympic Peninsula** is the northwesternmost corner of the contiguous 48 states – a remote, exotic, and wildly beautiful region within easy reach of both Seattle and Victoria, British Columbia, Canada. It is set apart from these places not merely by Puget (pronounced "*pyew*-jet") Sound and the Strait of Juan de Fuca, but by its climate, its geology, the mystery of its peaks and forests, and by the natural rhythms that guide the pace of life.

From **Edmonds**, due north of Seattle, a ferry crosses the short, scenic distance across the sound to **Kingston** ⑥⑧ on the peninsula. From here, it is a lovely drive west and north to the peninsula's northeastern tip at the entrance to Puget Sound.

At the heart of the peninsula are the majestic **Olympic Mountains**, snow-streaked even in summer. Long a subject of myth, these mountains remained unexplored until the 1890s, when an expedition from Seattle set off in search of man-eating savages. Even the peninsula's Native Americans avoided venturing into the interior, fearing the wrath of mighty

Sol Duc Falls, Olympic Peninsula.

Thunderbird, who was believed to reside atop Mount Olympus. Today, the mountains are preserved and protected in a near-wilderness state as part of Olympic National Park, which comprises 923,000 acres (374,000 hectares) of the peninsula, most of it inland but also including a 50-mile (80km) strip of Pacific Ocean coastline. Only a few roads venture into the park, and these only peripherally. In fact, the park proper is surrounded by the **Olympic National Forest**, which makes it difficult to reach. Because the peninsula is largely under some form of Federal jurisdiction, there is considerable conflict with the lumber industry.

The Olympic Peninsula sustains the rainforests of the Hoh, Quinault, and Queets river valleys; the glacial peaks of the Olympics; and the rugged Pacific coastline as well as lumber towns, fishing villages, and nine Native American reservations.

Charming **Port Gamble**, the first town along the route, is an authentic lumber town reflecting a bygone era. Just beyond it, a bridge crosses the Hood Canal – the work of glaciers rather than men. At the town of **Discovery Bay**, State 20 veers off and up to Port Townsend.

Victorian town

Port Townsend ⑥⑨, first settled in 1851, is the peninsula's oldest town and an attractive base. Sea captains and storekeepers from back East made their homes here, and it was quick to become a boomtown, built in anticipation of being linked with the Union Pacific Railroad and consequently becoming the major seaport of the Northwest. All this came to pass – for Seattle, not Port Townsend. After the bust, settlers tore up the train tracks, closed down the banks and departed for more prosperous parts.

Left behind is the best example of a Victorian seacoast town north of San Francisco. Declared a National Historic District, Port Townsend has become a haven for artists and is also

the headquarters of the **Northwest School of Wooden Boatbuilding** (tel: 360-385-4948; Mon–Fri), where a dying art has been revived.

US 101 loops around the peninsula like a misshapen horseshoe, open at the bottom. In the north, it passes through Olympic National Forest and on to the lumber towns of the "West End." The region between Discovery Bay and Port Angeles has been called the "banana belt," sitting as it does in the rain shadow of the Olympics. Farmers here see an average rainfall of only 17 inches (43cm) compared with upwards of 140 inches (356cm) on the other side of the mountains. Irrigated farms are a common sight along this stretch, as are madrona trees, twisted and terracotta in color.

Small towns and a rainforest

The towns along the way are small and distinctive. **Blyn** is gone before you can say "Little Brown Church of Blyn," its one and only landmark. Just north of **Sequim** (pronounced *skwim*), on the Strait of Juan de Fuca

Hiking in the verdant Olympic National Forest.

Victorian B&B in Port Townsend.

Second Beach, Olympic National Park.

(explorer De Fuca thought this was the Northwest Passage), is **Dungeness**, where the Dungeness crabs are landed.

The plants of several major lumber companies are located at **Port Angeles**, and the smell of wood permeates the air; here you can catch big cruise boats to Victoria, British Columbia, on gorgeous Vancouver Island. Port Angeles is the gateway to **Olympic National Park** ⑦ (tel: 360-565-3130; www.nps.gov/olym; daily). Head up to Hurricane Ridge for stunning views of Mount Olympus and its surrounding glaciers. Heading west, US 101 traces Elwha Creek, enters the National Forest and winds down to crystalline Lake Crescent within the park. The highway is lined with towering evergreens, the roadside carpeted with ferns, as you continue west toward the ocean and the rainfall amounts suddenly begin rising again.

West End

Logging is a way of life in the peninsula's "West End" and evidence of this is everywhere: clearcut hillsides denuded of all trees, reforested plantations, and logging trucks barreling down the roads. Most of the big trees are long since gone now, and what remain are usually – though not always – off-limits to these lumber companies.

US 101 passes through the towns of **Sappho** and **Forks**. The village of **La Push**, on the **Quilayute Indian Reservation**, is reached by way of La Push Road (Route 110) from Forks. Those who live here fish for a living, and those who visit here visit for the fishing. If La Push were not so unpretentious, it would surely proclaim itself driftwood capital of the world: its beach is beautiful at night, a string of warming campfires and sea-stacks visible through the perpetual mist.

The temperate rainforests west of the mountains are the finest of all the sights in the national park. They are the only ones in North America and contain some of the tallest timber in the world. Most accessible of these awe-inspiring forests is the **Hoh River Valley**, located south of Forks and inland on Hoh River Road. Most awesome are the ancient evergreens – western red cedar,

Sitka spruce, Douglas fir, and western hemlock – shrouded with club moss, filtered by light, surrounded by ferns and the sound of the river. It is an eerie, overgrown, magical place, barely touched by the presence of man – with one exception.

John "The Iron Man of Hoh" Huelsdonk came to the Hoh Valley from Iowa in 1891. Discouraged by all who met him, he nevertheless poled his canoe up the wild river and made his home in this forest. What he could not carry by canoe, such as his cast-iron stove, he strapped to his back. Hence the nickname – and the birth of a legend. The Iron Man died and is buried in the forest he so loved, as is his wife.

US 101 continues south to another wide, driftwood-strewn shoreline at **Ruby Beach**; look for rock oysters and starfish clinging to the rocks when the tide is out. On the south side of the park, the **Quinault Rainforest** offers accessible hiking trails through the big trees.

Land's end

You can't get any farther northwest in the continental United States than isolated **Neah Bay**. Forking off the loop of US 101 at Sappho, State 113 and then State 112 wind their way to the ocean along the strait. Vancouver Island is now visible in the distance. Neah Bay is the ancestral and current home of the fine **Makah Indian Nation**, whose presence here for at least 3,000 years has been confirmed by archeologists. Once renowned whale and seal hunters who took to the sea in cedar canoes, the Makah still live off the ocean, though the catch today is more likely to be salmon. On entering town, a sign proclaims: "Makah Nation – a treaty tribe since 1855." The Makah do not underestimate the importance of this treaty, which guarantees their territorial and fishing rights, which to them means survival.

Neah Bay is also a gateway to one of America's most splendid stretches of wilderness coastline. A network of gravel and dirt roads goes part of the distance, but to reach land's end it is necessary to go on foot. If you want some adventure, drive as far as you dare and then hike the precipitous trail down to pretty **Shi-Shi Beach** and simply gaze out to sea. Be aware of time – and tide-tables – as the water rushes in quickly around here.

The trail to **Cape Flattery** is shorter and less dangerous. It descends an intricate stairway of tree roots through the forest, a clearing, and a stand of huckleberry bushes before reaching the cliff's edge. Look out over Cape Flattery, knowing you stand as far northwest as possible in the lower 48 states of the US – and that you have reached the end of a journey that began, thousands of miles ago, beside a different ocean in busy Boston Harbor.

Then retrace your steps back to Seattle, or follow US 101 around the rest of the peninsula and down to the town of Aberdeen, where you can, if you wish, drive all the way to Mexico on US 101 and Highway.

Young buck in the Hoh Rainforest.

A SHORT STAY IN SEATTLE

Seattle is youthful and friendly, business-minded, busy, and beautiful: a city of the 21st century. Here's a list of the not-to-be-missed attractions.

Glide into the **Seattle Center**, home of the Space Needle, on the monorail and explore its many attractions, from theaters and a children's museum to the excellent **Pacific Science Center**. It also hosts the famous **Bumbershoot music festival** each Labor Day weekend.

The **Seattle Aquarium** features 200 varieties of fish native to Puget Sound, plus environments simulating rocky reefs, sandy seafloors, eelgrass beds, and tide pools. It's one part of the vibrant Waterfront area, which also has ships, piers, stores, and restaurants.

Bruce Lee, Seattle's founding fathers and other famous folk lie in the cemetery on **Capitol Hill**, an eclectic neighborhood of coffeehouses, funky shops, hip bars, and restaurants. The renowned **Seattle Asian Art Museum** stands in Volunteer Park, where there are great city views from the water tower.

Set in a Frank Gehry building, **Experience Music Project** (**EMP**) is a rock music museum conceived by Paul Allen of Microsoft fame, featuring artifacts like Eric Clapton's guitar, state-of-the-art technology, and interactive exhibits. It stands adjacent to the very cool **Science Fiction Museum**, whose exhibits are out of this world.

From spy planes to supersonic jets and a Space Shuttle trainer, explore more than 85 aircraft at the fascinating **Museum of Flight**. Then head for the **Future of Flight Aviation Center** in **Everett**, with hands-on exhibits, and take the Boeing Tour to watch these famous airplanes being assembled.

"The Mountain" (as it is known by locals) is in **Mount Rainier National Park**, just outside of the city. A single road loops through miles of parkland and timbered canyons.

Built for the 1962 World's Fair, the Space Needle offers the best views of the city and surrounding hills from its observation deck with 360 views.

Like the Space Needle, the Monorail dates from the 1962 World's Fair. Trains run between Seattle Center and downtown's Westlake Center.

Sunfish Fish & Chips is a long established, Greek-influenced chippy along the beach at Alki.

The oldest part of the city, Pioneer Square's 19th-century buildings are now showcases for shops and bars.

THE EMERALD CITY

Seattle is constantly rated as one of the most livable US cities. With a diverse population, rich cultural life and wealthy industries (Boeing, Starbucks, Microsoft), all situated amid awesome scenery, who wouldn't want to live here? By the time it was named for Native American chief Sealth, the laid-back lifestyle associated with the city had long been in place; tribes like the Salish and the Duwamish had been living peacefully here for years. As do its residents now, surrounded by water and mountains, working hard, playing easy, and drinking gallons of strong coffee. If the future of America is anywhere, it is probably right here.

esigned by Robert Venturi, the Seattle Art Museum holds a ghly regarded collection of Northwest Indian art, paintings modern artists, and an Australian Aboriginal Gallery.

IMPORTANT INFORMATION

Population: 610,000
Dialing code: 206
Website: www.visitseattle.org
Tourist information: One Convention Place, 701 Pike Street, Suite 800, WA 98101 (no drop in); tel: 206-461-5840

JUN ILLINOIS 75

Old license plates make great souvenirs.

OHIO
GPF·397
MONTGOMERY

APR

CPI

GRAND

M
H
LAND OF ENCHANTMENT
☼24832
NEW MEXICO USA

T-

RT

GRAND

SEAT BELTS FASTENED?
8536 RS
73 OHIO

BICENTENNIAL
76

4T

AUG ARIZONA
CDW✶399
GRAND CANYON STATE AZ87

A

RJ

GRA

ONA
725
NYON STATE AZ 94
G429189

19 OKLAHOMA
E 14795
1776. BICENTENNIAL

RIZ 69 AZ 72
Y 73263
3036
YON STATE

Vermont
56AF6
Green Mountain State

NTANA FEB
3731
G SKY 77
185734

LAND OF ENCHANTME
H 75
19 NEW MEXICO

NA 73 AZ77
F 05992
348
NYON STATE AZ78
8N 0975

88 WYOMIN
2
1 633
TRUCK

A cattle rancher.

Moonrise over the US Capitol building, Washington, DC.

THE CENTRAL ROUTE

A detailed guide to the Central US, with principal
sites clearly cross-referenced by number to the maps.

Civil War memorial.

I
t is perhaps fitting to begin a journey across America from
the nation's capital of Washington, DC; the many museums and landmarks that give a glimpse into the country's past do much to set the scene for the rest of your trip
west. We've chosen a "south-central" course that combines
enough history and beauty to sate any traveler's appetite.

The history lesson begins as soon as you leave
Washington, heading first west and then sharply
south along Skyline Drive and the Blue Ridge Parkway through the
Appalachian Mountains of Virginia. This was Stonewall Jackson ter-
ritory and the route is sprinkled with Civil War sites.
Interstate 40, which we'll be following for much of the
trip, continues into North Carolina and through the Great
Smoky Mountains, taking you past the fine old homes of
Knoxville, Tennessee before reaching Nashville, the capital
of Tennessee and of country music.

From there, it's truly into small-town America as you
hit Arkansas, stopping in Little Rock, with its impressive
state capitol building, historic district, and hot springs.
Then into Oklahoma where we pick up Route 66. Some
know Route 66 from legend, others from childhood, when
every weathered telegraph pole and zany-shaped motel
was a milestone on a journey into a wonderland, whose
roadside attractions included snake pits, live buffaloes, and
Indian dancers.

Fuel brand inspired by Route 66.

Oklahoma's piece of Route 66 passes through many interesting small
towns, but also some bigger ones, such as Oklahoma City. You'll cross
the Texas Panhandle before heading into New Mexico, visiting the attractive city of Santa Fe. The state has a wealth of ancient pueblos, homes
of early Native American inhabitants. As you cross into Arizona, you
enter the Navajo Nation; the route passes by the Petrified Forest National
Park before reaching Flagstaff, the gateway for the incomparable Grand
Canyon. You'll cross some desolate countryside in western Arizona, and
again in eastern California's Mojave Desert, before you start seeing signs
of civilization as you head into the urban sprawl of Los Angeles. With
some 2,900 miles (4,700km) behind you, the Pacific Ocean beckons.

A SHORT STAY IN WASHINGTON, DC

Planned as a city of monuments and memorials, the nation's capital is also one of its most beautiful. Here's a list of the not-to-be-missed attractions.

Tours of the **White House** are very restricted, but its Visitor Center at the Department of Commerce, 15th and E streets NW, provides a good sense of the building's history since 1792.

Whether you wish to retrace the path of Martin Luther King Jr, whose "I Have a Dream" speech came from these steps, or simply take a look at the huge statue of Abraham Lincoln, the **Lincoln Memorial** celebrates the liberty sought by the founding fathers.

Set aside time to explore the world's largest museum and research complex. The **Smithsonian Institute** exhibits outstanding collections of artifacts and fine arts in 19 museums and galleries including the National Museum of American History, the National Museum of the American Indian, and the National Portrait Gallery.

The **Vietnam Veterans Memorial**, at Bacon Drive and Constitution Avenue, lists on polished granite the names of more than 58,000 American soldiers killed in the 1960s conflict.

At first a strategic stronghold in the Civil War, the **Arlington National Cemetery** contained 16,000 headstones by the end of the struggle. The eternal flame at the grave of John F. Kennedy honors the fallen president, and the Tomb of the Unknowns commemorates the nameless soldiers felled in battles over the past 100 years.

Exhibits at the **National Air and Space Museum** range from the Wright Brothers' *Flyer* to the Apollo 11 spacecraft, and includes a planetarium and an IMAX theater.

The striking granite sculpture of the **Martin Luther King, Jr Memorial** at Independence Avenue and West Basin Drive is surrounded by seventeen quotes from the Civil Rights leader.

The **World War II Memorial** on the Mall between the Washington and Lincoln Memorials, honors those Americans who fought for their country.

Basilica of the Immaculate Conception and the dome of the Capitol.

The Smithsonian Institution's Mary Livingston Ripley Garde It lies between the Arts and Industries Building and the Hirshhorn Museum and Sculpture Garden.

pen-air fish market on Maine Avenue, where dozens of ndors along the Washington Channel hawk fresh seafood.

IMPORTANT INFORMATION

Population: 581,500
Dialing code: 202
Website: www.washington.org
Tourist information: 901 Seventh Street NW, Fourth Floor, Washington, DC, 20001; tel: 800-422-8644

The White House in winter.

THE NATION'S CAPITAL CITY

A visit to Washington, DC, is nothing less than a lesson in history, literally a living history, since the President of the US lives here. The city also has a unique beauty, the credit for which should go to George Washington. The new president insisted on creating a new city as the nation's capital, a place as grand as Paris or London. With this in mind, he hired French architect Pierre Charles L'Enfant to create a "city of magnificent distances." L'Enfant's plan was only partially realized, but Washington *is* magnificent and the distances between monuments deceptively large; bring a good pair of walking shoes.

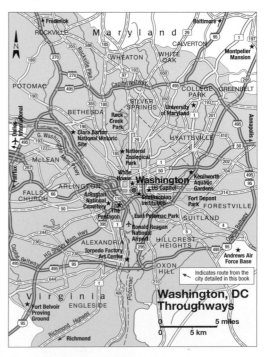

Washington, DC
Throughways

WASHINGTON, DC TO ARKANSAS

This route traces the essence of Americana:
Civil War battlefields, Native American reservations
in pine-scented mountains, blues and country
music in Memphis and Nashville, and
pioneer history in Arkansas.

O ur route begins in **Washington, DC ❶** (see page 180), the first leg of which explores Northern Virginia and the Appalachians to Winston-Salem, North Carolina. Some of the route requires driving I-66 and I-81, but the secondary roads parallel the interstates and are generally more scenic, less busy, and without 18-wheelers.

Leaving Washington on I-66, look for the **Virginia Welcome Center** west of Fairfax. You will find information about every possible site, lodging, or activity in the "Old Dominion."

Manassas

Take Exit 47B to visit **Manassas National Battlefield Park ❷** (tel: 703-361-1339; www.nps.gov/mana; daily) the spot of two great Confederate victories during the Civil War – the First and Second Battles of Manassas (or locally, Bull Run). Ten hours of deadly fighting on July 21, 1861, resulted in a Union defeat, but the cost was horrific: 3,000 Union casualties and 2,000 Confederate. Spectators arriving in carriages from Washington planned to picnic while watching what they expected to be an afternoon of colorful heroics. They were overwhelmed by the carnage, as were the troops who anticipated a day of almost schoolboy playground fighting.

It was here that General Thomas J. Jackson earned the nickname

"Stonewall," for sitting on his horse in the face of enemy fire "like a stone wall." The second Confederate victory one year later convinced General Robert E. Lee to cross into Maryland in an unsuccessful attempt to invade Pennsylvania. The Visitor Center has information about self-guided, ranger-led, and cellphone tours.

Toward Virginia's Mountains

The Civil War looms large in these parts, as Virginia was the site for more than half of its major battles. Almost

Main Attractions

Washington, DC
Manassas National Battlefield
Shenandoah National Park
Old Salem
Great Smoky Mountains
  National Park
Nashville
Memphis
Little Rock Central High School
  National Historic Site
Fort Smith

On stage at the Grand Ole Opry.

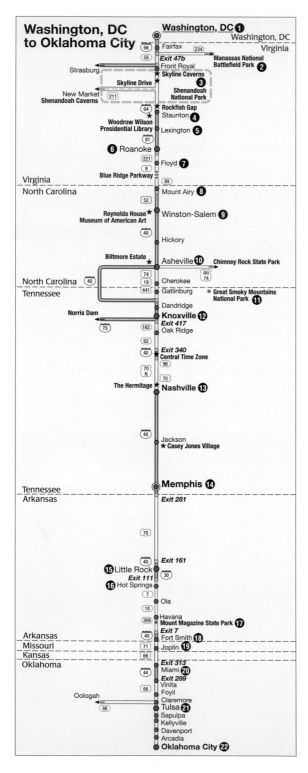

Washington, DC to Oklahoma City

Washington, DC ❶
Washington, DC
Virginia
Fairfax
66
55
Exit 47b
Front Royal
Skyline Caverns ❸
234
Manassas National
Battlefield Park ❷
Strasburg
Skyline Drive
Shenandoah
National Park
New Market
Shenandoah Caverns
211
64
Rockfish Gap
Staunton ❹
Woodrow Wilson
Presidential Library
Lexington ❺
81
❻ Roanoke
221
8
Floyd ❼
Blue Ridge Parkway
Virginia
North Carolina
89
52
Mount Airy ❽
Reynolda House
Museum of American Art
Winston-Salem ❾
40
Hickory
Biltmore Estate
Asheville ❿
Chimney Rock State Park
74
Alt 74
North Carolina
Tennessee
40
19
441
Cherokee
Gatlinburg
Great Smoky Mountains
National Park ⓫
Norris Dam
Dandridge
Knoxville ⓬
Exit 417
75
162
Oak Ridge
62
40
Exit 340
Central Time Zone
96
70
N
70
The Hermitage
Nashville ⓭
40
Jackson
Casey Jones Village
Tennessee
Arkansas
Memphis ⓮
Exit 281
70
40
Exit 161
⓯ Little Rock
Exit 111
⓰ Hot Springs
30
7
Ola
10
Havana
309
Mount Magazine State Park ⓱
40
Exit 7
Arkansas
Missouri
Fort Smith ⓲
71
Joplin ⓳
Kansas
Oklahoma
66
Exit 313
44
Miami ⓴
Exit 289
Vinita
66
Foyil
Oologah
Claremore
Tulsa ㉑
88
Sapulpa
Kellyville
Davenport
Arcadia
Oklahoma City ㉒

every exit off the interstate leads to the site of a skirmish, raid, or other event.

Even if this page of history does not appeal to you, it's a good idea to abandon the interstate and enjoy the more scenic and leisurely alternate route. Try taking Exit 23, turning left, and then right onto Route 55. Cattle graze near faded red barns; roadside stands sell fresh produce. In autumn, orchards sell apples by the bushel basket, along with apple desserts (look for apple-cinnamon doughnuts). This is also a center of Virginia's wine industry, and signs direct you to vineyards along the way. You can pick up a brochure for the Blue Ridge Whiskey and Wine Loop at most of them.

Around 70 miles (112km) west of Washington, DC at the junction of I-60 and I-81, on the eastern edge of the Shenandoah Valley is **Front Royal**. Like most of the small towns dotting the valley, it was once a bustling center for farmers and mountain folk, Improved transportation and communication, however, sapped much of the vitality from their economies. Located at the northern end of the Skyline Drive, a few miles north of the entrance to Shenandoah National Park, Front Royal fares better than most of the valley towns, providing food and services for tourists. The Front Royal **Visitor Center** at 414 East Main Street (tel: 540-635-5788; www.discoverfrontroyal. com; daily) has an enthusiastic staff and useful information about the area.

Shenandoah National Park

Settlers from Europe turned the fertile Shenandoah Valley into a successful agricultural area. During the Civil War, its meat, grain, leather, and wool supplied the rebels, and Union forces devastated the valley. After the war, the decline continued as logging, poor farming techniques, and a chestnut blight led to soil exhaustion and erosion.

In 1926, Congress created the **Shenandoah National Park** ❸ (tel: 540-999-3500; www.nps.gov/shen; daily). At the dedication in 1936, President

Roosevelt announced an experiment in land reclamation allowing the nearly one-third of the park's land which had been deforested by decades of logging and intense cultivation to be returned to its natural state. Between natural regrowth and a vigorous restoration program, cropland and pastures were replaced with oak, pine, mountain laurel, and berry bushes. Wildflowers and azaleas now brighten the landscape and wildlife has returned; the park now has the largest black bear population in the eastern United States. White-tailed deer stroll nonchalantly along the roads. Bobcats and coyote are sometimes sighted, and catbirds and junco fly overhead.

In 1939, **Skyline Drive** was completed. The 105-mile (169km) National Scenic Byway runs the entire length of the Shenandoah National Park. Aside from the entrance near Front Royal, there are three other access points, each about an hour from the next. The per-car fee ticket is good for a week. The speed limit is a leisurely 35mph (56kph) along the winding, two-lane road. Be in no hurry; you will want to pull off at the 82 overlooks and picnic locations for views of the **Shenandoah Valley** and **Shenandoah River** to the west and the **Piedmont Plateau** to the east.

At the **Dickey Ridge Visitor Center** (Apr–Nov; daily), you can purchase guides for hiking and identifying flora and fauna. The **Harry Byrd Visitor Center** at Mile Marker 51 tells about the creation of the park and the people who once lived there.

At some point, you should experience the forest from beyond the confines of your vehicle. At Mile Marker 50.7, stop for the short round-trip hike to **Dark Hollow Falls**. The 1.4-mile (2.25km) hike is a bit steep in places, but the wide, well-maintained trail leads to a 70ft (21-meter) waterfall, which is especially impressive during spring run-off.

You can finish the drive in one day, but if you want to linger, Skyland and Big Meadow Lodges and Big Meadow Campground are well-equipped and comfortable.

Underground scenery

The limestone rock under the Blue Ridge was eroded over eons of

FACT

There are mileposts on the west side of Shenandoah National Park's Skyline Drive, beginning with 0.0 at Front Royal and continuing to 105 at the southern end of the park. Park maps use these markers as a reference guide.

Magnificent view from a summit above Shenandoah Valley.

A young spotted fawn taking its first steps in Shenandoah National Park.

Savoring the Blue Ridge Parkway scenery from Raven's Roost.

geologic history by underground streams, leaving dozens of caverns nestled in the foothills near Front Royal. **Skyline Caverns** (tel: 540-635-4545; www.skylinecaverns.com; daily) **Luray Caverns** (tel: 540-743-6551; www.luraycaverns.com; daily), **Endless Caverns** (tel: 540-896-9494; www.endlesscaverns.com; daily), and **Shenandoah Caverns** (tel: 540-477-3115; www.shenandoahcaverns.com; daily; elevator service for guests with mobility issues) are all near **New Market**. If you are on Skyline Drive, take Route 211 West to reach both Luray and New Market.

In New Market, the **Virginia Museum of the Civil War** (tel: 866-515-1864 or 540-740-3103; www.vmi.edu/newmarket; daily) chronicles the conflict as it impacted the state. The Battle of New Market is most remembered for the 257 teenaged cadets from the Virginia Military Academy who fought there. Ten of the boys were killed, another 47 wounded.

Skyline Drive ends at **Rockfish Gap**. You can take I-64 to **Staunton** or opt for the more relaxed Route 250.

Staunton and Lexington

Staunton ❹, (pronounced "Stanton") tucked into the steep hillsides of the Appalachians, is a pleasant former mining town with buildings dating to the 19th century. The **Woodrow Wilson Presidential Library** (tel: 540-885-0897; www.woodrowwilson.com; daily) portrays the 28th president's political career and eight-year (1913–21) White House stint.

Don't miss a performance at **Blackfriars Playhouse** (tel: 540-885-5588 or 877-MUCHADO). The home of the American Shakespeare Company is an exact replica of the stage the Bard knew, and performances return to that time. The audience sits on the stage, lighting is from chandeliers, sets are minimal, and the actors play to the lively spirit of Elizabethan times. There are daily backstage tours. Also worth visiting is the **Frontier Culture Museum** (tel: 540-332-7850; www.frontiermuseum.org; daily), which compares transplanted farmsteads from Europe and West Africa with American frontier farms from 1750 to 1840 to demonstrate the merging of different traditions.

From Staunton take the I-81, or the more scenic US 11, to another town with deep connections to the Civil War. Attractive **Lexington** ❺, is where ol' Stonewall was teaching cadets at the Virginia Military Institute (VMI) shortly after its founding in 1831. The VMI Museum (tel: 540-464-7334; www.vmi.edu; daily) includes the coat Jackson was wearing when he was accidentally shot by his own men. It also has the mounted hide of his horse, Little Sorrel (which ranks very high on the tasteless and creepy scale), an extensive collection of 19th-century firearms, and seven medals of honor bestowed on VMI graduates.

In town, you can tour the **Stonewall Jackson House** (tel: 540-463-2552; www.stonewalljackson.org; daily), the only residence Jackson ever owned.

Jackson's commander, **General Robert E. Lee**, became president of **Washington College** after the Civil

War. In contrast to the discipline at VMI, his only "rule" was that "every student must be a gentleman." Lee and his family are interred in the crypt beneath the school's chapel. An excellent museum about the close ties between Virginia "aristocracy" and Lee's life after the war is in the chapel's basement. The remains of Traveler, Lee's beloved horse, are respectfully interred outside the chapel. The school was renamed **Washington and Lee College** after the General's death.

Lively Roanoke

Continue south on Route 11. It rolls through Virginia's alluring landscape to **Roanoke ❻**, a pleasantly relaxed and sophisticated city with the added bonus of its proximity to the Blue Ridge Parkway. Mill Mountain, topped by the huge, illuminated **Roanoke Star**, overlooks the city. The outstanding outdoor **City Market**, with about 50 stalls selling produce, plants, baked goods, and meats – all from local sources – operates daily in the heart of the city's historic district. The **Center in the Square** (tel: 540-342-5700; www.centerinthesquare. org) has museums focusing on science, regional history, and African-American culture, rooftop gardens, and the largest living coral reef in the East. The ultramodern **Taubman Museum of Art** (tel: 540-342-5700; www.taubmanmuseum.org; Tue–Sat and first Sun of the month) owes some of its design to Australia's Sydney Opera House. Inside, the comprehensive collection runs the gamut of artistic inspirations: folk and visionary art, US masters, and contemporary regional artists. Adjacent to the **Visitor Center** (tel: 800-635-5535; daily) is the **O. Wilson Link Museum** (tel: 540-982-5465, www.linkmuseum.org; daily), an evocative collection of photographic vignettes which record the last years of steam railroads.

Blue Ridge Mountains and music

eaving Roanoke, take US 221 south. coils up Bent Mountain, past Baptist

churches preaching redemption and houses flying the Confederate flag. Motorcyclists will be in heaven; RVers will need to stay in second gear. The trek ends in **Floyd ❼**, where Bluegrass music is in the air. Floyd is one of the venues for The Crooked Road, Virginia's Heritage Music Trail, a driving route through southwest Virginia. At the **Floyd Country Store** (tel: 540-745-4563; www.floydcountrystore.com; Tue–Sun) you can buy penny candy, a field guide to cows, bib overalls, eco-friendly cleaning supplies, and get a map of the Crooked Road. Musicians gather Thursday and Saturday evenings, and Sunday afternoons to jam. The town is a magnet for craft artisans; there are galleries, and almost weekly art and music fests.

Take Route 8 south for 6 miles (9.6km) to Tuggle's Gap and the **Blue Ridge Parkway** (www.blueridgeparkway.org). A National Scenic Byway, it connects the Shenandoah and Great Smoky Mountains national parks, passing through forests and past farms and crossroad hamlets. There are several scenic overlooks, but not as many

Long-established barbecue joint in Eureka Springs, Arkansas.

View of Roanoke from Mill Mountain.

TIP

Leave yourself plenty of time to enjoy the walking and hiking excursions offered along the way; even a tiny walk to a beautiful waterfall can relieve the tedium of driving.

as along Skyline Drive. Pick up a free guide at the **Rocky Knob Visitor Center** at Milepost 169.

Mabry Mill at Milepost 176 has a picture-worthy restored 1900-era gristmill and moonshine still. At Milepost 210, **The Blue Ridge Music Center** (tel: 276-236-5309; www.blue ridgemusiccenter.org; daily) recounts the story of the distinctive music of these mountains: bluegrass, ballads, gospel, and traditional songs played on fiddle, mandolin, guitar, and banjo. Musicians jam in the covered courtyard every afternoon.

Leave the Parkway at VA Route 89 and follow it southeast into North Carolina to **Mount Airy ❽**. The birthplace of the late Andy Griffith and setting for *Mayberry RFD* has a museum of Griffith's career and a recreation of the gas station, city hall, and sheriff's office.

Winston-Salem

Continue south on US 52 to **Winston-Salem ❾**. The city's history is split between the Moravian settlers who arrived in the 1750s and the R.J. Reynolds Tobacco Company, which

Cycling along the Blue Ridge Parkway.

began packaging tobacco in 1875. Even with the decline in US tobacco consumption, the factory still produces over 400 million cigarettes a day. The firm sponsors NASCAR's Winston Cup Series. The **Winston Cup Museum** (tel: 336-724-4557; www.winstoncupmuseum.com; Tue–Sat) is Mecca for NASCAR fans.

But the Moravians were here first at **Old Salem** (tel: 336-721-7300; Tue–Sun). Very slightly removed from the modern city, the "Salem" part of Winston-Salem is one of the most authentic and inviting living history districts in the US. A covered bridge transports you from the Visitor Center to the village. At its foot, the **Museum of Early Southern Decorative Arts** in the Frank L. Horton Museum Center (tel: 336-779-6140; www.mesda. org; Tue–Sun) has an "Antiques Road Show" feel to its collection. Each piece has a family-history tale of where it was made, when, by whom, and why,

Most of the Old Salem buildings are privately owned, and there are modern concessions. Air-conditioners hum behind houses and cars park on the streets. But costumed guides roam the village, and buildings operating as examples of the historic period feature hands-on demonstrations of daily life. Its old tavern is an upscale restaurant. The printing shop of John Christian Blum, founding publisher in 1828 of *The Farmers' and Planters' Almanac*, is one of the exhibit buildings. Be sure to stop at the **Winkler Bakery** for impossibly thin Moravian ginger cookies. And what of the giant-size metal coffeepot standing on the village green? Built by the sons of Salem's founders, Samuel and Julius Mickey, it was used to advertise their tinsmith's shop.

Costumed guides roam another restored Moravian village, **Historic Bethabara Park** (tel: 336-924-8191; www.bethabarapark.org; Tue–Sat) in a pleasant green setting off University Parkway. The open-air museum has a 1788 church, archeological ruins, and 20 miles (32km) of nature trails.

Reynolda House Museum of American Art (tel: 336-758-5150; www.reynoldahouse.org; Tue–Sun) is the former home of Katharine Smith and Richard Joshua Reynolds (founder of R.J. Reynolds Tobacco). The home, its gardens and adjoining Reynolda Village, in which the old buildings have been converted into shops, offices, and restaurants, are open to visitors. The Southeast Center for Contemporary Arts (SEECA) (tel: 336-725-1904; www.secca.org; Tue–Sun) is connected to the Reynolda Museum via an enclosed passageway. It is as contemporary as the Reynolda is traditional.

From Winston-Salem, I-40 is the highway west. About 73 miles (117km) along the route is the town of **Hickory**, the center of the state's furniture industry.

Asheville

With the Blue Ridge Mountains as a backdrop, **Asheville** ❿ enjoys great natural beauty. It also enjoys a gallery of elegant buildings commissioned by paternalistic businessmen in the early 1900s. They successfully promoted Asheville to investors. In the early years of the 20th century, the city was booming. When the Depression hit, it became the most indebted city in the nation. Rather than default, the Asheville community swore it would repay all loans; it signed the final check in the 1970s.

That economic disaster prevented Asheville from participating in the Urban Renewal projects of the 1960s, which saw many downtowns replacing classic buildings with "Nouveau Gulag" architecture. So the block-square Grove Arcade – the original indoor shopping mall – remains as it was when it was completed in 1923, and the surrounding streets retain their period charm. Only Miami has more Art Deco buildings. You will find no national retailers downtown; by community consensus, all businesses are locally owned. The River District along the French Broad River houses the studios of nearly 200 artists.

At the **Grove Park Inn Resort** (see page 411), you can tour the Grovewood Gallery of Regional Crafts and a collection of antique autos. The **Thomas Wolfe Memorial** (tel: 828-253-8304; www.wolfememorial.com; Tue–Sun) preserves the boardinghouse where Wolfe grew up and which he used in his novel *Look Homeward, Angel*. The unflattering novel about Asheville so angered residents (many of whom recognized their fictional selves) that it was banned in the city.

A winery, sporting activities, shops, and restaurants are all part of the immense landscaped property of the 250-room **Biltmore Estate** (tel: 800-411-3812; www.biltmore.com; daily). It is America's largest privately owned home. George Vanderbilt's vision took root in 1887, when he visited Asheville on vacation and became enchanted by the mountain scenery. Vanderbilt set out to create a mansion modeled after the French Loire Valley chateaux. The self-guided tour includes three floors and the basement. Inside you'll find 16th-century tapestries, many priceless antiques, and a banquet hall with a

TIP

Winston Salem's **Visitor Center** at 200 Brookstown Avenue (tel: 336-728-4200; Mon–Fri) distributes free maps and other information about the city and surrounding area.

Hiking in Shenandoah National Park.

Nicknamed 'The Batman Building' for its resemblance to the superhero's mask, the 32-story AT&T Building in Nashville is the tallest in the state of Tennessee.

Knoxville's springtime celebration, the Dogwood Arts Festival.

70-foot (21-meter) ceiling. The former village for employees is now a shopping district. All new buildings must reflect the original Tudor-style architecture, even the McDonald's, which has faux-marble floors and a fireplace.

Southeast of Asheville, near the intersection of US 64 and US 74A, is **Chimney Rock State Park**, a 1,000-acre (405-hectare) Natural Heritage Site including Chimney Rock itself. An elevator whisks visitors 26 stories to the top of the formation, 1,200ft (366 meters) above sea level. The waterfalls of majestic **Hickory Nut Falls** were the backdrop for the climactic scenes in the movie *The Last of the Mohicans*.

THE GREAT SMOKIES

Great Smoky Mountains National Park ⑪ (tel: 865-436-1200; www.nps.gov/grsm; daily), 16 of whose peaks exceed 6,000ft (1,800 meters), sprawls majestically over the North Carolina and Tennessee borders. Access on the North Carolina side is gained from the town of **Cherokee** by taking I-40W Exit 27 (US 74) from Asheville, then Exit 103 (US 19). The arrival in

Cherokee is jarring – with the 21-story Harrah's hotel and casino dominating the townscape. The resort is vital to the economy of the Cherokee Nation, whose reservation surrounds the town.

The town of Cherokee is the unofficial capital of the Eastern Band of the Cherokee. About 12,000 members of the tribe live on the Quallah Boundary, the name of the 56,000-acre (23,000-hectare) reservation that is adjacent to the national park.

A string of souvenir shops sell mass produced moccasins, beadwork, key rings, and other gee-gaws. Many schedule "Indian dances" for entertainment. The 11,000 years of documented Cherokee history is presented with dignity at the **Museum of the Cherokee Indian** (tel: 828-497-3481; www.cherokeemuseum; org; daily). An introductory film describes the Cherokee's use of stories and nature to define their place in the world, Displays explain their non-material social order, the visit to England by their leaders to meet George III, and their efforts to have their land recognized as an independent nation. Although the US Supreme Court upheld their claim in 1831, Jackson ignored it.

The **Qualla Arts and Crafts Center** (tel: 828-497-3103; www.quallaartsandcrafts.com; daily), next to the museum, is the oldest Native American arts co-operative in the country. Contemporary Cherokee artists display traditional and interpretive takes on pottery, fetishes, and both decorative and ceremonial objects. The **Oconaluftee Indian Village** (tel: 828-497-2111; May–Oct Mon-Sat) recreates life in a Cherokee village in the year 1760.

US 441 climbs out of Cherokee across the Great Smoky Mountains towards **Gatlinburg**. As you start the trek, a sign warns of "35 miles of steep, winding road." You soon reach the **Oconaluftee Visitor Center** for the Great Smoky Mountains National Park, which enjoys an impossibly beautiful location in a broad glade surrounded by the blue-grey mountains

There are many overlooks along the way. It is impossible to capture the views on camera, but you will try anyway. There's a stop light at the end of the forest; drive out of the greenery and you will abruptly find yourself in **Gatlinburg**, confronted with every chain restaurant and souvenir shop known to man. **Sky Lift Gatlinburg** (tel: 865-436-4307; www.gatlinburgskylift.com; Apr–Oct daily, Nov–Mar hours vary) lifts riders 1,000ft (459 meters) above the valley for peaceful views of the vast forest. There is free parking at the Visitor Center and a shuttle service into town.

Pigeon Forge, 4 miles (6.5km) away is home to Dollywood Theme Park (tel: 865-428-9488; www.dollywood.com; Apr–Dec) – the creation of Dolly Parton, the buxom country singer and actress – and more resort attractions. To bypass them turn on Route 449 and continue to the T-intersection at Dolly Parton Boulevard. Turn right to rejoin US 441.

Towards Knoxville

Driving northeast from Gatlinburg, you will pass through some pleasant countryside of hills and pastures for 23 miles (37km) to **Chestnut Hill**, home of **Bush's Baked Beans** (tel: 865-509-3077; www.bushbeans.com; Mon–Sat). The company's Visitor Center is on the highway. The brand is best known for a popular US television ad featuring Duke, a talking dog who schemes to sell the secret family recipe. There is a video virtual tour of the factory and the company's story (the recipe really does come from the family matriarch), a scale telling your weight in beans, and the opportunity to have your photo taken with Duke via backdrops. The café features Southern dishes and the "bean of the day."

From the Bush's Visitor Center, take Route 92 to **Dandridge**. The views along Lake Douglas will have you ready to buy lakefront property. From here, I-40 is a straight shot to **Knoxville** ⑫. Tennessee is proud of its musical heritage, and it starts at the **Visitor Center**

at 301 Gay Street (tel: 865-523-7263; daily) which is the location of *The Blue Plate Special*, a daily, live, free noon-time performance of traditional music broadcast over radio station WDVX.

In 1982, Knoxville was the site for the World's Fair, which attracted 11 million visitors from 30 countries and established Knoxville – considered an unlikely location for the event – as a sophisticated urban venue. The most attractive Downtown feature is an extensive park with a lake and rock-lined creek, which was created for the World's Fair. None of the buildings erected for the fair remain.

"Voices of the Land" at the **East Tennessee Historical Society** (tel: 865-215-8824; www.easttnhistory.org; daily) uses written and oral excerpts from diaries, letters, and official documents, which give the region's history a personal perspective. "Betsy," Davy Crockett's rifle is on display, as are relics of the Civil War (which locally quickly degenerated into personal vendettas), and of logging. Main Street in the **Old City** is a pedestrian shopping and business area. A few blocks

Breathtaking view across Great Smoky Mountains National Park.

All ages welcome at the annual Country Music Association (CMA) Festival in Nashville.

away, **12th Street** is an up-and-coming residential and entertainment district.

James White's Fort (tel: 865-525-6514; www.jameswhitesfort.org; daily) is the restored farm of Knoxville's founder. As many as 100 people, along with livestock, stayed inside the palisaded compound, which is not much bigger than a lot in a suburban housing development. Across the street, at the **Women's Basketball Hall of Fame** (tel: 865-633-9000; www.wbhof. com; May–Labor Day Mon–Sat, Labor Day–Apr Tue–Sat), you can watch videos of past moments of glory, as well as shoot some hoops. **Volunteer Landing** along the riverfront has a walking trail and the dock for a dinner cruise boat.

North of the city on US 441, the **Norris Dam** was the first to be built by the vast Tennessee Valley Authority, which brought electric power to this region in the 1930s. **Norris Lake**, acclaimed as one of the cleanest in North America, has several marinas and supports houseboats and fishing. There are trails and campgrounds in the surrounding woods. On Highway 61, the **Museum of Appalachia** (tel:

865-494-7680; www.museumofappalachia. org; daily) is "a living mountain village" and does a superlative job of interpreting rural Tennessee. The extensive collection of transplanted buildings, demonstrations of basic skills of daily life, personal items and the stories told by the owners make you deeply aware of how hard it was to survive in the mountains.

The Secret City of World War II

West of Knoxville at Exit 364 off I-40 is **Oak Ridge**, the "secret city" built in 1942; 75,000 people lived there in total secrecy to work on production of the first atomic bomb. The **American Museum of Science and Energy** (tel: 865-576-3200; www.amse.org; daily) tells the stories about life there, and includes a photo of guards frisking Santa. The rest of the museum is an explanation of nuclear energy and displays about the Y-12 National Security Complex, which is responsible for various aspects of nuclear activity, and dealing with nuclear vulnerabilities. Back on I-40, you enter the **Central Time Zone** just past Exit 340. Take Exit 268, turn right on to Route 96 to US 70 North. Turn left. You are now about 50 miles (80km) from Nashville. This rolling ride through the last of the mountains starts as a two-lane road on a thread-thin strip of land with steep ravines on one side. It levels out to pastures and cultivated fields where weathered, silver grey barns with faded red roofs pose for photos.

Just before you reach Nashville, stop to visit President Andrew Jackson's gracious and beautiful mansion, **The Hermitage** (tel: 615-889-2941; www. thehermitage.com; daily), and on whose grounds still stands the pre-existing farmhouse in which Jackson lived before becoming America's seventh president. He died there in 1845.

Nashville

In the 1850s **Nashville** ⓭ was considered the most refined and

sophisticated city in the South, calling itself "The Athens of the South." In 1897, the city built a full-scale replica of the **Parthenon** for its centennial celebration. It still commands its imposing location on a hill in Centennial Park, complete with a 420ft (12.8-meter) -tall, gilded statue of Athena. The building also serves as **Nashville's Art Museum** (tel: 615-862-8431; www.nashville.com/parthenon; Tue–Sun) with a permanent collection devoted to 19th- and 20th-century American artists.

The **Frist Center for Visual Arts** (tel: 615-244-3340; www.fristcenter.org; daily), located in the magnificent Art Deco former Post Office on Broadway, has no permanent collection. Instead, it stages three or four temporary exhibits at any time. Often they complement each other; just as often, they demonstrate the great variety of visual expression.

The **Tennessee State Museum** (tel: 615-741-2692; www.tnmuseum.org; Tue–Sun) is a comprehensive exploration of Tennessee history and culture from the days of the mastodon to the early years of the 20th century. The centerpiece of the museum is an illustrated

history of the Civil War accenting the role of Tennessee, a Confederate state. Occupying an entire floor are interactive exhibits with sound effects, film, battle flags, and personal effects of soldiers. There are also exhibits about the New South that Tennessee helped create during Reconstruction (the period after the Civil War), Davy Crockett's powder horn, and a Conestoga wagon in which some long-forgotten family from Virginia migrated to the state in about 1800.

Music City

Despite its other attractions, Nashville is known primarily as the epicenter for country music. Musicians, singers, songwriters, and performers have gravitated to the city since 1925, when radio station WSM began broadcasting the WSM Barn Dance show on Saturday nights. Two years later, it was renamed the **Grand Ole Opry** (tel: 615-871-OPRY or 800-SEE-OPRY; www.opry.com), a joking parallel to the program broadcasting classical opera which preceded it. In 1943, the show moved to **Ryman Auditorium** (tel:

TIP

Take a stroll along Nashville's Walk of Fame, found along the 1-mile stretch connecting downtown with Music Row. Star-and-guitar sidewalk markers commemorate Jimi Hendrix, Roy Orbison, and Emmylou Harris, amongst others.

Country rock star Charlie Daniels performing at the Grand Ole' Opry.

The Hermitage, Andrew Jackson's Tennessee home.

Country Music Hall of Fame.

615-889-3060; www.ryman. com; daily). With acoustics second only to the Mormon Tabernacle, it was originally built as the Union Gospel Tabernacle, hence the nickname of the auditorium as "The Mother Church of Country Music." But it staged theatrical and music performances of all genres from Katherine Hepburn to Caruso. The Opry moved to expanded, modern facilities in 1974, and the Ryman closed until 1994. It now hosts a schedule of musical performances in the classic theatre with its church pews and stained glass windows.

Today, the Grand Ole Opry is housed in a large, custom-built facility north of Nashville. To honor the Opry's history, a large circle of wood from the Ryman's stage is inlaid at the front of the new Opry stage. Performances are Friday and Saturday, with Tuesday shows during the summer. Every country artist dreams of

being invited to perform there; to be chosen as a member of the Opry roster is a career highlight.

The Ryman is a cornerstone of a district devoted to country music that is contained by Second to Fifth avenues and Church to Demonbreun streets. Broadway, between Second and Fourth avenues is lined with tiny honky-tonk bars that never close and where undiscovered musicians perform at all hours, each hoping that they'll be noticed by a passing talent agent. Stop at **Hatch Show Print** at 316 Broadway (tel: 615-256-2805; www.countrymusichalloffame.org/our-work; Mon–Sat). Since 1875, the company has produced handbills and posters for entertainers using wood block, letterpress techniques little changed from Gutenberg's press. Across the street, **Ernest Tubb Music Shop** (tel: 615-255-7503; www.etrecordshop.com; daily) opened in 1947. Its inventory, both CD and vinyl, is beyond comprehensive.

The **Country Music Hall of Fame** (tel: 615-416-2001; www.countrymusichalloffame.org; daily) occupies an entire city block along Demonbreun

Street. From above, the building is shaped like a bass clef; the windows mimic piano keys; the soaring northwest corner resembles the fins of cars from the 1950s. Allow at least three hours to even casually explore the exhibits. Starting with the origins of a music that deals with "real people and real lives," it honors singing cowboys and Western swing, Tennessee Ernie Ford and the television variety show *Hee-Haw*,(with the original cornfield set). Songwriters explain their inspiration, listening booths play classic and forgotten recordings. Elvis' gold Cadillac, scores of guitars from famous owners, and Taylor Swift's laptop are on display. In the center of the buildings, the Hall of Fame has bronze tablets honoring members of the creative and business communities who are dedicated to advancing country music. The random placement of the plaques in the circular hall demonstrates the equality of all of the members.

The **Johnny Cash Museum** (tel: 615-736-9909; daily) on Third Avenue honors the memory and career of one of country music's iconic performers.

The **Musicians Hall of Fame** (tel: 615-244-3263; www.musicianshalloffame. com, reopening 2013), meanwhile, is dedicated to the "studio musicians," those who accompany artists and stars and who are rarely recognized. The **Willie Nelson and Friends General Store**, near the new Opry, shows off Nelson's long career and sells all manner of Nashville and Nelson souvenirs.

Music Highway

Most of the towns along I-40 claim connection to some musical star. Exit 143 leads to **Loretta Lynn's Ranch** (tel: 731-668-1222; www.lorettalynn ranch.net; daily Apr–Oct, limited attractions Nov–Mar) with a replica of the "house in Butcher Holler" where the Coalminer's Daughter was born and tours of the 1837 plantation house she bought when she became a star.

Jackson, at Exit 82, claims Tina Turner, Isaac Hayes, and Carl Perkins. At **Casey Jones Village** (tel: 731-668-1222; www.caseyjones.com; daily), a museum and performance venue shows off all of the genres. Jackson was the home of John Luther Jones, nicknamed Casey, who entered into history when he rode his engine, *The Cannonball Express*, into the rear of a stalled freight train, slowing his train enough that all of his passengers survived. The house where he lived with his wife and three children is open for tours. The train depot is filled with articles about the Casey Jones legend and the history of Tennessee railroads. Hank Williams, Jr lives in nearby Paris.

The **West Tennessee Delta Heritage Center** at Exit 56 (tel: 731-779-9000; www.westtnheritage.com; daily) is a good place to stop to gather information about attractions throughout the region. If you have time, swing past The Minefield in **Brownsville** on South Main/Highway 54. Tennessee's largest outdoor sculpture, at first glance it looks like an electrical substation. A closer look shows it to be an ever-expanding, visionary reflection on life by self-taught artist Billy Tripp.

FACT

Interstate 40, the road that connects Nashville with Memphis, is known as "Music Highway."

Memphis: Music City USA

The gateway to the Mississippi delta, Memphis is home of the blues, Beale Street, and the memory of two kings: Elvis and Martin Luther.

The guest list at Memphis's ornate and venerable **Peabody Hotel** (pronounce it *ho-tel*) has included US presidents as well as General Robert E. Lee, but today's notables are the Peabody ducks. Every day at 11am, they take a ride in the elevator from their rooftop home to the lobby, waddle across a red carpet and, to the strains of John Philip Sousa, climb into the fountain, where they happily paddle around until 5pm when the performance is repeated in reverse.

Memphis is best known, of course, for **Graceland** (tel: 800-238-2000; www.eliv.com/graceland; Dec–Feb Wed–Mon), home and final resting place of Elvis Presley. The in-depth, self-guided audio tour covers the bottom floor and basement of the mansion. Other buildings contain his awards, and concert and movie memorabilia. Arrive early: on busy days, the wait for the shuttle to the mansion can be over an hour.

Beale Street music clubs.

Tributes to Elvis, Graceland.

Sun Studio (tel: 901-521-0664; www.sun studio.com; daily) was where "the King" recorded, but B.B. King, Ike Turner, and many other artists preceded him here. In recent years, Bono, U2, and Paul Simon have been Sun clients. Half-hourly tours are given. The **Stax Museum of American Soul Music** (tel: 901-946-2535; www.staxmuseum. com; Apr–Oct daily, Nov–Mar Tue–Sun) celebrates the musicians, like Aretha Franklin and Otis Redding, who lived, worked or are buried in the Memphis area called Soulsville, while the **Memphis Rock 'n Soul Museum** (tel: 901-205-2533; www.memphisrocknsoul.org; daily) on Beale Street has seven galleries that examine the history of the city's music.

There are plenty of other music venues, among them the **Center for Southern Folklore** (tel: 901-525-3655; www.southernfolklore.com; Mon–Sat), which puts the music in a larger cultural and social context. **Beale Street** is where it all began, and the street's bars and nightclubs swell with the strains of the Delta blues created by W.C. Handy (1873–1958).

On Mulberry Street, the **National Civil Rights Museum** (tel: 901-521-9699; www.civilrights museum.org; Wed–Mon) incorporates the Lorraine Motel where Martin Luther King, Jr was assassinated on April 4, 1968. The sight of the rumpled bed, breakfast tray, and a few objects in Room 306 – the last things Dr King saw before stepping onto the balcony – somehow make the event very personal. Other exhibits chronicle key moments in the American Civil Rights movement and global efforts towards human and civil rights.

Tennessee's music and cultural heritage rolls right on in to **Memphis ⓮** (see page 196).

ARKANSAS

At Memphis, the I-40 crosses the **Mississippi River** into Arkansas. With barely 3 million people in an area of 53,000 sq miles (138,000 sq km), much of Arkansas remains undeveloped, which accounts for one of its nicknames, "The Natural State." The state capital, Little Rock, has only 700,000 people; Fort Smith, the second largest, has 87,000.

Instead of taking the interstate, consider traveling US 70 west to Little Rock. Take time to observe some of the best of Arkansas' natural landscapes along this route – rich Delta bottomland, prairie, pine forests, and cypress swamps – before rejoining I-40 at Galloway at Exit 161.

Little Rock

The Arkansas River carves a gateway between the Ouachita and Ozark mountains to the delta at **Little Rock ⓯**. The city is, therefore, first and foremost a river city. **Breckling Riverfront Park** is a wonderful outdoor space with great walking along the water, a fountain that's filled with laughing kids and more than a few adults in hot weather, and the "Little Rock" after which the city is named.

Markham Street has hotels and the convention center. Cross Broadway, and the street becomes President Clinton Avenue. This is **River Market District,** the center of activity for tourists and entertainment. At the **Clinton Presidential Library** (tel: 501-748-0419; www.clintonlibrary.gov; daily), the self-guided tour includes the only full-scale replica of the Oval Office, a timeline of Clinton's career, and many of the gifts collected by the Clintons during their time in the White House. Outside, a refurbished railroad bridge is now a pedestrian walkway crossing the river to North Little Rock, a developing neighborhood.

Behind the library is the headquarters of **Heifer International** (tel: 800-422-0474; www.heifer.org; Mon–Sat). The charity develops self-sufficiency by giving livestock to poor communities in the Third World. The exhibits explain how this leads to better living conditions and social progress.

The **Arkansas Museum of Discovery** (tel: 501-396-7050; www.museumofdiscovery.org; Tue–Sun) is fun for kids but is equally great for adults, so much so that the museum has "adults only" nights. The Tornado Alley Theater places you inside a tornado shelter during a storm. Even knowing that it's not real, it is still very frightening.

Surrounded by the modern city, the **Historic Arkansas Museum** (tel: 502-324-9351; www.historicarkansas.org; daily) is a collection of the first buildings in Little Rock. The city's oldest structure, the **Hinderliter Grog Shop,** sadly no longer serves customers. The museum's pride is the printing press used to produce the state's first newspaper.

The modern history of Little Rock is inexorably linked to the ordered

TIP

You may want to roll down your windows when traveling through Arkansas: a highway department program has resulted in the planting of 600 kinds of wildflowers, some of which attract hummingbirds.

Re-living a Civil War battle in Arkansas.

Lunch break at a Civil War re-enactment event.

Paddle steamer on the Arkansas River, Little Rock.

desegregation of **Central High School**. In 1957, nine black students entered the school past scores of violent protesters. The city already planned to desegregate the high school that year, but the Governor swore that Arkansas schools would remain segregated. Inside The **Central High School Visitor Center** (tel: 501-374-1957; www.nps.gov/chsc; daily), interactive displays recreate the tension-filled weeks and includes recollections of the "Central High Nine" and others who were involved at the school and in the community.

The **Arkansas Arts Center** (tel: 501-372-4000; www.arkarts.com; Tue–Sun) is committed to building a collection of outstanding works on paper, from the Renaissance to the present. You can wander past art by Van Gogh, Cézanne, and Jackson Pollack. Contemporary crafts is another focus, with pieces from Dale Chihuly and Dorothy Gill Barnes.

A submarine is about the last thing you'd expect to find in the Arkansas River. But the USS *Razorback* is berthed at the **Inland Maritime Museum** (tel: 501-371-8320; www.aim. museum; Wed–Sun). The sub saw duty in the Pacific, during the Cold War, and in Vietnam before being decommissioned in 2001 after near 65 years of service. Guided tours show off the extremely complicated machinery and tight quarters the crew tolerated.

Hot Springs

The hour-long drive from Little Rock to **Hot Springs** ⑯ is purely functional. Take I-30W to Exit 111 and US 70. The last part of the drive goes through some steep mountain terrain; hikers can explore the trails around the resort town. There are several access points to the trailheads, which are clearly marked. Native Americans called Hot Springs "the Valley of the Vapors" for the steam rising from the thermal waters. By the 1880s it was an elegant resort town, when Bathhouse Row, with its elaborate spa houses, was completed. Today, two of the bathhouses still operate. Buckstaff Bathhouse (tel: 501-623-2308; www.buckstaffbaths. com; daily) gives traditional tub baths, while Quapaw Baths and Spa (tel: 501-609-9822; www.quapawbaths.com; Wed–Sun) has more modern atmosphere and amenities. **Hot Springs National Park** (tel: 501-620-6715; www.nps.gov. hosp; daily) encompasses Bathhouse Row. It preserves Fordyce Bathhouse; the self-guided tour includes bathing rooms, lounges, and the gym where Babe Ruth worked out. The former 1920 "Ozark Bathhouse" has new life as the **Museum of Contemporary Art** (tel: 501-609-9966; www.museumof contemporaryart.com; Wed–Sun). A small permanent collection is augmented by unique exhibitions of sculpture, photography, and multi-media.

Before there was Las Vegas, there was Hot Springs. In the 1930s and 1940s, this was the hangout of the famous and notorious. Al Capone and Lucky Luciano vacationed here. Many of the buildings that are shops now were speakeasies then. For an entertaining version of that era, visit the **Gangster**

Museum of America (tel: 501-319-1717; www.tgmoa.com; daily). Wearing fedoras and using just enough New York accent, guides tell stories – most of them true – about the decades when Hot Springs was synonymous with vice, corruption, and good times.

A few miles from town, **Garvan Woodland Gardens** (tel: 502-262-9300; www.garvangardens.org; daily) is a welcome break from the hustle of Hot Springs. Operated by the University of Arkansas' Department of Landscape Architecture, the gardens were once a timber clear-cut area. Restoration began about 40 years ago and the gardens are now a showcase of blooms, bulbs, and perennials, mature trees and shrubs, a koi pond, and flowing streams and waterfalls. There are golf cart tours for those with mobility issues.

Mount Magazine

The two-hour drive from Hot Springs to **Mount Magazine State Park** ⑰ goes through some of the loveliest scenery of the Ouachita National Forest. Leave Hot Springs on State 7 to State 10 and turn onto State 309 to the park. This is the crown jewel of Arkansas' superior state parks. The "Island in the Sky" is the highest peak in the state, rising 2753ft (839 meters) above the valley where Blue Mountain Lake shimmers. It's a natural destination for nature lovers, with dozens of hiking trails, facilities for rock climbing, backpacking, hang-gliding, and mountain biking. On the east side of the mountain, **Mount Magazine Lodge** (see page 413) has breathtaking views of the valley. From Hot Springs, take Route 7 north to Ola, switch to Route 10, then turn onto Route 309 in Havana. The 90-minute drive is one of the most scenic in the state.

Fort Smith

From Mount Magazine, take Route 309 north to I-40W to **Fort Smith** ⑱. The town revels in its "Wild West" heritage. The lovely restored Victorian mansion at 2 North B Street that houses the **Visitor Center** was once "Miss Laura's Social Club" – now on the National Register of Historic Places, this was once one of the town's more upscale bordellos (tel: 479-783-8888; daily). Many of the rooms are restored to

TIP

Stop by the Old State House museum in Little Rock, the place where Bill Clinton gave his election night victory speeches (tel: 501-324-9685; daily).

Wildflowers on a farm in Mountain Country.

FACT

Fort Smith features in *True Grit*, a novel by Charles Portis that inspired two movie adaptations.

Capitol building, Little Rock, where former US president Bill Clinton served five times as governor.

their "business" appearance, and staff cheerfully gives tours.

Fort Smith National Historic Site (tel: 479-783-3961; www.nps.gov/ fosm; daily) tells the rest of the lively history. The courtroom of "Hanging" Judge Parker and the jail where many of the defendants in the 13,490 cases he heard were incarcerated have been restored. Excellent displays tell about the hard, dangerous, violent, and exciting time when outlaws slipped across the river into "Indian Territory," followed by US Marshalls.

The **Fort Smith Museum of History** (tel: 479-783-7841; www.fort smithmuseum.com; Tue–Sun) pays more attention to the city's "respectable" times and its citizenry, who often maneuvred around the lawless residents. The old-time soda fountain is a good place for refreshment. Outside, hop onto a vintage **trolley** which circulates through the downtown historic district. The scenic railroad ride that chugs through the countryside is especially grand in the fall.

When Elvis Presley joined the Army, he reported to Fort Chafee, just south of Fort Smith, to the east of I-540. The **Chafee Barbershop Museum** (tel: 479-783-7841; Mon, Wed–Sat) is where he had that famous haircut. The barbershop is restored with the chair Elvis sat in and videos of the famous buzz cut. The Fort has played a major role in other events, including helping Vietnamese refugees and housing evacuees from Hurricane Katrina. The building has exhibits about those more important activities.

Fayetteville

Although I-40 will carry you all the way through the state of Oklahoma and on westward, it you are interested in a more colorful journey, we suggest taking the I-540 to **Fayetteville**, about an hour north of Fort Smith. The city is home to the University of Arkansas and the first house owned by Bill and Hillary Clinton when they were both instructors at the University. The **Clinton House Museum** (tel: 479-444-0066, Mon–Sat) is a modest, Tudor-style house on a side street near the school. Pull into the gravel driveway and knock on the front door.

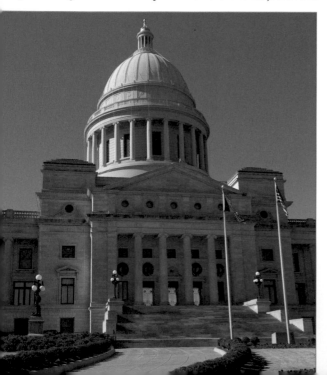

MUD ISLAND RIVER PARK

You can spend a very pleasant day at the **Mud Island River Park and Museum** (tel: 901-576-7241; www. mudisland.com; mid-Apr–Oct Tue– Sun), a scaled down version of the Mississippi River in a lovely setting on the river.

A model scaled to one step equals one mile means you can "walk" the entire 954 miles (1,535km) of the river, with accurate, real-time water levels and geographic, geologic, and historic details. Running the length of this island in the middle of the Mississippi, it takes about an hour to complete the journey.

There are small boats and bikes to rent, and a museum focussing on the days of the Mississippi riverboats, including a nearly full-scale paddle wheeler to explore.

Volunteers have great stories about how it took Bill six months to put tiles around the fireplace, a job he told Hillary would take a weekend.

Bentonville: Fine Art and Wal-Mart

Further along I-540, just below the Missouri line, is **Bentonville**, home of Wal-Mart. One of the storefronts facing the town square is the original five-and-dime store that Sam Walton ran and where his Wal-Mart plans were made. The store is now the **Wal-Mart Visitor Center** (tel: 479-273-1329; daily). After viewing a video tribute to Sam Walton and a promotional cheerleading piece about the firm, you go through many displays about the growth of Sam's empire and the operations today.

The Waltons are among the richest people in the country, worth several billion dollars. So when Alice Walton decided to build a museum dedicated to American art and history, she went on a cultural shopping spree that wowed the art world. (She purchased the Hudson River School landscape,

Kindred Spirits, by Asher B. Durand from the New York Public Library for a reported $35 million.) The result is the stunning **Crystal Bridges Museum of American Art** (tel: 479-418-5700; www.crystalbridges.org; Wed–Mon). Every "master" in American art from colonial to modern times is represented; you will see Charles Wilson Peale's portrait of George Washington and Andy Warhol's tribute to Dolly Parton. The building, designed by Moshe Safdie, is notable: eight linked pavilions bordering two large pools fed by the Crystal Springs, which gives the museum its name.

From here, continue north on US 71 into Missouri. At **Joplin** ⑲, you can pick up America's "Mother Road," Route 66, which cuts across the southeast corner of Kansas before entering Oklahoma. Parts of Joplin were devastated by a massive tornado that ripped through the southeast corner of the city in May 2011. Much of the area east of St John's Hospital where the twister first touched down is still a wasteland scoured clean by the winds.

TIP

You may want to roll down your windows when traveling through Arkansas: a highway department program has resulted in the planting of 600 kinds of wildflowers, some of which attract hummingbirds.

Bill and Hillary Clinton's former home in Little Rock.

Tempting rural road in Oklahoma.

OKLAHOMA TO NEW MEXICO

Take "a stroll on wheels" along Route 66 through
Oklahoma and the Texas Panhandle, then cruise
through Santa Fe and Albuquerque to Gallup.
The highway anthem begins here.

Main Attractions

Gilcrease Museum
Philbrook Museum of Art
National Cowboy & Western
  Heritage Museum
Oklahoma Route 66 Museum
Cadillac Ranch
Santa Fe
Albuquerque Old Town
Indian Pueblo Cultural Center
Acoma Sky City
El Morro National Monument

Oklahoma was the site of one of the most dramatic land rushes in the country in 1889. Today, the Sooner State, as it's known, is where we finally get to know 2,448-mile (3,940km) -long Route 66 (see page 35), the "Mother Road" of John Steinbeck's Grapes of Wrath, which has one of its longest drivable stretches in Oklahoma.

Be prepared to get lost. In some cases, the brown "Historic US 66" signs vanish, with little or no indication as to where the road has gone, or whether it has been subsumed by the nearby interstate. Time, patience, and guesswork are the keys to a successful trip – along with a reliable segment-by-segment map. Expect to take at least eight days to drive the whole route – from the road's origin in Illinois to the final mile in California. A thorough exploration will take longer.

ROUTE 66 INTO OKLAHOMA

Route 66 enters Oklahoma at **Quapaw** in the northeast corner, then traverses 400 miles (644km) of the state, running parallel to (or being replaced by) I-44 as far as Oklahoma City, where you pick up I-40 west through New Mexico, Arizona, and much of California.

Starting in 1817, Oklahoma became Indian Territory, where Native

Americans from tribal lands east of the Mississippi were forceably resettled by an expansionist US government. But after the creation of Oklahoma Territory and the subsequent Land Rush, Indian Territory was halved almost overnight and Oklahoma's tribes were forced to abandon communal ownership in favor of small individual plots. More than 65 Native American tribes are still represented in the state, and you will drive across numerous reservations as you follow Route 66 west.

Open-road relic along the Oklahoma leg of Route 66.

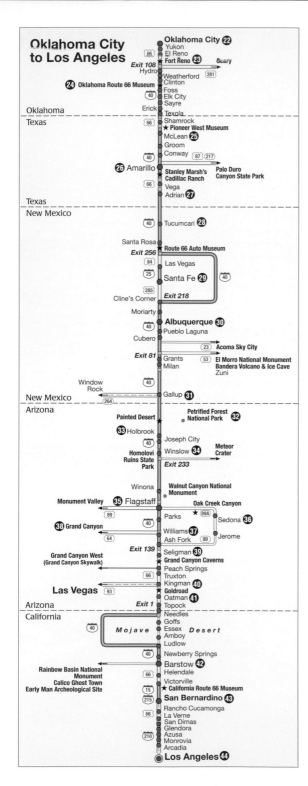

Oklahoma City to Los Angeles

Oklahoma City ㉒
Yukon
El Reno
Fort Reno ㉓ — Geary
Exit 108
Hydro
Weatherford (281)
Clinton
㉔ Oklahoma Route 66 Museum
Foss
(40) Elk City
Sayre
Oklahoma
Erick
Texas
Texola
Shamrock
(66)
★ Pioneer West Museum
McLean ㉕
Groom
Conway (87) (217)
(40)
㉖ Amarillo
Stanley Marsh's — Palo Duro
Cadillac Ranch — Canyon State Park
(66)
Vega
Adrian ㉗
Texas
New Mexico
(40) Tucumcari ㉘
Santa Rosa
Route 66 Auto Museum
Exit 256
(84)
Las Vegas
(25)
Santa Fe ㉙ (40)
(285)
Cline's Corner
Exit 218
Moriarty
(40)
Albuquerque ㉚
Cubero
Pueblo Laguna
(23) Acoma Sky City
Exit 81
Grants (53) El Morro National Monument
Milan — Bandera Volcano & Ice Cave
Zuni
Window
Rock (40)
New Mexico
Gallup ㉛
(264)
Arizona
Painted Desert
Petrified Forest
National Park ㉜
㉝ Holbrook
(40)
Joseph City
Homolovi
Winslow ㉞ — Meteor
Ruins State — Crater
Park
Exit 233
Winona
Walnut Canyon National
Monument
Monument Valley ㉟ Flagstaff
Oak Creek Canyon
(89)
Parks ★ (89A)
㊲ Grand Canyon (40) Sedona ㊱
Williams ㊲
(64) Ash Fork (89) Jerome
Exit 139
Seligman ㊴
Grand Canyon West
Grand Canyon Caverns
(Grand Canyon Skywalk)
Peach Springs
Truxton
(66)
Kingman ㊵
Las Vegas (93) Goldroad
Oatman ㊶
Arizona
Exit 1
Topock
California
Needles
Goffs
(40)
Mojave — Essex Desert
Amboy
Ludlow
(40)
Newberry Springs
Barstow ㊷
Rainbow Basin National — Helendale
Monument
(66)
Calico Ghost Town — Victorville
Early Man Archeological Site
(15)
★ California Route 66 Museum
(215)
San Bernardino ㊸
Rancho Cucamonga
(66)
La Verne
San Dimas
Glendora
(210)
Azusa
Monrovia
Arcadia
◉ Los Angeles ㊹

Miami to Claremore

The first major town you'll come to after entering Oklahoma, **Miami** ⑳ (pronounced "My-am-er"), is named for a local tribe (as is Quapaw). Located in what was once a prominent zinc mining region, Miami is still a commercial center and an early segment of Route 66 passes right through town. Miami's pride and joy is its restored Spanish Revival landmark **Coleman Theatre** (tel: 918-540-2425; www.colemantheatre.org; free tours Tue–Thurs, Sat), built in 1929, which still has its Wurlitzer organ. Look for **Waylan's Ku-Ku Burger**, a classic 66 drive-in, as you leave town.

Southwest of Miami, you can drive one of two stretches of original 9-foot-wide old alignment Route 66 "sidewalk highway" to **Afton**, named for the daughter of a Scottish railroad engineer after a river in Scotland. It's worth a stop to visit **Afton Station and Route 66 Packards** (tel: 918-257-4044; http://postcardsfromtheroad.net/afton.shtml; daily) a restored vintage DX gas station with a small Route 66 museum on First Street.

Vinita was founded in 1871 by Elias Boudinot, son of one of the Cherokees who sold ancestral lands to the US government, resulting in the Cherokee Trail of Tears mass migration in 1838. Boudinot renamed the community after a friend, Miss Vinnie Ream, who, at the age of 18, sculpted the lifesize Lincoln statue in the US capitol. Route 66 is still alive and kicking in Vinita. **Clanton's Cafe** (see page 441), opened in 1927, is the oldest continually owned family restaurant on Route 66 in the state, and you'll find many vintage 66 buildings in town.

Four miles (6km) east of **Foyil** is the world's largest totem pole. At 90ft (27 meters) tall, it is one of several sculpted by Ed Galloway in the 1940s. Foyil's main street sits on Oklahoma's first stretch of original Portland Cement concrete-paved Route 66. It's named after Andy Payne, the local man who won the 84-day "Bunion

Derby" in 1928, which required contestants to hike 2,400 miles (3,862km), from New York to Los Angeles, mostly along Route 66.

In **Claremore,** stop to visit the interesting **Will Rogers Museum** (tel: 918-341-0719; www.willrogers.com; daily). Eight galleries with interactive exhibits commemorate the Cherokee-born cowboy, vaudeville performer, social commentator, and renowned wit, one of Oklahoma's most famous native sons. The section of I-44 between Miami and Tulsa is known as the Will Rogers Turnpike. It's the subject of a folk song celebrating Route 66 by Woody Guthrie, who was born in Okemah, southeast of Oklahoma City, where the popular Woodyfest is celebrated every July.

Just outside Tulsa is **Catoosa,** home to a classic Route 66 roadside attraction: a large, smiling papier-mâché **Blue Whale** sculpture next to a swimming hole and picnic area popular with Tulsans. Adjoining **Molly's Landing Restaurant** (see page 440) is a scenic spot for a barbecue dinner before heading into Tulsa, where there's plenty more good food ahead in the cultural capital of Oklahoma.

Tulsa: birthplace of Route 66

Tulsa ㉑ (pop. 391,906), on the banks of the winding Arkansas River, was once known as the Oil Capital of the World. It paraded its wealth in a number of glorious, now-restored downtown Art Deco businesses and hotel buildings, and elegant mansion-filled neighborhoods such as Brookside, south of 11th Street on the post-1933 Route 66 alignment.

Plan on spending a day visiting Tulsa's two most important museums, which are housed in the former homes and extensive gardens of two men who made their money in oil but whose love of art and beauty created a lasting legacy in their hometown.

The **Gilcrease Museum** (tel: 918-596-2700; www.gilcrease.org Tue–Sun),

northwest of downtown, houses one of the largest collections of Western and Native American art in the US, the life's work of Thomas Gilcrease, who deeded his home and collection to Tulsa in 1955. Now part of the University of Tulsa, the museum includes the satellite Zarrow Center for Art and Education in the up-and-coming Brady Arts District downtown.

Also in the Brady Arts District is the **Woody Guthrie Center** (116 East Brady), which houses a major Guthrie archive, including the original lyrics to the singer's famous anthem, "This Land is Your Land." The archive was purchased for $3 million by the George Kaiser Family Foundation, and represents something of a homecoming for Guthrie, Oklahoma's prodigal son, in the year of the centennial of his birth.

The gorgeous **Philbrook Museum of Art** (tel: 918-749-7941; www.philbrook.org; Tue–Sun;), south of 11th Street, in a leafy neighborhood off Peoria Avenue, is housed in a 1927 Italian villa–style home and gardens built by Waite Phillips. The

TIP

1-44 is a turnpike, or toll road, between Miami, Oklahoma and Oklahoma City. Not all tollbooths are manned and automatic entries may require exact change, so be sure to carry plenty of quarters and dollar bills with you. Ask for and keep your receipt; if you get on and off to visit Route 66 towns, you'll get a refund at those exits.

Tulsa, Oklahoma.

wide-ranging art collection, which is displayed thoughtfully in its intimate home setting, includes many fine works by Native American and Southwestern artists, a passion of Phillips, whose former home in northeastern New Mexico, Philmont, is now another fine art museum. No matter your age or inclination, this is truly a romantic and inspiring place to visit. The European-style café overlooking 23 acres (9 hectares) of classical gardens created by Phillips himself, a renowned gardener, is a welcome respite from sticky heat in summer.

Tulsa's disappearance from Route 66 literature is perplexing, all the more so because, as Tulsa historian Michael Wallis, author of the best-selling *Route 66: The Mother Road*, says: Route 66 owes its very existence to the tireless efforts of Tulsa resident Cyrus Avery. Avery was the owner of a gas station and restaurant on Mingo Circle near the 11th Street Bridge (now Cyrus Avery Memorial Bridge) and was a driving force in getting Route 66 built in 1926.

After decades of neglect, Tulsa is finally getting round to promoting its important role in Route 66 history. Funds have been allocated to build gateway signs at the east and west ends of 11th Street, the main Route 66 drag through Tulsa, and to install interpretive kiosks, including one on 66's famed motor court motels. Already built is the **Cyrus Avery Centennial Plaza**, next to the Cyrus Avery Memorial Bridge. The plaza will have a Route 66 Interpretive Center and a large bronze statue entitled "East Meets West," depicting the Avery family in a Model T Ford encountering a horse-drawn carriage on its way back to Tulsa from the western Oklahoma oilfields.

Diners, motor courts, and wineries

After crossing the river, Route 66 continues through the rough-'n'-tumble of industrial West Tulsa to nearby **Sapulpa**, which became an important cattle shipping center with the arrival of the railroad (cowboy star Gene Autry once sang in the local ice-cream parlor here). Sapulpa was home to **Frankoma Pottery**, founded in

Back lawn of Philbrook Museum in Tulsa Oklahoma

1933 and located on an old alignment of Route 66. The pottery's closure in 2010 ensures that its attractive vintage ceramics – popular with Route 66 eateries like Norma's Diamond Café, which closed when its longtime owner died – are now collector's items.

The stretch of Route 66 between Sapulpa and Edmond is one of the longest and most scenic Route 66 segments in Oklahoma and a popular day trip destination. The country is rolling, and its lush greenery contrasts nicely with the bright red Oklahoma soil, fields of corn, and distinctive grain silos, a sign that you are still in the fertile confluence of the Midwest and South and have not yet reached the arid West.

The route follows the train tracks through **Kellyville** and **Bristow**. Don't miss the turnoff for **Depew**, a Route 66 near-ghost on the old alignment whose Main Street has been restored by Route 66 enthusiasts. This is an unexpected and charming photo op.

Stroud is certainly no ghost; in fact, it's roaring to life as the center of what is becoming Oklahoma wine country. You'll find several wine tasting rooms as you pass through town, but be careful about drinking and driving around here—Oklahoma's finest are often out in force, particularly on weekends. Best to stop a while and soak up any alcohol with a meal at the historic **Rock Café** (see page 441) in a 1939 redrock building in the center of town. The Rock Café is famous in these parts. It burned down in 2008, but its fans helped it rebuild, and it reopened (its owner, Dawn Welch, by the way, was the model for Sally in the movie *Cars*).

Its worth a quick stop at **Davenport** to drive its bumpy 1925 brickway to view the enormous murals depicting scenes from its past painted on the buildings. The Early Bird Diner on the corner is covered in license plates—a classic Route 66 montage.

The winding road through the pretty town of **Chandler** has a classic Route 66 feel. The **Lincoln Motel** (see page 413) with its cabins and garages, is a classic motor court motel, albeit one that has seen better days, but don't miss the innovative **Route 66 Interpretive Center** (tel: 405-258-1300; www.route66interpretivecenter.org; daily;) in the 1930s redrock building that once housed the armory, where the Route 66 experience includes lying on beds and doing a virtual Route 66 trip.

There are two major landmarks at the appropriately pastoral **Arcadia**: the large and distinctive restored 19th-century **Old Round Barn** (www.arcadia roundbarn.com;10am–5pm) and **POPS Diner** (see page 440) (www.route66.com; daily), a fun retro gas station and diner in a massive glass cantilevered building in the Deep Fork River Valley. POPS was designed by the same firm that created the Oklahoma Route 66 Museum in Clinton, and driving in here on a busy Saturday night feels just like arriving on the set of *Happy Days*.

Just past **Lake Arcadia** in Edmonds, Route 66 is a fickle customer as you enter the sprawling Oklahoma City

Oklahoma city

suburbs. Plan on getting on I-44 south to visit the state capital.

An exuberant state capital

Oklahoma City ㉒ sprang up overnight on April 22, 1889, when the Oklahoma Land Rush opened up the adjoining territory to settlement, attracting 50,000 hopeful prospectors. Its appeal for visitors today is its attractive **Downtown**, filled with renovated Art Deco bank buildings and boutique hotels, and the adjoining **Bricktown Historic District**, where restored warehouses house hip restaurants and nightclubs, as well as an unexpected treasure, the delightful **American Banjo Museum** (tel: 405-604-2793; www.americanbanjomuseum.com; daily) – a must-see for bluegrass fans.

Downtown has benefited from the planning genius of architect I.M. Pei who, in the 1960s and 1970s, helped develop the city's urban renewal plan, creating an elegant mix of lakes, parks, landscaped hills, distinct neighborhoods, and stylish buildings. Highlights are **Myriad Botanical Gardens** (tel: 405-297-3995; www.

myriadgardens.org; daily), a 17-acre (7-hectare) oasis with a seventh-floor illuminated Crystal Bridge housing a plant- and tree-filled tropical conservatory and waterfall; and **Oklahoma City Museum of Art** (tel. 405-236-3100; www.okcmoa.com; Tue–Sun), which has one of the country's most extensive collections of art glass by master glassblower Dale Chihuly.

Water, plants, light, and art also feature prominently in what, for many visitors, is Oklahoma City's most important destination: the poignant **Oklahoma City National Memorial and Museum** (tel. 405-235-3313; www.oklahomacitynationalmemorial.org; daily), commemorating the April 1995 bombing of the Alfred P. Murrah Federal Building, which killed 168 adults and children. At the memorial, which is managed and well interpreted by the National Park Service, the dead are remembered with 168 empty cast-bronze chairs on a grassy slope under a canopy of trees facing a reflecting pool. A surviving building to the north now houses the memorial museum. In front is the Survivor Tree, a large spreading oak that escaped destruction and is now a symbol of hope. Dusk, a reflective time of day, is a good time to visit. You can sit quietly with other pilgrims to Oklahoma's Ground Zero, watching birds swooping overhead and the lights beneath the chairs turn on, so that they appear to float ethereally between heaven and earth – an apt metaphor.

Classic neon, cows, and oil

Even more than Tulsa, Route 66 seems to hide in plain sight in OKC, but buildings on old alignments along 23rd Street and Beltline 66 are still visible. The 1930 **Milk Bottle Building**, just north of 23rd Street on an old alignment of Route 66, is the epitome of 66 roadside vernacular architecture, with its large milk bottle advertising local Braum's milk atop a 350-sq-foot (33-sq-meter) triangular building. Remarkably, it's still in business

The 'Welcome Sundown' statue at the National Cowboy & Western Heritage Museum.

– currently, as a Vietnamese sandwich shop.

Oklahoma's State Capitol (right on Route 66, at NE 23rd Street and Lincoln Boulevard) is unique in having a working oil pump on its grounds, a reminder that the city's wealth stemmed from a major gusher 75 years ago; oilfields still operate in the state. Cotton was once king here, but it's cattle ranching that predominates today. This heritage is celebrated at **Stockyards City**, a few minutes southwest of Downtown, off I-40, where ranchers and real cowboys have been coming since it grew up in the early 1900s as a place for apparel, equipment, supplies, and a good meal.

National Cowboy and Western Heritage Museum

If you're drawn to the cowboy lifestyle, check out the **National Cowboy & Western Heritage Museum** (tel: 405-478-2250; www.nationalcowboy museum.org; daily), just northeast of downtown, off I-44 (Exit 129). This sprawling museum feels over-scaled and rather "old school," and its

emphasis is on promoting contemporary and historic Western art, which might make it rather boring for kids (although there is a frontier town they can walk through). As always, the Hollywood Cowboy gets good treatment: movie posters of Gene Autry, Tom Mix, and John Wayne decorate one gallery, close to a larger-than-life statue of Ronald Reagan and the museum's famous centerpiece: the huge statue titled *The End of the Trail*, by James Earle Fraser.

Continue west either on Route 66 or on I-40; the two highways become one, anyway, about 40 miles (64km) out of the city. The Chisholm Trail, which was used to trail cattle to market, ran along what is now Ninth Street in tiny **Yukon,** just outside the OKC limits on 66 and hometown of country music star Garth Brooks. Sid's Diner and Johnnie's Grill in neighboring **El Reno** claim to be the home of that distinctive Oklahoma treat – the Fried Onion Burger. The

Fancy hood ornament on an antique Ford at a classic car rally.

Clinton, Oklahoma, has one of the best 66 museums along the historic route.

The historic first Phillips gas station in McLean, Texas.

El Reno Hotel, built in 1892 when rooms cost all of 50 cents a night, is now part of the Canadian County Historical Museum.

Chisholm Trail

Fort Reno ㉓ (tel: 405-262-3987; www. fortreno.org; daily) displays exhibits from the days when it served as a cavalry post during the Indian Wars. El Reno is now the headquarters for the Cheyenne-Arapaho tribe.

If you take Exit 108 off I-40, a short detour north on US 281 leads to **Geary**, bypassed by Route 66 in 1933 despite the locals' work in grading and graveling the road in the hope of enticing the route, and its dollars, through their town. Not far away is **Left Hand Spring Camp**, where Jesse Chisholm, who gave his name to the famous Chisholm Trail, is buried. The trail, which stretched 250 miles (400km) from San Antonio to Abilene, was first laid in 1860, when buffalo still roamed nearby. Twenty years later, when the trail was more or less abandoned, it had seen the passage of more than 10 million cattle.

Steep hills and historic gas stations

Near where I-40 intersects with US 281 is the 3,944ft (1,202-meter) -long "pony bridge" crossing the South Canadian River, a multiple simple-span bridge typical of the type used in the construction of Route 66. In addition to offering superb vistas of the river, the William H. Murray Bridge starred in a scene in John Ford's 1940 movie version of *The Grapes of Wrath*.

The hill leading to the bridge is so steep that Model T Fords – their engines generating more power in reverse – had to climb it backward (something that was also a problem on New Mexico's infamous La Bajada Hill on the pre-1938 Route 66 alignment, between Santa Fe and Albuquerque).

Continuing west on I-40, just north of Exit 88 is Lucille's gas station and store at **Hydro**. Lucille ran the property for 59 years till her death in 2000, and it's still a sentimental stop for Route 66 regulars, some of whom had been buying gas and groceries here since 1941. In 2004, a local resident bought Lucille's and restored the exterior; he later opened Lucille's Roadhouse in nearby **Weatherford**, as a tribute to this 66 landmark and its longtime owner. Other Weatherford landmarks include a building with Greek columns (formerly a bank, now a dress shop) and the century-old Lee Cotter's Blacksmith Shop, where the **General Thomas P. Stafford Air and Space Museum** (tel: 580-772-5871; www.staffordmuseum.com; daily), with fighter jets and moon rocks, commemorates Oklahoma's premier astronaut.

A Mother Road museum

You really begin to feel like you're traversing the old road at sleepy **Clinton** (pop. 8,852), where the state-sponsored **Oklahoma Route 66 Museum** ㉔ (tel: 580-323-7866; www.route66.org; Feb–Nov daily, Dec–Jan Tue–Sat) is the most comprehensive – and memorable – of many similar places found along the famous highway. In 2012, it underwent a major renovation to improve its audiovisual exhibits in each of the rooms dedicated to a single decade in the history of Route 66. Kids will love the computer game that allows you to stick to a Route 66-era daily budget while traveling across country. Each room has scrapbooks containing headlines of the era and typical family memorabilia.

There are photographs of the road's construction in the 1920s. In the 1930s, Oklahoma was still "dry," and the rise of the bootlegger prompted a corresponding increase in the number of law enforcement officers, who are pictured in their intimidating uniforms. A typical garage from the same era – with its glass-topped Red Crown gasoline pump – flanks pictures of a few of the three million Okie migrants in their battered trucks bearing "California or Bust" signs. The photos of trucks, crammed with furniture, bedding, pots and pans, and crated chickens, typify the Dust Bowl years, when parched farmlands induced the westward-flight of almost one-fifth of the state's population.

A Greyhound bus and a VW bus evoking the hippies-on-the-road era of the 1960s are among the vehicles on show, the "bug" illuminated by fluorescent lighting in a room whose walls display Sixties album covers from Sinatra and Dina Shore to Hank Williams and Chuck Berry.

A poster promoting a one-time rattlesnake show, a map made by a retired postmaster with franking stamps from every post office along the route, a glass case of souvenirs from long-vanished gift shops, a diner, and a video running quaint family movies on an endless loop are also part of the museum tour, which climaxes with a nostalgic and heart-tugging movie celebrating the ongoing romance of the road and its characters and places, written and narrated

by road historian Michael Wallis (you can also rent an audio tour of the museum by Wallis).

Grapes of Wrath towns

The ghost town of **Foss** and the Old Town Museum complex at **Elk City** of relocated old buildings (misleadingly dubbed the National Route 66 Museum – it's not) might draw you off the road after leaving Clinton. When the US Highway 66 Association held its convention in Elk City's Casa Grande Hotel in 1931, more than 20,000 enthusiasts attended. The hotel is now the **Anadarko Basin Museum of Natural History** (tel: 580-243-0437; tours by appointment). Songwriter Jimmy Webb ("Up, Up, and Away") was born here.

Sayre is also alarmingly empty these days, but the town has a rather grandiloquent courthouse, which featured fleetingly in the movie *The Grapes of Wrath*. The small, fairly ordinary town of **Erick** and the almost deserted **Texola** have each – at different times by different surveys – been declared as sitting on the 100th

Big Texan – that famous "72-ounce steak" eatery in the Texas Panhandle.

meridian, the longitudinal arcs running through both the North and the South poles that are used as geographical definitions.

On the stretch heading through Erick, Route 66 is renamed Roger Miller Boulevard – a tribute to its songwriting ("King of the Road") native son, who is celebrated in a small downtown museum.

THE TEXAS PANHANDLE

As you make your way west across the high plains of Oklahoma, which merge into the Texas Panhandle, the air becomes drier, the prairie grass shorter, and the hills turn into eroded buttes and mesas. There's an overwhelming sense of insignificance in the face of the wide, open space stretching as far as the horizon. As might be expected in Texas, there is also a palpable feeling of having arrived in the real West, reflected in the expansive confidence of its residents.

At **Shamrock**, Texas, don't miss the lime-green-and-sand-colored Art Deco masterpiece, the **U Drop Inn**

(now a tourism office; www.shamrock-texas.com), and adjoining gas station with matching tower. Early gas stations had to fight hard for customers in a competitive market, and the filling pump station took many forms. One, on the site of Albuquerque, New Mexico's present-day Lobo Theater, was shaped like a giant chunk of ice.

Picturesque, sleepy **McLean** (pop. 814), which describes itself as "the heart of old Route 66," feels like the backdrop to *The Last Picture Show*. Here, an old Phillips 66 gas station has been restored by volunteers and is one of a surprisingly small number along the route (there are none at all in Arizona). The Phillips Petroleum Company records some of the many erroneous explanations people have offered for the "66" in the company's name. Michael Wallis claims to have the real story from Phillips himself in his book: Phillips was traveling 66mph (106kph) on Route 66, when the new name came to him.

Barbed wire: the devil's rope

At the **Devil's Rope Museum** (tel: 806-779-2225; www.barbwiremuseum.com; Tue–Sat), the "rope" in question is barbed wire, a large rusty ball of which sits outside. Although the museum has only a small selection, more than 8,000 different types exist. In the mid-1800s, there were hundreds of competing designs, but it was Joseph F. Glidden's patent for fencing material, consisting of barbs wrapped around a single strand of wire, that eventually dominated.

The unpaved section of Route 66 between Alanreed and **Groom** has always been a problem for unwary drivers. Jericho Gap, as it was known, "was notorious for bogging down cars and trucks in a black gumbo mud every time it rained," according to 66 guidebook authors Bob Moore and Patrick Gauwels. As you get to Groom, be on the lookout for the

Mascot outside the Big Texan steak ranch.

huge leaning water tower defying gravity beside the road.

Palo Duro Canyon

Just before Amarillo (where local rancher J.F. Glidden invented his barbed wire), turn south on US 87 to visit **Palo Duro Canyon State Park** (tel: 806-488-2227; www.palodurocanyon. com), dubbed Texas's Grand Canyon and closely associated with the legendary cattleman Charles Goodnight. Goodnight – inventor of the chuckwagon and once owner of the largest ranch in Texas – was the first rancher to move into the Panhandle in the 1870s. Chuckwagon tours beginning or ending with "cowboy" breakfast or dinner are offered on the rim of the canyon, where part of an Indiana Jones movie was filmed.

Amarillo

Dusty Amarillo ㉖, redolent with the smell of feedlots, stages regular rodeos (tel: 800-692-1338). Route 66 fans know it for its big-and-cheesy **Big Texan Steak Ranch** (see page 442), a fun roadside attraction offering 72oz (2kg) steaks free to anybody who can eat one (along with the sides) within an hour. The city's one-way traffic system can be confusing, but you'll be back on Route 66 proper if you follow Sixth Street, which leads into "**antique row**," where plenty of Route 66 shops and modern cafés entice visitors with their colorful signage, such as the Golden Light Café.

Just west of town is **Cadillac Ranch**, the much photographed chorus line of graffiti-covered Cadillacs, an art installation by the Ant Farm and funded by local art patron Stanley Marsh. The Cadillacs, with their rear ends sticking out of the earth, are literally in the middle of a field, south of I-40. To get closer, look for a frontage road parallel to the interstate, where you can park free and walk through a gate to take your snapshots of the cars.

Midpoint of Route 66

Vega is largely a ghost now, but you can still see old buildings roadside, including the restored 1926 Magnolia Gas Station and the Vega Motel, which is now closed. Tiny **Adrian** ㉗ has one big claim to fame: it sits at the exact halfway point of the Mother Road: 1,139 miles (1,833km) to Chicago and 1,139 miles to Los Angeles. A sign announcing this fact can be found at the west end of town, right across from a restaurant that has been operating on Route 66 since its earliest days, the **Midpoint Café** (see page 441), a classic diner famous for its homemade pies.

NEW MEXICO

Nothing can prepare you for the pleasure of your first encounter with the aesthetic beauty of New Mexico, a high-desert landscape of dun-colored earth, sagebrush, dwarf pinyon and juniper trees, floating mesas, and distant high volcanic peaks. A big yellow sign announcing "Welcome to New Mexico, Land of Enchantment" is an invitation that generations of

Tinkertown, the amusingly eccentric roadside attraction packed with curiosities, is located a few miles east of Albuquerque on old Route 66.

Cadillac Ranch, just outside Amarillo, Texas.

TIP

Remember to set your watch back an hour as you cross the border between Texas and New Mexico and move from the Central to Mountain time zone.

dreamers along Route 66 have happily accepted – many have never left.

The country here, the Llano Estacado (Staked Plains) – a high plateau covering 33,000 sq miles (85,430 sq km) – is one of the hottest, flattest areas of the continental US. Spanish explorer Francisco Vasquez de Coronado unsuccessfully combed the region for the fabled Seven Cities of Cibola back in 1540, expecting to uncover unimaginable hoards of gold and silver. Instead, he discovered innumerable Native American pueblos, where the glitter came from micaceous adobe homes and pottery and jewelry shaped by tribal craftspeople from local turquoise. Nineteen of the pueblos still exist and can be visited today.

Tucumcari curios and neon

Route 66 extends more than 300 miles (483km) across the state along I-40. On its eastern end, the road crosses and re-crosses I-40 before running through **Tucumcari** ㉘ ("two miles long and two blocks wide"), where the **Tee Pee Curio Store** (1944) is one of the oldest souvenir shops

along the route. Every conceivable type of souvenir item turns up here, and in dozens of independently run shops in one small town after another along the route: pop-up art of paper buildings, old postcards, caps, jackets, scarves, traffic signs, sheriff's badges, playing cards, mugs, glasses, paperweights, ashtrays, earrings, belt buckles, money clips, and even baby bibs bearing the 66 logo.

Homely Tucumcari once trumpeted its "thousands of motel rooms" on ubiquitous "Tucumcari Tonite" signs. With the decline in traffic, that is no longer the case, but the town is home to a famous motel veteran of the highway, the historic **Blue Swallow**, famous for its bright neon sign and old-style garages. It was run for decades by Lillian Redman, a kind and charitable innkeeper who was given the motel as an engagement present by her future husband. Now a bit worn but slowly upgrading under energetic new owners, it remains a nostalgic destination for Route 66 buffs.

Santa Rosa

Santa Rosa, famous for its sparkling freshwater lakes, maintains strong links to Route 66. Its **Route 66 Auto Museum** on Will Rogers Boulevard (tel: 575-472-1966; www.route66auto museum.com; daily) displays classic cars, and the town hosts a Route 66 Festival every September. Joseph's Bar and Grill has been serving burgers and New Mexican food to Route 66 travelers since 1956 (look for its historic Fat Man sign, which was moved from the 1935 Center Café, a Route 66 landmark, when it closed in 1991).

A detour to Santa Fe

Just past Santa Rosa, at Exit 256 from I-40, is a major Route 66 detour that you won't want to miss. The old pre-1938 alignment of Route 66 swings north on US 84, crosses the Pecos River, and passes through tiny Hispanic villages toward Las Vegas,

Jemez Mountains in northern New Mexico.

New Mexico, before turning sharply west to reach **Santa Fe** ㉙, the oldest state capital in the US.

Santa Fe was the end of the Santa Fe Trail, which, beginning in 1821, ran between the Santa Fe Plaza for almost 800 miles (1,290km) to Kansas City, Missouri, and was the major Western trade and immigration route until the railroad arrived in the 1880s. You can still follow the old Route 66 alignment to the Santa Fe Plaza on Old Santa Fe Trail (Pecos Trail exit from I-25), along Water Street, out on Cerrillos Road (Highway 14), and south through Santo Domingo Pueblo and Algodones to Albuquerque; it was decommissioned in 1938, when a straighter route through Albuquerque superseded it and cut 126 miles (200km) off the journey.

Today, the traditional adobe buildings in Santa Fe's attractive historic downtown district, with their flat roofs and large portals, are filled with intriguing museums, superb restaurants, small inns, lively bars, art galleries, and unique boutiques selling Southwestern arts and crafts. Santa Fe is known as the "City Different" because of its unique blend of Spanish history, Native American influences, and contemporary artistic culture, which make the city one of the most popular destinations in the Southwest.

A historic tricultural mecca

The heart of Santa Fe is its **Plaza**, which dates to the founding of the city by Spanish settlers from Mexico around 1610. With its bandstand and wrought-iron benches, it's a good place for people-watching and has free outdoor concerts in summer. Stretching along the north side is the **Palace of the Governors** (tel: 505-476-5100; www.palaceofthegovernors.org; Memorial Day–Labor Day daily), which has Pueblo vendors selling high-quality jewelry, pottery, and other crafts beneath its portal. The seat of regional government for

300 years by successive administrators from Spain, Mexico, and the US (as well as, briefly, local Pueblo during the 1680 Pueblo Revolt), the palace is the oldest public building in the country. It's now part of the **New Mexico History Museum** (tel: 505-476-5200; www.nmhistorymuseum.org), a fascinating interactive museum that opened in 2009. In the next block is the **New Mexico Museum of Art** (tel: 505-476-5072; www.nmartmuseum.org), with works by Southwestern artists. All three museums (and the Museum of Indian Arts and Culture on Museum Hill) are part of the **Museum of New Mexico** (www.museumofnewmexico.org; all museums Memorial Day–Labor Day daily, early Sept–late May Tue–Sun; four-day museum pass is good for four museums, free Fri 5–8pm).

Nearby is the **Georgia O'Keeffe Museum** (tel: 505-946-1000; daily; www.okeefemuseum.org). Inspired by the light and landscapes, the artist made northern New Mexico her home. The museum holds the largest collection of her works.

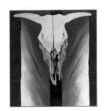

'Cow's Skull: Red, White and Blue' by Georgia O'Keeffe; visit a museum devoted to the artist in Santa Fe, New Mexico.

Painting the Santuario de Nuestro Señor de Esquipulas, in Chimayó, New Mexico.

East of the Plaza is the **Museum of Contemporary Native Arts** (tel: 888-922-IAIA; www.iaia.edu/museum Memorial Day–Labor Day daily, early Sept–late May Wed–Mon;) in the Santa Fe-style historic post office building. Run by the Institute of American Indian Arts, it contains the largest collection of contemporary Native American art in the country. Opposite is the **Cathedral Basilica of St Francis**, whose founding archbishop, Jean Baptiste Lamy, buried below the altar, was the model for Willa Cather's novel, *Death Comes to the Archbishop*.

Just past the cathedral is **Loretto Chapel** (tel: 505-982-0092; www.lorettochapel.com; daily) with its "Miraculous Staircase." South of the river is Santa Fe's oldest section, home to the attractive and much-photographed **San Miguel Mission** (tel: 505-983-3974; daily) and the **State Capitol**, or **Roundhouse** (tel: 505-986-4589; Mon–Fri). Even this governmental seat is an art gallery, with works by New Mexico artists on its circular walls.

Museum of Indian Arts and Culture.

Art town

Art is everywhere in Santa Fe. **Canyon Road**, off Paseo de Peralta, the ring road around downtown, was once a burro track used by local residents but is now lined with art galleries housed in historic adobes (Friday night is Art Walk night, when many galleries stage openings). West of the Plaza, South Guadalupe Street leads to **The Railyard**, the city's newest arts and entertainment district, with native gardens and modern warehouses containing a year-round farmers' market and art galleries and the Rail Runner train, linking Santa Fe and Albuquerque.

Off Old Santa Fe Trail is Museum Hill, home to the delightful **Museum of International Folk Art** (tel: 505-476-1200; www.internationalfolkart.org) Tue–Sun, daily in summer; as well as the **Museum of Spanish Colonial Arts** (tel: 505-982-2226; www.spanishcolonialblog.org; daily), **Wheelwright Museum of the American Indian** (tel: 505-982-4636; www.wheelwright.org; daily), and impressive **Museum of Indian Arts and Culture** (tel:

505-476-1250; www.indianartsand culture.org; Museum of New Mexico hours).

The city makes a good base for visiting other highlights in northern New Mexico, including the Eight Northern Pueblos; the Santuario de Chimayó, "the Lourdes of America"; Puyé cliff dwellings at Santa Clara Pueblo and those at nearby Bandelier National Monument, as well as artsy Taos, to the north via the Rio Grande Gorge.

Toward Albuquerque

You can drive I-25 south, which parallels the old alignment to Albuquerque, or pick up the new alignment by heading south through scenic Galisteo Basin on US 285 to I-40. At the junction, you can't miss the roadside emporium **Cline's Corners**, in business since the 1930s, at a spot that founder Roy Cline described as "the coldest, the meanest, the windiest place on Highway 66."

The longest remaining stretch of Route 66 in New Mexico runs through **Moriarty**, a dusty ranch town. Nostalgic reminders here include a Whiting Brothers Gas Station and the huge 1960s "rotosphere" rotating neon Sputnik sign atop the still-popular El Comedor de Anayas restaurant (see page 442). This is one of only 264 remaining rotospheres created by Warren Milks between 1960 and 1971 and thought to be the only one on Route 66 still in use.

The State Fairgrounds in Albuquerque were the site of the 2001 75th anniversary celebration of Route 66. Post-1938 Route 66 bisects **Albuquerque** ❸⓪, running past the University of New Mexico at Nob Hill on what is now Central Avenue. The Civic Center, the tourist office, and a handful of vintage buildings lie across the Atchison, Topeka, and Santa Fe railroad tracks just past Second Street in downtown Albuquerque. A multi-million dollar revitalization project has transformed this stretch of the route into a vibrant Downtown scene with neon, theaters, nightclubs, hotels, and restaurants. A notable landmark is the **KiMo Theater**, built in 1927 in a fusion of Pueblo Revival and Art Deco styles.

Lunch on the plaza at La Hacienda, Albuquerque.

A 20ft (6-meter) arrow pierces the ground outside a store in Gallup, New Mexico.

Albuquerque's Old Town

Two miles (3km) farther west, before you reach the Rio Grande and the western edge of the city, **Old Town**, with its attractive shops and restaurants, is one block to the north of Central Avenue, its plaza dominated by the adobe **San Felipe Church** (1706). Five flags have flown over this plaza: Spanish, Mexican, Confederate, the Stars and Stripes, and that of New Mexico.

In the heart of Old Town are the **Albuquerque Museum of Art and History** (tel: 505-243-7255; www.cabq.gov/museum; Tue–Sun), the shuddery **American International Rattlesnake Museum** (tel: 505-242-6569; www.rattlesnakes.com; daily), and the **Turquoise Museum** (tel: 505-247-8650; www.turquoisemuseum.com; Mon–Sat), which will shed some light on jewelry purchases. Nearby are the **New Mexico Museum of Natural History and Science** (tel: 505-841-2800; www.nmnaturalhistory.org; daily) with its planetarium, and the **Explora** (tel: 505-224-8300; www.explora.us; daily), a hands-on learning center for kids. To the west of Old Town is the

The 1950s-style 66 Diner in Albuquerque.

Albuquerque BioPark (tel: 505-764-6200; www.cabq.gov/biopark; daily), with a zoo, aquarium, and botanical garden.

If you don't have time to actually visit a pueblo, the next best thing is the excellent **Indian Pueblo Cultural Center** (tel: 505-843-7270; www.indianpueblo.org; daily), which has galleries telling the stories of each of the 19 pueblos. It has a gift shop, Native American foods restaurant, and free traditional Native American dance performances on weekends. At the other end of the spectrum is the **National Museum of Nuclear Science and History** (tel: 505-245-2137; www.nuclearmuseum.org; daily). Whatever your politics, it presents an intriguing look at the Atomic Age and New Mexico's role in developing the atom bomb.

Acoma Sky City

West of the Duke City, Route 66 passes through **Laguna Pueblo** (tel: 505-552-6654), with its early 18th-century church, and through **Cubero**, where an apocryphal tale claims that Ernest Hemingway wrote *The Old Man and the Sea* in a motor court motel. A side road heads south a few miles to **Acoma Sky City**, which, perched on a mesa 367ft (112 meters) overhead, claims to be the oldest continuously occupied village in the country (Taos Pueblo also makes that claim). Tribal members lead guided tours from the attractive new **Sky City Cultural Center** (tel: 800-747-0181; www.acoma skycity.org) up to the Old Pueblo and its historic church and village, explaining its complex history. The cultural center has an excellent small museum and a restaurant serving regional foods and Starbucks coffee.

Grants (named after three brothers) feels like a Route 66 town. In the mid-20th century it was a center for uranium mining, a history that can be explored in the **New Mexico Mining Museum** (tel: 505-287-4802; Mon–Sat). The multiagency **Northwest New Mexico Visitor Center** (tel:

505-876-2783; www.nps.gov/elma/plan
yourvisit), just south of I-40, has information about nearby national parks
(remote Chaco Culture National
Historical Park is to the north and will
require at least a day trip) and other
regional attractions.

Your best bet is to detour south
on Highway 53 between Grants and
Gallup for a taste of this glorious country of sandstone mesas and ancient volcanic lava flows from nearby Mount
Taylor. **Bandera Volcano and Ice
Cave** (tel: 888-423-2283; www.icecaves.
com; daily) and **El Malpais National
Monument** (tel: 505-783-4774; www.
nps.gov/elma; daily) both offer a look at
the volcanic features of the area, but
the highlight of the scenic highway is
El Morro National Monument (tel:
505-783-4226; www.nps.gov/elmo; daily),
a sandstone promontory covered in
the carved petroglyphs and painted
pictographs made by centuries of
travelers who stopped here to drink
the water at the pool below the rock.
These included Native Americans,
Spanish explorers, and the US Army
Camel Corps, as well as pioneers heading west in the mid-19th century and
railroad surveyors. A trail leads to a
ruined pueblo atop the rock.

Just before you reach Gallup,
the highway passes through **Zuni**,
the largest pueblo in the state. The
pueblo is famous for its Our Lady of
Guadalupe Mission dating from 1629
and intricate silver jewelry skilfully
inlaid with turquoise and coral.

Gallup's movie star hangout

Although its redrock setting is glorious, the spit-and-sawdust railroad
town of **Gallup** ㉛ isn't pretty to look
at. It is however a classic Route 66
town, one that you should not miss.
The highlight, on the east end of town,
is **El Rancho Hotel and Motel**, built
in 1937 by Raymond E. Griffith, who
passed himself off as the brother of
movie pioneer D. W. Griffith. From
the beginning, the hotel was a favorite
with movie stars shooting on location;

by the 1960s, at least 15 movies had
been shot using the hotel as headquarters, among them *Sundown*, *Streets of
Laredo*, and *The Hallelujah Trail*.

Gallup tags itself "Where the Indian
Southwest Begins" and remains a
major trading center for the Navajo,
or Diné – 300,000 in number – who
live on the 9,817-sq-mile (25,426-sq
km) adjoining **Navajo Nation**. The
Navajo capital of **Window Rock** is 25
miles (40km) northwest of Gallup, just
across the border in Arizona, on State
Route 264.

Native American artifacts such as
rugs, jewelry, and other crafts can be
bought at longtime trading posts like
Richardson's and Ortega's in downtown Gallup, a 12-block area around
Hill Avenue and Fourth Street. The
century-old **Rex Hotel** (tel: 505-863-
1363) is now a museum, and the historic railroad station is occupied by
a cultural center staging ceremonial
dances nightly in summer. If you're
here in August, check out the world-
famous Intertribal Indian Ceremonial,
an enormous powwow held in
Redrock State Park, east of town.

*Swapping gas for leg
power on a desert road.*

*Frank Lloyd Wright Spire,
Scottsdale.*

ARIZONA TO LOS ANGELES

Wigwam motels, gorgeous gas stations, soda fountains that work – the cruise along Route 66 continues, taking in ghost towns and the Grand Canyon along the way.

The Mother Road becomes difficult to follow just over the border from New Mexico into Arizona, so if cruising the length of Route 66 is not a priority, you can remain on I-40 through Holbrook, Arizona. Approximately 25 miles (40km) inside the state, Exit 330 from I-40 leads into **Petrified Forest National Park** ㉜ (tel: 928-524-6228; www.nps.gov/pefo; daily), whose 220,000 acres (89,000 hectares) are littered with giant petrified logs. More than 200 million years ago, the region was a swampy, tropical zone in which mineral-rich soil helped to preserve the fossilized bones of prehistoric animals. In the northern section of the park is the **Painted Desert Inn National Historic Landmark**, now a museum and bookstore (no lodging).

Dinosaur statues line the road on the way to **Holbrook** ㉝, whose outstanding attraction is the roadside **Wigwam Motel** (see page 415), a long-standing favorite (particularly with kids) on Route 66. Each of the 15 cozy rooms is inside its own tall, stone tepee built by owner John Lewis' father in the 1940s from plans by architect Frank Redford. He allowed seven similar motels around the country to be built from his plans, stipulating only that each be equipped with a radio that played 30 minutes for 10 cents.

Parked outside the tepees is the family collection of 1950s Fords and

Buicks, while inside the main building a small museum exhibits chunks of petrified trees, Native American artifacts, and rifles and powder horns from the frontier days. A Visitor Center and historical museum can be found in the **Historic Navajo County Courthouse** (tel: 928-524-6558; daily), built in 1898, on Navajo Boulevard (Route 66), which runs through the center of town. Native American dances are performed nightly on the courthouse lawn in summer. The local trading posts are a good place to buy

Main Attractions

Petrified Forest National Park
Meteor Crater
Monument Valley
Sedona
Grand Canyon
Grand Canyon Skywalk
Kingman Route 66 Museum
Las Vegas
Route 66 "Mother Road" Museum
California Route 66 Museum

1920s Route 66 gas station, Cool Springs.

TIP

If you want a letter to be carried via the Hashknife Posse in the spirit of the old Pony Express, send it, stamped, in the first two weeks of January. Put that envelope in another stamped envelope addressed to the Holbrook Postmaster, Pony Express Ride, Holbrook, AZ, 86025. In the lower left-hand corner write: *Via Pony Express.*

Apache baskets, silver and turquoise jewelry, and pottery.

Pony Express

The spirit of the short-lived but legendary Pony Express, whose demise was sealed by the telegraph system some 150 years ago, is kept alive in Holbrook by the Navajo County Sheriff's posse, who carry mail to Scottsdale (near Phoenix) in late January every year.

Under a contract with the US Postal Service, the 40-strong "Hashknife Posse" carries out a tradition begun in 1954, when a similar posse carried to the state governor an invitation to attend a stampede. An estimated 20,000 letters (sent in by admirers throughout the world) are hand-stamped with the official ride logo and franked with a Pony Express postmark before being sent off in mailbags relayed by the riders every few miles in the course of the 200-mile (320km) journey.

The posse's name is derived from The Hash Knife Outfit, a branch of the third-largest cattle company in the country, which began shipping out

Homolovi Ruins State Park.

thousands of cattle after 1881 when the life-changing railroad began to go through here.

Holbrook's preserved **Blevins House** across from the Santa Fe depot was the scene of a spectacular shootout on September 4, 1887, when the county sheriff went to arrest a horse thief and was wounded while gunning down several members of the thief's family. Nearby are the notorious Bucket of Blood Saloon, the 1910 J&J Trading Post and the one-time Campbell's Coffee House (now a Rexall drug store), which became famous for its "Son of a Bitch stew."

Anasazi ruins

Five miles (8km) off I-40 near **Joseph City** ("Joseph Small Town" would be more appropriate) is the Jack Rabbit Trading Post, with its original crouching rabbit sign, while 16 miles (26km) farther on, a turn north on State Route 87 – just before you get to Winslow – will take you to the extensive 14th-century Anasazi site of **Homolovi Ruins State Park** (tel: 928-289-4106; www.azstateparks.com; daily). The name Homolovi is the Hopi word for "Place of the Little Hills."

Winslow ❸ achieved fame from its inclusion in the Eagles' hit "Take It Easy," written by Jackson Browne. The song refers to "Standin' on a corner in Winslow, Arizona," and visitors pour into town to do just that at Standin' on the Corner Park (Kinsley and Second streets), where there is a bronze statue of a man with a guitar. The lyric goes: *Well, I'm standing on a corner in Winslow, Arizona/Such a fine sight to see/It's a girl, my Lord/In a flatbed Ford/Slowing down to take a look at me.*

Until the 1960s, Winslow – born with the arrival of the railroad in 1880 – was the largest town in northern Arizona, but business began to fade when it was bypassed by the interstate. Its rebirth began with the renovation of Downtown, and, most notably, **La Posada** (tel:

928-289-4366), the 1930 Fred Harvey railroad hotel (see page 415).

South of Winslow off SR 99, Anasazi petroglyphs can be admired in **Chevelon Canyon**, west of town, to which tours are conducted from Rock Art Canyon Ranch (tel: 928-288-3260; May–Oct, advance reservations required). Anglers know the area well for its rainbow and (more enticingly) brown trout that live in the lake and creek here.

About 20 miles (32km) west on I-40, Exit 233 leads south to **Meteor Crater** (tel: 928-289-5898; www.meteorcrater.com; daily tours), a 600ft (183-meter) -deep hole almost a mile across created by the impact of a meteorite nearly 50 centuries ago. Astronauts were trained here before the moon visit, and the Astronaut Park has an Apollo Space Capsule. The museum has exhibitions documenting the history of meteorites impacting the earth and a theater recreating those impacts as if you were at ground zero. Back on the main road heading west, the ghost town of **Two Guns** sits on an abandoned portion of Route 66.

Although **Winona** features in Bobby Troup's "Route 66" song (it rhymes with "Arizona"), it's actually a dead-end, and what Route 66 historian Tom Snyder calls "a one-blink town." Near Winona, 7 miles (11km) before Flagstaff, is the **Walnut Canyon National Monument** (tel: 928-526-3367; www.nps.gov/waca; daily), where a short hike down a paved trail reveals ancient cliff dwellings that fell into disuse hundreds of years ago.

The skeleton of a sickle claw dinosaur at the Museum of Northern Arizona in Flagstaff.

Flagstaff

The only large town in northern Arizona, **Flagstaff** ㉟ is a staging point for trips to the Grand Canyon, 80 miles (129km) to the north. The trip up US 89 and then along State Route 64 is longer, but more scenic, than the shorter route from Williams farther along the highway. Two of Flagstaff's museum attractions, the **Pioneer Museum** (tel: 928-774-6272; www.arizonahistoricalsociety.org/museums; Mon–Sat) and the **Museum**

Navajo shepherd by the 'ear of the wind' formation in Monument Valley, a Navajo Tribal Park.

MONUMENT VALLEY

A 182-mile (293km) journey from Flagstaff, Arizona, leads to one of the most famous sights in the Southwest. Monument Valley is easily recognized from far away thanks to scenes from countless Westerns, especially those by director John Ford, who often used it as the backdrop for his movies. With its serene rock formations dominating the surrounding desert plains, the valley's mesas were not just attractive to Hollywood, but also served as significant religious monuments for local Native Americans. Medicine men once climbed the Rain God Mesa – home to a sacred burial ground – to pray for rain. The Totem Pole formation served as a center for mythical incidents in folklore, while the Yei-Bi-Chei resembles holy Navajo figures performing a traditional dance. Like the Grand Canyon or Sedona, the timeless mystery of these rocks is humbling. What seems an impossible creation is the result of ageless erosion of the sandstone and shale, which leaves the harder stone intact. Monument Valley lies entirely within the Navajo Nation reservation, and the tribe conducts tours through its desolate beauty. Catch a sunrise or sunset at the Visitor Center (tel: 435-727-5870), from which many famous formations can be seen. To venture further into Monument Valley, you'll need to obtain a permit (tel: 928-879-6647) from the Navajo Nation. Visit www.navajonationparks.org for further information.

QUOTE

Don't Take A Curve At 60
Per We Hate to Lose A
Customer.

Burma Shave

*On Route 66 near
Winslow.*

of Northern Arizona (tel: 928-774-5213; www.musnaz.org; daily), are not far apart on Fort Valley Road, or from US 180, which also leads to the canyon. Flagstaff's other attractions are either in or near the historic and attractive downtown railroad district, through which Route 66 runs. The city stages a Route 66 Days celebration each September with live music, a parade of classic cars, and displays of arts and crafts.

On the way into Flagstaff from the direction of the east, be sure to stop by the **Museum Club** (tel: 928-526-9434; daily), a 1931 roadhouse which in Prohibition days began as a "zoo" filled with stuffed animals. Now listed on the National Register of Historic Places, it is a popular dance club by night and dozens of country music stars have performed in the Southwest's largest log cabin. Nearer to Downtown are the **Lowell Observatory** (tel: 928-774-3358; www.lowell.edu; daily) and the richly furnished 40-room **Riordan Mansion** (tel: 928-779-4395; daily), set in an attractive park.

Opposite the train station on Leroux Street, you'll find the remarkable **Weatherford Hotel** (see page 415), which opened its doors on the first day of 1899. That day, it welcomed among its scores of distinguished guests the publisher William Randolph Hearst, President Theodore Roosevelt, and lawman Wyatt Earp. The bar boasts an antique counter that came from Tombstone, and the ballroom is named for Western author Zane Grey, who stayed here while writing *Call of the Canyon*.

A young reader of Zane Grey's books was one Cecil B. DeMille, who concluded that Flagstaff sounded like a good place to launch his movie career. When he arrived in the town from the East, however, it was snowing, and DeMille decided to continue on the train to Los Angeles, thus altering the course of movie history forever.

An attractive side trip from Flagstaff is along State Highway 89A through the spectacular **Oak Creek Canyon** to the upscale artist community of **Sedona ㊱**, 28 miles (45km) south. It is surrounded by stunning red rock

formations that have also been a magnet for film directors, as well as for New Age types who are drawn to its mystical "vortexes." Further south is another artist's haven, **Jerome**, a former ghost town named after a defunct copper mine, with attractive Old West buildings.

Back on Route 66

Between Flagstaff and Williams, Route 66 is mostly unsurfaced and not very well maintained, but has the distinction of containing the highest point of the route at 7,300ft (2,225 meters) above sea level, about a mile or two before **Parks**. The Parks in the Pines general store has been in business for more than 80 years. Nearby are the remains of the **Beale Wagon Road Historic Trail**, a sturdy 120ft (37-meter) -wide track constructed in 1857 on which pioneers could safely travel as far as the Colorado River.

Back on I-40, the next town, **Williams** ❸, as well as its main street on Route 66 and the nearby mountain, were all named for Bill Williams (1787–1849), an early fur trapper whose statue stands at the west end of town. The excellent *Route 66 Magazine* was once published here, the last town on Route 66 to be bypassed by I-40.

Near the Williams railroad depot (which also houses an interesting museum) is the restored **Fray Marcos Hotel** (now the Grand Canyon Railway Hotel; see page 415), originally a unit of the once-ubiquitous Harvey House chain, which an English immigrant, Fred Harvey, established in the 1880s along the route of the Santa Fe line, revolutionizing the then-abysmal standards of railway food. One of Harvey's basic rules was that the coffee – served by smiling "Harvey Girls" in black dresses and spotless white aprons and bows – was re-made every two hours, even if the urn was still full. For 75 cents, customers could choose from seven entrees and take second helpings, too.

A tan-colored 1953 Cadillac and life-size cutouts of James Dean and Marilyn Monroe sit outside **Twisters**, a self-proclaimed "back-to-the '50s diner" that displays hundreds of

Desert songbird.

Monument Valley is an iconic American West landscape and an epicenter of Navajo culture.

snapshots of families taken along the route, along with an old glass-topped Sky Chief gasoline pump that has been converted into a holder for typical road souvenirs.

Sit here for 20 minutes or so and immerse yourself in pure, unadulterated kitsch. A menu offers a dozen different shakes, malts, floats, and cherry phosphates. For those seeking more conventional fare, the best-known restaurant in town, **Rod's Steak House**, has been serving customers along Route 66 for more than half a century.

The Grand Canyon

Williams is the main departure point for the **Grand Canyon** ❸❽ (tel: 928-638-7888; www.nps.gov/grca). The Grand Canyon Railway (tel: 800-843-8724) departs here for the canyon every morning. The five-hour round-trip – by vintage steam locomotives in summer, diesel locomotives the rest of the year – allows for three hours' sightseeing at the canyon, but is a worthwhile trip in itself (particularly for families), complete with strolling

Grandview viewpoint on the Grand Canyon's south rim.

cowboy musicians and, on the return trip, a "train robbery."

The South Rim of the Grand Canyon, which can also be reached by traveling about 40 miles (64km) north on US 180 from Williams, is open around the clock every day of the year, although the Visitor Center and most park facilities operate only from 8am to 5pm. A good place to start your visit is at the Canyon View Information Plaza opposite Mather Point. This spacious center has wall-size maps, exhibits, and guides that set the canyon in a larger context and help you get oriented. Park rangers are on hand to answer questions. From here, continue west to Grand Canyon Village, a hub of tourist facilities.

Free canyon shuttle buses operate from March through November from the village, west along the 7-mile (11km) Hermits Rest Route, giving visitors access to nine of the best canyon overlooks and a hiking trail along the canyon rim. Private cars are only allowed along this stretch of road in winter. At **Trailview Point**, you can look back at the village and

the **Bright Angel Trail** switchbacking down to the river. In the morning, mule trains plod into the canyon, bearing excited greenhorns who may wish they'd gone on foot when the day is done. Other recommended points along Hermits Road are **Hopi**, **Mohave**, and **Pima**. From each vista different isolated buttes and "temples" present themselves, many with fanciful names bestowed by early explorers. The road ends at **Hermits Rest**, which has a gift shop, concession stand, and restrooms. Returning to the village, another road, **Desert View Drive**, follows the canyon rim for 25 miles (40km) to the east. Overlooks along the way display still more spectacular canyon scenery.

The Grand Canyon is one of the world's great natural wonders, and it's worth staying at least one night to appreciate the spectacular views at different times of day, as the formations take on different colors and moods. To reserve accommodations at one of the Grand Canyon lodges, call 303-297-2757. Be sure to book early, as rooms are highly prized.

Beyond Williams

From Williams, 19 miles (31km) west along I-40, it's worth getting off the busy road to visit somnolent **Ash Fork**, which was a stagecoach depot until the arrival of the railroad in 1882. This was also a regular stop along Route 66 until the town was bypassed by the bigger thoroughfare; a Confederate flag flies over the Route 66 Grill. One of the adorable Harvey Girls lived nearby until her death, and she donated several artifacts from the defunct Harvey House chain to a fledgling museum located in a vast, empty warehouse beside the tourist office.

Seligman

Returning briefly to the interstate, it's advisable to leave it again at the Crookton Road exit for the longest and most nostalgic section on the entire Historic 66 Highway. It's quite simple to remain on it all the way to the California border at Topock, a distance of about 180 miles (290km).

You won't miss **Seligman** **39**, whose main thoroughfare and Route 66 are

Stomachs and gas tanks fueled here at Delgadillo's Snow Cap Drive-in, Seligman, Arizona.

Delgadillo's Snow Cap Drive-In, Seligman.

Clark Gable and Carole Lombard were married in Kingman, Arizona.

Route 66 as it passes through Seligman.

lined with strangely compelling gift shops devoted to the highway's history, which carry every conceivable type of souvenir, from US 66 highway signs, Mother Road license tags and oil company signs, to old Coca-Cola posters and bottles – as well as the now-familiar inscribed mugs, glasses, and T-shirts. One of these is the Delgadillo Route 66 Gift Shop (tel: 928-422-3352), which also doubles as a Visitor Center. Here you can pick up a leaflet that will take you on a 20-minute walking tour that takes in colorful remnants of the town's Route 66 heyday. These include the Rusty Bolt Souvenir and Gift Shop with its collection of vintage cars, and Delgadillo's Snow Cap Drive-In, a Route 66 landmark that serves classic road fare and kitsch in equal measure.

Twenty-five miles (40km) west of Seligman is the deep **Grand Canyon Caverns** (tel: 928-422-3223; www.gc caverns.com; daily), into which early visitors paid 25 cents to be lowered 150ft (46 meters) by rope. Today, there's an elevator and illuminated paths on which to walk.

Grand Canyon Skywalk

Peach Springs is the tribal headquarters of the Hualapai Nation, whose lands encompass the western end of the Grand Canyon. **Grand Canyon West** (tel: 928-769-2636; www.grand canyonwest.com; daily) is 242 miles (389km) from the entrance at the South Rim – nearly as long as the canyon itself. Here the Hualapai have built the phenomenal Grand Canyon Skywalk, a U-shaped glass-bottomed walkway that extends from the edge of a clifftop out into the air above the canyon, giving visitors a hawks-eye view of the surroundings and the Colorado River, 4,000ft (1,220 meters) below. It's not for those with vertigo, nor for those on a budget. On top of the pricy Skywalk fee, visitors must purchase a Hualapai tour package to gain access to the site, but it's a fun day of activities and a unique opportunity to walk on air and see the canyon from a new perspective.

Access to Grand Canyon West, 70 miles (112km) north of Kingman, is via minor roads. The last 21 miles (34km) are on unpaved gravel surface,

so those with low-clearance vehicles or RVs should use the Park and Ride coach service available at the site.

Kingman ④ is where the tubby, gruff-voiced movie star Andy Devine was born. The main street is named after him, and on this and the adjoining Beale Street are the oldest buildings, including the old Beale Hotel where Clark Gable and Carole Lombard were married in March 1939. Kingman's **Route 66 Museum** is located in the visitor center (tel: 928-753-9889; http://www.gokingman. com; daily), and one of its exhibits is a re-creation of a small-town Main Street, complete with a 1950s yellow Studebaker car. The **Mojave Museum of History and Arts** (tel: 928-753-3195; www.mohavemuseum.org; Mon–Sat) displays attractive turquoise jewelry and a re-created Hualapai dwelling, among other historical artifacts.

Heading west, the highway takes on a desolate, rocky wilderness appearance – an indicator of what's to come; be sure you have good brakes. Before long, the road is climbing between jagged peaks in a series of seemingly endless switchbacks and scary, blind curves to the 3,500ft (1,067-meter) -high summit at **Sitgreaves Pass** (named, like the Beale Wagon Trail, for a mid-19th-century Army surveyor), before beginning an equally twisting and turning segment down into the tiny town of Oatman.

Oatman and its quirks

On the way down into Oatman, you'll pass **Goldroad**, the site of a mine that produced $2-billion-worth of gold in its early years, but closed down in 1907 when gold prices dropped.

Hundreds of wild burros turned loose by early miners roam the mountains, occasionally straying across the highway and wandering into **Oatman** ④, proving irresistible camera fodder for photographers and inspiring the name of the Classy Ass gift shop, next to the Oatman Hotel, which sells jewelry made from rocks and sand dollars and other one-of-a-kind gifts. Oatman looks exactly the way you'd imagine an ancient Western town to look, with sagging wooden shacks

Map on page 204

TIP

The "almost" ghost town of Chloride, Arizona (10 miles/16km north of Kingman) is a fitting venue for the Old Miners' Day. Join in the Old West festivities – mock gunfights, pie baking contests, a parade, food booths, and more. Held the last Saturday in June. For further information call 928-565-9419.

Sheep Hole Pass on Amboy Road.

lining the solitary unpaved street, on which amusing mock gunfights are conducted daily.

Across the street from Fast Fanny's (selling clothes, sunglasses, and postcards), a bed on wheels promotes the annual Great Oatman Bed Races, which are held every January. Summer temperatures can reach 118°F (48°C), prompting the annual Sidewalk Egg Fry every Fourth of July (magnifying glasses permitted).

The worn and characterful 1902 **Oatman Hotel** (tel: 928-768-4408) no longer rents rooms, but it will be forever famous as the place where Clark Gable and Carole Lombard spent their honeymoon night in Room 15, after being married in Kingman, and the simple room is preserved as a sort of shrine to the glamorous Hollywood couple with pictures of the pair on the walls and a pink nightdress draped over a chair. On the ground floor is an ice-cream shop and a bar and restaurant popular with the locals.

Twenty miles (32km) of desert scrubland lies between Oatman and **Topock**, where the Colorado River

marks the California border. Route 66 comes to a dead-end at Moabi Regional Park with its lake and boat rentals – a refreshing stop after the long drive in the hot sun.

CALIFORNIA

As the car heads ever closer toward the setting sun, spare a thought for those migrants from the early days of Route 66 for whom crossing the border into the "promised land" became an ordeal. Faced with an influx of refugees from the Dust Bowl states, Californians were worried about the impact on property prices and already poorly paid jobs. In some places guards were posted at the border and scores of exhausted migrants were turned away. It's a story that is still familiar today, albeit at a different border.

Sadly, once in California, much of the old Route 66, apart from a few parched stretches through the Mojave Desert, has been largely supplanted and is submerged beneath a welter of busy freeways to re-emerge only in occasional short stretches or as the main routes through towns such

DETOUR TO LAS VEGAS

A desert drive of 101 miles (163km) from Kingman, Arizona, on US 93 leads straight to Sin City. At latest count, nearly 40 million visitors spend over $9 billion annually on gaming alone in this capital of frivolity, greed, and gluttony – not to mention plain old fun. For a long time after gambling was legalized in 1931, Las Vegas remained a sleepy desert town. It took visionary underworld hit man Bugsy Siegel to free this seething neon dragon. In 1946, Siegel opened the Flamingo Hotel, sparing no expense in mob finances for its plush interior, which sported a flashing pink neon facade and set a new standard in sheer swank.

From a high-roller's point of view, Las Vegas is divided into two parts. First is the Strip, where modern hoteliers vie with each other to offer the latest in accommodation extravaganzas, with hotels replicating Venice, Paris, Rome, ocean liners, and Egyptian pyramids.

Then there's Downtown – the original Vegas – also known as Glitter Gulch. As for gambling, either way you lose, but Downtown casinos are said to afford better odds. The best advice is simply enjoy it: win, lose or draw, there's nothing quite like the Strip at night, ablaze with electric light and self-indulgence. For more information, contact the Las Vegas Convention and Visitors Authority at 702-892-0711; www.visitlasvegas.com.

as Barstow, Victorville, and Rancho Cucamonga.

Needles

In the first town you'll come to in California, **Needles**, Route 66 passes through the business section and along Broadway. Past the Amtrak terminal, the defunct 1906 Fred Harvey House, known as El Garces and regarded as the crown jewel of the chain, is now just a part of the station. Harvey Girls lived in the upper floors. Trained in neatness and courtesy, the girls signed a contract of employment agreeing not to marry for a year, and lived on the upper floors of the hotel.

The **Needles Regional Museum** (tel: 760-326-5678; Mon–Sat) has a fanciful collection of stuff guaranteed to raise a grin: vintage clothes, old jars and bottles, obsolete currency, pictures curling with sepia, cartridge shells, and Native American artifacts. The Fort **Mojave Tribal Center** (tel: 760-629-4591) adjoins the tribe's resort, casino, golf course, and Colorado River marina. A February Pow Wow celebrates Native American culture.

In World War II, General George Patton established an army training center in the Mojave, realizing that a familiarity with its harsh terrain would prepare the troops for the forthcoming Africa campaign, and indeed, conditions are similar. The US Army National Training Center is still headquartered at Barstow, 145 miles (233km) due west of Needles.

The route from Needles to Barstow can be traveled swiftly on I-40, but the old Route 66 runs north of the interstate and heads through **Goffs** before diverting south through the barely existing communities of Essex, Amboy, and Bagdad (famous for its landmark café, inspration for the 1987 film Bagdad Café and, earlier, another Harvey House). Tiny **Essex** was featured on NBC's *Tonight Show* in 1977, claiming to be the only town in America without television. A Pennsylvania company promptly donated the necessary equipment. About a mile from **Amboy** (now a ghost town owned by preservationist Albert Okura and featuring a closed-down café and gas station, once a

Keep your eyes peeled for snakes when hiking in the desert – a rattler taken by surprise may not give you a warning before striking.

Bright lights of Las Vegas.

FACT

Barstow's Route 66 Mother Road Museum has a special exhibit devoted to the large number of Hispanic people who traveled along Route 66 when migrating west from New Mexico.

favorite with filmmakers) is an extinct volcano known as the **Amboy Crater**.

Ludlow, where Route 66 links up once more with the interstate, was once a boomtown served not only by the Santa Fe railroad, but also by two others (local lines bearing ore from Death Valley), and in fact was named for a Central Pacific repairman. The 1940s Ludlow Cafe building is derelict, as is the abandoned Ludlow Mercantile Building (1908) down by the railroad tracks, but the newer Ludlow Coffee Shop is usually bustling with activity. Water, always scarce in these parts, was at one time brought in to fill the steam trains by tank cars from **Newberry Springs**, 40 miles (64km) to the west (actual filming site of the cult movie *Bagdad Café*). There really are springs here, and they supplement the water supply from the region's numerous artesian wells.

At the State Agricultural Inspection Station, you may be asked if you are bringing any citrus fruits into California; it's a precaution against pests that might threaten the state's orange crop. Just before Barstow is

Daggett, whose landmark **Stone Hotel** (currently closed for renovation) was popular with Tom Mix and other movie cowboys. On show in the small Daggett Museum (tel: 760-254-2629; Sat–Sun) is a scale model of the California Edison Company's Solar One thermal plant (1981–1986) out in the desert. Giant mirrors focused the sun's energy on tanks of nitrate salt intended to convert water into the steam required to power a turbine generator.

Barstow

The Mojave Desert was a forbidding yet paradoxically inviting place in the 1870s when gold, silver, and borax were among the valuable metals and minerals that drew prospectors and miners from all over the country. The arrival of the Santa Fe railroad in 1883 connected – and in many cases created – isolated small towns, and the Mediterranean-style Santa Fe Depot at **Barstow** ㊷, and renovated 1911 Casa del Desierto (a former Harvey House and now a route 66 Museum), give some idea of the forgotten

Calico ghost town near Barstow.

splendor of the times. Gift shops and a McDonald's, at which customers eat in converted railroad cars, are among the station's attractions. Among the exhibits in the **Route 66 "Mother Road" Museum** (tel: 760-255-1890; Fri–Sun) are archival and contemporary prints by photographers who have captured images of the road and its icons. Many are available for purchase.

With the arrival of the pre-World War II National Old Trails Highway, the predecessor to Route 66, Barstow's importance as a transportation center was quite literally cemented. Sitting at the major junction of I-15 and I-40, it has shown little sign of decline. Midway between Los Angeles and Las Vegas, it is a convenient rest stop for drivers on their way to and from the resort city. The older Route 66 motels are to the west end of town. Watch for the El Rancho, built with railroad ties, and whose 100ft (30-meter) -high neon sign has been a landmark since the early days of the highway.

The **Mojave River Valley Museum** (tel: 760-256-5452; www.mojaveriver valleymuseum.org; daily) and the **Desert Discovery Center** (tel: 760-252-6060; www.desertdiscoverycenter.com; Tue–Sat) will together answer all your questions about the desert – past and present.

Side trips from Barstow

One worthwhile side trip from Barstow is to the **Rainbow Basin** (tel: 760-252-6000; daily), where a 4-mile (6km) loop road circles an area filled with fossilized animal remains and fringed by multicolored cliffs; another is to **Calico Ghost Town** (tel: 800-8622-5426; daily), 11 miles (18km) to the east, whose prosperity between 1881–96 came from mining a $12-million seam of silver, a boom that was supplemented by the discovery of borax nearby.

When both "cash crops" gave out, the town's 22 saloons closed one after another as the population drifted to other areas to seek their fortunes, but many of the old buildings have been rehabilitated, and such tourist attractions as wagon rides, mock gunfights, and gold panning were introduced. A few miles to the east at the town of **Calico**, the **Archeological Site** (tel:

Joshua tree in the Mojave Desert.

760-252-6000; www.blm.gov; Wed–Sun) displays relics from the Pleistocene era, which was approximately 50,000 years ago.

Victorville

It's an uneventful 40-mile (64km) drive on a good road (which parallels I-15) to Victorville, where Route 66 is merely another city street. **Victorville** began as a mining camp in the 19th century and became a magnet during Hollywood's golden age for moviemakers attracted by its "Western" feel. For a while, it also attracted the Roy Rogers-Dale Evans Museum, where the galleries glittered with the husband-and-wife cowboy stars' sequined costumes, before the museum moved to the country-music town of Branson, Missouri.

The **California Route 66 Museum** (tel: 760-951-0436; www.califrt66museum.org; Mon, Thurs–Sat) offers a final fix for westbound travelers who haven't yet had their fill of ephemera from the Mother Road; the museum building itself was once a roadhouse called the Red Rooster Cafe.

Its premier exhibit is Hula Ville, an example of the folksy roadside attractions once found all along Route 66. In the mid-1950s, a man named Miles Mahan decided to drive nails into fence posts and hang from them all the bottles left behind by transients. Later, he rescued a huge metal sign of a dancing hula girl and arranged for her to tower over the fences, practically stopping traffic along the route. Locals began to donate other items to Mahan's "Cactus Garden," and in time Hula Ville became a Route 66 high desert legend.

San Bernardino

South of Victorville, I-15 heads over the 4,300ft (1,310-meter) Cajon Summit, which, after taking the Oak Hill exit, brings you to Mariposa Road and the **Summit Inn**, a long-time Route 66 landmark that has been serving diners since 1952. Apart from a brief stretch, I-15 has subsumed much of the old route, but you're on it if you follow Cajon Boulevard into **San Bernardino ㊸**, a Mormon town in the 1850s, and once a major citrus center. It's the gateway to the mountainous **San Bernardino National Forest**, more than 600,000 acres (243,000 hectares) of wilderness dominated by 11,500ft (3,505-meter) -high Mt San Gorgonio, the highest in Southern California. Deep in the forest are the well-known resorts of **Big Bear** and **Lake Arrowhead**, known hideaways for Hollywood stars. State Route 18, romantically known as the Rim of the World Drive, is the lofty 40-mile (64km) highway that leads to these destinations.

Rim of the World Drive

With panoramic views, switchback turns and lots of overlooks, **Rim of the World Drive** is particularly exhilarating to do on a motorcycle. The best stretch is the 25-mile (40km) run from Redlands up the hill toward **Big Bear Lake**.

Kitsch mementos of the Mother Road.

Back down on the ground in San Bernardino itself, the classy old (1928) **California Theater**, on West Fourth Street, is worth noting. Head out of town on Mt Vernon Avenue past some aged motels and a hard-to-miss Santa Fe railroad smokestack, and eventually you will pass the tepees of another Wigwam Motel (1950) along Foothill Boulevard. This leads into **Rancho Cucamonga** and begins with a series of large and anonymous shopping malls, but at the corner of Vineyard Avenue there is a glimpse of earlier times, with an old-fashioned Mobil station from the 1920s sitting on the opposite corner to the historic Thomas Winery building. Once a popular stop on Route 66, the winery is a state landmark, designated as the oldest commercial winery in California and the second-oldest in the country. Sadly, the Thomas vineyards fell victim to development in the 1960s, but the premises are now occupied, appropriately, by The Wine Tailor, which sells custom wines.

Further down is the historic **Sycamore Inn**, a huge, rustic log palace and steak house on the site of an 1848 trailside inn that catered to the Gold Rush adventurers. In 1858, it became a stop along the route of the Butterfield Stage.

Past **Claremont**, where the old route suddenly moves upscale with a grassy median and eucalyptus trees, are a few eating places that old-timers might remember. There's Wilson's restaurant (now La Paloma) at **La Verne**; the Pinnacle Peak Steak House, where they cut off customers' ties, at **San Dimas**; and the Golden Spur Restaurant (which began as a hamburger stand over 80 years ago) in **Glendora**.

There are many old motels and eateries along this part of Route 66, including the Derby Restaurant and Rod's Grill in **Arcadia**, and in **Monrovia**, the distinctive one-story Aztec Hotel. This hotel dates from 1925, when it was built by architect Robert Stacy-Judd in a pseudo-Mayan style to catch the attention of motorists along the route.

The end of the road

Just before **Los Angeles** ⓬ proper, Route 66 becomes what is now the Pasadena Freeway, but which started life in the closing days of 1940 as the Arroyo Seco Parkway, the first freeway in a bold, new experiment that was eventually to cover the entire state of California with a network of similarly fast highways. Continue driving and take the Sunset Boulevard exit, then head west along Sunset until it joins Santa Monica Boulevard, which runs all the way to the Pacific Ocean. Here, in Palisades Park overlooking the beach, a modest plaque commemorates the western terminus of this famous American road.

Nobody can recall seeing a Burma Shave sign in Santa Monica itself, where Route 66 ends, but if the company had ever put one there it would probably have been the one that read *If You/Don't Know/Whose Signs/These Are/You Can't Have/Driven Very Far!*

TIP

If you happen to be in Long Beach in August, check out the outdoor waterfront Jazz Festival, just south of Los Angeles. Greats like Poncho Sanchez and Michael Franks and classic Motown musicians have featured in past years. For details: www.longbeachjazzfestival. com; tel: 562-424-0013.

Santa Monica, Los Angeles.

A SHORT STAY IN LOS ANGELES

The city of fantasy and film, LA has endless sun, an easy ambiance, and, of course, Hollywood. Here's a list of the not-to-be-missed attractions.

The Hollywood Museum is the place to pay homage to the achievements of the silver screen. Included are displays on history, personalities, and Max Factor movie make-up innovations.

Part amusement park, part working film studio, **Universal Studios Hollywood** is one of the most visited sites in LA. Go behind the scenes to see sensational stunts and special effects, or face dinosaurs and vengeful mummies on heart-pounding thrill rides.

Lined with jewelers, designer studios, upmarket fashion, and accessories boutiques, **Rodeo Drive** in Beverly Hills is one of the most exclusive shopping addresses in the world.

Watch a parade of stars – the celestial kind – at the landmark **Griffith Observatory**. Like the famous Hollywood sign, it stands in Griffith Park which extends for miles and has far-reaching views over LA and the San Fernando Valley.

The **GRAMMY Museum** celebrates modern music, with four floors of interactive exhibits about popular artists and songs and their impact on the world.

Art lovers should not miss the **Los Angeles County Museum of Art**. Its displays of costumes, pottery, silverware, and decorative arts, as well as paintings and sculpture from all eras, are augmented by the new **Broad Contemporary Art Museum** on campus, designed by Renzo Piano.

L.A. Live is the city's hottest entertainment destination, with the Nokia Theatre, music clubs, restaurants, and more, next to Downtown's premier sports venue, the **Staples Center**.

Historic and modern-day injustices of racism and prejudice are the focus of the thoughtful **Museum of Tolerance** on West Pico Boulevard.

Sidney Grauman, who "invented" the movie premiere, designed Grauman's Chinese Theatre in the 1920s. Its main attraction is the forecourt with stars' hand- and footprints.

The stars that make up the Walk of Fame on Hollywood Boulevard.

View over LA from the Griffith Observatory.

CITY OF ANGELS

In 1781, Father Junípero Serra named a dry, dusty settlement after St Francis of Assisi's first church, St Mary Queen of the Angels. No one could have conceived that this hot, arid place would turn into glittering Los Angeles, the capital of moviedom and a world-famous synonym for glamor and fun. Residents of most big cities pretend to be blasé in the presence of celebrities, but Angelenos really are: movie stars are the stock-in-trade here, as common as scarlet-suited guardsmen in London or yellow cabs in New York. LA is also a city of adventure and innovation: Disneyland, rollerblading, beach culture, West Coast rap music – it all started here.

ade famous by Billy Wilder's magnificent melodrama, nset Boulevard is an important avenue in the evolution of llywood.

IMPORTANT INFORMATION

Population: 4 million
Dialing codes: 213, 310, 323, 562, 626, 714, 818, 949
Website: www.discoverlosangeles.com
Tourist information: LA Visitor Info Center, 685 South Figueroa Street, CA 90017; tel: 213-689-8822; Bollywood branch, 6801 Hollywood Boulevard; tel: 323-467-6412.

Los Angeles Throughways

0   10 miles
0   10 km

Indicates route from the city detailed in this book

A farmer surveys his day's work baling hay.

Texas rancher.

THE SOUTHERN ROUTE

A guide to the South and the Southwest, with principal
sites clearly cross-referenced by number to the maps.

All-American classic.

Sit back and enjoy the ride on the Southern route across the continent. The pace is leisurely, as you meander down a Georgia street lined with trees draped in Spanish moss, relax on a Texas beach, or kick up your cowboy boots in a Tombstone, Arizona saloon.

Our nearly 2,500-mile (3,900km) journey through the South departs from Atlanta, capital of the "New South" and home of slain civil rights leader Martin Luther King. Atlanta is home to well-known global corporations like CNN, but its attractive woodsy setting, foodie leanings, and numerous visitor attractions make it a great jumping-off point. After a detour in charming Macon, the route speeds south along the Civil Rights trail to the architecture-rich state capital of Montgomery, Alabama, and on to oil-rich Mobile on the Gulf of Mexico. From here, you'll be following the Gulf through hurricane-devastated Mississippi and Louisiana, stopping in New Orleans, a sensory explosion of sights and sounds, soulful food, gracious architecture, and resilient citizens defying the odds after Hurricane Katrina.

Louisiana has the highest alligator population.

West of the state capital of Baton Rouge, the highway crosses the country's largest swamp into Cajun Country, one of the cultural highlights of the trip. Ease into rambunctious Texas by dipping your toes in the Gulf on the resort island of Galveston before driving north into Houston, famed for its space program but also an art destination of note. Superb live music is the draw in the dynamic state capital, Austin. The highway rolls through wildflower-strewn Hill Country before reaching San Antonio, renowned for its historic missions, Alamo, and downtown River Walk.

It's a long haul to El Paso, as the highway follows the Rio Grande, the US border with Mexico, passing through dusty border towns with Wild West links. River trips among beautiful canyons and wildlife viewing draw nature lovers to spectacular Big Bend National Park, just south of Marfa, a rising art and cultural destination in ranch country.

After El Paso and its Mexican sister city of Ciudad Juárez, it's on to New Mexico, with its contrasting scenery, ancient cultures, and modern high-tech weaponry and atomic history. The highway crosses the Continental Divide en route to Arizona, where the Old West survives in places like Tombstone and Bisbee. In Tucson and Phoenix, indulge in some pampering at a spa resort before heading across the Mojave Desert to San Diego, California.

A SHORT STAY IN ATLANTA

Atlanta is bold, brash, and self-confident – a cosmopolitan island surrounded by rural Georgia. Here's a list of the not-to-be-missed attractions.

Atlanta's main attractions are walkable, clustered around the small **1996 Centennial Olympic Park** in **Downtown**. There's plenty for families at the dynamic **Georgia Aquarium**, which has the world's largest fish tank; Imagine It! The **Children's Museum of Atlanta**; and the **New World of Coca-Cola**. The worthwhile **Inside CNN Atlanta tour** offers a fascinating behind-the-scenes look at newscasting.

Underground Atlanta is filled with shops and watering holes and stretches six blocks above and below ground. **Little Five Points**, meanwhile, has shops specializing in everything from New Age crystals and vintage clothes to music and books and serves as the hub for Atlanta's excellent **MARTA** transportation system.

Midtown, centered on 10th and Peachtree streets, is Atlanta's fast-growing arts district. Highlights are the light-filled **High Museum of Art**, designed by Richard Meier, showcasing Rodin sculptures, works by Picasso and Matisse, and big traveling exhibits, and the 1929 **Fox Theatre**, a Moorish-style movie palace, best seen on a tour with the Atlanta Preservation Society.

Gone With the Wind author **Margaret Mitchell** is a hometown literary hero. The modest apartment where the pioneering journalist wrote her one masterpiece is open daily for tours.

Piedmont Park, surrounded by tree-shaded streets and old homes, is a Midtown favorite. Its northside has a a Botanical Garden while the south side hosts a Saturday Green Market (May–Dec) and an April Dogwood Festival.

Uptown's ritzy **Buckhead** district contains beautiful homes, restaurants, and a Whole Foods Market. The **Atlanta History Center** is a hidden gem. Nestled amid 33 acres (13 hectares) of wooded trails and gardens, it covers the Civil War and other local history and offers tours of the **Tullie Smith Farmhouse** and **Swan House mansion**.

Vintage vending machines at the World of Coca-Cola.

Discover more about the Civil Rights leader at Martin Luther King National Historic Site. The four-block Sweet Auburn District includes King's birth home (shown), his tomb and the church in which the King family preached.

A studio tour of CNN headquarters shows the professionals at work.

CAPITAL OF THE NEW SOUTH

Atlanta is a city alert to opportunity. This is not just because it was burned down during the Civil War – Atlanta has always been this way. Winning the bid for the 1996 Olympics was just the beginning; now Atlanta is an urban phenomenon, exuding prosperity, self-confidence, self-absorption, and constant reinvention. Don't be fooled by all the construction, though: Atlanta retains a Southern graciousness and is very welcoming. Its population is diverse – it has the second-largest gay population in the US – and, once you get used to navigating streets without good signs, you will quickly feel at home and want to linger.

The Buckhead District is the center of Atlanta's nightlife.

IMPORTANT INFORMATION

Population: City: 420,003; Metro: 5,626,400
Dialing codes: 404, 770, 678
Website: www.atlanta.net
Tourist information: Atlanta C & V Bureau, 233 Peachtree Street, Suite 1400, GA 30303; tel: 404-521-6600; open Mon–Fri

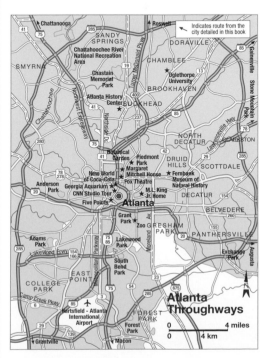

Freight train at a crossing.

ATLANTA TO NEW ORLEANS

The mournful whistle of freight trains, small towns on hot summer nights, and grand, glorious antebellum towns characterize this trip through Georgia and Alabama.

For more than a century after its cataclysmic encounter with historical destiny – as the focus of the Confederacy during the American Civil War (1861–65) – the South set itself apart from its conquerors (the Federal Government, or Union), stubbornly continuing to identify with the antebellum days on the Cotton Belt. Finally – and in part unwillingly, as a result of the changes forced upon it by the civil rights campaigns of the 1950s and 1960s – a "New South" is emerging. While there is still truth in the popular image of the region as a poor, undeveloped, and uneducated rural backwater, many of its urban communities have recast themselves beyond recognition, as high-tech high-achievers to match any in the nation.

NEW SOUTH MEETS OLD SOUTH IN GEORGIA

Nowhere is that more true than in the cities of Georgia, particularly its dynamic capital **Atlanta ❶** (see page 244), on the broad Piedmont Plateau of its north-central region. Home to global corporations from Coca-Cola to CNN, Atlanta justly claims to be the heart of the "New South." Nonetheless, it has managed to retain the more appealing aspects of its past, such as the South's traditional mannered gentility and famed flair for hospitality.

Summit Skyride cable car on Stone Mountain, Georgia.

Macon, too, on the "fall line" that runs from Augusta to Columbus separating northern Georgia from the Coastal Plain, has prospered without losing sight of its heritage, while Savannah, on the Savannah River close to the Atlantic Ocean, surrounds its stunning, antebellum city center with modern industry and shipping activity.

Banking, manufacturing, media, military installations, and tourism may have come to dominate its cities, but much of the rest of Georgia remains rural. Agricultural produce such as the

Main Attractions

Hay House
Little White House State Park
Carver Museum
Civil Rights Memorial
Bellingrath Gardens
Walter M. Anderson Museum of Art
Beauvoir
The French Quarter

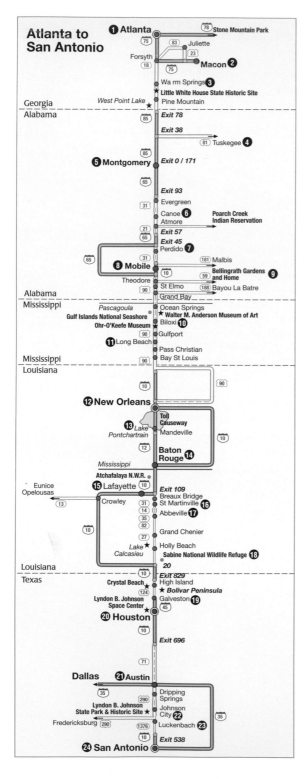

Atlanta to San Antonio

❶ Atlanta

⑦⑧ Stone Mountain Park

⑦⑤

⑧③ Juliette

Forsyth

②③

⑱

⑦⑤

Macon ❷

Wa rm Springs ❸

★ Little White House State Historic Site

Georgia

West Point Lake

Pine Mountain

Alabama

★

⑧⑤ Exit 78

Exit 38

⑧⑤

⑧① Tuskegee ❹

❺ Montgomery

Exit 0 / 171

⑥⑤

Exit 93

③① Evergreen

Canoe ❻

Poarch Creek

Atmore

Indian Reservation

②①

⑥⑤ Exit 57

Exit 45

Perdido ❼

③① ⑱① Malbis

❽ Mobile

⑥⑤

Bellingrath Gardens ❾

⑩ ⑤⑨ and Home

Theodore

St Elmo ⑱⑧ Bayou La Batre

⑨⓪

Grand Bay

Alabama

Mississippi

Pascagoula Ocean Springs

Gulf Islands National Seashore ★ Walter M. Anderson Museum of Art

Ohr-O'Keefe Museum ⑨⓪ Biloxi ❿

Gulfport

⓫ Long Beach

Pass Christian

Mississippi ⑨⓪ Bay St Louis

Louisiana

⑩ ⑨⓪

⓬ New Orleans

Toll

⓭ Causeway

Lake Mandeville ⑩

Pontchartrain

⑫

Baton

Mississippi Rouge ⓮

Atchafalaya N.W.R.

Eunice ⓯ Lafayette ⑩

Opelousas Exit 109

⑬ Breaux Bridge

Crowley ③① St Martinville ⓰

⑭ Abbeville ⓱

③⑤

⑩ ⑧②

Grand Chenier

②⑦

Lake ★ Holly Beach

Calcasieu Sabine National Wildlife Refuge ⓲

Louisiana 20

Texas ⑩ Exit 829

Crystal Beach ★ High Island

⑫④ ★ Bolivar Peninsula

Lyndon B. Johnson Galveston ⓳

Space Center ★ ④⑤

⓴ Houston

⑩

Exit 696

⑦①

Dallas ㉑ Austin

③⑤ Dripping

②⑨⓪ Springs

Lyndon B. Johnson Johnson ③⑤

State Park & Historic Site ★ City ㉒

Fredericksburg ②⑨⓪ ①③⑦⑥ Luckenbach ㉓

⑩ Exit 538

㉔ San Antonio

state's trademark peaches and sweet Vidalia onions, together with lumber, cattle, and poultry, continue to figure prominently in the economy.

Throughout Georgia, expect hot, humid days and pleasant nights from May through September, temperate comfort in April and October, and cool to cold temperatures November through March, with occasional frigid northerly winds, even snow. Georgia blooms most beautifully in the spring, which is ideal visiting season. Southern Georgia, on the Coastal Plain, is balmiest, often sweltering in summer.

If finding parking in downtown Atlanta leaves you crying for escape, take a trip 7 miles (11km) east of I-285 on US 78 to **Stone Mountain Park** (tel: 770-498-5690; www.stonemountainpark.com; daily), a recreation complex with seasonal attractions, including an ice rink, golf course, campground, hotels, waterslides, boating, fishing, tennis, wildlife trail, "Scenic Railroad" ride, and reconstructed plantation. Stone Mountain's plantation showcases buildings from throughout the state.

The park sprawls around its eponymous landmark: **Stone Mountain**. The exposed portion of this granite giant occupies a volume of 7.5 trillion cubic ft (213 million cubic meters) and is thought to be almost 3 million years old. Its gestation period was long, as igneous rock struggled to push through the surface. Stone Mountain's thrust to the sky is a fine metaphor for the concrete explosion of modern Atlanta after its razing by the Union army.

The mountain itself, smooth but for light pocks in the surface, is spectacle enough. Its focus, however, is the **Stone Mountain carving**, over 50 years in production, depicting Confederate leaders Jefferson Davis, Robert E. Lee, and "Stonewall" Jackson. The sculpture, which spreads 147ft (45 meters) across and towers 400ft (122 meters) above the ground, was completed in 1972.

Macon

Heading southeast out of Atlanta on I-75, you'll begin to encounter what the Federal Writers' Project called "the rolling character of the land [which] makes for undulations in the roadways, the fields, and the pine forests that border them. The clay hills are deeply gullied by erosion and their red color against the dark pines of the wooded regions creates a perpetually vivid landscape." Some 80 miles (130km) after leaving the "big city," I-75 takes a sharp turn to the south and straight into the heart of **Macon** ❷ (it rhymes with "bacon"); you can venture into the city from either I-75 or I-16, which continues southeast to Savannah. In recent years, Downtown has experienced something of a cultural resurgence, sparked not only by the largest number of listed historic antebellum mansions and civic buildings in Georgia but also Macon's deserved reputation as a music mecca: it is the hometown of rock-and-roll legends Little Richard, Otis Redding, the Allman Brothers, and REM, among others.

The Old South

Macon's marvelous historic buildings were spared destruction during the Civil War by a simple ruse. In 1864, when General Sherman and his troops fired into the city across the Ocmulgee River, the return fire suggested a substantial resistance. But the troops that diverted Sherman and his all-too-tragic torch toward Savannah were not Confederate regulars, just old men and young children.

The architecture that has been preserved and restored is incredibly diverse, yet thoroughly Southern. As one resident puts it: "When people from outside the South come to find the 'Old South,' it's not in Atlanta, which is too new, nor is it in Savannah, which by virtue of its settlers and design is closer to a European city. The Old South is right here in Macon."

During the "cotton boom" of the early 19th century, cotton kings built lavish homes in the early Federal style with classical touches. These were followed by structures in the Greek Temple style adapted to the climate. Over the years, waves of commercial

Macon is the epitome of the Old South.

expansion inspired forays into new styles for mansions and civic and commercial buildings. Italianate Revival, Roman Revival and Academic Revival experiments carried through to the 1920s. Among fine examples open daily to visitors are the huge **Hay House** (tel: 478-742-8155; www. georgiatrust.org/historic_sites/hayhouse) on Georgia Avenue, and **Cannonball House** (tel: 478-745-5982; www.cannon ballhouse.org) on Mulberry Street, scarred by a shot from Sherman's artillery and now appropriately housing a **Confederate museum**.

All can be enjoyed at their best in March each year, when the Cherry Blossom Festival celebrates the simultaneous flowering of Macon's pride and joy, the incredible 300,000 Japanese cherry trees that have been planted along the downtown streets.

The **Macon Visitor Information Center** (tel: 478-743-3401; www. maconga.org; Mon–Sat) on Martin Luther King Boulevard has a film introducing Macon narrated by Little Richard, interactive exhibits, and offers walking tours of Macon's historic

homes and museums. Although sadly, Macon's Music Hall of Fame has now closed, the **Georgia Sports Hall of Fame** (tel: 478-752-1585; www.gshf.org; Tue–Sat), celebrating Georgia athletes such as record home run hitter Henry "Hank" Aaron and golf legend Bobby Jones, remains a popular destination on Cherry Street.

A bridge honoring Macon's best-known hometown musical legend, Otis Redding, leads away from Downtown across the Ocmulgee River to **Ocmulgee National Monument** (tel: 478-752-8257; www.nps.gov/ocmu; daily). This small, peaceful national park doesn't do much to toot its own horn but is one of Macon's undiscovered treasures. It preserves ceremonial mounds, cornfields, and other remnants of the powerful Mississippian Mound Building culture that thrived here between AD 900 and 1100.

A museum inside the 1930s Art Moderne Visitor Center along with trailside exhibits interpret the lifeways of the Mississippians. Children will enjoy going inside the 42ft (12.8-meter) diameter reconstructed earthlodge. With its thunderbird-shaped altar, firepit, and banquette seating, the semi-subterranean structure resembles the great kivas found at Chaco Canyon in New Mexico, one of the Mississippians' far-flung trading partners.

Whistle Stop Cafe

Taking US 23, which winds northward from Macon along the Ocmulgee River, affords an appealing taste of rural Georgia. Tiny **Juliette**, 20 miles (32km) along, was reinvigorated in the early 1990s, when its air of picturesque deep-woods dereliction made it the perfect location for the movie *Fried Green Tomatoes at the Whistle Stop Café*, based on Fannie Flagg's original novel. The actual **Whistle Stop Cafe** (tel: 478-992-8886; www.whistlestopcafe. com; daily), built for the film beside a still-used country railroad station, was almost destroyed by a flood in 1994.

The Italianate Revival Hay House, Macon.

It has definitely seen better days and the food has mixed reviews, but it still attracts tourists making a pilgrimage to eat the Southern specialty of tempura-style green tomatoes.

From Juliette, pick up State 83 east, then State 18, which winds all the way to the Georgia-Alabama border. The bucolic town of **Warm Springs ❸**, approximately an hour east of Juliette, is nestled amid the foothills of Pine Mountain. It grew to fame as a therapeutic center for polio sufferers in the 1920s, when then-New York Governor Franklin Roosevelt, who suffered from polio himself, began using the warm mineral springs to ease his symptoms. Roosevelt opened a hospital with therapeutic pools, now a private internationally recognized polio facility (the pools are not open to the public).

In 1932, the year before winning the presidency, Roosevelt built a six-room cottage at Warm Springs that served as a regular retreat, where he took the waters, formulated his New Deal policies, and eventually died on April 12, 1945. **Little White House State Park** (tel: 706-655-5870; www.gastateparks.org/

LittleWhiteHouse; daily) has a museum on FDR and makes a fascinating stop. This part of Georgia is worth savoring. Using Warm Springs or nearby Franklin D. Roosevelt State Park as a base, you can hike, camp, fish, horse-back ride, and rest up before entering Alabama, a short way to the west on I-85.

ATLANTA TO SOUTHWEST ALABAMA

Alabama and much of the land to its west passed through several hands before it was taken over by the United States in the late 18th century. Labyrinthine colonial struggles involving the Native American "Five Nations" (Cherokee, Seminole, Muscogee, Chickasaw, and Choctaw) mark Alabama's early history, and its coat of arms displays the emblems of the five non-native nations that successively held sovereignty over it: France, Great Britain, the United States, the Confederacy, and again the United States.

The last two of these regimes, of course, have left the clearest stamp on Alabama, named for the Alabama River, itself named after a Native

Labor Day crowds prepare to watch the laser show at Stone Mountain. On the side of the mountain is the Confederate Memorial Carving, depicting three heroes from the Civil War: President Jefferson Davis, General Robert E. Lee and General Thomas J. Jackson.

The earth lodge at Ocmulgee National Monument.

American tribe. Alabama rose to its economic apex during the cotton boom of the 19th century, and has been markedly reluctant to let go of the memory of its Confederate heyday. Only following bitter campaigns in the 1990s did the state capitol building in Montgomery finally cease to fly the Confederate flag. The state has seen better days, economically and socially, but its natural resources, hard-working citizenry, and enduring pride refuse to admit decline.

Although in principle the **Chatta-hoochee River** delineates the boundaries of Georgia and Alabama, in fact, at this point, you cross the Alabama state line a short way west of the river. Even then, you don't join the rest of Alabama on Central Time – one hour earlier – until you're beyond the Lanett Valley here.

Tuskegee and black education

After rolling through a forested area along I-85 westbound, you can turn off at Exit 38 to **Tuskegee ❹** via State 81 south and State 126 west. Tuskegee

Booker T. Washington statue 'Lifting the Veil of Ignorance', Tuskegee.

is the site of Booker T. Washington's **Tuskegee Normal and Industrial Institute**, which is one of the few institutions of higher learning for American blacks that existed during the 19th century.

In the words of the leading black intellectual, W.E.B. DuBois, Booker T. Washington was "the greatest man the South produced since the Civil War." Handsome, politically deft, and enormously inspired, Washington believed in cooperation with the ruling whites and in practical education to serve the needs of the black masses concentrated in the South. Washington's policy of avoiding confrontation made enemies among other educated blacks and "liberal whites," but he kept Tuskegee alive from 1881 to 1915.

While the institute remains very much active, much of its historic campus has been preserved with the aid of the National Park Service. Its centerpiece is the **Carver Museum** (tel: 334-727-3200; www.nps.gov/tuin; daily), named after the black agricultural chemist George Washington Carver, who worked and taught on campus from 1896 until his retirement to The Oaks in Tuskegee, where he died in 1943.

A former slave, Carver had abandoned artistic aspirations to forge the pioneer science of industrial agriculture. His discoveries saved the Southern economy from collapse after the boll weevil infestation of 1919 destroyed the cotton industry. Many of his "bulletins" are displayed in the museum; through such works as *How To Grow The Peanut and 105 Ways of Preparing It for Human Consumption*, a black man saved a region whose elite had oppressed and would continue to oppress his race. The museum also shows two 30-minute films about Carver and Washington that detail the history of the institution and of their struggles without shying away from the controversies that surround them.

Among Carver's interests were polio therapies, which brought him to the attention of Franklin Roosevelt. In

1939, Roosevelt visited Tuskegee, and shortly thereafter, Tuskegee became the pilot training base for the first all-African-American 99th Pursuit Squadron.

In 1998, neighboring Moton Field was redesignated **Tuskegee Airmen National Historic Site** (tel: 334-724-0922; www.nps.gov/tuai; daily) to celebrate the lives of these unsung heroes of World War II. Hangar No. 1 has an Orientation Room, where you can view a four-minute video on the Tuskegee Airmen, and a museum re-creates some of the sights and sounds of Moton Field during the 1940s, including two World War II–era aircraft. A visitor center has exhibits and five films on the airmen, as well as views of the airfield. An annual Tuskegee Airmen Fly-In is held here every Memorial Day weekend, featuring historic aircraft, aeronautical displays, and exhibits.

Montgomery

Back on I-85 south, travel 41 miles (66km) from Tuskegee to the boundary of **Montgomery** ❺. Alabama's capital city consists of a small, surprisingly quiet downtown area surrounded by wide outlying neighborhoods whose names smack of agricultural gentility. While the prairie muds are still rich, Montgomery bases its livelihood on government services, construction, and manufacturing. It also benefits from the patronage of the US Air Force, whose elite members are frequently assigned to **Maxwell Air Force Base** on the site of famed aviators Wilbur and Orville Wright's flight school.

The state government complex on Goat Hill has several extraordinary public buildings in the gleaming white antebellum style that simply take your breath away. The marble-columned **State Capitol** (tel: 334-242-3935; Mon–Sat) is one of the country's only state capitols designated a national historic landmark: the place where Confederate president Jefferson Davis took his oath of office.

Two grand structures stand across Washington Street from the Capitol: the **First White House of the Confederacy** (tel: 334-242-1861; www.firstwhitehouse.org; Mon–Sat) and the imposing **Alabama Department of Archives and History** building (tel: 334-242-4435; Mon–Sat; www.archives.alabama.gov; Mon–Sat). The White House, relocated from its original site at Bibb and Catoma streets, was the home of Confederate president Jefferson Davis during Montgomery's stint as first capital of the Confederate States of America. This rebel nation was comprised of the 13 states and territories that seceded from the United States in 1860 and 1861 over the issue of states' rights – among them the right to maintain slavery. Davis has been eclipsed in history by Confederate General Robert E. Lee, but in the South he is still revered as an emblem of distinction and self-determination,

This shack's climbing vine, known as kudzu, was brought from Asia and used by the government to stop soil erosion. It is now virtually unstoppable, smothering thousands of acres of land.

Civil Rights Memorial, Montgomery.

The Greek Orthodox Malbis Memorial Church.

Quiet spot on a Gulf coast beach.

as evidenced by the bumper sticker "Don't Blame Me – I Voted For Jefferson Davis."

The neoclassical Archives Building is a rich storehouse of Native American arts, Confederate history, and state development. It once housed a diverse collection of performing outfits belonging to hometown music legend Hank Williams, Sr. They, and Williams' baby-blue 1952 Cadillac, now take center stage at the enormously popular **Hank Williams Museum** (tel: 334-262-3600; www. thehankwilliamsmuseum.com; daily) on Commerce Street. Literature buffs won't want to miss the delightful **F. Scott and Zelda Fitzgerald Museum** (tel: 334-264-4222; www.fitzgeraldmuseum.net; Wed–Sun) where the author of *The Great Gatsby* and his wife lived after meeting in Montgomery during World War I.

Civil rights sites

Barely a hundred yards down from the Capitol is **Dexter Avenue King Memorial Baptist Church**, whose 26-year-old pastor, Rev. Martin Luther King, Jr, was thrust somewhat unwillingly into the limelight in December 1955, when he was invited to spearhead the civil rights campaign known as the Montgomery Bus Boycott after Montgomery resident Rosa Parks refused to give up her seat to a white man. A mural inside the church, "Montgomery to Memphis, 1955–1968," commemorates the long struggle for dignity and equality. Outside the Southern Poverty Law Center nearby, the powerful **Civil Rights Memorial** (tel: 334-956-8200; www.splcenter.org/civil-rights-memorial; Mon–Sat) designed by Maya Lin (who was also responsible for the celebrated Vietnam Veterans Memorial in Washington, DC), honors King and 40 other martyrs of the movement. A small but well-thought-out visitor center has a stirring audio-visual presentation and an interesting bookstore.

Backroads Alabama

Interstate 85 into Montgomery dovetails into I-65 and continues south

into the rural glades of southwestern Alabama. Along the way, the radio bands are striped with black contemporary music, pop, country, gospel, sermons, and jazz. The soil deepens again to red, where it had been sandy and gray in the "Black Belt" through the midsection of the state.

Deeper exploration of rural Alabama is definitely recommended, and US 31 is a good place to start. Branching away from the interstate near the cute little town of **Evergreen**, US 31 arcs through Escambia and Baldwin counties, grazing the northwesternmost edge of Florida near Atmore and Perdido. The land surrounding towns such as Castleberry – "Home of the Alabama Strawberry" – is dotted with small green ponds and spread with groves of pine and oak. Cattle graze on the muddy soil, and farmhouses call forth images of peaceful backwaters.

Before reaching **Atmore**, you pass through **Canoe** ❻, where you might see a horse and buggy along one side of the road as a 100-car-long freight train whistles by on the other. Atmore is weary-palmed, open-fielded, and railroad-tied, with churches signposted in all directions off the highway. Eight miles (13km) north of Atmore, you'll find the 2,340-member **Poarch Creek Indian Reservation**, the only reservation in Alabama and the only one whose members have never been forcibly moved from their original homeland. You can learn more about Poarch Creek history and culture at its large, eye-catching **Wind Creek Casino** (tel: 866-WIND-360; www.windcreekcasino.com) near the interstate, which has gambling, four restaurants, and a hotel.

Alabama wine

Continue on I-65 along a 13-mile (21km) stretch before the next exit (Exit 45) to **Perdido** ❼. Just south of the highway, the fruit of Jim and Marianne Eddins's gumption and perseverance continues to thrive: **Perdido Vineyards** (tel: 251-937-9463; www.perdidovineyards.net; Mon–Sat). Winemaking in Alabama, once a great domestic industry, was effectively killed by Prohibition. Even afterward, Baptist leaders maintained that drinking – let alone manufacturing – alcohol was next to ungodliness. The Eddins family dared the opposition and began their muscadine vineyard in 1971, marketing the grapes to a Florida winemaker. When that arrangement fell through, Perdido Vineyards began producing its own wine in 1979.

The muscadine varieties grown at Perdido – scuppernongs, higgins, nobles, and magnolias – are from a tough vine indigenous to the southeastern United States. Perdido's table wines, which may be sampled at the vineyard, are mostly sweet wines with a few drier varieties, including an extra-dry white that is reminiscent of some California wines. The Perdido venture met with initial hostility from the community, but its success and the subsequent attention it brought to

Pristine Alabama gulf shoreline.

TIP

Mobile, Alabama's historic Downtown features many architectural gems designed by Rudolph Benz in the early 1900s. A walking tour for the area around Dauphin Street includes a number of these buildings, many of which have filigree ironwork similar to that found in New Orleans' French Quarter.

Dauphin Street, downtown Mobile.

Baldwin County considerably warmed their reception.

Baldwin County is subject to a "pressure-cooker" climate, hot and prone to extremes of humidity. Nature has been hard on American farmers for centuries, but the environment was very attractive to a settlement of Greeks who came to the shores of Mobile Bay before World War II. Under the leadership of a Greek Orthodox priest named Malbis, the community established the lushest plantation in the county. When Malbis died in Nazi hands after he returned to Greece, the community carried out his plan to build an Orthodox Church in what is now the town of **Malbis**, between US 31 and I-10, 4 miles (6km) east of Mobile Bay. The church was constructed from materials imported from Greece and includes stunning tile work and stained glass.

MOBILE TO NEW ORLEANS

The coastline of the Gulf of Mexico, arcing from northwest Florida to southeast Texas, can well lay claim to the title of "the American Riviera"

– though less reverently, it's also known as "the Redneck Riviera." Not so much a Côte d'Azur as a Côte de Blanc, the Gulf Coast spreads its white sands beside warm waters stocked with fine shrimp, oysters, and other delicacies. While never quite rank ing as an international destination, the superb beaches of Gulf Coast Alabama, Mississippi, and Texas have attracted vacationers from the South and Midwest since the mid-19th century. Tourism, gambling, and fishing are the economic mainstays of the region, but they have been impinged upon by hurricanes and the growth of the oil industry, which often drills and explores within sight of the sunbathers. Whatever the ecological effects of oil retrieval may be, the petrochemical industry has been crucial to the survival of cities such as Mobile, Alabama.

Former French capital

Interstates 10 and 65 and US 90 (which pick up from US 31) all straddle the mouth of the Mobile River, as they cross westward from Baldwin County into the port of **Mobile** ➑

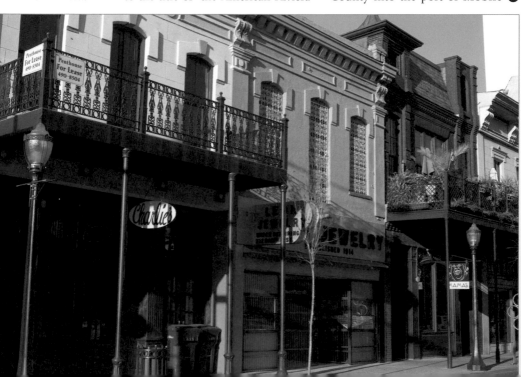

(pronounced "Mo-beel"). Mobile's locale on river and gulf has made it the most contested area in all of Alabama's twisted power struggles, and to this day it feels resolutely atypical of a state that outsiders regard as the most insular in the South. That sense of rich cosmopolitan diversity is hardly surprising; after all, Mobile began life in 1703 as the capital of the French colony of Louisiana, which covered a far larger, if not all that precisely defined, area than the modern state of the same name.

A pair of illuminated skyscraper spires make up a distinctive skyline, but Mobile's colonial past remains evident everywhere. Parallels with Louisiana in general, and New Orleans in particular, range from the intricate iron grillwork that adorns the city's balconies to the oysters and gumbo sold in its restaurants. Most striking of all is Mobile's Mardi Gras, which predates its more famous counterpart in New Orleans. Arrive the week before Lent, and you'll be dazzled by the parades and costumes, but throughout the year telltale strings of colored Mardi Gras beads festoon the live oaks and telephone wires in Downtown.

A stroll along downtown avenues such as lower **Government**, **Church**, and **Dauphin streets** is much the best way to get a flavor of Mobile. Pick up a historic walking tour brochure at the south end of Royal Street, at the city's Visitor Center, which is housed in a partial replica of the 1724 **Fort Condé** (tel: 251-208-7569; daily), whose cannons now point forlornly across a concrete underpass. Across the street, **Mobile Museum of History** (tel: 251-208-7569; www.museumofmobile. com; daily) is housed in an Italianate building and has good exhibits on local history. From there, a short walk will take you through stately historic districts that flourish with magnolia, azalea, and oak, all of which thrive in the semi-tropical climate. In a familiar pattern, serious commerce has fled to the outlying malls, and the old department stores have closed down. Downtown does, however, have a plethora of hip cafés, clubs, and restaurants, and a restored *grande dame* hotel – the 1852 Beaux Arts-style **Battle**

Crest of the Historic Development Commission in Mobile, Alabama.

Overlook Lake, Bellingrath Gardens.

TIP

The popular Blessing of the Shrimp Fleet takes place in early May in Bayou La Batre, a fishing town near Mobile, Alabama.

House (see page 417) – established on the site of Andrew Jackson's military headquarters during the War of 1812.

Semi-tropical jungle

Government Street becomes US 90 as it pulls away from Mobile Bay and widens into the usual mall-motel-and-fast-food sprawl. On reaching the town of **Theodore**, you'll spot a huge billboard directing you south on State 59 to **Bellingrath Gardens and Home** ❾ (tel: 251-973-2217; www.bellingrath.org; daily), "The Garden For all Seasons." All the hype – "Incomparable," "One of the World's Most Beautiful Year-Round Gardens" – turns out to be pretty much true. Originally a semi-tropical jungle serving as a fishing camp along the Fowl River, the land was purchased by Walter Bellingrath, who made his fortune as the first bottler of Coca-Cola in Alabama. Mr and Mrs Bellingrath landscaped 65 acres (26 hectares) of the 905-acre (367-hectare) plot, sculpting an evolving, living work of art to surround their magnificent riverfront home. Azaleas, roses, hibiscus,

Fat crabs from the warm waters of the Gulf.

chenille, chrysanthemums, poinsettias, lilies, violets, and dogwood are all part of the "rapturous floral beauty." The Oriental-American Garden, honking geese, flamingos, and teeming bayou will charm where the gift shop and restaurant depress; renting a taped tour is an unnecessary distraction. This attraction is out of the way. Allow half a day for a visit.

Gulf wildlife and art in Ocean Springs

US 90 is the "old highway" along the Gulf Coast from Florida to Louisiana. You'll have to decide for yourself whether the potted roads, frequent traffic lights, dreary trailer parks, and gritty fishing ports such as Grand Bay and Bayou La Batre close to Mobile merit taking the slow route the whole way, or whether you want to drive the more efficient and pleasantly grassy freeway some of the way and get off at US 90 communities that interest you.

If you're taking I-10, **Pascagoula** is your best bet to exit and pick up US 90 as it heads west through Biloxi and Gulfport. Just before reaching Biloxi,

you'll pass through the delightful beach town of **Ocean Springs**, a cultural mecca with the intimate feel of California's Carmel that seems almost out of place amid the working-class towns of the Gulf. The pretty, compact downtown – a haven for artists – offers unique boutiques, eateries, cafés, and art galleries, and makes a relaxing spot to linger over lunch or a cup of coffee.

If you only visit one small-town art museum on this whole Southern Route, make it Ocean Springs' super **Walter Anderson Museum of Art** (tel: 228-872-3164; www.walter andersonmuseum.org; daily). Local boy Anderson (1903–65), a classically trained artist who developed mental health problems, was a passionate recorder of the natural treasures along the Gulf Coast shoreline. His moving artwork combines an inner turmoil reminiscent of Van Gogh with the subtly colored but detailed natural forms found in Georgia O'Keeffe's artwork, all of it expressed in thousands of jewel-like watercolors of his beloved Mississippi Gulf Coast. A huge mural in the adjoining community center,

containing numerous spiritual references and natural motifs, was designated a National Treasure in 2005. Among the 900 works in the collection are ceramics by Walter's brothers Peter, founder of Shearwater Pottery, and James, a noted painter and ceramist.

At the east end of Ocean Springs, you'll find the Mississippi branch of **Gulf Islands National Seashore** (tel: 228-875-9057; www.nps.gov/guis; daily) – the other branch is in Florida. Its pleasant boardwalk trail offers glimpses of the Gulf and bayous that so entranced Anderson. The visitor center has exhibits and information. This is a good place for nature lovers hoping to view ospreys and other birds and to relax in an unspoiled setting.

Mailbox with tiny Confederate flag in the deep South.

Biloxi

Just across the bridge from Ocean Springs is **Biloxi** ❿ (pronounced locally: "bluxi"), the second base of operations for the French government of the Louisiana Territory, when

Hard Rock and Beau Rivage casinos in Biloxi.

TIP

Gulf Islands National Seashore offers a rare unspoiled look at the natural history of the gulf in charming Ocean Springs, an arts town near Biloxi, Mississippi. Ospreys nest near the Visitor Center and the boardwalk trail through the bayous and gulf shore.

Beauvoir Mansion, Biloxi.

it moved from Mobile. Founded in 1699 across the Biloxi Bay from its present location, the city sits on a peninsula cut by two bays and the Gulf of Mexico, which has created a popular beach. In the 1800s, Biloxi had a reputation as a posh winter resort, but its bayou-front stately homes are mostly gone now, largely due to a succession of severe storms that have made direct hits on Biloxi. Hurricane Camille wreaked severe damage in 1969, then, in 1998, Hurricane Georges caused further widespread destruction. Then in August 2005, Hurricane Katrina devastated the resort town, killing residents and uprooting homes and businesses.

More heartache for Gulf residents came with the April 2010 Deepwater Horizon explosion and oil spill, which in addition to killing workers on a Gulf oil platform operated by British Petroleum, polluted area beaches, killed birds and other wildlife, impacted tourism, and ruined the livelihoods of numerous Gulf residents. A major cleanup operation and strong advertising campaign promoting the Gulf's clean beaches (including a visit

from President Obama) went some way toward allaying tourism fears, but fisheries and small Gulf businesses are still counting the costs.

Biloxi's big gambling resorts have survived it all, demonstrating the strong corporate incentives at play here, as well as a fierce North-versus-South politics that saw Republican governors like Mississippi's Haley Barbour and Louisiana's Bobby Jindahl emphasizing recovery through private enterprise rather than long-delayed government handouts.

Today, Biloxi is roaring back to life. Along with gambling resort mainstays like the Hard Rock (see page 418) and Beau Rivage, a Jimmy Buffet Margaritaville Resort opened in May 2012 to much fanfare. Sweeter still is the November 2011 opening of the $38 million **Ohr-O'Keefe Museum** (tel: 228-374-5547; www.georgeohr.org; Tue–Sat;), a museum and cultural center designed by celebrated architect and artist Frank Gehry and dedicated to Biloxi's "mad potter" George Ohr.

Incidentally, state laws only allow for gambling on boats, not on land,

so the huge structures you see from the road are in fact just the hotel and restaurant segments of the operation, while the actual gaming takes place on "barges" situated behind. Once inside, however, you can't tell where building ends and barge begins.

Gulfport and Long Beach

Thankfully, Biloxi still holds one genuine historical attraction – though it, too, suffered enormous damage during Hurricane Katrina and only reopened in 2008. The white-columned 1852 oceanfront mansion of **Beauvoir** (tel: 228-388-4400; daily), the last home of Confederate president Jefferson Davis, serves as a showcase for his possessions, and also as a wide-ranging Confederate museum. Five of the seven buildings on the 51-acre (20-hectare) estate were destroyed by Katrina, and the lengthy process of restoration still continues. But Davis's enduring appeal for diehard Southerners is demonstrated daily by the huge outpouring of support for restoring the home and rebuilding its **Jefferson Davis Presidential Library** on the site of the old one. Guides here offer eyewitness accounts of Hurricane Katrina destruction and mince no words in expressing their feelings about the proud South and Beauvoir's historic importance. A visit here is truly an education for any outsider.

If it's beach fun you're after, continue along the coast on US 90, where the golden strands of **Gulfport** and **Long Beach** ⑪ are lined with kiosks that rent out jet skis, beach tractors with inflatable wheels or simply multicolored beach parasols. One final community, the intriguingly named **Pass Christian**, once harked back to more gracious days in Mississippi, with the Gulf on one side of US 90 and an avenue of live oaks whose branches intertwined above the highway to create a cool green tunnel. It was a popular retirement community until Hurricane Katrina destroyed

over 2,000 homes, permanently altering the town. Recovery here is still ongoing and, as with Gulfport and Long Beach, if you're looking for a non-chain hotel or restaurant, you're pretty much out of luck.

US 90 then curves sharply away from the coast and crosses the Bay of St Louis, where a bridge terminates in lovely **Bay St Louis**, "Gateway to the Gulf Coast." With little warning, the road forks: State 609 takes the northwestern way toward I-10 and a National Aeronautics and Space Administration (NASA) test site; US 90 slides southwestward. Both bring you shortly to Louisiana. Eight miles (13km) of bridges form I-10 from shore to shore – from St Tammany "Parish" (as counties are called in Louisiana) into Orleans Parish. As the car crosses on **Lake Pontchartrain Causeway**, you feel you're dipping and climbing through the water itself. Suddenly, wistful **New Orleans** ⑫ (see page 262) rises from the opposite shore of **Lake Pontchartrain** ⑬, a crescent of skyscrapers amid a green lake of oak.

(see page 262)

FACT

Pass Christian was named for a nearby deepwater pass commemorating Nicholas Christian L'Adnier who lived on nearby Cat Island in 1746.

Drawbridge on the Lake Pontchartrain Causeway, gateway to New Orleans.

New Orleans: The Big Easy

Anchor of the Gulf Coast, cradle of
jazz, home of exotic food – this is
without doubt the most fascinating
city in the South.

Curling around a mighty bend in the Mississippi,
New Orleans (Noo-*Orlens*) is known as the
"Crescent City" – the home of jazz, blues, and complex Creole food, blending French, Latin, and
Caribbean influences. Since 1857, it has also been
synonymous with Mardi Gras, whose private balls,
flamboyant float parades, masks, and glittering
costume jewelry capture the towering gothic spirit
of this unique American city.

Not even the devastating Category 5 Hurricane
Katrina, which narrowly missed hitting New Orleans
in August 2005, stopped Carnival the following
year. But it came close. The levees that protect New
Orleans from the surrounding watery domain failed
in more than 50 places during the subsequent
storm surge, flooding 80 percent of the city for
weeks. Remarkably, the Vieux Carre, or **French**

St Louis Cathedral.

Quarter, and other historic areas along the river,
the high ground on which the French government
had wisely built the original walled city in the
1700s, were spared.

Several Katrina Disaster Tours, guided by locals
who witnessed the storm first-hand, escort visitors
to view the damage at levees along the canals and
slow rebuilding efforts in neighborhoods that one
lakeside resident describes as being like Beirut.
Many of the 1,836 fatalities were in the Ninth Ward,
the poorest part of the city, where residents
couldn't afford to leave. Thousands of displaced
residents remain in FEMA trailers; many more have
left for good, radically reducing the population. If
you are interested in volunteering while here, visit
www.volunteerlouisiana.gov.

In the French Quarter, between Canal Street and
Esplanade, though, it's business as usual – an
eerie contrast with outlying neighborhoods. The
heart of the French Quarter is **Jackson Square**,
fronted by **St Louis Cathedral** (1794). The sidewalks here are the domain of street musicians,
portrait artists, and fortune tellers – not to mention the "Lucky Dog" hot-dog sellers, their carts
shaped like garish giant sausages, immortalized in
John Kennedy Toole's comic masterpiece *A
Confederacy of Dunces*. To either side are the red-
brick **Pontalba Buildings** (1849), the oldest apartment buildings in the US. The **Cabildo** and
Presbytere (tel: 504-568-6968; daily), two excellent state museums, flank the cathedral itself,
housed in cupola-topped Colonial structures.
Among their treasures are Napoleon's death mask
and the room in which the 1803 Louisiana
Purchase was signed.

The main drag (in every sense) is Bourbon Street,
a pedestrian circus at all hours. In contrast to
Bourbon, one block toward the river, parallel Royal
Street hosts an array of classy galleries and antique
shops as well as formal restaurants such as
Brennan's – legendary for its breakfasts – and the
Court of Two Sisters, whose shaded courtyard is a
perfect jazz brunch spot, (both restaurants on page
444).

Along **Decatur Street**, the riverfront thoroughfare, tourist dollars are mined enthusiastically at
souvenir shops and restaurants and the mall-ified
French Market and **Jackson Brewery**. It's all
accompanied by the deafening blare of tunes
played on the whistle of the **Steamboat *Natchez***,
which offers daily sightseeing cruises on the
Mississippi. For an appealing half-mile or so, the
aptly named "Big Muddy" is lined first by a wooden

boardwalk known as the "Moonwalk," then by grassy parks, one of which contains the well-stocked Aquarium of the Americas (tel: 800-774-7394; Tue–Sun). A small free ferry crisscrosses the river to the island of **Algiers**, an interesting vantage point on the city.

Lafitte's Blacksmith Shop at 941 Bourbon Street, the tumbledown brick smithy where the pirate Lafitte plotted many a high-seas escapade, is an atmospheric if almost impenetrably gloomy bar that makes an appropriate starting point for nightly walking tours of "Haunted New Orleans," while the stately Napoleon House at 500 Chartres Street, allegedly the focus of a scheme to rescue the exiled emperor from St Helena and bring him to the United States, is another ravishingly Stygian bar with its own courtyard café.

All along Bourbon Street, talented house bands entertain diners at cafés and restaurants. The spot for traditional jazz is Preservation Hall (tel: 504-522-2841; www.preservationhall.com), a tiny, dilapidated hall on St Peter Street whose appearance belies the famous musicians who nightly toot their horns here. At legendary clubs like Tipitina's (tel: 504-566-7095), featured in Jim Jarmusch's movie *Down by Law*, you'll see local bands like the Radiators tearing up the dance floor.

Best with spicy gumbo, jambalaya, and crawfish étouffée is ice-cold Abita beer, Louisiana's own brew. The definitive local liquor drinks are Sazerac and Ramos Gin Fizz; a rum-based Hurricane at Pat O'Brien's; or a cooling Pimm's Cup at the Napoleon House. New Orleans is famous for its chicory coffee. It is traditional to enjoy creamy café au lait with beignets – donuts drowned in powdered sugar – at the 24-hour sidewalk **Café du Monde** in the French Market, a great people-watching spot.

West of the Vieux Carré, the **Warehouse District** is New Orleans' up-and-coming arts district. Among its boutique hotels and contemporary restaurants like Cochon (see page 444), whose Cajun Southern pork dishes celebrate everything but the squeal, you will find art galleries and the **Louisiana Children's Museum** (tel: 504-523-1357; www.lcm.org; May–Sept daily, Oct–Apr Tue–Sun), and the **National World War II Museum** (tel: 504-527-6012; www.ddaymuseum.org; daily). Beyond the Central Business District, the home of the **Louisiana Superdome** – a good trip to take by tram – is the lush and wealthy **Garden District**, where antebellum houses stand amid the azalea and dogwood, and baroque oak trees shade marvelous structures built in Greek Revival, Renaissance, and Victorian styles.

Bourbon Street, at the heart of the French Quarter.

Cajun musician.

NEW ORLEANS TO SAN ANTONIO

Cruise across what is claimed to be "the longest
bridge in the world," take an alligator-enhanced trip
through Cajun Country and end up in Cowboy Country.

This route from New Orleans to
the Texas border takes in, first,
Cajun Country and then the
state's capital. Leaving the city and
driving north, Lake Pontchartrain
is spanned by **Lake Pontchartrain
Causeway**, "the world's longest
bridge." The causeway is a 24-mile
(39km) double stripe of highway
propped above the surface of the lake.
For miles, nothing can be seen on the
horizon, and the camelback plunge
into the void is akin to crossing the
barren yet subtle plains of Texas.

On the trip north over the causeway to **Mandeville**, land initially
appears as a thin blue sliver on the
horizon, an airy gray-blue strip melting off the murky waters into the
sky. Gradually, it becomes more distinct, broader and deeper in color,
until it becomes the interface of
two great azure bodies: sea and
sky. If you choose to cross the Lake
Pontchartrain Causeway, it might be
best to do it when leaving the city.

A round-trip across the lake may be
a little overwhelming, and concentration can falter on the second stretch.
When the Causeway touches land in
Mandeville, it becomes US 190. Four
miles (6km) north of the lakeshore,
it interchanges with I-12, which runs
61 miles (98km) west to the capital of
Louisiana – Baton Rouge.

*ffic jam on Lake Pontchartrain
seway.*

Acadian bayous

Alternatively, follow the efficient but
gritty I-10 out of New Orleans and
cut through the boggy, baroque bayou
country on the southwest bank of Lake
Pontchartrain in St Charles and St
John the Baptist parishes. The highway
is stilted out of grass-fringed still water,
where the thin trunks that disappear
into the mire mimic the somber poles
that support the parallel powerlines.

Bayous – narrow, sluggish rivers
surrounded by wetlands – run in
veins throughout southern Louisiana,

Main Attractions
Lake Pontchartrain Causeway
New Louisiana State Capitol
Atchafalaya Swamp
Breaux Bridge
Jean Lafitte Scenic Byway
St Martinville
Port Bolivar Ferry
Bishop's Palace
Texas State Capitol
Lyndon B. Johnson State Park
Luckenbach

otherwise known as Acadiana. This expansive region is named after the Acadians, French Catholic refugees driven out of Nova Scotia by the British in the mid-18th century. Settling the Louisiana lowlands, mostly Spanish dominions, they were joined by Frenchmen fleeing the Revolution, and created a culture known as "Cajun" (a corruption of "Acadian").

Acadiana, stretching along the Gulf Coast to Texas and west from the Mississippi River up to Avoyelles Parish, has been described as "South of the South," although in many ways it's more conspicuously akin to the societies of the French and Spanish West Indies than to the traditional American South.

Baton Rouge

Interstate 10 meets the Mississippi River at the city of **Baton Rouge** ⓮, capital of Louisiana and the state's major port. Its French name means "red stick," apparently the "stick" being a tree, red either from the blood of animals hung there by Indians or from the stripping of its bark. In the latter case, the tree may have been used to mark the boundary of Houma and Bayou Goula Indian land. Although Baton Rouge abuts Acadiana, it has little to do with it, except for governing it and shipping its oil. The ambiance is definitely "Southern," and you'll notice, in comparison to New Orleans, a deepening of accent and of provincial ways. The rather quiet, laid-back tempo of the streets belies the intense industry and politicking at the city's heart.

The principal sights of Baton Rouge are the old and new trappings of government. The **Old State Capitol** (tel: 225-342-0500; www.louisianaoldstate capitol.org; daily free tours) was a Gothic folly constructed beside the Mississippi in 1849 that was derided by all, including writer Mark Twain. In contrast, the 34-story Art Deco **New Capitol** (tel: 225-342-7317; www.brgov.com; daily free tours), a national historic landmark, bestrides the north end of town like a scaled-down Empire State Building. The skyscraper was built in 1932 by Louisiana's infamous governor Huey Long, the so-called "Kingfish," who reigned supreme throughout the Great

Old State Capitol, Baton Rouge.

Depression. By all accounts a distasteful and corrupt man, Long was nevertheless an enlightened despot who brooked no opposition to his semi-socialistic rule for the "common man." Highways, schools, and hospitals were built; the unemployed put to work; the privileged heavily taxed. He was gunned down in the capitol in 1935 – a plaque on the exact spot admits that he may have been killed by his own bodyguards as they panicked in the face of a supposed assassin who never fired a shot. He is buried in the adjacent garden, alongside a larger-than-life statue.

The twin foundations of the city's wealth appear as you leave. From the huge **Baton Rouge Bridge**, on which I-10 crosses the river, you can see belching petrochemical refineries stretching into the distance. Down below stands Baton Rouge's port, the fourth most active in the nation thanks to being the farthest inland of all deep-water ports serving the Gulf of Mexico. That status was not achieved by chance; one of Long's most brilliant ploys to boost his own state was to build this very bridge too low for ocean-going vessels to continue any farther upstream.

West of the Mississippi, you re-enter Acadiana in West Baton Rouge Parish, and soon pass beyond into Iberville Parish. For the first time in this trip – but not the last, as you head toward the open spaces of the West – you're treated to spectacular scenery without having to leave the interstate. Here, it becomes the **Atchafalaya Swamp Freeway**, crossing America's largest swamp, dividing into two separate highways, supported on precarious concrete stilts and separated by an expanse of soupy open water that holds lozenge-shaped islets.

Drowned forests in the Bayou

To either side, the landscape is a magical melding of water and drowned forest, punctuated by clumps of trees, telegraph poles, and strangely shaped cypress "knees" (those parts of the root systems of cypress trees that poke out of the morass). Locals fish sedately, or even race speedboats, just below the highway, and every unidentified

'Gator in a glade, Atchafalaya.

TIP

The Cajun language includes many French words: *cher* dear one, *boudin* sausage, *lagniappe* something extra, *beignet* square donut found in New Orleans, *gris-gris* good luck charm or spell, *laissez les bon temps rouler!* let the good times roll!

piece of flotsam may potentially be an alligator. On the far side of the 20-mile (32km) -wide swamp, you find yourself safely back on terra firma. Louisiana-born residents draw a distinction between the Prairie Cajuns, who farm the soil of south-central Louisiana, and the Bayou Cajuns, the "half-man, half-gator" shrimp-fishing river-dwellers of the marshlands closer to the Gulf. In terms of what the rest of the world thinks of as being Cajun culture – the accordion- and fiddle-based Cajun music and spicy food – the two are not far apart.

Lafayette ⓯ 50 miles (80km) west of Baton Rouge, is the largest city in Acadiana, and, standing close to the hypothetical line that divides the prairies from the bayous, makes an ideal hub for exploring the region. It's a sprawling city, but, in addition to a number of excellent restaurant-cum-music-clubs, such as **Prejean's** and **Randol's**, it also holds a couple of entertainingly informative "living museums." The best, Vermilionville (tel: 337-233-4077; www.bayouvermilion. org; Tues–Sun), consists of an idealized

An Acadian accordion, handcrafted in Eunice.

village of 16 restored and transplanted 19th-century buildings where experts demonstrate traditional Cajun crafts.

Land of the Cajuns

The Texas border is barely 100 miles (160km) west of Lafayette, but the temptation to explore Cajun country will prove irresistible, as this is one of the most fascinating and culturally rich areas on the whole route. A short excursion north, for example, leads to the welcoming real-life prairie town of **Eunice**, and to **Opelousas**, home of Cajun music's blacker, bluesier counterpart – zydeco.

If it's a perfect taste of Acadiana you want, plan ahead and leave I-10 at exit 109 before you get to Lafayette to visit the delightful town of **Breaux Bridge**, which calls itself the Crawfish Capital of the World and has an almost English feel to it, with its tiny bridge, main street cafés, and antique shops. If you're here on a Saturday morning, don't miss the lively zydeco music and Cajun brunch at the famed restaurant/gallery **Café Des Amis** (tel: 337-332-5273; www.cafedesamis.com;

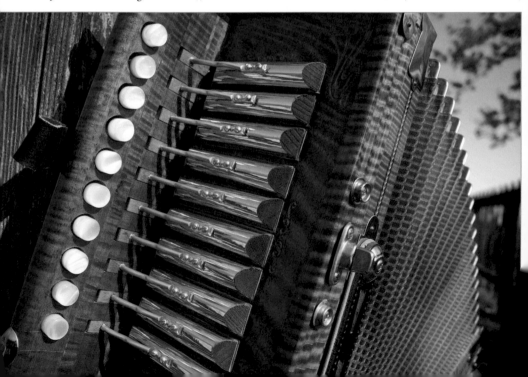

daily). Around the corner, on Main Street (State 31), at the **Coffee Break** café (tel: 337-442-6607; daily), there's a freewheeling Cajun jam session that attracts musicians young and old, a great place to pass the time as you load up on java for the drive ahead.

Driving the Jean Lafitte Scenic Byway

More ambitious travelers can continue on a long detour south to pick up State 82 to parallel the more interesting coast along the **Jean Lafitte Scenic Byway**. From Breaux Bridge, State 31 follows Bayou Teche another 11 miles (18km) south to **St Martinville** ⓰, one of the most unspoiled towns you will find in your travels in America. A former indigo plantation and Spanish holding, it was populated by Acadians and Frenchmen in the late 18th and 19th centuries, an era when its culture was so rich that its inhabitants nicknamed it "Petit Paris." After its transformation to a minor port on the bayou, St Martinville settled into its current form of small agrarian center, with visible Cajun and French roots.

Locals are glad to recite half-remembered and half-invented histories in small cafés, which might serve Coca-Cola and catfish *étouffée*. The town is infused with the legend of Evangeline (subject of a well-known Henry Wadsworth Longfellow poem), who allegedly walked from Nova Scotia to St Martinville in search of her lover.

The venerable **Evangeline Oak** next to the **St Martin de Tours** church (1765), where she arrived only to receive the news that her faithless sweetheart had married another, is now a riverside beauty spot where Cajun couples hold their wedding services, while the **Longfellow-Evangeline State Commemorative Area** preserves Acadian history in the interesting Acadian House Museum.

South of St Martinville, State 675 and then State 14 will take you west into Vermilion Parish and the attractive parish seat, **Abbeville** ⓱. Home to the Giant Omelette Celebration (www.giantomelette.org) in November, Abbeville consists of three interlocking and very sleepy squares, as well as a couple of oyster restaurants.

St Martin de Tours Catholic church.

Spanish moss is found draped over live oak trees. It is not really Spanish nor is it really moss; it is an air plant and a member of the pineapple family.

Cruising a bayou in a traditional Louisiana wooden boat.

Grazing cattle indicate solid ground, but the next field along may be a waterlogged rice paddy through which cranes and herons meticulously pick their long-legged way. Locals fish in the channels that run alongside the roadway, or wade through with shrimping nets.

The farther you go, the fewer signs of human life there are along this bleak and windswept drive, but the birds are a constant source of delight. The trees are bent at ever more acute angles as you approach the Gulf, and in places it feels as though you're having to force yourself through the thick tangles of Spanish moss that hang from overhead. This wispy, gray, romantic shroud is not a parasite but an epiphyte, an air plant, which draws no sustenance from its host, and is therefore equally at home dangling from telephone wires. Turn on the radio for company, and you'll find French- and English-language stations in equal measure, together with Spanish baseball commentaries from Houston as you come within earshot of that city.

Marsh trail

Seventy-two miles (116km) from Abbeville, highway signs announce that you're arriving in **Grand Chenier**, but apart from a few trailer parks and a Catholic church surrounded by praying statues, no recognizable town ever appears. Another 30 miles (48km) on, beyond a straggle of run-down motels and rudimentary restaurants catering to workers in the occasionally glimpsed oil refineries, the highway is interrupted by an on-demand platform ferry that shuttles a dozen vehicles at a time across the outlet of **Lake Calcasieu**. On the far side, the open ocean lies barely 50 yards (46 meters) off to your right, and mighty drilling rigs are visible far out to sea. It is said that early Spanish explorers would beach their vessels here to caulk their hulls with the mysterious black substance found oozing on the beaches –a boon for Louisiana, perhaps, but, especially after the BP oil spill in 2012, no incentive for a quick dip at **Holly Beach**. In any case, it's time to turn your wheel back inland. The coastal road ahead has been closed by

one Gulf storm too many, and to reach Texas you'll have to head 35 miles (56km) north to rejoin the interstate.

One final highlight remains, however, in the shape of the **Sabine National Wildlife Refuge** ⓲ (tel: 337-762-3816; www.fws.gov/refuges; daily), 9 miles (15km) up State 27. Exhibits in the Visitor Center and along the Wetland Walkway are a major draw. The trail starts beside the **Intracoastal Waterway** – a mind-boggling canal that spans almost the entire length of the state. The best times of year to see alligators sunning themselves along the Wetland Walkway are spring and fall.

EAST TEXAS TO SAN ANTONIO

Everyone has at least one picture of Texas. Tumbleweeds and cacti, oilfields, cowboy millionaires, humming border towns, cattle ranches: popular culture has disseminated a rugged, romantic vision of the largest of the Lower 48 states. Such familiar cultural snapshots, however, both over- and underestimate the sprawling diversity and vitality of Texas. This *is* where the West begins, but it's a West with no coherent definition. At the risk of oversimplifying, think of a passage through Texas as a microcosmic passage from East to West, with the point of transition coming at San Antonio, the westernmost of the state's major cities.

Within the compact urban triangle of Houston, Dallas–Fort Worth, and San Antonio is centered Texas's vast wealth and power. From Galveston through Houston to Austin, the Southern tour arcs through the heart of East Texas – its resort, its port, and the state capital. Wherever you go, note the change in the triangular yellow signs that elsewhere in the South advise motorists to "Drive Safely." Here, they read: "Drive Friendly." The name "Texas," after all, is derived from "Tejas," meaning "friendly" – the name given by the Spanish to the Native Americans they encountered.

Port Bolivar ferry

From the moment you enter Texas on I-10 from Louisiana, highway signs start to count down the mileage to New Mexico. Shortly after

FACT

Hurricane Ike in 2008 was the third costliest storm in US history, after Hurricanes Andrew and Katrina, doing $28.26 billion of damage in the US alone.

The "drowned forests" of Louisiana's bayous.

TIP

Bolivar Peninsula and nearby Galveston Island were hit hard by flooding during Hurricane Ike, which took lives, destroyed buildings, left behind mountains of debris, and closed businesses and attractions. Crystal Beach next to the Bolivar Ferry is rebuilding and is attracting vacation renters again, and many of the attractions on Galveston Island have since reopened. For more information and ferry status, check the Crystal Beach website (www.crystalbeach.com) and Galveston Convention and Visitors Bureau website.

Flock of pelicans over wooden beach houses in Galveston.

the state line, Exit 877 branches off to the town of Orange, and the first sign you will see for El Paso shows it as an incomprehensible 857 miles (1,379km) distant. You'll feel ready to leave this nondescript stretch of highway long before the first city of any size – Houston, 110 miles (177km) – and you're well advised to return to the Gulf coast as soon as possible and head for the historic island resort community of **Galveston** .

By far the most enjoyable way of reaching Galveston is to take the free 20-minute Port Bolivar ferry across Galveston Bay. As you approach Exit 829, look for the billboard that lets drivers know it's in operation, and if so, take the scenic island route rather than the straight-shot I-45 south from Houston by picking up State Route 124 South to the ocean at Winnie.

As you cross first Spindletop Bayou and then Elm Bayou, little about this marshy landscape suggests you've left Louisiana. Rice and even crawfish farms stand on either side of the highway, while indefatigable little oil pumps diligently bob

away, atop mounds of scrubby gulf vegetation. About 20 miles (32km) south, a humpback bridge crosses the Intracoastal Waterway at **High Island**. High Island's unique salt-dome geography allows trees to grow that serve as stopovers for thousands of neotropical migratory birds during spring migrations. In fact, this tiny hamlet is a birding hotspot, with no less than four bird sanctuaries run by Texas Audubon.

State 87 runs the 27-mile (43km) length of Bolivar Peninsula to dead-end at the ferry terminal for Galveston. This once was a wild barrier island, a boon for those with a taste for nature in the rough. Sparsely inhabited on its eastern end and growing rapidly into a high-end resort community on its west end – by 2008, Bolivar Peninsula had a permanent population of 3,800 residents and attracted thousands of local vacationers.

All that ended abruptly in September 2008, when Hurricane Ike, a category 2 storm with winds up to 110mph (178kph), made a direct hit on East Galveston, creating a massive storm surge that inundated the Bolivar Peninsula. The destruction on Bolivar was almost total, flattening homes and businesses and blowing debris into Galveston Bay. The historic Bolivar lighthouse, which survived the Great Storm of 1900, was destroyed. The peninsula remains a hushed, haunting, Hiroshima-like landscape covered in sand and debris. Cleanup is continuing, and residents of Crystal Beach – many of whom rode out the storm against advice from officials – are rebuilding and determined to stay. Nearly one-third of the 3,000 houses that were destroyed on the peninsula have been or are being rebuilt, and the vacation rental market is thriving once again.

Galveston's pirates and beaches

Galveston grew to prominence during the early 1800s as a seaport a headquarters for the pirate Lafitte, of New Orleans fame. I local economic boom that followed the Civil War, it flowered into a fully fledged city, becoming Texas' leading manufacturing center and, by 1899, the largest cotton port in the world. Galveston had the first telephone system in Texas, the first newspaper, electric lights, golf course, brewery, and Ford dealership, while the Strand (named for the street in London), thanks to its profusion of great commercial houses, was renowned as "The Wall Street of the Southwest."

Houston's port has entirely overshadowed the island's, but Galveston remains an active shipping center and is heavily involved with the vacation industry. Of its 32 miles (51km) of beach, the most popular stretch lies on the Gulf side of the island, along Seawall Boulevard. This broad thoroughfare is lined on its inland side by numerous sprawling motels and fast-food restaurants, while the beach itself is interrupted by a succession of privately owned piers that jut out into the ocean.

There's lots of family-style entertainment in Galveston. In Downtown, you'll find **Texas Seaport Museum** (tel: 409-763-1877; www.tsm-elissa.org; daily), featuring the **tall ship *Elissa***. **Ocean Star Offshore Drilling Rig and Museum** (tel: 409-766-7827; www.oceanstaroec.com; daily) has a unique working replica of an offshore oil rig. **Galveston Railroad Museum** (tel: 409-765-5700; www.galvestonrrmuseum.com; daily), at the foot of the Strand, is located in a looming early 20th-century skyscraper, the former home of American National Insurance Company founded by wealthy Galvestonian William Moody Jr.

Moody's name is associated with several places on the island. On Broadway, the 1895 **Moody Mansion** (tel: 409-762-7668; www.moodymansion.org; daily), built in a Romanesque style, was the family home for 50 years. While over on the island's quieter northwest side, a family bequest created the sprawling **Moody Gardens** (tel: 800-582-4673; www.moodygardens.com; daily), a

The tall ship 'Elissa', built in 1877 by Alexander Hall & Co. in Aberdeen, Scotland, is now part of the Texas Seaport Museum in Galveston.

Dolphin statue on Galveston's seawall.

Houston: Space-Age City

Once an oil town, Houston now houses a wide range of high-tech industries and quintessentially Texan self-confidence.

Houston, the nation's fourth largest city, boasts that the first word uttered by the first man on the moon was – you guessed it – "Houston." Mission Control Center is the city's prime tourist attraction. **Space Center Houston** (tel: 281-244-2100; www. spacecenter.org; daily), the official Visitors Center for **Johnson Space Center**, is located on NASA Road 1, off I-45, about 25 miles (40km) south of Houston. A guided tram tour takes visitors through a campus of structures containing moon rocks and astronauts, into the Mission Control Center and full-scale replicas of the Space Shuttle used for training. Named for the Sea of Tranquility, the base for the 1969 *Apollo* moonshot, Tranquility Park, in downtown Houston at Bagby and Walker streets, is landscaped to look like Tranquility Base, with craters and mounds, fountains, reflecting pools, and copper tubes representing rockets taking off.

View of Houston's skyline from a trail in City Park.

More deserving of the name "Tranquility" is the hushed art temple of **Rothko Chapel** (tel: 713-524-9839; www.rothkochapel.org; daily), located on Sul Ross in the Museum District. American abstract expressionist Mark Rothko was commissioned by collectors Dominique and John de Menil to create 14 of his oversized trademark colorwash paintings for this chapel for nondenominational worship and meditation. More of the de Menil couple's extensive art collection can be viewed at the gorgeous **Menil Collection** (tel: 713-525-9400; www.menil. org; Wed–Sun), which houses arts and artifacts of mankind from the earliest days to the present.

The galleries of Houston demonstrate how "black gold" has enriched the state of Texas through the purchase of works of art. The Matisse bronzes that turn their backs to you at the **Museum of Fine Arts Houston** (tel: 713-639-7300; www. mfah.org; Tue–Sun) at Main and Bissonet streets make their case about Houston's attitude toward the norm. The MFAH's collection is particularly strong in American paintings. Across the street is the **Contemporary Arts Museum Houston** (tel: 713-284-8250; www.camh.org; Tue–Sun), dedicated to contemporary works. At Hermann Park is the **Museum of Natural Science** (tel: 713-639-4629; www.hmns.org; daily), with a walk-through greenhouse aflutter with butterflies, a giant-screen theater, and a planetarium. George Observatory, a satellite facility of the Museum of Natural Science is located in Brazos Bend State Park, approximately an hour's drive south of Downtown.

An emblem of Houston's appreciation for size is the unbelievable **Astrodomain**, comprising the Astrodome stadium (one of the various structures labeled the "Eighth Wonder of the World"); Astroworld (a 100-ride amusement park); and Astrohall (the world's largest one-level convention facility). The discount booklet CityPass includes entry to five major Houston attractions. For more information, log on to www.visithoustontexas.com.

Johnson Space Center on NASA Parkway.

242-acre (98-hectare) educational complex used heavily by Texas schools. It has three themed glass pyramids containing a Rainforest, an Aquarium, and a Museum/IMAX theater; landscaped waterfront gardens; and a huge hotel/convention complex.

East End architecture and food

The historic Strand has undergone a familiar renovation into tourist attraction, arguably losing its soul in the process, but the East End Historical District, bounded roughly by Broadway, Mechanic, 19th and 11th streets, remains unspoiled. Here, Victorian homes stand, intermixed with buildings that betray neoclassical, Renaissance, and Italianate influences. Bungalows rest in the shade cast by oleanders, oaks, maples, and palms, and are slightly raised from the ground out of respect for the gulf. Post Office and Church streets are particularly lovely. Several of the town's best contemporary eateries are located on 14th Street. On the corner of Broadway and 14th is **Bishop's**

Palace (tel: 409-762-2475; www.galvestonhistory.org/1892_Bishops_Palace.asp; daily), a turreted Gothic fantasy rated as one of the top historic buildings in the US by the American Institute of Architects. It was built for the wealthy Gresham family in 1886 by famed Galveston architect Nicholas Clayton.

Galveston is 50 miles (80km) south of Houston, but the buildup to the megalopolis begins as soon as you cross back to the mainland on the I-45 Causeway, to be confronted by massed ranks of smoke-belching oil refineries.

From there on, strip malls and garish billboards line the interstate for the full 27 miles (43km) up to the Sam Houston Tollway, which circles the entire city at a distance of around 20 miles (32km). As you pass beneath its stacked and spiraling freeways and connecting concrete loops, the futuristic downtown skyline of **Houston** ⓴ (see page 274) finally rises on the northern horizon.

Well-sheltered Austin

If you see Texas as a microcosm of the whole country, then it's as you head

Shrimp boats in Galveston's dock.

EAT

Austin's premier barbecue restaurant is the family-run Salt Lick (tel: 512-858-4959; www.saltlickbbq.com; daily), famous for smoked pork ribs, sausage, and brisket from family recipes.

Bank of America Plaza and Renaissance Tower, Dallas.

west of Houston that you leave the South behind and enter the Great Plains. The state capital, **Austin** ㉑, is approximately 150 miles (240km) west, but as I-10 runs directly to San Antonio instead, along a slightly more southerly route, reaching Austin entails at least 40 miles (64km) of driving off the interstate. Whichever route you choose will be much the same, a relaxing cruise through the lush plains and gently rolling hills of the German- and Czech-influenced "ranch country" that lies within the Houston–Dallas–San Antonio triangle. Probably the most bucolic option is to leave I-10 at exit 696, near little Columbus, and join State 71 as it meanders back and forth across the equally sinuous Colorado River (not the one that carved the Grand Canyon) all the way up to Austin.

Austin itself nestles amid verdant woodland in the middle of an agricultural paradise that's unique among the many Texan climates and terrains. Sheltered from the humid heat that sweeps in waves over Houston, this locale is ideal for ranching and recreation. Unlike Houston, and despite having experienced similarly phenomenal growth, Austin is fairly well contained. Exit between Martin Luther King, Jr Boulevard and 83rd streets from I-35, and you'll be in the middle of a walkable downtown. For most visitors, the experience of the city is confined to the area from First Street and the Colorado River up to 24th Street and the heart of the **University of Texas** (UT) at Austin along Guadalupe Avenue.

High tech and outlaws

Austin manages the difficult double act of being not only Texas's political capital but also its true cultural capital. Having attained that distinction during the 1960s, when it was a hippie mecca, it went on to spearhead the "outlaw country" movement of the 1970s, when country singers like Willie Nelson, Waylon Jennings, and Jerry Jeff Walker first came to prominence. Its reputation as a center for live music and the arts no doubt contributed to its 1980s growth as "the Silicon Valley of Texas," when more and more high-tech and financial firms relocated here.

DETOUR TO DALLAS

A 195-mile (314km) drive along I-35 from Austin leads to Dallas, which, with 1.2 million residents, attracts visitors with its sky-high architecture, quality art collections, and high-end shopping malls. The city grew up around a cabin built by trapper John Neely Bryan beside the Trinity River, which Bryan believed to be navigable for trade all the way to the Gulf of Mexico. It wasn't, but the Houston and Texas Railroad soon brought people and commerce. The pioneer era comes alive at Dallas Heritage Village (tel: 214-421-5141; Tue–Sun; www.dallasheritagevillage.com), which preserves 38 historic structures in a living history museum. Extravagance rules at the flagship Neiman Marcus department store, whose Christmas catalog once contained a page entitled "How to Spend a Million Dollars." But that extravagance has also led to wonderful art collections, such as the Meadows Museum on the Southern Methodist University campus (tel: 214-768-2516; www.smu.edu/meadowsmuseum; daily), home to the largest collection of Spanish art outside Spain. Darker history plagues Dallas. Its most visited site is the former Texas School Book Depository, where Lee Harvey Oswald shot President John F. Kennedy in 1963. The Sixth Floor Museum overlooks Dealey Plaza, where the president was assassinated. Dallas Convention and Visitors Bureau (tel: 214-571-1000; www.visitdallas.com).

That process, of course, brought with it an influx of young urban professionals, and one need look no farther than **Sixth Street** to see the impact of aggressive consumerism on the culture. Experiencing the same gentrification as San Francisco's Haight Street, formerly gay-dominated Sixth Street is still a good place to bar-hop, but not nearly as much of a community as it used to be. Construction, moreover, has become a constant in Downtown – so much so that locals joke that Austin's native bird is the "crane."

Despite its changing face, Austin retains much of its laid-back, tolerant spirit. At the University of Texas – with over 50,000 students, the largest university campus in the state – the counter-cultural element will always have its place. At heart, it's still got long hair and a beard, though it might also have a Mercedes, a top-of-the-line road bike, and a kid. Hardly surprising, then, that Austin is home base for **Whole Foods Market**, the natural foods giant whose luxurious headquarters in Downtown has become a tourist destination in itself.

Austin is the Live Music Capital of the US. Some 200 venues offer everything from hard-edged country, "new music," ska, classical, and blues to R&B and jazz, and Downtown is host to the popular South-by-Southwest (SXSW) Music Fest every March. Theater and literary events are numerous, while good bookstores, record stores, cafés, and Tiffany glass restaurants rub shoulders with low-down, funkier spots. Above all, local legends have persisted despite the changes – for example, **Scholz Garten** (tel: 512-474-1958; www.sholzgarten.net; daily). Scholz Garten was founded in 1866, 16 years before construction began on the Capitol building. You can find good food here, along with unpretentious charm and heartfelt music.

Acoustic band playing at the Continental Club in Austin.

Lone star capitol

Scholz Garten is a few blocks from the **State Capitol** (tel: 512-463-0063; www.tspb.state.tx.us; daily tours) and the lower edges of UT, two major sources

Austin by night.

of business. The Capitol itself is unmistakable, a local pink-granite version of the nation's Capitol in Washington, DC. Its white, classical interior focuses on the great rotunda, commemorating the six governments that reigned supreme over Texas (Spain, France, Mexico, the Confederate States, the United States, and, most proudly, the Republic of Texas). Above, at the apex of the dome, is the lone star that is the state's emblem: independence, self-determination, and singularity.

Information on touring the Capitol Complex is available at the **Capitol Visitors Center** (tel: 512-305-8400; daily), located in the distinctive castle-like building southeast of the Capitol that housed the General Land Office in the mid-1800s. The enjoyable **Bob Bullock Texas State History Museum** (tel: 512-936-8746; www.thestoryoftexas.com; daily), behind the Capitol, is housed in an attractive modern building constructed from the same pink granite as the Capitol. Its soaring atrium contains three floors of well-presented audio-visual exhibits covering Texas's Native American, Spanish, and American history, as well as an IMAX theater.

Hill Country

Historic San Antonio is barely an hour's drive southwest of Austin on I-35, but there's a diverting half-day's sightseeing to be had if you make your way between the two along the **Texas Hill Country Trail** to the west instead. At first, leaving Austin, the "trail" – in reality, US 290 – crosses a somewhat dreary Western landscape of thin grassland. Beyond **Dripping Springs**, the road starts to climb through a rich rolling terrain of open meadows sprinkled with profuse wildflowers, and then starts to undulate through **Johnson City** ㉒, 50 miles (80km) west of Austin, and pastoral countryside.

Johnson City acquired its name long before local boy Lyndon Baines Johnson became the 36th President of the United States, following the assassination of John F. Kennedy in 1963. Even so, LBJ (who shared his initials with wife Lady Bird Johnson) is the big story here. His downtown birthplace and the LBJ Ranch in nearby

Texas State Capitol building guarded by a Texas Ranger statue.

Stonewall, to which the couple retired after the Vietnam War put an end to his political career, are now part of **Lyndon B. Johnson State Park and Historic Site** (tel: 830-644-2252; www. tpwd.state.tx.us/state-parks/lyndon-b-johnson; bus tours of ranch and birthplace daily). Incidentally, the glorious **Lady Bird Johnson Wildflower Center** (tel: 512-232-0100; www.wildflower.org; Tue–Sun) in Austin showcases the First Lady's passion for Texas' spectacular wildflowers, easy to understand if you visit the Hill Country in spring.

Everywhere there is evidence of the German settlers who were attracted here in the 1800s. The main street of touristy **Fredericksburg**, another 32 miles (51km) west, for example, calls itself "Hauptstrasse" and is lined with pseudo-Teutonic beer gardens and bakeries, while numerous German-named farms along the intervening highway, like "Der peach garten," sell German-style wines and liquors.

Lukenback to San Antonio

Wander through the real Hill Country down to San Antonio by getting off US 290, 4 miles (6km) east of Fredericksburg, and taking State 1376 south. The backroad passes within a few feet of the tiny village of **Luckenbach** ㉓ (tel: 830-997-3224; www.luckenbach texas.com; daily), another 4 miles (6km) on. Unless you know where to look, however, you'll miss it altogether; the unmarked turning comes immediately before South Grape Creek. A much-loved ghost town – more of a joke town, really – Luckenbach was bought in its entirety by humorist Hondo Crouch in 1970, and made famous by a No. 1 Country & Western hit, recorded in 1976 by Willie Nelson and Waylon Jennings, that featured the refrain "Let's Go To Luckenbach, Texas."

Hundreds of country fans now do just that, to while away an afternoon in the bar inside the diminutive post office as the postmaster cracks corny jokes and sings songs, and perhaps buy a souvenir uch as a stuffed armadillo drinking a

bottle of Luckenbach beer. Willie Nelson hosts a picnic here on July 4th each year, while most summer weekends there's some sort of large-scale concert in the dancehall. From Luckenbach, State 1376 continues south toward San Antonio by way of some beautiful hills, where you're liable to startle wild deer grazing beside the highway. Ten miles (16km) northeast of the city limits, it meets I-10/US 87 at Boerne.

San Antonio ㉔ at first seems deceptively pastoral – not far from the interstate, luxurious Italianate villas perch on isolated rocky knobs that look like Tuscan hill towns. Soon enough, however, you're forced to run the gauntlet of the manic freeways entailed in reaching every large American city; just before it finally spits you out into Downtown, the interstate for no reason splits alarmingly into two separate highways, one stacked on top of the other.

General store, post office and saloon dating from 1849 in Luckenbach, Texas.

Jam session in the saloon of Luckenbach's general store.

The Rio Grande flows through Big
Bend National Park, Texas.

SAN ANTONIO TO SOUTHERN NEW MEXICO

Davy Crockett and Billy the Kid are only two of the people who left their mark on the lands that border Mexico and the Rio Grande.

O f all the major cities in Texas, El Paso and San Antonio are the oldest. El Paso began as the first Spanish mission in the future state, while it was in San Antonio that American Texas was born and almost lost back to Mexico at the Alamo. Stretching between the two is the vast expanse of **Trans-Pecos Texas**, a largely barren yet subtly beautiful mountainous desert. There is a timeless quality to the landscape that stands in marked contrast to the booming spectacle of the metropolitan east.

In the anchor cities, Hispanic culture consistently revitalizes itself much more effectively than in Galveston, Houston, or Austin. El Paso and adjoining Ciudad Juárez are bound as a Mexican/American metropolis, a popular gateway to the American Southwest.

Cradle of Texas liberty

San Antonio ㉔, the "Cradle of Texas Liberty," was the Spanish capital of Texas before Mexico won its independence from Spain in 1821. Mexico was essentially an absentee landlord. It began opening the territory of New Spain to settlement by anyone who would develop the land, including immigrants from the fledgling United States. American Stephen F. Austin, whose father Moses had received a land grant from Spain in 1820,

inherited it and, in 1822, led a group dubbed the Old Three Hundred to settle Los Brazos River. Before Austin's pilgrimage, there were 3,500 persons of European descent in San Antonio and La Bahia. By 1836, 30,000 Anglos, 5,000 black slaves, and 4,000 Mexicans populated Texas.

In the late 1860s, when Spaniards first came to the San Antonio River Valley, which cradles modern San Antonio, they found it occupied by the Payaya people, hunters who supplemented their catches with the fruits

Main Attractions

The Alamo
Big Bend National Park
Chinati Foundation
Museum of the Big Bend
Chamizal National Memorial
White Sands National Monument
Cloudcroft
Mescalero Apache Indian Reservation
La Mesilla Plaza
Gila Cliff Dwellings National Monument

Tribal ceremonial, Gallup.

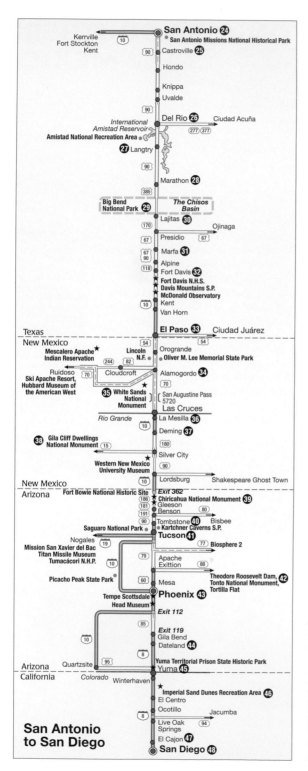

San Antonio to San Diego

of the pecan and mesquite trees and prickly pear cactus. The Payaya cooperated readily with the Europeans, but the Apache, who controlled the plains to the north, took more convincing, and the nomadic Comanche were always a threat.

Intent on securing their claims in the area, and on taming people they considered godless heathens, the Spanish established a military barracks, or *presidio*, and a mission on the west bank of the San Antonio River in 1718. By 1793, Mission San Antonio de Valero had been relocated to the east bank and secularized, and Mexican troops were transferred there to protect the pueblo that had grown up on the riverbanks. Renamed *El Alamo* (the Cottonwood), it became a crucial fortification.

Remember the Alamo

The infamy of the converted mission arose much later, during the early American frontier period, and involved an ill-conceived standoff with the forces of Mexican president General Antonio Lopez de Santa Anna, the self-styled "Napoleon of the West," on March 6, 1836. Mexico's 5,000 troops were met by 187 (or 186, depending on who you ask) "Texian" martyrs-to-be. In the words of memorializer Frank J. Davis, "All dead within one sanguinary hour; yet the heroes of the Alamo are deathless."

"Remember the Alamo!" was adopted as the Texan battle cry, and revenge came swiftly. Seven weeks later, Santa Anna was defeated in a mere 18 minutes at the Battle of San Jacinto, and the Texas Revolution culminated with the declaration of the newly independent Republic of Texas.

Davy Crockett

Riddled with as many contradictions as bullet holes, The Alamo (tel: 210-225-1391; www.thealamo.org; daily;) is nonetheless an essential destination. The Alamo's defenders during the battle were, after all, recen arrivals from foreign countries that included England, Ireland, Scotland, even Denmark – as well as the United States – while their 26-year-old commander, William B. Travis from South Carolina, wrote three days before he died that "the citizens of this municipality are all our enemies."

His associates included opportunists such as Jim Bowie, remembered for his namesake knife (though the museum here can only rustle up one of his less-celebrated spoons), and the legendary Davy Crockett, a three-term Congressman from Kentucky who sought his fortune in the West after the evaporation of his presidential ambitions. The independent Texas for which they fought and died survived just nine years before being subsumed by the United States.

A plaque on the front door of the graffiti-etched **Alamo Shrine**, originally the mission's chapel, requests "Be quiet friend, here heroes died to blaze a trail for other men." Most visitors focus on taking photos of the famous exterior of the shrine, then repair first to the lovely garden, shaded by everything from myrtles to a mescal bean tree, then the all-important souvenir shop. On sale are such reverent mementos as Alamo mugs, belts, patches, playing cards, pencils, plaques, postcards, dishware, license-plate frames, pins, coasters, caps, tote bags, and erasers.

Note: There are five missions in San Antonio. The Alamo is managed by the Daughters of the American Revolution, while the other four, also worth visiting, are preserved as **San Antonio Missions National Historical Park** (tel: 210-534-8833-1001; www.nps.gov/saan; daily) and managed by the National Park Service.

The River Walk

Though San Antonio is an enormous desert city, you'd never know it as you amble along the lively, pedestrianized **Paseo del Rio**, or River Walk, an inspired tourist attraction that has done wonders for the rough-around-the-edges Downtown. An original and elegantly simple concept, River Walk was instigated in 1939 as part of Franklin Roosevelt's New Deal.

The Alamo, symbol of the Republic of Texas.

The hand-operated Los Ebanos Ferry is the last of its kind on the Rio Grande.

San Antonio's River Walk.

The plan called for confining the San Antonio River into a tight and very narrow little channel as it loops through the city center, paving and landscaping both banks, and garnishing them liberally with restaurants, patio cafés, stores, and gardens.

River Walk stands roughly 10ft (3 meters) lower than the busy Downtown streets. Flat-bottomed cruise boats ply gently along the river itself, and at night, in particular, when it's all low-lit, the effect is magical. There's even an open-air theater, the ingenious **Arneson River Theatre**, where the stage is arranged on one side of the river while the audience watches from a stucco Spanish-style amphitheater of benches on the opposite bank.

Downtown San Antonio holds several other worthwhile attractions. The beautifully restored **Spanish Governor's Palace** (tel: 210-224-0601; www.spanishgovernorspalace.org; Tue–Sun), a tranquil gem, is located near the original site of Spain's Presidio de Bexar (1722), the **Plaza de Armas**, where a sign notes that

in the Republican era (1836–45), the grounds had already become a busy market teeming with "noisy vendors of vegetables, fresh eggs, chili peppers, and live chickens. . . ."

UTSA Institute of Texan Cultures (tel: 210-458-2300; www.texancultures.com; Tue–Sun), in Hemisfair Park, takes an entertaining look at the many different peoples, from Comanches to Czechs, who have contributed to the cosmopolitan blend of modern Texas. There's also a glorious evocation of the cowboy past; one early African-American *vaquero* is quoted as saying "we loved to work cattle so much we'd just be sittin' around cryin' for daylight to come."

Miles, mesas, and mountains

It's an exhausting 500-mile (800km)-long haul between San Antonio and El Paso, not recommended as a one-day drive. It's quickest to stick to I-10, but to experience the desolate border country you'll need to take US 90 out of San Antonio and head south toward Del Rio, where the legendary Rio Grande forms the US-Mexico border. Plan on

taking two or three days and exploring the dusty backcountry, including the arty towns in the Alpine–Marathon–Marfa–Fort Davis quadrangle and nearby Big Bend National Park, one of the country's most remote yet stunning national parks.

As you leave San Antonio, there's a parched quality to roadside grasslands that presages desiccation ahead. At first, however, agriculture maintains a foothold. Historic **Castroville 25**, 15 miles (24km) along on US 90, proclaims itself to be "The Little Alsace of Texas," and has several Alsatian restaurants. **Hondo** feels like the Great Plains, with huge fields of corn and wheat, while **Knippa** – "Go Ahead and Blink, Knippa is Bigger than You Think" – is devoted to stone quarrying.

The Great Depression hit Southwest Texas pretty badly, but Uvalde was fortunate to have President Franklin Roosevelt's vice president, John Garner, as a hometown boy. Among Garner's local projects were **Garner State Park**, a riverfront park created in 1941 by the Civilian Conservation Corps (CCC), and the **Aviation Museum at Garner Field**, a World War II training base that displays old bombers and other aircraft. The **Briscoe-Garner Museum** (tel: 830-278-5018; www.cah.utexas.edu/museums/garner.php), located in the former Garner home, is now run by the University of Texas and is completing renovations. Its new name honors Garner and former Governor Dolph Biscoe, both Uvalde-born. Exhibits are temporarily on display in First State Bank in Uvalde.

The Rio Grande

The US Border Patrol is an ever-vigilant presence along the border. Across most of Texas, the desert makes a far more effective barrier against illegal entrants from Mexico than does the Rio Grande. Rather than monitor every inch of the river, therefore, Border Patrol simply erects roadblocks along the few highways that lead away

from it. Be sure to have citizenship papers in hand at all times.

Past Uvalde, US 90 dwindles to a single lane. **Del Rio 26** is home to Laughlin Air Force base and malls catering to day-trippers from the adjacent Mexican town of **Ciudad Acuña**, but apart from a couple of 19th-century buildings, there's not much to divert tourists.

A further 12 miles (19km) northwest, **Amistad National Recreation Area** (tel: 830-775-7491; www.nps.gov/amis; daily), the "third-largest international man-made lake in the world," was created by the completion of Amistad Dam, a huge curving wall of concrete jointly dedicated by the presidents of the US and Mexico in 1969. Above this point, the Rio Grande is officially a "Wild and Scenic River," but you won't get any glimpses of the "wild" river until you reach Langtry and beyond, in Big Bend.

Another 30 miles (48km) northwest, the highest highway bridge in Texas crosses the deep gorge of the Pecos River, just before its confluence with the Rio Grande. It's worth stopping to

Map on page 282

TIP

Roadblocks and checkpoints by the US Border Patrol are commonplace along the US-Mexico border, so foreign travelers should always keep their papers handy. Passports, photo IDs, or green cards are required if you cross into any Mexican border town.

Morning on the border river – the Rio Grande is known as the Rio Bravo in Mexico.

British actress Lily Langtry, for whom it's said the eccentric Judge Roy Bean named the tiny Texas town of Langtry.

Black bears roam the rugged terrain of Big Bend National Park.

admire this, the first of the many western canyons to come and to envy the eagles and falcons that soar so majestically above it.

Beyond the Pecos you've reached true desert, and confirmation that you're in the Wild West arrives soon enough in historic **Langtry** ㉗..This semi ghost town was home to Judge Roy Bean, a storekeeper who was appointed Justice of the Peace here in 1882. Known as the "Law West of the Pecos," Judge Bean exacted swift frontier justice, despite an ignorance of all legal matters. His saloon-cum-courtroom, a hundred yards shy of the dry-as-bones canyon of the **Rio Grande**, is now a tiny state-run museum and information center. A dusty store offers lukewarm coffee and snacks. Take advantage: this is the only available sustenance in the 120 empty miles (193km) between Langtry and Marathon.

Until you come to **Marathon** ㉘, you've added time but no extra mileage to your trip by taking US 90 rather than I-10. This is where you'll have to decide whether to detour down to Big

Bend – a decision best contemplated after a night in the luxury of the restored **Gage Hotel** (see page 420), the first really appealing accommodation since San Antonio.

Big Bend National Park

Spectacular **Big Bend National Park** ㉙ (tel: 432-477-2370; www.nps.gov/bibe; daily) is so out of the way that if you do happen to be nearby, you owe it to yourself to go. The 40-mile (64km) drive south to the park entrance on US 385 is best done at sunset or early morning, when the long shadows play over a landscape as entrancing as Shangri-la. You head straight toward a misty wall of mountains, only to shimmy around them at the last minute and confront another equally alluring range on the horizon.

Once inside the park, watch for the cute but feisty desert boar known as javelinas crossing the road: they have very poor eyesight. Thirty more miles (48km) brings you to the main Visitor Center, an essential information stop, and one of only two places in this vast park where you can fill up with gas during business hours. The prime destination, the mountain-ringed **Chisos Basin**, lies another 12 miles (19km) beyond. A scenic road – too narrow for large RVs – climbs steeply into the park's central cluster of mountains, through a labyrinth of towering rocks guarded by tall yucca plants flanked by talus slopes speckled with eye-popping pink-blossomed cacti and other desert succulents. A succession of steep hairpin bends then drops into the grassy basin that holds the park's lodge, campground, and the store. Be aware: Big Bend is bear and mountain lion country, and you should learn what to do if you encounter these shy but majestic wild creatures. That also goes for rattlesnakes, which have been known to curl up on the doorstep of the motel rooms. The highest elevation in the park, Chisos Basin is the park's premier hiking area. From the campground, a superb hike takes yo

on a 4.4-mile (7km) round-trip trail to the **Window**, a gap in the mountains with views across an eerie desert landscape of buttes and mesas.

River-rafting trips

State 170 west of the park, the **River Road**, is one of Texas's most attractive highways – a rare opportunity to drive along the Rio Grande in all its glory. It reaches the river 17 miles (27km) south of the Terlingua/Study Butte turn-off, at the small resort of **Lajitas** ⓾, which specializes in river-rafting trips through high-walled Santa Elena Canyon into the park. For 50 miles (80km) from Lajitas, the River Road sticks close to the river, sometimes scrambling over high sandstone outcrops, at other times meandering through well-watered fields. Cattle can often be seen grazing in Chihuahua, Mexico, and in several places the river is shallow enough for them to wade across. There's another chance to cross into Mexico at **Presidio**, where **Ojinaga** on the far side holds a couple of seafood restaurants plus cut-rate opticians and pharmacies.

Big Bend country

From Presidio, a 61-mile (98km) drive north on US 67 returns you to US 90 at **Marfa** ㉛. The ranch town is celebrated as the location for the 1956 movie *Giant* – James Dean, Elizabeth Taylor, and other stars took over Downtown's charming **El Paisano** hotel as headquarters. In the 1970s, Marfa gained a new kind of fame when the late Donald Judd, a New York City native, began installing overscaled art projects in historic buildings around town. Judd's legacy is now safeguarded by the **Chinati Foundation** (tel: 432-729-4362; www.chinati.org), which, Wednesday through Sunday, offers morning and afternoon tours by reservation to installations. The town has become a haven for hip East Coast urban artists, many of whom have sensitively restored historic buildings for art galleries, eateries, bookstores, even a local public radio station. The wail of locomotives flying through town is often the only sound in this quiet West Texas backwater.

There are more art, restaurants, and lodgings in the small college town of

Hikers on a Big Bend trail.

Mission of Nuestra Señora de Guadalupe (Our Lady of Guadalupe), Ciudad Juárez, Mexico.

Alpine, 25 miles (42km) east of Marfa. The excellent **Museum of the Big Bend** (tel: 432-837-8143; www.sulross. edu/museum; Tue–Sun) on the campus of Sul Ross State University has exhibits on the natural and cultural history of the Big Bend area.

State 17 heads north to **Fort Davis** ㉜, in the Davis Mountains. **Fort Davis National Historic Site** (tel: 432) 426-3224 ext. 220; www.nps.gov/foda; daily), the best-preserved 19th-century fort in the West, adjoins **Davis Mountains State Park**, a pretty valley with lovely oak-shaded campgrounds. From here, it's a beautiful mountain drive on State 118 to return to I-10 at Kent. En route, you'll pass right by the entrance to **McDonald Observatory** (tel: 432-426-3640; www. mcdonaldobservatory.org; visitor center: daily), one of the largest astronomical observatories in the world.

El Paso

Once on 1-10, it's roughly two and a half hours to El Paso, gaining an hour as you enter Mountain Time. On the way, you will pass through

Van Horn, an historic crossroads of the old Bankhead Highway and the Old Spanish Trail. **El Paso** ㉝, a gritty, working-class city of 665,568, which spreads around the base of the Franklin Mountains, lies in the oldest European-settled area of Texas. In the 16th century, Spaniards first crossing the Rio Grande to explore their territories in New Mexico headed along El Paso del Norte – the Pass of the North – which sent the river through a break in the mountain ranges. Soon the trading route of El Camino Real (The Royal Road) was extended from south of Chihuahua City, Mexico, to what is now Santa Fe, New Mexico, by conquistador Juan de Oñate.

When the Spanish colonists were driven out of New Mexico by the Pueblo Indian Revolt of 1680, a dispirited column of refugees regrouped here, around an adobe Franciscan mission they called Ysleta del Sur. Its founder, Fray Garcia, is commemorated in Downtown's Pioneer Plaza with a 14ft (4-meter) statue by internationally known sculptor David Houser.

DETOUR TO MEXICO

Ciudad Juárez, across the bridge from El Paso, Texas, is probably the most interesting Mexican border town outside of Tijuana, south of San Diego. But whereas San Diego is sleek and efficient, confirming the US's superior grasp of the modern world, the difference between El Paso and Ciudad Juárez is definitely in Mexico's favor. El Paso is a rather desolate, depressing city, whereas Juárez, the biggest city in the state of Chihuahua, is vibrant and colorful. Bullfights and bright souvenirs make a strong impression right away, as does lush Chamizal Park, a counterpart to El Paso's memorial. Juárez Museum of History, occupying a dazzling historic building, traces the area's development, with special attention paid to the Mexican Revolution and the Mexican hero Pancho Villa. Our Lady of Guadalupe Mission explores the rich religious tapestry of the country. Juárez's food is wonderful and spicy, but don't drink the water, or eat ice cream or ice cubes. It's certainly worth a day trip to experience another country, but make sure you have all valid documents: a passport or proof of citizenship with photo and a green card to reenter the US, if necessary. If you stay in Mexico more than 72 hours, or travel beyond the border zone (La Frontera), you'll need a Tourist Card, available at the border.

It took 12 years for the Spaniards to reconquer New Mexico under De Vargas, during which time the towns of Ysleta and El Paso had sprung up around the mission. El Paso gradually absorbed Ysleta, but was itself split in two after the designation of the Rio Grande as the United States-Mexico border. The US city remained El Paso and the Mexican city was dubbed Ciudad Juárez. El Paso's strategic location has made it a travelers' stop for centuries. The Gold Rush '49ers passed through on their way to fortune in California. Refugees, desperados, and tourists have all met here. Today, it is best known as a major gateway to Mexico.

Much of El Paso's history involved gunfights. The notorious Marshall Dallas Stoudenmire and John Wesley Hardin were on many a winning end before finally biting the dust (John Wesley Hardin is buried in Concordia Cemetery). There's a lot of dust to bite in El Paso. Its climate is singularly dry, although rain is not unknown. The city is uniformly beige in look and feel. Its shanty dwellings clinging to barren hillsides have more in common with nearby Mexico than the United States.

El Paso is an inexpensive city, but there's little here to justify it as a destination. Tourism is mainly channeled to its environs and up to **Ranger Peak** in the Franklin Mountains. The **Tigua Indian Reservation**, a living pueblo of the oldest identifiable Native American tribe in Texas, is on the eastern edge of the city, while **Ysleta Mission**, one of three Spanish missions in El Paso restored and run by El Paso Mission Trail Foundation (tel: 915-851-9997; daily tours; www.visit elpasomissiontrail.com), is in the Ysleta neighborhood in western El Paso. **Fort Bliss Military Reservation**, in the northeast, is the site of the largest Air Defense School in the "free world."

Cross-cultural relations

The Rio Grande is more of a fortified moat than a river in El Paso, but its political role as the natural boundary between Mexico and the US is important. That interesting story is told well at **Chamizal National Memorial** (tel: 915-532-7273; www.nps.gov/cham; daily), a little-known unit of the National Park System overlooking the river.

The memorial was established to commemorate the Chamizal Convention of 1963, a milestone in diplomatic relations between Mexico and the United States, which resulted in the peaceful settlement of a century-long boundary dispute. It wholeheartedly celebrates Mexico, with art and museum exhibits, regular cultural performances such as folkloric dance and mariachi music, and thoughtful ranger talks. For visitors in town for just a few hours, it's a safe way of experiencing a little of Mexico's infectious *Viva La Vida*, especially if you have neither the time nor the inclination to cross into Mexico itself.

El Paso – notorious as one of the weakest links in the "Tortilla Curtain" between the United States and Mexico – has a decidedly uneasy, schizophrenic relationship with its

TIP

Day-trippers to Ciudad Juárez will do better to walk across one of the three footbridges to Mexico. Driving across the border requires the purchase of additional Mexican insurance.

Corner café in a Mexican border town.

TIP

Carlsbad Caverns and adjoining Guadalupe Mountains national parks are 152 miles (244km) north of El Paso on US 62/180. Texas's highest mountains and New Mexico's most spectacularly decorated caves are worth an extra day for a detour.

The New Mexico Museum of Space History tells the story of the international space race.

sister city across El Rio. That friction has been exacerbated by gun violence and crime in Ciudad Juárez, primarily between the warring Sinaloa and Juarez drug cartels, prompting the US Consulate in Mexico to issue a Travel Alert to travelers. With 47,515 people having died in drug-related violence since President Felipe Calderon took office in 2006, you would be wise to be very careful if you cross the border.

Weigh the risks against the many pleasures of a quick visit: the vast majority of Mexican citizens are hard-working, law-abiding, and hospitable people, equally terrorized by violence, whose livelihood from tourism on La Frontera is being seriously undermined by a tiny minority. Expect a high military presence in Juárez: thousands of troops have been sent in by the Mexican government during the most recent major crackdown.

A major symbol of the tension between the US and Mexico is the construction of a 670-mile (1,078km) -long fence along the US-Mexico border – a $2.6 billion, 18ft (5-meter) -high, steel-and-mesh behemoth that passes straight through neighborhoods in El Paso, blocking the view of Mexico and invoking the Berlin Wall. The fence has been an effective barrier to illegal entry. Once, some 2,000 illegal aliens per day were caught and repatriated, but that figure has dwindled to almost nothing these days.

NEW MEXICO

Exiting El Paso, US 54 east skirts the eastern slopes of the Franklin Mountains. New Mexico arrives, with the minimum of ceremony, 10 miles (16km) out of El Paso, at which point US 54 contracts to a two-lane undivided highway with virtually no services the entire 83-mile (134km) stretch to Alamogordo and the Tularosa Valley.

New Mexico is among the youngest of US states (the 47th admitted to the Union), but it has one of the longest histories. At its eastern edge, near Clovis, archeologists have dug up beautifully carved arrowheads dating back 12,000 years. By the time the first Spanish *conquistadores* reached the valley of the Rio Grande, in 1540, the Rio Grande Valley held some 150 separate villages, or *pueblos*, each home to a distinct clan-based group specializing in certain handicrafts and trade items. The Spaniards named the infant colony New Mexico in the misplaced hope that it might yield similar treasures to the Aztec empire of Mexico.

By the late 16th century, *El Camino Real* (now US 85) extended along the Rio Grande from Mexico to Santa Fe, site of the oldest government building in North America and the oldest US capital. However, although New Mexico covered an area far greater than the modern state, including all of modern Arizona and much of Nevada, California, and Utah, until the Yankees arrived in 1846 it remained an impoverished provincial backwater, whose farmers had to battle against not only the unforgiving desert environment but also Navajo, Apache, and Comanche raiders.

Under American rule, New Mexico has attended to its somewhat mundane motto: *Crescit Eunde* ("It grows as it goes"). Railroading, ranching, and mining have all thrived on the state's rocky surface, warm valleys, and subterranean waters. A deliberate US policy during World War II of siting defense installations in remote landlocked locations has also brought unexpected dividends. It was in New Mexico that scientists developed and tested the first atomic bombs, and military facilities continue to play a major part in the state's economy. New Mexico is sparsely populated by just over 2 million people, most of them clustered in the major cities of Albuquerque, Santa Fe, and Las Cruces. Among its notable residents have been sworn enemies Pat Garrett and Billy the Kid, "king of the innkeepers" Conrad Hilton, novelist D.H. Lawrence, artist Georgia O'Keeffe, and United Forestry Service mascot, Smokey Bear.

New Mexico's affecting natural beauty and mesmerizing landscape have captivated everyone, from prehistoric and modern Native Americans, to generations of Hispanics and Anglo explorers, traders, ranchers, and artists, to modern new-age tourists drawn to cities such as Santa Fe, Albuquerque, and Taos. Even little green men from outer space seem to love it, if you believe the "evidence" on display in Roswell.

Alamogordo

As you drive the gorge between the Organ Mountains to the west and the Hueco Mountains to the east, you nick the edge of **White Sands Missile Range**. Roadside signs warn of unexploded ammunition lying in the desert, and advise you not to leave the highway. Just south of Alamogordo, in the Sacramento Mountain foothills, is **Oliver M. Lee Memorial State Park**, named for a state legislator with a colorful past. An immaculate 50-site campground makes a good base to

explore scenic Dog Canyon and Lee's ranch, once the largest in New Mexico.

After all that emptiness, **Alamogordo ③④** itself feels positively urban. It's actually a small desert town, with a population of 31,327 people, but counting among its population international rocket scientists, astronomers, and military brass, it has a sophistication all its own. Alamogordo is built atop a large 11th-century Native American pueblo that was abandoned in the 1300s when a long drought and Apache raiding made life too difficult. Earlier, the Jornada branch of the Mogollon culture left behind some 21,000 extraordinary petroglyphs, or incised rock art, on basaltic boulders at **Three Rivers Petroglyph Site**, north of Alamogordo, many of which have, sadly, now been defaced. The Mogollon were the first to learn farming, pottery, and masonry architecture from Mexico. They were subsumed into the more powerful Ancestral Pueblo (Anasazi) trading culture to the north by AD 1000.

Spaniards passed through, naming the valley for its fat (*gordo*) cottonwood

Apache crown dancer (or mountain spirit) at an Apache Changing Woman Ceremony to mark an Apache girl reaching puberty.

Oliver Lee Memorial State Park.

Would-be cowboys should visit the Hubbard Museum of the American West in Ruidoso.

The Southern New Mexico Ski Apache resort is located on the Mescalero Apache Indian Reservation.

trees (*alamos*). They settled on the Tularosa River and founded a presidio and mission in 1719 at **La Luz**, but Apache raiding soon forced them to move on. The arrival of the US Army at **Fort Stanton** in 1855 was the beginning of the end for Apache warriors. In the 1880s, they were forced to make peace and move to a reservation at nearby Ruidoso, allowing Anglo settlement in the Tularosa Basin.

In 1898, C.B. and John A. Eddy founded Alamogordo as a stop on their railroad line. Seduced by the forested valley and its commercial potential for lumber, the Eddys sold the railroad and settled down in Alamogordo to make their fortune from indigenous resources. Alamogordo grew as a trade center, but the development of White Sands Proving Ground and nearby Holloman Air Force Base radically recast the contours of the city. In the words of one local historian, "No longer was it a sleepy, peaceful land of *mañana* (tomorrow), but a hustling, bustling, fast-growing city."

Today, Alamogordo is dominated by the high-tech weaponry

community. It also harbors a tribute to the peaceful uses of technology in the exploration of space, in the shape of the **New Mexico Museum of Space History** (tel: 575-437-2840; www.nmspacemuseum.org; daily), standing prominently on the foothills at the edge of the valley. This well-conceived museum chronicles the international race for the stars, featuring a "Hall of Fame" of pioneers in space exploration, from early dreamers to the moon-walking astronauts of NASA's *Apollo* missions. After admiring space shuttle models, a lunar TV camera and samples of foods brought aboard *Apollo* and *Skylab* missions (including canned vanilla ice cream and dehydrated peach ambrosia), you can watch a video presentation of highlights from the *Apollo* 11, 12, and 14 moon landings, or simulate a space shuttle landing.

Cloudcroft to Mescalero

In summer, the 12,000ft (3,657-meter) Sacramento Mountains, east of Alamogordo, provide welcome relief from the 100°F (37.7°C) heat of the torrid Chihuahuan Desert, attracting visitors from southeastern New Mexico and West Texas. Scenic US 82 climbs abruptly from 4,350ft (1,325 meters) at Alamogordo to almost 9,000ft (2,740 meters) to reach **Cloudcroft** in Lincoln National Forest, just 20 miles (32km) later. Hiking, cross-country skiing, and camping are popular in the cool, piney national forest.

The quaint alpine village of Cloudcroft is known for its rental cabins and hiking trails. Historic **Cloudcroft Lodge**, built in 1899 in the Bavarian style, is a must-see: it even has a resident ghost. Sixteen miles (26km) south of Cloudcroft, in tiny Sunspot, is the **National Solar Observatory and Apache Point Observatory** (tel: 575-434-7000; www.nso.edu; May–Oct daily). Take a Saturday tour to find out how astronomers safely view the sun, using telescopes like the Dunn Solar

Telescope, a rotating instrument that rises 330ft (100 meters) from a subterranean chamber.

Just north of Cloudcroft is the **Mescalero Apache Indian Reservation**. A 28-mile (45km) drive through the reservation on State 244 passes through bucolic scenery, with shimmering little lakes and flower-filled meadows, and Apache cowboys riding the range. Any notions you may have of reservations as desolate or depressing places will evaporate. See if you can catch a rodeo in July.

The Mescalero are prosperous entrepreneurs; while parts of the reservation are closed to outsiders, the tribe operates successful commercial enterprises on adjoining lands. These include the region's grand resort, the **Inn of the Mountain Gods**, which shares its lovely lakeside setting with glitzy **Casino Apache**. The tribe's luxury winter-sports venue, **Ski Apache**, is set above busy little **Ruidoso**, home to Ruidoso Downs racetrack and **Hubbard Museum of the American West** (tel: 575-378-4142; www.hubbardmuseum.org; daily), an affiliate of the Smithsonian. From Ruidoso, US 70 drops back down to the Tularosa Valley to tribal headquarters at **Mescalero**, best known for its restored 1939 **St Joseph Apache Mission**. From here, Alamogordo is 46 miles (74km).

White Sands National Monument

Taking the optional detour described above, you'll enjoy mountain-top views of the most spectacular feature of the region: **White Sands National Monument** ⑤ (tel: 575-479-6124; www.nps.gov/whsa; daily). Located 15 miles (24km) southwest of Alamogordo, this stunning 144,458-acre (58,505-hectare) expanse is made up of gypsum sand blown in between the San Andreas and Sacramento mountain ranges and deposited as shifting dunes on this corner of the otherwise off-limits White Sands

Missile Range. The only access road, US 70–82, is regularly closed for up to two hours at a time, so that military personnel can drive their top-secret cargo along it in peace; inquire at local visitor centers before you set off, or better still, check the park website for alerts. As you approach White Sands, you may see eerie V-shaped stealth jets silently speeding through brilliant blue skies, as the glowing dunes rise from the base of the San Andreas Mountains.

The historic Visitor Center has wonderful Pueblo-style historic architecture and is a good place to pick up information before taking the 16-mile (26km) paved scenic drive that loops through the dunes. The deeper it penetrates into the heart of White Sands, the more the road surface is obscured by drifts of gypsum sand. The effect is both disorienting and remarkable. Gypsum is one of the most common compounds found on earth, but it's rarely seen on the surface because it dissolves readily in water. Surface sand elsewhere is almost always composed of quartz.

White Sands National Monument.

Sierra Blanca is the highest peak in Southern New Mexico at 12,005ft (3,659 meters).

Trinity Site National Historic Landmark.

At midday, the sands are a blinding white, reflecting so strongly they sting the naked eye. As you clamber over the dunes, occasionally pocked by the slither marks and pawprints of nocturnal wanderers, periodically remove your sunglasses to appreciate the hallucinatory expanse fully. As the afternoon cedes to evening, the sands refract the light, breaking it down into a rainbow. The park is open until 10pm, a good time to hunker down quietly and hope to see some of the 500 different animals that populate the dunes, from coyotes and roadrunners to owls and skunks. There is also a sparse scattering of beautiful plant life, including the hedgehog cactus with its brilliant red flowers.

Concealed amid the roadless wastes of White Sands Missile Range, **Trinity Site National Historic Landmark** (www.wsmr.army.mil/PAO/Trinity/Pages/default.aspx) preserves the site where, in July 1945, scientists from the Manhattan Project in Los Alamos detonated the first US atomic bomb. If you're interested in seeing ground zero, a sobering site, you can attend an open house the first Saturdays of April and October, when visitors are accompanied by convoys of army vehicles to the detonation site from an inconspicuous gateway north of Alamogordo.

The Wild West

US 70 southwest slowly but surely rises out of the Tularosa Valley toward Las Cruces. For almost 30 miles (48km), as you head straight toward the sheer wall of the San Andreas range, a route through these mottled peaks seems like an impossibility. Eventually, the highway jinks to the right and climbs to its apex at **San Augustine Pass**, 5,720ft (1,740 meters) high and overlooking the valley that holds Las Cruces. Summiting the pass, you plunge down an exhilarating 3-mile (5km) slope to find yourself back in the Lower Rio Grande valley, where greens and browns evolve through shades and mixtures below the pearly blue peaks in the distance.

The route briefly engages **Las Cruces** before hooking into I-10 to Deming. Las Cruces – "the crosses" – acquired its name in 1830, after a caravan of travelers coming from Taos were ambushed and slaughtered, and white crosses were erected to mark their graves. Las Cruces is a bit homely on the outskirts but its regenerating downtown, New Mexico State University campus, and burgeoning business environment has made it New Mexico's fastest-growing city.

Cultural offerings include two good downtown art museums, both free: **Branigan Cultural Center** (tel: 575-541-2154; www.lascruces.org/museums; Tues–Sat) and **Las Cruces Museum of Fine Arts** (tel: 575-541-2155; www.lascruces.org/museum; Tue–Sun). The **New Mexico Farm & Ranch Museum** (tel: 575-522-4100; www.nmfarmandranchmuseum.org; daily), on the outskirts of town, highlights 3,000 years of farming and ranching in the area, and is a hit with kids. Spanish churro sheep, burros, longhorn cattle, and other traditional livestock are kept on the grounds. Demonstrations of weaving,

candle making, and other pioneer skills are presented regularly.

La Mesilla

The lovely town of **La Mesilla** ㊱, a short hop from downtown Las Cruces on State 28 and State 292 (Motel Boulevard), is the main attraction for area tourists. Its restored historic **Plaza**, dominated by an old gazebo, evokes the color and sounds of Old Mexico. This was where the Gadsden Purchase was sealed in 1854, establishing the current boundaries of Mexico and the United States, while a gift store in one corner was originally the courthouse where the notorious outlaw Billy the Kid was tried and sentenced to hang for murder in 1881. The Kid managed to escape before his hanging, but subsequently met his maker at the hands of Pat Garrett, near Fort Sumner; Garrett was himself murdered near Las Cruces in 1908. Vendors create a Mexican *mercado* (market) atmosphere and will be happy to sell you rugs, pottery, Native American jewelry, ceramics, and other souvenirs. One of Mesilla's most important annual events is April's **Border Book Festival**. Founded by renowned local Hispanic author Denise Chavez, it highlights the rich literature of the borderlands and is headquartered in the **Cultural Center of Mesilla** bookshop (tel: 505-523-3988; www.oldmesilla.org/ html/books; Fri–Sun), a former Mexican garrison dating to the 1840s. Look for the **Double Eagle Restaurant** (see page 446), set in a registered historic building and filled with antiques, and have a drink in its elegant Imperial Bar.

Across the Great Divide

A short distance out of Las Cruces on I-10 west, a double ribbon of landscaped orchards lines the narrow Rio Grande, which flows from its source in Colorado via Taos and Albuquerque. Beyond the shallow sandy ridge on the far side, the highway levels out to cross the windblown chapparal of Luna County, where increasing numbers of the ostrich-like state plant, the yucca, scrutinize travelers as they make their way westward. From here to the Arizona state line, freeway exits are commonly lined with frontier-style outlets for supposedly characteristic

La Mesilla town square.

goods. Behind false facades spring a trading post, Wild West town, or tepee, where moccasins, cactus jelly, and plant candy are sold to tourists.

Fifty-six miles (90km) out of Las Cruces, in New Mexico's "bootheel," is the truck-stop town of **Deming** ㊲, encircled by four short mountain ranges. Deming was of great strategic importance to railroad magnate Charles Crocker, who joined his Southern Pacific line to the Santa Fe Railroad. Early settlers included soldiers, professionals, merchants, and a large population of gunmen who dominated local affairs until the town was "cleaned up" in 1883. Housed in a historic 1917 armory building in the nondescript downtown, the **Deming Luna Mimbres Museum** (tel: 575-546-2382; daily) displays local history, including artifacts of the prehistoric Mogollon culture, whose Mimbres branch made spectacular black-on-white pottery for trade.

One exhibit re-creates frontier life, which, in the words of a guide, was "as you can see just by looking around, not easy here. This wasn't a luxury

place." Today, Deming is a homely desert town of just under 15,000, where retirees drive and walk slowly, shade trees shield against a fierce sun, and the enticing smell of roasting green chili from nearby Hatch, the country's leading grower of chili, perfumes the air every August.

Relics of the Mimbres

Rather than stay on dreary I-10 for the 60 miles (97km) west to Lordsburg, it makes sense to veer northward on US 180 toward the Gila Mountains. Between the 10th and 12th centuries, this region was home to the Mimbres branch of the Mogollon culture, the highland people who took ceramics from its earliest expression in the Southwest to an exquisite, and now highly collectable, art form – a precious trade item throughout North and Central America. Early archeologist and Mogollon specialist Jesse W. Fewkes has claimed that "no Southwestern pottery, ancient or modern, surpasses that of the Mimbres; and its naturalistic figures are unexcelled in any pottery from prehistoric America."

The Mimbres are named for the Mimbres River, which at lower elevations remains a bone-dry sandy *arroyo* (wash) most of the year. US 180 crosses it repeatedly en route to Silver City, 53 miles (85km) north of Deming. Now one of New Mexico's most popular historic art towns, **Silver City** has successively been the base for Native American turquoise miners, Hispanic silver miners, modern copper conglomerates, and now artists and nature lovers. Billy the Kid lived here as a child, but most of the town he knew was wiped out by a cataclysmic flood in 1895.

Western New Mexico University Museum (tel: 575-538-6386; www.wnmu.org; daily), 12th and Alabama streets, holds the world's finest collection of Mimbres pottery, decorated with black-on-white snakes, parrots, and other animal designs as well as abstract patterns. Each pot is thought to have belonged to a single

Gila Cliff Dwellings.

individual, and to have been buried with its owner, having first had a symbolic "kill hole" punched through its base.

Gila Cliff Dwellings

Allow a whole day to make the lengthy, winding, 88-mile (142km) round trip into the Gila Mountains on State 15 to visit **Gila Cliff Dwellings National Monument** ㊳ (tel: 575-536-9461; www.nps.gov/gicl; daily), where cliff dwellings built by a late phase of the Mogollon people in the 14th century are built in caves above the Gila River. A moderate 1-mile (1.7km) trail leads to the dwellings, where rangers conduct regular tours. Be sure to bring water and food: there's none at this remote spot.

State 90 runs 44 miles (71km) southwest from Silver City to rejoin I-10 at **Lordsburg**. Along the way, it crosses the Continental Divide, then descends slowly and gloriously to the vast alkali flats, or playas, in which Lordsburg seems to float alone. The largest settlement in Hidalgo County, Lordsburg sprawls languidly beside

the interstate and the Southern Pacific railroad tracks at the northern edge of the Pyramid Mountains. The train tracks themselves tell the story of modern Lordsburg, which eventually eclipsed neighboring **Shakespeare**. Shakespeare had been a stop on the great Butterfield Stagecoach Line run by the post office from St Louis, Missouri, to San Francisco, California, at the time Charles Crocker laid his railroad tracks.

Today, Shakespeare is a ghost town, preserved in its current state of decay after being abandoned for more profitable pastures. A short drive south on Main Street from Lordsburg, Shakespeare is the genuine item, although it *is* inhabited by surviving residents and owners Janaloo and Manny Hough, who open up the town for two weekends each month, conducting folksy one-hour tours at 10am and 2pm (tel: 575-542-9034; www.shakespeareghosttown.com). Several notable characters are known to have graced the dining room of its **Stratford Hotel**, including an escapee from Silver City jail: Billy the Kid.

Abandoned automobiles and gas pump in Mogollon, a ghost town near Silver City.

SOUTH ARIZONA TO SAN DIEGO

Celebrated for its ponderosa pine forests, Colorado River canyons, and Native American ruins in the north and in the Sonoran Desert, and for Tucson and Phoenix in the south, this part of the Southwest is fascinating to explore.

Water is precious in Arizona, but its name has nothing to do with aridity. It is likely derived from the local Pima word for "little spring place." There are, in fact, many "little spring places" secreted among the desert canyons and mountains of Arizona, as well as just about every climatic, topographic, and ecological variant found in the US.

For millennia, Arizona's Native American tribes clustered around precious water sources. In the north, among the mountains and canyons of the Colorado Plateau, the dominant Ancestral Pueblo culture farmed washes and tributaries of the Colorado River, while to the south, in the Sonoran Desert, the ancient Hohokam developed a complex agricultural civilization based on sophisticated irrigation canals in what is now Phoenix.

Heat, lack of water, and Native American incursions deterred Spanish, Mexican, then Anglo settlement. It was only with the development of sophisticated irrigation for farming and later, during World War II, air-conditioning, that Arizona began its spectacular growth. Much of the desert remains undeveloped. Though beautiful, the Sonoran and adjoining Mojave deserts are dangerously hot in summer. Balmy winter temperatures are peak season in southern Arizona, when you can expect to pay premium prices to enjoy its famous spa resorts, dude ranches, and historic hotels.

Sky islands and Fort Bowie

After leaving Lordsburg, New Mexico, on I-10, the Arizona state line is just 20 miles (32km) away. You're now driving close to the US-Mexico border, through Arizona's distinctive basin-and-range topography of "sky island" mountains interspersed with heat-hazed low desert. To the north are the Peloncillo Mountains, while to the southwest the towering Chiricahua

Main Attractions

Chiricahua Nat'l Monument
Tombstone
Amerind Foundation
Saguaro National Park
Arizona-Sonora Desert Museum
Mission San Xavier del Bac
Titan Missile Museum
Biosphere 2
Heard Museum, Phoenix
Yuma Territorial Prison State
  Historic Park

Heard Museum, Phoenix.

An empty road curving through Saguaro National Park. The tall, slim saguaro cactus flowers in the springtime with blossoms opening only in the cool desert night air.

Victims of the OK Corral shootout are buried in Tombstone's Boothill Graveyard.

Mountains march in serried ranks into Mexico and the Sierra Madre.

Until the late 1800s, these ranges offered protection from white settlers for the nomadic Chiricahua Apache, who, along with other Apache groups, had separated culturally and geographically from their Navajo relatives centuries earlier, after arriving from northwest Canada, making the mountains of southern Arizona and New Mexico their homeland.

The tragic confrontation between the Apache and the US Army during the Indian Wars is commemorated at Fort Bowie and nearby Chiricahua national monuments. Both can be reached by taking Exit 366 from I-10 at Bowie, then heading south on Apache Pass Road. A small parking lot at the monument marks the start of the hiking trail to **Fort Bowie** (tel: 520-847-2500; www.nps.gov/fobo; daily). Built in 1886, for the next 25 years the fort was the headquarters of a campaign that eventually drove the Apache from this

region altogether. As you walk the 3 miles (5km) up to its evocative ruined adobe walls, you seem at first to be in a dry, bowl-shaped depression entirely ringed by mountains. Eventually, however, you come to tranquil, well-wooded Apache Spring, teeming with wildlife, which made this spot so precious to the Apache, then to the fort, commanding wonderful views across the valley below.

Chiricahua National Monument

Another 8 miles (13km) of easy driving on the unpaved road leads to State 186. Head west from here to I-10 if you're in a hurry to reach Tombstone, by way of Willcox and Benson, but spectacular **Chiricahua National Monument** ㊴ (tel: 520-824-3560; www.nps.gov/chir; daily) lies a mere 14 miles (23km) east, and though a little off the beaten track, is the most magnificent spot on this part of the route for hiking, camping, and scenic drives.

Chiricahua's unique landscape has taken shape over millennia, as hardened deposits of ash from volcanic eruptions at Turkey Caldera 25 million years ago have been eroded by water, wind, and ice into hoodoo rocks. To view them, follow the 6-mile (10km) **Bonita Canyon Drive**, which climbs from the Visitor Center through lush **Bonita Canyon** to **Massai Point**, the start of a short nature trail and day hikes among the rocks. All the way up, alarmingly balanced stacks of rock loom precariously above the road, while the viewpoint at the top surveys a panorama of bizarrely shaped stone towers and columns.

With twice the rainfall of the Chihuahuan Desert below, these "sky islands" attract numerous plants and animals. Rocky Mountain and Sierra Madrean wildlife from both sides of the border use a natural corridor running through the mountains to Mexico, and Mexican species such as the rare Apache fox squirrel and and Chihuahua and Apache pines live side by side with

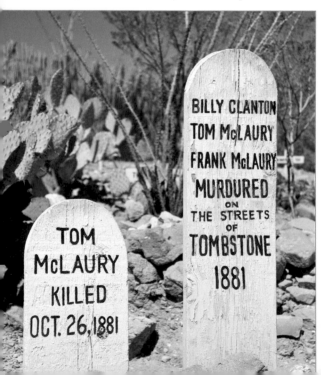

BILLY CLANTON
TOM McLAURY
FRANK McLAURY
MURDURED
ON
THE STREETS
OF
TOMBSTONE
1881

TOM
McLAURY
KILLED
OCT. 26,1881

species more commonly found north of the border. Of note are the birds that summer in Cave Creek, on the east side of the Chiricahua Mountains, near Portal. Top of every birder's list is the trogon, a Mexican native with a long, coppery tail and bright feathers. It returns from the Sierra Madre every May to raise its young at Cave Creek, along with sulphur-bellied flycatchers, tanagers, chickadees, and a variety of hummingbird species.

Heading westward on State 181, you pass the lovely **Dragoon Mountains**, a great place to hike and camp and visit **Cochise Stronghold**, a hideout used by Cochise. Continuing to Tombstone, you will drive south of Willcox Playa, which floods in winter to form a wetland that attracts up to 10,000 sandhill cranes, Canada and snow geese, and other migratory waterfowl.

Ahead are the dusty mining ghosts of **Gleeson, Courtland**, and **Pearce**. Pearce is now the only site with sizeable ruins (a mercantile store, post office, and jail). Its decrepit state belies the 1894 gold rush that occurred here and is indicative of the boom-and-bust

nature of mining in resource-rich Arizona. Today, one mining town is mining a different kind of gold – from tourists – the "Town Too Tough to Die": **Tombstone ④**.

Tombstone's OK Corral

Infamous Tombstone was named by founder Edward Schieffelin, as a retort to those who said his mad hunt for silver would end in his own tombstone. But Tombstone sat amid lands rich in silver, and strikes here led to dizzying growth, wealth, and some famous troublemakers. It went into sudden decline in 1886, when its main silver mine flooded, and today is a tacky but endearing tourist trap, cheerfully providing visitors with a sanitized and glamorized taste of the lawless days of the Wild West.

Like Pearce, Tombstone would probably be forgotten now save for the infamous shootout that took place at its **OK Corral** (tel: 520-457-3456; www. ok-corral.com; daily), which pitted Wyatt Earp, his brothers, and the consumptive dentist Doc Holliday against the Clanton and McLaury brothers. The latter were at the forefront of a cowboy

Tombstone actors ready for a showdown.

Tombstone's history is recalled in the local watering hole Big Nose Kate's Saloon.

TIP

If you plan to spend some time in southern Arizona, it might be worthwhile buying a Tucson Attractions Passport for $18 from the Tucson Visitor Center (www.visittucson.org). This contains 2-for-1 offers and discounts on a wide range of theatres, museums, state parks, and gardens, several of which are mentioned in this guide.

gang that allegedly engineered a series of stagecoach robberies, while the Earps – themselves no angels – represented establishment Tombstone. Political and personal clashes culminated in the legendary, bloody "Gunfight at the OK Corral" on October 26, 1881, which left three men dead.

Art, mines, and underground caverns

The OK Corral still stands on Allen Street, preserved as it looked on the fateful day, mannequins of the various participants posed in its yard, guns in hand. Staged gunfights take place here every afternoon, with actors re-creating the showdown and keeping the legend alive. Stagecoaches clatter evocatively past landmarks like the **Bird Cage Theatre,** where working girls plied their trade in 14 "cages" or "cribs" suspended from the ceiling, and **Tombstone Courthouse State Historic Park** (tel: 520-457-3311; http://azstateparks.com/parks/TOCO/index.html; daily), on East Toughnut Street, which has an excellent diorama model of the gunfight. The victims of the shootout rest (or try to) in

Cowboys rule in Tombstone.

kitschy **Boothill Cemetery** at the edge of town, on a dusty hillside, where their eternal slumber is disturbed by loud-speakers concealed amid the boulders that play mournful country music.

Things are more authentic, 24 miles (39km) south of Tombstone, in the delightful former mining town of **Bisbee** an attractive artist haven sprawled 3 steep miles (5km) across Mule Pass Gulch and Tombstone Canyon in the 5,000ft (1,500 meter) **Mule Mountains**. Its restored down-town Victorian mansions and buildings house comfortable historic hotels and B&Bs, restaurants, and an intriguing array of unique boutiques, art galleries, and antique stores. The **Queen Mine Tour** (tel: 1-866-432-2071; www.queenminetour.com; daily) takes you deep underground to see one of the most productive copper mines of the 20th century.

From Bisbee, take State 90 (which initially heads west and then takes a jog north in Sierra Vista) to meet up with I-10 at **Benson**. Don't miss **Kartchner Caverns State Park** (tel: 520-586-4100; http://azstateparks.com/parks/kaca/index.html; daily), just 9 miles (14km) south of I-10 off State 90. Hailed by many as the best of Arizona's state parks, its focal point is the recently discovered (1974) rare "living" limestone caverns that erosion has carved and decorated in the Whetstone Mountains. Tours are given daily, but numbers are limited in order to protect the cave's environment, so you must book ahead (tel: 520-586-2283). In addition to the cave, there is a world-class Discovery Center, 5 miles (8km) of hiking trails, a picnic area, campground, and hummingbird garden.

Another premier Southwest destination, at a rural location a few miles east of Benson, is the private **Amerind Foundation Museum** (tel: 520-586-3666; www.amerind.org; Tue–Sun), housed in a lovely hacienda-style ranch built by amateur archeologist William Fulton in 1937. An important research center, its museum displays an outstanding collection of

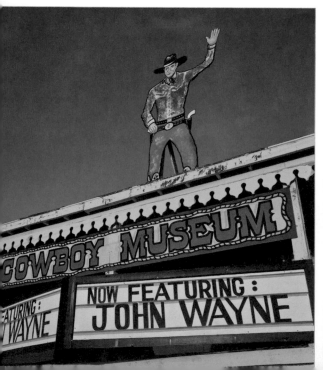

Native American art and archeological artifacts, as well as works by Western artists like Frederic Remington and William Leigh.

Tucson

From Benson, it's a quick 43 miles (69km) via I-10 to **Tucson ㊶** (pronounced "too-sawn"), a sprawling modern desert city of 980,000, with a well-preserved 18th-century Hispanic downtown, an excellent university, and stunning mountain-and-desert setting. Founded in 1776 as a Spanish settlement on Pima land, Tucson is the same age as the United States, though it only passed into American hands with the Gadsden Purchase of 1854.

Downtown Tucson, or the Old Pueblo as it is known locally, still centers on the area that was originally contained within the adobe walls of the Spanish *presidio*. This delightful spot is now dotted with artisans' shops, cafés, several good shade trees, and some extremely interesting architecture, anchored by **St Augustine Cathedral**, built in 1897, and the **Pima County Courthouse** with its mosaic tile

dome. Five historic homes stand on the grounds of the **Tucson Museum of Art and Historic Block** (tel: 520-624-2333; www.tucsonmuseumofart.org; Tue–Sun), whose collection features pre-Columbian, Hispanic, Western, and modern art.

Sonoran Desert wildlife and missions

For many visitors, Tucson's greatest appeal lies in the fantastic scenery that surrounds it. **Saguaro National Park** (tel: 520-733-5153; www.nps.gov/sagu; daily;) occupies two separate tracts of land to either side of the city proper. It was established to protect dramatic expanses of multiarmed saguaro (pronounced *sah-WA-row*) cacti. Although it's often considered emblematic of the Wild West, the saguaro – which can live for 200 years and grow to a height of 50ft (15 meters) – is native to the Sonoran Desert, only a small portion of which extends into Arizona from Mexico. The western segment of the park, the **Tucson Mountain District** (tel: 520-733-5158), holds an extraordinary "forest" of towering

Trail riding at White Stallion ranch, Tucson.

The purple prickly pear cactus is native to the Sonoran Desert.

Lake Pleasant Regional Park, near Phoenix.

saguaros, which take on an other-worldly magnificence at sunset.

Nearby, the expansive **Arizona-Sonora Desert Museum** (tel. 520-883-2702; www.desertmuseum.org; daily) is the best place to understand the flora and fauna of the Sonoran Desert. Walk through beautiful gardens of cacti and desert plants to view desert mammals, from prairie dogs to mountain lions, in naturalistic enclosures. One high-light is the walk-through aviaries, alive with darting, iridescent humming-birds, and the raptor free-flight dem-onstrations that take place twice a day from late October to mid-April.

The Mexican border at Nogales is 65 miles (105km) south of Tucson via I-19, a good place to enjoy shopping, Sonoran *ranchero*-style food, and lively *norteño* music. But even if you don't visit Mexico, it is worth driving down the lovely Santa Cruz River Valley from Tucson to Nogales. It's known as the **Mission Trail**, for the string of preserved missions on both sides of the US-Mexico border established by Italian Jesuit missionary Padre Eusebio Kino in the 1600s.

Just 9 miles (14km) from Down-town is famed **Mission San Xavier del Bac** (tel: 520-294-2624; daily). The ornate whitewashed mission church dates from around 1783 and is still in use. Both its resplendent facade and its intricately painted interior have been restored to their full glory. The "White Dove of the Desert," as it is known, was established by the Spanish in 1700 to minister to the Pima people, descend-ants of the early Hohokam tribe. The Pima are now known by the name they call themselves, Tohono O'odham. Their 2.8-million-acre (1.1-million-hectare) reservation sprawls west of Tucson to the Mexican border and adjoins **Organ Pipe Cactus National Monument** (tel: 520-387-6849; www.nps.gov/orpi; daily), a great place to enjoy desert backcountry.

Missions and missiles

Tumacácori National Historical Park (tel: 520-398-2341; www.nps.gov/tuma; daily), 40 miles (64km) south on I-19, preserves the remains of three mission churches built between 1691 and the early 1800s. Its small museum

details what mission life was like in the time of the Spanish padres. Nearby is the charming artists' colony of **Tubac**, a former mining town with a rich history and a popular February Festival of the Arts. **Tubac Presidio State Historic Park** (tel: 520-398-2252; http://azstateparks.com/parks/TUPR/index.html; daily) preserves part of the presidio erected by the Spanish in 1752.

Titan Missile Museum (tel: 520-625-7736; www.titanmissilemuseum.org; daily underground tours), near Green Valley, 16 miles (26km) south of San Xavier, is an entirely different experience. It preserves the only one of the 27 US Titan Missile II sites not to have been dismantled at the end of the Cold War. Operational July 1963 to November 1982, it held two missiles that were capable of being fired over 5,000 miles (8,000km) in less than 20 minutes.

Biosphere 2

Modern technology also created another Tucson area curiosity: **Biosphere 2** (tel: 520-838-6200; www.b2science.org; daily), near **Oracle**, 32 miles (51km) north of the city on State

77. Completed in 1991, Biosphere 2 was a private human experiment that went awry. It was designed as a 3-acre (1-hectare) hermetically sealed replica of Biosphere 1 – the planet Earth – albeit cunningly disguised as a giant terrarium – and its grand aim was to pave the way for colonization of Mars. To that end, a group of eight ex-actors and scientists – four men and four women – were locked into it for two full years, to see whether they could survive in a closed and self-sufficient environment. Now operated as a department of the University of Arizona's College of Science, tours are less exciting now that there are no "Biospherians" to be glimpsed, but you do get to go inside the huge and oddly beautiful structure, including its luxurious living quarters, and explore its multiple environments.

The Apache Trail

The quickest route between Tucson and Phoenix to the north is the long, flat 100-mile (160km) drive on I-10, which takes less than two hours. About 30 miles (48km) north of

Tumacácori National Historic Park.

FACT

Dateland, Arizona was
used as the site for two
of General Patton's
desert training camps in
the 1940s – Camp Horn
and Camp Hyder. Three
airstrips, built for training
B25 bombers, still exist.

*The hermetically
sealed environment of
Biosphere 2.*

Tucson, the interstate passes historic
Picacho Peak, a distinctive, fang-shaped volcanic promontory around
which the Battle of Picacho Peak,
the westernmost battle in the Civil
War, took place on April 15, 1862.
It's a great place to stop in spring to
photograph huge, orange carpets of
California poppies and other desert
wildflowers.

Alternatively, State 79 heads north
from Biosphere 2 on a parallel
course to Phoenix, east of the interstate. Known as the **Pinal Pioneer
Parkway**, it is lush with native vegetation, from the prickly pear and
saguaro cactus to the catclaw and
mesquite tree and is worth taking if
you have the time. It leads to **Apache
Junction**, east of Phoenix, the start of
the **Apache Trail**. This modern road
was constructed in 1905 to provide
access to **Theodore Roosevelt Dam**
㊷, the first of the great dams of the
West, built to quench the growing
thirst of nearby Phoenix. Named the
Apache Trail in the hope of encouraging tourism, it was hailed by
President Teddy Roosevelt, when he

dedicated the dam in 1911, as combining "the grandeur of the Alps,
the glory of the Rockies, and the
magnificence of the Grand Canyon."
Despite the hyperbole, it is indeed a
ravishing drive.

Shortly after leaving Apache
Junction, the Apache Trail passes the
touristy ramshackle **Goldfield Ghost
Town**, where you can take horse or
jeep rides amid the abandoned mine
machinery and false-front stores,
or simply buy a snack at the bakery. Beyond that comes your first
clear sighting of the **Superstition
Mountains**. The Spanish called
these peaks the "Mountains of Foam"
because of their effusive volcanic
ridges, but they're best known for
the legends that surround the Dutch
prospector Jacob Walz. He seems to
have struck a huge lode of gold in the
Superstitions in the late 19th century,
but no one who followed him on his
expeditions was ever seen again, and
the "Lost Dutchman Mine" remains
hidden to this day. The Superstition
Mountains have taken the life of many
an overly curious fortune-seeker.

The Apache Trail cuts into **Tonto National Forest**, where vistas and foot trails skirt the highway. The fun really begins as it winds its narrow way into the highlands. Drivers beware: you'll have to keep your eyes more on the road than the alpine rises, glorious vistas, and lush canyons. Saguaros and mesquite, dry riverbeds, and wave upon wave of mountain ridges follow a scenic overlook of the **Canyon River**. When you descend into the valley, pull up and strip down, because the blue waters are irresistible.

The trail is well paved for the 18 miles (29km) up to **Tortilla Flat**, a required stop for lovers of desert lore and witty western character. The essence of Tortilla Flat is sold in two forms: a postcard reading *Tortilla Flat/Pop. 6/30 Miles from Water/2 Feet from Hell!* and the hokey cans of Jack Rabbit Milk, "a balanced diet for unbalanced people."

Indian ruins, a temple and a university enclave

A hotel, post office, café/restaurant, gift shop, riding stable, curio shop, a legend, and a marvelous view – Tortilla Flat is a great place to stop for "the best chili in the West" and a "Howdy" from "the friendliest town in America." Admire the hundreds of dollar-bills tacked under business cards on the ceiling and walls of the café before you return to the sun-drenched desert. Roosevelt Dam lies another 30 miles (48km) up the precipitous but passable dirt road beyond Tortilla Flat. Above and behind it spreads **Roosevelt Lake**, the reservoir it created. The best views are from a steep hiking trail in **Tonto National Monument** (tel: 928-467-2241; daily; www.nps.gov/tont), just west of the dam on State 88.

That short but grueling hike culminates in a "cliff-dwelling" once occupied by the Salado culture, which disappeared from this area before the Apache arrived. Retrace State 88 into

the valley, where you'll pass through two unique suburbs, as State 88 becomes Main Street in Mesa, then Apache Boulevard in Tempe. **Mesa** contains Arizona's largest community of Latter Day Saints (Mormons), and you'll pass by their beautiful **LDS Temple.** It is closed to non-Mormons, but its Visitor Center (tel: 480-964-7164; http://www.lds.org/church/places-to-visit/mesa-arizona-temple-visitors-center) is open daily.

Tempe is home to Arizona State University, which anchors the south side of Phoenix with its lively Mill Avenue and postmodern buildings along the river. The beautifully designed **Tempe Center for the Arts** (tel: 480-350-2822; www.tempe.gov; Tue–Sat) is worth a stop. The community center houses two theaters, an art gallery, a restaurant with a view of Tempe Town Lake, an artificial lake impounded from the Salt River, and an adjoining riverwalk and sculpture garden. Turning left on University, you'll come to I-10, which quickly whisks you into the heart of **Phoenix** ❹ (see page 314).

A staple ingredient in this region, chilis are frequently hung in bundles to dry in the sun.

Petroglyph rock art at Signal Hill picnic area, Saguaro National Park.

Space cowboys should take a break from the road at the Outer Limits Restaurant, part of the Best Western Space Age Lodge, Gila Bend.

Dining at El Charro, Arizona's oldest Mexican restaurant, in Tucson.

PHOENIX TO SAN DIEGO

The 150 miles (240km) between Phoenix and the Colorado River, which marks Arizona's border with California, are interesting for the way the relatively green Sonoran Desert starts to yield to the more monochromatic Mojave Desert, your companion all the way to San Diego. You can stick with I-10 as far as Quartzsite, then change to US 95 south, or drop south much earlier, to meet I-8 at Gila Bend. Either way, your final destination in Arizona will be Yuma, where the words "furnace heat" might have been invented.

Quartzsite is only worth visiting if you're passing through in January or February, when up to a million sun-seeking, northern "snowbirds" (retirees in classic Airstream trailers and RVs) descend on the town for the **Quartzsite Powwow Rock and Mineral Show** (tel: 928-927-6325), a huge, open-air "flea market" for seekers and sellers of precious, semi-precious, and not-even-slightly-precious stones and gems of various shapes and sizes.

Otherwise, you'd do better to turn off I-10, 25 miles (40km) west of Phoenix, and take State 85 down to the I-8 truckstop of **Gila Bend**. (In fact, if you're in a hurry to get to the beach from Tucson, I-8 enables you to bypass Phoenix altogether.) Named for its location on a big bend in the Gila River, Gila Bend holds a predictable array of fast-food restaurants and motels, plus one outstanding exception. The **Best Western Space Age Lodge** (see page 422) is a marvelous 1950s-style folly, kitted out with kitsch Sputnik-shaped neon signs. Its **Outer Limits Restaurant**, which features a dazzling lunar-exploration mural, is well worth a stop for a bite to eat. The Visitor Center nearby, which doubles as a museum of local history, will confirm your suspicions that not a lot happens in Gila Bend. (The most exciting thing to happen in the area recently was, in fact, Prince Harry's stint in aircraft training in late 2011).

Signs on the interstate near Gila Bend warn that this is a "Blowing Dust Area," while bridges repeatedly cross "rivers" that are little more than dry

arroyos. Somehow, **Dateland** ⓜ, 50 miles (80km) west of Gila Bend, manages to grow a bumper annual crop of dates. If you're desperate for diversion, stop for a date shake or whatever other date-related product may strike your fancy in Dateland's solitary diner.

Mexico's Devil's Road to Yuma

There's plenty of notice that you're approaching **Yuma** ⓛ – its avenues are numbered a mile apart, thus you pass an Avenue 51E that's a full 50 miles (80km) east of downtown Yuma. Yuma is large, but it's not *that* large (about 91,000 people). The road climbs over the pass through the Gila Mountains and descends into the Colorado River valley, before there's any sign of life. That is, apart from the low-flying jets that screech overhead. Southwest Arizona is a proving ground for the US military, and the latest top-secret warplanes are constantly being tested above the barren desert that lies between I-8 and the Mexican border.

When Padre Eusebio Kino, the most tireless of all Spanish missionaries to the American Southwest, opened a trail in 1699 from Sonoita, Mexico, to what is now Yuma, he called the trail *El Camino del Diablo* – the Devil's Road. It seemingly led straight into the inferno. The town subsequently gained a long-standing reputation as one of the worst hellholes in the Wild West. Yuma smoulders to this day, but it has been tamed by the air-conditioner into a city fit for human beings. With some 339 days of sunshine and less than 4 inches (10cm) of rainfall annually, it made the *Guinness Book of World Records* as the "sunniest place on earth." All that heat has made Yuma a mecca for sun-seekers, and the gigantic sprawl of RV parks as you approach town in winter just might make you agree with Kino's description.

A historic ford on the Colorado River

Set just below the confluence of the Gila and Colorado rivers, Yuma has been known for centuries as the site of the only natural ford on the southern trail to the Pacific. As such, it was a crucial way-station on the road to

Numerous Hollywood films and television shows were shot at Old Tucson Studios.

California, even before the Gold Rush of 1849. Originally, local Quechan people held a monopoly on the lucrative river crossing, but as ever-greater numbers of starry-eyed miners demanded to be ferried into gold country, control was wrested away in some astonishingly bloodthirsty conflicts.

Fort Yuma Quechan Museum (tel: 760-572-0661; www.cba.nau.edu/caied/tribepages/Quechan.asp; daily) on the California bank preserves the 1859 fort built to protect travelers prior to the area coming under US control with the 1854 Gadsden Purchase. Ironically, it is now run by the Quechan Tribe, which uses the museum to interpret its culture.

When gold was also discovered *east* of Yuma, in 1858, the city blossomed into a port, where ore was transported by steamboat down the Colorado River and into the Gulf of California. After the mines dried up and the river was dammed, Yuma converted itself into an agricultural center, with help from irrigation technology. But it is still a crossroads, where I-8 from San Diego meets US 95. The gray railroad bridge that spans the Colorado

close to the prison was completed in 1915 as the "Ocean to Ocean" bridge that finally spared travelers the ferry ride across the river. But it was built for Model Ts, not four-wheel-drive vehicles, and the narrow bridge takes today's traffic one direction at a time.

A territorial prison and wetlands refuge

Thanks to diminished water flow, the Gila and Colorado now meet 5 miles (8km) upstream from downtown Yuma. The bluff that once overlooked their intersection is occupied by the surprisingly interesting **Yuma Territorial Prison State Historic Park** (tel: 928-783-4771; http://azstateparks.com/parks/yute/index.html; daily), which preserves the remaining structures of the most infamous prison in Arizona Territory, including its guardhouse, courtyards, cellblock, and notorious "Dark Cell" for solitary confinement. It housed a total of 3,069 convicts before its closure in 1909, three years before Arizona achieved statehood.

Inside the central building there's a rogues' gallery of photos of former

Cowboy at Rancho de los Caballeros.

inmates, including Pearl Hart, the prison's only female inmate, who was jailed for five years for robbery and released two years early when it was learned she was pregnant, presumably by one of her guards. The Hell Hole (no air-conditioning in these cells!) was so dreaded that at least a few desperadoes surely thought twice before pulling the trigger.

Yuma Crossing Heritage Area (www.yumaheritage.com) is an ambitious wetlands project that is gradually restoring 1,400 acres (560 hectares) of the riverfront, and birds and wildlife are returning, along with native plants and trees. You can walk the Yuma East Wetlands Trail for 3 miles, starting at Gateway Park. Volunteers offer guided walks on Saturday mornings.

The point from which the ferries once set off, down below on the fringes of Downtown, is now occupied by **Yuma Quartermaster Depot State Historic Park** (tel: 928-329-0471; http://azstateparks.com/parks/YUQU/index.html; Tue–Sun, closed June–Aug), formerly Yuma Crossing State Historic Park, which preserves the original river ford and the quartermaster depot. Living history demonstrations are offered by docents, recalling the bygone era when paddle-wheel steamers plied the Colorado. Outdoor interpretive exhibits can be found at Pivot Point Interpretive Plaza (daily) in the restored historic riverfront area, at the location where the first railroad train entered Arizona in 1877. The multiuse pathways provide a pleasant spot for strolling or cycling along the riverbank, linking the West and East Wetlands and other points of interest.

At the core of downtown Yuma, "**Old Yuma**" consists of a few blocks of sleepy but atmospheric Victorian-era buildings, such as the Sanguinetti House. Lutes Casino, on South Main Street, resembles a featureless barn on the outside, but the interior is bursting with memorabilia and bric-a-brac.

Camel Farm

Outside town is a surprising bit of Yuma history: camels. Camels have been a feature of the Western landscape since the late 1850s, when the US Army imported a batch of the

Prison gate at the Yuma Prison Historic Park.

Colorado River at Yuma on the Arizona–California border.

beasts to see whether they were any better equipped than horses and mules to negotiate Arizona's rough terrain. Though the camels produced amazingly high scores on their "endurance tests," they were prone to stampede and smelled atrocious. After the Civil War put them out of a job, they were set free, and became a nuisance until camel hunting became a brief but effective fad. Today **The Camel Farm** (tel: 928-627-7511; Tue–Sun am only) breeds a herd of drooling, slobbering, one-humped dromedaries along with other exotic animals.

CALIFORNIA

Over the Colorado River, down-at-heel **Winterhaven** provides a deceptively low-key introduction to California, the third-largest and most populous state in the nation. Northwest of here, the **Imperial Valley** – thanks to extensive damming and irrigation – is one of the most agriculturally productive regions on Earth. As you follow I-8 to the coast, however, it takes a while before the myth of California to be fulfilled. First, there is the desert to deal with.

The expansive Mojave has room for even the biggest of visions. Exit 164 leads to the **Center of the World** (tel: 760-572-0100; www.felicityusa.com), a unique site built by Jacques-Andre Istel, French-born author of the children's book *Coe: The Good Dragon at the Center of the World*. The Center of the World is marked on a plaque inside a pyramid in the town of Felicity, founded by Istel, who named it for his wife. In addition to the pyramid, there's a giant sundial whose gnomon replicates Michelangelo's Arm of God on the Sistine Chapel, the original staircase from the Eiffel Tower in Paris, and the incredible **Museum of History in Granite** (tel: 760-572-0100; www.historyingranite.org; call to check opening times), an ongoing project that captures the history of mankind on massive etched granite panels.

Algodones Dunes and a desert oasis

The **Algodones Dunes**, immediately west of the Colorado River, were every bit as much of an obstacle to early travelers as the river itself. This strip of deep, shifting sands stretches 40 miles (64km) north to south. It's only around 6 miles (10km) wide at this point, but for the first motorists to attempt to cross, this might as well have been the Sahara Desert. In 1915, a "Plank Road" of railroad ties was laid down to enable automobiles to rumble their way over. By 1925, when as many as 30 cars were using the road each day, it had deteriorated alarmingly. A two-lane paved highway, State 80, finally opened in August 1926; it has long since been superseded by I-8.

A small segment of the original plank road can still be seen by leaving the interstate 20 miles (32km) west of Yuma on Grays Well Road, to enter **Imperial Sand Dunes Recreation Area ㊻** (tel: 760-337-4400) immediately south. Roughly 4 miles (6km) along, parallel to the interstate and

Migrant worker harvesting lettuce near Yuma.

also to the very long **All American Canal**, the dried-out old planks descend a short slope. These arid dunes are now a raucous playground for the Californian youths who race their dune buggies and other off-road vehicles over the razor-edged inclines, while older "snowbirds" tan themselves sleepily beside their RVs.

Islands of irrigated green dotted with palms spell "oasis" at the end of the 58-mile (93km) tumble from Yuma to **El Centro**. Supposedly the largest city below sea level in the western hemisphere, and birthplace of the entertainer Cher, El Centro prospers quietly as a supply center for the Imperial Valley.

Beyond the reach of the canals, the vegetation all but disappears, and you enter the bare **Yuma Desert**. Scattered with only the occasional 14ft (4-meter) orange-blossomed ocotillo cactus, the desert floor appears to have undergone an unsuccessful hair transplant. The appropriately named **Ocotillo**, 28 miles (45km) west of El Centro, is no more than a flyblown little hamlet.

The mountain ranges that sweep down from the northwest just past Ocotillo are at first obscured by the dust, but soon you find yourself embarking on the very steep climb up their rocky flanks. The east- and westbound lanes of the interstate divide at this point, each plotting its own course across a terrain that consists of no more than piles of rust-colored boulders. Every few hundred yards stand roadside barrels filled with "Radiator Water," as the risk of overheating is so high. Atop a minor eminence at an elevation of 3,000ft (914 meters), 5 miles (8km) out of Ocotillo, the **Desert View Tower** commands a stunning view back across Imperial Valley. Constructed in 1922 using blocks of hewn granite, it holds an enjoyable jumble of exhibits on local history. Entering San Diego County at Mountain Spring, I-8 pulls south to skirt the Mexican border; a minor turn-off leads to the border town of **Jacumba**.

San Diego revealed

Near **Live Oak Springs**, 27 miles (43km) west of Ocotillo, the winds die down and the rises level off. Interstate 8 soon swoops to green valleys and into **Cleveland National Forest**, winding through Pine Valley and Alpine. As you drop toward Alpine, you should get your first glimpse of the Pacific Ocean, glinting on the horizon ahead. **El Cajon** ⓸⓻, 43 miles (69km) beyond Live Oak Springs, is a nicely landscaped city that marks the first major outpost of the San Diego metropolitan area. **La Mesa** follows, set picturesquely amid the hills that rise on El Cajon's western outskirts.

Past La Mesa, traffic on I-8 becomes increasingly congested; the overpass of I-15 is the portal to San Diego. As the interstate pushes out to the Pacific beaches, its shoulders open up onto shopping malls and numerous skyscraper hotels. A little further to the south, buildings arched by trees glimmer on the slopes. Behind them lies the sunny border city of **San Diego** ⓸⓼ (see page 322).

Performing at a Cinco de Mayo (Fifth of May) celebration.

Phoenix: Valley of the Sun

Business is booming in Phoenix, with plenty of industry, tourism, and golf courses. Just be sure to come in winter.

Phoenix may not have had any real ashes to rise from, but its founders were inspired by the knowledge that the merciless heat of the Salt River Valley had been overcome before. Between approximately 1100 and 1450, the Hohokam people successfully irrigated this region by means of a network of over 300 miles (480km) of canals. In 1867, Jack Swilling established modern Phoenix by simply redigging the waterways.

During World War II, the military used the desert for aviation training and revolutionized Phoenix by introducing air conditioning. Suddenly, life in the torrid Sonoran Desert was a year-round possibility, and the great migration was on. Now, Phoenix, with a metropolitan area population of 4.2 million people, is booming.

The city's setting is impressive. To the east soar the massive Four Peaks and Superstition Mountains, while the Sierra Estrella, sacred to the Maricopa and Gila River Indian Community, rides the southeast horizon. Hemming in the city north and south are lower mountain ranges, framing Camelback Mountain. Day hikes offer visitors an opportunity to witness the beauty (and silence) of the Sonoran Desert, but note: the average high temperature in Phoenix from June through August is 103°F (39°C). Peak tourist season is winter, when daily maximum temperatures hover around 70°F (21°C) and the valley's spa resorts and 200 golf courses fill with tourists.

Once lacking character, downtown Phoenix has transformed itself in recent years into an enticing venue. Its major cultural attractions and restaurants are located on or near the **Central Avenue** artery, which now has the appearance of a European boulevard anchored by the popular new 57-mile (92km) light rail network connecting Downtown with outlying communities.

Heritage Square, a block east of the Civic Plaza, preserves Victorian buildings in **Phoenix Heritage and Science Park** (tel: 602-262-5029; Tue–Sun). **Rosson House** (tel: 602-262-5029; Wed–Sat, closed mid-Aug through Labor Day), a striking red Victorian home built in 1895, stands out from the square's 11 buildings, while two of the city's hottest award-winning restaurants make the square a popular destination for foodies. Nearby **Arizona Science Center** (tel: 602-716-2000; www.azscience.org; daily;), a hands-on funhouse of science housed in a $50 million building designed by famed architect Antoine Predock, has 300 exhibits in five themed galleries on four floors, as well as a planetarium.

If you only visit one museum make it the spectacular **Heard Museum** (tel: 602-252-8848; www.heard. org; daily) at 2301 North Central Avenue. Founded in 1929 to house the Heard family's collection of American Indian art and artifacts, the museum's 12 galleries focus on interpreting Indian arts and crafts, both ancient and modern. Its signature exhibit is Home: Native People in the Southwest, which tells the story of Arizona's Indian tribes, then and now, through multimedia. It includes 250 historic Hopi kachina dolls collected by the late Republican senator Barry Goldwater and donated to the Heard. The classy **Phoenix Art Museum** (tel: 602-257-1880; wwwphx-art.org; Wed–Sun), around the corner from the Heard, has also recently expanded. Galleries display some 17,000 artworks by American, Mexican, and Asian artists, Southwest painters, as well as Western art by Moran and Remington.

The influence of famed architect Frank Lloyd Wright echoes throughout the **Arizona Biltmore**

Central Business District.

The Arizona Biltmore resort.

Resort (tel: 602-955-6600) at 24th Street and Missouri, 5 miles (8km) northeast of Heritage Park in swanky **Scottsdale.** Albert Chase McArthur, a former student of Wright, originally designed the building in 1929, but found himself in trouble and summoned the master for help. Wright probably gave more help than required, for the hotel is a delightful masterpiece from Wright's middle period. Wright stayed in Phoenix to found his architectural school and residence, **Taliesin West** (tel: 480-860-2700; www.franklloydwright.org; tours daily), in the Scottsdale foothills. Taliesin still bustles with architecture and design students, offering visitors not only a fascinating look at Wright's organic architecture but glimpses of how his legacy is being continued today.

Luxury spa resorts cluster around the foot of Camelback Mountain, a distinctive promontory in Scottsdale. High-end malls like **Fashion Square** are popular shopping destinations, along with **Old Town**, which has a number of galleries selling cowboy and Indian art. Don't miss the small **Scottsdale Museum of Contemporary Art** (tel: 480-874-4766; www.smoca.org; Wed–Fri), which features an installation by famed light artist James Turrell.

The huge new **Musical Instruments Museum** (tel: 48-478-6000; www.themim.org; daily) is located in northern Scottsdale. The vision of a retired CEO, it is a work-in-progress whose aim is to tell the story of music throughout the world through state-of-the-art exhibits. The entrancing **Desert Botanical Garden** (tel: 480-941-1225; www.dbg.org; daily) is located in **Papago Park** in southern Scottsdale. It displays 139 rare, threatened, and endangered species of plants from around the world as well as the Sonoran Desert, the world's largest collection of desert plants living in a natural environment.

South of the garden is the Salt River where you will find **Pueblo Grande Museum Archeological Park** (tel: 602-495-0901; http://phoenix.gov/recreation/arts/museums/pueblo/index.html; Oct–Apr Mon–Sat), preserving a rare 1,500-year-old Hohokam village ruin built on a mound within sight of the airport. It is an intriguing juxtaposition, one that is common throughout the Valley of the Sun.

African savanna re-created at Phoenix Zoo.

Highway 1 by Big Sur coast.

THE PACIFIC ROUTE

A guide to the Pacific Coast, with principal sites
cross-referenced by number to the maps.

On the road in California.

America's historic US 101 – which stretched from San Diego all the way up the coast through Oregon and Washington to the Canadian border, and eventually became, in part, today's California Highway 1 – has a history that is comparable with its more famous companion, Route 66. Until 1909, it had been a narrow, bumpy, dirt-surfaced track on which horse-drawn wagons and primitive autos competed for space. Then a concrete and macadam road began stretching north from the cities of San Diego and Oceanside.

The spiffy new road stimulated the rise of a phenomenon known as "car culture," epitomized in sunny California, which spawned all the enterprises that subsequently came to be associated with travel along the highway, such as gas stations, car dealers, motels, diners, and auto laundries.

The highway led visitors from all parts of the Pacific Coast to San Diego's Balboa Park for the 1915–16 Panama-California Exposition, enticed Hollywood movie stars and others to its pristine beaches, and lured those in search of a good time during Prohibition to Mexico's Tijuana.

In 1925, the road officially became US 101. Increased traffic spelled its doom, however, and by the end of the war a new four-lane highway, eventually to become Interstate 5, bypassed the old route. Today, the Pacific Coast Highway, often abbreviated to "PCH," and also known as El Cabrillo

Surfing at Zuma Beach, Malibu.

Trail, is a sometimes-scrappy, often sea-scented mixture of the old US 101, California Highway, and roaring Interstate 5. We have followed it here as faithfully as possible, stopping off at breathtaking sites like California's Big Sur and Hearst Castle and sometimes diverting inland and away from its charms to visit vibrant cities like Portland and Seattle. Along the way there are quaint Victorian-era towns, wineries, giant redwoods, romantic windswept beaches, historic sites such as Mission San Juan Capistrano, and countless opportunities to see a fascinating array of wildlife.

The Pacific Coast Highway's villages and towns – as well as much of its old structure – are still here, and for those who have time, and a romantic desire to reclaim an earlier America, following Highway 1 and historic 101 along to Seattle can lead to unimaginable pleasures.

A SHORT STAY IN SAN DIEGO

San Diego is a busy, elegant harbor town with a history unsurpassed in the state of California. Here's a list of the not-to-be-missed attractions.

Mission San Diego (1769) offers a peaceful sanctuary with fragrant gardens. A museum and walking tour tell the story of the "Mother of the Missions," while Mass is still celebrated in the basilica.

Old Town State Historic Park preserves the site of the original settlement where Spanish soldiers and their families lived until the early 1800s. Its historic adobe structures now house interesting small museums and shops, offering a glimpse of California as it was in the Spanish, Mexican, and early American periods.

Thar she blows! Board a **Hornblower yacht** at **Broadway Pier** for a 3.5-hour professionally guided whale-watching cruise, where you can expect to see sea lions, harbor seals, dolphins, and, between December and April, gray whales during their seasonal migrations between Alaska and Mexico. Scenic harbor and dinner cruises can be enjoyed all year.

From Dixieland jazz to haute cuisine, the old, restored **Gaslamp Quarter** offers some of the city's best entertainment and nightlife, as well as interesting Victorian architecture. Shopaholics should make a beeline for nearby **Horton Plaza**, which has around 150 upmarket shops.

In the heart of San Diego, 1,200-acre (490-hectare) **Balboa Park** is San Diego's major cultural destination, with 17 museums, theaters, beautiful gardens, art galleries, and more. A park pass, available at the visitor center, admits you to most of the museums, several in ornate old buildings. Have lunch at the rose garden, visit the **Spanish Village Art Center** and, afterward, soak up some culture at the **Starlight Bowl** or **The Old Globe theater**.

Hire a convertible and cruise the **59-Mile Scenic Drive**, which takes you through **Downtown**, **Balboa Park**, the beaches, **La Jolla**, and out to **Cabrillo National Monument** on **Point Loma** for fabulous views of the city and the open ocean.

Vessels of all sizes line the natural harbor of San Diego Bay, from yachts to the USS Midway aircraft carrier, now a museum.

The Cabrillo National Monument. The statue on Point Lom commemorates the first European landing on the West Coast

Hotel del Coronado. Eleven US presidents ha visited this characterful Victorian resort.

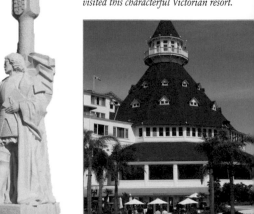

Swim, surf, and sunbathe on San Diego's sandy beaches.

THE BIRTHPLACE OF CALIFORNIA

Although Spaniard Juan Cabrillo was the first European to stake a claim to California in 1542, it wasn't until July 16, 1769, that it became a reality, when Padre Junípero Serra conducted a mass dedicating the newly created Mission San Diego de Alcalá on Presidio Hill (it was moved to its present site in Mission Valley five years later). History and luxury can be found in many parts of this harbor city, which has numerous upscale shops and 90 golf courses. San Diego's harborfront, the Embarcadero, can be touristy, but there are enough historic sites, cultural attractions, fine restaurants, shady walks, harbor cruises, and sandy beaches to appeal to the most discerning of visitors.

Historic Gaslamp Quarter of San Diego, the place to head to for entertainment, nightlife, shopping and dining.

IMPORTANT INFORMATION

Population: 1.3 million
Dialing codes: 619, 858
Website: www.sandiego.org
Tourist information: San Diego International Visitor Information Center, 1140 North Harbor Drive, San Diego, CA 92101; tel: 619-236-1212

SAN DIEGO TO LOS ANGELES

Beach towns, beach facilities, and beaches themselves – more than 20 of them – line this short stretch of coastline. Is it any wonder the bikini first became famous here?

The journey from seaside **San Diego ❶** (see page 322) to glittering Los Angeles is only around 125 miles (200km), but following the ragged coastal roads can take much longer than that short distance implies. It's also much more rewarding, as the coastal route meanders past Southern California's best beaches, prettiest towns, and most exclusive residential areas. For navigational purposes, the road signs along the way go by a variety of names – Highway 1, US 101, I-5 - but to most Californians, this mix of roads paralleling the ocean is known simply as the Pacific Coast Highway (PCH).

LA JOLLA TO OCEANSIDE

The first stop out of San Diego is **La Jolla ❷** (pronounced "la-hoy-ya"), a seaside community that once boasted "the richest zip code in America." This college community and upscale town can be reached in a few minutes by heading north up I-5, but a more scenic way is to start the drive to Los Angeles as you intend to proceed – using water as your navigator. From SeaWorld, take the road called SeaWorld Drive to West Mission Bay Drive, routes that curl along the bottom of **Mission Bay** itself. The road turns north (changing into Mission Boulevard) to parallel Mission Beach, then the livelier

Pacific Beach, before rolling into La Jolla. La Jolla has beautiful homes and a downtown area – which calls itself "the village" – filled with expensive shops, as well as a branch of San Diego's **Museum of Contemporary Art** (tel: 858-454-3541; www.mcasd. org; Thur–Tue). Described by writer Raymond Chandler as "a nice place for old people and their parents," La Jolla featured in Tom Wolfe's 1960s surfer novel *The Pump House Gang*. On the campus of the University of California is La Jolla Playhouse,

Main Attractions
San Diego
La Jolla
Birch Aquarium
Oceanside
Mission San Juan Capistrano
Laguna Beach
Newport Beach
Huntington Beach
Long Beach
Venice Beach
Santa Monica

Sunset over the San Diego coast.

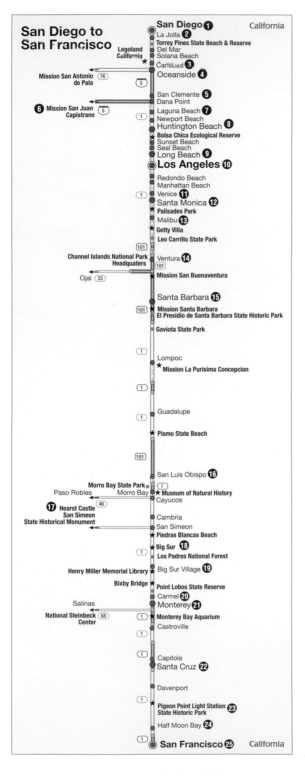

San Diego to San Francisco

Legoland California

San Diego ❶
La Jolla ❷
Torrey Pines State Beach & Reserve
Del Mar
Solana Beach
Carlsbad ❸
Oceanside ❹

Mission San Antonio de Pala (76)
(5)

❻ Mission San Juan Capistrano (5)
(1)

San Clemente ❺
Dana Point
Laguna Beach ❼
Newport Beach
Huntington Beach ❽
Bolsa Chica Ecological Reserve
Sunset Beach
Seal Beach
Long Beach ❾
Los Angeles ❿

Redondo Beach
Manhattan Beach
(1)
Venice ⓫
Santa Monica ⓬
Palisades Park
Malibu ⓭
Getty Villa
Leo Carrillo State Park
(101)

Channel Islands National Park Headquaters
Ojai (33)

Ventura ⓮
(101)
Mission San Buenaventura

Santa Barbara ⓯
(101)
Mission Santa Barbara
El Presidio de Santa Barbara State Historic Park

Gaviota State Park

(1)
Lompoc
★ Mission La Purisima Concepcion

(1)
Guadalupe
(1)
★ Pismo State Beach

(101)
San Luis Obispo ⓰

Morro Bay State Park
(1)
Paso Robles   Morro Bay
★ Museum of Natural History
Cayucos
❿ Hearst Castle (46)
San Simeon State Historical Monument

Cambria
San Simeon
★ Piedras Blancas Beach
★ Big Sur ⓲
(1)
Los Padres National Forest

Henry Miller Memorial Library ★ Big Sur Village ⓳
Bixby Bridge ★ Point Lobos State Reserve
Carmel ⓴
Salinas   Monterey ㉑
National Steinbeck (68)
Center (1)
★ Monterey Bay Aquarium
(1) Castroville

(1)
Capitola
Santa Cruz ㉒

(1)
Davenport

★ Pigeon Point Light Station ㉓
State Historic Park
Half Moon Bay ㉔
(1)
San Francisco ㉕   California

California

---

whose forerunner was founded by the late actor Gregory Peck. The caves carved into its coastal bluffs have long been a paradise for both deep-sea divers and cliff divers, and nearby **Black's Beach** was once legally – now illegally – a nudist beach.

At the north end of town, above Point La Jolla, is the renowned **Scripps Institution of Oceanography**, whose well-stocked **Birch Aquarium** (tel: 858-534-3474; www.aquarium.ucsd.edu; daily) offers whale-watching cruises in season. Among the more than 60 different habitats exhibiting marine life is a two-story sea-filled tank that replicates a kelp bed with all its familiar and unfamiliar creatures. Farther north and also by the sea is the **Salk Institute**, designed by the late Louis I. Kahn, perhaps one of America's most admired contemporary architects. The institute is named after its famous resident scientist, Jonas Salk, who devised the polio vaccine.

Torrey Pines Scenic Drive

La Jolla Shores Drive parallels Torrey Pines Road, which follows a winding hillside out of La Jolla through the affluent suburb of Torrey Pines – both named for the trees of that name, which are environmentally protected. The road accesses **Torrey Pines Scenic Drive**. Look for the windswept hillside that flying enthusiasts have been using to launch gliders over the ocean since the 1930s. **Torrey Pines Gliderport** (tel: 858-452-9858; www.sandiegofreeflight.com; daily) offers introductory lessons in paragliding; spectators are welcome. There's also a restaurant and flight sport shop at the site. **Torrey Pines State Reserve** (tel: 858-755-2063; www.torreypine.org; daily) and **Torrey Pines State Beach** are two places perfect for picnics.

Del Mar and Solana Beach

A series of small coastal roads, which together make up US 101, parallels I-5 as far as the town of Oceanside, where the mighty interstate takes over until it reaches Dana Point. From then on, PCH becomes Highway 1 more or less until it reaches San Francisco.

Both the coast road and the interstate lead to the community of **Del Mar**, which has an Amtrak Station. Its famous racetrack (tel: 858-755-1141) has attracted crowds since the 1930s. It was rescued from collapse by actor Pat O'Brien and singer Bing Crosby, who turned the track into one of America's most popular racing circuit venues. The season begins in July, a week after Del Mar's big fair ends, and runs until mid-September.

The track's sandy-colored main building, in a sort of California-meets-Mediterranean style, can be glimpsed from the interstate, but much of the town itself lies farther down the hill, beside the coast road. Head for Camino del Mar, with its art galleries, boutiques, and outdoor dining with oceanside views.

The road passes **Solana Beach**, with its futuristic-looking railroad station, and the north San Diego communities that make up Encinitas – Old Encinitas, New Encinitas, Leucadia, Cardiff-by-the-Sea, and Olivenhain – which run into each other along this stretch of coast. A profusion of stop signs and red lights can slow progress; otherwise, this is a pleasant stretch to drive, with plenty of roadside trees, the beach and the railroad track both near the road, and here and there a "Historic US 101" sign. Sweet-smelling **San Diego Botanic Gardens** (tel: 760-436-3036; www.sdbgarden.org; daily) in **Encinitas (formerly Quail Botanical Gardens)** may be worth a stop to admire the waterfall and extensive collection of exotic plants. The **San Dieguito Heritage Museum** (tel: 760-632-9711; www.sdheritage.org; Wed–Fri, last Sat of the month;) specializes in the history of the area – from the Diegueño tribe of 10,000 years ago to life today – and includes a fine collection of more than 8,000 photographs. The beach is a few blocks away; the railroad parallels the road to the east. At the north end of the community are the golden domes of the Self-Realization Fellowship temple.

TIP

Birch Aquarium at San Diego's Scripps Institution of Oceanography offers whale-watching cruises through its highly regarded aquarium, December to April. Tel: 858-534-3474 for more information.

These waters form part of the migratory path for whales.

TIP

One- and two-day "hopper" tickets allow admission to both Legoland and Sea Life Aquarium in Carlsbad, California. Buying online (www.legoland.com) removes the need to queue at the ticket booths.

Carlsbad

At **Carlsbad ❸**, the road runs along the beach and through the pretty downtown village, with its antiques stores and historic **Carlsbad Mineral Water Spa** (tel: 760-434-1887; www. carlsbadmineralspa.com), which reflects the heritage of its spa-town namesake in the Czech Republic. The region is known for flowers, particularly flowering bulbs, which it sells nationwide. Almost 50 hillside acres (20 hectares) are resplendent with brightly colored Giant Tecolote Ranunculus at **The Flower Fields at Carlsbad Ranch** (tel: 760-431-0352; www.theflowerfields.com; Mar–May), a big draw every spring. The **Museum of Making Music** (tel: 760-438-5996; www.themuseumofmakingmusic. org; Tue–Sun) spans a century of music-making in America. Exhibits include vintage instruments, samples of music from each era, and photographs and paintings.

Carlsbad's 128-acre (52-hectare) **Legoland California** (tel: 760-918-5346; www.california.legoland.com; June–Aug daily, Sept–May Thur–Mon) was the first Legoland theme park in the US. It used 120 million of its signature toy plastic bricks to depict such scaled-down landmarks as New York City and Washington, DC – as well as Castle Hill with an "enchanted walk" where children can search for hidden treasure. Also on the grounds is a waterpark and the Sea Life Aquarium.

Oceanside surf history

With almost 4 miles (6km) of white-sand beaches and "world-class surf," **Oceanside ❹** is an appropriate place to find the **California Surf Museum** (tel: 760-721-6876; www.surfmuseum.org; daily), which displays the evolution of surfboards from 16-footers weighing 200 pounds (90kg) to fiberglass creations known as "potato-chip boards."

There's a huge market among surfing dudes for memorabilia, making much of the museum's collection priceless. Famous surfing veterans such as Duke Kahanamoka are honored here.

Other interesting museums include that of **Oceanside Historical Society** (tel: 760-722-4786; www.oceanside

Sailboats in Avalon harbor, Santa Catalina Island.

historicalsociety.org; Thur–Fri, Sat by appointment;); **Oceanside Museum of Art** (tel: 760-435-3720; www.oma-online.org; Tue–Sun); and **Buena Vista Audubon Nature Center** (tel: 760-439-2473; www.bvaudubon.org; Tue–Sun), beside a lagoon on the highway south of town. Four miles (6km) inland from the beach is the lovely 1795 **Mission San Luis Rey de Francia** (tel: 760-757-3651; www.sanluisrey.org; daily), the largest of the 21 California missions. Nearby is **Heritage Park Village and Museum** (tel: 760-801-0645; park daily, buildings Sun), whose old buildings include the cottage that was once Oceanside's post office.

Watch for the **101 Cafe** (tel: 760-722-5220; www.101cafe.net; daily) as you drive through Oceanside. While the bright mural on its outside wall is a contemporary tribute to Highway 101, the diner itself is the real thing. Built in 1928, it is the town's oldest restaurant and is filled with memorabilia. Oceanside has more cafés and shops located in a pleasant man-made harbor, with a lighthouse that serves as a marina for several hundred boats at the north end. From here, boats run across to **Santa Catalina Island** (for information, contact the Catalina Island Chamber of Commerce and Visitors Bureau, tel: 310-510-1520; www.catalinachamber.com). Oceanside's pier, just north of Mission Avenue, is the longest recreational wooden pier on the West Coast. Hundreds of downtown walkways are marked with the mysterious O.U. MIRACLE, the name of contractor Orville Ullman Miracle, whose construction company submitted the winning bid in the 1920s to improve the community's streets.

OCEANSIDE TO LOS ANGELES

An interesting diversion from Oceanside is to drive inland along State Route 76 for a few miles to **Mission San Antonio de Pala** (tel: 760-742-3317; www.missionsanantonio.org; daily) on the Pala Indian Reservation. This is the only Californian mission still serving a Native American tribe. San Antonio has celebrated its Corpus Christi Festival, with an open-air mass, dances, and games, on the first Sunday of every June since 1816.

The United States Marine Corps occupies the coastal area north of Oceanside, where the coast road is incorporated into I-5 and the sea is half a mile away. Just north of the controversial San Onofre Nuclear Power Plant is **San Clemente ❺**, where former US president Richard Nixon, an Orange County native, set up a Western White House on his 25-acre (10-hectare) estate. This attractive town, with its Spanish Colonial-style red-tiled roofs and white stucco walls, prompted the *Los Angeles Times* to write in 1927: "If the charms of this place could be shown to the poor, snow-bound, wind-beaten people back East, there would be an exodus so great the hills above San Clemente would be covered like mushrooms."

Golf carts are used to get around on Santa Catalina Island.

The lovely Mission San Juan Capistrano.

Laguna Beach.

In 1925 the town's founder, a former mayor of Seattle named Ole Hanson, purchased and designed the community on what was then empty space. He is memorialized at **Casa Romantica Cultural Center and Gardens** (tel: 949-498-2139; www.casa romantica.org; Tue–Sun), his old home near the Parque Del Mar, as well as at the Ole Hanson Beach Club and Ole's Tavern.

Writing in the *San Clemente Journal*, Ann Batty claimed that it was San Clemente designers who first popularized the bikini on local beaches, of which there are many (bikinis *and* beaches). San Clemente and Doheny beaches allow camping for a small fee, and Doheny, Dana Point, Laguna Niguel, Irvine Coast, and Newport Beach all have marine life preserves (patrolled by state fish and game wardens) that are open to the public.

Dana Point and Catalina Island

Capistrano Beach and Doheny State Beach span San Juan Creek, just before **Dana Point**, where most of the buildings in the harbor complex are a lot younger than they look – although the overall effect is quite attractive. There are dozens of places to shop and eat, and whale-watching excursions depart from here in season (Dec– Mar). Dana Point's annual Festival of Whales is an amusing event, with its imaginative whale costumes, parade of clowns, jugglers, and antique cars, and lively street fair.

The **Ocean Institute** (tel: 949-496- 2274; www.ocean-institute.org; Sat–Sun), at the northern end of the harbor, commemorates Richard Henry Dana, whose seafaring exploits from here resulted in the novel *Two Years Before the Mast*, which became a 1946 movie starring Alan Ladd. **Catalina Island**, 22 miles (35km) of the coast, can be reached from here, too. This makes a fabulous day trip. Hour-long Catalina Express boat trips depart 30 times a day (tel: 800-481-3470; www.goto catalina.com) for the city of Avalon and town of Two Harbors.

San Juan Capistrano

Interstate 5 now veers away from the coast and heads inland to the town of San Juan Capistrano. Following it into town, Del Obispo Street leads to Camino Capistrano, on which sits celebrated **Mission San Juan Capistrano** ⑥ (tel: 949-234-1330; www.misssionsjc.com; daily), seventh in the chain of California missions founded by Franciscan padres in the late 1700s. There's a statue of Father Junípero Serra, now beatified, who founded this and eight other California missions. The Serra chapel behind the church is the oldest building still in use in the state of California. Pick up a free map that identifies and dates the chapel's treasures, including the bells to the left of the church.

San Juan Capistrano is most famous, of course, for its swallows, whose return signals the start of spring. Their scheduled arrival is on St Joseph's Day (Mar 19) and their departure for the warmer climate of Argentina on October 23. By some mysterious alchemy, the swallows have almost always been on time; their arrival here is marked by a week-long festival with mariachi bands leading a parade. Nevertheless, disappointed tourists sometimes arrive to find only pigeons.

Highway 1

Back on the coast, PCH now officially becomes Highway 1. It's been a while since the long-gone Serpentarium at **Laguna Beach** ❼ advertised *rattlesnake à la Maryland* on the reptile zoo's menu – today, this upscale beach community is full of art galleries and chic shops. Laguna was always a favorite of Hollywood's movie colony, and Mary Pickford, Bette Davis, Judy Garland, and Rudolph Valentino were just a few of the movie stars who maintained homes here.

The resort has established a worldwide reputation with its annual **Pageant of the Masters** each summer, at which well-rehearsed volunteers take up their roles in living reproductions of famous paintings.

Popular **Laguna Art Museum** (tel: 949-494-8971; www.lagunaartmuseum. org; daily) is a great place to see art; the city and local galleries organize a **First Thursdays Art Walk** (www.firstthursdaysartwalk.com), when some 40 galleries stay open from 6 to 9pm and offer music, food, drink, and entertainment; a free trolley is available, or you can walk. The Visitors Bureau located at 252 Broadway (tel: 949-497-9229; www.lagunabeachinfo.com; Mon–Fri) has information on other "heritage tours," such as the **Murphy-Smith Historical Bungalow** (tel: 949-497-6834; Fri–Sun), one of the few houses in downtown Laguna Beach remaining from the 1920s.

Whale-watching trips to view the gray whale migrations are popular here, but there is plenty for outdoors lovers to enjoy. Lace up your hiking boots and check out **Laguna Coast Wilderness Park** (tel: 949-923-2235; www.ocparks.com/lagunacoast), a native plant and wildlife refuge on Laguna Canyon Road; the worthwhile **Pacific Marine Mammal Center** (tel: 949-494-3050; www.pacificmmc. org; daily), which cares for sick and injured seals; **Laguna Outdoors** (tel: 949-874-6620), which offers guided trail hiking and mountain biking along the coast; or **Glenn E. Vedder Ecological Reserve** (tel: 949-497-6571; www.lagunabeachinfo.com), an underwater park at the north end of the main beach, where divers can explore marine life.

Balboa peninsula

Upscale **Balboa peninsula**, with its 6 miles (10km) of sandy shore, encloses a harbor filled with yachts and a large paddle wheeler moored beside the highway bridge. It's hard to miss **Balboa Pavilion** on Main Street – it was built in 1905 as a railroad terminal with a distinctive but totally unnecessary steeple. Behind it, if you get here early enough, you'll find fishing boats unloading their daily catch. Almost as old is the ferry that makes

Balboa Pavilion, Newport Beach.

the 3-minute trip from the end of Palm Street to **Balboa Island**, with its million-dollar homes and classy shops and cafés. The hour-long walk around the island along the sidewalk hugging the water's edge is enjoyable, particularly just before twilight.

On your way back across the narrow channel, someone will surely point out, on nearby islands, the former homes of John Wayne and cowboy hero Roy Rogers. From **Balboa Pier**, you can admire the kite-flyers, frisbee-throwers, and bodysurfers. Check out the restaurant at the end of the pier before finishing up at the Balboa Fun Zone, with its rides and video arcades.

Waves cascade over the breakwater in pretty **Newport Beach**. It's not a swimming beach; expert body-surfers are the only people with the right skills to negotiate this water. Kids will enjoy the hands-on experience at **Newport Harbor Nautical Museum** (tel: 949-675-8915; www.explorocean.org; Wed–Sun), while **Orange County Museum of Art** (tel: 949-759-1122; www.ocma.net;

Wed–Sun) is the premier visual arts center in Orange County, and you may be lucky enough to visit when a blockbuster art exhibition is on, such as the critically acclaimed *Picasso to Pollock: Modern Masterpieces from the Wadsworth Atheneum Museum of Art*. You can reach Catalina Island from Newport Beach on the *Catalina Flyer*; check with the tourist office (tel: 800-942-6278). In **Corona del Mar**, just to the south, the gardens of the **Sherman Library** and **Roger's Gardens** are pleasant places to pause.

Huntington Beach

Many communities around here jostle for the title "Surf City," but **Huntington Beach** ❽ stakes a strong claim. In 1994, it inaugurated a sidewalk **Surfers Walk of Fame** in the presence of its surf-fanatical congressman Dana Rohrabacher, and it also has an **International Surfing Museum** (tel: 714-960-3483; www.surfingmuseum.org; Wed–Sun).

The highway heads along the coast past Huntington State Beach and the state's longest municipal pier,

International Surfing Museum at Huntington Beach.

rebuilt in concrete after the original was destroyed by a fierce storm. Three blocks up Main Street and directly opposite the pier is **Plaza Almeria**, with an attractive collection of shops, restaurants, and homes. Farther uptown, another old mall, the **Huntington Beach Center**, is an entertainment and shopping complex.

Rail tycoon Henry Huntington introduced the railroad here in the late 1800s, and a subsequent oil boom brought prosperity to a town that ironically is now best known for its environmental awareness. Its 350-acre (140-hectare) **Central Park**, 50 percent of which is devoted to wildlife and greenery, is a mere hors d'oeuvre to the main entrée, the sprawling **Bolsa Chica Ecological Reserve** (tel: 714-846-3460), which preserves the vast coastal salt marsh that serves as a stopover for birds migrating between North and South America.

The best spot for birdwatchers is on the inland side of the highway between Golden West Street and Warner Avenue, opposite the entrance to the state beach. There are walking trails and plenty of parking. **Bolsa Chica Interpretive Center** (tel: 714-846-1114; daily), which offers bird checklists, is at Warner Avenue. Not far away, between Warner and Heil avenues, is the **Monarch Butterfly Habitat**, where rare migratory butterflies gather in the eucalyptus trees between November and March. Passing through the small, waterside community of **Sunset Beach**, you can't miss a huge wooden water tower beside the highway. It became a private residence years ago, but is a local landmark.

Seal Beach pier and Naples gondolas

At the Los Angeles County line, **Seal Beach**, an unspoiled enclave with an 80-year-old inn and a lengthy pier uncluttered with modern diversions, is the last place at which the ocean can be seen from the highway for many

miles. To the right of the highway at **Belmont Shore**, you can make a diversion along Second Street, which skirts the beach of Alamitos Bay. **Gondola Getaway** on East Ocean Beach Boulevard (tel: 562-433-9595; www. gondolagetawayinc.com; daily) operates hour-long tours in real gondolas along canals that pass the elegant homes of neighboring **Naples**.

Highway 1 goes inland here, bypassing Long Beach, San Pedro, and the Palo Verdes Peninsula to hit the coast again just south of Redondo Beach.

The Queen Mary in Long Beach

Although PCH bypasses **Long Beach ❾**, it's worth passing through town to see some of its attractions, which include the world's largest mural, a panorama of marine life that covers the entire surface of the Long Beach Arena on Ocean Boulevard. Other sights include the magnificent **Aquarium of the Pacific** (tel: 562-590-3100; www.aquariumofpacific. org; daily) and the venerable occan liner *Queen Mary* (tel: 800-437-2934

The famous Art Deco ocean liner in Long Beach, the Queen Mary, is home to a hotel, restaurants and bars.

Gondola tour in Naples.

or 562-435-3511; www.queenmary.com; daily), which made 1,000 transatlantic crossings and was a heroine of World War II before ending her journey here – moored in the harbor. The ship's history is a starry one, having been the carrier of choice for both celebrities and royalty; visitors can pretend to be the same by staying overnight in a cabin, or dine in the elegantly restored Art Deco Sir Winston's restaurant.

Long Beach has positioned itself as a sleek, modern city in recent years, and it certainly has a number of architecturally chic new structures. But it's also anxious to promote its historic downtown buildings from the early part of the 20th century. A walking tour map of more than 40 of these landmarks is available from the Visitors Bureau (tel: 800-452-7829; www.visitlongbeach.com). If you're traveling with kids, note that State 22 east from Long Beach hooks up with I-5 and leads to Anaheim, where the attractions include **Disneyland**, Knotts Berry Farm, Adventure City, and Medieval Times.

Rollercoaster at Knott's Berry Farm amusement park, Anaheim.

Venice canal.

Harbor tours

Headquarters of Southern California's fishing fleet, **San Pedro** once carried the distinction of being a genuine fishing port. The old town is long gone, replaced by an imaginatively designed pseudo-19th-century construction called Ports O'Call Village. Several blocks of saltbox-type weathered-looking shops and numerous restaurants are a pleasure to walk around. Harbor tours and fishing trips leave from here (as well as the *Catalina Express* and a beautiful classic sailing ship), and there are masses of free parking space. Green-and-white trolleys run along the waterfront, stopping at the World Cruise center, the maritime museum, Ports O'Call Village and the Frank Gehry-designed **Cabrillo Marine Aquarium** (tel: 310-548-7562; www.cabrillomarineaquarium. org; Tue–Sun).

San Pedro's **Cabrillo Beach** has earned a reputation as one of the best places in the area to go windsurfing, and beginners especially favor the sheltered waters inside the harbor breakwater. Between March

and September – twice a month, like clockwork – milky-white grunion fish ride in on the tide by the thousand to deposit their eggs in the sand.

On the **Palos Verdes** peninsula are multi-million-dollar Italianate villas and French châteaux overlooking the ocean. Abalone Cove, the beach west of Narcissa Drive, is an ecological preserve at the end of a steep path, perfect for divers and tide-poolers. Just past the Golden Shores mall is a lighthouse beside which, at the **Point Vicente Interpretive Center** (tel: 310-541-0334; www.sanpedro.com/sp_point/ptvicic. htm; daily), are long-lens telescopes for sighting passing whales (Dec–Apr), and an exhibit in which visitors can don earphones to hear the mournful voices of these loveable mammals.

About a mile farther on is the wood-and-glass **Wayfarers Chapel** (daily), designed by Frank Lloyd Wright's son, whose inspiration is said to have been Northern California's majestic redwood trees. The chapel was built in 1951 as a memorial to the 18th-century Swedish theologian Emmanuel Swedenborg. Walking around the peaceful gardens to the sound of songbirds, a fountain, and the gurgling stream is a very tranquil experience. There are services in the chapel at 11am every Sunday.

Beach towns

By now we are well and truly in **Los Angeles ❿** (see page 236), although most of this sprawling city's inland tourist attractions lie quite a ways farther north. LA's southern beaches are varied and linked by a combination of Highway 1 and minor roads. After its chances of becoming a major port were wrecked by its vulnerability to severe storms, **Redondo Beach** turned its attention to tourism. A Pacific Electric Railway developer hired a Hawaiian teenager called George Freeth to demonstrate surfing, and before long visitors were flocking to watch "the man who can walk on water."

In the 1930s, even bigger crowds were lured by the gambling ships moored offshore – the most famous being the *Rex*, which could accommodate 1,500 customers taking the 25 cents ride out to the boat from the town pier. Offshore gaming was outlawed by Congress in 1946, but a pier remains at the center of the town's colorful boardwalk. The current pier is horseshoe-shaped, after several predecessors were destroyed by storms, while Redondo Beach itself is a big draw for bodybuilders.

Follow Catalina Avenue from Redondo Pier to **Hermosa Beach**, an inland road leading past Kings Harbor Marina, opposite which an enormous ocean mural is painted on the wall of the power plant. Hermosa Avenue continues for quite a way one block from the beach. The beach itself stretches for eight sandy miles (13km) between Kings Harbor and **Marina Del Rey**, the longest uninterrupted stretch in Los Angeles County. There are pedestrian-only streets leading from Hermosa Avenue to the beach at every block. At 22nd Street, a good

LA'S PETERSEN AUTOMOTIVE MUSEUM

Lovers of automobiles and travel will want to make a sidetrip into Los Angeles to visit the **Petersen Automotive Museum**, one of the world's largest museums devoted exclusively to the history and cultural impact of the car. For when it comes to vehicles, no city knows them like Los Angeles, and no one can know Los Angeles without a vehicle.

This city, like few others, was designed for the car, and its endless miles of freeway tie it together the way rivers tie together London or Paris. With a board of advisors comprising high-profile enthusiasts like racing ace Parnelli Jones, the four floors of this $40 million museum detail everything you ever wanted to know about four wheels, and the culture that rides above them. The second floor houses racing and classic cars, hot rods, movie-star cars, and vintage motorcycles.

But the Petersen is not just about transportation; it's also about style. Although the museum has yet to host an exhibition on why balding old men buy flashy red sports cars, it does have rotating cultural exhibitions covering such novelties as low-riding cars, and the history of that quintessential American icon: the pick-up truck. The museum is at 6060 Wilshire Boulevard, tel: 323-930-2277 (CARS); Tue–Sun; www.petersen.org.

TIP

If you're passing through LA in September, visit the Greek Festival for a celebration of all things Hellenic, from ouzo and baklava to Greek dancing and raffles. Tel: 323-737-2424; www.lagreekfest.com.

neighborhood place to sit outside and watch the locals while drinking a cup of coffee is **Martha's 22nd Street Grill** (see page 447).

Hermosa is known for its nightclubs, Marina Del Rey for its child-friendly beaches. In between the two is **Manhattan Beach**, named by a homesick New Yorker who was living here in 1902, when it was a community of just a dozen families. Its population grew dramatically during World War II, when aircraft plants sprang up along Avalon Boulevard. In recent years, the Disney company has constructed a dozen enormous sound stages in what is still largely a commuter community of LA.

In the last few years, this part of Orange County has become second only to Hollywood as a venue for moviemakers, with its coastal piers especially attractive to the makers of television commercials. The scene down by the water resembles an old episode of *Baywatch*, with plenty of bronzed and beautiful joggers, rollerbladers, and volleyball players.

Venice and its canals

Just north of Marina Del Rey, the long pedestrian and bicycle path linking **Venice ⓫** (and **Venice Beach**) with Santa Monica is a lively hub of activity, especially in Venice itself, where you'll encounter rollerbladers of both sexes, rainbow-haired punks, magicians, fortune tellers, itinerant musicians, and pumped-up bodybuilders flexing their biceps at **Muscle Beach**. You can rent rollerblades on Windward Avenue or a bicycle on Washington Street (opposite the abandoned pier), or just sit at one of the sidewalk cafés and admire the passing parade. The most interesting place to grab a snack in Venice is probably the art- and artist-filled **Rose Café** (see page 449) on Rose Avenue. If you feel like getting away from the noise and the relentless body-beautiful activities, this is also a good spot from which to begin

exploring Venice proper, which is surprisingly different from the image normally associated with the place.

The lesser-visited town of Venice is much more charming than the beach. Take a stroll through the residential area around the inland canals, where a proliferation of bright flowers tumbles over sagging fences and ducks nestle under upturned boats on tiny jetties. Visitors can pick their way along rutted paths, over gentle hump-backed bridges and past lovingly tended gardens, admiring the variegated architecture, numerous birds, and floral displays.

More than 70 years after the death of Abbott Kinney, who acquired and reclaimed what was worthless marshland in anticipation of creating an "Italy in California," some of his vision still remains in what is probably the most pleasant walk in urban Los Angeles.

The original circulation system for the canals – a design that envisaged seawater pulsing through 30-inch (76cm) pipes with every fresh tide – proved unworkable, and the canals themselves became sand-clogged and

stagnant. In 1993, a $6 million over-haul dredged and refilled the canals, repaired the adjoining paths, and rebuilt some of the bridges.

Santa Monica Pier and the movies

Santa Monica **⑫** is a seaside resort where West LA meets the ocean. In the streets behind and the canyons above lie the most famous of Tinsel Town's attractions: Hollywood, Beverly Hills, Rodeo Drive. But down near the waterside, the "Bay City" of Raymond Chandler's novels is a pleasant place to be. The boulevards and side streets are attractive places to stroll and shop. The trendy **Third Street** pedestrian mall, lined with restaurants, stores, bars, and movie theaters, is usually filled with street performers by day and nightlife seekers after dark.

The town's landmark is the century-old **Santa Monica Pier**, which has an assortment of amusement arcades, fairground rides, souvenir stands, snack bars, and sedentary fishermen along its lengthy boardwalk. There's also a wonderful carousel with 44

hand-carved horses, which featured in the 1973 film *The Sting*. On either side is the wide, sandy beach bordered by a busy bicycle path.

Clifftop **Palisades Park**, a euca-lyptus-fringed grassy stretch along Ocean Avenue, overlooks the beach and offers views of boats and sunsets. The park is popular with the home-less – although their presence should not deter you from visiting. To one side is an information cabin for bro-chures and useful tips on where to catch local buses. Main Street, with its murals, shops, and numerous excellent restaurants, is also worth exploring. Looming over the corner with Rose Avenue is Jonathan Borofsky's giant sculpture, *Ballerina Clown*.

The mansions along the seashore at the northern end of Santa Monica were mostly built by moviedom's for-mer elite. The grandest, at 415 Pacific Coast Highway, was the 118-room compound designed for William Randolph Hearst and his paramour, Marion Davies. The house was sold to the owner of the Hotel Bel Air, who turned it into a beach hotel and club.

Hire a beachcruiser and cycle along the Venice Beach boardwalk.

Dusk falls over Santa Monica Pier.

view of San Francisco from Twin Peaks.

LOS ANGELES TO SAN FRANCISCO

This legendary stretch of Highway 1 takes in California's most famous attractions on the coast: extravagant Hearst Castle and fog-shrouded Big Sur.

The distance from Los Angeles to San Francisco is 380 miles (611km). Taking I-5 all the way means a city-to-city trip can be accomplished in around six hours, but that would be a pity. Highway 1 hugs the coast almost the entire way, presenting heart-stopping curves, breath-taking scenery, pretty inns, scenic sites, and two of California's best attractions – Hearst Castle and Big Sur. With all of this to savor, allowing two days rather than six hours makes far more sense.

LOS ANGELES TO SANTA BARBARA

The Pacific Coast Highway out of Los Angeles cruises through **Malibu** ⑬. Despite its reputation for hedonism, it's largely a residential community, where much of the beach has been cordoned off into the exclusive Malibu Colony. Don't miss **Getty Villa** (tel: 310-440-7300; www.getty.edu/visit; Thur–Mon). The original home of the Getty Museum was fashioned after an ancient Roman villa and now houses the Getty Center's superb collection of Greek, Roman, and Etruscan antiquities.

North of Malibu, there's a string of accessible beaches – **Point Dume**, **Zuma**, and **Leo Carrillo** – until the highway turns inland toward Ventura. Highway 1 merges with US 101 here, and you must leave it to visit

Ventura ⑭ itself, which has a heavily restored "Olde Towne." The 1782 **San Buenaventura Mission** (tel: 805-643-4318; daily) is pretty and worth a visit, and Ventura's harbor area has lots of seafood restaurants. Most of the town's sites are connected by trolley.

Channel Islands National Park

Ventura is headquarters for **Channel Islands National Park** (tel: 805-658-5730; www.nps.gov/chis; daily), which protects five offshore islands – Santa

Main Attractions
Malibu
Channel Islands
Santa Barbara
Pismo State Beach
San Luis Obispo
Morro Bay
Cambria
Paso Robles wine region
Hearst Castle
Piedras Blancas beach
Big Sur
Carmel
Monterey

Getty Villa, Malibu.

Barbara, Anacapa, Santa Cruz, Santa Rosa, and San Miguel. Transportation from the mainland is via commercial boat or chartered flight to Santa Rosa. You can hike and camp on all the islands; one of the most enjoyable is **San Miguel**, a premier spot for viewing six species of seals and sea lions. The National Park Service operates visitor centers in Ventura and on **East Santa Cruz Island**, at the **Scorpion Ranch Visitor Center,** in an 1866 ranch.

Inland along State 150, on the edge of Los Padres National Forest, is **Ojai** (pronounced "o-hi"), a sleepy artists' and writers' colony, near which the 1926 movie *Lost Horizon* was filmed. The town is centered around a main street on which a graceful tower offsets a row of unpretentious shops built under a covered veranda. Artifacts in the Ojai Historical Society Museum include those from prehistoric Chumash times through the ranching period to the days when heavyweight boxing champion Jack Dempsey cleared rocks from what became "Pop" Soper's training ranch.

Santa Barbara

In **Santa Barbara** ⓯, following a destructive 1925 earthquake, the city's policy of rebuilding in Spanish Colonial–style architecture – whitewashed adobe, red-tiled roofs, and iron grillwork – has created one of the most beautiful cities on the California coast. Celebrated as "Santa Teresa" in Sue Grafton's popular Kinsey Mulhone private eye stories, Santa Barbara is immediately recognizable. Largely, that's due to its unique geography, which juxtaposes the soaring, east-west-trending Santa Ynez Mountains with wildlife-rich beaches beneath steep cliffs, the sparkling waters of the Santa Barbara Channel, and a moneyed, laid-back lifestyle.

The 1782 **Mission Santa Barbara** (tel: 805-682-4713; www.santabarbara-mission.org; daily) may have one of the best locations of any California mission: at the start of the lush foothill drive known as the Riviera. Nearby is the tiny **Santa Barbara Museum of Natural History** (tel: 805-682-4711; www.sbnature.org; daily), which has an excellent Chumash tribe artifact

Zuma Beach, Malibu.

collection and a huge blue whale skeleton outside. A satellite, the **Ty Warner Sea Center**, is an aquarium located down on historic **Stearns Wharf**, at the bottom of State Street.

Nearby **Santa Barbara Harbor** is the spot to enjoy fresh-off-the-boat seafood. Daily whale-watching excursions are available here between Christmas and late March, as well as year round trips to Santa Barbara Island, critical habitat for elephant seals in winter and California sea lions in spring, and a good birdwatching venue.

Red Tile Walking Tour

Explore downtown Santa Barbara using the self-guided Red Tile Walking Tour booklet, available at the Visitor Center on Cabrillo Boulevard (tel: 805-965-3021; daily), the palm tree-lined seafront promenade. Two highlights include the handsome 1929 **Santa Barbara County Courthouse** (tel: 805-962-6464; www.santabarbaracourt house.org; daily), on East Anapamu, which has a lobby lined with mosaics and murals, grassy picnic areas, and one of the city's best views from

its rooftop; a block away is **Santa Barbara Museum of Art** (tel: 805-963-4364; www.sbmuseart.org; Tue–Sun), a treat for art lovers. Among its large collection of world-class art are many French Impressionist paintings, including more Monets than any museum on the West Coast, as well as an antiquities collection to rival the Getty.

El Presidio de Santa Barbara State Historic Park (tel: 805-965-0093; www. sbthp.org; daily), on Canon Perdido Street, housed the Spanish soldiers who protected Mission Santa Barbara. Tour the restored adobe chapel and other buildings, then have lunch in the charming 1920s shopping arcade of **El Paseo**, whose theater once featured a dancer named Rita Cansino, better known as Rita Hayworth.

SANTA BARBARA TO BIG SUR

After meandering through **Gaviota State Park** (tel: 805-968-1033; daily), Highways 1 and 101 turn inland and split. Continue on Highway 1 to sleepy **Lompoc**, home to **Mission La Purisima Concepcion** (tel:

TIP

For those interested in architecture, join the 1- to 1.5-hour leisurely walking tours led by the Architectural Foundation of Santa Barbara (tel: 805-965-6307; www. afsb.org). The Saturday tours at 10am (weather permitting) uncover hidden courtyards and look at architecture after the 1925 earthquake. A $10 donation is appreciated.

Mission Santa Barbara.

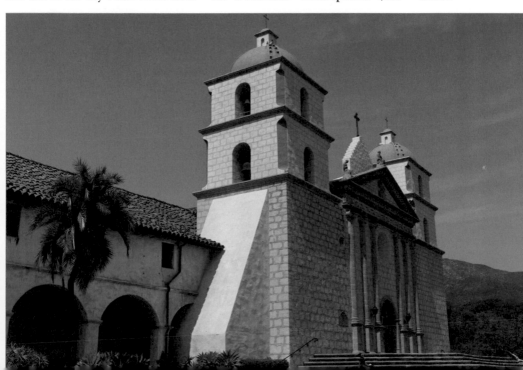

FACT

Santa Barbara author Ross McDonald was the first to use the fictionalized name of Santa Teresa for Santa Barbara in his mystery *The Moving Target* (1949). Writer Sue Grafton decided to use the name in her Santa Teresa mysteries featuring P.I. Kinsey Mulhone in homage to McDonald.

Dune buggy on Pismo Beach's sand dunes.

805-733-3713; daily), California's 11th mission. North of town, the landscape is dominated by agribusiness, including irrigated fields of broccoli, cauliflower, and strawberries, and extensive fields of flowers, which in season offer an extraordinary display of magentas, pinks, golds, and purples.

This continues past **Guadalupe**, a quiet, old-fashioned town with an Amtrak station and one-story buildings dating to the turn of the 20th century. Eighteen miles (29km) north, **Pismo State Beach**, once famous for its huge clams (still celebrated with a Clam Festival every October), has fabulous sandy shores stretching all around the bay and leads directly into San Luis Obispo, which is more or less the midway point between Los Angeles and San Francisco. Pismo is one of the few beaches where driving is allowed, so watch for dune buggies. Just before San Luis Obispo, keep an eye open for the extraordinary **Madonna Inn** (tel: 805-543-3000; see page 425), whose 109 rooms are individually decorated in memorably kitsch fashion.

The attractive, low-key college town of **San Luis Obispo** ⑯ (SLO) also has an 18th-century mission (tel: 805-781-8220; daily), with a downtown community located around its plaza. There's an **Art Center** (tel: 805-543-8562; Wed–Mon) and, across from the mission, the **County Historical Museum** (Wed–Sun, daily in summer).

Morro Bay

Morro Bay is dominated by its 576ft (176-meter) -high volcanic rock, a nesting site for peregrine falcons, which dive-bomb their prey at astonishing speeds of 175mph (282kph). You may catch glimpses of threatened snowy plovers if you hike and camp at popular **Montana de Oro State Park** (tel: 805-772-7434; www.slostateparks.com; camping reservations May–Sept;), southwest of town. Morro Bay has a beautiful, sweeping, sandy beach and a restaurant-fringed harbor. Note: the harbor drive deadends in both directions, and parking can be difficult. Follow it to the end below Morro Rock, where you

can watch sea lions and playful sea otters wrapping themselves in kelp. **The Museum of Natural History** (tel: 805-772-2694; www.slostateparks. com/natural_history_museum; daily) in **Morro Bay State Park** has exhibits on Central Coast wildlife and migratory Monarch butterflies. This short-lived beauty, with its amber and black wings, can be seen near Pacific Grove in winter.

Thirteen miles (21km) north, beyond the pretty town of **Cayucos**, is pastoral **Cambria**, set below the hills with its lovely Moonstone Beach. In between the two towns, State 46 winds east through the barren but beautiful hills of the Santa Lucia range, linking US 101 and **Paso Robles** (pronounced "paso **ro**-buls"). This is a charming, small, wine-producing region where most of the wineries offer free daily tastings. A map of local wineries is available from the Visitor and Conference Bureau (tel: 805-238-0506) in Paso Robles, not far from **Paso Robles Pioneer Museum** (tel: 805-239-4556; www.pasoroblespioneermuseum. org; Thur–Sun pm).

Hearst Castle

Back on the coast, the hamlet of **San Simeon** sits below late newspaper and movie tycoon William Randolph Hearst's 250,000-acre (101,171-hectare) estate, best known for its owner's ravishingly beautiful home, **Hearst Castle** ⑰ (tel: 800-444-4445; www.hearstcastle.org; daily). Perched on what Hearst called "The Enchanted Hill," so high the house is often wreathed in fog, this was once the largest private residence in the US. Today, it rivals Disneyland for California's most popular attraction.

Designed by architect Julia Morgan, the mansion began construction in 1919. Craftsmen labored for 28 years to create the twin-towered home, which Hearst then filled with carvings, furnishings, and works of art from European castles and cathedrals. (During his lifetime, Hearst accumulated one of the largest collections of private art in the world, with a value measured in the hundreds of millions of dollars.) All

Spanish Colonial-style architecture of Santa Barbara County Courthouse.

Central Californian hillsides turn a verdant green after spring showers.

TIP

The premier scenic drive in the Santa Barbara area heads over San Marcos Pass (State 154) to Los Olivos, for gorgeous views over the Santa Barbara Channel and the Santa Ynez Valley, the wine-growing region featured in the film Sideways. Continue west on State 246 through the Danish town of Solvang to Buellton to rejoin US 101. Loop back along the coast to Santa Barbara or continue north on 101.

Hearst Castle.

materials had to be brought up the coast by steamer, then hauled up that impossible hill. San Simeon's grounds were stocked with animals from all over the world, and Jean Harlow, Clark Gable, and other Hollywood royalty were invited to visit and stroll the beautiful gardens or enjoy the magnificent indoor and outdoor swimming pools.

Reservations are strongly recommended for one of the five daily tours leaving from the staging area below, some of which include the home movies of Hearst, whose lonely, lavish lifestyle was the subject of Orson Welles's most celebrated movie, *Citizen Kane*. Tour 1 is best for first-time visitors, as it offers an overview of the castle and main rooms. Although Hearst Castle is extremely busy, especially during the summer, the estate is efficiently run, and timed entry means you can go away and have a picnic on the beach below if the wait proves to be a long one. Unmissable.

Four miles (6km) north, Piedras Blancas is the birthplace each January of thousands of elephant seals. Well

into spring, from the walkway overlooking the beach, you can watch the young pups learning to swim. The sheer number of these long-nosed creatures is amazing, and nowhere else on the coast can you see them this close.

Big Sur

The 94-mile (151km) stretch of coastline between San Simeon and the Monterey Peninsula is known as **Big Sur** ⑱, a legendary wilderness of holistic healing retreats and remote homesteads inhabited by third-generation pioneers. The area was barely accessible to traffic until 1937, and even now the sheer cliffs of the Santa Lucia Mountains hugged by the highway occasionally slide into the sea, leaving residents in complete isolation until the road is rebuilt. There are no roads inland between Cambria and Monterey, so check road conditions before proceeding. Fill your tank, preferably in Morro Bay, as prices leap in Cambria and gas stations beyond are few – and expensive – along this stretch.

The dark, thicketed mountains rise steeply to the right; the foamy sea to the left constantly changes shape and color. Only the two-lane road separates the two, which means the curling ribbon of road has its own distinct weather pattern. For this read: fog. Although the sun may be shining brightly on the other side of the mountain, and can often be seen slatted through the trees, Highway 1 can be distinctly chilly, and the fog comes on quickly, obliterating the world for unexpected moments. Infrequent guardrails, looking suspiciously flimsy, are small comfort in the face of the menacing rocks below.

Driving here is not for the faint-hearted, but for those with a sense of adventure and time on their side, this stretch of the California coastline is one of the most exhilarating routes in the US. Traveling nonstop with good weather, you could arrive in Carmel in about three hours, but the best way is to pause, at least for lunch or dinner. This is especially important for the person at the wheel, as the view is fabulous, but

the road hazardous, and it can be frustrating (not to mention vertigo-inducing) if you don't take frequent stops. Luckily, scenic overlooks are numerous.

Coming from San Simeon, the hills begin gently enough, and the road is fairly easy to navigate. The first sight on the right is **Los Padres National Forest**, the southern tip of the coastal redwood belt, which contains several almost preternaturally beautiful state parks. **Julia Pfeiffer Burns State Park** and **Pfeiffer Big Sur State Park** have wonderful trails that lead up into the mountains or down toward the sea; Julia Pfeiffer Burns has a waterfall near McWay Cove, accessible via an easy hike.

Big Sur Coastline and Esalen Institute

Big Sur Village ⑲ is just a stop in the road, really, with a few shops, a post office, and a handful of lodgings and eating places. If you're planning to stay overnight in summer or on a weekend, book well in advance. Accommodations range from

TIP

Every Thursday night, part of San Luis Obispo's Higuera Street closes to traffic and transforms into a farmer's market and street fair with bands and entertainment.

The stunning rocky coastline of Big Sur.

campgrounds to luxury resorts and historic hostelries, such as Djeetjen's Big Sur Inn, a charming family-run rustic inn built in the 1930s that is a good place to have a meal and mingle with interesting locals.

Until 1945, Big Sur was mainly populated by ranchers, loggers, and miners, but soon after began to attract writers. The **Henry Miller Memorial Library** (tel: 831-667-2574; www.henrymiller.org; Wed–Mon), near spectacular **Nepenthe Restaurant**, where everybody goes for drinks at sunset, preserves works by and about the world-famous author, who called the area "the face of the earth as the creator intended it to look."

In 1962, Michael Murphy and Richard Price moved to Murphy's cliffside family ranch at Big Sur, with others attracted by the human potential movement. Their idea was to create a residential retreat and center for alternative humanistic education, exploring and integrating ideas from the East and West, to help build a better world. Named

Nepenthe restaurant overlooking Big Sur.

Esalen Institute (www.esalen.org), after the Esselen tribe who once used the famous hot springs on the property, the stunning setting and intellectually challenging environment quickly attracted leading pioneers in spirituality, bodywork, psychology, and New Age thinking, from Fritz Perls, Ida Rolf, and Milton Trager to Allan Watts and Buckminster Fuller. Today, the nonprofit institute offers 500 residential workshops a year, lasting from a weekend to a week, including all meals from the organic gardens, (clothing-optional) hot springs access, and the chance to receive one of the world's best massages. The property is off limits to non-workshop attendees, but occasionally, during the low season, its rustic lodgings are available for overnight stays. Check with the institute.

North of Big Sur is the area's crowning man-made achievement, **Bixby Bridge**. Spanning the steep walls of Bixby Canyon and often obscured by fog, the bridge was called an engineering marvel when it was constructed in 1932.

BIG SUR TO SAN FRANCISCO

Leaving the lush lands of Big Sur for the cities on the Monterey Peninsula can be a shock to the system. A way to ease this uncomfortable transition is to visit one last natural wonder on the way, the undramatic but still lovely **Point Lobos State Natural Reserve** (tel: 831-624-4909; www.parks.ca.gov/?page_id=571; daily). Miles of trails offer glimpses of deer, rabbits, sea lions, and sea otters. Robert Louis Stevenson is said to have been inspired to write *Treasure Island* while at Point Lobos. Several short footpaths traverse the rock-strewn headland, on which is one of two existing groves of ghostly Monterey Cypress trees.

Carmel and Monterey

Carmel ⑳, "Gateway to the Monterey Peninsula," once attracted famous artists and writers like poet Robinson Jeffers and photographer Edward Weston. It's a sign of the times that the cost of living here now makes pretty Carmel more of a place for selling creative works than making them. It's a classically beautiful little town, which has outlawed high-rises, neon signs, traffic lights, parking meters – anything possessing the foul taint of city life, including artificial house plants. Its residents include actors Clint Eastwood, who famously did a stint as the town's mayor, and Doris Day. Downtown is lined with upscale shops and galleries. **Mission San Carlos Borroméo del Río Carmelo,** otherwise known as **Carmel Mission** (tel: 831-624-1271; www.carmelmission.org; daily) and **Carmel Beach** are very appealing, and just to the north is **Pebble Beach**, home to the challenging golf course of the same name.

Motorcyclists are not barred from the peninsula's **17-Mile Drive**, which charges a hefty entrance fee to drive around admiring its luxurious private homes. These look, in fact, much like any other affluent American neighborhood, and given the proximity to the exquisite Big Sur coast, this is a drive you can probably miss.

Highway 1 runs almost the entire length of California. The Big Sur stretch is not for the fainthearted.

Paraglider along the coast on the Monterey Peninsula.

Inside the Carmel Mission.

Vintage clothing store, Santa Cruz.

Cannery Row in **Monterey ㉑**, at the north end of the peninsula, basks in the glow of John Steinbeck's brilliant novel of the same name. Steinbeck's world withered with the mysterious disappearance of the sardines in the mid-1940s, and today his legacy is celebrated in nearby **Salinas**, at the **National Steinbeck Center** (tel: 831-775-4721; www.steinbeck.org; daily).

Cannery Row has become a bit of a tourist trap. A visit is redeemed, however, by a few hours spent at the excellent **Monterey Bay Aquarium** (tel: 831-648-4800; www.montereybayaquarium.org; daily), one of the best in the world, which offers innovative exhibits and interpretation on the marine life found in a Grand Canyon–sized trench just offshore. Wall-length tanks house sharks, regal salmon, and schools of tiny fish amid beds of kelp that writhe with the simulated tides. Highlights include the Seahorses and Jellies exhibit. Try to time your visit to coincide with feeding time, when keepers in wet suits climb into the glass tanks and talk to spectators through underwater microphones. The sea otters are especially amusing.

Fisherman's Wharf is a delightful pier, lined with tourist shops, restaurants, and stands selling clam chowder in sourdough bread bowls. In the boat-filled harbor you'll see – and hear – resident seals. Inland from the pier, **Monterey State Historic Park** has 17 interesting museums and buildings from the town's days under Spanish, Mexican, and early American rule. Traffic on the stretch of coast north toward San Francisco can sometimes be horrendous. If so, you may wish to detour on State Highway 183 to **Castroville**, the "Artichoke Capital of the World," where the Giant Artichoke Restaurant serves the delicious deep-fried leaves.

Santa Cruz and Half Moon Bay

The communities in this heavily agricultural area of California have a

strong Mexican flavor, and all along Highway 1, you'll be surrounded by flat agricultural fields producing California's finest artichokes, cherries, and strawberries (all available fresh at roadside stands). The cute, colorful beach town of **Capitola** is a pleasant place for a stroll, its beach wall decorated with bright tiles. The university city of **Santa Cruz** ㉒ is famous for its century-old Beach Boardwalk, with a popular amusement park, thrilling roller coaster, and arcade games alongside the beach. Dine on yummy Dungeness crab in season in one of the restaurants on the pier, then drive along West Cliff Drive, lined with beautiful homes, to see surfers hitting the waves below the cliffs near the Santa Cruz Surfing Museum.

Farther up the coast is the attractive wide beach at **Scott Creek**, north of **Davenport**. Tan, black, and white cows graze in fields high on the cliffs before Highway 1 swoops down to **Waddell Creek** and driftwood-lined beaches (such as Bean Hollow State Beach and Pescadero State Beach) all

the way up to the Santa Cruz county line. Thin veils of fog sometimes obscure the view, but when it shifts (which it does every few minutes), drivers are rewarded by glimpses of **Pigeon Point Lighthouse** ㉓. At 115ft (35 meters), it is one of the tallest lighthouses in the country and has been in use since 1872.

Heading toward San Francisco, wide, flat fields lie between the highway and the coast. **Half Moon Bay** ㉔ is only half an hour's drive from the city and is famous not only for its pumpkins and nurseries but for the huge waves that pound its shores. Surfers from all around come to tackle the big ones – up to 40ft (12 meters) high – and the talk in the bars is of "mavericks" and "tubes." Sunday lunchtimes at Half Moon often include jazz or rock concerts.

With the city suburbs on the horizon, the coastline becomes rocky and untrafficked again. **Gray Whale Cove State Beach** or **Big Basin Park** are peaceful places for a final walk or picnic before hitting the big time – **San Francisco** (see page 350).

(see page 350).

TIP

From the boardwalk behind the fog signal building at Pigeon Point Lighthouse, just south of San Francisco, keep an eye out for gray whales on their annual migration back to Alaska from Mexico, between January and April. The lighthouse grounds are open to the public.

Bixby Bridge.

San Francisco: City By The Bay

San Francisco, Fisherman's Wharf, Chinatown, the Golden Gate Bridge – this city wins hearts straightaway and effortlessly.

Each visitor takes away a different memory of San Francisco: the steep street that drops off toward the bay, the fog drifting through the Golden Gate Bridge, the divine food, or the simple fun of a cable-car ride, admiring Victorian houses along the way.

Begin at **Union Square,** where a winged statue commemorates Admiral George Dewey's naval victory over the Spanish in 1898. **Chinatown Gate** appears just to the northeast. While it is no secret to tourists, crowds of Chinese residents vying for space on the sidewalk show the area still caters to locals. Tiny herb shops in mysterious alleys promise everything from rheumatism relief to the restoration of sexual prowess.

Chinatown ends where **North Beach** begins. While a few clubs still offer lap dances, critically acclaimed restaurants and posh nightclubs entice a different crowd altogether. But this traditional Italian neighborhood still attracts writers and artists, particularly to **City Lights** bookstore, once the rendezvous of Beat poets like Jack Kerouac and Lawrence Ferlinghetti.

To the east, **Telegraph Hill** rises above North Beach, offering spectacular views across San Francisco Bay. **Coit Tower** (tel: 415-362-0808; daily), with its momentous views and frescoes, crowns the hill and can be climbed. Follow Columbus Avenue to **Fisherman's Wharf**. Fishing boats put out before dawn; their catch determines the "special of the day" at restaurants clustered around the wharf. This is a "must" stop for all.

At the opposite end of the Embarcadero is another San Francisco landmark. Built in 1903, the **Ferry Building** survived the Great Fire and in its heyday was a hub for water transport between the bay communities. It has now been renovated to house the **Ferry Building Marketplace,** a foodie haven with a fantastic farmers' market and stalls selling gourmet foodstuffs. From here you can ride the vintage electric streetcars of the F-line to **Fisherman's Wharf** or along Market Street to the **Castro district**.

A mile offshore from San Francisco is windswept **Alcatraz Island** (boat tickets – tel: 415-981-7625; www.nps.gov/alca; daily), part of **Golden Gate**

Cable car trundles along Hyde Street.

The landmark Transamerica Pyramid.

National Recreation Area. Once home to such hardened criminals as Al Capone and the notorious Machine Gun Kelley, officials closed the prison in 1963, when repair costs grew too great. A tour of the prison is surprisingly rewarding, as much for its wildlife and historic buildings as its human past. Bring a sweater for the breezy boat ride over.

A ride on the **Powell-Hyde cable car** begins two blocks inland from Hyde Street Pier, offering a tour of Russian Hill's high-rise apartments and mansions. The cable car passes near the curvy section of Lombard Street often seen in movies and continues on to **Nob Hill**, called the "hill of palaces" by Robert Louis Stevenson.

At the corner of Washington and Mason streets, **San Francisco Cable Car Museum** (tel: 415-474-1887; www.cablecarmuseum.org; daily) exhibits the city's transit history alongside the operating machinery that pulls the cable cars through town.

The Financial District holds three landmarks. **The Embarcadero Center, the Bank of America building** – so tall its roof sometimes disappears in the fog – and the distinctive **Transamerica Pyramid**, with 48 floors the tallest building in San Francisco.

"South of Market," or **SoMa**, is a focal point for art galleries, cafés, nightclubs, and local theaters. **San Francisco Museum of Modern Art** (tel: 415-357-4000; www.sfmoma.org; Thur–Tue) spearheads the attractions, which also include the Yerba Buena Gardens, the Center for the Arts, the Cartoon Art Museum, the Museum of the California Historical Society, and the Foto-Grafix bookshop, which sells Ansel Adams books and prints. The **Asian Art Museum** (tel: 415-581-3500; www.asianart.org; Tue–Sun) is located in the Civic Center district. It contains 10,000 artifacts dating back 3,500 years.

Mission Street heads south into the heart of the **Mission district**, San Francisco's melting pot of Latin American cultures. The thick adobe walls of **Mission Dolores**, built in 1776, still form the oldest building in San Francisco that can be visited.

To the west lies the celebrated gay community of **the Castro**. Same-sex couples and rainbow flags fill the streets lined with table-hopping bars. It's a lively and fun area, regardless of your gender.

Farther west is the **Haight-Ashbury district**. Haight Street was once so gaudy and bizarre that tour buses full of goggle-eyed tourists ran up and down it. Like most such radical departures from the social norm, the hippie experiment fell victim to time and fashion. The neighborhood retains its anti-establishment roots, but today piercing shops and tattoo parlors replace flower power. It's still a popular stretch,

however, with great shopping and a wide range of inexpensive restaurants and cafés.

Golden Gate Park (tel: 415-831-2700; www.golden-gate-park.com), 3 miles (5km) long and almost half a mile wide, consists of tree groves dotted with lakes, meadows, windmills, and dells. Despite thousands of visitors, it's easy to find tranquility. In addition to peace, the Conservatory of Flowers offers sweet scents and botanical beauty, and the Music Concourse holds Sunday concerts.

California Academy of Sciences (tel: 415-379-8000; www.calacademy.org; daily) includes animal dioramas, 16,000 specimens of marine life at Steinhart Aquarium, and a laser light show at Morrison Planetarium. **The Japanese Tea Garden** claims to be the birthplace of the fortune cookie.

The beautiful and neoclassical **Legion of Honor** (tel: 415-750-3600; www.legionofhonor.famsf.org; Tue–Sun) is unmissable. At the entrance is one of five bronze casts of Rodin's *The Thinker*.

Golden Gate Bridge extends beyond Golden Gate National Recreation Area. A promenade goes through Crissy Field, a picnic area that belongs to the 1,480-acre (600-hectare) **Presidio**. In it stands the Plaster Palace, the rococo rotunda of the Palace of Fine Arts, housing the hands-on exhibits of the **Exploratorium** (tel: 415-561-0360; www.exploratorium.ed; Tue–Sun).

Street in the Castro district.

Drive-thru redwood tree, Klamath.

SAN FRANCISCO TO OREGON

The Pacific Coast Highway, also known as Highway 1,
threads its way past golden beaches, hot-tub
hideaways, famed wineries, and the tallest
living things on earth.

From San Francisco to the town of Crescent City, about half an hour's drive from the California-Oregon border, is 363 miles (584km). Beaches, wineries, and redwood forests are the attractions of this beautiful journey, with trees so massive you can even drive through a few of them.

PCH passes through windblown **San Francisco ㉕** (see page 350), traversing Golden Gate Park and Golden Gate Bridge, two units of 75,000-acre (30,351-hectare) **Golden Gate National Recreation Area** (tel: 415-561-4900; www.nps.gov/goga), the largest urban park in the world, preserving significant natural and cultural sites (including Alcatraz Island) in a setting that is hard to beat.

The pretty little harbor town of **Sausalito ㉖** is right off Highway 1/101, after Golden Gate Bridge and Marin Headlands. With its bustling marina, pricey waterside boutiques, and hillside mansions, it's a postcard-pretty place to stroll and enjoy seafood. Just north, Highway 1 (Shoreline Highway) heads west, twisting and turning to the coast.

South of the highway is **Green Gulch Farm Zen Center** (tel: 415-383-3134; www.sfzc.org), a popular retreat center that offers workshops, lectures, public meditation programs, and overnight accommodations on a gorgeous organic farm. Nearby are

Mount Tamalpais State Park (tel: 415-388-2070; daily) and the giant redwoods of 300-acre (120-hectare) **Muir Woods National Monument** (tel: 415-388-2595; www.nps.gov/muwo; daily) – both offering terrific hiking, sweeping views, and local history.

At rugged **Stinson Beach**, a popular beach destination for San Franciscans, the slow coast road heads north past **Bolinas Lagoon**, a rich wetland protected by Audubon, and on to spectacular **Point Reyes National Seashore** (tel: 415-464-5100; www.nps.gov/pore;

Main Attractions
Point Reyes National Seashore
Sonoma Valley
Napa Valley
Bodega Bay
Mendocino
Avenue of the Giants
Ferndale
Eureka
Redwood National Park

Wine tasting in Napa Valley.

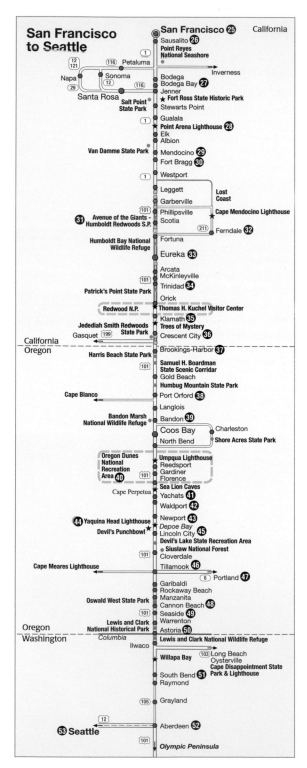

San Francisco to Seattle

San Francisco 25 — California
Sausalito 26
Point Reyes National Seashore
Petaluma 116
Napa 12/121
Sonoma 12
29
Santa Rosa 116
Salt Point State Park
Inverness
Bodega
Bodega Bay 27
Jenner
★ Fort Ross State Historic Park
Stewarts Point
Gualala
★ Point Arena Lighthouse 28
Elk
Albion
Van Damme State Park
Mendocino 29
Fort Bragg 30
Westport
Leggett — Lost Coast
Garberville
Phillipsville — Cape Mendocino Lighthouse
Scotia
Ferndale 32
Avenue of the Giants – Humboldt Redwoods S.P. 31
Fortuna
Humboldt Bay National Wildlife Refuge
Eureka 33
Arcata
McKinleyville
Trinidad 34
Patrick's Point State Park
Orick
Redwood N.P. — Thomas H. Kuchel Visitor Center
Klamath 35
Jedediah Smith Redwoods State Park — Trees of Mystery 36
Gasquet 199
Crescent City 37

California / Oregon

Brookings-Harbor 37
Harris Beach State Park
Samuel H. Boardman State Scenic Corridor
Gold Beach
Humbug Mountain State Park
Cape Blanco
Port Orford 38
Langlois
Bandon Marsh National Wildlife Refuge
Bandon 39
Coos Bay — Charleston
North Bend — Shore Acres State Park
Oregon Dunes National Recreation Area 40
Umpqua Lighthouse
Reedsport
Gardiner
Florence
Cape Perpetua
Sea Lion Caves
Yachats 41
Waldport 42
Yaquina Head Lighthouse 44
Devil's Punchbowl
Newport 43
Depoe Bay
Lincoln City 45
Devil's Lake State Recreation Area
Siuslaw National Forest
Cloverdale
Cape Meares Lighthouse
Tillamook 46
Portland 47
Garibaldi
Rockaway Beach
Oswald West State Park
Manzanita
Cannon Beach 48
Seaside 49
Warrenton
Lewis and Clark National Historical Park
Astoria 50

Oregon / Washington — Columbia

Lewis and Clark National Wildlife Refuge
Ilwaco
Willapa Bay — Long Beach
Oysterville
Cape Disappointment State Park & Lighthouse
South Bend 51
Raymond
Grayland
Aberdeen 52
Seattle 53
Olympic Peninsula

daily), the highlight of this scenic drive, with its sweeping shoreline, marine life, cows grazing on lush grass, and historic **Point Reyes Lighthouse** (tel: 415-669-1534; visitor center and lighthouse stairs: Thur–Mon). Plan on stopping for a meal or spend the night in inviting **Inverness**, which has several inns and a good deli and bakery.

The delicious milk from those grazing cows is the secret to the spectacular farmstead and artisan cheeses now being made in Marin. Some of the best come from **Cowgirl Creamery** (tel: 415-663-9335; www.cowgirlcreamery.com; daily), with creameries in Petaluma and Point Reyes Station where you can watch their award-winning cheeses being made. Prince Charles and wife Camilla visited in 2005, largely drawn by the excellent local foods in this region.

Wine country

You can take the road east from Point Reyes Station (or Highway 101 north from Sausalito through Novato) to **Petaluma**, turning east on Highway 116. After the upscale communities crowded around the bay, the beautifully open, rolling hills and farmland of Marin County make for a very enjoyable drive to historic **Sonoma**, hub of the Sonoma Valley wine country.

With numerous distinguished wineries and tasting rooms spread throughout the 17-mile (6.9-hectare) valley, Sonoma feels less hectic than its famous neighbor, Napa. Highlights include the Gloria Ferrer Champagne Caves, Château St Jean, and Buena Vista Winery, California's oldest winery, dating from 1857. A guide to wine-tasting throughout the valley is available from Sonoma Valley Visitors Bureau on First Street (tel: 866-996-1090; www.sonomavalley.com; daily).

On the east side of the mountains, Highway 29 runs through America's most renowned wine region, **Napa Valley**. Some 300 wineries lie cheek by jowl in this beautiful rolling landscape, ranging from boutique winemakers to vast corporate operations. It can be a little overwhelming for first-time visitors, so stop by the Napa Valley visitor center (tel: 707-226-7459; www.napavalley.com; daily) in **Napa** town center for a guide to tastings and tours.

There are tasting rooms in Napa itself, an attractive riverside town with good restaurants, gourmet food shops, and galleries. Pretty **St Helena**, with its lovely old homes and upscale shopping, is a favorite base. At the northern end of the valley, **Calistoga** is most appealing of all, with its mineral baths, arcaded Victorian-era main street, and casual air.

Bodega Bay, birds and beaches

Back on the coast, Highway 1 winds along beautiful Tomales Bay, passing oyster farms and rustic hamlets like Olema and historic Tomales, with its 1850s wooden buildings.

It's no coincidence that Alfred Hitchcock filmed his 1963 movie *The Birds* around **Bodega Bay** ㉗, where hundreds of bird species can be found. Brown pelicans are especially abundant. Just to the south and slightly inland, in the separate village of **Bodega**, you can see the schoolhouse and St Teresa's church that featured in the movie.

After **Sonoma Coast State Beach**, another really dramatic portion of the California coast begins, where Rivers End sits overlooking the mouth of the Russian River at **Jenner**. For miles, Highway 1 snakes around the canyon at ascending levels. The top of a subsequent canyon has been plugged with stone, making a bridge on which to site the road.

The road passes the timbered stockade of **Fort Ross State Historic Park** (tel: 707-847-3437; www.fortross.org; daily). For history buffs, it's worth exploring the cannon-studded fort, with its church and blockhouses – if only to wonder how 19th-century Russian otter hunters withstood the rugged winters in flimsy wooden buildings on one of the windiest parts of the coast. So well fortified were they that their Native American and Spanish neighbors left them alone. In 1842, after 30 years of relentless otter

Hot-air balloons over Napa Valley.

Napa and Sonoma valleys are great destinations for scenic roadtrips.

hunting (for furs), they sold out to rancher John Sutter and left.

At **Salt Point State Park**, the trees march down to the water's edge as you drive through this lovely pine-scented stretch. Off the highway, other beaches abound – such as Stump Beach and Fisk Mill Cove. Much of the time, you'll find yourself a solitary visitor, as swimming is unsafe due to rip tides and what the coast guards call "sleeper waves." **Stewarts Point** was once a "doghole" for schooners, so-called because of its anchorages, so tiny "only a dog could fit into them." After Pebble Beach, Stengel Beach, and 8 more miles (13km) of a winding two-lane road, a bridge across the Gualala River marks the end of Sonoma County.

Mendonoma

Mendonoma, a name derived from the adjoining counties of Sonoma and Mendocino, identifies the coastal region between the Russian River at Jenner and the Navarro River, north of Point Arena. A heterogeneous mix of Russians, Germans, and Spaniards settled **Gualala** (pronounced

"wah-lah-lah") in the 1800s, which by the middle of the last century had four sawmills and four bars. Wells Fargo and Western Union had offices in the Gualala Hotel, built by the town's founder in 1903, when a room with bath and ocean view cost $5. The writer Jack London stayed here a century ago, and things don't appear to have altered much. Since the last mill closed, tourism has filled the gap.

The town's name is a local Native American word that translates as "where the waters flow down," and you can paddle up the estuary of the Gualala River in a canoe or kayak, looking for the osprey, heron, kingfishers, and river otters that make their homes here. Many local artists reside in and around the town, which has numerous galleries, shops, and a full program of concerts and theatrical performances at **Gualala Arts Center** (tel: 707-884-1138; www.gualalaarts.org). Art and nature come together in the Art in the Redwoods festival in August and the Redwood Coast Whale and Jazz Festival in April.

A wooden Old West structure with a tower marks a general merchandise store at **Anchor Bay**. After this, the coast-hugging, sometimes lonely road seems mostly deserted. Fifteen miles (24km) of winding two-lane highway allow ample time to contemplate that state law decreeing that slow-moving vehicles must use a turn-off if five or more vehicles back up behind them.

Beyond the cute town of Point Arena, one of the truly great coastal experiences is **Point Arena Lighthouse ㉘** (tel: 707-882-2809; www. pointarenalighthouse.com; daily), the tip of which can be spotted at the beginning of the 2-mile (3km) diversion. A classically beautiful 111ft (34-meter) -high white tower with 145 steps, it replaced an earlier lighthouse damaged by the 1906 San Francisco earthquake. Its 2-ton (1,800kg) French-made Fresnel lens (floating on a tub of mercury) was itself replaced in the 1970s with an aircraft-type beacon. It is maintained by a nonprofit group of local citizens,

Point Arena Lighthouse.

and you can even spend the night in an adjoining vacation rental.

Miles of open pasture dotted with ramshackle barns and grazing cows follow Point Arena. Then the road dips, turns, climbs, and dives, winding through tiny **Elk** and **Albion**, pretty roadside communities on either side of the Navarro River, with sloping tracks down to the beach. Look down as the road crosses the Albion River Bridge for a lovely view of the river flowing out to meet the sea, with big rock outcrops framing the river's mouth just offshore. There's another pretty crossing at Little River as the highway twists and turns around high cliffs before descending to a leafy stretch past **Van Damme State Park** (which contains a "pygmy forest" of pines and cypresses), offering occasional glimpses of the sea.

Mendocino

The lovely old town of **Mendocino** ㉙ was established by New England whalers and is one of the most admired places on the coast. It is a big hit with day-trippers, but if you choose to linger and stay the night, you'll be rewarded with great restaurants (some with health-conscious menus), numerous small bed-and-breakfast inns, as well as art galleries, jewelry and gift shops, and quaint cafés. The entire village is on the National Register of Historic Places. Among several Victorian homes exhibiting period pieces are the 1854 **Ford House Museum and Visitor Center** (tel: 707-937-5397; www.mendo parks.org; Fri–Mon) and the 1861 **Kelley House** (tel: 707-937-5791; kelleyhouse museum.org; June–Sept daily, Oct–May Fri–Mon). **Mendocino Art Center** (tel: 707-937-5818; www.mendocinoart-center.org; Wed–Sun;), founded by Bill and Jennie Zaca in 1959, showcases work by local and national artists. Paths lead along the cliffs overlooking Mendocino Bay with lovely views. Note: parking in Mendocino is tight.

North of Caspar, delightful **Mendocino Coast Botanical Gardens** (tel: 707-964-4352; www.gardenbythesea.org; daily) is worth a stop, if only to walk through the aromatic pine forest to the sea, enjoying the interplay of light and shade. It's a good place for whale-watching in season. Plants can

Statue in Mendocino.

On the road to Mendocino.

TIP

If you don't feel like making the fairly arduous four to five-hour round-trip drive to see the hidden attractions of California's Lost Coast, you can hire a guide in Ferndale; inquire locally for details.

Walking through wildflowers along the Lost Coast Trail.

be bought here, too. Nearby **Noyo Harbor** was once the biggest lumber port between Eureka and San Francisco. It's now a marina for sports fishing boats, along with a "fisherman's village" and plenty of restaurants.

Fort Bragg

An 1820 shipwreck led to the founding of **Fort Bragg** ㉚, when treasure seekers came to loot the wreckage and discovered the redwoods. A fort was built, and the Bureau of Indian Affairs established a reservation for the Pomo Indians. Lumber mills sprang up, along with a railroad to transport their product. When the 1906 earthquake devastated much of San Francisco, it was Fort Bragg's mills that provided the wood for rebuilding. The famous old "**Skunk Train**" (tel: 707-964-6371; www.skunktrain.com) that once carried lumber across the mountains to the sawmill at Willits has been a tourist favorite for years. It still follows the same picturesque route along the Noyo River and through redwood groves.

What remains of the original fort, along with surviving Victorian buildings, can be seen one block east of Main Street (Highway 1), near the Skunk Train depot at Laurel and Franklin. Both the 1892 **Guest House Museum** (tel: 707-964-4251; www.fort bragghistory.org; May–Oct daily, Nov–Apr Thur–Sun), with displays on local history, and award-winning **North Coast Brewing Company** (tel: 707-964-2739; www.northcoastbrewing.com), a pioneer in the microbrewery movement founded in 1988, are on Main Street. Fort Bragg is an unpretentious working town that also blossoms with nurseries, one of which grows millions of trees for reforestation projects.

The Lost Coast

Pretty hamlets and gorgeous views of crashing breakers and surf mark the winding coastal road beyond Fort Bragg. North of **Westport**, after 22 miles (35km) of dramatic, picturesque coastline, Highway 1 takes a final look at the sea before heading 25 miles (40km) inland. Here, it merges with US 101 at Leggett and – apart from a brief stretch near Eureka – disappears forever.

The relatively inaccessible (and often unpaved) coastal road travels through primitive **Sinkyone Wilderness State Park** (limited facilities) on the celebrated **Lost Coast**, an area of "black sand beaches and old-growth forests on a wall of windswept peaks," as one writer noted. Beyond the state park, in **King Range National Conservation Area** (www.blm.gov/ca/st/en/fo/arcata/kingrange/index.html), 35 miles (56km) of coastal trails and six campgrounds are managed by the Bureau of Land Management.

Once slated for an extension of Highway 1, the coast can be visited via a loop road picked up at the town of Weott, north of Leggett. The narrow side road crosses the Mattole River at Honeydew, heads through Petrolia, the site of the state's first but disappointingly unproductive oil strike, and follows the coast north to Ferndale, where it veers inland again to rejoin US 101.

Avenue of the Giants

South again, Highway 1 climbs through coastal redwood forest and merges into US 101 at **Leggett**, where you'll find redwood figures carved with chainsaws (Big Foot is a favorite) and **Confusion Hill** (tel: 707-925-6456; www.confusionhill.com; daily). The latter is a classic Forties roadside attraction that kids and adults will enjoy, including a funicular ride up the mountain, the world's tallest carved totem pole, a house made out of a redwood log, and a gravity house, where water runs uphill, a golf ball climbs a slope, and a chair prevents you from getting up without using your arms. Some of the effects are obviously optical illusions, but the owner says there are things he still hasn't figured out.

Containing several restaurants and motels, **Garberville** is a pleasant little place to break your journey before heading into redwood country proper. Farther north, at **Phillipsville**, the 31-mile (50km) **Avenue of the Giants ③** offers an irresistible alternative to US 101, to which it runs

parallel, allowing occasional on-off access. Some trees here are more than 300ft (91 meters) tall and 20ft (6 meters) in diameter. "From them comes silence," wrote John Steinbeck.

A handful of buildings is all that remain of two small towns that straddled the route until they were washed away by floods in 1964. Otherwise, the route through this stupendous 50,000-acre (20,250-hectare) redwood forest shows no signs of human habitation. A series of small groves is dedicated to various groups and individuals that have fought to preserve this magnificent enclave. They are places for contemplation. "We do not see nature with our eyes," wrote William Hazlitt, "but with our understandings and our hearts." Many of the trees on the east side were planted in the 1980s, as reforestation projects. Near the town of **Myers Flat** is the **Drive-Thru Tree**, a favorite with children and tourists. Before Weott, **Humboldt Redwoods State Park Visitor Center** (tel: 707-946-2263; daily) offers useful

The drive-thru Chandelier tree in Leggett.

Avenue of the Giants.

interpretive exhibits about coastal redwoods (*Sequoia sempervirens*), which attract arborphiles from around the world.

Redwood trees

Redwood has long been prized for its density and deep color, and despite slumps in the building industry and competition from more common trees such as cedar, it remains in demand. The logging industry, which grew up with the Gold Rush, made hardly a dent in the redwood belt until the advent of chainsaws in the 1940s, paving the way for acres of redwoods to be clearcut in a single day. It takes 40 years to raise a stand of redwoods for pulp, press board, and other uses, and 500 years to develop the fine grain and blood-red tint that have made the wood so popular. Conservationists estimate that trees are logged at two and a half times the rate of regeneration.

The redwoods inspire not only passing tourists but also constitute the entire livelihood of the Humboldt community. Sculptors carve timbers

into life-sized grizzly bears for sale at the roadside. Others, for a pretty hefty admission fee, show off the stout trunks growing in their backyards. Huge logging trucks carrying both raw timber and finished boards along the highway are a constant reminder that the trees in this area are an economic necessity as well as a natural wonder.

Fortuna Depot Museum (tel: 707-725-7645; www.sunnyfortuna.com; June–Aug daily, Sept–May Thur–Sun) features local logging and railroading history. Located on a back road between Fortuna and Eureka is minuscule **Loleta**, celebrated for cheese and ice-cream production. Its factory, which featured in the 1982 movie *Halloween III: the Season of the Witch*, makes supermarket ice cream in loads of varieties for 11 different companies.

Ferndale's Victorian history

Ferndale ❷, on the Eel River west of US 101 (reached by turning west off the highway, just north of Fortuna) has so many brightly painted Victorian stores and houses – many of which have been converted into enticing bed-and-breakfasts – the whole town has been designated a state historical landmark. The elaborately turreted and gabled **Gingerbread Mansion Inn** on Berding Street is outstanding, and the town's oldest building, the 18-room **Shaw House Inn** (see page 423), is fashioned after Nathaniel Hawthorne's *House of the Seven Gables*. The year-round mild climate encourages enthusiastic gardening – don't be surprised if you see cypress topiaries shaped like giant gumdrops; it's that kind of town.

At the top of Main Street is the 110-year-old **Victorian Inn** (see page 423). Also notable is **Ferndale Emporium**, farther down the street, which serves genteel afternoon teas from Thursday to Saturday. You can learn more about the town's history in the **Ferndale Museum** (tel: 707-786-4466; www.ferndale-museum.org; June–Sept Tue–Sat, Oct–May Wed–Sat).

Walking through the majestic groves in Humboldt Redwoods State Park.

A top-hatted driver offers rides around town in a horse and carriage, while there's a genuine soda fountain on Main Street. Understandably, Ferndale attracts moviemakers, who use its setting for movie and TV dramas. The town is also the birthplace of the delightful Kinetic Sculpture Race, which sees its people-powered models competing in the annual three-day race from Arcata.

Cape Mendocino Lighthouse and Eureka

The drive south along the Lost Coast from Ferndale follows the old stagecoach route known locally as Wildcat Road, climbs high into the hills, then, after 30 miles (48km) of twists and turns, descends to cross the Bear River and arrive at the defunct community of Capetown. Off the deserted black sand beach is the immense Sugarloaf Rock and nearby Steamboat Rock, which resembles a big tanker stranded at sea.

Cape Mendocino is the westernmost point in California. **Cape Mendocino Lighthouse** was completed in 1868 only after a two-year

struggle to bring materials in by sea and haul them up the steep cliff. Although it warned countless vessels of the treacherous waters, at least nine ships were wrecked off this rugged shore during its 83-year history. Decommissioned in 1951, the wind and sea would have claimed the lighthouse, too, but it was rescued and restored in 1999 and now stands in a park at the edge of Point Delgado (open Memorial Day–Labor Day when guides are available).

Ferndale's Victorian architecture.

Back on the main road, Highway 101 returns to the coast at Humboldt Bay, where it passes several of 10 units of **Humboldt Bay National Wildlife Refuge** (www.fws.gov/humboldtbay; daily). As a key stop on the Pacific Flyway, it provides protected wetland habitat for tens of thousands of migratory water birds, including Aleutian cackling geese and shorebirds.

The biggest coastal city on the California coast north of San Francisco, **Eureka ㉝** (pop. 27,217) and its **Old Town** on the waterfront often stands

The Gingerbread Mansion Inn in Ferndale is named for the lavishly ornamented style of Victorian architecture.

The highly embellished Carson Mansion in Eureka was designed by San Francisco architects Samuel and Joseph Newsome.

Eureka is known for its sizeable number of Victorian buildings.

in for Fog City in movies. Early guests at the landmark **Eureka Inn**, a massive Tudor Revival mansion built in 1922, included Laurel and Hardy, Shirley Temple, John Barrymore, and Britain's Winston Churchill, who stopped in Eureka to visit an old friend who was editing the local paper. After closing for six years, it underwent renovations and reopened in 2010 under new owners. The town's distinctive 1886 **Carson Mansion** – built by a lumber baron with a yen for gables, towers, and turrets – is generally regarded as the handsomest Victorian building in the state, if not in the entire West. It is now a private club.

At **Blue Ox Millworks** (tel: 707-444-3437; Mon–Sat; www.blueoxmill.com), a working Victorian sawmill, visitors can watch craftsmen at work and see how much of the characteristic "gingerbread" ornamentation for such houses was crafted. The old Carnegie Library on F Street, with its wonderful balconies and redwood pillars, has been converted into the enjoyable Morris Graves Museum of Art (tel: 707-442-0278; www.humboldt

arts.org; Wed–Sun). It is named for painter Morris Graves, a founder of the Northwest School of Art in the Pacific Northwest, who, prior to his death in 2001, donated a substantial portion of his personal art collection, including some of his own works, and the use of his name to help with the creation of the museum. Other attractions include **Clarke Historical Museum** (tel: 707-443-1947; www.clarkemuseum.org; Wed–Sat), with its collection of weapons, Native American crafts, and Victoriana, and across the bay, on a peninsula, **Humboldt Bay Maritime Museum** (tel: 707-444-9440; www.humboldtbaymaritimemuseum.com; Tue–Wed, Fri–Sat), with its lighthouse memorabilia.

Next door to Humboldt Bay Maritime Museum is the famous **Samoa Cookhouse** (see page 447), which is the last remaining example of the 1890s lumber camp cookhouses, whose rules included eating as much as you could for a fixed price and helping yourself to anything within reach as long as one foot remained on the ground. Today, huge meals are served family style at long tables – and the same rules apply.

EUREKA TO OREGON

Arcata, just north of Eureka, has been called "the Galapagos of North America," because the number of bird species found here is greater than anywhere else in the state. The focus of all this birding activity is **Arcata Marsh and Wildlife Sanctuary** (tel: 707-822-8184; www.arcatamarsh.org; daily), a 307-acre (124-hectare) wetland that has been created by the city's innovative wastewater treatment plant on Arcata Bay (which produces more than half of California's oyster crop).

Among the birds thriving at the sanctuary, which is on the Pacific Flyway, are endangered Aleutian geese, once down to less than 1,000 in number, but rebounding with federal protection. Other notable birds found here are marbled godwits,

white-tailed kites, and cinnamon teals. Birdwatchers from all over the country converge on the town for Godwit Days every April, when field trips and workshops are offered. Rookery Books and a coffee company advertising "our coffee is for the birds" indicate the level of interest in our feathered friends. The Chamber of Commerce on G Street, two blocks north of the plaza, publishes a free bird list. Also on G Street, Humboldt State University's **Natural History Museum** (tel: 707-826-4479; www.humboldt.ed/natmus; Tue–Sat) exhibits everything from butterflies to dinosaur tails.

Arcata was founded by a group of miners from the Trinity River region in 1849 and grew up around the 1857 **Jacoby Building** on the plaza, built of masonry during an era of timber construction by a merchant serving the goldmines upriver. Elegantly restored and refitted, it now houses stylish shops, a railroad museum, and two of the town's best restaurants. A self-guided walking tour booklet of old Victorian homes is available at the chamber.

McKinleyville, the fastest growing town in Humboldt County, is also the nearest one to the misnamed Eureka-Arcata airport. It claims to have the world's tallest single-tree totem pole (at the shopping center). Its 30-acre (12-hectare) **Azalea State Natural Reserve** (tel: 707-488-2041; daily), which blooms in spring, can be reached via a trail off North Bank Road (take the Central Avenue exit from US 101).

Moonshine Beach and Wedding Rock

After traveling in tandem for the last 100 miles (161km), Highway 1 splits from US 101 at **Moonshine Beach**, just north of the airport, and for 20 or so delightful miles (32km), it runs along the coast through the lovely clifftop village of **Trinidad** 34 (pop. 367), named by a Spanish explorer in 1775 and the site of a small museum.

Fill up here; this is the last gas station on this scenic stretch.

Farther north is **Patrick's Point State Park** (tel: 707-677-3570; daily), where you can admire seals basking on the rocks off Rocky Point and explore tide pools at low tide. The park was named for an Indian scout who settled here in 1851. **Wedding Rock** is a popular site for marriage ceremonies conducted to the sounds of crashing waves below. The rock got its name from the park's first caretaker, Vieggo Andersen, whose marriage to his housekeeper in 1933 began a popular custom. Scenes from Steven Spielberg's *Lost World* were filmed in the parking lot. Nearer to the highway is the site of the old Yurok village, where you'll see an old canoe made of a tree trunk that was hollowed out by fire near a native plant garden. Camping is allowed, and for those who enjoy the luxury of "glamping," you can even rent a Mongolian *yurt* (a comfortable circular tent with a wooden-floor).

About 14 miles (22km) north of Patrick's Point, on the highway before Orick, stop at **Thomas H. Kuchel**

TIP

If you're stopping off in California's Patrick's Point State Park, hike the Rim Trail, a 4-mile (6.5km) round-trip walk that follows an old Indian pathway over the park's bluffs. Steeper spur trails lead off the main route to points jutting out into the ocean, affording amazing views.

Café on Arcata Plaza, Arcata.

TIP

Contact the long-established Tributary Whitewater Tours (tel: 800-672-3846) to experience whitewater rafting on the Smith River in northern California. This can only be done between March and May and the difficulty level varies from III (moderate) to V (extremely difficult).

Roosevelt elk stag on Gold Bluffs Beach.

Visitor Center (tel: 707-465-7765; daily) for information on hiking and camping in **Redwood National Park** (tel: 707-465-7335; www.nps.gov/redw; daily) and three state parks – Prairie Creek Redwoods, Del Norte Coast Redwoods, and Jedediah Smith Redwoods – protecting 132,000 acres (53,418 hectares) of redwoods between here and Crescent City.

The redwoods can reach heights of more than 360ft (110 meters) and are the tallest living things on Earth. Fossil records indicate that millions of years ago, when the climate was warmer and wetter, the trees were found throughout the northern hemisphere. Today, only isolated patches of redwoods remain, mainly in California and China.

Near **Orick**, once a major logging center, turn onto the signposted Newton B. Drury Scenic Parkway through **Prairie Creek Redwoods State Park** (tel: 707-464-6101), a long avenue of incredibly tall trees. If you are interested in hiking, stop for information at **Prairie Creek Visitor Center** and take one of several trails that leave from here. If you

continue driving, you'll probably see the resident herd of Roosevelt elk, which has a tendency to graze beside the highway. These animals should be treated with respect because they can be unpredictable. A worthwhile sidetrip is to drive down the narrow, potholed Coastal Trail along **Golden Bluffs Beach** (a good place to picnic, explore tide pools, bird, and watch whales). The trail goes through dense woodland to **Fern Canyon**, a magical ravine bordered on either side by sheer, fern-carpeted cliffs.

Chainsaw tree sculptures

Just before **Klamath** ⑤, US 101 parallels the broad **Klamath River**, formerly used by Yurok Indians and now a haven for salmon and steelhead fishermen. For a spectacular view of where the river meets the ocean, take the Requa Road on your left to an overlook 600ft (183 meters) above the water. (This side road dead-ends after a few miles.) Gold mines farther up the Klamath River were once served via Klamath from steamers that brought supplies up the coast from San Francisco. Today, the river is popular for jet boat tours from Klamath to see such wildlife as elk and bears. Huge likenesses of legendary lumberjack Paul Bunyan and his blue ox, Babe, and chainsaw-sculpted trees herald the popular tourist spot **Trees of Mystery** (tel: 800-638-3389; www.treesofmystery. net; daily).

A trail leads past some unusual groupings: nine trees growing from one root structure to form the so-called **Cathedral Tree**; a dozen others growing from a single Sitka Spruce trunk. Admission is charged to each trail, but the absorbing museum, with its large collection of Yurok Indian costumes and crafts, is free. The **Sky Trail** nearby is a 1,570ft- (480-meter)-long lift that offers treetop views of the redwoods.

US 101 continues through **Del Norte Coast Redwoods State Park**, the smallest of the state parks. The

highway hugs the coast around many attractive bays before beginning a lengthy climb, where traffic along the narrow road is controlled by solar-powered lights. Tall trees flank most of the final 10 miles (16km) into Crescent City, until the sea comes into view once again just before town.

Redwood preservation and fur trapper history

Crescent City **36**, named for the shape of the bay on which it sits, sprawls somewhat unattractively behind an interesting harbor replete with restaurants, a seafood market, and the **Northcoast Marine Mammal Center** (tel: 707-465-6265; www.northcoastmmc.org), where distressed seals and sea lions are rehabilitated. West of the harbor, **Battery Point Lighthouse** (tel: 707-464-3089; summer daily, Oct–Apr Sat–Sun) can be visited at low tide and contains a museum with photographs of some of the shipwrecks off this treacherous coast.

When environmentalist John Muir visited Crescent City in 1896, he went out on a logging train to see "the work

of ruin going on." Some of the redwoods, he observed, were up to 200ft (61 meters) high and 20ft (6 meters) in diameter, yet two men could chop them down in a single day. His experiences led him to fight for the redwoods' preservation.

Jedediah Smith Redwoods State Park (tel: 707-458-3018), the 10,000-acre (4,050-hectare) state park to the east, is named after Jedediah Smith, the fur trapper who first explored the region in the 1820s. It's a great place for hiking, camping, and picnicking, and fishing, swimming or white-water rafting in the spectacular and turbulent Smith River, California's only undammed river system. Stop at **the Jedediah Smith Visitor Center** (May–Sept) in Hiouchi for information on visiting the state park. The US Forest Service office (tel: 707-457-3131) in **Gasquet** provides maps and information Six Rivers National Forest and reserving a night in the remote fire-lookout cabin atop Bear Basin Butte. Whether you head north from Crescent City or Gasquet, in less than 25 miles (40km), you'll be in **Oregon**.

On the shore, Crescent City.

Fishing at the mouth of the Columbia River, near Astoria, Oregon.

OREGON TO WASHINGTON

The rugged 400-mile (644km) Oregon coast is famous for basaltic cliffs, historic lighthouses, and pullouts offering views of migrating gray whales all along its coastline and into Washington.

rusty US 101 trundles up the Oregon coast into the state of Washington, offering some of the best coastal scenery in the United States. Rural and more rugged than California, this section of 101, which is signposted "PACIFIC COAST SCENIC HIGHWAY," brings you into dramatic proximity with cliffs, beaches, wildlife, and attractive state parks.

BROOKINGS-HARBOR TO WALDPORT

The southern part of the Oregon Coast – the **Siskiyou Coast** – begins calmly enough, with a drive through farmland. Ships are beached on dry land – first, a huge one beside the aptly named Ship Ashore Motel, then an old tugboat converted into a souvenir store just south of **Brookings-Harbor** ③⑦. Brookings, located at the mouth of the Chetco River, is the larger of the two communities. The sports-fishing fleet is anchored here, and it also contains the local visitor information bureau (tel: 800-535-9469; www.brookings harborchamber.com).

Brookings is a popular retirement spot, as it's in the "banana belt," with winter temperatures often reaching 65°F (18°C). The scientific explanation for this is that the town's south-east-to-northwest geographical layout combines with constant low-pressure thermal troughs that pull down the

highly compressed air following a storm system. One consequence is that the area is famous for its spring blooms. It produces most of the country's Easter lilies, and the city's 33-acre (13-hectare) **Azalea Park** (tel: 541-469-1100) attracts visitors every spring, especially on Memorial Day weekend, when there's an Azalea Festival.

Some of Oregon's most spectacular coastal scenery is protected in **Samuel H. Boardman State Scenic Corridor** (tel: 800-551-6949), just north of town. The state park runs for about 12

Main Attractions

Boardman State Park
Coquille River Lighthouse
Coos Bay
Oregon Dunes
Sea Lion Caves
Yachats
Newport
Depoe Bay
Portland
Cannon Beach
Astoria

Rounding up horses in Oregon.

TIP

Sites on public lands along Oregon's Pacific Coast require a pass. The **Oregon Pacific Coast Passport** (www. fs.usda.gov) is available as a one-day, five-day, or annual pass and covers entry, parking, and day use fees at all state and federal fee sites. Washington's **Discover Pass** (http://www. discoverpass.wa.gov) allows unlimited access to state lands. If you plan on visiting a lot of federally managed lands on your travels, invest in an annual **Interagency Pass** ($80).

View of the coastline at Brookings-Harbor.

miles (19km) past exposed cliffs, sparkling coves, and offshore rock formations such as Arch Rock and Natural Bridges. March brings daffodils, May the wild azaleas, and July the snow lilies, while every month of the year brings eager photographers.

Whale watching sites

North of Brookings-Harbor, near **Harris Beach State Park** (tel: 541-469-2021), is one of 28 places on the Oregon coast to be designated a whale-watching site. The whale-watching station is manned by some of the 450 trained volunteers who take part in Oregon's Whale Watching Spoken Here program every winter, headquartered at Depoe Bay's excellent Whale Watching Center on the seawall.

Gray whales leave the Bering Sea to head south to their breeding grounds in the protected lagoons of Baja California from mid-December to January, then make the return journey to Alaska starting in March, as soon as the newborn calves are old enough to survive the dangerous journey. It is a grueling 10,000-mile (16,000km)

round trip, at a speed of around 5mph (8kph). The whales typically stay 5 miles (8km) offshore, and during peak migration pass by at a rate of 30 whales per hour. You are almost guaranteed a sighting, if you time your visit right – a real thrill.

Kissing Rock

US 101 soon crosses the **Thomas Creek Bridge**, the state's highest at 345ft (105 meters), then a string of dune-backed beaches begins just before Pistol River. The best of these are around the rather eye-catching **Kissing Rock**, popular with windsurfers, between Meyers Creek and Gold Beach. The latter's name dates from the 1850s, when prospectors discovered that the sands around the mouth of the Rogue River were salted with gold dust.

Today, several companies offer excursions in powerful hydro jet boats up this wild and scenic river through a beautiful, pristine landscape teeming with wildlife; its upper reaches encompass dramatic canyons hundreds of feet deep. Sportfishing for salmon and steelhead trout can

be arranged, as well as ocean fishing, and horses can be rented for riding on the beach. At **Gold Beach**, a laid-back town large enough for a couple of good restaurants, make time to visit **Curry Historical Society Museum** (tel: 541-247-9396; www.curryhistory. com; Feb–Dec, Tue–Sat;). Highway 101 then crosses the graceful Patterson Memorial Bridge over the Rogue River to continue up the coast.

Seven miles (11km) north, at **Nesika Beach**, the highway parallels the shoreline. Low-lying, tree-covered hills flank the right-hand side and marshland sits between road and sea. Massive moss- and lichen-covered rocks stick out of the water, and around **Humbug Mountain** the scenery is particularly stunning. Towering mountains taper down to the road, which flanks a series of bays enlivened by crashing white surf.

Westernmost city in the US

Keep an eye out on the right for the painted dinosaur outside the **Prehistoric Gardens** in the rainforest. Perched on scenic bluffs, **Port Orford**

38 is the westernmost city in the contiguous United States, and was a major lumber shipping port more than a century ago. Just offshore, past the battered Shack Art Studio, is a wooded island called **Battle Rock**. In 1851, the island's original party of settlers was besieged by local Native Americans who resented the newcomers' claim to the land. A month later, a larger white group arrived and took possession.

From here, there's a beautiful view of the coast back to Humbug Mountain. Take a lingering look at Port Orford's lovely bay, because it will be your last uninterrupted view of the ocean for nearly 100 miles (161km), although frequent "COASTAL ACCESS" signs dot the highway. Northeast of town, on Elk River Road, is the **Elk River Fish Hatchery**, where salmon smelts are raised.

Lighthouses and lazy countryside

From here, you can make a 6-mile (10km) side trip to **Cape Blanco State Park** and take tours of its historic **Hughes House** and **Lighthouse**

Stegosaurus exhibit at Prehistoric Gardens.

TIP

Stop in the small parking area provided on the west side of Riverside Drive in Oregon's Bandon Marsh National Wildlife Refuge (tel: 541-347-1470) to find the observation deck. This refuge is one of the best places to spot rare shorebirds, such as the Mongolian plover, as well as being an oasis for bald eagles and the California brown pelican.

(tel: 541-756-0100; Tue–Sun; tours in Memorial Day–Labor Day only). The lighthouse sits on the cliffs, 245ft (75 meters) above the sea, and was the first in the state to be outfitted with a first-order Fresnel lens in 1870. It is operated by the Bureau of Land Management. Next comes **Langlois**, located in serene countryside filled with grazing cows and sheep. There are many lonely sheep ranches in the surrounding hills, and knitters will find a factory outlet selling wool among Langlois's small shops.

Miles of bright yellow gorse line the approach to **Bandon** ㉟, twice destroyed by fire in the last century; a brick chimney on the site of the old bakery stands as a memorial just off the highway. Artists' homes and studios and craft shops surround Bandon's **Old Town** area. **Bandon Historical Society Museum** (tel: 541-347-2164; www.bandonhistorical museum.org; Mon–Sat) includes an exhibit about cranberry cultivation, which has been taking place in nearby bogs for more than a century – ever since the early settlers learned

Coquille River Lighthouse.

the technique from local Native Americans. The town celebrates with a Cranberry Festival every fall, and you can tour cranberry farms by appointment. Near Bandon is charming **Coquille River Lighthouse** (tel: 541-347-3501; tours daily, May–Oct), accessed through **Bullards Beach State Park** (tel: 541-347-2209), a large family-oriented state park.

Coos Bay is a major lumber shipping port, with warehouses and stacked logs lining the road. Even its Mill Casino, run by the Coquille Tribe, is in a converted sawmill. Back in 1850, Captain Asa Simpson established a sawmill and shipyard here, which built about 50 vessels before the end of the century. On a smaller scale, you can tour the **Oregon Connection** factory (tel: 541-267-7804; www.oregonconnection.com), one of the oldest myrtlewood factories on the Oregon coast, where you can see logs fashioned into bowls, goblets, and other products.

A 24-mile (39km) drive east leads to **Golden and Silver Falls State Natural Area** (tel: 800-551-6949), a hidden gem in the coastal forests with 100ft (30-meter) waterfalls. On the coast, the fishing village of **Charleston** is a good place for fresh crab and seafood at Fisherman's Wharf. Continue south on the scenic **Cape Arago Beach Loop** for stunning sea views and vantage points for spotting seals, sea lions, and whales. Cape Arago is home to elephant seals, known for their deep diving skills – up to 4,000ft (1,200 meters). The loop encompasses three state parks, including **Shore Acres State Park** (tel: 541-888-4902), formerly the gardens of the spacious house belonging to lumber baron Louis J. Simpson, Asa's son.

Oregon Dunes

Across the magnificent McCullough Bridge spanning Hayes Inlet is Coos Bay's neighbor, **North Bend**. Stop in at **North Bend Welcome Center** (tel: 541-756-4613; www.visittheoregoncoast.

com/cities/northbend) for visitor information and find out more about **Coos Historical and Maritime Museum** (tel: 541-756-6320; www.cooshistory.org), which is currently building an attractive new cultural center to interpret local history.

Oregon Dunes National Recreation Area ❹ begins at North Bend and protects a broad expanse of towering sand dunes up to 500ft (152 meters) high, which block access to the coast for 40 miles (64km). There are 11 different places offering beach access, at least one of which, **Spinreel** (watch for the highway sign) offers a chance to rent dune buggies (tel: 541-759-3313; www.ridetheoregondunes.com) and cavort in the sandy wilderness. The dunes are constantly sculpted into different shapes by wind and water and are a refuge for a rich variety of animals and plants, including red and yellow salmonberries, thimbleberries (similar to raspberries), wild strawberries and, in the fall, huckleberries. At the **Umpqua Dunes Trailhead** (watch for the highway sign), you can park the car and climb the dunes.

Dune buggy ride along the Southern Oregon coast.

"Glamping" enthusiasts (luxury campers) will be glad to learn that camping facilities here include spacious Mongolian *yurts*: structurally supported domed tents with plywood floors, lockable doors, comfortable beds, and light and heating. They are designed to withstand high winds and retain heat in winter. You'll find them throughout the Oregon State Park System, from rustic to deluxe (tel: 800-551-6949 for information and reservations). In summer, take a 5-mile (8km) side trip to visit **Umpqua Lighthouse State Park** (tel: 541-271-4118). The 1894 lighthouse is 65ft (19 meters) high and its lens has a distinctive red-and-white flash. It replaced the 1857 lighthouse that had been built here.

Lower **Umpqua Bay** is said to be the most fertile place for big softshell clams, some weighing around half a pound (220 grams). The delicious Dungeness crab is found in the Winchester Bay area, where the Umpqua River meets the ocean. Shops sell crabbing equipment and bait.

Oregon Dunes National Recreation Area.

Salmon Harbor to Gardiner

Just before **Salmon Harbor** (unsurprisingly the largest salmon fishing port on the Oregon coast), keep an eye out for the Rusty Frog Gallery to your right and then cross the bridge into **Reedsport**, which is located at the midpoint of Oregon Dunes NRA.

Here you'll find **Umpqua Discovery Center** (tel: 541-271-4816; www.umpquadiscoverycenter.com; daily), an attractive hands-on education center that interprets the dunes and much else besides. Also in Reedsport is **Oregon Dunes NRA Visitor Center** (tel: 541-271-6000; Wed–Fri) on US 101, run by the US Forest Service, which publicizes preservation efforts, issues bird checklists (there are five different types of seagull alone), and can help you book campground sites (tel: 541-271-3611). A mile or two to the east, on State 38, visitors can admire herds of Roosevelt elk at the pleasant **Dean Creek Elk Viewing Area**, which is also a haven for bald eagles, osprey, and blue herons.

Continuing north, Highway 101 passes through **Gardiner**, with a historic district of quaint buildings and a pioneer cemetery. The **Tsunami Art Gallery** (tel: 541-271-1597; Tue–Sun), which contains the bronze sculpture studio of Mack Holman and features sculptures, pastels, porcelain, bronze, and oil paintings.in the old Gardiner General Store is aptly named, given the number of "tsunami hazard zone" signs along the coast. Thankfully, the Pacific Northwest coast was not damaged by the Japanese Tsunami in 2011, but debris continues to wash ashore, and you'll see debris collection sites along the coast. Glimpses of lakes and mountains appear through the pines along the pretty forest-lined road. There are numerous campgrounds, and the dunes continue all the way to Florence.

Florence and Sea Lion Caves

Florence has a picturesque harbor with some very old buildings as a backdrop. It's especially pretty when the rhododendrons display their vivid pink blossoms in late spring. In the Old Town, **Siuslaw Pioneer Museum** (tel: 541-997-7884; www.siuslawpioneermuseum.com; May–Sept Labor Day daily, Feb–Apr, Oct–Dec Tue–Sun) has old photographs and household items. When landslides block US 101 to the north (as happened for months early in 2000), it's the last chance to turn inland before Waldport. If traffic conditions have been bad, check with the Oregon Department of Transportation (tel: 888-275-6368; www.oregon.gov/odot), because even when the road is "closed," it's sometimes open for an hour or two each day, usually early morning and early evening.

Eleven miles (18km) north of Florence is the 1894 **Heceta Head Lighthouse** (tel: 866-547-3696; tours Memorial Day–Labor Day weekend, Thur–Mon) in Heceda Head State Park. The lighthouse is closed for renovations until August 2013, but the

Florence's harbor.

park is still open. Just before the lighthouse is **Sea Lion Caves** (tel: 541-547-3111; www.sealioncaves.com; daily), the world's largest sea cave, at the bottom of cliffs accessed by an elevator. Only a wire screen separates visitors from hundreds of Steller's sea lions, the closest you'll get to their underground lair. Harbor seals (which have spotted coats) and elephant seals are the most common pinnipeds on this coast; neither has external ears – as opposed to sea lions. The latter can also rotate their hind flippers and walk on land.

Cape Perpetua is the highest point (803ft/245 meters above sea level) on the Oregon coast. **Cape Perpetua Visitor Center** (tel: 541-547-3289), run by the US Forest Service, is an excellent place to stop, enjoy a ranger-led program, and get maps and suggestions for hikes in Siuslaw National Forest. Its overlook has a terrific view – the highway looks like a thin sliver of silver ribbon threading along the coast. Note: You will need to purchase a $5 National Forest Day Pass for recreation in Northwest national forests, available at Forest Service visitor centers and kiosks.

Cape Perpetua Visitor Center is 2 miles (3km) south of the curiously named **Yachats** ❹, an attractive and laid-back resort town nestled between the mountains and the sea, has beach trails, richly populated tidepools, and good fishing. Once known for the multitude of smelts (a silvery sardine-like fish) that spawned here, the numbers have steadily declined in recent years and the community now has to import the fish from California for its annual Smelt Fry in July.

Waldport ❷ sits at the mouth of the Alsea River, which arrives at the ocean from its origin in Siuslaw National Forest, and US 101 enters the town over the huge bay bridge. Waldport is mainly known for its fishing, crabbing, and clamming. It's also a good base for hiking.

WALDPORT TO SEASIDE

Look to the right while crossing Yaquina Bay into **Newport** ❸: the section below the bridge is Newport's **Historic Bayfront**, where the attractions include old taverns, gift shops, a harbor filled with fishing boats, and a trio of commercial attractions, including **Undersea Gardens** (tel: 541-265-2206; www.marinersquare.com; daily), an aquarium where divers cavort behind glass. Across the bay, **South Beach** has the larger and well-known **Oregon Coast Aquarium** (tel: 541-867-3474; www.aquarium.org; daily), whose famous former resident, Keiko the orca, starred in the film *Free Willy*.

To reach the Bayfront, turn off the main street at the traffic light (opposite the Mazatlan Mexican restaurant in a gray, wooden building) and head down Hurburt Street. Farther on through town, several streets lead west to the seaport with its pedestrian promenade and historic murals. One block farther, Third Street leads to **Nye Beach**, at one time the Oregon Coast's major draw and still a worthy destination to visit **Newport Visual Arts Center**

Yachats covered bridge crosses the North Forks of Yachats River in Lincoln County, Oregon.

Heceta Head Lighthouse.

(tel: 541-265-6540; www.coastarts.org; Tue–Sun), with excellent art exhibits, including one called Washed Ashore, in 2012, featuring artworks made from coastal debris, a major theme following the 2011 Japanese Tsunami. The center also has a memorial to the famed composer Ernest Bloch, who spent the last decades of his life at his home at nearby Agate Beach.

On US 101, opposite Newport Visitor Center (tel: 541-574-2679), the ornate **Burrows House**, a boarding house from the 1890s, is part of the **Oregon Coast History Center,** run by Lincoln County Historical Society to interpret central Oregon coastal history. Just outside town is the much-photographed **Yaquina Head Lighthouse** ❹, built in 1873 and part of the BLM-run **Yaquina Head Outstanding Natural Area** (tel: 541-574-3100; grounds and interpretive center daily; lighthouse tours: Thur–Tue).

About 5 miles (8km) north of Newport, don't miss the signs for **Devil's Punchbowl**, where a huge stone basin fills dramatically – and noisily – as the tide crashes in. Waves are higher in the Pacific than the Atlantic because the wind blows uninterruptedly over a larger distance. The study of waves – whose height is measured as the distance between the highest point (crest) and lowest point (trough) – is understandably one of great interest to coastal communities.

Oregon's whale watching capital

Cape Foulweather was named in 1778 by British navigator Captain James Cook. It was his first sighting of the American mainland after he had "discovered" Hawaii. The winds here, 500ft (152 meters) above the ocean, can reach 100mph (161kph). The small gift shop sells the much-prized green glass bubbles that have drifted here from fishermen's nets all the way from Japan. Lincoln City launches its own floats every year at its Festival of Glass.

The awesome cliffs and headlands are basalt, formed by molten lava hitting the ocean eons ago and hardening instantly. Sometimes, this instant cooling creates oddly shaped rock structures known as pillow basalt,

Hiking on Cascade Head.

which can be seen offshore near Cape Foulweather and at **Depoe Bay**, a pretty resort that claims to be the world's smallest navigable harbor. Depoe Bay is Oregon's Whale Watching Capital, and the state-run **Whale Watching Center** (tel: 541-765-3304; daily) on the seawall is a terrific place to learn about whales. A resident pod of gray whales spends the summer feeding in the kelp beds off Depoe Bay. Boats in the harbor offer whale-watching and fishing tours, and this is your best bet on the Oregon coast to get out on the water.

At high tide, seawater shoots skyward through two rock formations known locally as the **Spouting Horns**. Visitors get a close-up look at the wave action just by walking along the sea wall, which runs the full length of the town. When a storm is about to hit, everyone heads to a Depoe Bay restaurant for a full-frontal view, complete with sound effects.

Lincoln City

Trawling for glass floats, collecting driftwood and studying tide pools are all popular pastimes along this stretch of low-key coast. Tide pools could be regarded as miniature ocean habitats, where some creatures wait in anticipation for the waves to wash in their lunch. Orange and pink starfish, urchins and sea anemones can usually be seen among the tiny fish that dart about the shallows, while rocky residents such as long-tapered mussels and white barnacles cluster on the rocks.

Lincoln City 45 has 7 miles (11km) of beaches, including a half-mile-wide strand when the tide is out at Siletz Bay. It's home to a cluster of antique stores and second-hand bookstores, as well as Chinook Winds Casino for night-time action and a factory outlet center for daytime shopping. The tiny D River links nearby **Devil's Lake** with the ocean, providing both freshwater and oceanside fun. North of town, **Cascade Head** is a good place to see falcons, hawks, bald eagles, and other raptors, which use their keen eyesight, outstanding hearing, and amazing speed to hunt and kill their prey, then eat it using large clawed feet and hooked bills.

Rooms at the Cannery Pier Hotel in Astoria have fabulous views of the Columbia River.

Portland: City of Roses

A ride-for-free transit system, stunning scenery, and micro-breweries everywhere – no wonder Portland smells like roses.

Light railway in Downtown.

Portland is a famously livable city. It has always prided itself on its bike-and-pedestrian friendliness and trees-and-parks image. In a city that boasts 247 parks and recreational sites, including 196 neighborhood parks, the largest is 6,000-acre (2,438-hectare) **Forest Park,** the fifth largest municipal park in the US.

Portland Regional Arts and Culture Council (tel: 503-823-5111; Mon–Fri; www.racc.org) promotes the arts in the city through education, public sculpture, and grants and is a good first stop for information about museums and art galleries. One popular public space for the arts is **Pioneer Courthouse Square** in Downtown, which hosts more than 300 programs events a year. Its "Weather Machine," an earth-shaped sphere by local artist Terence O'Donnell on a 25ft (8-meter) column, comes to life with a musical fanfare at noon each day.

View over Portland and Mount Hood.

Top art spots include **Portland Art Museum** (tel: 503-226-2811; Tue–Sun; www.pam.org) and the **Museum of Contemporary Craft** (tel: 503-223-2654; Tue–Sun; www.museumofcontemporarycraft.org). Portland's quirkiest attraction is the Church of Elvis (24 hours), a coin-operated shrine offering marriage counseling and more. For those interested in history, **Portland Development Commission** (tel: 503-823-3200; Mon–Fri; www.pdc.us) produces a map showing interesting historical and architectural sites and offers private guided walking tours.

The city's efficient transit system embraces a 300-block "Fareless Square" Downtown, where passengers ride free on buses or the light rail system. Washington Park subway is within easy access of many major attractions, including **Oregon Zoo**, the **World Forestry Center, Hoyt Arboretum,** and the **Children's Museum.** A streetcar system links Downtown with the **Pearl District** (an area colonized by local artists) and the **Nob Hill** neighborhood, with its fine Victorian and Georgian mansions. In the historic **Skidmore District**, there's a large weekend open-air market with live entertainment. Portland also has more microbreweries and brewpubs than any other city in the nation.

Oregon history comes to life in **Oregon History Museum (**tel: 503-222-1741; Tue–Sun; www.ohs.org) and in **Pittock Mansion** (tel: 503-823-3623; Feb–Dec daily), the 1914 home of the founder of Portland's well-regarded daily newspaper, *The Oregonian*. Literary pursuits are popular in rainy Portland, and no visit here is complete without a trip to famous **Powell's Books,** an independent bookstore in Downtown.

At the **Oregon Museum of Science and Industry** (tel: 503-797-4000; Tue–Sun and Mon during school holidays; www.omsi.edu), you can experience a simulated earthquake. East of Portland is the basaltic Columbia Plateau, formed by hardened lava from erupting Cascade volcanoes like Mount Hood and later carved by Ice Age flooding and the now-dammed Columbia River into a spectacular gorge. The breathtaking cliffs, waterfalls, wildlife, and historic sites preserved in **Columbia Gorge National Recreation Area** make a perfect day trip.

Pastured dairy farms

The highway passes through the wonderful, fresh-scented **Siuslaw National Forest**, its highest peak, Mount Hebo, ascending to 3,000ft (914 meters). The highway skirts residential **Neskowin** and then heads inland, passing meadows of grazing cows (which outnumber people in this pastoral county) owned by the 180 working farms that provide the milk for the delectable Tillamook cheese. After **Cloverdale**, with its colorful rustic buildings, sturdy wooden barns and springtime daffodils catch the eye before the towns of Hebo and Beaver appear.

Tillamook Air Museum (tel: 503-842-1130; daily; www.tillamookair.com), a couple of miles south of town, is housed in an enormous hangar containing World War II vintage planes and a welcome 1940s-style café. **Tillamook ⑯** is justly famous for its huge, pristine **Tillamook Cheese Factory** (tel: 503-815-1300; daily; www.tillamookcheese.com; daily), which offers free tours of its manufacturing facility. You can admire a life-size, painted plaster cow, beribboned with a computer

chip that has replaced the old cowbell. A wall chart lists "udderly amazing" facts such as that 2,600 pints of blood pass through the udder to produce one pint of milk and that a cow yields 10,000 gallons of milk in her lifetime. Help yourself to the free cheese samples, because it's a sure bet that you're bound to buy something in the tempting Aladdin's Cave that calls itself a gift shop. Not to be outdone, the **Blue Heron French Cheese Company** (tel: 503-842-8281; www.blueheronoregon.com; daily) offers wine with its cheese tastings. Needless to say, the Dairy Parade is a major event each June.

West of Tillamook, a detour along 20-mile (32km) **Three Capes Scenic Drive** takes you to the "Octopus Tree" – a Sitka spruce with multiple trunks – and **Cape Meares Lighthouse**, built in 1890 with a lens imported from Paris. An early lighthouse keeper wrote of the harrowing all-night horse-and-buggy trip required to reach a doctor in Tillamook, a trip that today takes about 16 minutes.

Two miles (3km) out to sea is **Tillamook Lighthouse**, situated on

FACT

Portland is the hometown of Matt Groening, creator of the long-running TV series *The Simpsons*. A number of the animated characters are named after city sites and streets.

Sports fishing boat in Garibaldi Harbor.

Cannon Beach.

a solitary rock amid crashing waves that in 1934 roared into a maelstrom, climbing more than 100ft (30 meters) high to engulf the entire building. "Terrible Tilly" was how lighthouse keepers used to describe the building. Life on the rock was too hazardous to allow families to accompany staff to their jobs, who were rotated every three weeks and allowed 96 days' leave each year to recover. The lighthouse was decommissioned in 1980.

For a taste of big-city life, take a detour from Tillamook along State Route 6 east to the "City of Roses," otherwise known as **Portland ④** (see page 376). Past Tillamook, the highway hugs the 13-sq-mile (34-sq-km) shallow bay, which is rarely deeper than 6ft (2 meters). Estuaries such as this, where fresh water mingles with that of the ocean, are especially inviting to plant and marine life. Eelgrass provides shelter and nourishment to crabs as well as young salmon and other small fish; mudflats harbor gourmet treats for the stately great blue heron, which can often be seen prospecting for dinner.

Garibaldi ghosts and Cannon Beach

Garibaldi is named for the 19th-century Italian liberator. Its down-home attractions include the battered Ghost Hole Tavern, the Lumberman's Memorial Park, **Garibaldi Museum** (tel: 503-322-8411; www.garibaldimuseum. com; May–Oct Thur–Mon), and annual Crab Races, which presumably take place sideways.

At the cute, old-fashioned resort of **Rockaway Beach**, a red caboose beside the highway houses the tourist office (tel: 503-355-8108; Mon–Fri, albeit sporadically). Freight trains loaded with lumber can occasionally be seen running on the roadside track, which follows the course of the Nehalem River. Tiny **Wheeler** has antiques shops and a wildlife viewing area along the bay in the town center.

After the long climb from **Manzanita**, there are spectacular ocean views from an overlook where **Oswald West State Park** begins. Down to the trestle bridge over the canyon, Tillamook County ("the land of cheese, trees, and gentle breeze") comes to an end just before the tunnel.

Oregon's most iconic natural landmark can be found at **Cannon Beach ④**, where 235ft (72-meter) -high **Haystack Rock is** home to nesting tufted puffins in spring and summer. Cannon Beach, named for a cannon washed ashore after an 1846 shipwreck, is an attractive artists' haven, with over a dozen visual arts studios and galleries. The vision of colorful stunt kites soaring overhead is matched only by the tranquil scene of families and friends gathering round campfires on the beach as the silhouetted rock fades into the sunset.

Cannon Beach sponsors an annual Sandcastle Day in June and a dog show on the beach in October, with contests for best bark, Frisbee catch, and owner/dog lookalike. There's even a Stormy Weather Arts Festival (indoors) in November. The visitor center (tel: 503-436-2623; www.

cannonbeach.org) can suggest plenty of things to do, but the big draw is strolling along the beach and investigating tide pools on this magnificent section of the Oregon coast.

Historic Seaside

On the north side of town, Ecola State Park has beautiful views of the coastline and Haystack Rock. Eight miles (13km) north of Cannon Beach, US 101 descends into **Seaside ❹** (pop. 6,476), the largest resort town on the Oregon Coast. It is bisected by the Necanicum River, with its historic downtown area on the western side of Broadway. A wide sandy beach is flanked by a pedestrian promenade, where you'll find the **Aquarium** (tel: 503-738-6211; daily). Three blocks farther north is **Seaside Historical Society Museum** (tel: 503-738-7065; www.seasidemuseum.org; Mon–Fri).

It was at Seaside that members of the Lewis and Clark exploration party set up a camp to make salt by boiling seawater. After their epic journey west brought them to the mouth of the Columbia River and the Pacific in 1805, the expedition hunkered down for a cold, wet winter. They built **Fort Clatsop**, a 50-sq-ft (5-sq-meter) stockade with a parade ground and two rows of small cabins, southeast of what is now Warrenton and named it for the local Native Americans, who brought whale meat to trade (Clark cooked and ate some, describing it as "very palatable and tender").

The replica of the fort in **Lewis and Clark National Historical Park** (tel: 503-861-2471; www.nps.gov/lewi; daily), which protects Lewis and Clark sites on both the Oregon and Washington sides of the river, helps visitors imagine the challenging conditions. Its summer living history program features buckskin-clad rangers demonstrating daily life during the period. Another fort, located in nearby **Fort Stevens State Park,** was built to defend the mouth of the Columbia River during the Civil War.

ASTORIA TO ABERDEEN

Astoria ❺ – 22 miles (35km) north of Seaside – was once known as "the salmon canning capital of the

Haystack Rock at Cannon Beach.

A serene corner of the lovely Portland Japanese Gardens.

TIP

Waikiki Beach is where the North Jetty meets the cape in Washington's Cape Disappointment State Park. This is an ideal place for storm watching as the waves crash into the cliffs, with Cape Disappointment lighthouse in the background. It's only a few miles from Ilwaco and great for photos.

world," and in an 1872 book, Frances Fuller Victor was able to write: "The immense numbers of all kinds of salmon, which ascend the Columbia annually, is something wonderful. They seem to be seeking quiet and safe places to deposit their spawn, and thousands of them never stop until they can reach the great falls of the Snake River, more than 600 miles (966km) from the sea." As late as 1915, fishermen were taking 21,000 tons of salmon from the river. But then came the giant dams. The protest by the Cayuse Tribe that it would abrogate their rights by eliminating most of the salmon sadly turned out to be true. Some salmon runs have declined 85 percent from what they once were, despite the production of 170 million fish each year by artificial hatcheries. Only here, at the mouth of the Columbia, can you experience the untamed river.

The mighty Columbia

At its most powerful, the Columbia thrusts 150 billion gallons (682 billion litres) of water a day through the sandbars into the Pacific Ocean, a torrent that has capsized at least 2,000 boats in the two centuries since John Jacob Astor's Pacific Fur Company created the first American settlement on shore. In recent years, the Federal government has dredged a 40ft (12-meter) channel and placed long jetties at each side to narrow the channel, but despite constant dredging and other attempts to tame the river at its mouth, it remains one of the most dangerous sandbars in the world. The weather so consistently stirs up stormy seas that the Coast Guard set up its National Motor Lifeboat School at the tip of Cape Disappointment, where waves sometimes reach 30ft (9 meters) in height. For all that, this is a spectacular place, and cruise boats regularly call at Astoria, depositing hundreds of passengers at the 17th Street Dock, used regularly by Coast Guard cutters.

Columbia River Maritime Museum (tel: 503-325-2323; daily) is all about shipwrecks, lighthouses, fishing, navigation, and naval history. Much of Astoria's history is reflected in its

Pushing off for a kayaking trip on Long Island Slough, Willapa National Wildlife Refuge.

handsome Victorian houses, which fall into particular styles: Italianate, whose overhanging eaves have decorative brackets and tall or paired windows and doors, or Queen Anne (multiple roof lines, towers and turrets, paneled doors, and stained glass). An interesting example of the latter is the **Captain George Flavel House**, dating from the 1880s, on Eighth Street (tel: 503-325-2203; daily).

It's a steep, winding drive past the historic homes up the hill to the **Astoria Column**, with its 164 winding steps, each one individually sponsored. The Great Northern Railroad and Vincent Astor, great-grandson of Jacob Astor, were responsible for installing the 125ft (38-meter) -high tower in 1926. The views, of course, are stupendous, but once back on the ground you'll be glad to warm up in the hut as you buy a postcard.

WASHINGTON STATE'S DISCOVERY COAST

It took three weeks for the Lewis and Clark exploration party to cross the wide mouth of the Columbia River and set up another camp near today's **Chinook** on the Washington coast ("the Discovery Coast"). Motoring across the 4-mile (6km) -long bridge linking Oregon and Washington is one of the great thrills of driving this Pacific Coast route, even (or perhaps especially) in a fog. It climbs steeply above the water, as seagulls swoop overhead with keening cries and the wind reaches almost gale force.

US 101 continues past a bird-filled wildlife refuge to the attractive, unspoiled town of **Ilwaco**, with its murals and **Columbia Pacific Heritage Museum** (tel: 360-642-3446; www.columbiapacificheritagemuseum.org; Tue–Sun). The expedition stayed for three lonely months in this isolated area.

Ilwaco sits at the bottom of the Long Beach peninsula – 28 miles (45km) of sandy beach – which gets nicer the farther north you go. In the southwest corner, in **Cape Disappointment State Park** (tel: 360-642-3078), **Fort Canby** guarded the mouth of the Columbia for almost a century before it became part of the state park in 1957. Built in 1856,

FACT

John Jacob Astor was a German immigrant who became the first multi-millionaire in the States. He made his fortune from real estate, opium, and fur trading, from which he created the Pacific Fur Company.

Crown Point overlooking the gorge of the Columbia River.

Cape Disappointment Lighthouse is the oldest operational lighthouse on the West Coast. So treacherous was Cape Disappointment that another lighthouse had to be built in 1898 at nearby **North Head** (tel: 360-902-8844 for times of May–Sept tours). There's a very interesting **Lewis and Clark Interpretive Center** (daily), where you can study biographies of members of the original party and entries from the actual journals they kept. This excellent park overlooks 28 miles (45km) of sandy beach that was voted top beach in Washington.

Nearby **Long Beach** is a perennially popular beach resort with weekenders from Seattle and Portland. It specializes in good, old-fashioned seaside fun and games and doesn't put on any airs or graces. Beaches on the peninsula are popular for clamming. **Nahcotta** and **Oysterville** at the northern end became prosperous from oyster gathering before the crop was overharvested, and some fine Victorian homes remain from those days. **Willapa Bay Interpretive Center** (Memorial Day–Labor Day Fri–Sun), in a replica of an oyster house in Nahcotta, explains the history. **Leadbetter Point State Park**, in Willapa Bay separating the point from the Pacific, is also a wildlife refuge where waterfowl stop over on their way south.

South Bend and Raymond

Back on "the mainland," US 101 crosses the Naselle River and a number of sloughs (inlets) before arriving at **South Bend** 🟡, which sits on a bay at the mouth of the Willapa River. Signs announcing oysters for sale in what calls itself the "oyster capital of the world" are a reminder that a century ago tons of these succulent bivalves were harvested by Native Americans, and now find a ready market in the gourmet restaurants of Seattle, Portland, and San Francisco. Also in search of the same is the black oystercatcher, a bird whose long red bill helps it open the shellfish once it has found them.

Two ancient wooden warehouses contain a shipwright and an ironworks in South Bend, which stages its annual Oyster Stampede every May. South Bend's neighbor, **Raymond**, is an unspoiled sort of place, with a library built in the style of a timbered English cottage, its art-glass panes depicting fairy-tale characters.

Cranberry bogs and lumber towns

Architecturally, Raymond's pride and joy is the old courthouse, with its spiral staircase and stained-glass dome. "A gilded palace of reckless extravagance" was how the local paper described it when the courthouse first went up in 1910. Life-size metal silhouettes of sculptured animals and historical figures form the **Wildlife Heritage Sculpture Corridor**, which runs through the town along Highway 101. Four miles (6km) east of Raymond on State 6 is the (marked) grave of Willie Kiel, a 19-year-old who died of malaria just before the family wagon train left Missouri in 1855. Preserved in whisky

Diver with a sunflower sea star.

in a lead casket by his doctor father, the body came along for the trip and was buried atop a grassy knoll, which is now crowned with towering cedars.

Access to beaches here is via State 105, which runs past the Shoalwater Indian Reservation and the cranberry bogs between North Cove and Grayland. Cranberries blossom in late June, and **Grayland** holds its annual cranberry festival in October, following the harvest.

Between Raymond and the lumber town of Aberdeen, US 105 bends and twists through a forest of mist-shrouded pines. Large tracts have been devastated by clearcutting, while others are covered in monocultural new plantings that give the forest a monotonous look. The road emerges just south of town, beside the century-old Weyerhaeuser sawmill, which recently closed as a result of the economic downturn. When the bridge over the broad Chehalis River is raised, vehicles must wait to continue their journey.

Like its Scottish namesake, **Aberdeen ㊿** sits at the confluence of two rivers. It is known for **Grays Harbor**, the seaport that grew up after Robert Gray sailed in on the *Lady Washington* in 1788 to help arrange fur trading between the Pacific Northwest and China. A replica of the 170-ton ship is used for educational trips, but is usually on show in the harbor, and more about the town's early days can be explored in **Aberdeen Museum of History** (tel: 360-533-1976; www.aberdeen-museum.org; Tue–Sun). By the time the first mill was built in 1852, the government was making treaties with the Native American tribes of the region and Aberdeen was developing into a rowdy, honky-tonk shipping town.

On to Seattle

US 101 reaches the end of the journey that began all the way south in sunny San Diego with a flourish, by looping around the magnificent Olympic Peninsula (see page 168), ending up not far from Seattle. This is a real highlight of the trip, so try not to miss it. If you do decide to head straight for **Seattle ㊿** (see page 172) from Aberdeen, you can take US 12 to **Olympia**, then hop on I-5N.

Pacific Ocean fish and crabs find a ready market in Seattle and Portland.

Metal figures along the Wildlife-Heritage Sculpture Corridor in Raymond.

The General's Highway, Sequoia National Park, California.

INSIGHT GUIDES TRAVEL TIPS
UNITED STATES ON THE ROAD

TRANSPORTATION

GETTING THERE AND GETTING AROUND

GETTING THERE

Most travelers arriving in the United States do so by air. The routes in this book begin and end at major US cities with international airports: New York to Miami (Atlantic route); Boston to Seattle (Northern Route); Washington, DC to Los Angeles (Central Route); Atlanta to San Diego (Southern Route); Los Angeles to San Diego (Pacific Route). From here, connecting flights can be made all over the US to secondary cities and towns. It is also possible to arrive by ship. Transatlantic crossings include service between Southampton and New York on the Queen Mary 2; also, several "positioning voyages" (allowing cruise ships to switch from Mediterranean or Baltic to Caribbean service) are scheduled between European and Florida ports in autumn.

Important Note: Non-US residents from Visa Waiver countries such as the UK are required to submit information about themselves online to the Department of Homeland Security and be pre-approved for travel to the US at least three days before they travel (see page 468).

Atlanta

Hartsfield-Jackson Atlanta International Airport (tel: 404-530-6600; www.atlanta-airport.com), located 10 miles (16km) from Atlanta, is the world's busiest. International passengers arrive at Concourse E. The terminal has six concourses with 151 domestic and 28 international gates; international passengers arrive at Concourse E. There are over 200

Airlines

Air Canada: tel: 888-247-2262; www.aircanada.com
AirTran Airways: tel: 800-247-8726; www.airtran.com
American: tel: 800-433-7300; www.aa.com
British Airways: tel: 800-247-9297; www.british-airways.com
Delta: tel: 800-221-1212; www.delta-air.com
Frontier Airlines: tel: 800-432-1359; www.flyfrontier.com
KLM: tel: 800-618-0104; www.klm.com
Lufthansa: tel: 800-645-3880; www.lufthansa.com
Southwest Airlines: tel: 800-435-9792; www.southwest.com
Spirit Airlines: tel: 800-772-7117; www.spirit.com
United Airlines: tel 800-864-8331; www.ual.com
US Airways: tel: 800-428-4322; www.usairways.com
Virgin Atlantic: tel: 800-862-8621; www.virginatlantic.com

food and beverage, retail and high-end outlets, with more planned in the future.

Boston

Logan International Airport handles more than 1,100 flights daily, with more than 30 carriers serving the airport. It is the northern terminal of the world's busiest airline market: the Boston–New York–Washington, DC run. Delta Airlines, US Airways, and JetBlue run shuttles between these airports. Logan has four terminals (A, B, C, and E; for some reason, there is no D). Note that domestic

and international flights of the same airline do not necessarily use the same terminal. There is a free shuttle bus service between the terminals.

Los Angeles

Los Angeles International Airport (LAX) is the city's main airport. It is the sixth-busiest airport in the world and serves most of the world's major airlines. LAX is 17 miles (27km) from Downtown and a short drive to Santa Monica and other locations along the coast. Free shuttle buses connect its nine terminals. An information booth is located on the departure level of the Tom Bradley International Terminal, which offers a language translation link for non-English speakers. Other convenient airports serving the metro area with domestic flights include **Bob Hope Airport** (BUR) serving the San Fernando Valley; **John Wayne (Orange County) Airport** (SNA) is 35 miles (56km) south of Los Angeles in Santa Ana, convenient for Disneyland; and **Long Beach Municipal Airport** (LGB).

Miami

Miami International Airport is the city's primary airport. It is sometimes also called Wilcox Field, and is one of the key airports serving the Southern United States as well as other Central and Latin American destinations. Miami International is about a 30-minute drive from Downtown, though traffic congestion at peak times can lengthen this considerably. Currently, there are eight concourses that serve almost all major domestic and international carriers. Information booths have Miami maps and can provide info about buses and shuttles to and from the airport via the train and Tri-Rail lines. Alternately, the Fort Lauderdale airport in Broward County (FLL) can be used and is only 30 minutes north of Miami. Other airports are inconveniently distant, making Miami International or Fort Lauderdale the best choices for incoming travelers.

New York City

New York's two major airports, **John F. Kennedy International** (JFK) and **LaGuardia**, are both in Queens, east of Manhattan on Long Island, respectively 15 and 8 miles (24km and 13km) from Midtown. Driving time to/from Kennedy is estimated at 90 minutes, but heavy traffic can often double this, so leave lots of time if you're catching a flight. LaGuardia is used only for shorter US domestic and some Canadian routes, and does not have any intercontinental flights.

San Diego

San Diego International Airport (tel: 619-400-2404; www.san.org), also called Lindbergh Field, is 3 miles (5km) northwest of downtown San Diego, about a 5-minute drive from the city center. It is served by all the major domestic carriers and many international airlines. Free transportation between the airport's three terminals is provided on the Airport Loop Shuttle Bus system; color-coded parking shuttles also run between parking areas and the airport terminal. Volunteer Airport Ambassadors in green polo shirts provide assistance to travelers around the airport and at the information booths in the baggage claim areas in Terminal 1 (tel: 619-231-7361) and Terminal 2 (tel: 619-231-5230) from 6am to 11pm daily.

Seattle

Seattle-Tacoma International Airport (SEA), known locally as Sea-Tac, is served by domestic carriers and several major international airlines. It is 14 miles (22km) south of Seattle city center, about a 25-minute drive depending on traffic. The airport has a central terminal and two satellite terminals for international flights, which are linked by a rail transit system. An airport information booth is located in the baggage claim area across from carousel 12 and is open daily from 6am until 2am.

Washington, DC

The city is served by three regional airports. **Ronald Reagan Washington National Airport** (or simply National, as it's often still called) is closest to the city, just 4 miles (6.4km) across the Potomac in Virginia. **Dulles Airport** is also in Virginia, 26 miles (42km) from DC. **Baltimore-Washington International Airport** (or BWI) is 40 miles (64km) north in the city of Baltimore in Maryland and about an hour by car. **Reagan National** offers mostly domestic service and also flights to and from some Canadian cities. Dulles and BWI are both international airports. Domestic flights through BWI are generally considerably less expensive than flying into Reagan National.

GETTING AROUND

The United States is so huge that, for most people, the only logical way to get around is by flying. Many flights connect through hub cities, served by major airlines. A number of regional airlines fly into smaller cities. A large road network offers a variety of driving options: rapid **interstate** and US **highways**, **scenic state routes**, and **slow county**, **forest**, and **Native American reservation backroads**.

Federal and state highways are paved and kept free of snow by snow plows in winter. Rural backroads, which are maintained by towns, may be either paved or gravel and are also plowed, with the exception of some remote routes closed in winter. Even those gravel roads kept open all year can become impassibly muddy after heavy rains, making four-wheel drive a wise choice. Other transportation options include **trains**, operated nationally by Amtrak, and

light rail within and between local cities. **Buses** operated by Greyhound crisscross the country, usually operating out of an easily accessible downtown depot with links to local transport.

By Air

If it is too impractical because of long distances to drive to the destinations listed here, an easy alternative is to fly. Airlines that serve the airports in the major hub cities include American, Delta, Southwest, United, and US Airways.

You can also fly into cities along the routes, including Charleston, Savannah, and Tampa; Mobile, New Orleans, Houston, and Phoenix, San Francisco, and Portland; Buffalo, Chicago, Minneapolis/St Paul, Sioux Falls, Spokane. Smaller cities are often served by regional airlines.

Airport Security

Since September 11, 2001, air travel in the US has changed drastically. Expect delays departing US airports due to recent Homeland Security anti-terrorism rules. These are apt to change, so check before flying. Leave gifts unwrapped, and take laptops out of bags for inspection by Transportation Security Administration (TSA) personnel. Consider wearing slip-on shoes as all footwear must be removed and scanned by x-ray machines.

Passengers are allowed one carry-on resealable 1-quart (1-liter) clear plastic bag, which can contain liquids, gels, or aerosols in containers of 3 ounces or less. The contents in the plastic bag must be sealed and may be subjected to x-ray inspection separate from the carry-on bag.

Allow plenty of time at the airport to clear security. Arrive at least one hour before departure for flights within the

Flying into Logan International Airport, Boston.

TRANSPORTATION

ACCOMMODATIONS

EATING OUT

ACTIVITIES

A – Z

US; two hours for international flights. Expect searches and questions to be asked, and do not attempt to carry any sharp objects in your hand luggage. This includes scissors, nailclippers, penknives, and other seemingly innocuous items.

By Train

Although passenger services were greatly curtailed in the latter part of the 20th century, it is still possible to travel the length and breadth of the continent by rail. **Amtrak** is the major rail passenger carrier in the US. Its network links many cities, but sadly bypasses many more. However, there are still some excellent trans-continental and coastal routes that glide through breathtaking scenery and often feature on-board entertainment, such as Native American storytellers and local historians. It's also possible to find Amtrak trains that allow you to take your car with you, such as the Auto Train between Lorton, Virginia, near Washington, DC, and Sanford, north of Orlando. You will also find an increasing number of light-rail options once you arrive in major cities.

Train passes

Passes for unlimited travel on Amtrak over a fixed period of time are available only from a travel agent in a foreign country. Proof of non-US residency is required. For information about Amtrak's services, call 800-872-7245 or visit: www.amtrak.com.

By Bus

The national bus line, Greyhound, as well as a number of smaller charter companies, provide an impressive network of ground travel throughout the country, offering daily service to major towns and cities. Routes and schedules are subject to change; it is a good idea to check all arrangements with local stations in advance.

Most cities also have municipal bus systems. As both Greyhound and municipal stations are often situated in somewhat squalid areas, try to stay alert and do not wander too far, particularly after dark. Plan your journey for daylight arrival if possible. On the whole, the buses themselves are safe and reasonably comfortable; choosing a seat near to the driver may discourage unwanted attention.

For reservations and local bus station details, telephone 800-229-9424, or visit www.greyhound.com.

Bus passes

A Greyhound Discovery Pass offers unlimited travel to 2,600 destinations. Details are available at www.discoverypass.com.

By Car

The American love affair with the car is reflected in the excellent network of roads that has sprung up since World War II creating access to the remotest areas. If you're in a hurry, the larger interstates are your best bet, with their fast, direct routes, 24-hour services, and year-round maintenance. But you will see more of the real America and its people if you drive at least some of the time on its folksy "blue highways." This book's routes offer a combination of both experiences.

Car rental agencies are located at all airports, in cities, and large towns; they are very hard to find in more remote areas of the US West. In most places you must be at least 21 years old (25 at some locations) to rent a car and you must have a valid driver's license and at least one major credit card. More agencies are accepting debit cards these days, but may hold back as much as $500 on the card to cover rental. Inquire at the time of reservation to avoid nasty surprises.

Be sure to check insurance provisions before signing anything. Cover is usually $15–25 per day. You may already be covered by your own auto insurance or credit card company, however, so check with them first. **Loss Damage Waiver** (LDW) or **Collision Damage Waiver** (CDW) is essential. Without it, you'll be liable for any damage done to your vehicle, regardless of fault. You are advised to pay for supplementary liability insurance on top of standard third-party insurance. Be sure to walk around the rental car slowly, check it for existing damage, and make sure the agent notes any dents or dings before leaving the lot.

US rental car rates are excellent ($35/day average for a compact), if you return the car to the original location. One-way rentals are much more expensive: $100/day average. Good deals may be found in the US by checking online and booking through either a company or travel website.

Distances and Driving Times

The routes in this book are not designed to be driven straight through, so how long you take to drive

Car Rental Companies

Contact details for major nationwide car rental agencies are listed below. Check the *Yellow Pages* for a full list of firms.
Alamo: tel: 800-222-9075; www.goalamo.com
Avis: tel: 800-831-2847; www.avis.com
Budget: tel: 800-527-0700; www.budget.com
Dollar: tel: 800-800-4000; www.dollar.com
Enterprise: tel: 800-261-7331; www.enterprise.com
Hertz: tel: 800-654-3131; www.hertz.com
National: tel: 800-227-7368; www.nationalcar.com
Thrifty: tel: 800-367-2277; www.thrifty.com

them is entirely up to you: preferably, the slower the better. If you do decide to drive the whole route at once, allow two weeks for coastal routes and a month for cross-country routes so that you can spend two to three nights at major destinations and single nights in between. Where possible, the drives in this book are planned so that there are reasonable driving distances between towns and cities. Driving no more than 200 miles (320km)/day or four hours allows you to get the driving done in the morning, allowing you some of the afternoon to see the sights.

On cross-country routes across the West, you will inevitably have a few days of 500-mile (800km) pushes across empty highway to reach the next destination. Do a bit of planning and try to find a way of breaking up the journey to avoid burning out and having roads and towns blurring into one another.

Not counting stops, visits to attractions, side trips, traffic delays, and low-speed highways, the routes in this book could, theoretically, be driven Jack Kerouac–style straight through in the following time frames:
Atlantic Route: New York to Key West (1,761 miles/2,836km, allow 32 driving hours minimum)
Northern Route: Boston to Cape Flattery (4,095 miles/6,590km, allow 55 driving hours minimum)
Central Route: Washington, DC to Los Angeles (2,922 miles/4,702km, allow 42 driving hours minimum)
Southern Route: Atlanta to San Diego (2,572 miles/4,139km, allow 40 driving hours minimum)
Pacific Route: San Diego to Seattle

(1,399 miles/2,251km, allow 30 driving hours minimum).

For detailed information on mileage between key cities along the route, see mileage charts at the back of the book.

RV Rentals

No special license is necessary to operate a motor home (or recreational vehicle – RV for short), but they aren't cheap. When you add up the cost of rental fees, insurance, gas, and campgrounds, you may find that renting a car and staying in motels or tent camping is less expensive. Keep in mind, too, that RVs are large and slow and may be difficult to handle on narrow mountain roads. If parking space is tight, driving an RV may be very inconvenient. Access to some roads may be limited. For additional information about RV rentals, call the **Recreational Vehicle Rental Association**, www.rvra.org; tel 703-591-7130.

Open Road Survival Skills

It is essential to inform yourself properly about the area you are traveling in, including weather and road conditions, and be prepared to change your plans at the first hint of potential danger, such as blizzards, heavy thunderstorms, and tornadoes.

Traveling in remote backcountry on foot is not recommended for solo women, but if you do, leave a note inside the car about your planned return time and don't hike off-trail or otherwise invite problems. It helps to know a few survival skills suitable for the terrain, including first aid, if you're traveling alone, especially in desert and mountain areas of the West.

It goes without saying that you should drive a reliable vehicle and carry plenty of supplies, including any medications, first aid kit, spare tire and gas, a gallon of water per day, nutritious food, emergency flares, warm clothing, and a cellphone.

Desert travelers: the single most important precaution you can take is to tell someone your destination, route, and expected time of arrival. Check tires carefully before long stretches of desert driving. Heat builds pressure, so have them at slightly below normal air pressure. The desert's arid climate makes carrying extra water – both for passengers and vehicles – essential. Carry at least one gallon per person per day. Keep an eye on the gas gauge. It's

a good idea to gas up whenever you have an opportunity and have more than you think you need. Remember, if you should have car trouble or become lost, do not strike out on foot. A car, visible from the air and presumably on a road, is easier to spot than a person, and it affords shelter from the weather. Wait to be found. Mountain drivers are advised to be equally vigilant. Winter storms in California's Sierra Nevada and Washington's Cascades occasionally close major roads, and at times chains are required on tires. Conditions often change fast, so check the weather forecast regularly and phone ahead for road conditions before you depart.

AAA Membership

Anyone spending a significant amount of time driving US highways is strongly advised to join the Automobile Association of America (AAA or Triple A). Benefits include emergency breakdown service, excellent road maps, travel literature, and personalized trip planning. Premier level offers towing up to 200 miles (320km) from breakdown site – important if you are in the middle of nowhere – and lock-out, refueling, and jumpstart service. Insurance is also available through the association, which has a reciprocal arrangement with some of the automobile associations in other countries. Telephone 800-874-7532 or visit www.aaa.com.

Bikers in the Valley of Fire State Park, Nevada.

By Motorcycle

For those with *Easy Rider* dreams, touring by motorcycle may be an inspiring option. Harley-Davidson and other major motorcycle vendors also offer rentals in some locations in the US. If you do decide to ride a motorcycle on any of the routes in this book, be conservative: you won't be able to cover as much ground as in a car in a day (probably no more than 250–300 miles/320–480km) to allow plenty of time for visiting attractions. And inevitably, you'll be riding on scenic highways and backroads off the Interstate, so factor that in, too. Vital clothing includes a helmet, stiff boots, and, in cool weather, leather chaps to cut down on road abrasion, should you take a spill. There are several organizations for enthusiasts of particular motorcycle makes, from Harley-Davidson to BMW. Several homegrown websites offer ideas on US motorcycle traveling.

By Bicycle

Bicycle touring is gaining in popularity in the US. It's definitely the slow option of seeing the country, but that's not a bad thing in this age of rapid transit. Most cyclists average little more than 10–15mph (16–24kmh), so your best bet is to cover a short scenic segment of any of the routes in this book, if you choose the bicycle option, and stick to areas

with clustered attractions, scenery, and lodging/food services.

Atlanta

Public Transportation
From the airport: Hartsfield-Jackson Atlanta International Airport is 10 miles (16km) from Downtown, farther to Midtown and Buckhead on the north side. Many hotels offer courtesy buses from the airport. Shared-ride shuttles provide service into the city: The Atlanta Airport Shuttle (tel: 404-941-3440; www.taass.net) serves downtown Atlanta, $16.50 one way. Taxis are usually $30 plus tip. Public transportation from the airport to the city and within the metropolitan area is much cheaper and extremely safe, clean, and reliable.
Rapid Transportation/buses: Metropolitan Rapid Transit Authority (MARTA) is a rapid-rail and bus system comprising local bus service and north–south and east–west rail lines intersecting at the main Five Points Station in downtown Atlanta. Train stations are designated N, S, E, W, or P, denoting their compass points (P represents the current single station Proctor Creek line). The Hartsfield International Airport Station is designated Airport S7 and is the final stop on the South line. The trip to downtown Atlanta takes just 17 minutes. Trains operate daily 4:45am–1am. A one-way ticket costs $2.50. You can also buy a Breeze card and add value to it for your time in Atlanta. For more information, log on to www.itsmarta.com.
National buses: Greyhound operates from the depot at 81 International Boulevard NW, tel: 800-231-2222.
National rail: Amtrak trains run from Peachtree Station, 1688 Peachtree Street NW, tel: 404-881-3060.

Private Transportation
Atlanta – sprawling, suburban, and subject to extremes of weather – is not ideally suited for extensive walking tours.
Car rental: car rental companies may be found at the airport and/or Downtown.
Taxis: Taxi companies are numerous. Hotels are always good places to find a taxi. Flat-rate fares within Downtown, Midtown, or Buckhead zones are $8, $2 each additional person. Outside the Business District, the following fares apply: first 1/8 mile, $2.50; each additional 1/8 mile, 25 cents;

waiting, $21 an hour. Flat-rate fare from the airport to Downtown: $30, to Buckhead: $40. Fares are subject to 4 percent Georgia sales tax. Tel: 404-351-1111 for more information.

Boston

Public Transportation
From the airport: Logan International Airport, just 3 miles (5km) from downtown Boston, is closer to town than any other major airport in the nation: this refers to distance and not to time. Traffic can back up at the tunnels under the harbor connecting the airport and city. The Massachusetts Bay Transportation Authority's (MBTA) Blue Line from Airport Station is the fastest way to Downtown (about 10 minutes) and to many other places as well. Silver Line buses also serve downtown. Free shuttle buses run between all the airport terminals and the subway station. Cabs can be found outside each terminal. Fares to Downtown should average about $20, including tip, providing there are no major traffic jams. Airways Transportation buses leave all terminals every half hour for downtown and Back Bay hotels, and several major bus companies, including Bonanza, Concord Trailways, Peter Pan, and Vermont Transit, serve many outlying suburbs and distant destinations.
Rapid transit: Boston's subway system (the "T") offers good value. A seven-day Link Pass, good for unlimited travel on subways, local buses, short-distance commuter rail, and inner harbor ferries costs $15; information at www.mbta.com.
City buses: The majority of the MBTA's 160-plus bus routes operate feeder services linking subway stations to neighborhoods not directly served by the rapid transit system. Some crosstown routes connect stations on different subway lines without going into Downtown. Only a few MBTA buses actually enter downtown Boston, and most of these are express buses from outlying areas. The basic MBTA bus fare is under $1.50.
Intercity buses: Several intercity bus companies serve Boston. The two largest, Greyhound (800-229-9424), and Peter Pan (800-237-8747), have frequent daily services from New York City and Albany, NY, as well as services from points within New England.
Commuter rail: The MBTA Commuter Rail extends from downtown Boston to as far as 60 miles (100km) away

and serves such tourist destinations as Concord, Lowell, Salem, Ipswich, Gloucester, and Rockport. Trains to the north and northwest of Boston depart from North Station; trains to points south and west of the city leave from South Station. All south side commuter trains, except the Fairmount Line, also stop at the Back Bay Station. For information on trains from any of these stations, telephone 617-222-3200.
National rail: Amtrak Passenger trains arrive at South Station (Atlantic Avenue and Summer Street, 800-872-7245; TDD: 800-523-6590) from New York, Washington, DC, and Philadelphia, with connections from all points in the nationwide Amtrak system. They also stop at Back Bay Station (145 Dartmouth Street).

Private Transportation
Boston, it is justly claimed, is a walker's city – a good thing, for it is certainly not a driver's city. Early city planners laid streets along cow paths, Native American trails, and colonial wagon tracks, linked by crooked little alleys. However, in the middle of the 19th century, impeccable grid systems were introduced in the Back Bay, South End, and, to a lesser degree, South Boston. If you attempt to drive, be aware that being stuck in a traffic jam, getting lost, and then being unable to find a parking space is about par for the course. Public parking facilities are found at Government Center; Post Office Square; the Public Garden; the Prudential Center; on Clarendon Street near the John Hancock Tower; and elsewhere. Private lots are scattered here and there.
Car rental: Most agencies have offices at the airport and/or Downtown.
Taxis: Taxi stands are common at popular tourist sites. Companies to call include: Checker Taxi, tel: 617-536-7500; Red Cab, tel: 617-734-5000; Town Taxi, tel: 617-536-5000.

Los Angeles

Public Transportation
From the airport: Public transportation is found on LAX's lower level, which is where arriving passengers claim baggage. At this level, there are stops for taxis, LAX shuttles, buses, courtesy trams, and vans in front of each airline terminal. Information boards about ground transport are located in all the baggage claim areas, and they are very easy to understand. Shuttles

from the airport are reasonably priced; the fare varies depending on your destination. Among the companies operating 24 hours a day are FlyAway Bus Service, tel: 866-435-9529; Prime Time Shuttle, tel: 310-536-7922; and The SuperShuttle, tel: 877-770-4826. Hopping in a taxi at LAX should be avoided if at all possible. Los Angeles' cabs are very expensive – more so than most US cities – and are almost never found driving the streets looking for customers. Free shuttle service is now provided to the Metro Green Line's Aviation Station. Pick up is on the Lower/Arrival level under the LAX Shuttle sign. Check out the Metro Bus and Metro Rail routes and schedules on 323-466-3876; www.metro.net.

Metro: Los Angeles County Metropolitan Transportation Authority, known as **Metro**, serves an area of 1,433 sq miles (3,711 sq km). With around 2,200 buses and four rail lines, Metro Rail currently operates over 73 miles (117km) of subway and light rail lines, with nearly 100 stations stretching from North Hollywood south to Long Beach, and from the coast east to Pasadena, serving many key visitor destinations. The Metro Red Line subway serves Hollywood, Universal Studios, and several downtown locations. The Metro Blue Line runs from Downtown to Long Beach. The Metro Gold Line connects with the Red Line and runs to Pasadena. The Metro Green Line serves Los Angeles Airport. The Metro Orange Line serves the San Fernando Valley with Metroliner buses. The Purple Line runs from Union Station (downtown) to Koreatown along Wilshire Boulevard. The Expo Line runs to Culver City.

For information on **Metro Rail** and **Metro Bus**, tel: 323-466-3876 or use the trip planner on their website: www.metro.net. The base fare is $1.50 plus 35 cents for transfers. Bus drivers do not give change, so you must have the exact fare or a token. The **Metro Day Pass**, which allows unlimited bus and rail journeys, is good value at $5. You can buy them on the bus, or at vending machines in rail stations. Buses and rail lines operate from 4am to after midnight, though night services are less frequent.

The DASH **shuttle system** (tel: 213-808-2273; www.ladottransit.com) operates Downtown during daytime hours, linking major businesses and the civic and entertainment centers. It costs 50 cents per ride and transfers are free. Separate DASH systems operate around Hollywood and other

parts of the city, while the Runabout is a similar service operating in Long Beach.

Private Transportation

The most efficient way to get around Los Angeles is to rent a car. Rental agencies may be found at the airport, your hotel and in various locations around the city. Cars often can be delivered to you. Car rental companies all charge basically the same price.

Taxis: Taxis are fairly expensive and you will rarely find them cruising the streets but they can be ordered or found at airports, train stations, bus terminals, and at major hotels.

Try: Yellow Cab Co, tel: 310-817-6823 or Independent Taxi, tel: 213-483-7660. The LA Checker Cab Co, tel: 213-482-3456 also offers vans with wheelchair lifts. An average fare from the Los Angeles Airport to downtown Los Angeles would be at least $46, plus tip.

Miami

Public Transportation

From the airport: Miami International Airport is 7 miles (12km) from Downtown. SuperShuttle (tel: 305-871-2000) operates between the airport and major hotels. Metrorail's Orange Line connects the new Airport Station with downtown Miami and points south, and connects with the Green Line to points north. Several Metrobus routes also serve the Airport Station. Train fare $2. A taxi fare to Downtown costs about $22 to downtown; $32 to Miami Beach, plus tip. **Rapid transit:** Metrorail is an elevated rapid transit system connecting Downtown with Dadeland and Hialeah. The Metromover monorail system circles the Downtown area. Metro-Dade Transit runs both (tel: 305-770-3131). Single fares $2.

City buses: Metro-Dade Transit also runs the Metrobus fleet from stops indicated by distinctive blue and green signs. Single fares under $2. **Intercity buses:** The main Greyhound terminal is at Bayside Station, 4111 NW 27th Street (tel: 305-871-1810). **Commuter rail:** The Tri-Rail (tel: 800-874-7245) service links Miami-Dade with Palm Beach, Broward, and the airport.

Trains: Amtrak trains run from the Miami Terminal (tel: 305-835-1223).

Private Transportation

Miami is not a difficult city to negotiate by car but try to avoid weekday rush-hour snarls. Parking

in the Miami Beach area can be scarce and restrictions are stringently imposed by a fleet of super-efficient tow-trucks. Fortunately, Miami Beach is a delightful place to explore by foot. Most of the car rental companies have offices at Miami International airport or Downtown. Check the *Yellow Pages* for a full list of firms.

Ports: Florida has several major cruise ship ports, with Miami and Port Everglades leading with the most sailings. Others include Port Canaveral, Palm Beach, St Petersburg, Tampa, Port Manatee (in Tampa Bay), and Madeira Beach and Treasure Island (just north of St Pete Beach). The Port of Miami is the largest cruise port in the world. Seven cruise lines carry more than 1.5 million passengers a year into the port, which represents over two-thirds of all cruise passengers worldwide. The port is just a five-minute ride from Downtown and Miami Beach. Tel: 305 371-7678.

Taxis: Taxis are relatively plentiful in South Beach with fares under $5 per mile (1.6km). They can also be found at airports, train stations, bus terminals and the major hotels, or ordered by telephone. Call Yellow Cab Co (tel: 305-444-4444); Metro Cab (tel: 305-888-8888); or Flamingo Taxi (tel: 305-759-8100).

New York City

Public Transportation

From the airport: AirTrain is an airport rail system that connects JFK and Newark airports with the subway and rail networks, at Howard Beach (A train) and Sutphin Boulevard (E, J, and Z train) subways and at Jamaica Long Island Railroad station for JFK, and at a special airport rail station in Newark. At each airport, AirTrain runs every few minutes and takes about 10 minutes from each terminal. Traveling between JFK and Midtown Manhattan by AirTrain and subway takes about one hour; traveling from Newark (by AirTrain and then Amtrak or NJ Transit train to Penn Station) can take only 30–45 minutes. For AirTrain information contact (JFK) tel: 973-961-6000; www.airtrainjfk.com; (Newark) tel: 888-397-4636; information: tel: 888-397-4636; www.panynj.gov/airtrainnewark.

New York Airport Service (tel: 212-875-8200; www.nyairportservice.com) buses run between both JFK and LaGuardia airports and Manhattan. Pick-up and drop-off points include: Port Authority Bus Terminal, Penn Station, and Grand Central Terminal, with a transfer service available to or from Midtown hotels. Buses from JFK run 6.15am–11.10pm.

From LaGuardia, the M60 bus to upper Manhattan subway stations operates 5am–1am, while **Triboro Coach** bus Q-33 runs to 74th St subway stop in Jackson Heights, Queens, from which various trains run to Manhattan.

Newark Liberty Airport Express (tel: 877-8-NEWARK www.coachusa. com) operates express buses daily between Newark airport and Manhattan, stopping at the Port Authority Bus Terminal, Grand Central, and Fifth Ave, at 42nd Street. Buses run 4am–1am.

There are several minibus services from all three airports to Manhattan. A big plus is that they take you door-to-door, direct to hotels or private addresses, but this can be slow, with many stops. SuperShuttle (tel: 212-258-3826;800-258-3826 www. supershuttle.com) offers a frequent service. It can be booked online, at airport ground transportation centers or from courtesy phones at the airports.

Rapid transit and buses: Subways and buses run 24 hours, less frequently after midnight, with the fare payable by token or (buses only) exact change, as well as by MetroCard pass (available at subway ticket booths), which allows free transfers within two hours of use. Unlimited-ride passes are good for seven days or 30-day passes are also available, as is a day pass sold at newsstands, hotels, and electronic kiosks in some subway stations. For general bus and subway information and for other details about the MetroCard pass call: 718-330-1234; http://www.mta.info/metrocard/mcgtreng.htm has details. Greyhound buses run from the Port Authority bus terminal, 41st, and Eighth Avenue (tel: 800-229-9424).

Trains: National rail trains arrive and depart from Manhattan's two railroad terminals: Grand Central Terminal and Pennsylvania Station. City buses stop outside each terminal and each sits atop a subway station. Amtrak information, tel: 800-872-7245.

Private Transportation
Car Rental: Driving around Manhattan is not much fun although, should the need arise, there is a wide range of firms available at airports from which cars can be rented.

Taxis: All are metered, cruise the streets randomly and must be hailed, although there are official taxi stands at places like Grand Central Terminal.

Be sure to hail an official Yellow Cab, not an unlicensed "gypsy" cab. One fare covers all passengers up to four (five in a few of the larger cabs). After 8pm there is a 50¢ surcharge on all taxi rides. Telephone 212-302-8294 for lost property or to make a complaint.

San Diego

Public Transportation
From the airport: Various shuttle services operate from San Diego International Airport to Downtown and are reasonably priced. Shuttle service companies include Advanced Shuttle, tel: 800-719-3499 and Sea Breeze Shuttle, tel: 619-297-7463. The Metropolitan Transit System bus route 992 travels from the airport to Downtown.

City buses and trolleys: City buses and the San Diego Trolley are run by San Diego Metropolitan Transit System (tel: 619-685-4900; www. transit.511sd.com). Fares start at $2.25 for buses and $2.50 for trolleys, exact change required. Day passes cost $5 and include both bus and trolley routes. The **San Diego Trolley System** has three lines; the Blue Line travels from Downtown to the Mexican border at San Ysidro, the Orange Line travels Gillespie to Downtown, and the Green Line travels Santee to Old Town. Trolleys operate daily from 5am until midnight. Some bus services run later, but routes vary.

Trains: Amtrak (tel: 800-872-7245; www.amtrak.com) trains run from the Santa Fe Depot at 10850 Kettner Boulevard to Los Angeles with stops along the coast. **The Coaster** (tel: 800-262-7837; www.transit.511sd. com) is an express rail commuter service that runs between downtown San Diego and Oceanside.

Private Transportation
Unlike Los Angeles, San Diego is a relatively easy city to explore with or without a car. However, as in most big cities, journeys are best planned around the weekday early morning and late afternoon crush. Parking is generally easy to find and for the most part moderately priced. Most of the major car rental agencies have offices at the airport and in the downtown area.

Taxis: Try any of the following or check the *Yellow Pages* for a full list of companies – Orange Cab, tel: 619-291-3333; San Diego Cab, tel: 619-226-8294; Airport Yellow Cab of San Diego, tel: 619-234-6161.

Traveling to Tijuana, Baja California, Mexico
About 300,000 people visit Tijuana over the border on the Baja Peninsula every year. In the past, US citizens did not need a passport to travel to Tijuana for the day, but new Homeland Security border security rules now require that US citizens as well as non-citizens carry a valid passport (some US state-issued enhanced driver's licenses with embedded microchips are permitted) and, if applicable, an alien registration card (green card), to reenter the country. Be sure you have these in hand before making the trip to avoid big headaches.

US car insurance is not valid in Mexico, so it's essential to obtain short-term car insurance at one of the many sales offices just north of the border if you plan on driving in Mexico. Crossing into Mexico is easy, with immigration officers at both sides usually just waving you along.

Because driving is not easy in Tijuana for those unfamiliar with the city (and the Spanish language), many drivers park in San Diego's San Ysidro, crossing into Tijuana via the elevated pedestrian walkway. Avoid leaving your car in the parking places of merchants unless you want to have it towed away by police. There's an all-day secure lot off the "Last Exit US parking" ramp – turn right at the stop sign to the Tijuana side. Cheap taxis and buses are available.

Return Crossing: Reentering the US is generally a much more tense experience than entering Mexico, as US Border Patrol officers scrutinize who is entering the country very carefully. Expect long lines, especially in busy vacation periods, and plan accordingly. Finally, keep your wits about you while visiting Mexico to avoid getting caught up in any unrest or areas of high-crime activity. It's best to keep to well-traveled areas and particularly avoid driving at night.

Seattle

Public Transportation
From the airport: Buses provide the least costly method of transportation between Seattle-Tacoma (Sea-Tac) Airport and downtown, and are a welcome alternative to dealing with the heavy traffic on I-5. The 194 is the most direct, bringing passengers downtown in about 30 minutes. The 174 makes local stops on its way downtown. The quickest connection between Sea-Tac and downtown is via Central Link Light Rail (www.

soundtransit.org; tel: 888-889-6368). Bus or van companies that link the airport with metropolitan Seattle or Bellevue include:

The Gray Line Downtown Airporter (tel: 206-426-7532)

Shuttle Express (tel: 425-981-7000)

Capital Aeroporter (tel: 206-244-0011)

Quick Shuttle (tel: 800-665-2122)

Yellow Cab (tel: 206-622-6500) provides a taxi service to and from the airport. From the airport to Downtown (or vice versa) costs about $32 plus tip.

National buses: The Greyhound terminal is located at 811 Stewart Street (tel: 800-231-2222).

National trains: The Amtrak station is at Third Avenue and S. Jackson Street (tel: 800-872-7245)

Public Transportation: Metro Transit (tel: 206-553-3000; www.metro.kingcounty.gov) operates commuter rail, buses, and water taxis.

Monorail: The Monorail tel: 206-905-2620; www.seattlemonorail.com), which was built for the 1962 World's Fair, runs every 15 minutes between Seattle Center and Fourth and Pine streets to Westlake Center. The ride is just under 1 mile (2km) and takes only 90 seconds. It's clean and spacious with large windows.

Ferries: The Washington State Ferry system (tel: 800-843-3779; www.wsdot.wa.gov/ferries), the largest in the country, covers the Puget Sound area, linking Seattle (at Pier 52) with the Olympic Peninsula via Bremerton and Bainbridge Island. State ferries also depart from West Seattle to Vashon Island and Southworth, and from Edmonds, 7 miles (11km) north of Seattle, to Kingston on Kitsap Peninsula. They also go from Anacortes, 90 miles (145km) northwest of Seattle, through the San Juan Islands to Victoria, on Canada's Vancouver Island. Passengers to Canada need a passport. The Black Ball Ferry (tel: 360-457-4491) departs from Port Angeles on the Olympic Peninsula to Victoria, BC, four times a day in summer and twice daily the rest of the year. Ferries carry cars.

Private Transportation

When the weather is fine, Seattle is a very pleasant city to walk about in – it is hilly, but many of the sights may be toured comfortably on foot. Heavy traffic congestion and scarce, expensive parking make driving in the center a less attractive option. Many of the major car rental agencies have offices at Seattle-Tacoma Airport or in the downtown area. Consult the *Yellow Pages* phone book for a full listing of rental firms.

Washington, DC

Public Transportation

From National: There's a Metro subway station here, easily accessible from the airport terminal with quick service into DC (about $6). You can also take a taxi, available curbside when you pick up your bags, with fares that range from $10 to $30.

From Dulles: Take a Washington Flyer Taxi directly into the city, which will cost about $50. Bus service runs about every 30 minutes and costs $8. Buy your bus ticket at the kiosk on the airport Arrivals level. The Washington Flyer Motor Coach leaves every 30 minutes from Arrivals Level door 4 and connects to the Metro for $9.

From BWI: A taxi from this airport, which you can hail at the curb near the baggage claim, will cost about $60 into DC. You can also take the free shuttle bus to the nearby Amtrak rail station (800-872-7245, or visit www.amtrak.com) and take the train into DC's Union Station for about $30, but you may have a wait, depending on the train schedule.

SuperShuttle: You can pick up one of these dependable blue mini-vans at any of the airports and share a ride into the city. Cost from Dulles and BWI into DC is about $25, from National about $20. When you're ready to fly home, schedule a pickup to the airport by phoning 800-258-3826 (Blue Van). **International Limousine** is one of the city's oldest limo services, available 24 hours. Tel: 202-388-6800 or visit www.internationallimo.com.

Metro: A $7.80 one-day Metrorail pass provides all-day subway travel after 9.30am.

City buses: Metrobus (tel: 202-637-7000) operates a comprehensive but confusing network of routes covering the city and outlying areas. You need exact change to board. The express service between Dulles and downtown is $3 and runs every 30 minutes.

National buses: Greyhound buses operate out of the station at 1005 First Street NE (800-231-2222).

National rail: Amtrak runs from Union Station, 60 Massachusetts Avenue NE (800-872-7245).

Private Transportation

Washington, DC is compact enough to make it one of the best cities in the country for exploring on foot.

Car rental: Another good way to get around – particularly if you are interested in some of the worthwhile day trips – is to rent a car. You can do this at the airport, your hotel, or any car rental agency,

Parking: A very few hotels in town offer free parking, but most charge a daily fee, which is in the $50/day range. Many hotels on the outskirts also charge, but generally in the $20/day range. Parking around DC is difficult on the street and expensive in parking lots.

Taxis: Long-distance taxi fares are steep; in the District, fees are $2.16 per mile, with a $25/hour "wait fee," which kicks in whenever the cab is moving at less than 10 mph (16kph). There's also a $1 gas surcharge. For planned trips, reserve a taxi at least an hour in advance of departure. Two of the major taxicab companies are: Diamond Cab, tel: 202-387-6200 and Yellow Cab, tel: 202-544-1212.

Washington DC's metro.

ACCOMMODATIONS

HOTELS, MOTELS, BED AND BREAKFAST, NATIONAL PARKS

Choosing Accommodation

Hotels and Motels

Chain hotels and motels are reliable, convenient, and often reasonably priced, but tend to lack character. In general, prices range from $50 to $150 depending on the location, the season, and additional amenities. Resorts and large hotels are often located on spacious properties outside Downtown and cater to guests who want everything onsite, from pools, spas, health centers, and sporting facilities to restaurants and snack shops, high-end shopping, ATM machines, business and meeting facilities, and in-room amenities such as fridges, microwaves, and coffeemakers. Their friendly, all-in anonymity may be just what you require when your nervous system needs to come down from the occasionally overwhelming sensory input of a long road trip.

Boutique inns and small historic hotels, on the other hand, are often located in converted historic buildings in Downtown. They offer B&B-like charm along with big-hotel sophistication and a surprising number of amenities, such as spas, fine dining, and in-room extras like Jacuzzi baths and robes. Their downtown location can make them a bit noisier than outlying hotels, and you'll usually pay more. But it's definitely worth it, if your budget allows, as these unique inns tend to be memorable and offer a quick way of getting to know more about the history and ambiance of a town – a boon if you're only in an area for one night.

Watch for hidden fees at luxury hotel chains. Most lodgings – even

small ones – offer wireless internet in rooms but beware of hefty access fees (up to $12.95/day) at major hotels. Phone connection charges are also often charged. You can usually access wireless internet for free in the lobby and use a pay phone there, if you don't have a cellphone. It is also common for large resorts to tack on a daily fee to cover guests' use of facilities such as the swimming pool, spa facilities, and shuttle service. Be sure to ask when booking. Many hotels in larger cities will also charge a nightly parking fee, which can quickly push up a bill. Reservations made on the internet generally offer the best deal, but you can also call and ask specifically about special weekend or corporate rates and "package deals." Motels, such as Best Western, offer a discount for AAA and AARP members. Book your room by credit card and secure a guaranteed late arrival, in case of any delays in your travel plans. A list of telephone numbers to make reservations at major chains in the US follows.

Bed and Breakfasts

B&Bs tend to be more personal than hotels. In some cases, you're a guest at a person's home where the accommodations are fairly simple and may involve a lot of interaction with family and other guests; in others, the rooms are in separate (large) historic homes or inns decorated with antiques, quilts, art, and other period furnishings. Before booking, also ask whether the room has a private bathroom, telephone, television, and wireless internet access. Inquire about breakfast, too. The morning meal is included in the price but may be anything from a couple of muffins

to a multicourse feast. For more information contact:
Bed-and-Breakfast Inns ONLINE
909 N. Sepulveda Boulevard, 11th Floor, El Segundo, CA 90245.
Tel: 800-215-7365 or 310-280-4363
www.bbonline.com

Budget Accommodations
Hostelling International
Second Floor, Gate House, Fretherne Road, Welwyn Garden City, Herts., AL8 6RD, England

Tel: 01707-324170
www.hihostels.com
Hostelling International/American Youth Hostels
8401 Colesville Road, Suite 600, Silver Spring, MD 20910
Tel: 301-495-1240
www.hihostels.com
YMCA
YMCA of the USA
Association Advancement, 101 N. Wacker Drive, Chicago, IL 60606
Tel: 800-872-9622
www.ymca.net
YWCA
1015 18th Street NW, Suite 1100, Washington, DC 20036
Tel: 202-467-0801
www.ywca.org

National Parks

Lodgings inside popular parks such as Grand Canyon, Yosemite, and Yellowstone sell out a year in advance, so it's essential to book as soon as possible. Reservations are handled through the park's concessionaire, a company operating under license with the **National Park Service** to manage accommodations, food service, gift shops, tours, and other services. Information is available on the park's website or by calling direct. For general park information, contact:
National Park Service
Department of the Interior

1849 C Street NW, Washington, DC 20240
Tel: 202-208-3818
www.nps.gov

Campgrounds

Most state and national parks, US Forest Service areas, and some Bureau of Land Management sites have developed campgrounds. National Park Service campgrounds typically offer groomed tent and RV campsites with water, hookups, barbecue grate, picnic table, and a restroom with flush toilets; state parks usually also offer showers, electrical hookups, campstore, and other facilities.

Fees average $14 per site. You'll often find "primitive" campgrounds in remote areas of national parks and national forests, where there may be designated campsites but only a pit toilet and often no water or other facilities. Such sites are usually less expensive ($5–10).

National forests also allow free "dispersed camping" away from trails and destinations. At primitive sites, expect no facilities and bring everything you need, including a gallon of water per person per day, nutritious food, and the means to practice "leave no trace" camping.

If you plan on overnighting in national park backcountry or wilderness, you'll need to register with the park's backcountry office in person to receive a permit and a designated campsite. This may be free (although not necessarily): rangers use it to restrict backcountry numbers, safeguarding the resource and visitor experience of solitude. Most campgrounds are busy from mid-June to September (winter in Florida). Be sure to make advance reservations for popular coastal state park campgrounds, especially those in California and Florida and the Northwest. Reservations for state park campgrounds and those under National Park Service or US Forest Service management may be made by logging onto www.reserveamerica.com or www.recreation.gov; tel: 877-444-6777; International: 518-885-3639. Reservations may be made up to six months in advance. Note: most NPS campgrounds still operate on a first-come, first-served basis, so be sure to arrive early in the day to get a spot.

Private RV campgrounds are typically very developed and more expensive and offer additional facilities such as coin laundries, pools, playgrounds, and restaurants. An extensive nationwide network of such sites is run by **Kampgrounds of America (KOA)**; tel: 406-248-7444; www.koa.com. Another good resource is *Go Camping America* at www.gocampingamerica.com.

On Golden Bluffs beach, Redwood National Park, California.

ATLANTIC ROUTE

New York

New York City
The Carlyle
35 E. 76th Street, NY 10021
Tel: 212-744-1600
www.thecarlyle.com
Posh, reserved, and serene in its
elegance, The Carlyle remains one of
the city's most highly acclaimed luxury
hotels. Home of Café Carlyle and
Bemelmans Bar, two of the city's most
enduring and upscale evening spots.
The Carlyle is a favorite with visiting
royalty. **$$$**

Hotel Pennsylvania
401 Seventh Avenue (at 33rd Street), NY
10001
Tel: 212-736-5000
Vast hotel, with 1,700 rooms, across
from Madison Square Garden and
Penn Station, the Pennsylvania
donated its phone number to the 1938
Big Band hit *Pennsylvania 6-5000* and
offers good-value packages with few
frills. **$$$**

Comfort Inn Manhattan
42 W. 35th Avenue, 10001
Tel: 212-947-0200
The Choice Hotels group has about
a half-dozen properties under the
Comfort, Clarion, and Ascend brands.
Comfort and Clarion are rather
standard, but their locations are
excellent, and their rates are among
the more "affordable" for Manhattan.
The Ascend brand is decidedly more
upscale, with prices to match. **$$$**

Pod Hotels
145 E. 39th Street, NY 10016
Tel: 212-865-5700
230 E. 51st Street 212-355-0300
If all you want is a place to sleep and
shower, these are worth checking out.
Rooms are as small as 50 sq ft (4.6
sq meters), but are bright, smartly
furnished, and have most modern tech
amenities. Some share baths. The
public areas are gathering places for
guests. **$$**

Murray Hill East Suites
149 E. 39th Street, NY 10016
Tel: 212-661-2100
Good value for longer stays. Each suite
has a kitchen, which you can stock
inexpensively from local stores. **$$**

**New York International Youth
Hostel**
891 Amsterdam Avenue (at W. 103rd
Street), NY 10025
Tel: 212-932-2300
Accommodations in dormitory-style
rooms range from $29 upwards per
person per night; $3 less for IYH
members. **$**

Washington Square Hotel
103 Waverly Place, NY 10011
Tel: 212-777-9515
www.wshotel.com
An almost century-old hotel that offers
the perfect Village locale. The rooms
are small but nicely appointed. In a
former incarnation, this was the seedy
Hotel Earle, where Papa John wrote
the 1960s rock classic *California
Dreaming*. **$$**

New Jersey

Basking Ridge
Olde Mill Inn
225 Route 202, NJ 07920
Tel: 908-221-1100
www.oldemillinn.com
Located 8 miles (13km) southwest
of Morristown, just driving onto the
grounds of this traditional American
inn soothes nerves jangled by north
New Jersey traffic and commotion.
More like a family country retreat
than a hotel. Many of the rooms
have balconies overlooking the
courtyard garden; some have drive-up
accessibility. There are several "PURE"
rooms for guests with allergies, a
guest library, a restaurant and a pub.
And instead of the sorry in-room coffee
machines with powdered java, the
rooms have Keurig coffee makers.
$$-$$$

North Bergen
Days Inn
2750 Tonnelle Avenue, NJ 07047
Tel: 201-348-3600
Parking is free, and there are
options for van service to downtown
Manhattan ($12 round trip), and
nearby ferry, bus, and commuter train
services. The rooms are clean and
comfortable, there is a full-service
restaurant, and the staff is well-
versed about how to navigate New
York. **$$**

Lambertville
Chimney Hill Farm Estate
207 Goat Hill Road, NJ 08530
Tel: 609-397-1516
www.chimneyhillinn.com
An impressive gabled fieldstone house
located in the hills 5 miles (8km)
from Lambertville. Candlelit country
breakfasts and many other nice
touches. **$$-$$$**

The Inn at Lambertville Station
11 Bridge Street, NJ 08530
Tel: 609-397-4400
www.lambertvillestaion.cmo
The only waterfront hotel in
Lambertville, each room in this
boutique hotel has an unobstructed

view of the wide, placid river. Suites
have gas fireplaces. The one-night
packages are particularly good value,
with room, discount voucher for the
upscale indoor or casual riverfront
restaurants, and in-room continental
breakfast. **$$-$$$**

Morristown
The Madison Hotel
1 Convent Road, NJ 07960
Tel: 973-285-1800
www.themadisonhotel.com
In the heart of Morristown, this is
particularly attractive for executive
travel and sensibilities. High-
end beddings, concierge service,
full fitness center, indoor pool,
complementary business center,
parking, and shuttle van service in the
immediate area. **$$-$$$**

Princeton
Nassau Inn
10 Palmer Square, NJ 08542
Tel: 609-921-7500
www.nassauinn.com
Located in the heart of Princeton –
Palmer Square – Nassau Inn has been
welcoming notables to the town since
1756. The large (200-plus rooms),
full-service hotel still tries to maintain
a B&B ambiance, and it generally
succeeds. In fact, the B&B package is
a good deal. Pet friendly. **$$**

Pennsylvania

Philadelphia
Alexander Inn
12th and Spruce streets, PA 19107
Tel: 215-923-3535
www.alexanderinn.com
Popular city-center boutique hotel with
48 designer rooms done up in the Art
Deco style of the great cruise ships;
there's art work everywhere; stained
glass and wood molding in the lobby.
Rates do not fluctuate with season or
demand. **$$**

The Rittenhouse Hotel
210 W. Rittenhouse Square, PA 19103
Tel: 215-546-9000
Tel: 800-635-1042
This AAA 5-diamond hotel
earns every carat with elegantly
comfortable rooms, a spa, views
of the city from the terrace, marble
bathrooms, and an attentive and
warmly welcoming staff. Rittenhouse
Square, the heart of Philadelphia,
is just outside the doors. Rooms
are huge, starting at 450 sq ft (4 sq
meters). Far from pretentious, the
hotel has family packages. **$$-$$$**

Thomas Bond House
129 S. Second Street, PA 19106
Tel: 215-923-8523
www.thomasbondhousebandb.com
The only accommodation in the Independence National Historic Park, the 12 rooms in this 1769 building are furnished in the style that Ben Franklin and friends would have appreciated. Especially since the rooms in the B&B have modern conveniences as well as period trappings. Make reservations early; the place fills quickly, especially in summer. **$$**

Maryland

Annapolis
Historic Inns of Annapolis
58 State Circle, MD 21401
Tel: 410-263-2641
www.historicinnsofannapolis.com
Three inns in buildings from the colonial era located in the historic district overlooking the State House, Church Circle, Main Street and the city dock. Reservations at The Maryland Inn, Governor Calvert House, and the Robert Johnson House are handled through a central booking service, but you can choose the property you prefer. Each captures the charm and history of colonial Annapolis, but with all of modern touches and creature comforts. **$$**

Baltimore
Admiral Fell Inn
888 S. Broadway, MD 21231
Tel: 410-539-2000
www.admiralfell.com
Pleasing proportions and custom-crafted Federal-style furnishings characterize this well-preserved Fells Point inn. The Admiral Fell has received many accolades for its New American cuisine and award-winning wine cellar. Guests are offered free parking and transportation to local attractions. **$$$**
Celie's Waterfront Inn
1714 Thames Street, MD 21231
Tel: 410-522-2323
www.celiesinn.com
Perfectly located on the brick street facing the Fells Point waterfront, it's a perfect merger of colonial atmosphere with modern amenities. Most of the rooms overlook a private courtyard, but the shared rooftop deck overlooks the waterfront. In the heart of the lively action of Fells Point. **$$–$$$**
Mount Vernon Hotel
24 W. Franklin Street, MD 21201
Tel: 410-727-2000
www.mountvernonbaltimore.com
A well-appointed, quiet, sophisticated hotel located in Mt Vernon, steps

from the Walters Art Galley, Peabody Conservatory, and Antiques Row. **$$$**

Virginia

Charlottesville
Cavalier Inn
105 N. Emmet Street, VA 22905
Tel: 434-296-8111 or 888-882-2129
www.cavalierinn.com
In the heart of the university district. Clean, bright, spacious rooms in University of Virginia colors and themes, of course. Full hot breakfast. The seasonal outdoor pool is especially welcome in humid Virginia summers. Availability reflects school calendar. **$**
Silver Thatch Inn
3001 Hollymead Drive, VA 22911
Tel: 434-978-4686 or 800-261-0720
www.silverthatch.com
This delightful clapboard home is one of the oldest buildings in central Virginia (c.1780). Accommodations comprise seven guest rooms all with private baths and several with canopy beds and fireplaces. The uniquely appointed rooms are named after early Virginian-born presidents. There are three dining rooms and a bar. **$$**

Fredericksburg
Richard Johnston Inn B&B
711 Caroline Street, VA 22401
Tel: 540-899-7606; 877-557-0770
On the main street of Fredericksburg's historic district, this house witnessed the Revolution and Civil War and retains the serene period ambiance of the past. Seven rooms and two suites in the Johnston Inn; a renovated property, the Caroline House, at 528 Caroline Street, has three romantic rooms with Jacuzzis. **$$–$$$.**

Richmond
The Grace Manor Inn
1853 W. Grace Street, VA 23220
Tel: 804-353-4334
www.thegracemanorinn.com
A grand Southern mansion located one block from Monument Avenue in the Fan District. Four large, two-room suites; walking distance to many museums and restaurants. Three-course breakfast and outdoor saltwater pool. **$$**

North Carolina

Chapel Hill
Carolina Inn
211 Pittsboro Street, NC 27516
Tel: 919-933-2001
www.carolinainn.com
This elegantly furnished historic inn calls itself "The University's

Living Room," as it is located on the campus. It's a good base for exploring downtown Chapel Hill and the shops and restaurants of Franklin Street. Very eco-friendly in furnishings, amenities, and operations. **$$–$$$**

Durham
King's Daughters Inn
204 N. Buchanan Boulevard, NC 27701
Tel: 919-354-7000; 877-534-8534
www.thekingsdaughtersinn.com
Historic preservation and green construction techniques were equally important when this 1920 historic building – once a dormitory for single, aging women – was renovated into a 17-room, boutique B&B. Each room is individually designed and furnished. Across the street from Duke University and in Trinity Park (one of Durham's oldest neighborhoods) it is a pleasant urban retreat. **$$**

Fayetteville
Holiday Inn – Fayetteville/Bordeaux
1707 Owen Drive, NC 28304
Tel: 910-323-0111
www.ichotels.com
Large, older property with very clean, comfortable rooms in a good location, a nice onsite restaurant, and outdoor pool. The hotel is close to the highway, convenient to attractions, and popular with groups. **$–$$**

Greensboro
Studio Six
2000 Veasley Street,
I-40E, Exit 217, NC 27407
Tel: 336-294-8600
www.staystudio6.com
Great value, extended stay hotel. All rooms are small suites with full kitchens. There is a coin-operated guest laundry, an outdoor pool and grill area. Wi-fi is available for a small fee. Pet friendly. ($6) **$**

Manteo
Tranquil House Inn
405 Queen Elizabeth Street, NC 27954
Tel: 252-473-1587
www.1587.com
Built in the style of the grand 19th century inns, with cypress woodwork, and beveled and stained glass, and four-poster beds. Right on the waterfront, overlooking sailboats in Shallowbag Bay on the Outer Banks. **$$**

PRICE CATEGORIES

Price categories are based on the average cost of a double room for one night:
$ = under $110
$$ = $110–250
$$$ = more than $250

TRANSPORTATION

ACCOMMODATIONS

EATING OUT

ACTIVITIES

A – Z

Nags Head
First Colony Inn
6720 S.Virginia Dare Trail, NC 27959
Tel: 252-441-2343 or 800-368-9390
www.firstcolonyinn.com
Perfect Outer Banks beach retreat. Classic three-story, "shingle style" inn, built in the 1930s that retains the charm, but with modern amenities. A wide, two-story veranda encircles the garden. **$-$$**

Wilmington
Front Street Inn
215 S. Front Street 28401
Tel: 910-762-6442; 800-336-8184
www.frontstreetinn.com
Twelve suites with 14ft (4-meter) ceilings, arch windows, and maple floors. Second-floor suites overlook the Cape Fear River. Each suite reflects the personality after whom it is named: Hemingway, Jacques Cousteau, Molly Brown, and others. **$$**

The Wilmingtonian
101 S. Second Street, NC 28401
Tel: 910-343-1800 or 800-525-0909
www.thewilmingtonian.com
All-suite hotel in the heart of the historic district comprised of three restored buildings (including an 1841 mansion) and a hotel built in 1994 specifically for the movie industry. The balconies on all floors overlook a courtyard garden with a fishpond. Some rooms reflect rustic Southern ambiance; some are nautical; the "Cinema" House is themed around classic movies or stars. **$-$$**

Winston-Salem
Augustus Zevely Inn
803 S. Main Street, NC 27101
Tel: 336-748-2999; 800-928-9299
www.winston-salem-inn.com
Only lodging in Old Salem. Restored to its mid-19th century appearance with antiques and accurate reproductions of Moravian furnishings. Pets welcome. **$$**

The East Bay Inn, Savannah, Georgia.

Brookstown Inn
200 Brookstown Avenue, NC 27101
Tel: 336-725-1120
www.brookstowninn.com
Exposed brick walls and wooden beams reveal the inn's 1837 origins as a textile mill. Wine and cheese reception, and cookies and milk at bedtime each evening adds to its charm. A short walk from the restored Moravian village of Old Salem, for which they sell admission passes. **$-$$**

South Carolina

Beaufort
Rhett House
1009 Craven Street, SC 29902
Tel: 843-524-9030 or 800-480-9530
www.rhetthouse.com
Plantation house bordering the Intercoastal Waterway. Built in 1820 and restored following the Civil War, the inn features stately white columns, broad verandas, rocking chairs, and period decor. Many rooms have fireplaces, private balconies, and whirlpool baths. Afternoon tea is offered. **$$**

Charleston
Francis Marion Hotel
387 King Street, SC 29403
Tel: 877-756-2121
www.francismarionhotel.com
Built in 1924 to be the grandest and largest hotel in the Carolinas, it continues to be one of the most elegant and amenity-heavy lodgings in town complete with valet parking, day spa, fitness center, and piano lounge. Ask for a room with a harbor view. Many packages. **$$**

Governor's House Inn
117 Broad Street,
SC 29401
Tel: 843-720-2070 or 800-720-2070
www.governorshouse.com
Attention to detail, elegant decor, and exceptional service are hallmarks of this historic inn. Originally the residence of Governor Edward Rutledge, the youngest signer of the Declaration of Independence, the house still retains an air of tradition with its broad veranda, chandeliers, numerous fireplaces, and spacious rooms. In the center of the historic district and close to many landmarks and restaurants. **$$$**

Shem Creek Inn
1401 Shrimpboat Lane,
Mt Pleasant SC 29464
Tel: 843-881-1000 or 800-523-4951
www.shemcreekinn.com
Just across the Cooper River Bridge from downtown Charleston. A serene setting; all rooms (which are furnished more like downtown luxury lodgings than a waterfront inn) have private balconies with views of the creek and Charleston Harbor. **$$**

Georgetown
Harbor House Bed and Breakfast
15 Cannon Street,
SC 29440
Tel: 843-546-6532
www.harborhousebb.com
The only waterfront lodging in town. Built in 1740 on a bluff overlooking Sampit River, Harbor House has the original heart-pine floors and eight fireplaces, and is surrounded by live oaks that were saplings when the house was built. Sailors say the distinctive red roof can be seen four miles out at sea. Lowcountry dishes such as shrimp and grits, sweet potato pancakes, and crab hors d'oeuvres are served in the afternoon. All rooms are on upper floors, and there is no elevator. **$$**

Myrtle Beach
Caravelle Resort
6900 N. Ocean Boulevard,
SC 29577
Tel: 800-507-9145
www.thecaravelle.com
Large, family-friendly, family-owned resort that's been around since the beginnings of Myrtle Beach's development as a resort. Nine buildings include studios, condos, and suites with kitchenettes and ocean views. Many have private balconies overlooking the beach. **$$**

Coral Beach Resort
1105 S. Ocean Boulevard, SC 29577
Tel: 843-448-8412
www.coral-beach.com
Full service oceanfront resort with nicely furnished guest rooms and public areas. Facilities include indoor and outdoor pools, saunas, whirlpool, restaurant, and lounge. Disabled access. **$$$**

Georgia

Brunswick
Hostel in the Forest
PO Box 1496, GA 31521
Tel: 912-264-9738
www.foresthostel.com
Since 1975, this hostel has offered beds in tree houses or geodesic domes. Amenities include tranquility and natural beauty. **$**

St Simons Island
The Lodge on Little St Simons Island
PO Box 21078, GA 31522
Tel: 912-638-7472
www.littlestsimonsisland.com
This unique lodge, set on an unspoiled barrier, hosts only 30 overnight guests. The only way there is by boat. Price includes three Southern meals and on-island activities. Idyllic. **$$$**

Savannah
East Bay Inn
225 E. Bay Street, GA 31401
Tel: 912-238-1225
www.eastbayinn.com
A historic bed-and-breakfast, this 28-unit restored 1853 warehouse features large, Georgian-style rooms, high ceilings, brick interior walls, and classic furnishings. **$–$$**
The Gastonian
220 E. Gaston Street, GA 31401
Tel: 912-232-2869
www.gastonian.com
Selected as one of the finest B&Bs in the world by several hospitality associations and guest surveys, the Gastonian has 17 intimate guest rooms in two adjoining houses built in 1868. All have working fireplaces; some have whirlpool baths. **$$**
Inn at Ellis Square
201 W. Bay Street, GA 31401
Tel: 912-236-4440; 877-542-7666
www.innatellissquare.com
Called "The Grand Lady of Bay Street," the 1851 has period Southern charm, but also a pool, fitness room, lounge, and garage parking – an amenity most hotels don't offer in a city where parking is at a premium. Nicely situated in the Riverfront District. **$–$$**

Florida

Big Pine Key
Bahia Honda State Recreation Area
36850 Overseas Highway, FL 33043
Tel: 305-872-2353
www.floridastateparks.org/bahiahonda/default.cfm
Three duplex cabins set on stilts overlooking the bay have cooking facilities and private baths, and comfortably sleep four to six people. **$$**

Big Pine Key Fishing Lodge
33000 Overseas Highway, Big Pine Key, FL 33043
Tel: 305-872-2351
A diverse range of 16 accommodations includes mobile homes, rooms in the lodge, two-floor lofts, and six canal-front motel efficiencies. **$**
Deer Run Bed and Breakfast
Long Beach Road, FL 33043
Tel: 305-872-2015
www.deerrunfloridabb.com
Spacious guest rooms with ocean views located in two houses near the bay. Deer roam the surrounding native wooded land (also a good birdwatching area). Amenities include a full vegetarian breakfast, Jacuzzi on the beach, porches, and private balconies. **$$$**

Bradenton
Silver Surf Gulf Beach Resort
1301 Gulf Drive N., FL 34217
Tel: 941-778-6626
www.silverresorts.com
An older but well-maintained facility just across the road from the beach offers 50 clean, basic rooms; some on the main floor have patios. Amenities include a private sand beach, heated pool, and use of beach chairs and umbrellas. Scooter, bicycle, wave runner and boat rentals. **$$**

Clearwater Beach
Amber Tides Motel
420 Hamden Drive, FL 33767
Tel: 727-445-1145
www.ambertides-motel.com
Small motel with clean and cozy rooms, efficiencies, and one-bedroom apartments. There's a nice pool and a courtyard. Bike rental and fishing trips available. Note: a minimum two-to-three-night stay may be required. **$**
East Shore Resort Apartment Motel
473 East Shore Drive, FL 33767
Tel: 727-442-3636
www.eastshoreresort.com
Waterfront resort offers nicely appointed and spacious one- and two-bedroom suites, all with living and dining rooms, full kitchens and two TVs. Ground level units have private porches and water views. Guests can use the barbecue grills and the resort's private 60ft (18-meter) fishing pier. Units are rented by week or month, although nightly stays are permitted when rooms are available. **$$**

Fort Myers
Mantanzas Inn
414 Crescent Street, FL 33931
Tel: 239-463-9258

www.matanzasinn.com
Nicely situated waterfront lodging in the downtown district offers accommodations ranging from small motel units to three-bedroom canal-front villas with balconies. There's a restaurant on site, as well as a marina, pool spa, and rooftop bar. **$–$$**

Homestead
The Hotel Redland
5 S. Flagler Avenue, FL 33030
Tel: 305-246-1904
www.hotelredland.com
New owners are giving some modern touches to this historic, downtown hotel built in 1904 to accommodate passengers traveling on the Flagler Railroad. All but two of the thirteen rooms are on the second floor, and all have private baths, TV, and internet. There are a restaurant and bar on site. **$**

Key Largo
Jule's Undersea Lodge
51 Shoreland Drive at MM 103.2, FL 33037
Tel: 305-451-2353
www.jul.com
A unique two-bedroom lodge 21ft (6.4 meters) beneath the sea. Originally built as a mobile undersea laboratory, accommodations are a tad small but surprisingly comfortable. Each of the two bedrooms has a 42in (107cm) round window looking onto the sea, hot and cold shower, and TV/VCR. The only way to get there is by scuba diving. The price includes all gear and unlimited diving. Reserve well in advance. **$$$**
Kona Kai Resort , Gallery and Botanic Gardens
97802 Overseas Highway at MM 97.8, FL 33037
Tel: 305-852-7200
www.konakairesort.com
Each of the 13 elegantly appointed rooms and one- and two-bedroom suites at this waterfront resort has its own ground floor entry and overlooks the tropical gardens or Florida Bay. **$$–$$$**

Islamorada
Lime Tree Bay Resort Motel
PO Box 839 at MM 68.5, Long Key, FL 33001
Tel: 305-664-4740
www.limetreebayresort.com
Delightful cottages, apartments and

PRICE CATEGORIES

Price categories are based on the average cost of a double room for one night:
$ = under $110
$$ = $110–250
$$$ = more than $250

tastefully decorated motel rooms on the Gulf of Mexico, 17 miles (27km) past Key Largo on the way to Key West. Amenities include a private sandy area with beach chairs, hot tub, pool, small water sports rental concession, and snorkeling. Little Italy Restaurant is on the premises. **$–$$**

Key West
Hostelling International – Key West
718 S. Street, FL 33040
Tel: 305-296-5719
www.keywesthostel.com
Located two blocks from the waterfront, and a part of Seashell Motel, the mixed dorm rooms are very basic, but the most affordable in Key West. There is an outdoor courtyard, a barbecue pit, a pool table, bicycle rental, and laundry facilities. **$**
The Marquesa Hotel
600 Fleming Street, FL 33040
Tel: 305-292-1919
www.marquesa.com
This late 19th-century landmark has been lovingly restored to its original splendor. Tucked in the heart of Key West's Historic District, four handsome buildings encircle two swimming pools and luxurious tropical gardens. Amenities include marble baths and fine dining in the adjoining Café Marquesa. **$$$**
Southernmost Hotel Collection
1319 Duval Street, FL 33040
Tel: 305-296-6577
www.southernmostresorts.com
The properties in this Key West collection include a quaint oceanfront B&B in Old Town, the southernmost resort on the beach, and the southernmost hotel in the US. **$$**

Kissimmee
Sevilla Inn
4640 W. Irlo Bronson Highway, FL 34746
Tel: 407-396-4135
www.sevillainn.net
All 51 units in this well-maintained, two-story motor inn close to Walt

Disney World have microwaves and fridges. There is a heated pool, and a laundry facility. **$**

Miami
Hotel Beaux Arts Miami
255 Biscayne Boulevard Way, FL 33131
Tel: 305-421-8700
www.marriott.com
The lobby of this small boutique hotel within the J.W. Marriott Marquis is on the 39th floor, and everything goes up from there, offering ultramodern rooms with spectacular views and the latest technology (including iPads and automatic drapes). Breakfast is included, but parking is $35/night. **$$$**

Miami Beach
Astor
956 Washington Avenue, FL 33139
Tel: 305-531-8081
www.hotelastor.com
Understated stylishness is the hallmark of this trendy South Beach Art Deco hotel. Bedrooms – mostly suites – and their wall-to-wall marble bathrooms come in muted creams and beiges. The pool is striking, and the restaurant, Casa Firoentina, prepares fine Tuscan cuisine. **$$**
Cardozo
1300 Ocean Drive, FL 33139
Tel: 305-535-6500
www.cardozohotel.com
Owned by Gloria Estefan and her husband, Emelio, this Streamline Moderne Art Deco masterpiece is bathed in purple neon at night. A lively bar, seductive dining terrace, and 43 eye-catching bedrooms with hardwood floors, iron beds, and zebra-striped furniture. **$$**
Clay Hotel Hostelling International – Miami Beach
1438 Washington Avenue, FL 33139
Tel: 305-534-2988
www.clayhotel.com
Comfortable and affordable lodgings in the heart of the Old Miami Beach Art Deco District and just two blocks from

the beach. Amenities include kitchen, laundry facilities, lockers/baggage storage, and restaurant. The semi-private rooms are a great bargain. **$**
The Marlin Hotel
1200 Collins Avenue, FL 33139
Tel: 305-695-3000
Built in 1939, this spectacular and very hip Art Deco hotel offers rooms ranging in size from 200 to 1390 square feet; sophisticated technology allows guests to control everything from mood lighting to a pre-loaded movie on the 60in (1.5-meter) flat-screen TV. The hotel is also home to South Beach Studios, where many famous artists have recorded. **$$**
The Tides
1220 Ocean Drive, FL 33139
Tel: 305-604-5070
www.tidessouthbeach.com
This sleek white oceanfront block contains a small luxury hotel of immaculate taste. The giant, minimalist bedrooms have mischievous postcards with the message "Let's make love at The Tides," and each has uninterrupted views of the ocean and the beach, with telescopes for birding... or to spy on sunbathers. Also a good-sized swimming pool. **$$$**

Orlando
Embassy Suites – Lake Buena Vista
8100 Lake Avenue, FL 32836
Tel: 407-239-1144
www.embassy-suites.com
Spacious suites with in-room movies, fitness center, whirlpool, steam room, and family fun center. Free breakfast and transportation to Walt Disney World. **$$**
Floridays Resort Orlando
12562 International Drive, FL 32821
Tel: 407-238-7700
www.floridaysresortorlando.com
Floridays' 432 spacious, condominium-style two- and three-bedroom suites have fully equipped kitchens, two bathrooms (one with a Jacuzzi tub), and private balconies. One of the two pools on the 20 landscaped acres is for kids; the other is for those wanting a bit of quiet time. A shuttle to Disney World and Orlando is included in the daily resort fee of $12.25. **$$**
Walt Disney World All-Star Resorts
The cheapest rooms within Walt Disney World.
www.disneyworld.disney.go.com
All Star Movies Resort
Tel: 407-939-7000. **$**
All Star Music Resort
Tel: 407-939-6000. **$**
All Star Sports Resort
Tel: 407-939-5000. **$**

Loews Don CeSar Hotel, Saint Petersburg Beach, Florida.

Art of Animation Resort
Tel: 407-938-7000. **$**
Pop Century Resort
Tel: 407-938-4000. **$**

St Augustine
Kenwood Inn
38 Marine Street, FL 32084
Tel: 904-824-2116
www.thekenwoodinn.com
This time-honored three-story B&B, a
Queen Anne Victorian built between
1865 and 1886, has 13 comfortable
rooms and is close to the seafront and
other attractions. The rate includes
an excellent breakfast and there's a
lovely pool and courtyard. **$$**

St Petersburg
The Pier Hotel
253 Second Avenue N., FL 33701
Tel: 727-822-7500
www.thepierhotel.com
The city's oldest hotel, in the heart of
the downtown waterfront district, first
opened its doors in 1921 and was
completely renovated in 2001. Many
of the 33 rooms have microwaves,
refrigerators, and wet bars; some have
the original clawfooted ladies' soaking
tubs. Rate includes an expanded
continental breakfast and two-hour
evening reception with free beer and
wine. Parking is $6/night. **$$**

Saint Petersburg Beach
Loews Don CeSar Hotel
3400 Gulf Boulevard, FL 33706
Tel: 727-360-1881

www.loewshotels.com/Don-CeSar-Hotel
Splendidly situated overlooking the
Gulf of Mexico, this sprawling pink
froth of a hotel has 277 rooms and
suites, many with private terraces
and spectacular views. There are two
pools, a full service spa, restaurant,
bar, and several ground-level shops.
$$$

Sanibel Island
Blue Dolphin Cottages
4227 West Gulf Drive, FL 33957
Tel: 239-472-1600
www.bluedolphincottages.com
Family-owned, gulf-front mini-resort
on a quiet part of the island with
motel rooms as well as efficiency
and one-bedroom cottages set in
a lush tropical setting; some are
directly on the beach. Guests have
complimentary use of bicycles, lounge
chairs, and outdoor barbecues. **$$**
South Seas Island Resort
5400 South Seas Plantation Road, Captiva,
FL 33924
Tel: 239-472-5111
www.southseas.com
On Sanibel Island's sister island,
this sprawling resort village is part
of a 330-acre (121-hectare) wildlife
preserve on the Gulf of Mexico.
Accommodations range from villas to
condominiums to cottages to private
homes, and family-friendly amenities
include a water park and a host of
watersports, numerous restaurants, a
tennis complex, and a beach perfect
for shell collecting. **$$**

Tampa
Holiday Inn Express Hotel Suites – Tampa USF-Busch Gardens
2807 E. Busch Boulevard, FL 33612
Tel: 813-936-8200
www.ichotelsgroup.com
Modern and clean rooms, a good pool
and close to tourist attractions and
restaurants. **$$**
Sailport Waterfront Suites
2506 N. Rocky Point Drive, FL 33607
Tel: 813-281-9599
www.sailport.com
All-suite lodging on a small island
overlooking Tampa Bay. Family suites
have bunk beds for the kids; there
are also workspaces for business
travelers, and barbecue grills for
guests. **$$**
Wyndham Tampa Westshore
700 N. Westshore Boulevard,
FL 33609
Tel: 813-289-8200
www.wyndhamhoteltampa.com
Convenient location with a good
onsite restaurant and spacious rooms.
Also close to the airport, stores, and
restaurants. **$$**

Tarpon Springs
Tarpon Shores Inn
40346 US Highway 19N, FL 34689
Tel: 727-938-2483
www.tarponshoresinn.com
Good-value rooms with LCD TVs
and air-conditioning; some with
microwaves and refrigerators.
Facilities include pool, indoor Jacuzzi
and laundry facilities. **$**

NORTHERN ROUTE

Massachusetts

Boston
Boston Harbor Hotel
70 Rowes Wharf, MA 02110
Tel: 617-439-7000
www.bhh.com
Board the airport water shuttle at
Logan, and seven minutes later, step
into the luxury of the city's foremost
waterside hotel. Bedrooms all have
either harbor or skyline views.
Eighteen rooms are specially designed
for the disabled guests. A museum-
quality art collection decorates the
public areas. **$$$**
Lenox Hotel
61 Exeter Street at Boylston, MA 02116
Tel: 617-536-5300
www.lenoxhotel.com
Modest and moderate traditional
family hotel built in 1900. Bedrooms,
some with functional fireplaces, have
been redecorated in French Provincial,

Oriental or Colonial decor. Just a few
steps from the Prudential Center and a
block from the subway. There are two
restaurants onsite, and the popular
and very chic City Bar is open nightly
until 2am. **$$**
The Liberty Hotel
215 Charles Street, MA 02114
Tel: 617-224-4000
www.libertyhotel.com
Much of the original 1851 Charles
Street Jail was incorporated by
architects in designing the city's most
unique hotel, which opened in 2007.
But there's nothing austere about the
appointments, which are a vibrant
blending of the understated and the
elegant. Most of the well-appointed
and thoroughly modern guestrooms
are in an adjoining 16-story tower.
$$$
Omni Parker House
60 School Street, MA 02018
Tel: 617-227-8600

www.omnihotels.com
Reportedly the oldest continuously
operating hotel in America (since
1855), it's right Downtown on the
Freedom Trail. The 551 renovated
rooms range from "economy petite"
singles to luxury suites. **$$–$$$**

Cambridge
The Charles Hotel
1 Bennett Street, MA 02138
Tel: 617-864-1200
www.charleshotel.com
A modern Harvard Square hotel with
294 airy, neo-traditional rooms, some
overlooking the river. Home to the
popular Regattabar jazz club which

PRICE CATEGORIES

Price categories are based on the average
cost of a double room for one night:
$ = under $110
$$ = $110–250
$$$ = more than $250

draws nationally known jazz artists. **$$$**

Harvard Square Hotel
110 Mount Auburn Street, MA 02138
Tol: 617-864-5200
www.hotelsinharvardsquare.com
A six-floor motel in the heart of
Harvard Square; all rooms with
picture windows. Onsite parking is
available but there is a charge. The
Inn at Harvard, on the grounds of
Harvard University, is the hotel's sister
property. **$$**

Mary Prentiss Inn
6 Prentiss Street, MA 02140
Tel: 617-661-2929
www.maryprentissinn.com
Tastefully appointed Greek Revival
B&B. Some of the 20 rooms have
antique armoires and four-poster
beds. Made-to-order breakfasts served
outside on the terrace in summer.
Situated on a residential street
between Harvard and Porter Squares.
Free Wi-fi and parking. **$$–$$$**

Concord

Colonial Inn
48 Monument Square, MA 01742
Tel: 978-369-9200
www.concordscolonialinn.com
The historic main inn and its newer
wing, a guesthouse, a cottage and two
other houses offer 56 rooms, the latter
three more suited to longer stays.
The main 1716 inn on Concord's
town common has 15 rooms and
the Village Forge Lounge, where
live entertainment takes place from
Wednesday through Sunday evenings.
$$

Longfellow's Wayside Inn
72 Wayside Inn Road, Sudbury, MA 01776
Tel: 978-443-1776
www.wayside.org
Close to Concord, the country's
oldest operating inn has been
providing hospitality since 1716.
Each of the nine traditionally
furnished guest rooms has a private
bath and phone; rooms number nine
and ten have classic low ceilings and
wide-board floors. Sunday brunch
is served from September through
June; breakfast, lunch and dinner
daily. If the weather is nice, opt for
the outdoor patio. **$$**

Gloucester

Bass Rocks Ocean Inn
107 Atlantic Road, MA 01930
Tel: 978-283-7600
www.bassrocksoceaninn.com
Stay in one of the 51 rooms in the
Oceanfront, Seaside or Stacy Houses,
whose rooms all look out to sea. The
Oceanfront and Seaside Houses have
balconies or patios. Free bicycle use,

heated pool, and complimentary
breakfast. **$$–$$$**

Harborview Inn
Stacey Boulevard, 71 Western Avenue, MA
01930
Tel: 978-283-2277
www.harborviewinn.com
A comfortable house-turned-B&B near
the Fisherman Memorial statue. Three
rooms and three suites, all with private
bath and some with an ocean view.
Complimentary continental breakfast.
$–$$

New Hampshire

Claremont

Claremont Motor Lodge
16 Beauregard Street,
NH 03743
Tel: 603-542-2540
www.claremontmotel.com
This classic motel 2 miles from
downtown has rooms with cable
TV and internet access; some also
include kitchen facilities. Free
continental breakfast. **$**

Portsmouth

Inn at Strawbery Banke
314 Court Street, NH 03801
Tel: 603-436-7242
www.innatstrawberybanke.com
An elegant older house with seven
well-proportioned rooms spread over
two floors, each with a sitting room.
$–$$

**Residence Inn Portsmouth/
Downtown/Waterfront**
100 Deer Street, NH 03801
Tel: 603-422-9200
www.marriott.com
The city's newest hotel, next to the
harbor, has 128 suites with full
kitchens on five floors, and an indoor
pool. **$$–$$$**

Wolfeboro

Wolfeboro Inn
90 N. Main Street, NH 03894
Tel: 603-569-3016
www.wolfeboroinn.com
A thoroughly modernized and
picturesque 19th-century waterfront
inn with an inviting tavern. Stay in
the modern, rather than the historic,
part of the inn if you want a balcony
overlooking Wolfeboro Bay on Lake
Winnipesaukee. Guests can dine on
the patio in summer. **$$**

Maine

Cape Elizabeth

Inn by the Sea
40 Bowery Beach Road, ME 04107
Tel: 207-799-3134
www.innbythesea.com

Large, rambling carbon-neutral coastal
resort with 57 luxury rooms, suites,
and cottages, all with porch or deck
with ocean view. Rooms come with
flat-screen TVs. Amenities include
spa, gym, pool, bar, and a restaurant
serving fresh and local produce. Set
on 5 acres (2 hectares) of grounds
certified as a wildlife sanctuary, the inn
is popular with guests traveling with
their dogs. **$$$+**

Cornish

Cornish Inn
2 High Road, PO Box 266, MA 04020
Tel: 207-625-8501
www.cornishinn.com
Lovely early 1800s colonial house
at the base of the White Mountains.
A light breakfast is included.
The restaurant and bar are open
Wednesday through Sunday. **$–$$**

Kennebunkport

1802 House B&B
15 Locke Street, ME 04046
Tel: 207-967-5632
www.1802inn.com
This secluded hideaway minutes
from central Dock Square and next
to Cape Arundel golf course has six
warm, intimate guest rooms with
wood-burning fireplaces, antiques,
and original artwork. The private tiled
bathrooms feature whirlpool baths.
Three-course breakfast served.
$$–$$$

Ogunquit Beach

The Beachmere Inn
62 Beachmere Place, ME 03907
Tel: 207-646-2021
www.beachmereinn.com
Intimate, stylish, and eco-friendly
Victorian inn with wonderful coastal
views and a small private beach. 10
minutes south of Wells. Many rooms
have private balconies or decks
and four also have wood-burning
fireplaces. **$–$$**

The Dunes on the Waterfront
PO Box 917, 518 Main Street,
ME 03907
Tel: 207-646-2612
www.dunesonthewaterfront.com
Established in 1936, The Dunes
features 17 well-kept guest rooms and
19 traditional New England cottages
set in trim open grounds overlooking
the tidal river. Located just south of
Wells. Heated outdoor pool. Seasonal
opening. **$$**

Portland

Inn at St. John
939 Congress Street, ME 04102
Tel: 207-773-6481
www.innatstjohn.com

Dockside Guest Quarters in York, Maine.

Although it's at the western edge of downtown and about 1.7 miles from the Old Port, for the budget-conscious this 1897 Victorian charmer is well worth the walk. The 39-room inn has spacious and comfortable rooms ranging from value (shared bath) to luxury (private bath with jetted tub). Continental breakfast is included, and there are plenty of restaurants close by. **$**

Inn on Carleton
46 Carleton Street,
ME 04102
Tel: 207-775-1910
www.innoncarleton.com
A beautifully restored Victorian home in the center of Portland's historical district. This B&B has six rooms, four with private baths and showers, two with showers only. **$–$$**

Pomegranate Inn
49 Neal Street, ME 04102
Tel: 207-772-1006
www.pomegranateinn.com
A tranquil hideaway set in the Western Promenade historical district. Five of the eight rooms have working fireplaces, all have private bathrooms. The room on the first floor comes with access to a private garden. **$$–$$$**

York

Dockside Guest Quarters
22 Harris Island Road, ME 03909
Tel: 207-363-2868
www.docksidegq.com
Situated on a private peninsula surrounded by sweeping views. Rooms and suites are located in several buildings across the seven acres; the Maine House has large balconies. There is a restaurant, and the buffet breakfast included in the price. **$$**

Vermont

Arlington

Arlington Inn
Route 7A, VT 05250
Tel: 802-375-6532
www.arlingtoninn.com
An elegant B&B Greek Revival mansion with comfortable Victorian-style furnishings in the five guest rooms. More rooms available in the Carriage House, some with Jacuzzis, and in the Old Parsonage, which has some units with private porches. Restaurant and gardens. Located between Bennington and Manchester. **$$–$$$**

West Mountain Inn
River Road (off Route 313), VT 05250
Tel: 802-375-6516
www.westmountaininn.com
This 150-year-old inn on 150 acres overlooking the Battenkill Valley, has built a well-deserved reputation for its warm hospitality. The antiques-filled rooms are spacious and elegantly appointed with traditional accommodations in the main building, and two-bedroom apartments in the Historic Mill. Breakfast is a standout, and dinner is served nightly. Trails for hiking and cross-country skiing, game room, fishing, and the resident llama ranch amuse all ages. **$$–$$$**

Bridgewater Corners

October Country Inn B&B
362 Upper Road, PO Box 66, VT 05035
Tel: 802-672-3412
www.octobercountryinn.com
All 10 rooms in this cozy farmhouse have private baths and air-conditioning. The inn is on a back road, about 5 miles (8km) from the Killington ski area. Outdoor pool. Dinner available. **$–$$**

Dorset

Barrows House
Route 30, VT 05251
Tel: 802-867-4455
www.barrowshouse.com
An 18th-century Federal-style inn (plus eight other buildings) with homey touches in the 28 rooms, and a well-regarded restaurant. Outdoor pool, tennis courts. Bicycle and cross-country ski hire available. Located 6 miles (10km) north of Manchester. **$$**

Dorset Inn
8 Church Street (Route 30), VT 05251
Tel: 802-867-5500
www.dorsetinn.com
One of the state's oldest inns – and reliably enjoyable – opened in 1796. There are 25 graciously appointed rooms, a spa, and an award-winning

restaurant. Breakfast is included. **$$–$$$**

Fairlee

Silver Maple Lodge and Cottages
520 US Route 5 S., VT 05045
Tel: 802-333-4326
www.silvermaplelodge.com
A handsome old farmhouse with eight comfortable lodge rooms and a further seven rooms in well-fitted rustic, knotty-pine cabins (some with working fireplaces). Thirteen units have private baths. **$–$$**

Killington

Inn of the Six Mountains
2617 Killington Road, VT 05751
Tel: 802-422-4302
www.sixmountains.com
A 103-room modern resort hotel with a Rockies feel; everything, including the central fieldstone hearth, is lavishly overscale. Close to skiing and hiking trails. Two pools, hot tubs, and spa. **$–$$**

Mountain Meadows Lodge
285 Thundering Brook Road, VT 05751
Tel: 802-775-1010
www.mountainmeadowslodge.com
Large eco-friendly lakeside 19th-century farmhouse and adjacent three-story lodge offering 17 rooms with private baths, and some with balconies overlooking the lake. Extensive cross-country/hiking trails (the Appalachian Trail crosses the property). Farm animals wander the grounds and rowboats, canoes, and kayaks can be hired. Children under 12 years of age stay free. **$$**

Manchester Village

1811 House (owned by Equinox Resort)
3567 Main Street, Route 7A, VT 05254
Tel: 877-854-7625
www.equinoxresort.com/accommodations
A Federal manse that is the former home of Abraham Lincoln's granddaughter. Thirteen spacious, antiques-filled guest rooms, some with canopied beds, fireplaces, and private porches, all with flat-screen TVs. The three cottage rooms have wood-burning fireplaces. Located at the north end of Manchester Village. Access to Equinox Resort's spa and pool. **$$–$$$**

Reluctant Panther Inn
West Road, VT 05254

PRICE CATEGORIES

Price categories are based on the average cost of a double room for one night:
$ = under $110
$$ = $110–250
$$$ = more than $250

Tel: 802-362-2568
www.reluctantpanther.com
Spacious and luxurious
accommodations – including suites
with two fireplaces and private
entrances – make this complex
of several buildings on the village
outskirts a premier choice. The
candlelit restaurant and adjoining pub
serve upscale regional cuisine. $$$
The Equinox
3567 Main Street, Route 7A, VT 05254
www.equinoxresort.com
A grand old hotel with 195 renovated
and stylishly furnished rooms.
Amenities include three restaurants,
a bar, a tavern. The hotel also offers
plenty of sporting activities including
off-road driving instruction, fly fishing,
golf, falconry, archery, and clay target
shooting. $$$

Middlebury
Middlebury Inn
14 Court Square, VT 05753
Tel: 802-388-4961
www.middleburyinn.com
Since 1827 this handsome brick
lodging with restaurant in the heart of
town has been providing hospitality
to travelers. Those looking for a
traditional inn experience will want to
opt for a room in the main inn or the
1825 Porter House Mansion rather
than the modern annex. $$
Swift House Inn
25 Stewart Lane, VT 05753
Tel: 802-388-9925
www.swifthouseinn.com
An elegantly detailed 1814 Federal
house with 20 luxurious guest rooms;
the Carriage House features spacious
rooms with whirlpool baths and the
Gate House has a wraparound porch.
Restaurant, steam room, and sauna.
Breakfast is included and dinner is
served from Wednesday through
Sunday in season (Thur–Sun Nov–
May). $$

Quechee
Quechee Inn at Marshland Farm
Quechee Main Street, VT 05059
Tel: 802-295-3133
www.quecheeinn.com
With wilderness trails, cross-country
skiing, biking, and canoeing, this
meticulously restored but completely
updated 1793 inn has much to offer
those seeking an active holiday.
Breakfast is included; reservations for
dinner recommended. $$–$$$

Ripton
The Chipman Inn
Route 125, VT 05766
Tel: 802-388-2390
www.chipmaninn.com

Small, gracious historic B&B inn with
eight appealing rooms, a tranquil
atmosphere, and a friendly resident
cat. Main lounge has a private bar.
Children 12 and over welcome. $–$$
Weston
The Inn at Weston
Route 100, VT 05161
Tel: 802-864-6789
www.innweston.com
Located 20 miles (32km) from
Manchester in an iconic Vermont
village – home to the famed Vermont
Country Store and Weston Playhouse
– the inn is a romantic hideaway
featuring antique furnishings and
four-poster beds. Two suites have
balconies and fireplaces. The dining
room offers imaginative contemporary
cuisine and an impressive wine list.
Ask to see the innkeeper's spectacular
orchid collection. $$$

Windsor
Juniper Hill Inn
153 Pembroke Road, VT 05089
Tel: 802-674-5273
www.juniperhillinn.com
On the National Register of Historic
Places, this 1902 Greek Revival
mansion B&B, set on a broad lawn,
has 16 elegantly appointed rooms
furnished with Queen Anne and
Edwardian pieces. Dine on the
restaurant's regional specialities
in the same room Teddy Roosevelt
did. Hilltop setting near Ascutney
Mountain, outdoor pool. Full breakfast
included; dinner Thursday through
Monday. Children 12 and over
welcome. $$–$$$

Woodstock
Kedron Valley Inn
4778 South Road, South Woodstock, VT
05071
Tel: 802-457-1473
www.kedronvalleyinn.com
The 25 rooms in this B&B, an inn since
1828, are spread throughout the main
inn, tavern building, and a log cabin;
many have fireplaces and Jacuzzis
or private decks. The restaurant is
exceptional – book in advance if you
want dinner (Thur–Mon in summer
and Thur–Sun in winter). The ski
lodge-style building behind the main
inn attracts families, who also enjoy
the two-acre swimming pond. $$
Woodstock Inn and Resort
14 The Green (Route 4), VT 05091
Tel: 802-457-1100
www.woodstockinn.com
The Rockefellers' homage to country
inns past includes 142 bedrooms,
a library and three restaurants. The
decor is corporate/country with
modern furniture. Facilities include

indoor and outdoor pools, tennis
courts, golf, health club, racquetball
and squash courts, and a downhill ski
area. $$$

New York

Buffalo
Lenox Hotel and Suites
140 N. Street, NY 14201
Tel: 716-884-1700
www.lenoxhotelandsuites.com
Historic hotel offering guest rooms and
luxury suites. Rooms come equipped
with refrigerators and microwaves,
while some of the suites contain
kitchens. $$
Lord Amherst Hotel
5000 Main Street, NY 14226
Tel: 716-839-2200
www.lordamherst.com
Well-maintained motel close to
shopping malls. Exercise room, heated
outdoor pool, restaurant, and free
Wi-fi. $

Canandaigua
Morgan Samuels Inn
2920 Smith Road, NY 14424
Tel: 585-394-9232
www.morgansamuelsinn.com
This stately English-style mansion
with tree-lined approach invites you
to unwind in civilized comfort. The inn
stands in extensive wooded grounds
and is furnished with oil paintings and
antiques. $$

Cooperstown
The Inn at Cooperstown
16 Chestnut Street, NY 13326
Tel: 607-547-5756
www.inatcooperstown.com
A distinctive Second Empire-style
inn in a central location designed by
Henry J. Hardenbergh, known for his
New York City projects – the Dakota
Apartments and Plaza Hotel. Built in
1874 as an annex to the plush Hotel
Fenimore, the inn has 18 spotless,
modern rooms and suites. $–$$
(includes buffet breakfast)

Fredonia
The White Inn
52 E. Main Street, NY 14063
Tel: 716-672-2103
www.whiteinn.com
Dignified older inn furnished
with antiques and reproductions.
Restaurant offers excellent American
cuisine with top-quality, fresh
ingredients. $–$$

Geneva
Belhurst Castle
4069 Route 14 S., NY 14456
Tel: 315-781-0201

www.belhurst.com
A choice of 14 rooms, some with Jacuzzis, in a 19th-century castle overlooking Seneca Lake. Property has two restaurants and its own winery. **$-$$**

Niagara Falls
Sheraton At The Falls
300 Third Street, NY 14303
Tel: 716-285-3361
www.starwoodhotels.com/sheraton
Swanky and central. This huge hotel has nearly 400 rooms available, a Grille serving breakfast and a Sports Bar serving lunch and dinner. Facilities include a small gym, indoor pool, and casino. **$$**
Hostelling International – Niagara Falls
1101 Ferry Avenue, NY 14301
Tel: 716-282-3700
www.hihostels.com
The hostel occupies a historic Georgian-style home within walking distance of the Falls. Amenities include kitchen, internet access, onsite parking, laundry facilities, and luggage and bike storage. **$**

Rome
Quality Inn Rome
200 S. James Street at Erie Boulevard, NY 13440
Tel: 315-336-4300
Good location. Rooms come with microwaves and refrigerators. Amenities include laundry facilities, outdoor pool, exercise room, restaurant, and free internet access. Disabled access rooms available. **$**

Saratoga Springs
Batcheller Mansion Inn
20 Circular Street, NY 12866
Tel: 518-584-7012
www.batchellermansioninn.com
A marvelous High Victorian Gothic inn, impeccably preserved. This fantastic B&B features eight elegantly appointed rooms and one suite, a living room with grand piano, French windows, and shaded porches. Price includes hot breakfast, but be aware weekend rates are higher during the racing season (July–Sept). No guests under 16. **$$**
Caffe Lena
47 Phila Street, NY 12866
Tel: 518-583-0022
www.caffelena.org
Founded in 1960 and widely-considered the oldest continuously operating coffeehouse in the United States, Caffe Lena has played host to some of America's most beloved musicians including Bob Dylan and Arlo Guthrie. Now a non-profit

organization, the café is still a stage for live music, offering a warm welcome to anyone passing through. **$-$$**

Syracuse
Hostelling International – Syracuse
535 Oak Street, NY 13203
Tel: 315-472-5788
www.hihostels.com
Attractive hostel occupies an enormous old house in the center of Syracuse. Amenities include self-catering kitchen, laundry facilities, and baggage storage. **$**
Park View Hotel
713 E. Genesee Street, NY 13210
Tel: 315-701-2600
www.theparkviewhotel.com
Centrally located opposite Foreman Park, with spacious rooms, a gym, coffee and wine bar, and the elegant 1060 restaurant. **$$**

Utica
Red Roof Inn
20 Weaver Street, NY 13502
Tel: 315-724-7128
www.redroof.com
Spotless, well-fitted rooms and friendly service. Restaurants and shopping close by. Children 17 and under stay free when sharing a room with an adult family member. **$**

Pennsylvania

Erie
Downtown Erie Hotel
18 W. 18th Street, PA 16501
Tel: 814-456-2961
www.downtowneriehotel.com
Central location, with cable TV in the rooms and internet access in the lobby and lounge. Outdoor pool and complimentary continental breakfast. **$**

Ohio

Cleveland
Glidden House Hotel
1901 Ford Drive, OH 44106
Tel: 216-231-8900
www.gliddenhouse.com
Attractive historic hotel on the Case Western Reserve University campus and close to the city's museums. Stylish rooms with plasma screen TVs. Dine on Mediterranean cuisine in the Carriage House restaurant, often accompanied by live music. Wheelchair-accessible rooms. **$$**
Wyndham Cleveland Hotel at Playhouse Square
1260 Euclid Avenue, OH 44115
Tel: 216-615-7500

www.wyndham.com/hotels
Convenient location and adjacent to the theater district. Nicely decorated rooms, restaurant, lounge, indoor pool, and fitness center. Wheelchair-accessible rooms are available. There is a complimentary shuttle service to local attractions. **$$**

Sandusky
Baraboo, Wisconsin and Sandusky
Kalahari Waterpark Resort
1305 Kalahari Drive, WI 53913
OR
7000 Kalahari Drive, OH 44870
Tel: 877-525-2427
www.kalahariresorts.com
At 173,000 square feet, Kalahari's Ohio resort is the largest in the United States. Both locations offer and indoor water park with swimming pools, hot tubs, slides, and body boarding. The resorts are designed to look like the Kalahari Desert in Southern Africa with artificial fountains, trees, and animals. Tacky for some tastes, but kids seem to like it.
Hampton Inn Sandusky-Central
6100 Milan Road, OH 44870
Tel: 419-609-9000
www.hamptoninn3.hilton.com
Fifty comfortable rooms with free internet access plus the usual amenities, close to Cedar Point Amusement Park, the safari park, and indoor and outdoor waterparks. Complimentary hot breakfast, fitness room, indoor pool, and Jacuzzi. **$$**

Toledo
Mansion View Inn
2035 Collingwood Boulevard, OH 43620
Tel: 419-244-5676
www.mansionviewtoledo.com
Located in the historic old west end district, this striking 1887 mansion has four B&B rooms decorated in Victorian style. Sitting room has DVDs, videos, TV, and books. **$$**

Indiana

Nappanee
Inn at Amish Acres
1600 W. Market Street, IN 46550
Tel: 574-773-4188
www.amishacres.com
A chance to enjoy some of life's quiet pleasures: porch rockers, checkerboards, and twining flowers. All rooms have cable TV and Amish

PRICE CATEGORIES

Price categories are based on the average cost of a double room for one night:
$ = under $110
$$ = $110–250
$$$ = more than $250

TRANSPORTATION
ACCOMMODATIONS
EATING OUT
ACTIVITIES
A – Z

patterned quilts; 16 have hot tubs. Disabled-access rooms. Outdoor pool, free internet access, and continental breakfast served. **$–$$**

South Bend
The Oliver Inn
630 W. Washington Street, IN 46601
Tel: 574-232-4545
www.oliverinn.com
A B&B in a very pretty early 20th-century house with corner porches, bay windows, and trim gardens. The wood-burning fireplace and live piano music add to the flavor of the common areas. **$–$$**

Valparaiso
The Inn at Aberdeen
3158 S. State Route 2, IN 46385
Tel: 219-465-3753
www.innataberdeen.com
Comfortable guest rooms with Jacuzzis and balconies. Full gourmet breakfast, evening dessert, unlimited beverages, and snacks. Garden has a gazebo. **$$**

Michigan

Dearborn
Victory Inn
23730 Michigan Avenue, MI 48124
Tel: 313-565-7250
www.avictoryhotels.com/dearborn
All rooms in this Downtown inn come with cable TV, free internet access, refrigerator, and microwave. There is an an outdoor pool and free continental breakfast. **$**

Illinois

Chicago
Hotel Cass
640 N. Wabash Avenue, IL 60611
Tel: 312-787-4030

Chicago's landmark Drake Hotel.

www.casshotel.com
Great location on the Magnificent Mile for this central hotel within walking distance of Nacy Pier, John Hancock Center, and Millennium Park. Rooms come with free internet access, high-definition flat-screen TV, and complimentary breakfast. **$$**
The Drake Hotel
140 E. Walton Place, IL 60611
Tel: 312-787-2200
www.thedrakehotel.com
This elegant, updated landmark hotel has hosted everyone from the Queen of England to Japanese emperors, heads of state to Pope John Paul II. Luxurious rooms with Italian marble bathrooms, two ballrooms, a gym, and a shopping arcade featuring Chanel and the jewelry designer Georg Jensen. Four restaurants, including the nautically themed, celeb-favorite, seafood specialty Cape Cod Room, where Marilyn Monroe carved her initials in the bar – reservation recommended. **$$$**
Park Hyatt Chicago
800 North Michigan Avenue, IL 60611
Tel: 312-335-1234
Towering 67 stories above Michigan Avenue, the Park Hyatt Chicago is smack in the center of downtown and just five minutes' walk from attractions like John Hancock Center and Museum of Contemporary Art. Contemporary cool abounds here in this renovated landmark hotel: a massive lobby with soaring black columns, reproduction Eames furniture in the rooms, and oversize soaking tubs. Round this off with the luxurious spa and rooftop outdoor NoMi lounge, which is always abuzz with activity. Request a room facing Lake Michigan for a real treat! **$$$**
The Whitehall Hotel
105 E. Delaware Place, IL 60611
Tel: 312-944-6300
Perfectly located, European-style hotel restored to its original 1920s beauty. Rooms have mahogany furniture and 300-thread count Egyptian cotton sheets. Italian restaurant, pizza bar and lounge where the Beatles once drank. **$$$**

Wisconsin

Dodgeville
Best Western Quiet House & Suites
1130 N. Johns Street, WI 53533
Tel: 608-935-7739
www.bestwestern.com
Located only 3 miles (5km) from a state park, this hotel's rooms come with cable TV, internet access, microwave, and refrigerator. Free

continental breakfast, indoor and outdoor pools. **$–$$**
Don Q Inn
3658 State Route 23 N., WI 53533
Tel: 608-935-2321
www.fantasuite.com
Don Q has 21 themed rooms (**$–$$**), from geisha to safari, tacky to random, plus 35 standard rooms (**$**). Pool and free continental breakfast. **$–$$**
House on the Rock Inn
3591 Highway 23, WI 53533
Tel: 608-935-3711
www.thehouseontherock.com
A modern inn situated 7 miles (11km) south of the unique House on the Rock, echoing some of its features. An attractive lounge opens onto a deck overlooking the outdoor pool. Indoor pool includes children's play area. Continental breakfast included. **$–$$**

Madison
Hotel Red
1501 Monroe Street, WI 53711
Tel: 608-819-8228
www.hotelred.com
Madison's only independent boutique hotel, the Red has 48 modern suites with soaking tubs, kitchenettes and patios. The Bauhaus-inspired steel-and-glass structure was designed by a local architect, and Wisconsin artisans crafted many of the hotel's interiors. Relax with a glass of wine on the outdoor patio at The Wise, Hotel Red's new American-style restaurant, and watch the bikers and joggers breeze by.
Mansion Hill Inn
424 N. Pinckney Street, WI 53703
Tel: 608-255-0172
www.mansionhillinn.com
A mid-19th-century Romanesque Revival mansion situated in the historic district. Tastefully furnished with fine antiques. Expect a warm welcome and attentive service. No children under 13. **$$$**

Richland Center
Park View Motel
511 W. Sixth Street, WI 53581
Tel: 608-647-6354
www.pvrcmotel.com
Fifteen basic but well-maintained units with refrigerator, microwave, TV, and wireless internet. Opposite a public park and pool. **$**
Spring Green
The Usonian Inn
E5116 Hwy 14, WI 53588
Tel: 608-588-2323, 877-876-6426
www.usonianinn.com
Inspired by Frank Lloyd Wright's Taliesin Estate, this hotel spread across three acres is listed on the National Historic Register; rooms have

fridge, coffee maker, and free Wi-fi. There is a wine and beer shop in the lobby and the hotel tries to adhere to sustainable practices. $$

Bloomington
About 20 minutes south of Minneapolis on 35W.
Hotel Sofitel
5601 W. 78 Street, MN 55439
Tel: 952-835-1900
Luxury, contemporary-style accommodation close to the Mall of America, with an impressive French restaurant, bar, and fitness center. $$

Le Sueur
Cosgrove House
228 S. Second Street, MN 56058
Tel: 507-665-2500
Four B&B rooms, each with their own bath. Equipped with air-conditioning and laundry facilities, and serves a full breakfast. $–$$

Minneapolis
W Minneapolis - The Foshay
821 Marquette Avenue, MN 55402
Tel: 612-215-3700
www.starwoodhotels.com
Soaring 447ft (136 meters) over the city, W Minneapolis The Foshay blends Art Deco architecture with sleek style and is just steps from the Walker Art Center and Guthrie Theatre. The 229-room hotel has a Prohibition Skybar on the 27th floor and a top-floor observation deck. $$–$$$
The Depot Renaissance
225 S. Third Avenue, MN 55401
Tel: 612-375-1700
www.marriott.com
Well-maintained, comfortable rooms near city center. Housed in a restored train depot, close to the Light Rail, with restaurant, bar, gym, indoor waterpark, and seasonal indoor skating rink. Also, pet friendly (for a fee.) $$
Evelo's B&B
2301 Bryant Ave S., MN 55405
Tel: 612-374-9656
Pleasant bed and breakfast in well-preserved Victorian house. Four rooms, all with air-conditioning and TV, share two bathrooms. No children. $
Graves 601 Hotel
601 First Avenue N., MN 55403
Tel: 612-677-1100
www.graves601hotel.com
Swanky boutique hotel in the warehouse district, Graves 601 offers 255 rooms and 6 suites with free Wi-fi, an award-winning restaurant and cocktail lounge and an onsite gym. $$–$$$
Nicollet Island Inn
95 Merriam Street, MN 55401
Tel: 612-331-1800

www.nicolletislandinn.com
Prime riverside location with 24 individually appointed rooms and top-notch restaurant featuring local cuisine. The bread and desserts are prepared daily onsite. $$

Pipestone
Historic Calumet Inn
104 W. Main Street, MN 56164
Tel: 507-825-5871
www.calumetinn.com
The Calumet Inn is right in the middle of Main Street in downtown Pipestone. Rooms are charming, service is excellent, and there is a simple yet dependable restaurant at the hotel that serves breakfast, lunch and dinner. Close to Pipestone National Monument. $$

St Paul
The St Paul Hotel
350 Market Street, MN 55102
Tel: 651-292-9292
www.saintpaulhotel.com
Historic, landmark hotel located in city center, overlooking Rice Park. Luxurious rooms, restaurant, café, and lobby bar, rooftop fitness center, and complimentary local transport. $$$

South Dakota

Badlands National Park
Cedar Pass Lodge
20681 SD Highway 240, SD 57750
Tel: 877-386-4383
www.cedarpasslodge.com
Escape from life's hectic pace and stay in a cabin with air-conditioning and bathroom but no phone or TV to distract you (cabins, built for the 2012 season, have flat-screen TV's and are slightly more expensive.) Buffalo tacos served in the restaurant. Located just past the Ben Reifel park Visitor Center. Open mid-April to mid-October. $

Deadwood
Bullock Hotel
633 Main Street, SD 57732
Tel: 800-336-1876
www.historicbullock.com
Well-restored Victorian hotel in historic town with 24-hour gaming, 28 rooms, and breakfast and brunch available. Reputedly haunted by Seth Bullock, Deadwood's first Sheriff! $$
Historic Franklin Hotel
700 Main Street, SD 57732
Tel: 605-578-3670
www.silveradofranklin.com
Located on Deadwood's historic Main Street, this lovely old hotel was built in 1903 and is now thoroughly restored. Amenities: air-conditioning,

television, parking, restaurant, bars, and casino. $
Penny Motel
818 Upper Main Street, SD 57732
Tel: 605-578-1842
www.pennymotel.com
Minutes from historic Downtown. Amenities include internet, laundry facilities, parking, and patios with gas grills. Casino and restaurant located next door. Continental breakfast offered. $

Interior
About 30 miles south of Wall, South Dakota on 90, then 240.
Circle View Guest Ranch B&B
20055 E. Highway 44, SD 57780
Tel: 605-433-5582
www.circleviewranch.com
Stay on this third-generation, family-run, 3,000-acre (1,214-hectare) working cattle ranch, located on top of a butte with amazing views of the stunning scenery. Eight rooms with private bathrooms. Serene and lovely. Guest kitchen and games room. Cooked breakfast. $

Mitchell
Kelly Inn and Suites
1010 Cabela Drive, SD 57301
Tel: 605-995-0500
www.kellyinnmitchell.com
Good value for money. All rooms have refrigerators, microwaves, and internet access. Some family and wheelchair-accessible rooms. Exercise room and spacious indoor pool. $

Pierre
River Lodge
713 W. Sioux Avenue, SD 57501
Tel: 605-224-4140
www.riverlodgesd.com
Convenient, family-owned, and situated only one block away from the Missouri River. Continental breakfast included. Freezer space for fishermen's catches. Cookies await your arrival. Pet friendly. $

Rapid City
Best Western Ramkota Hotel
2111 N. LaCrosse Street, SD 57701
Tel: 605-343-8550
www.bestwestern.com
Spacious rooms plus 33 two-room suites for families. Free internet access and parking. Indoor pool, fitness room, restaurant and bar, and indoor waterpark. $$

PRICE CATEGORIES

Price categories are based on the average cost of a double room for one night:
$ = under $110
$$ = $110–250
$$$ = more than $250

Hotel Alex Johnson
523 Sixth Street, SD 57701
Tel: 888-729-0708
www.alexjohnson.com
Commissioned by rail tycoon, Alex Johnson, said to be a great admirer of Native American culture. An intriguing blend of German and Plains tribe influences. Don't miss the chandelier fashioned from war lances. Restaurant open during the summer. **$$**

Sioux Falls
Brimark Inn
3200 W. Russell Street,
SD 57107
Tel: 605-332-2000
www.brimarkinn.com
Just a few miles outside of Sioux Falls city centre, this motor inn offers a seasonal outdoor pool and laundry facilities on-site. A daily continental breakfast with cereal, juice, and coffee is served, and free Wi-fi is available throughout the property. Elmwood Golf Course is nearby. **$**

Spearfish
Spearfish Canyon Lodge
10619 Roughlock Falls Road, Lead, SD 57754
Tel: 877-975-6343
www.spfcanyon.com
Fifty-four rooms in a stone and wood, old west-style lodge nestled against cliffs. Hot tub on the balcony, lounge, bar, and restaurant. Ideal for outdoor types, with fishing, snowmobiling, birdwatching, and hiking opportunities on the doorstep. **$$**

Wall
America's Best Value Inn
201 S. Boulevard, SD 57790
Tel: 605-279-2127
www.abvi-wall.com
Save the pennies and stay in these clean and comfortable rooms fitted with cable TV and wireless internet. Continental breakfast and heated outdoor pool. **$**

Wyoming

Big Horn
Spahn's Big Horn Mountain Bed and Breakfast
50 Upper Hideaway Lane, SD 82833
Tel: 307-674-8150
www.bighorn-wyoming.com
This traditional mountain lodge has a peaceful location on the side of a mountain, with stunning views of the surrounding Big Horn range. Guest bedrooms in the main house are decorated with country quilts and oak furniture, and there are cozy cabins with front porches. **$$**

Cody
Irma Hotel
1192 Sheridan Avenue, WY 82414
Tel: 307-587-4221
www.irmahotel.com
Built in 1902 by Buffalo Bill Cody for his daughter, Irma, the hotel still retains the flavor of the Old West. Amenities include air-conditioning, television, restaurant and gift shop. **$–$$**

Gillette
White House Inn B&B
2708 Ridgecrest Drive, WY 82718
Tel: 307-687-1240
Email: whitehouseinn@vcn.com
Attractive, renovated inn with columned front porch. Formerly the Jost House Inn Bed & Breakfast, the White House Inn offers a traditional atmosphere with modern amenities and comfortable beds. Each suite has private bathroom. **$–$$**

Grand Teton National Park
Jackson Lake Lodge
Grand Teton Lodge
Highway 89, 5 miles (8km) North of Moran, WY 83013
Tel: 307-543-2811
www.gtlc.com
An eco-friendly, luxury lodge with stunning views of the lake and the Teton Range from its huge lobby windows, this large resort has 385 rooms in the main lodge and surrounding cottages. It has a swimming pool, playground, Western art, and other amenities. **$$–$$$**
Signal Mountain Lodge
Inner Teton Park Road, Moran, WY 83013
Tel: 307-543-2831
www.signalmountainlodge.com
At the only resort set on the shores of Jackson Lake in Grand Teton National Park, accommodation is in country-style rooms in the main lodge, modern bungalows and one- and two-room rustic log cabins with pine furniture. Deluxe lakefront units are also available **$$–$$$**

Greybull
Yellowstone Motel
247 Greybull Avenue, WY 82426
Tel: 307-765-4456
www.yellowstonemotel.net
Warm, comfortable rooms and suites at the base of the Big Horn Mountains, 100 miles (160km) east of Yellowstone National Park. Amenities include a putting green, heated pool, and restaurant next door. **$–$$**

Jackson
Buckrail Lodge
110 E. Karns Avenue, WY 83001

Long hours on the open road merit a luxury stopover.

Tel: 307-733-2079
www.buckraillodge.com
Large, comfortable cedar-log rooms with cathedral ceilings and western decor. Set in spacious grounds in quiet residential neighborhood with good views, Jacuzzi, and cable TV. **$–$$**
Rustic Inn at Jackson Hole
435 N. Cache Street, WY 83001
Tel: 307-733-2357
www.rusticinnatjh.com
Luxury log cabins in peaceful park setting near a quiet elk refuge but also convenient to Town Square. Amenities include a restaurant and wine bar, heated outdoor pool and Jacuzzi, spa, gym, and complimentary Wi-fi. **$$$**

Lovell
TX Ranch
20 Crooked Creek Road, WY 82431
Tel: 406-484-6415
www.txranch.com
Guests help out with duties on this working cattle ranch situated at the foot of Pryor Mountain. Tents, horses, gear, and food provided. **$$**

Sheridan
Apple Tree Inn Motel
1552 Coffeen Avenue, WY 82801
Tel: 307-672-2428
Family-run, affordable motel at the foot of the Big Horn Mountains. Rooms feature free Wi-fi, refrigerator, microwave, cable TV, shaded play area and barbecue grill. There are also pet friendly rooms available. **$**
Trail's End Motel
2125 N. Main Street, WY 82801
Tel: 307-672-2477
www.trailsendmotelwy.com
A few blocks from Downtown, the Trail's End is an excellent budget choice. The spacious rooms are

spread over several buildings, and the complimentary breakfast is better than you'd get in many more expensive hotels. There's also a lively bar (nonsmoking) and a restaurant, both of which are popular with locals. **$**

Montana

Bozeman
Mountain Sky Guest Ranch
Box 1219, Emigrant, MT 59027
Tel: 406-333-4911
www.mtnsky.com
This secluded ranch, overlooking the lovely Paradise Valley about 30 miles (48km) from Yellowstone National Park in southwestern Montana, offers 30 rustic one to three bedroom cabins which date back to 1929; many have fireplaces and picture windows or porches. Amenities include horseback riding and instruction, children's programs, fishing, tennis, pool, and hot tub. **$$$**

Columbia Falls
Meadow Lake Resort
100 St Andrews Drive, MT 59912
Tel: 406-892-8700 or 800-689-6579
www.meadowlake.com
Luxurious resort comprising vacation homes, combos, and inn rooms. Amenities include golf course, tennis and fitness center, a children's program, indoor and outdoor pools, a spa, restaurant, and lounge. **$$–$$$**

Coram
Glacier General Store and Cabins
10630 Highway 2 E., MT 59912
Tel: 406-871-3746
www.glaciercabins.net
Nestled just off the highway in the mountains surrounding Glacier National Park, the four spacious and well-appointed cabins have kitchenettes, and large front porches. Chuck, the owner, knows the area well and is delighted to provide guests with tips. **$**

Helena
Sanders-Helena's Bed and Breakfast
328 N. Ewing, MT 59601
Tel: 406-442-3309
www.sandersbb.com
One of the area's most highly regarded inns has seven spacious rooms with private baths, brass beds, and large windows overlooking Helena and the mountains beyond. A full breakfast is served in the handsome wainscoted dining room. **$$**

Elkhorn Mountain Inn
1 Jackson Creek Road, Montana City, MT 59634
Tel: 406-442-6625
www.elkhorninn.com
Elk antlers adorn the lobby of this rustic inn outside Helena at the base of the Elkhorn mountains. Rooms and three suites are attractively furnished and affordable, and there is a recreation area with trails behind the property. **$–$$**

Kalispell
Kalispell Grand Hotel
100 Main Street, MT 59901
Tel: 406-755-8100
www.kalispellgrand.com
In this fine old historic downtown hotel, guests can take either the grand oak staircase or the "grand lift" to comfortably furnished modern rooms on the second and third floors. All rooms have private baths, and there are larger family rooms and some suites with jetted tubs. **$–$$**

Livingston
63 Ranch
PO Box 979, MT 59047
Tel: 406-222-0570
www.63ranch.com
Opened in 1863, the ranch became, in 1982, the first dude ranch in the state declared a National Historic Site. It's set on 2,000 acres (810 hectares) in the Absaroka Mountain, adjoining Gallatin National Forest and about 50 miles (81km) north of Yellowstone National Park. Amenities include horseback riding and instruction, fishing, overnight trips. The weekly rate includes use of a saddle horse for six days, entertainment, meals, and lodging. **$$$**

Missoula
Goldsmith's Bed and Breakfast Inn
809 E. Front, MT 59802
Tel: 406-728-1585
www.goldsmithsinn.com
Quiet seven-bedroom riverfront Victorian close to the University of Montana and the historic downtown. Rooms have individual amenities such as a fireplace, hot tub or deck. **$$**

America's Best Value Inn
420 W. Broadway, MT 59802
Tel: 406-728-4500
www.mountainvalleyinnmissoula.com
A simple, pleasant, and inexpensive motel in the center of Missoula, just a few blocks' walk or drive from the main downtown shops, restaurants, and bars. Amenities include covered parking, coffee throughout the day, afternoon cookies, wireless internet, and a small exercise room. **$**

Polson
Best Western KwaTaqNuk Resort
49708 Highway 93, MT 59860
Tel: 406-883-3636
www.kwataqnuk.com
This 112-room waterfront resort on Flathead Lake has many first-rate facilities including a casino with more than 250 slot machines, two pools, whirlpool, fine dining restaurant, and a gift shop. The marina offers cruises on the lake. **$$$**

St Ignatius
Sunset Motel
32670 Highway 93, MT 59865
Tel: 406-745-3900
www.stignatiussunsetmotel.com
Well placed in the beautiful Mission Valley, this eight-room hotel has spacious "rustic" rooms, each with a small fridge, microwave, and a large window overlooking the valley. **$**

Whitefish
Duck Inn Lodge
1305 Columbia Avenue, MT 59937
Tel: 406-862-3825
www.duckinn.com
This pretty 15-room lodge by the river is an easy walk to downtown. The rooms are individually decorated and many have fireplaces, patios, Jacuzzi, and deep soak tubs. Phone calls anywhere in the US and Canada are free. Breakfast is included. **$–$$**

Idaho

Bonners Ferry
Best Western Kootenai River Inn and Casino
7169 Plaza Street, ID 83805
Tel: 208-267-8511
www.kootenairiverinn.com
Owned and operated by the Kootenai Tribe of Idaho, the complex houses a casino, luxury spa, restaurant, and an inn with spacious rooms, all with private balconies and sweeping views. Amenities include an indoor pool, fitness center, laundry facilities, video arcade, and a sun deck. **$$**

Coeur d'Alene
The Coeur d'Alene
115 S. Second Street, ID 83814
Tel: 208-765-4000
www.cdaresort.com
Luxury resort on scenic Lake Coeur d'Alene. The many first-rate amenities

PRICE CATEGORIES
Price categories are based on the average cost of a double room for one night:
$ = under $110
$$ = $110–250
$$$ = more than $250

include the world's only floating moveable golf green. Close to fishing, skiing, and other area attractions. **$$–$$$**

Sandpoint
The Lodge at Sandpoint
41 Lakeshore Drive, Sagle,
ID 83860
Tel: 208-263-2211
www.lodgeatsandpoint.com
On the shores of Lake Pend d'Oreille, the 29-room lodge built in 2007 combines an old-fashioned wooden rustic look with all the modern comforts like hot tubs, internet, movie library, and a terrific bar and breakfast room. The great room has a roaring fire and magnificent views. There are also two rustic cabins and a small house for rent. **$–$$$**

Washington

Ellensburg
Cedars Inn and Suites
1390 N. Dollarway Road, WA 98926
Tel: 509-925-9844
www.i-90inn.com
Located just off I-90's Exit 106, and a five-minute drive from downtown, this remodeled lodging is the kind of motel you dream of finding – comfortable, bright, very clean, and with a friendly staff, good-sized rooms, and inexpensive. **$**

Forks
Kalaloch Lodge
157151 Highway 101,
WA 98331
Tel: 866-525-2562
www.olympicnationalpark.com/accommodations
The Olympic National Park's Kalaloch Lodge, perched on a bluff overlooking the Pacific Ocean 35 miles (56km) south of Forks, offers simple but charming accommodations, with a choice of suites in the main Lodge; rustic cabins, many with fabulous views, fireplaces and kitchenettes; and the secluded Seacrest Building, with private patios/balconies. There's a full-service restaurant and small shop, but with no internet and very poor cellphone reception, this is for those who really like getting away from it all. **$–$$$**

La Push
Quileute Oceanside Resort
PO Box 67, WA 98350
Tel: 360-374-5267
www.quileuteoceanside.com
On the grounds of the Quileute Indian Reservation, this magnificently sited, oceanfront resort complex encompasses 33 deluxe ocean

front cabins, two 14-unit motels, a campground, and a full-service RV park. No TV or cell-phone access. **$$**

Leavenworth
Alpenrose Inn
500 Alpine Place, WA 98826
Tel: 509-548-3000
www.alpenroseinn.com
Intimate Bavarian-style B&B inn in scenic alpine setting. **$$**

Haus Rohrbach Pension
12882 Ranger Road, WA 98826
Tel: 509-548-7024
www.hausrohrbach.com
Cozy and convivial European-style pension with 10 rooms and suites perched high on a hill with views across the valley. Outdoor pool, year-round spa, and full breakfast. **$–$$**

Port Angeles
Red Lion Hotel
221 N. Lincoln Street,
WA 98362
Tel: 360-452-9215
www.redlion.rdln.com
On the shore of Hollywood Beach and overlooking the Strait of Juan de Fuca, the hotel has 186 room and suites, many with balconies overlooking the harbor. All have microwaves, refrigerators, coffeemakers, and free Wi-fi. Amenities include an outdoor pool, whirlpool, and fitness center. Breakfast buffet included; restaurant on premises. **$$**

Port Townsend
Palace Hotel
1004 Water Street, WA 98368
Tel: 360-385-0773
or 800-962-0741
www.palacehotelpt.com
A nicely restored historic downtown edifice, which was built by a retired sea captain in 1889. It has been decorated in original Victorian style. Amenities include free wireless internet, refrigerators and microwaves, and off-street private parking. **$–$$**

The Tides Inn
1807 Water Street, WA 98368
Tel: 360-385-0595
www.tides-inn.com
Charming hotel on the waterfront overlooking the beach and the bay, with view of the Cascades and Olympic Mountains. Several rooms have private Jacuzzis on the decks. **$–$$$**

Quinault
Lake Quinault Lodge
345 S. Shore Road,
WA 98575
Tel: 360-288-2900
www.visitlakequinault.com

Right on the shores of Lake Quinault and surrounded by the magnificent forests of Olympic National Park, the 1926 Lake Quinault Lodge offers a range of simple but comfortable accommodations aimed at those who come here to hike the trails and enjoy the scenery and the wildlife. The smart Roosevelt Restaurant is named for FDR who was staying here in 1937 when the idea of creating this National Park was suggested over lunch. **$$–$$$**

Seattle
Chelsea Station Inn
4915 Linden Avenue N., WA 98103
Tel: 206-547-6077
www.chelseastationinn.com
Close to the Woodland Park Zoo and Green Lake Park, this B&B has four elegant suites, all with master bedrooms, living rooms, dining rooms, kitchenettes stocked with local goodies, and luxurious baths. Breakfast is delivered to the suites each morning. **$$**

The Edgewater Hotel
Pier 67, 2411 Alaskan Way,
WA 98121
Tel: 206-728-7000
www.edgewaterhotel.com
Seattle's only luxury downtown waterfront hotel, with an atrium lobby, stone fireplaces, and mountain lodge decor. The highly regarded restaurant, Six Seven, features northwestern cuisine and has a lovely outdoor deck overlooking the water. Rates vary depending on water- or city-view rooms; the water view units tend to be quieter. **$$–$$$**

Inn At The Market
Pike Place Market, 86 Pine Street, WA 98101
Tel: 206-443-3600
www.innatthemarket.com
In Pike Place Market with splendid views of Elliott Bay, the hotel is surrounded by trendy shops, spa, and restaurants. The 70 rooms and suites have double-paned floor-to-ceiling bay windows that open, spacious bathrooms and free Wi-fi. **$$–$$$**

Shafer-Baillie Mansion
907 14th Avenue E., WA 98112
Tel: 206-322-4654 or
800-985-4654
www.sbmansion.com
Antique-furnished B&B in a Tudor-Revival mansion, set in spacious grounds on Millionaire's Row in Seattle's Capitol Hill. The eight second- and third-floor guest rooms and suites have rich oak and mahogany woodwork, antique and reproduction furniture, and Oriental rugs. Gourmet breakfast is included. **$$**

CENTRAL ROUTE

Washington, DC

The Channel Inn
650 Water Street SW, DC 20024
Tel: 202-554-2400
www.channelinn.com
Washington's only waterfront hotel, close to the marina restaurants, with large and simple but comfortable rooms. Amenities: good seafood restaurant, coffee shop, and outdoor pool, plus the Arena Stage, golf course, indoor and outdoor tennis courts are close by. **$$**

Liaison Capitol Hill
415 New Jersey Avenue NW, DC 20001
Tel: 202-638-1616
www.affinia.com
Great find; an upscale, boutique hotel with modern, sleek furnishings and around the corner from Capitol Hill. Large hotel (345 rooms), but very attentive staff; valet parking in the adjacent garage for about $50/ night. Amenities include "experience kits" -- for walking tours, yoga, and BYOB guidebook. Dog friendly; it has a room service menu for Fido. **$$**

Phoenix Park Hotel
520 N. Capitol Street NW, DC 20001
Tel: 202-638-6900 or 800-824-5419
www.phoenixparkhotel.com
Enter the square red-brick building and enter a 19th century Irish country estate. Rooms are small, but furnished with deep comforters, Irish linens, and turndown service. The popular Dubliner Pub can be reached through the lobby. **$$**

Virginia

Floyd
Hotel Floyd
120 Wilson Drive, WA 24091
Tel: 540-745-6080
www.hotelfloyd.com
A country-comfortable hotel in the bluegrass-echoing town near the Blue Ridge Highway. Solar and geo-thermal powered; all rooms are filled with locally made furniture and artwork. Pet friendly suite. **$–$$**

Lexington
Historic Country Inns
11 N. Main Street, VA 24450
Tel: 877-283-9680
www.lexingtonhistoricinns.com
This firm runs three inns in the area: two in the Lexington Historic District – the Alexander Withrow House and McCampbell Inn – and Maple Hall 6 miles (9km) to the north on 56 acres (22 hectares). All inns feature fireplaces, fine dining, trails, and pool. **$$**

Luray
Mayneview B&B and Greentree Inn
439 Mechanic Street, VA 22835
Tel: 540-743-7921
www.mayneview.com
The Mayneview. a former hunting lodge, was built by one of the discoverers of the Luray Caverns and was used as a stop on the Underground Railroad toward the end of the Civil War. Savor mountain views from the hot tub on the deck. Three of the five rooms have fireplaces. Located in 3 acres (1.2 hectares) of grounds with fine mountain views. The Greentree Inn is more private with three guest rooms, each with a fireplace, and more mountain views. **$–$$**

New Market
Blue Ridge Inn
2251 Old Valley Pike, VA 22844
Tel: 540-740-4136
www.blueridgeinn.com
Pleasant with cable TV and refrigerators. Set in 4 acres (1.6 hectares) of grounds, with a picnic area, barbecue, and play area. **$**

Roanoke
Hotel Roanoke and Conference Center
110 Shenandoah Avenue, VA 24016
Tel: 540-985-5900
www.hotelroanoke.com
Built in 1882, this fully restored, Tudor-style building overlooks Roanoke's lively downtown. All rooms have super plush bedding and Crabtree & Evelyn products. Allergy-free rooms are available. Very popular for meetings and conventions.

Days Inn Civic Center
601 Orange Avenue, DC 24016
Tel: 540-342-4551
www.daysinn.com/roanoke
Clean, large, standard rooms; convenient to the civic center and a quick trip to downtown. Big clean pool and excellent rates. $ Rates at the Days Inn Airport/I-81 are about $40/ night higher. **$$**

Skyline Drive
Skyland Resort; Big Meadow Lodge
Tel: 866-875-8456
www.nationalparkreservations.com
Two rustic lodges and several cabins deep in the park. TVs in the rooms, but no phones or internet (it is available in the lobbies). At Skyland, the rooms all have balconies overlooking the forest. **$–$$**

Staunton
Stonewall Jackson Hotel
24 S. Market Street,
VA 24401
Tel: 540-885-4848
www.stonewalljacksonhotel.com
Originally built in 1924, the hotel is a member of the Historic Hotels of America, beautifully restored and perfectly situated. Blackfriars Playhouse is next door and the rest of the town's attractions are around the corner. **$$**

North Carolina

Asheville
Asheville
Grove Park Inn Resort
Grove Park Inn
290 Macon Avenue,
NC 28804
Tel: 800-438-5800
www.groveparkinn.com
Built in 1913, this classic Grand Hotel exudes Southern charm in an incredibly beautiful mountainside setting overlooking Asheville. Huge – 512 rooms – with over a dozen themed suites. All the usual resort activities from golf and tennis to a full-service spa and fine dining are available. **$$$**

Cherokee
Comfort Suites
1223 Tsagli Boulevard,
NC 28719
Tel: 828-497-3500
www.comfortsuites.com/hotel-cherokee
Basic rooms, but within walking distance of the river, free hot breakfast (continental breakfast to-go available), microwave and fridge in all rooms, a mile from the Park entrance and Blue Ridge Parkway. Outdoor pool. Guest laundry. **$**

Harrah's
777 Casino Drive,
NC 28719
Tel: 828-497-7777
www.harrahscherokee.com
Luxury hotel with over 1,000 spacious, very comfortable rooms catering to the casino gamers far more than to those visiting for hiking in the mountains or discovering the Cherokee culture. **$$–$$$**

PRICE CATEGORIES

Price categories are based on the average cost of a double room for one night:
$ = under $110
$$ = $110–250
$$$ = more than $250

Tennessee

Dandridge
Mountain Harbor Inn
1199 Highway 139, IN 37725
Tel: 865-397-1313 or 877-379-1313
www.mountainharborinn.com
Twelve romantically themed suites and a getaway cabin, each with a view of the amazingly beautiful Lake Douglas. Rate includes breakfast buffet, intimate candlelit dessert, and sunset cruise. Jet ski and boat rental available. **$$–$$$**

Knoxville
Holiday Inn Downtown World's Fair Park
525 Henley Street, TN 37902
Tel: 865-522-2800
www.holidayinn.com
Well-appointed, well-situated hotel with free, secure underground parking, large indoor pool, hot tub, well-equipped fitness room, and guest laundry. Across the street from World's Fair Park, site of festivals and outdoor concerts. Walking distance to museums, Market Square.
Hotel St Oliver
407 Union Avenue, TN 37902
Tel: 865-521-0050
www.theoliverhotel.com
Located on Market Square in the centre of Downtown, the hotel features period furniture and antiques. Built in 1876 to serve as a bakery, it's been update and is now an exclusive boutique hotel with 28 rooms done up in comfortable chic Southern style with locally handmade furniture and original art. The Library Lounge is the gathering place for Knoxville's young professionals. **$$**

Memphis
Heartbreak Hotel
3677 Elvis Presley Boulevard, TN 38116
Tel: 901-332-1000
www.elvis.com/epheartbreakhotel
For the true Elvis aficionado, the hotel is within a sound-check of Graceland. Each room has 1950s-inspired furnishings with photos of The King and other Elvis touches. After touring the mansion and all of the exhibits in the complex, relax in the Jungle Room Lounge. **$$**
The Peabody
149 Union Avenue, TN 38103
Tel: 901-529-4000
www.peabodymemphis.com
Charming, elegant, and legendary, the rooms reflect historic Southern opulent ambiance. Top-rated by every group that rates hotels. **$$$**
River Inn at Harbor Town
50 Harbor Town Square, TN 38103

Tel: 901-260-3333
www.riverinnmemphis.com
This inviting boutique inn overlooking trails along the Mississippi greenbelt Mud Island feels miles from busy downtown Memphis. Windows in the 28 rooms and suites frame stunning sunsets over the Mississippi and include walnut armoires, floaty four-poster beds, desks, and Wi-fi. Guests are spoiled with champagne on arrival, homemade truffles, and port before bed, hot beverages in library sitting areas. Gourmet, silver-service breakfasts are included in the room rate. **$$$**
Sleep Inn at Court Square
40 North Front Street, TN 38103
Tel: 901-522-9705
www.sleepinn.com
Better than average furnishings and useful amenities for a budget chain in a location where most lodgings are high-end in luxury and price. Close to both I-40 and I-55, all rooms have a fridge and microwave; there's a guest laundry. The trolley that circuits through the tourist areas stops just outside. Ask for a river view room. **$**

Nashville
Best Western Convention Center
711 Union Street, TN 37219
Tel: 615-242-4311 or 800-657-6910
www.bestwestern.com
Best price in the most popular tourist area. About 10 minutes' walk to the Country Music Hall of Fame, Ryman Auditorium, Frist Center for the Arts. Clean rooms with nice details. Breakfast, clean guest laundry, fitness center, NY-style deli on site. **$–$$**
Daisy Hill Bed and Breakfast
2816 Blair Boulevard, TN 37212
Tel: 615-297-9795 or 800-239-1135
www.daisyhillbedandbreakfast.com
Tudor Revival-style house with three guestrooms with bathrooms. Beautifully decorated, with a communal living room, dining room, library, sunroom, porch, and garden. Full breakfast served. No children under 12. **$–$$**
The Hermitage Hotel
231 Sixth Avenue N., TN 37219
Tel: 615-244-3121; 888-888-9414
www.thehermitagehotel.com
Five-star elegance in a century-old hotel with all of the architectural glory of that age. Rooms are larger than most apartments, with marble bathrooms, down-filled duvets, and turn-down service. **$$$**
Millenium Maxwell House Hotel
2025 Rose Parks Boulevard, TN 37228
Tel: 615-259-4343
www.milleniumhotels.com
The three-star property is Nashville's

only music-themed hotel: the lobby and halls are filled with framed posters and pictures of stars, Country Music Television is on your TV when you arrive in your room. Outside of the downtown area, with a panoramic view of the skyline. Free parking and free shuttle into town. **$–$$**

Arkansas

Fort Smith
Holiday Inn City Center
700 Rogers Avenue, TN 72901
Tel: 479-783-1000
www.holidayinn.com
A five-story indoor waterfall and atrium are the features of this well-placed hotel, located next to the civic center and within a few steps of the National Historic Site and Museum of History. Spacious rooms, and excellent fitness center with indoor heated pool, sauna, and exercise equipment. **$–$$**

Hot Springs
The Arlington Resort Hotel and Spa
239 Central Avenue, AR 71901
Tel: 501-623-7771
www.arlingtonhotel.com
This full-service resort has been pampering visitors since 1875; previous guests include Al Capone. Facilities include an on-premises bathhouse with thermal water baths and massages (book well in advance!), three restaurants and beauty salon. **$–$$**
Wildwood 1884 B&B Inn
808 Park Avenue, AR 71901
Tel: 501-624-4267
www.wildwood1884.com
Carefully restored 1884 Queen Anne mansion with original woodwork, antiques, and stained glass. Some of the five rooms have porches. Ideal for couples due to the romantic focus. **$$**

Little Rock
Capital Hotel
Louisiana and Markham streets, AR 72201
Tel: 501-374-7474
www.capitalhotel.com
Beautiful Victorian hotel with stained glass skylight and grand staircase in the lobby, opulent rooms with regal furnishings catering to every creature comfort, and an attentive staff. **$$$**
The Empress of Little Rock
2120 S. Louisiana Street,
AR 72206
Tel: 501-374-7966
www.theempress.com
Designed for romance and relaxation, SPA suites with hydro-massage showers and aromatherapy. Elegant silver service breakfast for guests is served in the sun-filled dining room. **$$–$$$**

Rosemont B&B
515 W. 15th Street, AR 72202
Tel: 501-374-7456
www.rosemontoflittlerock.com
Comfortable, unfussy, en suite
Victorian rooms, most with fireplaces
or Jacuzzis in a 19th century
farmhouse in the Governor's Mansion
historic district. Swing and chairs on
the porch, garden, library. Vegetarian,
diabetic, and lactose-intolerant guests
catered for at breakfast. **$–$$**

Mount Magazine State Park Lodge
Route 309, Paris, AR 72855
Tel: 479-963-8502 or 877-MMLODGE
Just 200ft (61 meters) below the
summit of the highest peak in
Arkansas, each of the 60 rooms has
a balcony overlooking the magnificent
view of the Petit Jean River Valley and
Blue Mountain Lake. There are also 13
cabins scattered in the woods. Guests
enjoy an indoor pool also overlooking
the valley; there are several patios with
rockers and chairs, and nature trails.
The restaurant has the view, too. **$$**

Oklahoma

Chandler
Lincoln Motel
740 E. First Street, OK 74834
Tel: 405-258-0200
You can't miss this vintage motor
court, with its nicely landscaped
grounds, neon sign, and series of
buildings along a sweeping driveway.
The small rooms are two to a building
and are rather worn, but under the
supervision of friendly new owners,
are slowly being upgraded. All of the
rooms have fridges, TVs, and air-
conditioning. **$**

Miami
Buffalo Run Hotel
1366 US 69, OK 74834
Tel: 918-542-2900
www.buffalorunhotel.com
With its warm hardwood floors and
elegant stone fireplace in the lobby,
this attractive casino hotel owned
by the Peoria Tribe of Oklahoma, a
confederation of Kaskaskia, Peoria,
Piankesaw and Wea tribes, is a
fantastic value. The 100 rooms have
clean, relaxing decor and include
flat-screen TVs, desks, fridges,
microwaves, and free Wi-fi. Expanded
continental breakfast, pool, onsite
coffee shop and steakhouse. Concerts
and gaming in next-door casino. **$**

Oklahoma City
Colcord Hotel
15 N. Robinson Avenue, OK 73102
Tel: 405-601-4300
www.colcordhotel.com

This boutique hotel occupies a
restored 1910 Art Deco skyscraper,
a former office building adjoining
trendy Bricktown. Hushed, stylish,
window-wrapped rooms and suites
are party-sized, with sofas, marble
bathrooms, soaking tubs, 32in (81cm)
LCD TVs, and Wi-fi. There is also a gym
and a business center. The ground-
floor restaurant, Flint, offers delicious
meals in a stylish atmosphere,
including breakfast. **$$**

Grandison Inn at Maney Park
1200 N. Shartel, OK 73103
Tel: 405-232-8778
www.grandisoninn.com
Well-preserved, three-storey Victorian
B&B. Eight rooms, each with their
own bathroom, cable TV, and DVD
player. Help yourself to drinks and
home-baked dessert from the butler's
pantry. **$$**

Skirvin Hilton
1 Park Avenue, OK 73102
Tel: 405-272-3040
www.skirvinhilton.com
This restored 1911 *grande dame*
soars above downtown OKC in stately
splendor. Its 225 elegant rooms and
rotunda suites beckon weary business
travelers, with oak desks, large flat-
screens, free Wi-fi, huge, fluffy beds,
marble bathrooms, and coffeemakers.
The soaring lobby has historic photos
on the walls and stylish billowy
curtains. Park Avenue Grill offers good
Southwestern food and a piano bar.
$$–$$$

Stroud
Skyliner Motel
717 W. Main Street, OK 74078
Tel: 918-968-9556
This 1950 motel will please avid
66ers (you know who you are!), with its
vintage ambiance, neon sign, personal
touches, and what-you-see-is-what-
you-get vibe. An added bonus: it's
within walking distance of the famous
Rock Café. **$**

Tulsa
Campbell Hotel
2636 E. 11th Street, OK 74104
Tel: 918-744-5500
www.campbellhotel.com
This Route 66 boutique lodging
combines a lavishly renovated,
shopfront, boarding house setting,
across the road from the famous
Bama Pie Factory near UT, with
24 unique, artist-designed rooms
(the Route 66 room is, of course,
first choice). From the suitcases on
the walls in the lobby and vintage
roadsters in the corner showroom
(possible site of a future restaurant)
to the spa and sophisticated drinks

lounge, the Campbell exudes the
glamour but human scale of the
Mother Road. **$$**

Hotel Ambassador
1324 S. Main Street, OK 74119
Tel: 918-587-8200
www.tulsa.ambassadorhotelcollection.com
Originally built as accommodation for
oil barons while they waited for their
mansions to be built, this ornate and
comfortable hotel in the upmarket
Utica Square area offers spacious
rooms with Italian marble bathrooms.
Restaurant, library, and extensive
array of amenities. **$$**

Hotel Mayo
115 West Fifth Street, OK 74103
Tel: 918-582-6296
www.themayohotel.com
This 1925 jewel hopes to recapture
its glory days with an ambitious
renovation that reopened the long-
shuttered hotel. Rooms are rather
small and gloomy, and some street
noise does get in, but are luxuriously
kitted out, with enormous flat-screen
TVs and "green" features, like silky
Tencel sheets on cloud-soft beds. The
Art Deco lobby, rooftop bar, and onsite
Café Topeca, serving crepes, pastries,
and their own delicious, seed-to-cup
coffee, alone merit a visit. **$**

Vinita
Park Hills Motel and RV Park
Highway 60/66 2 miles west of Vinita, OK
74301
Tel: 918-256-5511
http://myweb.cableone.net/parkhills/
This modest but attractive motel
on the Mother Road has 21 clean,
standard-issue rooms, with A/C,
fridge, microwave, and cable TV. Large
fishing pond. **$**

Weatherford
**Best Western Plus Mark Motor
Hotel**
525 E. Main Street, OK 73096
Tel: 580-772-3325
www.bestwestern.com
This Best Western on Route 66 really
is a "plus," a welcome overnight stop
for weary travelers seeking friendly,
efficient TLC. Guest rooms define the
term "spotless," and include cable TV,
Wi-fi, fridge, microwave, coffeemaker,
quality bath amenities, and comfy
armchairs. Rate includes breakfast
in the adjoining coffee shop. Outdoor
pool. **$**

PRICE CATEGORIES

Price categories are based on the average
cost of a double room for one night:
$ = under $110
$$ = $110–250
$$$ = more than $250

Classic Route 66 motel sign, Flagstaff, Arizona.

Texas

Amarillo

Ashmore Inn and Suites
2301 I-40 E., Exit 72A, TX 79104
Tel: 806-374-0033
www.ashmoresuites-amarillo.com
This above-average hotel north of the interstate features all the usual room facilities, plus guest laundry, indoor pool, fitness center, and complimentary afternoon buffet and hot breakfast, all at a reasonable rate. **$**

Big Texan Motel
7701 I-40E, TX 79118
Tel: 806-372-5000
www.bigtexan.com/motel
This hokey Old West–themed motel, next to I-40 (bring earplugs) and the famed 66 roadside attraction Steak Ranch, comes complete with a false-front façade, but the shuttered rooms have a surprisingly attractive Texas feel, with good amenities, such as fridge, microwave, and coffeemaker, and a bathroom entered via café doors. Texas-shaped outdoor pool. **$**

Canyon

Buffalo Inn
300 23rd Street, TX 79015
Tel: 806-655-2124
This budget-conscious inn has run-of-the-mill rooms with A/C and Wi-fi near the Panhandle-Plains Historical Museum. There's a restaurant nearby. **$**

Shamrock

Shamrock North Holiday Inn Express
101 East 13th Street, TX 79079
Tel: 877 865 6578
www.hiexpress.com
The 65 rooms and suites at this Holiday Inn Express are nicely appointed and offer a comfortable night's stay to explore quaint Shamrock. Rooms include fridge, microwave, coffeemaker, cable TV, free Wi-fi. **$**

New Mexico

Albuquerque

Hi Way House
3200 Central SE, NM 87106
Tel: 505-268-3971
www.hiwayhousemotel.com
One of the last in the old Hi Way House chain founded in Phoenix in 1956 and seen along Route 66, this motel is in the popular Nob Hill district near UNM on Central (66), where you'll find a lot of good restaurants and shops. **$**

Los Poblanos Historic Inn and Cultural Center
4803 Rio Grande Boulevard NW, NM 87107
Tel: 505-344-9297
www.lospoblanos.com
This stunning 26-acre (10.5-hectare) estate was designed by Santa Fe-style architect John Gaw Meem for Congresswoman Ruth Hanna McCormick in 1934. The house is filled with *santos* and has six guestrooms with toiletries made from lavender grown on the onsite organic farm. The cultural center integrates art by Peter Hurd and Gustave Baumann, and peacocks stroll velvet lawns. **$$$**

Algodones

Hacienda Vargas Bed and Breakfast
1431 Highway 313 (El Camino Real), Algodones, NM 87001
Tel: 505-867-9115
www.haciendavargas.com
Choose from seven antique-filled Southwest-style rooms in this historic adobe on pre-1937 Route 66. Rooms have fireplaces, private entrances, and Jacuzzis. The Peña Suite, named for Amado Pena, favorite artist of the inn's original owner, displays the original 150-year-old wall through a glass casing called a "truth window." Beautifully landscaped. Gourmet breakfast. **$$**

Gallup

El Rancho Hotel and Motel
1000 E. Highway 66, NM 87301
Tel: 505-863-9311

www.elranchohotel.com
You'll feel like a Hollywood star in the comfortable rooms at this historic hotel. There's a variety of rooms and suites, some with balconies or kitchenettes, each decorated with signature Southwestern artwork. Hotel amenities include fitness room, pool, business center. It has a gift shop selling Native American arts and crafts and an old-fashioned coffee shop. **$–$$**

Las Vegas

Plaza Hotel
230 Old Town Plaza, NM 87701
Tel: 505-425-3591
www.plazahotel-nm.com
This gracious Victorian-era brick hotel overlooks the Old Town Plaza and is a popular destination. It has an attractive restaurant serving a Sunday brunch with live classical guitar, as well as good fine dining. The saloon is a good place to meet the locals. **$–$$**

Santa Fe

El Rey Inn
1862 Cerrillos Road, NM 87505
Tel: 505-982-1931
www.elreyinnsantafe.com
Set in lovely gardens, this 1930s motor court inn on the old Route 66 offers traditional and deluxe rooms, and Southwestern suites with fireplaces and kitchenettes. Amenities include pool, whirlpool, sauna, and complimentary continental breakfast. **$–$$**

Hotel Santa Fe
1501 Paseo De Peralta, NM 87501
Tel: 505-982-1200
www.hotelsantafe.com
Hotel Santa Fe is Santa Fe's only Native American–owned hotel (Picuris Pueblo) and is in the heart of the popular Railyard district. Stunning artworks by famed Apache sculptor Allan Houser and other artisans decorate the rooms and corridors, and Southwest archeology talks and Native American flute music take place in the lobby area. Amaya Restaurant specializes in Modern Native American cuisine; its prix-fixe menu is an exceptional value. **$$–$$$**

La Fonda Santa Fe
100 E. San Francisco Street, NM 87501
Tel: 505-982-5511
www.lafondasantafe.com
The 18th-century "Inn at the End of the Trail" was rebuilt in 1919 in the Pueblo Revival style that defines Santa Fe, and its rooms feature hand-painted wooden furniture and New Mexican art; some have fireplaces and balconies. Amenities include bars and restaurants, spa, fitness center, outdoor hot tub, heated swimming pool, and free Wi-fi. **$$–$$$**

Hotel St Francis
210 Don Gaspar Avenue, NM 87501
Tel: 505-983-5700
www.hotelstfrancis.com
This attractive Downtown boutique hotel, in a landmark building dating from the 1920s across the street from Café Pasqual's, has been completely renovated. It now exudes a stripped-down monastic calm befitting its name, but still offers a rich feast of food, drink, and elegance. **$$–$$$**

Tucumcari
Blue Swallow Motel
815 E. Route 66 Boulevard, NM 88401
Tel: 575-461-9849
www.blueswallowmotel.com
This old motor court motel and its landmark neon sign with signature blue swallow is still a popular stop on old Route 66. The garages are intact, but small rooms are now pretty worn. Highly motivated new owners are gradually upgrading them, with plush beds and sheets, antiques, and other improvements. **$**

Motel Safari
722 E. Route 66 Boulevard, NM 88401
Tel: 575-461-1048
Lovingly cared-for landmark motel on Route 66, opposite the Blue Swallow (see above). Rooms are clean and comfortable, with period lamps and furniture mixed with modern amenities. **$**

Arizona

Flagstaff
Hotel Monte Vista
100 N. San Francisco, AZ 86001
Tel: 928-779-6971
www.hotelmontevista.com

Wigwam Motel on Route 66 in Holbrook, Arizona.

This reasonably priced but a little threadbare 1926 hotel has 50 rooms and suites on four floors, with beautiful views over Flagstaff. Rooms are attractively furnished with antiques, and some are named celebrity guests who have stayed here. There's an excellent Thai restaurant in the former coffee shop downstairs, as well as a terrific local bar. **$–$$**

The Weatherford Hotel
23 N. Leroux Street, AZ 86001
Tel: 928-779-1919
www.weatherfordhotel.com
This 1899 hotel built of local sandstone by John Weatherford reflects Flagstaff's pioneer origins. Western author Zane Grey wrote novels In the turret room upstairs In 1908 (reopened ballroom upstairs is now named for him). Rooms are charmingly decorated in period style, and Charly's Pub downstairs is a perennial favorite. **$–$$**

Holbrook
Wigwam Motel
811 W. Hopi Drive, AZ 86025
Tel: 928-524-3048
Time your journey for an overnight stop in Holbrook and head for the Wigwam Motel. A night in a 1950s concrete tepee is a quintessential Route 66 experience. **$**

Jerome
Mile High Inn
309 N. Main Street, AZ 86331
Tel: 928-634-5094
www.jeromemilehighinn.com
A small, friendly inn occupying the 1899 Frontier-style Clinksdale Building, its compact rooms are attractively furnished with period antiques. There's relaxed dining downstairs at the Mile High Grill. **$–$$**

Peach Springs
Hualapai Lodge
900 Route 66, AZ 86434
Tel: 928-769-2230
www.grandcanyonwest.com/lodge
This attractive lodge is the only accommodation on the Hualapai Reservation, north of Kingman, and the main jumping-off point for tours of the reservation, river running trips, and Grand Canyon West's famous Sky Walk. It has an attractive, airy lobby with stone fireplace, a restaurant serving Native foods, and 60 pleasant rooms. Saltwater pool. Wi-fi. **$**

Sedona
Adobe Village Graham Inn
150 Canyon Circle Drive, AZ 86351
Tel: 928-284-1425
www.adobevillagegrahaminn.com
A stylishly furnished inn commanding spectacular views of the red rocks. In addition to the six deluxe guest rooms, there are four romantic *casitas* (cottages) with waterfall showers, bathroom fireplaces, and breadmakers. Includes early morning coffee, full breakfast, afternoon refreshments, and evening snacks. **$$–$$$**

Williams
Grand Canyon Railway Hotel
233 N. Grand Canyon Boulevard, AZ 86046
Tel: 928-773-1976
www.thetrain.com/grand-canyon-railway-hotel-williams-az-5686.html
Designed to resemble the historic Fray Marcos Hotel in the old train depot, this smart hotel has comfortable, classic rooms and suites with Southwestern accents. **$$**

Winslow
La Posada Hotel
303 E. Second Street, AZ 86047
Tel: 928-289-4366
www.laposada.org
This 1929 hotel was the last designed by famed Grand Canyon architect Mary Colter and built by the Fred Harvey Company for the Santa Fe Railway. Rooms are named after the many famous guests who stayed here in its heyday and are attractively furnished in Southwestern style (but avoid the railroad side; it can get a bit noisy). The Turquoise Room offers renowned dining using local foods. **$–$$**

PRICE CATEGORIES

Price categories are based on the average cost of a double room for one night:
$ = under $110
$$ = $110–250
$$$ = more than $250

Los Angeles
Bayside Hotel
2001 Ocean Avenue, Santa Monica, CA 90405
Tel: 310-396-6000
www.baysidehotel.com
Just across from the beach and minutes from the pier, with plush beds, flat-screen TVs, and a choice of ocean view, courtyard or economy rooms. Paid parking on first-come/first-served basis. **$$–$$$**

Hotel Oceana
849 Ocean Avenue, Santa Monica, CA 90403
Tel: 310-393-0486
www.hoteloceana.com
Oceanfront boutique hotel offers 63 elegantly appointed and chic rooms and suites. Meals are served in the sunroom or al fresco in the courtyard by the pool **$$$**

Los Angeles Marriott Downtown
333 S. Figueroa Street, CA 90071
Tel: 213-617-1133
www.marriott.com
Four hundred rooms and 69 suites with floor to ceiling windows providing panoramic city views. Executive floor, health club, business center, airport bus service, restaurants, pool, courtesy coffee, babysitting, foreign currency exchange. Fee for parking and in-room internet. **$$$**

O Hotel
819 S. Flower Street, CA 90017
Tel: 213-623-9904

www.ohotelgroup.com
Set in a historic 1920s building, the O is the first urban boutique hotel in downtown LA's financial district. The 67 rooms are well appointed in contemporary style with complimentary internet, plasma TVs, and ergonomic designer chairs. A daily $12 service fee includes deluxe continental breakfast, membership to Gold's Gym, and other amenities. **$$**

Residence Inn Santa Clarita
25320 The Old Road, CA 91381
Tel: 661-290-2800
www.residenceinn.com
Ninety suites, close to Six Flags Magic Mountain, 20 miles (33km) to Downtown LA. Free breakfast, room service, pool, exercise room, full kitchens, some fireplaces. **$$**

Sunset Tower Hotel
8358 Sunset Boulevard, West Hollywood, CA 90069
Tel: 323-654-7100
www.sunsettowerhotel.com
Art Deco landmark, and one-time home of such stars as Harlow, Gable, Monroe, and Flynn. Luxury rooms with period features and stylish lobby, bar, and restaurant, but it's the stunning rooftop pool that will take your breath away. **$$$**

Venice Beach House
15 30th Avenue, Venice, CA 90291
Tel: 310-823-1966
www.venicebeachhouse.com
Pretty, ivy-covered 1911 B&B in the heart of town and near the beach has

nine rooms with Wi-fi and continental breakfast; some share bathrooms. **$$–$$$**

Needles
Best Western Colorado River Inn
2371 W. Broadway, CA 92363
Tel: 760-326-4552
www.bestwestern.com
Spacious rooms and mini suites with large-screen TVs, microwaves, and refrigerators. Outdoor pool, sauna, and Jacuzzi area. Full breakfast at adjacent restaurant. **$**

San Bernardino
Hilton San Bernardino
285 E. Hospitality Lane, CA 92408
Tel: 909-889-0133
www.hilton.com
Spacious and comfortable guest rooms with high speed internet access and work desks; complimentary business center, heated outdoor pool with whirlpool, and a 24-hour fitness center. Restaurant/grill/bar on site. **$–$$$**

Wigwam Motel
2728 W. Foothill Boulevard, CA 92410
Tel: 909-875-3005
www.wigwammotel.com
The seventh and last of the Wigwam Motel chain, these Route 66 landmark tepees have wagon wheel headboards and checkered bedspreads, but have been updated with free internet, refrigerators, and TV. Pool and barbecue grill on site. **$**

SOUTHERN ROUTE

Atlanta
Atlanta Marriott Marquis
265 Peachtree Center Avenue, GA 30303
Tel: 888-855-5701
www.marriott.com
This contemporary downtown landmark hotel designed by architect John Portman is a beauty: the atrium lobby, with the 50ft (15-meter) color-changing "sail" of its iconic cocktail bar Pulse, has a volume of 9.5 million cu ft (269,010 cu meters), and visitors feel they've entered the rib cage of some mythical beast. The upgraded suites and rooms all have spectacular city views. The high-end amenities include in-room large work spaces and granite-top counters in bathrooms. **$$$**

Beverly Hills Inn
65 Sheridan Drive NE, GA 30305
Tel: 404-233-8520
www.beverlyhillsinn.com

This B&B – Atlanta's first – is in a 1929 building in ritzy Buckhead. It's British-owned and filled with antiques. Some of the 18 roomy suites have canopy beds; all have kitchenettes, making this a good choice for longer stays. Breakfast in the lovely conservatory is Expanded Continental. Pets with deposit. **$$**

Glenn Hotel
110 Marietta Street NW, GA 30303
Tel: 404-521-2250
www.glennhotel.com
Located in a converted 1923 building, next to CNN Center, the Glenn is Atlanta's first downtown boutique hotel. With its see-and-be-seen lobby bar and restaurant and rooftop Sky Lounge, dark night-club feel, and young, casual staff, it's aimed squarely at an urban hip crowd. An old-fashioned lift leads to low-lit corridors that feel more like art installations than thoroughfares. Rooms are tiny

but well planned with large windows, built-in wardrobes, desks, and lighting, and bathrooms with rain-flow showerheads. Onsite parking is a big selling point. **$$**

Westin Peachtree Plaza
210 Peachtree Street, GA 30303
Tel: 404-659-1400
www.starwoodhotels.com/westin
With its 1,068 pie-shaped rooms, this 73-story, circular high rise is an Atlanta landmark, and the tallest hotel in America to date. Designed by famed architect John Portman, the structure is a must-see for its liberal use of glass, in rooms and in the domed pool. Small pets allowed. **$$$**

Juliette
Jarrell 1920 House
Jarrell Plantation State Historic Site, 715 Jarrell Plantation Road, GA 31046
Tel: 478-986-3972
www.jarrellhouse.com

A unique backwoods experience in rural Georgia, this atmospheric bed-and-breakfast is housed in a listed structure built from heart-pine lumber milled on the Jarrell family plantation. Two bedrooms have adjoining bathrooms, TVs, and ceiling fans; one room has an antique queen and the other two antique double beds. Breakfast buffet. **$$**

Macon
1842 Inn
353 College Street, GA 31201
Tel: 912-741-1842
www.1842inn.com
This European B&B, a ravishing beauty even among Macon's many historic antebellum mansions, celebrates the finer things in life. Split between the main house and adjoining 1900 Victorian building, the 21 rooms all retain their historic elements but also have wireless internet, push-button gas fireplaces, and whirlpool baths. The warm welcome from long-serving staff includes proper afternoon tea, a substantial happy-hour spread of appetizers complete with mint juleps, and elegant gourmet breakfasts. You can walk to Hay House from here. **$$$**

Best Western-Riverside
2400 Riverside Drive, GA 31204
Tel: 912-743-6311
www.bestwestern.com
This 120-unit motor inn is a good deal in Macon. It has an antebellum facade, reasonably comfortable rooms with fridges, and other amenities, such as Wi-fi, a pool, and restaurant. **$**

Palmetto
The Inn at Serenbe
10950 Hutcheson Ferry Road, GA 30268
Tel: 770-463-2610
www.serenbe.com
Expect gracious Southern hospitality, from afternoon tea to treats at bedtime and gourmet breakfast, at this romantic country retreat on 284 acres (115 hectares), 32 miles (51km) southwest of Atlanta. Elegantly furnished rooms are available in the 1905 farmhouse and four cottages and include hardwood floors, window seats, and canopy beds. Walking distance to Serenbe Village with 900 acres (365 hectares) of trails, farm, and lake. **$$**

Warm Springs
Callaway Gardens
17800 US Highway 27, Pine Mountain, GA 31822
Tel: 706-663-2281
www.callawaygardens.com/resort/georgia-resort
This huge mountain resort has the feel of a national park, with its nature trails, biking and fishing, botanical gardens, shops and restaurants, wood-surrounded Mountain Creek Inn, and elegant Lodge and Spa. The reasonably priced inn sells out months in advance; rooms are usually available for the pricier Lodge. **$$$**

Mountain Top Inn and Resort
177 Royal Lodge Road, GA 31822
Tel: 706-663-4719
www.mountaintopinnga.com
You can rent a log cabin or stay in a lodge surrounded by Roosevelt State Park at this rustic retreat on Pine Mountain near Warm Springs. A popular place for weddings, this woodsy inn has a pool and restaurant. TVs but no telephones in cabins. **$$**

Alabama

Atmore
Royal Oaks Bed and Breakfast
5415 Highway 21, AL 36502
Tel: 251-368-8722
www.royaloaksbandb.com
This French-style country inn offers two-person apartments with private baths surrounded by gardens. The lovely peaceful setting is sometimes broken by the distinctive call of peacocks strutting near the pool. Farm-fresh eggs at breakfast in the morning. **$$**

Wind Creek Casino and Hotel
303 Poarch Road, AL 36502
Tel: 866-WIND360
www.windcreekcasino.com
This 17-story casino/hotel, near I-65 on the Poarch Creek Indian Reservation, is THE new luxury place to stay in the area. Its spacious rooms and suites have plump bedding, Native-made sweetgrass bathroom amenities, LCD TVs, and other extras. There are four restaurants including a global buffet. **$$**

Bayou La Batre
Bayou La Batre Inn and Suites
13155 N. Wintzell Avenue, AL 36509
Tel: 251-824-2020
www.bayoulabatreinn.com
Close to the beach with 40 comfortable rooms, this motel offers continental breakfast, a pool, and in-room microwaves and refrigerators. Hot tubs in some rooms. Restaurant adjacent. **$**

Mobile
Azalea House
115 Providence Street, AL 36604
Tel: 251-438-9921
www.theinnkeeper.com/bnb/10808
This Colonial home was built in 1904. Each of the three bedrooms has an en suite shower, TV, ceiling fan, and queen bed. Full breakfasts served. There is a spacious porch overlooking the beautiful grounds. **$–$$**

Malaga Inn
359 Church Street, AL 36602
Tel: 251-438-4701
www.malagainn.com
This unique downtown inn is set in a gas-lit courtyard and consists of two adjoining restored 1862 townhouses landscaped together with gardens and a patio. The 35 rooms and three suites are nicely decorated; many feature hardwood floors. Continental breakfast. **$$$**

Battle House Renaissance Mobile
26 N. Royal Street, AL 36602
Tel: 251-338-2000
www.marriott.com
Three hotels on this site have welcomed presidents and other history makers since 1852. The 1908 seven-story brick hotel, lavishly restored in 2007, has a massive circular lobby with spectacular stained-glass ceiling. Today's guests include many oil and shipping executives, and the 238 oversized rooms and suites feature masculine details such as dark-wood paneling and heavy brocade drapes as well as oversized bathrooms with tub and shower. Two restaurants onsite, bar, spa, and guests can play nearby at the Magnolia Grove Golf Course at a discount as part of the Robert Trent Jones Golf Trail. **$$$**

Montgomery
Red Bluff Cottage
551 Clay Street, AL 36104
Tel: 334-264-0056
www.redbluffcottage.com
This B&B is in a well-designed, comfortable, bluff-top cottage. It's on the busy edge of the historic Downtown, near I-65, but is remarkably peaceful at night. A large porch offers views of the Alabama River and State Capitol. The five themed rooms celebrate local history; the Great Gatsby Room, in particular, with original mementos belonging to Montgomery resident Zelda Fitzgerald, will inspire writers. Owners Barry and Bonnie Ponstein are eager hosts: guests can look forward to homecooked breakfasts, evening snacks, and lively discussions about the area. Phones and wireless internet but no TVs in rooms. **$$$**

PRICE CATEGORIES

Price categories are based on the average cost of a double room for one night:
$ = under $110
$$ = $110–250
$$$ = more than $250

Mississippi

Biloxi
Grand Biloxi Hotel
280 Beach Boulevard, MS 39530
Tel: 800-WIN2WIN
www.grandcasinobiloxi.com
This Harrah's-owned casino hotel was
rebuilt following Hurricane Katrina and
has reasonably priced guest rooms
with LCD TVs, beds with pillow-top
mattresses, and high-speed internet.
Spa, pool, and steakhouse onsite. **$**
Hard Rock Hotel
777 Beach Boulevard, MS 39530
Tel: 228-374-ROCK
www.hardrockbiloxi.com
The hotel's premium "crash pads"
feature "sleep like a rock" beds,
LCD TVs, plush robes, and Aveda
toiletries. It's pet friendly and there
are smoking and nonsmoking rooms.
There are concerts by big-name acts of
yesteryear in the Hard Rock Live venue
near the casino, low-cost country
music in the Roadhouse, and free
entertainment in the Hard Rock Cafe
along with the signature burgers. **$**

Gulfport
Magnolia Bay Hotel and Suites
9379 Canal Road, MS 39503
Tel: 228-822-9600
Under new ownership, this former
Crystal Inn has upgraded, attractive
rooms and good facilities, including
Wi-fi, complimentary hot breakfast,
pool, spa. It's close to Gulf beaches
and casinos. **$**

Long Beach
**Red Creek Inn Vineyard and Racing
Stable**
7416 Red Creek Road, MS 39560
Tel: 228-452-3080
www.redcreekinn.com
Fans of this lovely 1899 raised
French cottage on 11 wooded acres
(4.5 hectares) – the first B&B on
the Mississippi Gulf Coast – will be
pleased to know it survived Hurricane
Katrina. The three-story inn has three
main rooms: a honeymoon suite and
two attic rooms – areas between
rooms can be used as spillover low-
cost sleeping space for parties renting
main rooms. There are antiques, old-
fashioned wooden radios, and porch
swings throughout. **$**

Moss Point
Yellow House Bed and Breakfast
4401 Welch Street, MS 39563
Tel: 228-474-8927
www.yellowhouseofmosspoint.com
Formerly Moss Point Oaks Bed and
Breakfast, this 1870 B&B near Ocean
Springs is now under new ownership.

It has two guest rooms in one of
the oldest buildings in Moss Point,
and is surrounded by lush gardens
and wildlife habitat (this is a major
migratory birding area). Rooms are airy
and homey with antiques and four-
poster beds. **$$**

Ocean Springs
**Gulf Hills Hotel and Conference
Center**
13701 Paso Road, MS 39564
Tel: 866-875-4211
www.gulfhillshotel.com
This elegant hideaway hotel is on
an 18-hole golf course and was the
summer home of Elvis from 1951 to
1957. It has 52 beautifully calm rooms
and many amenities, including in-room
microwaves, fridges, coffee makers,
and wireless internet. Activities
include golf, tennis, and there's a large
pool. Snack bar. Deluxe continental
breakfast. Pet friendly. **$$**

Louisiana

Abbeville
Sunbelt Lodge
1903 Veterans Memorial Drive, LA 70510
Tel: 337-898-1453
www.sunbeltlodge.com
This budget motel has 99 basic
rooms and suites offering cable TV
with hbo; wheelchair-accessible
rooms are available. There's free
continental breakfast in the morning,
but the motel is close to shops and
restaurants. **$**

Baton Rouge
Hilton Baton Rouge Capitol Center
201 Lafayette Street, LA 70801
Tel: 225-3-HILTON
www.hiltoncapitolcenter.com
The former Heidelberg Hotel – a
favorite haunt of the Kingfish,
Governor Huey Long – has been
reborn as a sumptuous Hilton near
the State Capitol. It has 290 deluxe
spacious rooms and suites with ample
amenities, such as LCD TVs and sitting
areas. The atmospheric, brick-walled
Kingfish Restaurant serves steaks and
seafood. **$$**
The Stockade Bed and Breakfast
8860 Highland Road
Tel: 225-769-7358
www.thestockade.com
Named after a Union stockade that
occupied the site during the Civil
War, this sweet B&B is located in a
designated wildlife habitat near LSU.
The owner is an artist, and each of
the six comfortable guest rooms is
decorated with antiques and Louisiana
art and has a phone, fridge, TV, and
coffeemaker. Traditional Southern

breakfasts include grits, biscuits, and
all the fixin's or continental – your
choice. **$$**

Breaux Bridge
Bayou Boudin and Cracklin
100 W. Mills Avenue, LA 70517
Tel: 337-332-6158
www.bayoucabins.com
Breaux Bridge's first B&B is a
collection of 13 charming 19th-century
Cajun cabins with porches overlooking
Bayou Teche. Homemade Cajun treats
such as cracklin', boudin sausage,
hogshead cheese, and sweet pecan
pralines welcome guests. **$**

Eunice
The Seale Guesthouse
125 Seale Lane, LA 70535
Tel: 337-457-3753
www.angelfire.com/la2/guesthouse
This pretty guesthouse sits on 60
acres (24 hectares) of tranquil wooded
grounds. It has a large wraparound
porch and a reception that was once
robbed by Bonnie and Clyde. The
colorful rooms are tastefully decorated
with antiques in the main guesthouse
and a separate two-bedroom cottage.
Full continental breakfast. **$**

Lafayette
Bois des Chênes
338 N. Sterling Drive, LA 70501
Tel: 337-233-7816
www.boisdeschenes.com
Isn't it a joy to travel in rural America
and witness so much of the French
language? Award-winning historic
inn Bois des Chênes (the Oak Wood)
is a lovingly converted Civil War-era
Plantation carriage house close to the
city center. Its five elegant rooms have
four-posters and antiques. Louisiana
country breakfast served family style,
and yes, the host speaks French. **$$**
Hilton Lafayette
1521 Pinhook Road, LA 70503
Tel: 337-235-6111
www.hilton.com
This full-service high-rise Hilton is in
downtown Lafayette on the banks of
the Vermilion River. Some of its 327
luxurious rooms and suites have views
of the bayou; bathroom toiletries are
by Crabtree and Evelyn. There's a pool,
exercise facilities, spa, and high-end
restaurant Alexander's. **$$**

New Orleans
Bourbon Orleans
717 Orleans Street, LA 70116
Tel: 504-523-2222
www.bourbonorleans.com
This small French Quarter hotel is
an old-fashioned gem. Each room
and suite is uniquely decorated with

traditional Southern furnishings and has amenities like satellite TV, high-speed internet, and ergonomic desk chairs. It's built around a courtyard where cabanas encircle the pool. Rooms with balconies overlook Bourbon Street, but it is quieter on the courtyard side. Restaurant and lounge. **$$**

Chateau Hotel
1001 Chartres Street, LA 70116
Tel: 504-524-9636
www.chateauhotel.com
This small, tastefully furnished corner motel has a charming courtyard and 45 rooms around a pool. It's located in the residential Lower Quarter – a good choice for budget travelers. Daily continental breakfast. **$–$$**

Lafayette Hotel
600 St Charles Avenue, LA 70130
Tel: 504-524-4441
www.lafayettehotelneworleans.com
A 1916 gem, the very Gallic Lafayette's 44 beautifully understated rooms and suites have minibars, ottomans, easy chairs, and bookshelves; suites have wet bars, fridges, and some have four-posters and Jacuzzi baths. A few on St Charles Avenue open onto wrought-iron balconies – great during Carnival season. Offseason prices can be rock bottom; year round they are surprisingly moderate for what you get. Highly acclaimed Mikes on the Avenue restaurant is on the ground floor. **$–$$$**

Westin New Orleans Canal Place
100 Rue Iberville, LA 70130
Tel: 504-566-7006
www.starwoodhotels.com/westin
It's hard to top the views from the 29-floor Westin overlooking the Mississippi River and French Quarter. Linked to the upscale Canal Place shopping mall, the hotel reception on the 11th floor is reached via glass elevator and opens onto a lobby with panoramic vistas. The calming decor of the hotel – especially its oversized rooms – provides a welcome respite from the 24-hour action in the Vieux Carré. A great place to bring a client and seal a deal as you stare serenely at the Big Muddy. Rooftop pool, gym, onsite restaurant. **$$$**

Opelousas
Country Ridge Bed and Breakfast
169 Country Ridge Road, LA 70570
Tel: 337-942-3544
www.cajunbnb.com
This is a B&B in the traditional manner: the friendly owners offer weary travelers a laid-back setting and one of four spacious, super-clean guest rooms in their modern home.

Three have bathrooms and access to a Jacuzzi; all have Wi-fi and TVs. The landscaped pool area adjoins a thoroughbred horse farm. **$–$$**

St Martinville
The Old Castillo Hotel
220 Evangeline Boulevard, LA 70582
Tel: 337-394-4010
www.oldcastillo.com
This beautiful 1827 inn is in a listed building overlooking Bayou Teche and underneath the spreading branches of the famous Evangeline Oak. It has seven rooms with period antiques and wireless internet. Hot Cajun country egg breakfasts include bacon, beignets, and pain perdu with homemade jam. **$–$$**

Texas

Alpine
The Maverick Inn
1200 E. Holland Avenue, TX 79830
Tel: 432-837-0628
www.themaverickinn.com
This renovated historic motor court motel, complete with retro neon sign, poetically bills itself as a "Roadhouse for wanderers." The 18 rooms are small but exude a handsome West Texas machismo, with Mexican furnishings, and postmodern desert travel necessities like LCD TVs, fridges, microwaves, and wireless internet. Beds have high-thread linens and pillowtop mattresses. The lovely pool area is a great place to hang out. **$–$$**

Austin
Austin Motel
1220 S. Congress, TX 78704
Tel: 512-441-1157
www.austinmotel.com
Family owned since 1938, this authentic Fifties motel ("So close yet so far out") is retro-hip, green, and central, a few blocks south of Town Lake. A variety of rooms include small singles and two-room luxury suites. Onsite Mexican restaurant is a local favorite, and there's a kidney-shaped pool, of course. Two-night minimum on Fridays and Saturdays. **$$**

Driskill Hotel
604 Brazos Street, TX 78701
Tel: 512-474-5911
www.driskillhotel.com
This historic downtown landmark was built in 1886 as the showplace of cattle baron Jesse Driskill. Its huge columned lobby and stained-glass ceiling alone are worth a look. The 189 airy rooms span two wings and feature upscale amenities and unique hand-tooled furniture. There are workout facilities, business center,

bar, a gourmet restaurant, and café. Kid extras include cookies and milk, a deputy sheriff badge, and coloring book; pets stay for a fee and receive their own special pet bed. **$$**

Intercontinental Stephen F. Austin Hotel
701 Congress Avenue, TX 78701
Tel: 512-457-8800
www.austin.intercontinental.com
The 189 rooms and suites in this elegant, early 20th-century downtown hotel have dark-wood furniture, desk, couch, and coffee table, mini bar hidden in the TV cabinet, an enormous comfy pillow-top bed with fluffy linens and acres of pillows, and a spacious marble bathroom with vanity. High-speed internet in rooms; free Wi-fi in the lobby. On the ground floor, a substantial breakfast buffet is served in a dedicated airy café, and a bistro offers western food. The second-floor bar and restaurant, overlooking Congress, is a popular rendezvous for downtown businesspeople. Famous Intercontinental service doesn't disappoint: staff are knowledgeable, discreet, and friendly. **$$**

Castroville
Landmark Inn
402 E. Florence Street, TX 78009
Tel: 830-931-2133
www.visitlandmarkinn.com
Originally a mail stop on the Old San Antonio Road, this atmospheric 1850s inn is located in a state historic site and is less than a half-hour from San Antonio. Five romantically furnished suites have 1940s decor and mostly shared bathrooms. There's good bird- and butterfly-watching here. **$–$$**

Columbus
Country Hearth Columbus
2436 Highway 71S, TX 78934
Tel: 979-732-6293
www.countryhearth.com
This pleasant motel chain offers double and queen rooms with sofa beds, desks, and free wireless internet and in-room movies; some have microwaves and fridges. Eco-rooms with low-energy-usage are also available. Pool, hot breakfast included. Pet friendly. **$$**

El Paso
Camino Real Hotel
101 S. El Paso Street, TX 79901

PRICE CATEGORIES
Price categories are based on the average cost of a double room for one night:
$ = under $110
$$ = $110–250
$$$ = more than $250

Tel: 915-534-3000
www.caminoreal.com/elpaso
Reason enough to stop in El Paso, this handsome and sophisticated Mexican-owned border hotel has parts dating to 1912, including a simply amazing Tiffany-glass domed lobby, on a par with any of the other stately hotels you'll see on this trip. There are 359 spacious rooms and suites, a pool, sauna, and a fantastic bar and restaurant under the dome that is an unmissable experience. **$$**

Fredericksburg
Magnolia House
101 E. Hackberry Street, TX 78624
Tel: 830-997-0306
www.magnolia-house.com
This 1923 home is very welcoming. It has five rooms and suites, each with private bath, nice linens and towels, robes, cable TV, and wireless internet; suites have private entrances and fireplaces. Hot breakfasts are served on elegant tableware and include locally made sausage. **$$**

Galveston
Gaido's Seaside Inn
3802 Seawall Boulevard, TX 77550
Tel: 409-762-9625
www.gaidosseaside.com
Gaido's survived Hurricane Ike intact, and everyone is glad this popular inn, family run since 1947, is still in business. Many of its 104 rooms have a sea view and there's also a tiered flower garden. The adjoining restaurant is a big local favorite for authentic gumbo. **$**
Moody Gardens Hotel, Spa, and Convention Center
7 Hope Boulevard, TX 77554
Tel: 800-582-4673
www.moodygardens.com
This huge resort adjoining the popular theme park is a good family option and, since it's on the quiet, residential, northwest side of the island, received less Hurricane Ike impact than downtown locations. It has spacious, kid-friendly rooms, a big outdoor pool and "beach," a gift shop, snack shop, two restaurants, a spa and workout room, and access to Moody Gardens and a seasonal waterpark. **$$**

Hondo
Stony Ridge Ranch
326 PR 2323
Tel: 830-562-3542
www.stonyridgeranch.com
Located near popular Lost Maples State Park, this remote and special B&B offers a romantic getaway in its four wood cabins and custom log home but does all the cooking for you

with its sumptuous gourmet cooked breakfasts. Fireplaces and views of the Hill Country in each rental. Two-night minimum; closed Mon–Tue. **$$**

Houston
St Regis
1919 Briar Oaks Lane, TX 77027
Tel: 877-787-3447
www.starwoodhotels.com/stregis
Enjoy luxury accommodations, including 52 suites, located between the exclusive River Oaks neighborhood and Galleria. The Astro Floor features maître d' and butler service and interpreters. **$$$**
Sara's Inn on the Boulevard
941 Heights Boulevard, TX 77008
Tel: 713-868-1130
www.saras.com
This lovely Queen Anne mansion in the heart of the city has 14 beautifully designed rooms and suites with bathrooms, TVs, phones, wireless internet, and deluxe amenities. Extended continental breakfast, with breakfast buffet on weekends. **$–$$**
The Westin Galleria
5060 W. Alabama, TX 77056
Tel: 713-960-8100
www.westingalleriahoustonhotel.com
This stylish hotel is in the ritzy Galleria mall. Its superb facilities include an ice rink, pool, restaurant, and gym. **$$**

Lajitas
Lajitas Golf Resort and Spa
HC 70, Box 400, Terlingua, TX 79852
Tel: 432-424-5000
www.lajitasgolfresort.com
Luxury and backcountry living coexist at this high-end resort in a reconstructed frontier town just west of Big Bend National Park. Ninety-two elegant western-themed rooms and suites occupy an Old West hotel and saloon and buildings along the main street. There's also a 3-bedroom adobe house for rent. Guests enjoy golf, a pool, barbecues, float trips on the Rio Grande, and Country and Western dancing. There's an RV park, if you're camping. **$–$$$**

Marathon
Gage Hotel
101 Highway 90 W., TX 79842
Tel: 432-386-4205
www.gagehotel.com
Built as a private lodge by rancher Alfred Gage in 1927, this charming inn, a Texas Historical Landmark, is filled with western antiques; a modern adobe building was added in the early 1990s. Twenty brick guest rooms with private baths encircle a lovely courtyard with fountain, hacienda style; half have kiva-style fireplaces.

The 1927 historic hotel has 16 rooms with basins and private or shared bathrooms, and there are also three large casitas for rent on the property. Excellent onsite restaurant serves game and other western fare. **$$**

Marfa
El Paisano Hotel
207 N. Highland, TX 79843
Tel: 866-729-3669
www.hotelpaisano.com
The hacienda-style hotel that hosted Hollywood's finest during 1955's filming of Giant has dined out on its reputation for decades and is starting to look a little worn, which, depending on your perspective, may only add to its charm. Movie buffs will want to book the Rock Hudson Suite, where the actor enjoyed a rooftop terrace, fireplace, kitchen, sunroom, and a king-size bed. There's a lovely pool area, coffee shop, lobby gift shops, and the pleasant Greasewood Gallery, where you can see Western art that appeals to locals more than the modern art found elsewhere in Marfa. **$–$$**

New Braunfels
Gruene Mansion Inn
1275 Gruene Road, TX 78130
Tel: 830-629-2641
www.gruenemansioninn.com
This former cotton plantation home has been converted to a luxury inn with 25 antique-filled rooms scattered throughout restored barns and sheds. It overlooks Guadalupe River and is adjacent to Gruene Hall, the oldest dance hall in Texas. Breakfasts are bountiful. **$$$**

Presidio
Three Palms Inn
Old Highway 67N, TX 79845
Tel: 432-229-3211
This motor inn is a little worn these days, but Presidio is so small, it's lucky there's a motel here at all. There's a pool and cable television and a diner next door. Easy on the wallet. **$**

San Antonio
Drury Plaza Riverwalk Hotel
105 S. St Mary's Street, TX 78205
Tel: 210-270-7799
https://www.druryhotels.com
The superstar of the popular Drury Inn and Suites chain has an unbeatable location in the restored 1929 Alamo National Bank Building on the Riverwalk. Guests enjoy complimentary evening cocktails and hot breakfasts overlooking the Art Deco lobby, with its marble floors and inspiring art. Roomy suites have

kitchens, sitting rooms, LCD TVs, free Wi-fi, and long-distance phone. New Terrace rooms above the expanded Riverwalk (donated to the city as part of the restoration) have views but are close to the action and often noisier. **$**

The Historic Menger Hotel
204 Alamo Plaza, TX 78205
Tel: 210-223-4361
www.mengerhotel.com
Location, location: this 1859 hotel is located adjacent to the Alamo. Rooms are elegantly furnished with antiques, and several have Jacuzzis. The hotel's player piano and Menger Bar are famous. There's also a pool, fitness center, and fine-dining restaurant. **$$**

La Mansion del Río
112 College Street, TX 78205
Tel: 210-518-1000
http://www.omnihotels.com
The Spanish mission architecture and wrought-iron balcony rooms overlooking a quiet portion of the Riverwalk make this exceptional small hotel, a former 1852 school, a superior destination. **$$**

Terlingua
Big Bend Resort
At junction of Routes 118 and 170, TX 79852
Tel: 432-371-2218
www.bigbendresortadventures.com/lodging
Just west of the entrance to Big Bend National Park, this concessionaire-run resort offers 86 comfortable motel rooms and duplexes with kitchen facilities in several buildings; the VIP House, a full-facility rental; and an apartment. Conference center, pool, café, and RV park and campground. **$-$$**

New Mexico

Cloudcroft
The Lodge at Cloudcroft
1 Corona Place, NM 88317
Tel: 575-682-2566
www.thelodgeresort.com
Built in 1899 during the local timber-industry boom, this quaint lodge is a cool retreat for desert dwellers. The 59 finely appointed Victorian-style lodge rooms have antiques and romantic furnishings; the Governor's Suite is a favorite haunt for Rebecca, a former employee crossed in love. Rooms in the Pavilion, the original section of the Lodge, retain its rustic feeling with Adirondack log furniture, open rooms, and full breakfast. Pool, spa, restaurant onsite. **$$**

Las Cruces
Hotel Encanto de Las Cruces
705 S. Telshor Boulevard, NM 88011

Tel: 575-522-4300
www.hotelencanto.com
This luxury hotel is near all the main attractions in Las Cruces. It has 210 rooms and suites with Spanish Colonial decor, views, and full amenities such as comfy work areas, wireless internet, and fridges and microwaves on request. Onsite pool, spa, restaurant, bar, and salon. **$-$$**

Lordsburg
Comfort Inn and Suites
400 Wabash Street, NM 88045
Tel: 575-542-3355
www.comfortinn.com
Chains rule here but this one is newer than the others and has more attractive rooms and spacious suites with sitting areas. Indoor pool, hot tub, lobby fireplace, continental breakfast room, and free internet access. Book early: it's popular with Border Patrol. **$**

Mescalero
Inn of the Mountain Gods and Casino
287 Carrizozo Canyon Road, NM 88340
Tel: 888-324-0348
www.innofthemountaingods.com
Owned by the Mescalero Apache tribe, this famous resort hotel has been rebuilt on its original location on a lake facing 12,000ft (3,660-metre) Sierra Blanca peak, sacred to the Apache. Public spaces highlight Apache artwork. The 273 luxury view rooms and suites occupy their own tower. All are spacious with workspaces and soothing decor. The resort specializes in Native American-guided hunting, fishing, and horseback riding, boating, golf, and tennis. Onsite casino, fine-dining steak and seafood restaurant. No pets. **$$**

Old Mesilla
La Meson de Mesilla
1803 Avenida de Mesilla, NM 88046
Tel: 575-525-9212
www.mesondemesilla.com
Stay in a lovely boutique inn in historic Mesilla that also has one of the town's best restaurants. The remodeled rooms have pale walls, dark wood furnishings, and French doors leading to a wraparound veranda. Onsite pool, bocce ball court, fitness center, restaurant, bar. Breakfast included. **$$**

Pinos Altos
Bear Creek Motel and Cabins
88 Main Street, NM 88053
Tel: 888-388-4515
www.bearcreekcabins.com
Just north of Silver City, on the road to Gila Cliff Dwellings, these unique split-level cabins are built around

trees in the Gila National Forest. Each has a kitchen or microwave, fridge, TV, phone, fireplace or heater, air conditioning, and patio with rustic furniture and barbecue grate. Two-night minimum on weekends. **$$**

Ruidoso
Swiss Chalet Inn
1451 Mechem Drive, NM 88345
Tel: 505-258-3333
www.sciruidoso.com
This Swiss-style hotel is located in a cool, pine-clad forest and has 82 rooms with panoramic views of the Sacramento Mountains. Full breakfast, pool, hot tub, onsite steakhouse, and tavern. **$**

Silver City
Bear Mountain Lodge
2251 Cottage San Road, NM 88061
Tel: 575-538-2538
www.bearmountainlodge.com
This famous 1920s ranch hacienda was beautifully remodeled by The Nature Conservancy, whose Gila Preserve is nearby, and is a fantastic birding location. Now under new owners with an art background, it has added the popular Blue Dome Gallery, which displays work by local artists. Ten romantic rooms in the main lodge and adjoining building and a guesthouse are furnished with locally sourced furniture, handmade soaps, and nature items; several have Jacuzzi tubs. Café Oso Azul offers healthy gourmet breakfasts to guests, brunch on weekends, packed lunches, and dinner by reservation. **$$**

Arizona

Bisbee
Bisbee Grand Hotel
61 Main Street, AZ 85603
Tel: 520-432-5900
www.bisbeegrandhotel.com
Elegantly restored Victorian hotel with period decor in a small southern Arizona mining town. Amenities include parking, saloon, a billiard room with the only full-size pool table in Bisbee, and a free breakfast. **$-$$**

The Shady Dell
1 Douglas Road, AZ 85603
Tel: 520-432-3567
www.theshadydell.com
Nine vintage aluminum travel trailers have been kitted out with perfect

PRICE CATEGORIES

Price categories are based on the average cost of a double room for one night:
$ = under $110
$$ = $110–250
$$$ = more than $250

1950s kitsch at this one-of-a-kind motel on the edge of Bisbee. Old-style radios play big-band tunes and early rock 'n roll, and trailers have original working kitchens right down to the electric percolators. **$**

Gila Bend

Best Western Space Age Lodge
401 E. Pima Street, PO Box C, NM 85337
Tel: 928-683-2273
www.bestwesternspaceagelodge.com
The Space Age Lodge is like no other Best Western you've ever seen, the bedrooms having pictures from NASA on the walls and of course space-age lighting. There are even military aircraft in the public areas, alongside more conventional amenities like a pool and heated spa. **$–$$**

Phoenix

Arizona Biltmore
2400 E. Missouri Avenue, AZ 85016
Tel: 602-955-6600
www.arizonabiltmore.com
This impossibly elegant grand resort was designed in 1929 by a student of Frank Lloyd Wright and bears the unmistakable stamp of the master, whose Taliesin West architecture school is in nearby Scottsdale. A newer annex offers larger rooms for business travelers, but the historic hotel is the draw. The resort sits on 39 acres (16 hectares) of beautifully landscaped grounds adjoining the swanky Biltmore Fashion Park shopping center and has golf courses, biking, a fitness room, spa, pools (including one with historic tile and fountain), and restaurants. The New Western cuisine in Wright's is a memorable experience. **$$$**

Hermosa Inn
5532 North Palo Cristi Road, Paradise Valley, AZ 85016
Tel: 602-955-8614
www.hermosainn.com
Centrally located in a residential area between Phoenix and Scottsdale, this historic boutique inn is a delightful experience. It includes restored portions of the original 1930s adobe home and studio of cowboy artist Lon Megargee, which he later converted to a guest ranch and inn. The 34 airy casitas offer a refuge from the world amid lush walled gardens. Small pool, excellent small spa, the Last Drop Bar (in Megargee's former studio), and superb artisanal Western cuisine featuring organic produce from the property in the onsite dining room Lon's. **$$$**

Maricopa Manor
15 W. Pasadena Avenue, AZ 85013
Tel: 602-274-6302
www.maricopamanor.com

Spanish-style home built in the 1920s furnished with antiques and art and having just seven suites. All rooms are suites. Amenities include a pool with waterfalls, spa, and beautiful lush gardens that are a popular wedding venue. **$$$**

Scottsdale

The Phoenician
6000 E. Camelback Road, AZ 85251
Tel: 480-941-8200
www.thephoenician.com
The Phoenician is one of Scottsdale's premier resorts, set in 250 acres (100 hectares) and with no fewer than 10 restaurants and lounges to choose from, a spa, championship golf course, and numerous awards to its credit. **$$$**

Tombstone

Cochise Stronghold: A Canyon Nature Retreat
PO Box 232, Pearce, AZ
Tel: 520-826-4141
www.cochisestrongholdbb.com
Set on 15 acres (6 hectares) of forest land in the heart of historic Cochise Stronghold, this wilderness bed-and-breakfast built by John and Nancy Yates is the perfect place for nature lovers. Rent the suite in the attractive stone house, the Casita Manzana guesthouse, or indulge in a spot of "glamping" in a comfy Mongolian yurt that sleeps 10. In-room gourmet breakfasts are made from organic Ingredients grown onsite, but you need to bring your own food for other meals in this remote spot, or ask the Yates to provision. **$**

Tombstone Motel
502 E. Fremont Street, AZ 85638
Tel: 520-457-3478
www.tombstonemotel.net
With its clean, well-fitted rooms in a historic 1880s building, a stay at the Tombstone Motel ("rest in peace") channels the old western spirit of Tombstone. **$–$$**

Tucson

Arizona Inn
2200 E. Elm Street, AZ 85719
Tel: 520-325-1541
www.arizonainn.com
One of downtown Tucson's top lodgings, this elegant historic southwestern inn is just 5 minutes from the University of Arizona but feels like Its own oasis. Guest rooms and suites are tastefully furnished with antiques and are mainly in casitas, with patios and fireplaces, amid 14 acres (6 hectares) of manicured grounds and gardens. Outdoor pool, tennis courts, croquet, ping-pong,

massage, exercise room, fine dining on the patio, Audubon bar. Breakfast and afternoon tea or ice cream sundae included. Reserve well ahead. **$$**

Hotel Congress
311 E. Congress, AZ 85701
Tel: 520 622-8848
www.hotelcongress.com
Hotel Congress is idiosyncratic, inexpensive, fun, hip, and so historic (1919) that John Dillinger and his gang once stayed here. The excellent Cup Café, featured on the Food Network, offers well-priced globally inspired food and stays open late for those at the concerts in the hotel's music club, voted one of the 10 best rock clubs in the US. Be very selective about which room you stay in, due to noise levels from the club and nearby Amtrak station, and pack earplugs. **$**

Lodge on the Desert
306 N. Alvernon Way, AZ 85711
Tel: 520-320-2000
www.lodgeonthedesert.com
This in-town resort was first opened in 1936 and in summer 2009 received a massive make-over that has ensured it remains one of the top places to stay in the city. Most rooms have red-tiled patios and fireplaces, and facilities include a spa, pool, and outdoor hot tubs. Its restaurant highlighting Southwest cuisine is recognized as one of the best in Tucson. **$$–$$$**

Yuma

Best Western Coronado Motor Hotel
233 S. Fourth Avenue, AZ 85364
Tel: 928-783-4453
http://bwcoronado.com
One of the first Best Western hotels and the oldest still operating, the Coronado has comfortable rooms set around a flower-filled court. Still run by the same family (all Best Westerns are individually owned), it has an atmosphere and charm all its own, with a fascinating museum in the original reception building which doubled as the family's home. Rooms in one wing retain their 1950s-style furniture and there is a modern annex across the street. Features include a pool, great breakfast, free Wi-fi, and a vast free movie library. **$–$$**

La Fuente Inn and Suites
1513 E. 16th Street, AZ 85365
Tel: 928-329-1814
www.lafuenteinn.com
This contemporary inn has nicely landscaped gardens with fruit trees and flowers all surrounding a large pool. Other amenities include a fitness room, laundry, four BBQs, and a complimentary airport shuttle service. **$$–$$$**

Yuma Cabana Hotel
2151 S. Fourth Avenue, AZ 85364
Tel: 928-783-8311
www.yumacabana.com
The Cabana is an attractive little oasis with a quirky charm, due to the independent nature of the operation. It's very good value, relaxed, and the staff obviously enjoy working there.
$–$$

Calipatria
Calipatria Inn and Suites
700 N. Sorensen Avenue, CA 92233
Tel: 760-348-7348
www.calipatriainn.com
This privately run Spanish-style hotel is set in attractive grounds in Calipatria, in the heart of the Imperial

Valley, 26 miles (42km) from El Centro. It gets high marks as a surprisingly pleasant lodging, especially from birders who flock to the Salton Sea each winter to glimpse migratory waterfowl. The 41 rooms and suites all have cable TV, fridge, microwave, and Wi-fi; suites have spa tubs, sofa beds, and kitchenettes. Pool, continental breakfast, and onsite steakhouse. **$**

PACIFIC ROUTE

Arcata
Fairwinds Motel
1674 G Street, CA 95521
Tel: 707-822-4824
www.fairwindsmotelarcata.com
The Fairwinds Motel is a basic and clean motel right by the highway and in the heart of Redwoods Country. Facilities include free wireless internet, and it's just a short walk to Arcata Square and to the Arcata campus. **$$**

Big Sur
Big Sur Lodge
47225 Highway 1, Big Sur, CA 93920
Tel: 831-667-3110
www.bigsurlodge.com
Big Sur architect Mickey Muenning used the sea and the mountains as a backdrop to this lush resort, which is right in among the magnificent redwoods. At this lodge you will *not* find amenities like phones, TVs, or alarm clocks. **$$$**

Bodega Bay
Bodega Bay Lodge and Spa
103 Coast Highway 1, CA 94923
Tel: 707-875-3525
www.bodegabaylodge.com
The Inn is in an idyllic location with all rooms having balconies that look out across marshland toward the sea, with birds, frogs, and other wildlife all around. Rooms are spacious and romantic, with fireplaces. Lovely gardens lead to the fitness center and ocean-view pool. **$$–$$$**

Cambria
Pelican Cove Inn
6316 Moonstone Beach Drive, CA 93428
Tel: 805-927-1500
www.moonstonehotels.com
Just across the road from the beach with its seal rocks and pathways, the Pelican Cove is a few minutes outside the center of the lovely little town of Cambria. Rooms are spacious and elegantly furnished. Most have ocean

views of some kind. Guests are treated to a substantial cooked breakfast, afternoon wine and tea, and dessert and coffee in the evenings. There is a pool and gardens. **$$–$$$**

Carmel-by-the-Sea
Cypress Inn
Lincoln Street and Seventh Avenue, CA 93921
Tel: 831-624-3871
www.cypress-inn.com
Renowned for being co-owned by Hollywood legend Doris Day, who is also a great animal lover, the Cypress Inn is one of the most dog-friendly hotels on the Pacific Coast. Day's movie memorabilia lines the corridors, with some fun old film posters, and the Inn manages to be both chic and relaxed, with comfortable rooms and an excellent bar that's as popular with locals as with hotel guests. Downtown restaurants are a short walk away. **$$–$$$**
Vagabond's House Inn
4th and Dolores Street, CA 93921
Tel: 831-624-7738
www.vagabondshouseinn.com
The Vagabond Inn's 13 rooms, which are like luxury versions of rustic cabins, are grouped around a lovely, lush courtyard, where a waterfall plays day and night, a lovely sound to go to sleep to. The stylish rooms have king beds and cozy fires, and the complimentary breakfast is brought to your room. It's in a very quiet part of Carmel but only a short stroll to the town centre. **$$–$$$**

Eureka
Carter House Inn
301 L Street, CA 95501
Tel: 707-444-8062
www.carterhouse.com
The Carter House Inn is a collection of four romantic Victorian town houses on the edge of Eureka's historical district and a block back from the sea front. The Hotel Carter also contains the acclaimed Restaurant 301 (see page 447), where guests also enjoy

the complimentary and very tasty breakfasts. Rooms are spacious and successfully combine style with period charm, and with all modern comforts too. Bell Cottage and Carter Cottage are exquisitely decorated private retreats. **$$–$$$**

Ferndale
Shaw House Inn, 703 Main Street
Tel: 707-786-9958
www.shawhouse.com
This very charming bed-and-breakfast is in the town's oldest building, a delightful gingerbread affair surrounded by sumptuous gardens that attract abundant wildlife. The eight en suite rooms are decorated with period furnishings, including canopied beds and clawfoot tubs.
$$–$$$
Victorian Inn
400 Ocean Avenue, CA 95536
Tel: 707-786-4949
www.victorianvillageinn.com
This impressive inn was actually built from the local redwoods in 1890, and its Victorian style ensures high-ceilinged rooms that are filled with antique decor. The Village Inn also has its own on-site restaurant and bar. **$$**

Inverness
Ten Inverness Way Bed and Breakfast Inn
10 Inverness Way, CA 94937
Tel: 415-669-1648
www.teninvernessway.com
Located in a 1904 Craftsmen home in Inverness, an hour north of San Francisco, this is a nice, relaxed place from which to explore Point Reyes National Seashore and the lush hills of Marin County. Each of the inn's five rooms is named after a local hiking trail. Happy hour wine and cheese and

PRICE CATEGORIES

Price categories are based on the average cost of a double room for one night:
$ = under $110
$$ = $110–250
$$$ = more than $250

full hot breakfast are included in the room rate, but rooms are available without these for a reduced rate, if desired; however, that would be a great shame, as you are slap bang in a local foods haven. **$$**

La Jolla
The Lodge at Torrey Pines
11480 N.Torrey Pines Road, CA 92037
Tel: 858-453-4420
www.lodgetorreypines.com
The Lodgei a luxury retreat overlooking the Pacific Ocean and right next to the championship golf course at Torrey Pines. It has its own spa, swimming pool, and fine-dining restaurant. **$$$**

Laguna Beach
Casa Laguna Inn and Spa
2510 S. Coast Highway, CA 92651
Tel: 800-233-0449
www.casalaguna.com
Right on the Pacific Coast Highway, the Casa Laguna is a luxury mission-style inn with just 16 rooms, giving it an intimate and friendly feel. Some of the buildings used to be artists' studios, and the abundant greenery hides a pool, while inside there's a small spa and business center, free wine tastings, and a delicious gourmet breakfast. **$$–$$$**

Hotel Laguna
425S. Coast Highway, CA 92651
Tel: 800-524-2927
www.hotellaguna.com
The Hotel Laguna is right on the beach and many of its 65 guest rooms have a view of either the ocean or the gar-dens. There is a complimentary newspaper and continental breakfast, and a choice of restaurants. **$$–$$$**

Mendocino
Stanford Inn by the Sea
Coast Highway and Comptche Ukiah Road, CA 95460
Tel: 707-937-5615
www.stanfordinn.com
At this gorgeous retreat, you can be indulgent and environmentally conscious at the same time. Pine and redwood paneling and wood fires are a rustic backdrop to the comfortable rooms, which look out over organic gardens toward Mendocino Bay from private balconies. There's a cozy lodge and bar, and an inviting heated covered pool, yoga sessions, and spa service. **$$$**

Montecito
Montecito Inn
1295 Coast Village Road, CA 93108
Tel: 805-969-7854
www.montecitoinn.com

In the million-dollar neighborhood of Montecito just south of Santa Barbara, and just two blocks from Butterfly Beach, this Spanish-style historic inn was built by Charlie Chaplin and other Hollywood actors as a retreat. It has a very nice pool, spa, sauna, business centre, massage service, and exercise room. Some rooms have their own Jacuzzi tubs and some also have mountain views. Good restaurants and shopping within strolling distance along Coast Village Road. **$$$**

San Ysidro Ranch
900 San Ysidro Lane, CA 93108
Tel: 805-969-5046
www.sanysidroranch.com
This is a truly special rural hideaway, which is why so many celebrities have sought some privacy there. It has a fitness centre, a pool heated year-round, in-room massage services, yoga lessons, and 17 miles (27km) of hiking trails in the Santa Ynez Mountains from the front door. **$$$**

Monterey
Hotel Pacific
300 Pacific Street, CA 93940
Tel: 831-373-5700
www.hotelpacific.com
The Pacific is a luxury boutique hotel very close to Cannery Row, Fisherman's Wharf, and other Monterey attractions. The 105 guest rooms are all classified as suites, some being designated Romantic Fireplace Rooms. **$$–$$$**

Monterey Plaza Hotel and Spa
400 Cannery Row, CA 93940
Tel: 831-646-1700
http://montereyplazahotel.com
One of the largest and best hotels in Monterey, right in the heart of town on Cannery Row and overlooking Monterey Bay, this hotel has its own spa, and a choice of bistro, grill, or café dining. **$$–$$$**

Morro Bay
Embarcadero Inn
456 Embarcadero Street, CA 93442
Tel: 888-223-5777
www.embarcaderoinn.com
This peaceful inn features luxury rooms with private balconies, fireplaces, and attentive service. A good base for relaxing or touring local attractions. All rooms have bay view and some have hot tubs. **$$$**

Napa Valley
1801 First
1801 First Street, Napa, CA 94559
Tel: 800-518-0146
www.1801first.com
This luxury B&B inn is an indulgent treat, located right in Napa Town

itself. The architect-designed interior is cool and contemporary, yet it fits right into the classic details of this Victorian house built in 1903. Suites have fireplaces, canopies, and other romantic touches, and there are private cottages in the lush garden. Modern comforts include free wine and hors d'oeuvres in the afternoon, and three-course breakfasts to set you up for a hard day's wine-tasting in Napa Valley. **$$$**

Wine Country Inn
152 Lodi Lane, St Helena, CA 94574
Tel: 707-963-7077
www.winecountryinn.com
This gorgeous inn epitomizes Napa Valley's relaxed air of chic, with a friendly complimentary wine tasting in the afternoons and views over the neighboring vineyards. In addition to the luxurious guest rooms, several cottages offer the ultimate in privacy and pampering, with whirlpool baths beneath stained-glass windows, king-size beds, fireplaces, and patios. The Inn also has an outdoor pool and a hot tub, and superb fresh-cooked breakfasts. **$$–$$$**

Novato
Inn Marin
250 Entrada Drive, CA 94949
Tel: 415-883-5952
www.innmarin.com
There's a Southwestern feel to the rooms at the Inn Marin, which are decorated in warm reds and deep yellow colors. The bamboo coverlets and floors fit both with the hotel's design, and with its eco-friendly ethos. The 70 rooms and 4 suites border lovely spacious grounds with magnolia trees. Amenities include a swimming pool, complimentary Wi-fi and continental breakfast. Rickey's Restaurant (see page 448) is a must, with live jazz sessions at the weekend. **$$–$$$**

Pismo Beach
Spyglass Inn
2705 Spyglass Drive, CA 93449
Tel: 805-773-4855
www.spyglassinn.com
Stylishly refurbished with panoramic ocean view, dining room, and lounge, the Spyglass Inn is dramatically situated on the cliffs near Pismo Beach, and has its own spa and pool too. **$$$**

Redondo Beach
Portofino Hotel and Yacht Club
260 Portofino Way, CA 90277
Tel: 310-379-8481
www.hotelportofino.com
Located on a private peninsula close to Redondo Beach, the Portofino

Hotel and Yacht Club has its own pool, restaurant, views over the marina, and access to Gold's Gym nearby. **$$–$$$**

San Diego

Hotel del Coronado
1500 Orange Avenue, Coronado, CA 92118
Tel: 619-435-6611
www.hoteldel.com
World-famous Victorian-era landmark. As well as being a tourist attraction in its own right, the Coronado is also an exceptional hotel with its own tennis court, pool, spa, beachside cottages and villas, with nearby golf and boating. Coronado Beach was named America's Best Beach in 2012. **$$$**

Palomar San Diego
1047 Fifth Avenue, CA 92101
Tel: 619-515-3000
www.hotelpalomar-sandiego.com
The chicest hotel in the city, the Palomar San Diego (formely Sé San Diego and now a Kimpton boutique hotel) oozes designer style and luxury. Upper-floor rooms have a grand view over the city at night. Guests enjoy a personal welcome rather than a check-in, and a hotel tour to show off its every impressive feature like the hotel spa, the cool bar, the loanable laptops, the Saltbox restaurant, and rooftop bar. **$$$**

US Grant Hotel
326 Broadway, CA 92101
Tel: 619-232-3121
www.usgrant.net
The US Grant is a restored grand old historic hotel dating back to 1910, in the heart of the business, shopping, and nightlife areas downtown. In keeping with the name, there are no less than two Presidential suites, and all rooms have marble bathrooms with stone sinks. Even if you don't stay here, you can eat at the Grant Grill, which is also a San Diego landmark. **$$–$$$**

San Francisco

Hotel Boheme
444 Columbus Avenue, CA 94133
Tel: 415-433-9111
www.hotelboheme.com
Located on the site of a 19th century inn, Hotel Boheme has been more remodeled to echo the ambiance of 1950s North Beach. It has an abundance of bohemian charm and bags of history. Wonderful black-and-white photographs line the hallway. All rooms have free Wi-fi. **$$**

Hotel Vertigo
940 Sutter Street, CA 94109
Tel: 415-885-6800
www.hotelvertigosf.com
The setting for the Hitchcock movie *Vertigo*, this small city hotel is both

sophisticated and comfortable. The Plush Room Theater, which was once a Prohibition-era speakeasy, is now known for its cabaret. The location is its main selling point, though. **$$–$$$**

Red Victorian Bed, Breakfast and Art
1665 Haight Street, CA 94117
Tel: 415-864-1978
www.redvic.com
Perfect for the budget traveler, this B&B bills itself as "San Francisco's Living Peace Museum" and, in addition to bed and breakfast offers a Peaceful Café, a Peaceful Center, and a Peace Arts Gallery. As you'd expect, it's a friendly rendezvous, with each room reflecting a different theme, such as the Flower Child Room. The Summer of Love is not dead in some parts of San Francisco. **$$–$$$**

San Luis Obispo

Madonna Inn
100 Madonna Road, CA 93405
Tel: 800-543-9666
www.madonnainn.com
Well known for its eccentricity and bizarre decor, the Madonna Inn's 110 rooms are each radically different and have themes including Western, Hawaiian, Austrian, and even Safari and Sir Walter Raleigh! **$$–$$$**

Santa Barbara

The Cheshire Cat
36 W. Valerio Street, CA 93101
Tel: 805-569-1610
www.cheshirecat.com
This restored Victorian home offers a relaxed and pampered stay in the heart of Santa Barbara. Rooms are named after characters from *Alice in Wonderland*, including the Mad Hatter and the Queen of Hearts, and some have patios and in-room Jacuzzis. **$$–$$$**

Franciscan Inn
109 Bath Street, CA 93101
Tel: 805-963-8845
www.franciscaninn.com
The tiled roofs and white walls give a Spanish-mission look to this 1920s collection of buildings in a quiet part of Santa Barbara but only one block from the beach. Rooms are comfortable and spacious, and there's a heated pool open year-round, free Wi-fi and video library, fresh-baked cookies, and a freshly made continental breakfast – all welcome extras for a very reasonable price. **$$**

Santa Monica

The Embassy
1001 Third Street, CA 90403
Tel: 310-394-1279

www.embassyhotelapts.com
The Embassy Hotel Apartments have been in business since 1927 and the beautiful Mediterranean-style buildings sit among a lush garden where hummingbirds hover to greet arriving guests. The rooms are huge and have a kind of homely grandeur to them, with period furniture and kitchen facilities as there's no breakfast, but there are plenty of eating options nearby on the Third Street Promenade. **$$**

Sonoma

The Fairmont Sonoma Mission Inn and Spa
18140 Sonoma Highway, CA 95476
Tel: 707-938-9000
www.fairmont.com/sonoma
This pricey European-style spa in the heart of Wine Country has romantic rooms and suites, with marbled baths and plantation shutters. Its restaurant offers acclaimed fine dining and attentive service. **$$$**

Oregon

Astoria

Cannery Pier Hotel
10 Basin Street, OR 97103
Tel: 503-325-4996
www.cannerypierhotel.com
One of the top hotels in Oregon, this delightful hotel is located on the site of the former Union Fish Cannery, 600ft into the mouth of the Columbia River. It has unparalled views of the working river, the bridge, and Cape Disappointment Lighthouse. The public spaces have a soaring warehouse feel that reflects the sparkling light. The deluxe double-queen and king rooms, suites, and penthouse Pilot House are richly appointed with hardwood floors, fireplaces, spa tubs, balconies, and water views. Finnish sauna, hotel spa, and fitness room. **$$–$$$**

Clementine's Bed and Breakfast
847 Exchange Street, OR 97103
Tel: 503-325-2005
www.clementines-bb.com
A classic Italianate Victorian building with pretty English cottage gardens and a small library. The inn has five rooms with queen-sized beds, private bathrooms. One room has a gas fireplace. **$–$$**

PRICE CATEGORIES
Price categories are based on the average cost of a double room for one night:
$ = under $110
$$ = $110–250
$$$ = more than $250

Cannon Beach

Ocean Lodge
2864 S. Pacific Street,
OR 97110
Tel: 541-347-9441
www.theoceanlodge.com
This romantic lodge is tucked away
in a quiet corner of Cannon Beach,
right on the beach itself with views
of the town's famous Haystack Rock
from your private deck. It's a modern
creation but modelled on 1940s-style
rustic lodging, with all today's luxuries
included in the lovely rooms, like
a vast, free DVD library and wide-
screen TVs, free internet, fireplaces,
and Jacuzzis in many of them too.
An indulgent right, right down to the
homemade cookies in the lobby.
$$–$$$

Depoe Bay

Inn at Arch Rock
70 NW Sunset Street, OR 97341
Tel: 541-765-2560
www.innatarchrock.com
Picturesquely set on a bluff, with 12
of its 13 airy rooms offering dramatic
ocean views, this lovely white-washed
wood bed-and-breakfast is a terrific
value. It's a wonderful base for
explorations in Oregon's capital of
whale watching, or just relaxing with a
book on the inn's own private beach.
Gourmet breakfast and organic coffee.
$$–$$$

Gold Beach

Tu Tu' Tun Lodge
96550 N. Bank Rogue River Road,
OR 97444
Tel: 541-247-6664
www.tututun.com
A few miles inland from Gold Beach
on the banks of the Rogue River,
this beautiful lodge has luxurious
rooms, an acclaimed restaurant,
spa, sociable atmosphere, and
opportunities for hiking, fishing,
kayaking, golfing, or doing nothing
but watching ospreys and bald eagles
from your balcony. Each of its rooms
have relaxing river views, and some
have fireplaces and an outdoor
soaking tub. **$$–$$$**

Newport

Elizabeth Street Inn
232 SW Elizabeth Street, OR 97365
Tel: 541-265-9400
www.elizabethstreetinn.com
This modern bluff-top hotel has
ocean-view rooms, all with fireplaces,
balconies, fridge, microwave, coffee
maker, and robes. Northview rooms
look toward nearby Yaquina Head
Lighthouse, and there are also family
rooms. Pool. Jacuzzi. Hot breakfast

buffet. Homebaked cookies at 8pm,
and hot salmon chowder at 5pm in the
cooler months. **$$**

North Bend

The Mill Casino Hotel and RV Park
3201 Tremont Avenue, OR 97459
Tel: 541-756-8800
www.themillcasino.com
This former lumber mill has been
wonderfully converted into a hotel
and casino by the local Coquille tribe,
whose art can be seen in the gift
shop. There are panoramic views of
Coos Bay from every attractive suite;
corner suites in the tower have huge
baths with whirlpool tubs. The hotel
has a fitness room, indoor pool and
two outdoor spas, a business center,
and several bars and restaurants
in the casino. As with most tribal-
owned casino resorts, it's beautifully
appointed but very reasonably priced.
$–$$

Portland

The Benson Hotel
309 SW Broadway, OR 97205
Tel: 503-228-2000
www.bensonhotel.com
The Benson is a historic hotel, built in
1912, in the heart of Downtown and
close to the Pearl District. There's a
fitness center, business center, and
full-service dining in the Gaucho
steakhouse. **$$$**

Mark Spencer Hotel
409 SW 11th Avenue, OR 97205
Tel: 503-224-3293
www.markspencer.com
The Mark Spencer dates back to
1907 when it was opened in the
Theater District, and it still attracts
a lot of visiting actors and artists
today. Guests receive complimentary
continental breakfast and a copy of
the *New York Times* to read with it.
$–$$

Yachats

Overleaf Lodge and Spa
280 Overleaf Lodge Lane, OR 97498
Tel: 541-547-4880
www.overleaflodge.com
This relaxing lodge and spa is right
on the beach, a few minutes from
the center of this appealing little
town, one of the Oregon Coast's
hidden gems. A variety of room styles
feature fireplaces, whirlpool tubs,
patios or balconies and big picture
windows overlooking the sea. Outside
the spacious lobby lounge you can
walk out along the coastal footpath
and enjoy the sandy bays and rock
pools, while at night the sound of
the pounding surf lulls you to sleep.
$$–$$$

Grayland

Walsh Motel
1593 State Route 105, WA 98595
Tel: 360-267-2191
http://westport-walshmotel.com
This attractive little seaside motel has
12 standard units and a further 12
beachside units, some with fireplaces
and Jacuzzis, some with kitchens.
$$–$$$

Long Beach

Adrift Hotel and Spa
409 Sid Snyder Drive, WA 98631
Tel: 360-642-2311
www.adrifthotel.com
This eco inn with 80 rooms is in the
heart of the Long Beach peninsula. It
has a hip, stripped-down, industrial
chic aesthetic, so it may not be for
everyone, but for those who love
the less-is-more approach, it will be
perfect. Ask for an oceanview room.
Onsite bar and fourth-floor restaurant
serving southern coastal Italian
cuisine. Pet friendly. **$–$$**

Raymond

Seaview
Enchanted Cottages
Tel: 360-642-8606
www.enchantedstay.com
These three remodeled vacation
cottages are on the scenic Long Beach
peninsula at Seaview and offer a chance
to decompress and do your thing in
one of Washington's favorite coastal
getaways. Serendipity sleeps 5, the
Captain's Cottage sleeps 2, and the
Hollyhock sleeps 2 plus one small child,
and 2-3 of the cottages can be rented at
once for family reunions. **$–$$$**

Tokeland

Tokeland Hotel and Restaurant
100 Hotel Road
Tel: 360-267-7006
www.tokelandhotel.com
Built in 1889, the Tokeland is the
oldest seaside hotel in Washington
and on the National Register of Historic
Places. The large, creaky building
overlooks Willapa Bay and has the
feel of Grandma's house, with its large
fireplace in the lobby and homey rooms
and beds with quilts. Bathrooms are
separate from the rooms. No Wi-fi. The
restaurant serves homecooked local
food meals. A very good value. **$**

PRICE CATEGORIES

Price categories are based on the average
cost of a double room for one night:
$ = under $110
$$ = $110–250
$$$ = more than $250

EATING OUT

RECOMMENDED RESTAURANTS, CAFES, AND BARS

WHERE AND WHAT TO EAT

All-American

All-American (really German) mainstays like hot dogs and burgers and pretzels are associated with ballparks, corner stands, bars, and fast-food places throughout the country. In New York, look for Jewish deli favourites like corned beef, pastrami, and sour pickles; and thin-crust Neapolitan pizza. In Chicago, Polish-style sausages and Italian deep-dish pizza are local favorites. In Philadelphia, Philly Cheese Steaks explode out of hoagie rolls while in New Orleans, enormous muffaletta sandwiches, crammed with Italian sliced meats, olives, and dressing, are a specialty at Johnny's in the French Quarter, also home to the city's famous po'boy sandwiches stuffed with everything from fried oysters to alligator sausage.

Barbecue

Slow-cooked barbecue leans heavily on pork in the South and East but, invariably, beef in the West. Each region has its own style and fan base. You'll find aged beef with a smokey tomato sauce in Texas and "pulled" (shredded) pork in vinegar-based sauces in the South: Memphis, Tennessee, famous for its barbecue, offers both wet and dry versions.

Coastal America

Coastal America is a haven for fresh seafood – from lobster and clams in New England and grouper on the Gulf to snapper in California and Dungeness crab and salmon in the Pacific Northwest. Inland mountain lakes, rivers, and streams in the Rockies and the Cascades and the Mississippi Delta support rainbow trout, striped bass, catfish, and numerous other delicate freshwater fish.

The Pacific Coast's huge Asian population has led to a lighter fusion cuisine from California to Washington, combining traditional meat and fish with Chinese, Japanese, Vietnamese, and Thai flavors that linger in the mouth.

Southern Food

Southern food, while playing up deep-fried chicken, boiled ham, collard greens, hush puppies, grits, pecan and sweet potato pie, and other "po' folks" foods, has a fusion all its own. The region's Latin, Afro-Caribbean, and French roots are major influences, with the latter's rich Continental-style cuisine as the main fine-dining option.

Rich meets spicy in New Orleans, with its complex gumbo stews and smothered Cajun dishes like crawfish étoufée, and in Florida, where

Deep-dish pizza in Chicago.

Floribbean cuisine combines fresh fish, local citrus and other fruits, and West Indian spices.

Mexican and Southwestern

Mexican food is ubiquitous – sometimes authentic, but often involving quantities of meat and cheese in "Tex-Mex" concoctions that are a far cry from simple tortillas, tamales, and enchiladas. In Cowboy Country, blowout steak dinners are accompanied by the fixings – baked potatoes, sweetcorn, and coleslaw.

Out West, look for delicious, low-fat, grass-fed bison, venison, elk, and other game accompanied by wild greens, pinyon nuts, and wild berries, mainstays of Native American cuisine that have a growing following.

Road Food

Road food is a subject unto itself. Never pass up a slice of homemade pie made from local fruit in farm states like Arizona, Georgia, and Washington; backwoods barbecue, fried green tomatoes, and boiled peanuts in the South; and filled sweet pastries called kolaches in Texas Hill Country. Lastly, when you're traveling hundreds of miles a day, the most important meal of the day is breakfast. Even the lowliest truck stop or diner can fuel you properly for your travels with pancakes, waffles, and creative egg dishes for under $10. Reason enough to get up in the morning.
Note: many of the restaurants are in popular tourist destinations. To avoid long waits, make advance reservations whenever possible.

An American burger ought to feature in at least one meal.

ATLANTIC ROUTE

Burger, fries, and a beer.

New York

New York City
Carnegie Deli
854 Seventh Avenue at 55th Street
Tel: 212-757-2245
www.carnegiedeli.com
A pilgrimage site in the heart of Midtown, this is one of New York's most famous Jewish delicatessens, where the corned beef sandwich is a must. No credit cards. **$$**

Excellent Dumpling House
111 Lafayette Street (just below Canal Street)
Tel: 212-219-0212
www.excellentdumplinghouse.com
Unpretentious, unadorned and on the outskirts of Chinatown proper; always packed with locals and devoted visitors who love its no-nonsense atmosphere, reasonable prices, and stellar dumplings (especially the vegetable dumplings, steamed or fried). No reservations, but there's sometimes a short wait; best for mid-afternoon lunch. No credit cards. **$$**

Il Vagabondo
351 E. 62nd Street, between First and Second avenues
Tel: 212-832-9220
www.ilvagabondo.com
Like sharing a meal in an Italian town – classic Italian dishes in a place filled with locals, most of whom are hanging around the indoor bocce ball court. Consider the menu, but the waiter's advice is never to be ignored. **$$$**

Oyster Bar
Lower level, Grand Central Terminal
Tel: 212-490-6650
A New York institution and a must for seafood lovers. The best fresh oysters

and clam chowder in town, and you can sit at a counter, dining room or salon. **$$–$$$**

The Little Owl
90 Bedford Street
Tel: 212-741-4695
www.thelittleowl.com
This hip, upbeat, corner bistro in Greenwich Village is the essence of the New York neighbourhood hangout. The seasonal menu is lively without being uber chic; fresh seafood shares the menu with comfort food like gravy meatball sliders. Beer and wine only. **$$$**

Union Square Café
21 E. 16th Street
Tel: 212-243-4020
www.unionsquare.com
Possibly the friendliest service in New York and some of the best new-American cuisine anywhere. Reservations are difficult as this very popular restaurant's innovative menu attracts a hip crowd. Definitely call ahead. **$$$**

New Jersey

Morristown
The Famished Frog and The Side Bar
18 Washington Street
Tel: 973-540-9601
www.famishedfrog.com
In the mood for a sports bar and game of darts or foosball? That's the Famished Frog, a cheerful watering hole. Rather have a casual meal and sample brews from an amazingly long list of ales, lagers, stouts and barley wines? The Side Bar, on the other side of the wall, is calling your name. **$$**

Pennsylvania

Chadds Ford
Bistro on the Brandywine and Brandywine Prime
1623 Baltimore Pike 19317
Tel: 610-388-8090
www.bistroonthebrandywine.com
Located right on Route 1, in the heart of the Brandywine Valley, within a musket shot of the battlefield and the Brandywine Museum. The old stone building (on the right-hand side of the road) has been a tavern since 1736. After the Battle of Brandywine, the building was so "plundered" by the British that the owners were exempt from taxes. Bistro does French-inspired casual fare, stone hearth pizza, soups and salads. Brandywine Prime does steaks, chops, and other heartier fare at dinner only. **$–$$$**

Lambertville
Cross Culture
13 Klines Court
Tel: 609-397-3600
www.crosscultureindiancuisine.net
Well prepared Indian food in a nicely decorated room. The menu is smallish and explains each dish for those unfamiliar with the cuisine. The lunch special is a particularly good deal. BYOB. **$**

Philadelphia
Cuba Libre
10 S. Second Street
Tel: 215-627-0666
www.cubalibrerestaurant.com
Built to resemble an outdoor Cuban café in the 1940s, the menu has traditional and "nuevo" Cuban dishes. **$$**

Jim's Steaks
400 S. Street
Tel: 215-928-1911
www.lebecfin.com
Many cheese-steak connoisseurs consider this funky little place the tastiest in town. **$**

Lacroix at Rittenhouse Hotel
1210 W. Rittenhouse Square
Tel: 215-546-9000
www.lacroixrestaurant.com
Award-winning restaurant at the hotel, equal amounts of fresh seasonal ingredients and innovative uses of those ingredients to create a fresh menu. The Tasting and three-plate menus both bring the restaurant into an affordable price range. **$$$**

Le Bec-Fin
1523 Walnut Street
Tel: 215-567-1000
www.lebecfin.com
Regarded as one of the finest restaurants in the country, this very expensive French favorite near Rittenhouse Square garners rave reviews from critics and clients alike. Reservations required. Á la carte menu served at the downstairs bistro. **$$$**

Maryland

Annapolis
Carrol's Creek Restaurant
410 Severn Avenue
www.carrolscreek.com
Tel: 410-263-8102
Located on "restaurant row" east of the city harbor. Sophisticated treatment of Chesapeake standards – crab, scallops, rockfish, cream of crab soup. – with a view of the Bay. Extensive wine list. **$$$**

Chick and Ruth's Deli
165 Main Street
Tel: 410-269-6737
www.chickandruths.com
An institution, known for huge sandwiches named for politicians and local celebrities. Elected officials know they've "made it" when they're on the menu. Always crowded; always good. **$**

Baltimore
Bo Brooks
2701 Boston Street
Tel: 410-558-0202
www.bobrooks.com
The place to go for a crab feast. If you don't know how to crack and pick crabs, the friendly staff will teach you. If the weather cooperates, there are few better ways to spend an afternoon then spending it with crabs, slaw, corn on the cob and a Natty Bo (National Bohemian beer, a local brew). **$$–$$$**
Cafe Hon
1002 W. 36th Street
Tel: 410-243-1230
In Hampden, where film director John Waters draws inspiration for his unique, quirky view of the world. "Hi, Hon" is the universal greeting in Bawlmer – the local corruption of the city's name. Cafe Hon serves local favorites: crab cakes, meat loaf, chili, chicken pot pie, and homemade potato chips coated with Old Bay seasoning. **$–$$**
Jimmy's
801 S. Broadway
Tel: 410-327-3273
Where Fell's Point residents gathers in the pre-dawn hours – on their way to work or on their way home – and the rest of the day, as well. Famous for massive breakfasts served by friendly waitresses and good, diner food the rest of the day. Definitely fancy and definitely worth the visit. **$**
Tapas Adela
814 S. Broadway
Tel: 410-534-6262
www.tapasadala.com
Extensive menu of Spanish small plates designed to be shared by a group. You can nibble and sip from their wines from Spain and South America all night. **$$–$$$**

Virginia

Charlottesville
C&O Restaurant
515 E. Water Street
Tel: 434-971-7044
www.tapasadala.com
Imaginative dishes with a French influence served in an attractively converted rail workers' layover. Try the sliced, marinated, and seared flank

steak. Elegant but casual atmosphere. **$$**
Millers
109 W. Main Street
Tel: 434-971-8511
www.millersdowntown.com
An old-style and pleasantly smoky atmosphere bar. Formerly a drugstore specializing in "Miller's Tonic" in the early 1900s. The current Millers dispenses great cheeseburgers and a nice grilled chicken salad. Sit on the outdoor patio with bubbling fountain. **$**

Fredericksburg
Sammy T's
801 Caroline Street
Tel: 540-371-2008
www.sammyts.com
One block from the visitor center, Sammy's storefront restaurant serves sandwiches, burgers, and salads, plus a good vegetarian and vegan selection. **$**

Lexington
The Red Hen
11 E. Washington Street
Tel: 540-464-4401
www.redhenlex.com
One of the first farm-to-table restaurants, featuring the bounty of the Shenandoah Valley. Menu changes almost daily; wines are chosen to truly enhance the meal. **$$–$$$**

Richmond
Millie's Diner
2603 E. Main Street
Tel: 804-643-5512
With only 44 seats in this 1940s-era brick storefront, it's not uncommon to have to wait, but curb your impatience. The flavours and care with which the chefs in the open kitchen prepare the southern standards is worth it. Another bonus: the incredible jukebox with thousands of 45s. **$$**
The Tobacco Company
1201 E. Cary Street
Tel: 804-782-9555
www.thetobaccocompany.com
A landmark in the historic Shockoe Slip District, this converted four-story tobacco warehouse serves classic steaks, chops, and seafood in two distinct areas: a formal and elegant dining room or a garden veranda setting. **$$–$$$**

Roanoke
Roanoker
2522 Colonial Avenue
Tel: 540-344-7746
www.theroanokerrestaurant.com
A local favourite since it opened in 1941, this Southern diner serves up big portions of traditional down-home

Southern classics and comfort food from family recipes. **$–$$**

North Carolina

Chapel Hill
Spanky's
101 E. Franklin Street
Tel: 919-967-2678
www.spankysrestaurant.com
Buzzing restaurant in the student district serving sandwiches, seafood, and pasta. Spanky's club sandwich is a favorite with both locals and visitors. **$**

Durham
Bullock's Bar-B-Cue
3330 Quebec Drive
Tel: 919-383-3211
www.bullocksbbq.com
Tommy Bullock started working at the family restaurant as a kid when it opened in 1950. After all that time, he's got the recipe down pat. You can order off the menu, but go "family style." The food never stops coming: Brunswick stew, chopped Bar-B-Cue, fried chicken, hush puppies, string beans, greens, banana pudding, and sweet tea. Closed Sun/Mon. **$**

Fayetteville
Luigi's
528 N. McPherson Church Road
Tel: 910-864-1810
www.luigisnc.com
Casually upscale, with all of the beloved Italian favorites excellently well prepared as well as rack of lamb and steaks. Probably the best wine list in town. **$$–$$$**

Greensboro
M'Coul's
110 W. McGee Street
Tel: 336-378-0204
www.mcoulspub.com
An authentic Irish pub in an atmospheric 1892 building. Solid pub grub and many imported drafts. Outdoor courtyard and upper level terrace seating. **$**

Mount Airy
Snappy Lunch
125 N. Main Street
Tel: 336-786-4931
www.thesnappylunch.com
The Snappy Lunch is known for its hefty pork chop sandwich -– a

PRICE CATEGORIES

Price categories are for an average cost of dinner and a glass of wine, before tip:
$ = under $20
$$ = $20–40
$$$ = more than $40

cornucopia of juicy meat, condiments, and trimmings. Plenty of atmosphere too. **$**

Wilmington

Elijah's Restaurant

2 Ann Street
Tel: 910-343-1448
www.elijahs.com
Award-winning seafood chowder and other delectable, equally praiseworthy dishes. The adjoining oyster bar with outdoor covered patio faces Cape Fear. **$$**

Winston-Salem

The Old Fourth Street Filling Station

871 W. Fourth Street
Tel: 336-724-7600
www.theoldfourthstreetfillingstation.com
Located in a former filling station, this combines a welcoming atmosphere and great food. Very comprehensive menu, from salads and wraps to grilled salmon, pasta, and pork tenderloin. **$$**

South Carolina

Charleston

Poogan's Porch

72 Queen Street
Tel: 843-577-2337
www.poogansporch.com
A Lowcountry, Southern cooking restaurant in a Lowcountry, Southern setting. Dine on the porch of the old Victorian house or in the high-ceilinged dining room, both with white tablecloths and silverware, taking you to another, more elegant time. But the food is as Southern as it gets: farm-to-table buttermilk fried chicken, she-crab soup with sherry, homemade biscuits, pimento cheese straws, and a 1,500-bottle wine cellar. **$$–$$$**

Georgetown

Limpin' Jane's

713 Front Street
Tel: 843-485-4953
www.limpinjanes.com
Casual restaurant accessible from the boardwalk over the river or the street. Exposed brick walls and deep booths keep things cool in summer and cozy in winter. Lots of Lowcountry standards, good sandwiches. A definite seafood emphasis, but nice choices for meat-eaters. **$$**

Myrtle Beach

Omega Pancake and Omelet House

2800 N. Kings Highway
Tel: 843-626-9949
Favorite breakfast spot for tourists and locals alike. Cheerful service and all the coffee you want, from a pot on your table. **$**

Sea Captain's House

3002 N. Ocean Boulevard
Tel: 843-488-8082
www.seacaptains.com
Venerated seafood restaurant voted "Best" in the resort four years in a row. Extensive menu, all fresh. Deck seating, and most indoor rooms have a view. When very busy, service can be a little slow. **$$**

Georgia

Brunswick

Right on Q BBQ

2809 Glynn Avenue
Tel: 912-264-0047
www.rightonqbbq.com
Melt-in-your-mouth ribs, sweet potato fries, collard greens…southern barbecue doesn't get much better than this. Kids eat free Monday through Thursday. **$**

Sonny's BBQ

5328 New Jessup Highway 31525
Tel: 912-264-9184
www.sonnysbbq.com
Very convenient to I-95, you can get ribs, pork three ways, and the usual list of traditional Southern favorites. **$–$$**

Midway

Angie's Diner

510 N. Coastal Highway
Tel: 912-884-3663
Solid comfort food includes fried bologna sandwiches, biscuits and sausage gravy, and huge stacks of fluffy pancakes. **$**

St Simons Island

Palmer's Village Café

223 Mallory Street
Tel: 912-634-5515
www.palmersvillagecafe.com
Comfortable and casual spot where the creative breakfast menu shines. Specials include green eggs and ham, and challah bread French toast. **$**

Gnat's Landing

310 Redfern Village
Tel: 912-638-7378
www.gnatslanding.com
Casual sea shack atmosphere with excellent fresh seafood served in an open-air deck under a canopy roof. Seafood gumbo, sandwiches, and deep-fried pickles. **$$**

Savannah

The Distillery

416 W. Liberty Street
Tel: 912-236-1772
www.distillerysavannah.com
Well-placed near the Visitor Center, the building was a distillery until Prohibition. That it is now serves over

100 craft beers seems fitting poetic justice. The kitchen considers the burgers, sandwiches, salads, and noshes as important as the brews. Deep-fried Moon Pie dessert ought to be illegal! Equally popular with locals and tourists. **$**

Mrs Wilkes' Boarding House

107 W. Jones Street
Tel: 912-232-5997
www.mrswilkes.com
Southern-style communal dining, the old boarding house way. Pass the biscuits and fried chicken, and get there early. Lunch only. **$**

Wiley's Championship BBQ

4700 US Highway 80E 31410
Tel: 912-201-3259
www.wileyschampionshipbbq.com
The essence of southern barbecue. Within four years of opening, Wiley and Janet McCreary stopped participating in barbecue competitions, because they'd won all of them. The tiny storefront in a little strip shopping center usually has a cluster of people waiting for a table inside or out. Smoked ribs, sausage, chicken, and brisket, pulled pork, "best beans on the planer,' macaroni and cheese, collards, sweet potato casserole, and sweet tea. **$**

Florida

Bradenton

Anna Maria Oyster Bar

6696 Cortez Road W.
Tel: 941-792-0077
www.oysterbar.net
It's oysters…raw, Rockefeller, or fried… along with a huge menu of moderately priced dishes including peel-n-eat shrimp, chowders, and fresh fried fish platters. Happy hour 11am to 5pm and 8pm until closing. This family-friendly restaurant offers special kids' menus. **$–$$**

Fire and Stone Pizza

10519 Cortez Road W.
Tel: 941-792-5300
The draw here is the scrumptious "Endless" Artisan Pizza Bar, with a huge selection of toppings, 24-item salad bar, homemade soups, and ice cream with a choice of toppings…and all for under $10. **$**

Clearwater Beach

Kaiko Sushi Bar and Japanese Restaurant

2475 McMullen Booth Road
Tel: 727-791-6640
www.kaikosushibar.com
This award-winning restaurant, a local staple for more than 15 years, serves first-rate sashimi, sushi, teriyaki, and other authentic Japanese dishes.

Wash down some gyoza (sautéed beef dumplings) with a cup of warm sake. **$$**

Fort Myers
The Veranda
2122 Second Street
Tel: 239-332-2065
www.verandarestaurant.com
For more than 30 years this charming restaurant in two historic downtown homes has been a popular choice for Southern regional cuisine. In nice weather opt for a table al fresco. **$$$**

Gainesville
Paramount Grill
12 Southwest First Avenue
Tel: 352-378-3398
www.paramountgrill.com
The owner/chef at this chic downtown eatery carefully crafts sophisticated dishes such as grilled tandoori-spiced salmon. **$$$**

Jacksonville
Matthew's
2107 Hendricks Avenue
Tel: 904-396-9922
www.matthewsrestaurant.com
The five-course chef's tasting menu, which allows diners to interact with the chefs while they're cooking, is a fine introduction to the innovative and varied menu, served in a chic, stylish setting. Early dining and four-course menus are also offered. The wine cellar holds up to 2,000 bottles. **$$$**

Key Largo
Tasters Grille and Market
Tavernier Towne Center, MM 91, Tavernier
Tel: 305-853-1177
www.tastersgrille.com
The chef melds Caribbean, Asian, Lowcountry and Mediterranean flavors

Authentic fish house in Key West.

to prepare an eclectic menu of tasty treats. **$$–$$$**

Key West
Blue Heaven
729 Thomas Street
Tel: 305-296-8666
www.blueheavenkw.com
Relaxed, time-tested and popular café serving West Indian-style breakfasts, lunches, dinners, and authentic Key lime pie. Dining outdoors here is like being invited to someone's backyard party; there's often live music, and strolling chickens. **$**

Camille's
1202 Simonton Street
Tel: 305-296-4811
www.camilleskeywest.com
With a menu that changes daily, this funky, laid-back restaurant has been a local favorite for more than 20 years. Specialties include pecan waffles, stone crab cakes, chicken salad, and, of course, Key lime pie. **$–$$**

Louie's Backyard
700 Waddell Avenue
Tel: 305-294-1061
www.louiesbackyard.com
Fine Caribbean-American cuisine in a romantic setting with old Key West ambiance. Start with a glass of wine and roasted clams on the upper deck. **$$$**

Pepe's Cafe
806 Caroline Street
Tel: 305-294-7192
http://pepescafe.net
Excellent hand-cut steaks, succulent oysters, and fragrant, fresh-baked breads, indoor and outdoor dining and a very popular bar at the town's oldest restaurant, which serves up three delicious meals daily. **$$**

Marathon
Butterfly Café at Tranquility Bay Resort
2600 Overseas Highway, Mile Marker 48.5
Tel: 305-289-7177
www.tranquilitybay.com
Fine, family-friendly dining in a tropical setting close to the sea. Fresh seafood reigns supreme here, as does the Key lime pie. **$$$**

Herbie's
6350 Overseas Highway, Mile Marker 50.5
Tel: 305-743-6373
Fresh seafood served in a laid-back Keys ambiance. Opt for a seat at one of the picnic tables and tuck into an order of conch fritters and fish tacos. Landlubbers will like the burgers with homemade buns. **$–$$**

Miami
Casa Juancho
2436 SW. Eighth Street

Tel: 305-642-2452
www.casajuancho.com
Authentic Spanish fare includes a large selection of tapas, imported cheeses, and paellas, as well as elegantly prepared seafood and prime beef dishes. Entertainment is provided by roving musicians. **$$$**

Joe's Stone Crab Restaurant
11 Washington Avenue
Tel: 305-673-0365
www.joesstonecrab.com
This longtime South Beach favorite, in business since 1913, features the prized and delectably sweet stone crab. But a bevy of other offerings include Maine lobster, grouper, and several landlubbers' options. Reservations not accepted. **$$$**

La Rosa
4041 NW Seventh Street
Tel: 305-541-1715
www.rosarestaurant.com
Cuban-influenced specialties include arroz con pollo, sweet potato stuffed with shredded beef, and homemade ice cream. The friendly waitstaff is happy to make suggestions, and the nightly piano music adds to the delightful ambiance. **$$**

News Cafe
800 Ocean Drive, Miami Beach
Tel: 305-538-6397
www.newscafe.com
Very fashionable 24-hour café/restaurant/bar/newsstand whose kitchen prepares Middle Eastern dishes, paninis, and good egg breakfasts. Sit at one of the outdoor tables and enjoy the passing parade. **$–$$**

Scotty's Landing
33381 Pan American Drive, Coconut Grove
Tel: 305-854-2626
www.sailmiami.com/scottys.htm
A salty, casual shack with fish treats such as she-crab soup and conch fritters, and a million-dollar view of Biscayne Bay. It can be tricky to find: ask for directions. **$**

Versailles Restaurant
3555 SW Eighth Street, Little Havana
Tel: 305-444-0240
www.versaillesrestaurant.com
For more than 30 years a destination for delicious Cuban cooking in a wonderfully festive atmosphere. Open daily for breakfast, lunch and dinner; Sunday breakfast buffet (9am–11:45am) is not to be missed. **$**

PRICE CATEGORIES

Price categories are for an average cost of dinner and a glass of wine, before tip:
$ = under $20
$$ = $20–40
$$$ = more than $40

Orlando
Earl of Sandwich
Downtown Disney, 1750 East Buena Vista Drive
Tel: 407-938-0250
www.earlofsandwichusa.com
This aptly named, family friendly, and often-busy fast food chain specializes in hot sandwiches, including their signature Original 1762 – roast beef, cheddar and horseradish sauce; but also offers salads, wraps, desserts and breakfast sandwiches. **$**

Fulton's Crab House
Downtown Disney, 1670 North Buena Vista Drive, Lake Buena Vista
Tel: 407-939-3463
www.fultonscrabhouse.com
Lunch and dinner served aboard an authentic three-deck riverboat which stays moored at Downtown Disney. Seafood specialties with fresh fish flown in daily include an excellent raw bar. **$$$**

Kres Chop House
17 W. Church Street
Tel: 407-447-7953-7625
www.kresrestaurant.com
This very stylish downtown restaurant with a classic steak house menu serves some of the best beef in the area. Good desserts (try the chocolate bread pudding) as well. **$$$**

Victoria and Albert's
Disney Grand Floridian Resort
4401 Grand Floridian
Tel: 407-939-3463
www.victoria-alberts.com
For a big night out, this may be the best spot in town. The surroundings are elegant (jackets required), the service is excellent, and the menu – offerings change regularly – includes an option of a six-course prix fixe with wine pairings is superb. **$$$**

St Augustine
O'Steen's Restaurant
205 Anastasia Boulevard
Tel: 904-829-6974
www.osteensrestaurant.com
The fried shrimp, deep fried oysters, and homemade clam chowder make this casual spot worth the often-long wait. No credit or debit cards. **$**

Raintree
102 San Marco Avenue
Tel: 904-824-7211
www.raintreerestaurant.com
The diverse, intercontinental menu at this meticulously restored 1879 Viictorian home-turned-restaurant blends Mediterranean, American, and Asian cuisines. Seating is available in the interior garden atrium, dining room, or outdoor courtyard. **$$**

Tampa
Columbia Restaurant
2117 E. Seventh Avenue
Tel: 813-248-4961
www.columbiarestaurant.com
Authentic Cuban cuisine and nightly flamenco dancing in an atmospheric building make this Ybor City destination, founded in 1905, a must. **$$–$$$**

Osteria Natalina
3215 S. Macdill Avenue
Tel: 813-831-1210
Chain restaurants who like to brag about making diners feel like family would do well to visit this small restaurant, where patrons do indeed feel like long-lost relatives. And what do you do when relatives visit? Feed them, of course… treats like grilled calamari, homemade lasagna, and freshly prepared pasta. And since the proprietor and his family hail from the seaside Italian town of Rimini, he takes particular pride in preparing incredibly tasty seafood specialties. **$$**

Venice
K.T. Deli
454 E. Venice Avenue
Tel: 941-488-9567
Toan Nguyen and his wife, Kim, serve up a huge selection of sandwiches ranging from gyros to Ruebens to philly cheese steaks. But the standout is the Vietnamese Banh Mi sandwich, packed with succulent pork and fresh vegetables, and the sublime homemade eggrolls. **$$**

NORTHERN ROUTE

Massachusetts

Boston
Casa Razdora
115 Water Street (Financial District)
Tel: 617-338-6700
www.casarazdora.com
It's only open for lunch and there's limited seating, but this is the place to get a wonderful sub, panini, or home-made pasta. A perfect picnic stop. **$**

A hot dog with everything on it – the American way.

Durgin Park
340 Faneuil Hall
Market Place
Tel: 617-227-2038
www.durgin-park.com
Yankee cooking – especially prime rib and clam chowder – attracts flocks of tourists to this legendary old dining hall Reservations accepted except on Saturdays when the wait can be long. **$$–$$$**

Hamersley's Bistro
553 Tremont Street
(South End)
Tel: 617-423-2700
www.hamersleysbistro.com
One of Boston's early bistros, opened more than 20 years ago, is still one of its most popular. The cuisine is solid New England, with a nod to French bistro fare. And the dish that helped to build Hamersley's reputation, roast chicken with garlic, is still on the menu. Reservations not accepted for patio seating, which is the place to be on a beautiful night. **$$$**

Legal Sea Foods
www.legalseafoods.com
26 Park Plaza
Tel: 617-426-4444
Copley Place, 100 Huntington Avenue
Tel: 617-266-7775
Long Wharf, 255 State Street
Tel: 617-742-5300
Prudential Center, 800 Boylston Street
Tel: 617-266-6800
Logan Airport: numerous locations
Seaport, 225 Northern Avenue
Tel: 617-330-7430

What started as a small Cambridge fish store has blossomed into a national chain with a justly deserved reputation for serving a tremendous selection of the freshest fish available. **$$–$$$**

Pizzeria Regina
11½ Thacher Street (North End)
Tel: 617-227-0765
www.reginapizzeria.com
Although it has opened numerous branches, none rivals the original location, which serves what many aficionados consider the best pie in Boston. **$$**

Cambridge
East Coast Grill and Raw Bar
1271 Cambridge Street (Inman Square)
Tel: 617-491-6568
www.eastcoastgrill.net
A stylish, wildly popular spot for innovative grilled seafood (often topped with exotic spice rubs or fruit salsas), creative salads, barbecue and fiery "pasta from hell." Margaritas help ease the often-long wait for a table. **$$**

Rialto Restaurant
Charles Hotel, 1 Bennett Street
Tel: 617-661-5050
www.rialto-restaurant.com
Chef Jody Adams has earned international accolades for her flavorful melding of New England ingredients with regional Italian touches in a coolly elegant dining room. Monday is $1 oyster night. **$$$**

Concord
80 Thoreau
80 Thoreau Street
Tel: 978-318-0008
www.80thoreau.com
Hip, contemporary, and well-prepared New American cuisine in the middle of historic Concord. The Minute Men might have laid down their arms for an order of pappardelle with rabbit ragu. Dinner only. **$$–$$$**

Gloucester
Dog Bar
65 Main Street
Tel: 978-281-6565
www.dogbarcapeann.com
Cozy neighborhood restaurant with a small but varied pub-style menu ranging from seafood to burgers to flat bread pizza, served in a dramatic granite-walled hideaway. Dine al fresco in the summer. Entertainment most nights: check the website for their schedule. **$$**

Franklin Cape Ann
118 Main Street
Tel: 978-283-7888
www.franklincafe.com

Upscale bistro with a popular wine bar, blending fresh fish and local produce to prepare creative Modern American dishes such as cornmeal-crusted catfish. **$$**

The Rudder Restaurant
73 Rocky Neck Avenue
Tel: 978-283-7967
www.rudderrestaurant.com
A rollicking, deservedly popular waterfront restaurant in the Rocky Neck artists' colony. The specialty is fresh fish delivered right to the dock. Lobster served on the patio can't be beat. **$$**

Ipswich
Clam Box
246 High Street
Tel: 978-356-9707
www.ipswichma.com/clambox
One of the best places in the region for fried clams, harvested right on the famed Ipswich flats in season. You can't miss it – it's housed in a building shaped like a clam box. Order inside and dine outside at one of the picnic tables. **$**

Lexington
Daikanyama
43 Waltham Street
Tel: 781-860-9388
www.dkyama.com
Well-prepared sushi, sashimi and other Japanese dishes served by kimono-clad waitresses in a small, friendly spot. **$$**

La Boniche
143 Merrimack Street, Lowell
Tel: 978-458-9473
www.laboniche.com
An intimate restaurant serving creative French fare in a landmark Art Nouveau building. Open for lunch and dinner. The Tuesday through Thursday prix fixe three-course dinner draws a loyal clientele. Closed Sun–Mon. **$–$$**

New Hampshire

Meredith
George's Diner
10 Plymouth Street
Tel: 603-279-8723
www.georgesdiner.com
No-nonsense, fresh New England grub featuring such staples as corn chowder and chicken croquettes, and tasty, attractively priced nightly specials. **$**

Portsmouth
Golden Egg
960 Sagamore Avenue
Tel: 603-436-0519
www.goldeneggrestaurant.com

Although renowned for its great breakfasts…the eggs Benedict are a knockout…lunch at this very popular local eatery is also terrific, and the desserts are all homemade. Open daily from 6am to 2pm. **$**

Portsmouth Gas Light Company
64 Market Street
Tel: 603-430-9122
www.portsmouthgaslight.com
A local favorite for its delicious brick-oven pizza, wood-fired bistro cuisine and old-timey ambiance – it's in an 1837 building, which housed the city's first utility. The ground floor restaurant shares a lunch and dinner menu with the café on the open, upper deck, where there's live music in season. **$** (for the basement pizza joint), **$$** (for the restaurant)

Maine

Kennebunkport
50 Local
50 Main Street, Kennebunk
Tel: 207-985-0850
www.localkennebunk.com
Two-dollar tapas every Tuesday D only; closed Mon. One of the area's newest and most popular restaurants, a casually comfortable spot right in town, offers French bistro dishes with an American take, and draws extensively on local suppliers both on land and sea. The menu changes often, but diners are pretty sure to find a fine selection of local cheeses, lobster carbonara, and mac and cheese with roasted truffle oil. **$$**

The Clam Shack
2 Western Avenue (on the bridge)
Tel: 207-967-3321 (information); 207-967-2560 (take out)
www.theclamshack.net
Superlative fried clams, lobster rolls and other seafood favorites served on fresh baked buns and dispensed from a simple hut. Dining is al fresco (sit on wooden benches or lobster crates), and lines can be long at lunchtime. Open May to early October. **$**

Ogunquit Beach
Barnacle Billy's
Perkins Cove
Tel: 207-646-5575
www.barnbilly.com
Serves lobster galore plus chicken and clam chowder. Dine on the outside deck right on the edge of Perkins Cove.

PRICE CATEGORIES

Price categories are for an average cost of dinner and a glass of wine, before tip:
$ = under $20
$$ = $20–40
$$$ = more than $40

The next-door restaurant, Barnacle Billy's Etc (tel: 207-646-4711), is the pricier option. **$–$$**

Portland
Back Bay Grill
65 Portland Street
Tel: 207-772-8833
www.backbaygrill.com
Imaginative regional and New American dishes are prepared fresh daily in the open kitchen of this charming restaurant in an attractive century-old building. The wine list, which includes a fine selection of ports by the glass, is extensive and the desserts, including chocolate polenta cake and nougat parfait, are excellent. Dinner only. Closed Sun. and Mon. **$$–$$$**
Becky's
Hobson's Wharf, 390 Commercial Street
Tel: 207-773-7070
www.beckysdiner.com
Downtown diner with all-day breakfasts and hearty homestyle platters of fried seafood, turkey, meatloaf, and lobster rolls. Small, friendly, and very popular. Open daily. **$**

Wells
The Steakhouse
1205 Post Road/Route 1
Tel: 207-646-4200
www.the-steakhouse.com
Consistently voted one of the best steakhouses in the whole of New England, this busy restaurant serves hand-cut, well-aged prime and choice beef, as well as a variety of chicken and seafood dishes, including Maine lobster, of course. Open late March to mid-December. Dinner only; closed Mon. **$$**

Arlington
Arlington Inn
Route 7A
Tel: 802-375-6532
www.arlingtoninn.com
Fairly formal candlelit restaurant creating New England and Continental dishes such as lobster pie and beef Stroganoff prepared with local meats and produce. The tavern offers less expensive fare. Closed Mon. **$$$**
West Mountain Inn
River Road (off Route 313)
Tel: 802-375-6516
www.westmountaininn.com
New American fare featuring local and organic produce in a low-beamed paneled dining room at a romantic but family-friendly inn. A fixed-price multi-course dinner, with numerous menu options such as pan seared Atlantic

salmon with braised local ramps (a kind of wild scallion), is served nightly. Reservations necessary. **$$$**

Dorset
Chantecleer Restaurant
Route 7a, E. Dorset
Tel: 802-362-1616
www.chantecleerrestaurant.com
The Swiss chef at one of the area's favorite restaurants prepares Swiss and French provincial dishes such as veal scaloppini Schnitzel in a handsomely renovated dairy barn. A three-course special ($$) is offered. Reservations recommended. Dinner Wed–Sun. **$$$**
Dorset Inn
8 Church Street/Route 30
Tel: 802-867-5500
www.dorsetinn.com
Uncomplicated but excellent bistro-style seasonal fare in a 1796 hostelry. Offerings might include roast turkey croquettes or grilled veal paillard. Part of the Vermont Fresh Network, thereby supporting farmers and serving the best local produce. Service in the dining room or tavern. **$$**

Fairlee
Fairlee Diner
Route 5
Tel: 802-333-3569
Neat little diner with a classic diner menu, good-sized servings, and sometimes long waits. Breakfast omelettes are a popular choice, as are the burgers and strawberry rhubarb pie. **$**

Killington
Choices Restaurant
2820 Killington Road
Tel: 802-422-4030
choices-restaurant.com
Chef Claude specializes in rotisserie, with entrées such as filet mignon with Saga blue cheese, and rack of lamb. Lively 30-something bar scene. The deck is lovely on a warm, summer's night. **$$**

Manchester
Marsh Tavern
Equinox Resort, 3567 Main Street
Tel: 802-362-4700
www.equinoxresort.com
Well-prepared New England fare with a deft Continental touch served in an historic building that offers diners a sense of history along with their martinis and prime rib. Live entertainment, a lighter menu, and outdoor seating in the lounge. **$$–$$$**
Up for Breakfast
4935 Main Street
Tel: 802-362-4204

A popular choice for pancakes doused with Vermont maple syrup, delicious omelettes and fabulous French toast, along with freshly squeezed fruit juices. Jammed on the weekends but well worth the wait. **$**

Middlebury
Fire and Ice Restaurant
26 Seymour Street
Tel: 802-388-7166 or 800-367-7166
www.fireandicerestaurant.com
Since 1974 this deservedly popular restaurant with seating in a myriad of cozy nooks has been a favorite for prime rib, fresh fish, and unlimited trips to the 55-item salad bar. There's a special room with movies to keep children occupied while parents dine. The Moose Tavern offers a pub menu. **$$**

Quechee
Parker House Inn and Bistro
1792 Main Street
Tel: 802-295-6077
www.theparkerhouseinn.com
Tasty New England fare with a Mediterranean flair in a eclectically furnished brick Victorian mansion in the village. Al fresco dining overlooking the river. **$$**
Simon Pearce Restaurant
The Mill, 1760 Main Street
Tel: 802-295-1470
www.simonpearceglass.com
Fine country cuisine with Irish touches set in an old riverside mill. Dine on a covered terrace (glass-enclosed in winter) overlooking the falls. Extensive wine list. **$$**

Woodstock
The Prince and the Pauper Restaurant
24 Elm Street
Tel: 802-457-1818
www.princeandpauper.com
An in-town institution for more than 30 years serving an eclectic dinner menu that spotlights locally sourced products. Among the highlights – house-smoked salmon and roast duckling. Options include prix fixe and bistro (not available Sat) menus. **$$–$$$**

Buffalo
Anchor Bar
1047 Main Street
Tel: 716-883-1134
www.anchorbar.com
Family-run restaurant, originally established in 1935, famous for inventing spicy chicken wings in the early 1960s (now widely known as

Buffalo wings). It's worth stopping at this casual eatery if only to see what all the fuss is about! **$**

Encore
492 Pearl Street
Tel: 716-931-5001
www.encorebuffalo.com
Spread over two floors, this eatery specializes in steak and sushi. Located in the theatre district near Shea's Performing Arts Center, with bare brick walls and a modern, casual feel. Closed Sunday. **$–$$**

Laughlin's Hearty Bistro
333 Franklin
Tel: 716-842-6700
www.laughlinsrestaurant.com
In the heart of downtown Buffalo, this dark, swanky bistro serves a number of local specialties including spicy Buffalo wings with blue cheese and celery and the venerable Beef on Weck (shaved, juicy roast beef served on a salty kummelweck roll with horseradish.) Yum. **$$**

Lockport
Cammarata's
6336 Robinson Road
Tel: 716-433-5353
www.cammaratas.com
This Italian restaurant offers a varied menu catering for everyone, with prime rib steak, seafood, and pasta. Fish fry on Fridays. **$–$$**

Rome
Teddy's Restaurant
851 Black River Boulevard
Tel: 315-336-7839
www.teddysrestaurantny.com
Teddy's offers casual dining and friendly service with a menu featuring popular American and Italian fare including pizza, pasta, paninis, and seafood – and don't forget to ask about the soup of the day. L & D Mon–Sat. **$–$$**

Saratoga Springs
Wheatfields Bar and Restaurant
440 Broadway
Tel: 518-587-0534
www.wheatfields.com
Wholesome, freshly made pasta dishes ranging from chicken and seafood to vegetarian and gluten-free options. Pizza and salads also served. **$$**

Schenectady
Blue Ribbon Restaurant
1801 State Street
Tel: 518-393-2600
www.blueribbonrestaurant.com
Hometown diner with friendly service and large portions of comfort food. Family-run and well-loved with tasty

sandwiches and omelettes. Blue Ribbon is known for its award-winning cheesecake. **$**

Clinton's Ditch
112 S. College Street
Tel: 518-346-8376
www.onefortheditch.com
Casual place offering range of steak, burgers, pasta, pizza, and seafood, plus lighter bites for lunch. **$**

Syracuse
Empire Brewing Company
Armory Square, 120 Walton Street
Tel: 315-475-2337
www.empirebrew.com
Housed in a smartly converted old grocery warehouse with much exposed stone and brick, this popular microbrewery has a long list of beers and an eclectic menu with the focus on locally sourced ingredients. **$**

The Mission
304 E. Onondaga Street
Tel: 315-475-7344
www.themissionrestaurant.com
Mix of Mexican and South American cuisine with tacos, enchiladas and quesadillas, including meat, seafood, and vegetarian choices. Formerly a Methodist church, this building sits on an underground tunnel that fugitive slaves on the Underground Railroad used as a refuge. **$–$$**

Pennsylvania

Erie
Colony Pub and Grille
2670 W. Eighth Street
Tel: 814-838-2162
www.colonypub.com/
Three dining rooms including multiple fireplaces and jazz music some nights. Great seafood and steaks plus full bar. Locally owned and operated since 1955. **$–$$$**

Ohio

Cleveland
Fire Food and Drink
13220 Shaker Square
Tel: 216-921-3473
http://firefoodanddrink.com/
Located at historic Shaker Square, this chic spot serves up Sunday brunch like no other. Think lemon soufflé pancakes, fresh fruit salad, and a zesty Bloody Mary. The farm-to-table menu at Fire has been so popular with Clevelanders that Chef Doug Katz opened a second restaurant at the world-famous Cleveland Museum of Art in autumn 2012 (called Provenance). **$$–$$$**

Lolita
900 Literary Road

Tel: 216-771-5652
http://lolitarestaurant.com
Mediterranean style eatery by famous Chef Michael Symon. Small plates, artisanal cheeses and incredible wine list. **$$–$$$**

Toledo
Tony Packo's
1902 Front Street
Tel: 419-691-6054
www.tonypackos.com
Hometown diner with friendly service and large portions of comfort food. Family-run and well-loved with tasty sandwiches and omelettes. Blue Ribbon is known for its award-winning cheesecake. **$**

Indiana

South Bend
The Vine
103 W. Colfax
Tel: 574-234-9463
www.thevinesb.com
Pleasant, fairly upmarket restaurant with a menu designed to appeal to all palates, with an unfussy range of sandwiches, pizza, pasta, meat, and fish. Closed Sunday. **$**

Valparaiso
Strongbow Inn
2405 E. US 30
Tel: 219-462-5121
www.strongbowinn.com
In business for over half a century. Good home-style steaks and seafood dishes and specializing in turkey. Few vegetarian options. **$$**

Michigan

Dearborn
Ciao Ristorante
1024 Monroe Street
Tel: 313-274-2426
www.ciaodearborn.com
Traditional Italian food. Wide range of pizza, pasta, meat, and fish for very affordable prices. **$–$$**

Crave Restaurant and Sushi Bar
22075 Michigan Avenue
Tel: 313-277-7283
www.cravelounge.com
Casual dining in the lounge or on the patio. Mediterranean and Asian fusion cuisine served in elegant surroundings where the young and fashionable go. Nightly

PRICE CATEGORIES

Price categories are for an average cost of dinner and a glass of wine, before tip:
$ = under $20
$$ = $20–40
$$$ = more than $40

entertainment varies from live jazz to DJs to dancers. **$$**

Illinois

Chicago
Alinea
1723 N. Halsted Street
Tel: 312-867-0110
www.alinea-restaurant.com
Chef Grant Achatz is known for his innovative, tasty takes on variable comfort foods. Widely considered one of the top restaurants in the United States – if not the world – Alinea is a must for gastronomes. Housed in a converted townhouse in Lincoln Park, the atmosphere is easygoing, but the menu is serious stuff. **$$$**
Pizzeria Uno
29 E. Ohio Street
Tel: 312-321-1000
Now part of the Uno Chicago Grill franchise, this was where Chicago Deep Dish pizza was born. **$**
The Pump Room
1301 N. State Parkway
Tel: 312-229-6740
www.pumproom.com
Adjoining Ian Schrager's Public Chicago Hotel (former Ambassador East), the historic Pump Room restaurant that once drew the likes of Elizabeth Taylor, Marylyn Monroe, and Frank Sinatra has been modernized but is still the hottest place in town. (Sinatra's private booth remains, for old time's sake). The Pump Room's kitchen is overseen by Jean-Georges Vongerichten, winner of a 2011 James Beard Award, who turns out organic takes on classic comfort food. Come evening, the restaurant bar becomes a trendy nightspot. **$$–$$$**
Twin Anchors Restaurant and Tavern
1655 N. Sedgwick Street
Tel: 312-266-1616
www.twinanchorsribs.com
Among the best ribs in Chicago. Great burgers too. Pleasant neighborhood watering hole in the old town. **$–$$**

Wisconsin

Madison
Dotty Dumpling's Dowry
317 N. Frances Street
Tel: 608-259-0000
www.dottydumplingsdowry.com
Excellent burgers that can be customized to your liking and tasty milk shakes. Dotty's also has an extensive beer list, a fun décor and a cheerful atmosphere. **$**
Essen Haus
514 E. Wilson Street

Tel: 608-255-4674
Excellent German food, a long list of beers, and staff in German national dress. Rollicking good fun. **$$**
Merchant
121 South Pinckney Street
Tel: 608-259-9799
www.merchantmadison.com/
Sandwiches, salads and small plates in a contemporary setting. Craft cocktails and over 40 bourbons at the bar. **$$**

Minnesota

Mankato
Mexican Village Restaurant
1630 E. Madison Avenue
Tel: 507-387-4455
www.mexicanvillagemankato.com
Pleasant, rustic-style restaurant featuring homemade fajitas (chicken, steak, and shrimp), chimichangas, and burritos, plus vegetarian options. **$**

Minneapolis
Buca di Beppo
1204 Harmon Place
Tel: 612-288-0138
Generous portions of Italian fare with hard-to-resist desserts. Friendly service; amusing decor. **$–$$**
Kramarczuk's East European Deli
215 E. Hennepin Avenue
Tel: 612-379-3018
www.kramarczuk.com
Founded by a Ukrainian couple in the 1970s, this Eastern European deli specializes in cabbage rolls, varenyky, and sausages. Onsite bakery. **$**
Nye's Polonaise Room
112 E. Hennepin Avenue
Tel: 612-379-2021
Hearty Polish-American fare and an old school karaoke piano bar – all in one. Go figure. The piano man plays your tune as you croon to the crowd. What's more, the food is fantastic. **$$**

Vintage drink sign in California.

St Paul
Café Latte
850 Grand Avenue
Tel: 651-224-5687
www.cafelatte.com
Soups, salads, sandwiches, and fragrant hearth-baked breads, as well as full afternoon tea and award-winning desserts. Pizzas available in the attached wine bar. **$**
Mickey's Dining Car
36 W. Seventh Street
Tel: 651-222-5633
www.mickeysdiningcar.com
Classic, vintage diner in the heart of town serving up American fare like grandma used to make. Omelettes, BLT's, and lots of grease. Just go for the people-watching alone. You'll be glad you did. **$**
St Paul Grill
St Paul Hotel, 350 Market Street
Tel: 651-224-7455
www.stpaulgrill.com
Classy, upmarket restaurant with a select menu of mainly steaks, chops, and fish. Includes a bar serving rare scotches, whiskies, and cognacs, alongside an enviable wine list. There is also a great view of Rice Park. **$$$**

South Dakota

Deadwood
Jakes
677 Main Street
Tel: 605-578-1555
www.themidnightstar.com
Casual dining on the top floor of Kevin Costner's casino, Midnight Star. Small, if varied, menu including Cajun seafood and veal osso bucco. Strong wine list. **$$**

Lead
Cheyenne Crossing Cafe
21415 US Highway 14A
Tel: 605-584-3510
Scenic spot for tucking into a rib-sticking breakfast any time of day. Grocery store also on the premises. **$**

Mitchell

Chef Louie's Steak House
601 E. Havens Street
Tel: 605-996-7565
Not much to look at from the outside but don't let that put you off. This modern, family-friendly restaurant serves a varied menu, mainly steaks, which are excellent. **$$**

Pierre

La Minestra
106 E. Dakota Avenue
Tel: 605-224-8090
www.laminestra.com
Italian restaurant serving freshly made pasta and steaks handcut to order. Plenty of fish, calzone, and salad options for non-meat eaters. **$–$$**

Rapid City

Firehouse Brewing Company
610 Main Street
Tel: 605-348-1915
www.firehousebrewing.com
Microbrewery serving "pub-grub" and variety of handcrafted beers. Located in the city's former fire station and spread over two floors. Live music daily throughout the summer. **$**

Sioux Falls

K Restaurant
401 E. Eighth Street and Railroad Center
Tel: 605-336-3315
Contemporary cuisine with seasonal ingredients In the East Bank neighborhood. Buzzy atmosphere, upmarket food and always busy. **$$**

Minerva's
301 S. Phillips Avenue
Tel: 605-334-0386
Popular with locals and serving a range of prime-cut steaks, seafood, and pasta. One of the few places in the city to get decent seafood. **$–$$**

Spearfish

Bay Leaf Café
126 W. Hudson Street
Tel: 605-642-5462
www.bayleafcafe.net
Friendly and informal café in historic building serving a variety of well-prepared dishes from Alaskan seafood and Greek favorites humus and falafel, to rib-tickling and plate-filling buffalo steaks. **$–$$**

Wyoming

Cody

The Noon Break
927 12th Street
Tel: 307-587-9720
Cheerful breakfast and lunch spot serving Western, Mexican and Tex-Mex dishes. Beware of the chili. **$**

Gillette

Humphrey's Bar and Grill
408 W. Juniper Lane
Tel: 307-682-0100 or 877-360-6751
www.humphard.net
Lively sports bar with an excellent salad bar. Large array of snacks, sandwiches, fajitas, and burgers. **$**

Jackson

The Blue Lion
160 N. Millward Street
Tel: 307-733-3912
www.bluelionrestaurant.com
Long-established local favorite in an older, renovated building. Excellent regional menu and continental nightly specials including rack of lamb, elk, seafood, and vegetarian options. Sumptuous homemade desserts. Dine indoors or al fresco. **$$$**

Snake River Grill
84 E. Broadway
Tel: 307-733-0557
Unusual offerings include steak tartare pizza, but the real draw – for carnivores – are the bone-in rib eye, ginger-soy short ribs, and a massive elk chop. Local trout and Alaskan halibut also star. The menu varies with the season. **$$$**

Sundance

ARO Family Restaurant
205 E. Cleveland Street
Tel: 307-283-2000
Well-prepared food such as burgers, steaks, Mexican selections, served in warm atmosphere. Excellent value. **$**

Montana

Bozeman

Chickpea Café
25 North Wilson
Tel: 406-551-2007
www.chickpeabozeman.com
Authentic Middle Eastern cooking just a block from Main Street. Specialties include kebabs, *murget dijaj* (chicken stew), shawarma sandwiches, and vegetarian options. **$**

Helena

Lucca's
56 N. Last Chance Gulch
Tel: 406-457-8311
www.luccasitalian.com
Excellent Italian cooking with dishes such as double-cut lamb chops, and pan-seared calamari, served by a friendly waitstaff in a warm, romantic setting. **$$$**

Windbag Saloon
19 S. Last Chance Gulch Street
Tel: 406-443-9669
Sample the lively atmosphere and

wide range of microbrewery beers in this popular local spot. Good burgers and a terrific prime rib sandwich. **$–$$**

Kalispell

Moose's Saloon
173 N. Main Street
Tel: 406-755-2337
www.moosessaloon.com
The genuine article, with rustic tables and booths, sawdust on the floor, a lot of unusual beers on tap, and a family-friendly environment. Great pizzas, sandwiches, and a soup and salad bar at lunchtime. **$**

Missoula

Food for Thought
540 Daly Avenue
Tel: 406-721-6033
Across the street from the University, this popular spot serves the biggest breakfasts in town, as well as lunches and freshly prepared salads. **$**

The Old Post
103 W. Spruce
Tel: 406-721-7399
www.oldpostpub.com
"Hey, it's more fun to eat in a bar than to drink in a restaurant" – that the motto of this lively pub and it's definitely true, making it a Downtown favourite. There's a wide choice of local beers on tap, good food like fish tacos, black beans and rice, surf 'n' turf, and teriyaki chicken stir-fry. **$**

Whitefish

The Shak
669 Spokane Avenue
Tel: 406-730-1070
www.shakbbq.com
Succulent Southern fried chicken, melt-in-your-mouth ribs, and lots of tasty sides. Good news for twosomes: the Half Feast gets you some of most everything. **$**

Idaho

Bonners Ferry

Under the Sun
7178 Main Street
Tel: 208-267-6467
www.ultimateidaho.com
Lunch is served daily from 11am to 3pm at this organic bistro with a European ambiance. Homemade breads, scones, and paninis are among the offerings. **$**

PRICE CATEGORIES

Price categories are for an average cost of dinner and a glass of wine, before tip:
$ = under $20
$$ = $20–40
$$$ = more than $40

TRANSPORTATION

ACCOMMODATIONS

EATING OUT

ACTIVITIES

A – Z

Coeur d'Alene

Cedars Floating Restaurant
1 Marine Drive
Tel: 208-664-2922
www.cedarsfloatingrestaurant.com
Warm and welcoming restaurant
moored on Lake Coeur d'Alene affords
panoramic views at dinner nightly.
Extensive, nicely balanced menu
featuring very fresh, expertly prepared
fish and choice beef. Entrees include a
salad bar. **$$–$$$**

Sandpoint

Forty-One South
41 Lakeshore Drive, Sagle
Tel: 208-265-2000
www.41southsandpoint.com
Overlooking Lake Pend d'Oreille.
The timber-framed building with
wood-paneling provides a smart-
casual background to some very
smart cooking, with dishes such as
honeycomb salmon, and duck confit.
There's also a splendid array of
desserts. Shoga Sushi Bar is also on
the premises. **$$$**

Washington

Ellensburg

The Palace Café
Fourth Avenue and Main Street
Tel: 509-925-2327
http://thepalacecafe.net
In business since 1892, this old-
fashioned place with a laid-back
ambiance and friendly service serves
classic favorites including burgers
and halibut and chips; the dinner
prime rib packs in hungry crowds.
$–$$

Forks

Sully's Drive-In
220 North Forks Avenue
Tel: 360-374-5075
The burgers are juicy, the onion rings
crunchy, and the milk shakes frothy
at this fast food eatery. Try the Bella
Burger. **$**

Lake Quinault

Roosevelt Dining Room
Lake Quinault Lodge, 345 South
Shore Road
Tel: 360-288-2900
www.quinaultrainforest.com
The lodge's formal dining room is
named for President Teddy Roosevelt,
who was dining here when the idea for
creating Olympic National Park was
first suggested. The feel is still old-
fashioned, with romantic low lighting.
The menu focuses on seafood: its
signature dish is cedar plank salmon
for two, though meat eaters can enjoy
steak and prime rib. There is also an

excellent wine list and dessert menu.
$$$

Leavenworth

Café Christa
801 Front Street
Tel: 509-548-5074
www.cafechrista.com
A pleasant café right on the city
square, serving central European
cuisine in an atmosphere of old-world
charm. **$$**

Port Angeles

First Street Haven
107 E. First Street
Tel: 360-457-0352
A very cozy, old-fashioned spot for
homemade baked treats, hot off the
griddle pancakes, delectable quiches,
and a fine selection of luncheon
specials. **$**

Port Townsend

The Silverwater Café
237 Taylor Street
Tel: 360-385-6448
www.silverwatercafe.com
A local favorite for more than 20 years,
the café specializes in fresh seafood
and produce. The fish and chips they
built their reputation on is still on the
menu, along with a hearty cioppino,
pastas, and braised lamb shank.
$$–$$$

Seattle

Cafe Campagne
1600 Post Alley, Pike Place Market
Tel: 206-728-2233
www.cafecampagne.com
This classic Parisian brasserie
serves regional cuisine (and freshly
baked baguettes) in an ambiance
reminiscent of a French marketside
café. Sausage, smoked salmon,
and duck confit are just a few of the
specialties handcrafted in-house.
The patio affords a terrific view of the
marketplace. **$$–$$$**

The Pike Brewing Company
1415 First Avenue, Pike Place Market
Tel: 206-622-6044
www.pikebrewing.com
Handcrafted beers and ales and
classic pub fare are served in a
sometimes hectic environment.
Entrees, made whenever possible
with fresh local ingredients, include
grass-fed beef burgers, corned beef
and cabbage, and the house special –
pizza. **$–$$**

Ray's Boathouse
6049 Seaview Avenue NW
Tel: 206-789-3770
www.rays.com
Truly a local establishment, from
the wonderful view of Puget Sound

to elegant preparation of local
ingredients in this upscale eatery. The
café offers the same views and less
expensive fare. **$$$**

Salty's on Alki
1936 Harbor Avenue SW
Tel: 206-937-1600
www.saltys.com
The star here is the huge selection of
fresh seafood, but it's the al fresco
dining and view of the city skyline
across the bay that steals the show.
Saturday and Sunday brunch buffet is
a standout. **$$$**

Salumi
309 Third Avenue S.
Tel: 206-621-8772
www.salumicuredmeats.com
It's all about the home-cured meats
at this tiny spot where hungry hordes
cheerfully wait in line for specialties
such as pork cheek and porchetta
sandwiches. There's limited seating,
or order the "sampler" to go and have
a picnic. **$**

Thoa's Restaurant and Lounge
96 Union Street
Tel: 206-344-8088
www.thoaseattle.com
Seattle chef Thoa (pronounced
"Twa") Nguyen's smart downtown
restaurant serves contemporary
Vietnamese cuisine that combines
Pacific Northwest ingredients with
traditional flavors. Fresh, light, and
inspiring. **$$**

Sequim

Three Crabs Restaurant
11 Three Crabs Road
Tel: 360-683-4264
www.the3crabs.com
Situated right on the beach for more
than 50 years, this informal restaurant
offers a fine view of the harbor and
a fine selection of their own freshly
harvested fish. But Dungeness crab is
king. **$–$$**

Spokane

**Ginger Asian Bistro and
Sushi Bar**
1228 South Grand Boulevard
Tel: 509-315-5201
A small, busy spot with sometimes
uneven service that serves up some
of the city's tastiest and freshest
Japanese fare. The hearty luncheon
bento box is a crowd pleaser. **$$**

Wild Sage American Bistro
916 W. Second Avenue
Tel: 509-456-7575
www.wildsagebistro.com
Award-winning and creative fare at
a classically turned out bistro in the
heart of town. Specialties include
coconut curry pasta, and pan-seared
duck breast. **$$–$$$**

CENTRAL ROUTE

Washington, DC

There has been an explosion of "food trucks" that set up near the busier Metro stations at lunchtime, vending every type of cuisine you could want, amazingly well prepared in tiny mobile kitchens. A DC dining phenomenon. Try L'Enfant Plaza, Union Station, Navy Yard, and Metro Center. www.foodtruck fiesta.com is a real-time locator for the trucks.

Bistro du Coin
1738 Connecticut Avenue
Tel: 202-234-6969
www.bistroducoin.com
Authentic French country cooking, rarely seen in restaurants, proving that "peasants" can eat like royalty. Cassoulet, tartines (open-face sandwiches), and many kinds of mussels. **$$**

Market Lunch
225 Seventh Street SE
Tel: 202-547-8444
It's no surprise there's a fight to get in here for Saturday breakfasts. The crab cakes and homemade bread are superb, and the prices are cheap. You have a better chance of getting a seat for a weekday lunch. Don't expect to pay with plastic. **$**

Ristorante i Ricchi
1120 19th Street NW
Tel: 202-835-0459
www.iricchi.net
Traditional Tuscan restaurant serving fresh, simple, and hearty cooking. Bread, meat, and fish cooked and grilled in the dining room's wood-burning stove. Wonderful sage and ricotta-stuffed tortellini, flavorful sauces for pastas and risottos, and excellent seafood. **$$**

Tunnicliff's Tavern
222 Seventh Avenue SE
Tel: 202-544-5680
Across from Eastern Market, this is a neighborhood hangout, serving good burgers and other bar staples. Also open for breakfast: try the Eggs Benedict. **$**

Virginia

Arlington

Ray's Hell-Burger
1713 Wilson Boulevard, Arlington
Tel: 703-841-0001
www.rayshellburger.com
Owner Michael Landrum couldn't have wished for better publicity than when President Barack Obama and Vice-President Joe Biden directed their motorcade to his well-regarded burger bar and ordered two 10oz burgers with spicy mustard for lunch. **$**

Front Royal

Soul Mountain
300 E. Main Street
Tel: 540-636-0070
Varied Southern, Cajun, and Caribbean food, ranging from jerk chicken with coconut rice to lobster ravioli. Food is freshly prepared so you can dictate the level of spice required. Separate barbecue menu available. Open Wednesday through Sunday. **$**

Linden

The Apple House
4675 John Marhsall Highway (Route 55)
Tel: 540-636-6329
www.theapplehouse.net
A country store around 5 miles (8km) east of Front Royal, known for its pulled pork and barbecue, and for its apple desserts. There are free samples of apple-cinnamon doughnuts. You can and should buy a bag to go. **$**

New Market

Southern Kitchen
4576 S. Congress Avenue (Highway 11)
Tel: 540-740-3514
Diner serving Virginia southern cooking: Great fried chicken, salty country ham, peanut soup, and other regional favorites. **$**

Staunton

Cranberry's Grocery and Eatery
7 South New Street
Tel: 540-885-4755
Very popular stop serving tasty, healthy wraps, smoothies, quiches, and salads to both vegetarians and carnivores. Gluten-free and no trans-fats or high-fructose corn syrup anywhere in the kitchen or in any product served in the grocery side of the store. Lots of Thai and Mediterranean flavors, as well as a great BLT (bacon, lettuce, and tomato sandwich). Try the French toast fruit wrap at the Sunday brunch. **$**

Zynodoa Restaurant
115 E. Beverly Street
Tel: 540-885-7775
The menu changes daily at this fine dining restaurant that deals nearly exclusively with local farmers and growers. The results are creative and delicious: garden vegetables with house-made fettuccini with eggplant puree and anise cream; duck confit ravioli with Makati mushrooms and spring onions, pecan and maple cheesecake. Attentive, friendly staff share the mission of farm-to-table at the gourmet level. **$$**

North Carolina

12 Bones Smokehouse
5 Riverside Drive
Tel: 828-253-4499
www.12bones.com
Arguably, one of the best barbecue places in a state where barbecue is a religion. In the River Arts District. Lunch only. **$–$$**

Asheville

City Bakery Cafe
60 Biltmore Avenue
Tel: 828-252-4426
www.citybakery.net
A popular all-rounder. Family-owned enterprise serving artisan, organic bread, European-style pastries and cakes. **$**

Chai Pani
22 Battery Park Avenue
Tel: 828-254-4003
www.chaipani.net
Featuring Indian street food and home cooking. The owner's mom flew in from Mumbai to teach the chef her secrets. Good vegetarian selection. **$**

Tennessee

Cherokee

Granny's Kitchen
1098 Painttown Road (US 19N)
Tel: 828-497-5010
www.grannyskitchencherokee.com
Family is in the kitchen and greeting customers at this country buffet that's as popular with locals as it is with tourists. The buffet highlights Southern home cooking with occasional Native American offerings (one of the owners is a member of the Cherokee tribe.) There's also a huge salad bar. Closed Mon. **$**

Jackson

Old Country Store Buffet
Casey Jones Village
Tel: 731-668-1223
www.caseyjones.com/oldcountrystore
Dedicated to preparing and serving all of the traditional Southern foods people have heard about but have never found or tried. Not just fried chicken and pulled pork, but cracklin' cornbread fried while you watch, collards, fried green tomatoes, okra, and – of course – banana pudding,

PRICE CATEGORIES

Price categories are for an average cost of dinner and a glass of wine, before tip:
$ = under $20
$$ = $20–40
$$$ = more than $40

and sweet tea. Decor is all about the region's music history. **$$**

Knoxville
Calhoun's
400 Neyland Drive
Tel: 865-673-3355
www.calhouns.com
Enjoy excellent barbecue ribs (voted best in America) and a fine river view, being situated right on the riverfront, and an outdoor deck. **$**

Memphis
Automatic Slim's
83 S. Second Street
Tel: 901-525-7948
www.automaticslimsmemphis.com
Menu offers lamb and pork chops, honey-glazed chicken, duck, and pasta, all with an exotic twist. Martini list as long as your arm. **$$**
Currents River Inn at Harbor Town
50 Harbor Town Square
Tel: 901-260-3300
www.riverinnmemphis.com
Rich continental food is executed with New Orleans-style flair and close attention to detail in this lovely corner dining room overlooking the Mississippi. The waitstaff – several drawn from Eastern Europe – are discreet and knowledgeable. The chef visits the farmers' market in season: look for local tomatoes, field greens, blue goat cheese, and Tennessee Cheddar. Try the Gulf bouillabaisse to start, followed perhaps by seared sea bass and scallop. Leave room for a Key Lime Tasting of pie, sorbet, and cheesecake. **$$$**
Johnny G's Creole Kitchen
156 Beale Street
Tel: 901-528-1055
Great Cajun/Creole cooking from a tiny kitchen with flair by chef Antonio. (You can watch). Po'boys, crab-stuffed peppadew peppers, and jambalaya. Deep-fried strawberries served on a pillow of whipped cream drizzled with chocolate. **$**

Nashville
Loveless Cafe
8400 Highway 100
Tel: 615-646-9700
www.lovelesscafe.com
"Hot biscuits and country ham." Loveless Café serves authentic Southern cooking using locally sourced ingredients. With a choice of first-class preserves, ham, and red-eye gravy, breakfast is a real treat. Generous portions and abundant atmosphere. A local favorite for over 60 years **$**
Pancake Pantry
1796 21st Avenue S. 37212
Tel: 615-383-9333

www.thepancakepantry.com
Get there very early, or you will wait in a line that stretches around the corner. Twenty-three different varieties of pancakes and many syrups, plus Tennessee bacon, sausage, country ham, omelets, and homemade hash browns. A waitress-written theme song was performed at the Grand Ole Opry. **$**
Rippy's
429 Broadway
Tel: 615-244-7477
www.rippysbarandgrill.com
Sit at the bar, listen to live country music from the tiny stage, and enjoy excellent ribs and fixin's. Upstairs, there's an outdoor deck overlooking the action of the honky-tonks. **$$**
Valentino's Ristorante
1907 West End Avenue
Tel: 615-327-0148
www.valentinosnashville.com
Fine Northern Italian cuisine at reasonable prices. Consistently voted one of Nashville's best Italian restaurants for its good service and elegant but casual atmosphere. **$$**

<h2>Arkansas</h2>

Fayetteville
Penguin Ed's Bar-B-Que
230 S. East Avenue
Tel: 479-521-3663
www.penguineds.com
Congenially cramped wooden quarters; order via a red phone at each table. Racks of ribs and big portions of pulled pork, chicken, brisket, bologna served as sandwiches or dinners with sides like baked beans and macaroni and cheese. Don't miss the fried pies. **$–$$**

Fort Smith

Hot Springs
Belle Arti Italian Ristorante
719 Central Avenue
Tel: 501-624-7474
www.belleartigroup.com
Fine Italian dining in the center of the Bathhouse District. The usual offerings, but many refreshing, original dishes on the Chef's Family Menu. **$$**
McClard's Bar-B-Q
505 Albert Pike
Tel: 501-623-9665
www.mcclards.com
Run by descendants of the founders, this place has been serving savory, well-seasoned barbecue since 1928. Everything is made from scratch on the premises, while the recipe for the sauce is a closely guarded secret. **$**
Mooyah's
3954 Central Avenue

Tel: 501-520-5000
www.mooyah.com
Claims to serve the best burgers, fries, and shakes in the world. Maybe not that good, but definitely worth considering as a top contender. Everything is cooked to order in the open kitchen. **$**
Rolando's
223 Garrison Avenue
Tel: 479-573-0404
www.rolandosrestaurante.com
Nuevo Latino cuisine with its Caribbean, Cuban, and Mexican influences. The guacamole alone is worth the trip. Beautiful presentations and massive portions. **$$**
Little Rock
Boscos Restaurant and Brewing Company
500 President Clinton Avenue
Tel: 501-907-1881
www.boscosbeer.com
Steps from the River Front Walk, the cool, inviting brewpub – featuring their own ales – has a larger-than-usual menu with brick-oven pizza, duck spring rolls, and planked salmon. There is a jazz brunch on Sunday. **$$**
Doe's Eat Place
1023 W. Markham Street
Tel: 501-376-1195
www.doeseatplace.net
A favorite of Bill Clinton, Chef Lucille Robinson attended the first inauguration ball. Choice-cut steaks. Choose from T-bone, porterhouse, and sirloin, accompanied by fries and Texas Toast. Tamales, shrimp, and salmon are also available on the dinner menu, while burgers and pasta dishes are an addition to the lunch menu. **$$**

<h2>Oklahoma</h2>

Arcadia
Pops Diner
660 W. Highway 66
Tel: 405-928-7677
www.route66.com
Famous for its 66ft (20-meter) neon soda bottle out front, this distinctive *Happy Days*-style diner is inside a combined gas station/convenience store whose glass walls are lined with 700-plus different soda varieties (all for sale). Huge burgers and sinfully good milk shakes attract everyone from bikers to Mom and Pop. **$**

Catoosa
Molly's Landing
3700 N. Highway 66
Tel: 918-266-7853
www.mollyslanding.com
Steak and seafood are "on the barby" at this locally popular, award-winning

restaurant in a log cabin next to the Blue Whale landmark, just southeast of Tulsa. $–$$

Chandler
Steer Inn Family Restaurant
102 N. Oak Street
Tel: 405-258-3155
www.steerinnrestaurant.com
This family-run chain, with branches in Chandler, Cushing, and Mannford, serves up burgers, sandwiches, steaks, and barbecued pork, ribs, and chicken. Lunch buffet Mon–Fri, plus evening all-you-can-eat buffets Tuesday through Saturday, accompany the regular menu. $

Claremore
Hammett House Restaurant
1616 W. Will Rogers Boulevard
Tel: 918-341-7333
www.hammetthouse.com
Enjoy tasty, fresh meals prepared with loads of Southern family hospitality. In addition to standard family fare, the large menu offers an array of salads and soups, as well as many homemade pies, including (hallelujah!) a sugarless apple pie. $–$$

Davenport
Early Bird Café
N. Broadway (Highway 66)
Tel: 918-377-2209
Located at the turnoff for historic Davenport, this endearing hole-in-the-wall decorated with license plates dishes up good Mexican specials, such as *migas* (eggs scrambled with tortillas and salsa) and *pollo con arroz* (chicken with rice), alongside All-American diner fare. Finish with a homemade pastry or cobbler. $

Depew
Coach's Corner
325 Main Street (Route 66)
Tel: 918-324-5656
An all-you-can eat lunch buffet (all day on Saturdays) and plenty of stick-to-the-ribs entrées, sandwiches, nachos, and pizzas attract hungry 66ers to this lively diner in the semi ghost town of Depew, especially on weekends. Homemade pies. $

El Reno
Robert's Grill
300 S. Bickford Avenue
Tel: 405-262-1262
Hometown of the original Fried Onion Burger, Robert's has been operating since 1926 in a tiny white-washed building with red trim. A gem for road food aficionados, who vie for one of the 14 stools at the counter, and co-creator of the World's Largest

Hamburger every Memorial Day. $
Johnnie's Grill
301 South Rock Island Avenue
Tel: 405-262-4721
Another classic Route 66 diner in El Reno famed for its fried onion burgers and local version of a Coney Island hot dog. Breakfast is good here, too, and includes something called an Arkansas Sandwich, two pancakes layered with scrambled eggs. $
Sid's Diner
300 S. Choctaw Avenue
Tel: 405-262-7757
Famed for its fried onion burger, this cheap and cheerful burger shack is also popular for its own version of a Coney Island hot dog topped with meaty chili and a uniquely piquant and sloppy coleslaw. $

Oklahoma City
Cattlemen's Steakhouse
1309 S. Agnew Avenue
Tel: 405-236-0416
www.cattlemensrestaurant.com
Located in the middle of historic Stockyards City, this famous steakhouse (reputedly used as the stake in a bet) is the oldest restaurant in OKC. It's the first choice, even in a city known for beef, to tuck into a dinosaur-sized aged steak that would make even Fred Flintstone happy. $–$$
Flint
15 North Robinson Avenue (inside Hotel Colcord)
Tel: 405-605-0657
www.flintokc.com
This high-concept restaurant feels like an escapee from Scottsdale, Arizona, but its well-conceived New American dishes and stylish ambiance have been an instant hit with locals. Healthy renditions of eggs at breakfast and burgers, fish and chips, salads, and sandwiches at lunch join globally inspired meat and fish dishes at dinner. $$–$$$

Stroud
Rock Café
114 W. Main
Tel: 918-968-3990
www.rockcafe66.com
This classic Route 66 eatery is back after a fire; it, and its lively owner Dawn Welch (who inspired Sally in the movie Cars), are as popular as ever. The draw here is the tasty burger, which is lovingly flipped on Betsy the Grill, 73 years old and a survivor of the fire. $

Tulsa
Brookside by Day
3313 S. Peoria Avenue
Tel: 918-745-9989
Ask a local for their favorite weekend

brunch spot and "BBD," as it's known, is what you'll hear again and again, popular for its hometown atmosphere and generous waffles with fresh fruit, eggs benedict, and classic fry-ups and fixings. Combine with a trip to the equally tasty Philbrook Museum nearby. $
Juniper
324 E. Third Street
Tel: 918-794-1090
www.junipertulsa.com
Chef-owner Justin Thompson's farm-to-table Blue Dome eatery is fresh, creative, and on its game. Try the juicy pan-fried free-range Tahlequah chicken with brussels sprout 'slaw and mash, the delicate brown-butter trout, and local Bixby greens and artisan cheeses. The cooked-to-order blueberry-lemon bread pudding with mint crème anglaise is heaven on a plate! $$
Ollie's Station Restaurant
W. 41st and Southwest, Boulevard
Tel: 918-446-0524
www.olliesstation.com
This fun, café-style place has good food and 10 model trains chugging merrily around and through scale-model cities. $

Vinita
Clanton's Cafe
319 E. Illinois Street
Tel: 918-256-9053
www.clantonscafe.com
This classic Route 66 eatery is known for its chicken-fried steak. It also serves that regional classic: "calf fries" (aka testicles). $

Yukon
Braum's
1304 S. 11th Street
Tel: 405-354-2619
www.braums.com
With branches throughout Oklahoma, this family-run drive-in sells tasty organic burgers and ice cream made using meat and milk from its own large dairy herd in Tuttle (tours available). A local tradition for decades, it's also a good spot to pick up groceries (including Braum's meat and dairy) in their own stop-'n'-shop. $–$$

Texas

Adrian
Midpoint Café
305 W. Historic Route 66, Exit 22 I-40

PRICE CATEGORIES
Price categories are for an average cost of dinner and a glass of wine, before tip:
$ = under $20
$$ = $20–40
$$$ = more than $40

Tel: 806-538-6379
Located exactly halfway along
Route 66, this attractive diner is
one of the route's oldest eateries.
With enthusiastic new owners, its
longtime reputation for hospitality,
huge burgers, and "very good
pie" continues. This is a remote
spot, so note their opening hours:
8:30am–4pm daily. The famous
photo-op is across the road. **$**

Amarillo
Big Texan Steak Ranch
7701 I-40E
Tel: 806-372-6000
www.bigtexan.com
The shtick here? If you can eat a 72oz
steak plus side dishes in under an
hour, you don't pay. Smaller portions
of beef, bison, even rattlesnake are
available in the cavernous Western
dining room, where piped-in Willy
Nelson vies with real-life crooners
singing "Yellow Rose Texas." A fun
experience. **$$**

Tyler's Barbeque
2014 Paramount Boulevard
Tel: 806-331-2271
www.tylersbarbeque.com
This hugely popular barbecue spot
specializes in brisket and ribs
smoked over Texas mesquite, which
the owner honed to perfection while
traveling cross-country with his huge
portable barbecue rig.
$–$$

New Mexico

Albuquerque
Frontier Restaurant
2400 Central Avenue SE
Tel: 505-266-0550
www.frontierrestaurant.com
Located opposite UNM, this starving-
student diner is a Duke City legend
(replete with pictures of the Duke
himself, John Wayne, on the walls).
Massive breakfast burritos and
other New Mexico classics
smothered in red and green chili
roll out fast and furious. And wait
'til you see their famed cinnamon
rolls! **$**

Kelly's Brew Pub
3222 Central Avenue SE, Albuquerque,
NM 87106
Tel: 505-262-2739
www.kellysbrewpub.com
Located in the 1939 Jones Company
Ford service station on Route 66,
this Nob Hill pub is one of a couple of
good microbreweries in town (Marble
Brewery, Downtown, is also winning
raves). Grab a seat outside, quench
your thirst, load up on pub grub, and
watch the world go by. **$**

Las Vegas
**Charlie's Spic n' Span Bakery and
Café**
715 Douglas Avenue
Tel: 505-426-1921
This always-busy hometown favorite
pulls them in with its huge servings of
piping hot *huevos* with red and green
chili, homemade tortillas, stuffed
carne adovada sopaipillas, tacos, and
other New Mexican specials. Leave
room for one of Charlie's famous
éclairs, cream puffs, or donuts, and a
cup of joe to go. **$**

Moriarty
El Comedor de Anayas
Route 66
Tel: 505-832-4442
www.elcomedordeanayas.com
In business for six decades, this
family-run restaurant has the last
operating rotosphere (rotating neon
sign) on Route 66. It dishes up
hometown chat and plentiful Mexican-
American food. Former New Mexico
governor Bruce King was a regular
here until his death in 2009. Photos of
the affable gov line the walls. **$–$$**

Santa Fe
Café Pasqual's
121 Don Gaspar Avenue
Tel: 505-983-9340
www.pasquals.com
Katherine Kagel's globally inspired
Mexican eatery is snugged into a tiny
former drugstore, where the decor
and celebratory atmosphere is as
uplifting as the food. Any meal here
yields endless happy memories, but
breakfast is phenomenal. Try the
huevos rancheros, with the most
complex red chili you've ever tasted,
or the classic Yucatán breakfast dish
huevos motuleños. **$–$$$**

Cowgirl BBQ
319 S. Guadalupe Street
Tel: 505-982-2565
www.cowgirlsantafe.com
The Cowgirl is a longtime favorite in
the Railyard, delivering hearty food at
affordable prices in a lively Western-
meets-adobe atmosphere that kids as
well as adults love. Meat is the thing:
try the barbecue, or maybe a steak or
spicy jerk chicken. Live music outside
at happy hour in summer. **$$**

Harry's Roadhouse
96 Old Las Vegas Highway
Tel: 505-989-4629
www.harrysroadhousesantafe.com
An arty roadhouse with an eclectic
menu, Harry's is a popular local
rendezvous. Breakfast eggs come
with homemade turkey sausage
and homemade salsa; lunch and
dinner run the gamut from juicy bison

burgers to Moroccan couscous and
catfish, followed by a slice of co-owner
Peyton's heavenly pies. Efficient staff
keep the line moving. **$–$$**

Restaurant Martin
526 Galisteo Street
Tel: 505-820-0919
www.restaurantmartin.com
Star Santa Fe chef Martin Rios calls
the sensuous food at his luminous
South Capital restaurant "Progressive
American," but it feels like California
and France got married in Santa
Fe and invited the whole family to
celebrate. Classical techniques enliven
but don't weigh down meat and fish
dishes, and desserts are masterfully
whimsical. **$$–$$$**

Tune-Up Café
115 Hickox Street
Tel: 505-983-7060
A tiny neighborhood joint run by
husband-and-wife veterans of
the Santa Fe food scene, Tune-Up
has a loyal following for its Central
American twists on New Mexican
dishes and emphasis on fresh, organic
ingredients. Try anything with the
delectable *mole* sauce, the airy chili
relleno, or perhaps a *pupusa*, a fried
Salvadoran turnover made of *masa*,
filled with spiced steak or veggies, and
fried. Budget-friendly and sensational.
$–$$

Arizona

Flagstaff
**Black Bart's Steak House and
Musical Revue**
2760 E. Butler Avenue
Tel: 928-779-3142
www.blackbartssteakhouse.com
Oh go on, you know you want a big
steak and some country music over
your gravy and potatoes. Indulge. **$$**

Cottage Place Restaurant
126 W. Cottage Avenue
Tel: 928-774-8431
Set in a bungalow-style residence built
in 1909, this is one of Flagstaff's best
fine-dining establishments. Go all out
for the six-course tasting menu with
wine pairings, or come early for the
lighter Twilight menu. **$$–$$$**

Holbrook
Joe and Aggie's Cafe
120 W. Hopi Drive
Tel: 928-524-6540
www.joeandaggiescafe.com
Good Mexican dishes are prepared
with homemade red and green chili
from an old family recipe. The chili
rellenos are a local favorite, and even
the T-bone steaks are served with
rice, beans, and chili on top. If that
doesn't fill you up, polish it off with an

apple burrito topped with ice cream. **$–$$**

Sedona
L'Auberge De Sedona Restaurant
301 L'Auberge Lane
Tel: 928-282-1661
www.lauberge.com/dining
So good they named a whole street (well, lane) after it. The French cuisine at this elegant restaurant at L'Auberge de Sedona Inn and Spa is top-notch, matched only by its delicious setting on Oak Creek. **$$$**
Shugrue's Hillside Grill
671 Highway 179
Tel: 928-282-5300
www.shugrueshillside.com
Featuring a health-conscious American menu in the ideal Sedona setting, looking onto the red rocks, Shugrue's is operated by Chef Michael Mullins and his family and is a popular dining spot with locals. Steak and seafood are good bets, but there are a number of vegetarian and vegan options, too. **$$–$$$**

Williams
Rod's Steak House
301 E. Route 66
Tel: 928-635-2671
www.rods-steakhouse.com
Rod's is a much-loved Route 66 dining landmark in Williams. The menu is die-cut in the shape of a steer, one of many souvenir items at this all-American restaurant. **$$**
Twisters
417 E. Route 66
Tel: 928-635-0266
www.route66place.com/Twisters_50_s_Soda_Fountain_s/32.htms
Roll up for some great burgers and shakes at this 1950s soda fountain

on Route 66. The decor is real vintage Americana (bring your shades) complete with jukebox. This is a great spot for the whole family. **$**

Winslow
Falcon Restaurant
1113 E. Third Street
Tel: 928-289-2628
This Route 66 family restaurant serves humungous portions of down-home favorites like chicken-fried steak, accompanied by homemade salsa verde. **$**

California

Los Angeles
Chin Chin
8618 Sunset Boulevard
Tel: 310-652-1818
www.chinchin.com
This Chinese café in West Hollywood's Sunset Plaza is a prime people-watching spot, with indoor and outdoor dining. Great dim sum and noodle dishes; the classic Chicken Salad is a crowd pleaser. **$–$$**
Grand Central Market
317 S. Broadway
Tel: 213-624-2378
www.grandcentralsquare.com
Bustling shoppers, neon signs, and varied produce – it's a feast for the eyes at the city's oldest and largest open-air market, where vendors offer a tremendous selection of foods ranging from tacos to kebabs. **$**
JiRaffe
502 Santa Monica Boulevard
Tel: 310-917-6671
www.jirafferestaurant.com
Innovative California cuisine at this hip scene, which has been a local favorite for more than 16 years. Monday prix

fixe bistro night draws the crowds. **$$–$$$**
Musso and Frank's
6667 Hollywood Boulevard
Tel: 323-467-7788
www.mussoandfrank.com
Hollywood's oldest restaurant dates back to 1919. Its decor and menu of old faithfuls, from steaks and chops to macaroni and cheese, would still be familiar to the Hollywood giants who have dined here over the decades. **$$**
Porto's Bakery and Café
315 N. Brand Boulevard, Glendale
Tel: 818-956-5996
www.portosbakery.com
Since opening their tiny bakery in 1960, the Portos have grown their family business into a beloved local institution. Their Cuban sandwiches, baked goods, and other Cuban dishes are legendary. **$**
Providence
5955 Melrose Avenue
Tel: 323-460-4170
www.providencela.com
Seafood is the star at this upscale establishment. The servers are knowledgeable yet pleasant, and the atmosphere formal but friendly. To really get a sense for what the kitchen can do, opt for the chef's tasting menu with wine pairings. **$$$**

Rancho Cucamonga
Magic Lamp Inn
8189 Foothill Boulevard
Tel: 909-981-8659
www.themagiclampinn.com
The eponymous neon magic lamp denotes a Route 66 landmark which has been offering "fine dining and cocktails" since 1955. The traditional menu features prime aged steaks and shrimp scampi. **$–$$**

SOUTHERN ROUTE

Georgia

Atlanta
The Dining Room
Ritz-Carlton Hotel, 3434 Peachtree Road
Tel: 404-237-2700
www.ritzcarlton.com/atlanta/dining
One of only three US restaurants to receive Mobil's five stars, this elegant Buckhead eatery tops the list of Atlanta fine-dining places. Choose from an á la carte or six-course seasonal tasting menu paired with wines from the restaurant's award-winning wine list. A once-in-a-lifetime dining pleasure. **$$$**
The Varsity
61 N. Avenue

Tel: 404-881-1706
www.thevarsity.com
Opened in 1928, this drive-in burger-and-Coke joint is one of Atlanta's most famous restaurants. Classics include chilidogs, onion rings, fried fruit pies, and shakes. **$**

Jackson
Buckner Family Restaurant and Music Hall
I-75/US 36
Tel: 770-775-6150
www.bucknersfamilyrestaurant.com
Homestyle fried chicken suppers and barbecue are served family style in a cavernous dining room in this rural restaurant, where gospel music

accompanies old-fashioned food. Dessert is usually homemade Georgia peach cobbler. **$**

Macon
Marco Ristorante Italiano
4581 Forsyth Road
Tel: 478-405-5668
www.marcomacon.com
This elegant fine-dining restaurant's Italian owner has brought authentic

PRICE CATEGORIES

Price categories are for an average cost of dinner and a glass of wine, before tip:
$ = under $20
$$ = $20–40
$$$ = more than $40

Italian cuisine to Lil' Macon. Try branzino, Italian sea bass, veal ravioli with wild mushroom ragout, and end with a gelati sampler. **$$$**

Alabama

Mobile
Cafe 615
615 Dauphin Street
Tel: 251-432-8434
www.cafe615mobile.com
Popular with locals for its bottomless Champagne brunch on Sundays, 615 occupies a lovely, contemporary space on historic Dauphin Street. It's a great place to land for New Southern food that does inventive things with grits and seafood. The menu has a light touch, a boon after so much fried road food. **$$**

Wintzell's Oyster House
605 Dauphin Street
Tel: 251-432-4605
www.wintzellsoysterhouse.com
Fresh oysters done every which way have starred on the menu of this corner pub in downtown Mobile for 70 years. A bit raucous but sidewalk dining makes for great people-watching, especially around Mardi Gras. Branches at eight locations in Mobile. **$**

Montgomery
Lek's Railroad Thai
300 Water Street
Tel: 334-269-0714
www.thaiemeraldlek.com
Vegetarians celebrate! This authentic Thai restaurant in the historic Union Station has lots of veggie offerings as well as sushi and traditional Thai dishes. **$$**

Martin's
1796 Carter Hill Road
Tel: 334-265-1767
www.martinsrestaurant.org
A local favorite for 70 years, Martin's is famous for its fried chicken and is just the place when you want comfort food. Open lunch and dinner but closes very early and isn't open on Saturdays. **$**

Mississippi

Biloxi
Hard Rock Cafe
777 Beach Boulevard
Tel: 228-374-7625
www.hardrockbiloxi.com
The Hard Rock has seven restaurants to choose from, so if you're in a hurry, you should find something here to suit your taste. The casual 24-hour restaurant offers huge breakfasts, and the Hard Rock Cafe is, of course, famous for its trademark burgers and rock memorabilia. **$–$$$**

Gulfport
Port City Cafe
2418 14th Street
Tel: 228-868-0037
This appealing storefront café serves traditional Southern food. The owner is always willing to stop and chat. **$**

Ocean Springs
The Shed BBQ and Blues Joint
7501 Highway 57
Tel: 228-875-9590
www.theshedbbq.com
This eclectic barbecue spot is nationally known for its pulled pork, smoked sausage, and other barbecue. The junkyard atmosphere offers a certain *je ne sais quoi*. **$**

Louisiana

Abbeville
Dupuy's Oyster Shop
108 S. Main Street
Tel: 337-893-2336
www.dupuysoystershop.com
Established in 1869, this highly acclaimed oyster and seafood restaurant is the real deal for homecooked Cajun food. **$–$$**

Baton Rouge
Drusilla Seafood Restaurant
3482 Drusilla Lane
Tel: 225-923-0896
www.drusillaplace.com
A local favorite for seafood, steaks, and Cajun food. A good place to try shrimp remoulade, gumbo, crawfish étouffée, and their acclaimed seafood eggplant gratin. A real spirit of Louisianan *lagniappe* (a little bit more). **$–$$**

Breaux Bridge
Cafe Des Amis
140 E. Bridge Street
Tel: 337-332-5273
www.cafedesamis.com
Famous for its Zydeco Breakfast on Saturdays, featuring Cajun food, Zydeco music, and dancing, Cafe Des Amis is a great place to sample local color. Its location in a historic building near the bridge is perfect. Try one of the many crawfish dishes and Cajun breakfast treats like *couche couche*, a corn cereal batter with sweetened milk and *oreilles de cochon*, cornmeal donuts shaped like pig's ears. **$–$$**

Eunice
Ruby's Cafe
221 W. Walnut Avenue
Tel: 337-550-7665
This tiny backstreet café is the real deal. It serves up generous portions of well-flavored Cajun food for next to nothing. Try an authentic *ponce* (pork roast stuffed with sausage) or fried shrimp over rice washed down with Louisiana-style chicory coffee. **$**

Lafayette
Prejeans
3480 NE Evangeline Tramway (1-49N)
Tel: 337-896-3247
www.prejeans.com
Famous for its live Cajun music and award-winning chicken and sausage, smoked duck, and seafood gumbos, Prejeans is touristy but the food is worth running the gauntlet of tour buses to sample. **$–$$**

New Orleans
Antoine's
713 St Louis Street, French Quarter
Tel: 504-525-8045
www.antoines.com
This French Creole restaurant has been run by the same family since 1840. Dishes such as Oysters Rockefeller originated at Antoine's. Many dishes are sensational, especially the Baked Alaska. **$$$**

Brennan's
17 Royal Street
Tel: 504-525-9711
www.brennansneworleans.com
A mainstay since the 1940s, Brennan's features the full gamut of classic NOLA fare, including gumbo, etoufee, and turtle soup. The 10 rich Crescent City egg dishes include several featuring Holland rusks instead of English muffins (try the house special, Eggs Hussarde, made with poached eggs with Canadian bacon, Marchand du Vin sauce, topped with Hollandaise sauce). The tradition here is to drink wine with breakfast. Somehow in New Orleans it doesn't seem out of place. **$–$$**

Cochon
930 Tchoupitoulas Street
Tel: 504-588-2123
www.cochonrestaurant.com
A homage to everything porcine on the bayou, Cochon's chef-owner Donald Link has a French-inspired way with *boucherie*. The menu showcases traditional Cajun hog dishes, but you'll also find game and local seafood. It's located in a light-filled corner building in the Warehouse District. Unsuitable for vegetarians. **$$$**

Court of Two Sisters
613 Royal Street
Tel: 504-522-7261
www.courtoftwosisters.com
This restaurant in the French Quarter is a New Orleans institution, famous for its lovely historic courtyard setting and Jazz Brunch Buffet. The music

and ambiance are perfect, but the buffet brunch tends to suffer from overambition and underperformance. Stick with can't-fail egg dishes like Eggs Benedict, and try their home-churned ice cream with dessert. Open for breakfast, lunch, and dinner. **$-$$**

St Martinville

Josephine's Creole Restaurant
830 S. Main Street
Tel: 337-394-8030
Bona fide Creole and Cajun cooking using time-honored family recipes are the secret to Josephine's success. Locals swear this is the best place to eat. Try the shrimp and chicken stews, stuffed turkey wings, and stuffed Creole bread. Expect a wait, as it's always busy. **$$**

Texas

Austin

Threadgill's Old No. 1
6416 N. Lamar Boulevard
Tel: 512-451-5440
www.threadgills.com
This famed Texan roadhouse café is located on the site of a 1933 gas station whose owner helped start the live-music scene in Austin. The original building was where Janis Joplin cut her musical chops. A branch, located next to the famous 1970s live-music venue Armadillo World Headquarters in South Austin, was opened in the 1990s. There are lavish servings of Southern cuisine and live music at both venues. **$**

Wink
1014 N. Lamar Boulevard
Tel: 512-482-8868
www.winkrestaurant.com
Wink is located in a quiet corner but still manages to make a lot of noise among foodies. Its chef-owners do clever things with seasonal game, fish, and produce from local sources, using herb-infused oils, emulsions, and vegetable purées to draw out the natural flavors. Try sautéed onaga with escarole and sorrel aïoli or grilled black buck antelope. The elegant Wink Trio – lemon meringue pot, crème brûlée, and El Rey chocolate cake – makes a fitting finale. Reservations recommended. **$$$**

El Paso

The Dome Restaurant
101 S. El Paso Street
Tel: 915-534-3010
This upmarket dining room is located in the elegant Camino Real Hotel, where the chef's innovative seafood and wild game creations have a huge following. They are matched by the majestic Tiffany glass dome that gives the restaurant its name. **$$$**

L&J's Café
3622 E. Missouri Avenue
Tel: 915-566-8418
This atmospheric hole-in-the-wall across from the Concordia Cemetery, where John Wesley Hardin is buried, is a legitimate historic attraction in its own right. It's been dishing up the best Mexican food in El Paso for a century and has a loyal following. **$**

Fort Davis

Hotel Limpia Dining Room
100 State Street
Tel: 432-426-3241
www.hotellimpia.com
This dining room has a country ambiance befitting its historic hotel setting. It serves Texas classics such as steaks, seafood, and homemade pies. **$$**

Fredericksburg

Altdorf Restaurant and Beer Garden
301 W. Main Street
Tel: 830-997-7685
www.altdorfbiergarten-fbg.com
Housed in an 1847 landmark building on Main Street, Altdorf's supplies plenty of *oompah* for the hordes. If you're looking for an atmospheric beer garden with German music, beer, and international grub, this is the place. **$**

Galveston

Mosquito Cafe
628 14th Street
Tel: 409-763-1010
www.mosquitocafe.com
This lovely bistro feels Californian, with its light wood beams and excited foodie fervor. The owner is, in fact, Californian and has demonstrated his commitment to food and community by feeding clean-up crews from 2008's Hurricane Ike. The changing, globally inspired menu includes creative salads, fresh fish tacos, mesquite-grilled salmon, and signature desserts. The Sunday brunch is a popular local hangout. **$-$$$**

Houston

Dessert Gallery Bakery Café
3600 Kirby Drive, Suite D
Tel: 713-522-9999
www.dessertgallery.com
Sara Brook's original Dessert Gallery moved to new digs up the road in 2009, but she still makes some of the sexiest cupcakes, cakes, and cookies around. The Gallery also sells sandwiches, wraps, and box lunches, if sugar ain't your thing. Second location in Post Oak. **$**

The Grove Restaurant
1611 Lamar Boulevard
Tel: 713-337-7321
www.thegrovehouston.com
Perfectly located in Houston's newest park, 11-acre (4.5-hectare) Discovery Green, the Grove has an enviable leafy treehouse setting. The blond-wood room makes an elegant backdrop for inspired dishes like duck meatloaf, Gulf fish in parchment, or shrimp and scallop brochette, but basic burgers, soup, and sandwiches are done well, too. Closed Mondays. **$$-$$$**

RDG + Bar Annie
1728 Post Oak Boulevard
Tel: 713-840-1111
www.rdgbarannie.com
Following on from the success of Café Annie, Robert Del Grande has tweaked the concept at this new rendition in the same lovely Galleria location and continued to draw kudos for the best Southwest food in Houston. To start, try the smoked oysters, grilled squab with foie gras butter, or seared avocado salad with queso fresco and radish, and follow with red chili-daubed rabbit with red mole enchiladas. **$$$**

Marathon

12 Gage in the Gage Hotel
10 Highway 90 W.
Tel: 432-386-4205
www.gagehotel.com
The elegant dinner restaurant in this historic hotel has won raves for its rustic New Southwestern food. Earthy dishes draw heavily on fresh game meats, such as buffalo tenderloin and grilled quail, and Gulf seafood, prepared using authentically Mexican cooking techniques to create salsas from fire-roasted tomatoes and chilis and dry spice rubs. The adjoining Buffalo Bar specializes in tequilas. **$$$**

Marfa

Cochineal
107 W. San Antonio Street
Tel: 432-729-3300
www.cochinealmarfa.com
Marfa's best dinner restaurant is owned by seasoned restaurateurs from NYC. Their creativity and expertise comes through in perfectly prepared steaks, flash-cooked Gulf seafood, and other globally inspired dishes made from fresh local ingredients. Reservations

PRICE CATEGORIES

Price categories are for an average cost of dinner and a glass of wine, before tip:
$ = under $20
$$ = $20–40
$$$ = more than $40

recommended. Closed Wednesdays and Thursdays. **$$$**

San Antonio
Casa Rio
430 E. Commerce Street
Tel: 210-225-6718
www.casa-rio.com
This enduring Riverwalk favorite serves large portions of tasty Mexican food. Their tasty tortilla soup made with chicken is a nice light bite. **$**
Chart House Tower of the Americas
701 Bowie Street
Tel: 210-223-3101
www.toweroftheamericas.com/charthouse
Enjoy the Chart House's famously good steaks, prime rib, and seafood while taking in the spectacular views from the revolving Tower of the Americas in Hemisfair Park. **$$$**

New Mexico

Cloudcroft
Rebecca's
The Lodge at Cloudcroft, 1 Corona Place
Tel: 575-682-2566
www.thelodgeresort.com
Named after the resident ghost, Rebecca's features fine Southwestern and continental cuisine in an elegant dining room with a view into the meadows. **$$**

Mescalero
Wendell's Restaurant
287 Carrizozo Road
Tel: 888-324-0348
www.innofthemountaingods.com
Located in the sumptuously rebuilt Inn of the Mountain Gods, Wendell's celebrates Apache cowboy country with the kind of awesome certified Angus beefsteaks you'd expect. Fresh local elk, free-range chicken, and seafood options like sea bass are also available. Also serves breakfast and lunch. **$–$$$**

Mesilla
Double Eagle Restaurant
On the Plaza, Old Mesilla
Tel: 575-523-6700
www.double-eagle-mesilla.com
Set in a historic building dating from the 1840s, this atmospheric restaurant is filled with antiques from the days of the Old West. The menu features steaks from the restaurant's own ageing room, as well as gourmet poultry and seafood dishes with New Mexican flavors. **$$$**
Meson de Mesilla Restaurant
1803 Avenida de Mesilla
Tel: 575-525-9212
www.mesondemesilla.com
Savor Spanish, Italian, and French cuisine by acclaimed chef Joseph

Hilbert at this Pueblo-style boutique inn. Try the green chili corn chowder to start, followed by pistachio-crusted halibut or perhaps elk chop with seared foie gras. Open for dinner only from Wednesday through Saturday. **$$$**

Pinos Altos
Buckhorn Saloon and Opera House
32 Main Street
Tel: 575-538-991
www.buckhornsaloonandoperahouse.com
An authentic Wild West setting greets diners at this famous historic spot enroute to Gila Cliff Dwellings. White-linen-and-candlelight service in the main dining room enhances offerings such as bison burgers, New York strip steak with green chili, and prime rib. There's live blues or folk several nights a week in the dark bar, and melodramas in the adjacent Opera House on Friday and Saturday. **$$–$$$**

Ruidoso
Cafe Rio Pizza
2547 Main Street (Sudderth Drive)
Tel: 575-257-7746
Design a first-rate pizza from scratch at this hip little pizzeria. But don't stop there. The eclectic menu at this charming spot includes Portuguese kale soup, roasted garlic, spanokopita, baked clams, and jambalaya. No credit cards. **$**

Silver City
Diane's Restaurant and Bakery
510 N. Bullard Street
Tel: 575-538-8722
www.dianesrestaurant.com
Lace curtains, hardwood floors, and starched white linens add refinement to this relaxed eatery on the historic main street, an oasis of fine internationally inspired dining in southwestern New Mexico. At dinner, try an appetizer of spanokopita followed by Seafood Thai Curry. Lunch options include excellent quiche or green chili alfredo pasta. Diane's homemade bakery items are worth a special trip. Brunch on weekends. **$$**

Arizona

Phoenix
Barrio Café
2814 N. 16th Street
Tel: 602-636-0240
www.barriocafe.com
This lively James Beard–nominated restaurant in the up-and-coming foodie area of the Barrio just east of Downtown is one of the most enjoyable experiences in town and worth seeking out. Southern Mexican

dishes include complex *moles* and Cochinito Pibil, the famous Yucatan dish of marinated pulled pork cooked in a banana leaf until succulent, rarely cooked outside the Yucatan. Leave room for rich desserts like *flan* and *churros* with hot chocolate. **$–$$**
Christo's
6327 N. Seventh Street
Tel: 602-264-1784
www.christos1.com
One of the top Phoenix restaurants, chef-owner Christo's Italian food is elegance personified and a place where you can settle in and enjoy good food accompanied by jazz. Try the moist sea bass or the fresh and light pasta pomodoro. **$$**
Pizzeria Bianco
623 E. Adams Street
Tel: 602-258-8300
Chef-owner Chris Bianco helped found Slow Food Phoenix. His popular pizzeria is in a small historic building in Heritage Square, and there's always a wait for the pizzas topped with fresh, locally sourced vegetables. Sandwiches are available at his Pane Bianco bakery on Central. The man is a phenomenon. **$–$$**

Tucson
El Charro
311 N. Court Avenue
Tel: 520-622-1922
www.elcharrocafe.com
El Charro is legendary in Tucson and now has several outlets, but the restaurant in the historic Presidio district downtown dates back to the 1890s. Be sure to ask for their tequila list, and try their delicious sun-dried meat – their Carne Seca plate has been voted one of the best 50 dishes in the US. There's also a courtyard for outdoor dining. **$$**
The Grill at Hacienda del Sol
5601 N. Hacienda del Sol Road
Tel: 520-529-3500
www.haciendadelsol.com
Many Tucsonans say this is the city's best eating place, out at the intimate and historic Hacienda del Sol resort. Their Sunday brunch is definitely one of the best anywhere, and the romantic views of the foothills in the evening from the Terraza del Sol combine with dishes like Tasmanian ocean trout or expertly cooked rack of lamb, and one of the best wine lists in the country. **$$$**

Yuma
The Garden Cafe
250 Madison Avenue
Tel: 928-783-1491
www.gardencafeyuma.com
These lush gardens punctuated

with sweet-smelling flowers and birdsong were once part of the historic Sanguinetti House estate. Now they make a delightful setting for an al fresco lunch or breakfast. Dishes range from homemade quiche, soup and enormous salads, to scrumptious tri-tip steak and grande burritos. Excellent desserts. **$**

Market Wine Bar and Bistro
1501 S. Redondo Center Drive
Tel: 928-373-6574
www.marketwinebarbistro.co
This upscale but casual bistro and wine bar is in the new Radisson Hotel, a short drive from Downtown. The atmosphere is fun and colorful, with boutique wines and a menu inspired by Mediterranean cuisine with a fresh seafood catch flown in daily. **$$–$$$**

River City Grill
600 W. Third Street
Tel: 928-782-7988
www.rivercitygrill.com
This innovative restaurant offers healthy global fusion cuisine in a neighborhood bistro. The menu includes wild-caught seafood specials like gumbo, crab cakes, tequila snapper, and sushi, as well as grass-fed beef steaks, pasta, and organic veggies. **$–$$$**

California

El Centro
Exotic Thai Bistro
1461 S. Fourth Street
Tel: 760-353-0008
Located in a strip mall, this attractive Thai restaurant is a cut above most

dining choices in unpromising El Centro. Try the pad thai. **$**

La Mesa
Brigantine Seafood Restaurant
9350 Fuerte Drive
Tel: 619-465-1935
www.brigantine.com
Enjoy the popular lounge and oyster bar, or a seafood meal in the nautical-themed restaurant or outdoors on the lush garden patio. **$$**

Marieta's Restaurant
8949 La Mesa Boulevard
Tel: 619-462-3500
You'll find an array of authentic southern California-style Mexican dishes and friendly service at this neighborhood restaurant. You'll even be serenaded at your table. **$**

PACIFIC ROUTE

California

Big Sur
Deetjen's Big Sur Inn Restaurant
48865 Highway 1
Tel: 831-667-2378
www.deetjens.com
The country pub ambiance in the cozy restaurant of this historic inn hasn't changed since it was created by a British woman in 1939. Breakfasting on the famed eggs benedict by the fire on a cool, foggy coastal morning is one of the great Big Sur experiences. Dinner showcases local produce and is truly special. **$–$$$**

Nepenthe
48510 Highway 1
Tel: 831-667-2345
www.nepenthebigsur.com
This landmark restaurant on Highway 1 opened in 1949 and is still operated by the same family. It serves simple but delicious favorites like Ambrosia Burger and Three Berry Pie and has a lovely gift shop. The real reason to come here is the fabulous views over Big Sur. **$$**

Bodega Bay
Lucas Wharf Restaurant
595 Highway 1
Tel: 707-875-3522
www.lucaswharfrestaurant.com
Fresh seafood is the specialty at this restaurant, with a range of dishes such as blackened snapper and risotto with jumbo prawns. Note that it can close as early as 8pm. **$$**

Calistoga
All Seasons Bistro
1400 Lincoln Avenue

Tel: 707-942-9111
www.allseasonsnapavalley.net
Black-and-white tile flooring and red ceiling give it a retro look, but the cuisine at this casual restaurant is anything but. The menu features creative dishes based on fresh seasonal ingredients from local producers, grown organically, and paired with premium wines for a memorable meal. **$$$**

Cambria
Black Cat Bistro
1602 Main Street, Suite C
Tel: 805-927-1600
www.blackcatbistro.com
Chef-owner Deborah Scarborough's international cuisine emphasizes fresh, local, and organic. Try the Cayucos Abalone, salad of local greens, or the homemade soup. Follow with an entrée like Chipotle Wood Acres Shrimp and Linguini or flat-iron steak, and end with the Central Coast Creamery cheese plate or perhaps the salted caramel tart. A good place for vegetarians. **$–$$$**

Carmel-by-the-Sea
Dametra Café
Between Dolores and Lincoln streets on Ocean Avenue
Tel: 831-622-7766
www.dametracafe.com
Diners queue every night to enjoy the relaxed dining atmosphere created by the affable owner and his team in the kitchen, as they produce stunning versions of authentic Mediterranean dishes. The long, narrow dining room takes you back to the Med, too, with ocher walls

and a happy buzz from the close-set tables. **$$$**

Eureka
Restaurant 301
Carter House Inn, 301 L Street
Tel: 707-444-8062
www.carterhouse.com
Regarded as one of the best restaurants in Northern California (with one of the best wine lists, according to *Wine Spectator*), this small yet spacious hotel restaurant offers a changing menu of sophisticated dishes. You can opt to take a five-course Discovery Menu, including optional paired wines for each dish. **$$$**

Samoa Cookhouse
Off Highway 101 across the Samoa Bridge
Tel: 707-442-1659
Eat like a South Sea Islander at this Northern California landmark on the outskirts of Eureka. Hefty breakfasts, lunches, and dinners are served family-style at long tables where you help yourself. Save room for the hot apple pie. **$**

Hermosa Beach
Martha's 22nd Street Grill
25 22nd Street
Tel: 310-376-7786
It's only open for breakfast and lunch, but Martha's is an extremely popular award-winning café close to the beach that won't disappoint. Go for any of the

PRICE CATEGORIES

Price categories are for an average cost of dinner and a glass of wine, before tip:
$ = under $20
$$ = $20–40
$$$ = more than $40

breakfast omelets featuring avocado or perhaps the stuffed french toast. Homemade scones and real coffee will hit the spot for a snack. A great spot for soaking up the rays and people watching. **$**

Laguna Beach
Las Brisas
361 Cliff Drive
Tel: 949-497-5434
www.lasbrisaslagunabeach.com
Sit on the outdoor patio or in the dining room of this beautifully situated restaurant and enjoy excellent Mexican cuisine and seafood dishes accompanied by stunning views of the ocean. **$$–$$$**

Mendocino
Ravens Restaurant
Stanford Inn, Coast Highway and Comptche Ukiah Road
Tel: 707-937-5615
www.ravensrestaurant.com
The Stanford Inn's highly acclaimed vegetarian restaurant is open to non-guests too, and even if you're not vegetarian, if you're interested in food you should dine here at least once. The rustic decor is smart but relaxing, the wine list extensive, and the delicious food, such as the signature Sea Palm Strudel, original. **$$$**

Monterey
Abalonetti
57 Fisherman's Wharf
Tel: 831-373-1851
www.abalonettimonterey.com
As well as some of the best clam chowder and calamari on Fisherman's Wharf, Abalonetti's stands out as one of the few to have really good terraces overlooking the bay, where you can watch the seals and sea lions swimming and also enjoying their own fish dishes. **$$**

Morro Bay
Galley Seafood Bar and Grill
899 Embarcadero Morro Bay
Tel: 805-772-7777
www.thegalleymorrobay.com
Popular for its fresh, local seafood, but there's plenty here for vegetarians and meat lovers, too. The setting right on Morro Bay is perfect. **$–$$$**

Napa
The Bounty Hunter
975 First Street, Napa Town
Tel: 707-226-3976
www.bountyhunterwinebar.com
The lively Bounty Hunter bar makes full use of the wines in its adjoining wine shop, with a list that includes 40 wines by the glass and over 400 you can

purchase to drink or take home. The food is impressive, too, especially their trademark Smokin' BBQ Platter. **$$**

Novato
Rickey's Restaurant and Bar
Inn Marin, 250 Entrada Drive
Tel: 415-883-5952
www.rickeysrestaurant.com
Part of the Inn Marin but livelier than any hotel restaurant you've ever seen, Rickey's has live jazz on Friday and Saturday nights (booking advised), lots of tables, a fun feeling, and food that isn't fancy but goes down well – like pan-seared scallops or filet mignon with bacon-mashed potatoes. **$$–$$$**

Oceanside
101 Cafe
631 S. Coast Highway
Tel: 760-722-5220
www.101Cafe.net
Oceanside's oldest restaurant is a real roadside diner, decked out with 1950s memorabilia and serving great burgers, omelets, and classic diner dinners from 6.30am till midnight daily. Try a peanut butter malt. It's the bee's knees! **$**

Pescadero
Duarte's
202 Stage Road
Tel: 650-879-0464
www.duartestavern.com
With a beautiful historic setting on a remote stretch of coast, this casual tavern serves everything from sandwiches for beachgoers to family Sunday dinners with all the trimmings, but do not miss the cream of artichoke and cream of green chili soups – get one of each. **$**

San Diego
Rock Bottom Brewery
401 G Street
Tel: 619-231-7000
www.rockbottom.com
Set in a former Studebaker showroom in the Gaslamp Quarter, this brewpub serves great handcrafted beers and great food to go with them. Live music and dancing every weekend. **$–$$**

True Food Kitchen
7007 Friar's Road, Suite 394
Tel: 619-810-2929
www.truefoodkitchen.com
Located in Fashion Valley Mall, this attractive eatery is the latest in a well-received chain founded by renowned wholistic doctor Andrew Weil. It specializes in light, tasty Mediterranean and Asian renditions of colorful, antioxidant-rich foods with small amounts of fish, meat, and cheese. The Tuscan Kale salad is a big hit. **$–$$**

San Francisco
Greens
Building A, Fort Mason Center
Tel: 415-771-6222
www.greensrestaurant.com
Organic produce from Green Gulch Valley Farm near Mount Tam, seasonal specials, and a mesquite grill are the cornerstones of this world-famous vegetarian restaurant. Alongside some of the most inspired and meticulously executed veggie food you've ever tasted are spectacular views of the Golden Gate Bridge. Sunset is the perfect time to eat. **$$$**

House of Nanking
919 Kearny Street, Chinatown
Tel: 415-421-1429
www.houseofnanking.net
House of Nanking is Fog City's most popular Chinese restaurant, a Nob Hill tradition where the cramped seating, dark Irish Pub atmosphere, and pushy service are part of the charm. People come from miles around for the food, which is best enjoyed in a large group. **$**

Masa's
648 Bush Street, north of Union Square
Tel: 415-989-7154
www.masasrestaurant.com
Perhaps the most expensive and critically lauded restaurant in all of San Francisco, Masa's is the perennial winner in the city's top restaurant polls. It specializes in California French cuisine, and it does it very well indeed. **$$$**

Santa Barbara
La Super-Rica Taqueria
622 N. Milpas Street
Tel: 805-963-4940
Jaded taqueria aficionados meet their match in this tiny barrio eatery, which emphasizes a varied and unusual mix of flavors, some quite intense (hot), with not a boring burrito in sight. Try the soft tacos and eat on the covered patio with the eclectic clientele. This landmark was Julia Child's favorite local restaurant. **$**

Olio e Limone
11 W. Victoria, Suite 17
Tel: 805-899-2699
www.olioelimone.com
The wine cellar visible behind a glass wall in the dining room, combined with the white walls and tile floors, sets a cheerful Mediterranean scene at this always busy place. The mouthwatering wonderful Italian food is perfectly prepared and presented, with dishes like pumpkin ravioli. Excellent service by Italian waiters. **$$$**

Shoreline Beach Café
801 Shoreline Drive
Tel: 805-568-0064

www.shorelinebeachcafe.com
Eat a juicy burger or fresh-caught fish tacos in the café or from the takeout window at this reliable, budget-conscious café right on lovely Ledbetter Beach. A favorite with students at the nearby community college and locals for decades, it's the perfect spot to relax with friends "SB style." **$**

Santa Monica
Fig
101 Wilshire Boulevard
Tel: 310-319-3111
www.figsantamonica.com
This intimate restaurant in the Fairmont Miramar Hotel has a cool modern take on food and decor. The flavorful offerings include foie gras with fig sauce, expertly prepared fresh fish, beef served with minty tasting micro-greens, and strawberry shortcake with strawberry ice cream for dessert. **$$$**

Trinidad
Larrupin' Cafe
1658 Patricks Point Drive
Tel: 707-677-0230
www.larrupin.com
This unique dinner restaurant features California French cuisine using organic meat and produce, with many vegetarian offerings. Hobbit comfort in an enchanting woodsy setting, three-course dinners are a delight from appetizers to dessert. Make reservations weeks in advance, if possible, or you might miss out. Closed Thursdays. Live jazz Wednesdays and Sundays. **$$**

Venice
Rose Café and Market
220 Rose Avenue
Tel: 310-399-0711
www.rosecafe.com
A perfect local spot for brunch on the weekend, this beachside café is airy and bright and offers terrific egg dishes. Try Eggs San Pietro, poached eggs served on an English muffin with prosciutto, smoked ham, and béarnaise sauce. The coffee is hot and strong, and there's an in-house bakery turning out delectable treats. **$**

Oregon

Astoria
Bridgewater Bistro
20 Basin Street, Suite A
Tel: 503-325-6777
www.bridgewaterbistro.com
Housed in a large, renovated warehouse below the bridge, this attractive modern bistro is a renowned seafood restaurant that takes gluten-free dishes seriously. Almost 80 percent of the menu is GF. **$**

Cannon Beach
The Warren House Pub
3301 S. Hemlock Street
Tel: 503-436-1130
You can eat either in the family-friendly restaurant at the front, where there's often a wait for a table, or in the simpler bar at the back, with its pool table. Both places have good wine and beer lists, and the menu has a lot of good plain but tasty seafood, such as oyster burgers. **$$**

Coos Bay
Benetti's
260 S. Broadway
Tel: 541-267-6066
www.benettis.com
A family-run Italian restaurant with great service and fantastic food, Benetti's is always busy. There's family dining downstairs and an adult dining room upstairs, overlooking the bay and the boardwalk. **$$**
Fisherman's Wharf
Charleston Boat Basin, Dock D
Tel: 541-888-8862
There's no better place for fresh crab and seafood, which you can purchase right on the dock from local fishermen. They will pack you a box of crab to go – perfect for a picnic by the sea as you drive the Cape Arago beach loop. **$**

Gold Beach
Spinner's
29430 Ellensburg Avenue, Highway 101
Tel: 541-247-5160
www.spinnersrestaurant.com
Good service and a buzzing atmosphere are the hallmarks of this seafood, steak, and chophouse, set in a large, rustic wooden building with windows overlooking the shore. Great food, from bison burgers to prime rib to cedar-planked wild salmon. **$–$$**

Newport
Café Stephanie
411 NW Coast Street
Tel: 541-265-8082
A local favorite in Newport's Nye Beach district, breakfasts are the big draw here. Try a breakfast burrito or eggs any style with Stephanie's Potato Tornado, a mound of roasted red potatoes, red peppers, and grilled onions, covered with melted cheese. Both come with a side of fresh fruit and a house-baked scone. **$**

Portland
Bread and Ink Café
3610 SE Hawthorne Boulevard
Tel: 503-239-4756
www.breadandinkcafe.com
Situated in the center of Portland's historic Hawthorne shopping and arts district, this longtime favorite for breakfast, lunch, or dinner has cheerful service and dishes lovingly cooked with fresh ingredients that are locally sourced as much as possible. The onsite bakery turns out some delicious pastries. **$**
Jake's Famous Crawfish
401 SW 12th
Tel: 503-226-1419
www.jakesfamouscrawfish.com
A Portland landmark for 110 years for its mouthwatering seafood, Jake's has been voted one of the top 10 seafood restaurants in the nation. It's always busy, but it's worth the wait. **$$**

Yachats
The Drift Inn
124 Highway 101 N.
Tel: 541-547-4477
www.the-drift-inn.com
The historic Drift Inn is one of the best local eateries, with a bar down one side, a small stage where musicians play every night, and seating in booths. Their halibut fish and chips plate is perfect, and there are unusual dishes like "figs in a blanket" and vegetarian choices among the steak and seafood specials. **$$**

Washington

Long Beach
The Depot
208 38th Place
Tel: 360-642-7880
www.depotrestaurantdining.com
Located in the historic Clamshell Railroad Train Station in Seaview, this little "restaurant that could" is a winner for its casual fine dining with the seasons. Everything from Young's Bay king salmon to paella with fresh Willapa clams to cobbler made with eastern Washington peaches turns up on the changing globally inspired menu. **$$–$$$**

Olympia
La Petite Maison
101 Division Street
Tel: 360-754-9623
www.lapetitemaisonrestaurant.com
A foodie haven for fresh seafood and decadent desserts, you can't go wrong with this popular Olympia restaurant. **$$**

PRICE CATEGORIES

Price categories are for an average cost of dinner and a glass of wine, before tip:
$ = under $20
$$ = $20–40
$$$ = more than $40

ACTIVITIES

FESTIVALS, THE ARTS, NIGHTLIFE, SHOPPING, AND SPECTATOR SPORTS

FESTIVALS

January

First Peoples World's Fair and Powwow: Thunder in the Desert (Tucson, Arizona)
Tribes from around the country gather for this big powwow which includes parades, fashion shows, and equestrian events. Tel: 520-622-4900.
Orange Bowl (Miami, Florida)
The final game between Florida's two best college football teams. New Year's Day. Tel: 305-341-4702.
Westminster Kennel Dog Show (New York)
The US version of Britain's Crufts Dog Show, this two-day event at Madison Square Garden and Piers 92/94 attracts the cream of the canine crop to the Big Apple. www. westminsterkennelclub.org.

February

San Antonio Stock Show and Rodeo (San Antonio, Texas)
The largest junior rodeo and stock show in the US features family entertainment, competitions, horse shows and stock auctions. Tel: 210-225-5851.
Groundhog Day (Punxsutawney, Pennsylvania)
More than 30,000 people descend on Gobblers Knob to see whether groundhog Punxsutawney Phil sees his shadow, denoting six more weeks of winter. Hayrides, parades, ice and chainsaw carving, and other entertainment. www.groundhog.org.
Mardi Gras (Mobile, Alabama; New Orleans, Louisiana; Galveston, Texas, etc.)
Gulf cities celebrate Mardi Gras. Mobile has the oldest Mardi Gras celebration (1703) but New Orleans is the most famous and long-running, from January 6 (Epiphany) to the day before Ash Wednesday in February. Highlights are parades of colorful, exotic floats created by competing "krewes," eating, drinking, dancing, and mayhem. Tel: 251-208-2000 (Mobile) and www.neworleansonline. com (New Orleans).
Madison Winter Festival (Madison, Wisconsin)
Madison's hardy residents descend on frigid Capitol Square to enjoy ice and snow sculptures, tubing hill, snowboard rail jam, and world-class cross-country ski racing and snowshoeing; www.winter-fest.com.

March

South by Southwest (Austin, Texas)
This 10-day live-music festival, one of the country's largest, welcomes more than 2,000 different acts on more than 90 stages around Austin. A concurrent independent moviemaking conference rounds out offerings. www. sxsw.com.
Tennessee Williams New Orleans Literary Festival (New Orleans, Louisiana)
Five days of readings, dramatizations, lectures, and walking tours featuring renowned actors celebrate the *Cat on a Hot Tin Roof* author. Tel: 1-800-990-FEST.
Miami International Film Festival (Miami, Florida)
A 10-day feast of international films, with an emphasis on independent entries and those from Latin America. Tel: 305-237-FILM.

National Festival of the West (Scottsdale, Arizona)
This extravaganza pays homage to the old west. Jamboree with a multitude of activities including a musical jamboree, trade show, film festival, cookout, and Buffalo Soldiers re-enactment. Tel: 602-996-4387.

April

Boston Marathon (Boston, MA)
Runners from around the world gather to race in one of the country's most popular marathons. Tel: 617-236-1652.
National Cherry Blossom Festival (Washington, DC)
Commemorating Japan's 1912 gift of 3,000 cherry trees to the US, this festival heralds the advent of spring in the nation's capital. Tel: 877-44BLOOM.
Crossroads Film Festival (Jackson, Mississippi)
An inspiring cross-fertilization of Blues music and independent film makes this one of the biggest arts gatherings in Mississippi. www. crossroadsfilmfestival.com.
San Francisco Women's Film Festival (San Francisco, California)
A four-day festival honoring documentaries, animation, video, experimental films, and other movies made by women. www. womensfilminstitute.squarespace.com.
Doo Dah Parade (Pasadena, California)
This spoof parade features 1,500 participants. Some of the most famous include the Briefcase Marching Drill Team, the Hibachi Marching Grill Team, and the Invisible Man Marching Band. Berkeley also has its own Doo Dah Parade. www. pasadenadoodahparade.com.

May

Beale Street Blues Festival
(Memphis, Tennessee)
Three days of concerts by the nation's top blues performers, on the Mississippi River. Tel: 901-525-4611.
Cinco de Mayo (various US cities)
Festivals featuring parades, food, music, and folkloric dancing are held in Hispanic communities throughout the US to commemorate Mexican liberation from French occupation in 1862.
Key West Fishing Tournament (Key West, Florida)
A fish fest in Ernest Hemingway's old hometown, held March through November. Tel: 305-296-6601.
Route 66 Fun Run Weekend
(Seligman to Topock)
A classic car "run," with a festival in Kingman. Hualapai barbecue, booths, entertainment, classic car judging, and a leisurely Sunday morning ride on Route 66. Tel: 928-753-5001.
Sweet Auburn Springfest (Atlanta, Georgia)
The largest African-American festival in the region features more than 300 entertainers in downtown Atlanta. www.sweetauburn.com.

June

Corn Dances (Santa Abna, Tesuque, and other Pueblos, New Mexico)
One of the most important dances of the year prays for rain to ensure a good harvest. Tel: 505-843-7270.
Mariachi USA (Los Angeles, California)
Held at the Hollywood Bowl, this festival features a huge array of Mexican mariachi bands. www.mariachiusa.com
Juneteenth (various US cities)
Begun in Galveston, Texas, in 1865, Juneteenth is the oldest celebration in the US marking the end of slavery and celebrating African-American culture. Events throughout the US. www.juneteenth.com.
Solstice Celebration (Santa Barbara, California)
This wildly popular festival was the brainwave of local artists and has a free-spirited Mardi Gras-like feel, complete with gorgeous floats, extraordinary costumes and masks, dancing, face painting, and street food. The parade is held on the second day of the three-day event. Tel: 805-965-3396.

July

Fourth of July (throughout US)
Fireworks, cookouts, parades, and entertainment, from concerts to rodeos, mark American Independence Day celebrations.
Folkmoot USA (North Carolina)
More than 200 groups from 100 countries highlight international folk arts in the mountains of western North Carolina. Tel: 877-FOLK-USA.
Taste of Buffalo (Buffalo, New York)
One of the country's largest food festivals attracts more than 450,000 visitors to downtown Buffalo in upstate New York. Tel: 800-BUFFALO.
Olympic Peninsula Music Festival
(Quilcene, Washington)
Starting in July, several months of weekend concerts in an old barn attract classical music lovers to the Olympic Peninsula. Tel. 360-732-4800.
Bite of Seattle (Seattle, Washington)
Sample offerings of more than 100 local food vendors. Wash food down with some local brews, and enjoy entertainment presented on seven stages at this three-day celebration. Tel: 425-283-5050.

August

Burning Man Festival (Black Rock City, Nevada)
For a week every August, a temporary "city" of up to 45,000 participants arises in the scorching Mojave Desert to make art together and build community, culminating in the burning of a 52ft (15-meter) -high pagan effigy. Tel: 415-TO-FLAME.
Bumbershoot (Seattle, Washington)
The largest of its kind, Seattle's premier arts festival takes up residence below the Space Needle to offer three days of superb music on several stages, arts and crafts, food booths, and other activities over Labor Day Weekend (which may fall in early Sept.). Tel: 206-673-5060.
Santa Fe Fiesta (Santa Fe, New Mexico)
The oldest such celebration in the US, this festival commemorating Santa Fe's Spanish founding fathers features horseback parades, floats, a children's and pet parade – and the other Fiesta: the burning of Old Man Gloom, Zozobra – over Labor Day weekend. (which may fall in early Sept.). www.santafefiesta.org.
116th Street Festival Carnival Del Barrio (New York City)
A fun two-day open-air festival celebrating Hispanic and Caribbean arts, food, and culture. Tel: 212-243-1177 or 917-748-2264.
Retro on Roscoe (Chicago, Illinois)
A huge neighborhood weekend street festival featuring three stages of live entertainment, an antique car show, and an arts and crafts show. Tel: 773-665-4682.
Indian Market (Santa Fe, New Mexico)
For two days Santa Fe's Plaza is transformed into the US's largest open-air market when Native American artists from 100 tribes compete in a juried show; others set up booths along nearby streets. Book hotels well ahead. Tel: 505-983-5220.

September

Farm Aid (Chicago, Illinois)
This successful annual concert series raises funds for US small farms and features superb country rock music by founders Willie Nelson, John Mellencamp, Neil Young, Dave Matthews, and others. Tel: 800-FARM-AID.
East LA Mexican Independence Day Parade (Los Angeles, California)
The country's oldest Mexican independence day celebration includes a colourful parade. Tel: 310-914-0015.
Bluegrass FanFest (Nashville, Tennessee)
More than 60 musicians take to the stage to celebrate bluegrass music and choose a champion fiddler on the last weekend in September. Tel: 615-256-3222.

October

Albuquerque International Balloon Fiesta (Albuquerque, New Mexico)
The world's largest gathering of hot-air balloons is staged over this nine-day festival. Tel: 888-422-7277 or 505-821-1000.
Great Grapes! Wine, Food, and Arts Festival (Charlotte, North Carolina)
Visitors gather in Symphony Park to raise a glass to fine local wines (more than 200 to chose from), feast on gourmet foods, and enjoy musical entertainment. www.uncorkthefun.com.
Rock Shrimp Festival (St Mary's, Georgia)
This one-day fest in historic St Mary's, pays tribute to the Gulf's abundant rock shrimp with 5k/10k races, parade, entertainment, food, arts and crafts, and rock shrimp dinners. Tel: 800-868-8687.

November

New York Marathon (New York City)
Watched by two million spectators,

the largest marathon in the US attracts over 100,000 entrants competing for $600,000 in prize money. www.nycmarathon.org.

Dia De Los Muertos – Day of the Dead (Hispanic communities in the US)

Sugar skulls and food offerings adorn home altars and family gravesites in Hispanic communities on this day of celebrating those who have passed on.

Macy's Thanksgiving Day Parade (New York City)

More than 3.5 million fans line the streets to cheer a huge contingent of more than 10,000 parade participants, including the nation's best marching bands. Tel: 212-494-5432.

December

Christmas New Orleans Style (New Orleans, Louisiana)

A month-long Christmas celebration featuring guided walks of the decorated French Quarter and Reveillon holiday meals reminiscent of those from the 1800s. Tel: 504-522-5730.

Canyon Road Farolito Walk (Santa Fe, New Mexico)

Farolitos (brown bag candle lanterns) show the way to the Holy Family on Christmas Eve. Attracts thousands to historic Canyon Road to stroll, sing carols, drink hot cider, and celebrate the holiday. Tel: 800-777-2489.

New Year's Eve in Times Square (New York City)

More than 1 million celebrants pack into one of the city's major tourist destinations to watch the ball drop at midnight. www.timessquarenyc.org.

First Night (Boston, Massachusetts)

The oldest and largest celebration of the arts in New England takes place on New Year's Eve when more than 1,000 artists in venues throughout the city perform. The evening culminates with fireworks over the harbor. Many cities throughout the country hold similar celebrations. Tel: 617-542-1399.

OUTDOOR ACTIVITIES

The United States has a huge number of national, state, county, and city parks; lakeside recreation areas; and nature preserves. There is plenty of scope for walking, swimming, fishing, cycling, boating, and participant sports.

Water and wind

Coastal areas and parks on larger lakes are your best bet for water activities **Deep-sea charters** offer fishing for grouper, sailfish, and tarpon in Florida and halibut, tuna, and salmon on the Pacific Northwest coasts. **Surfing** is big along wave-pounded beaches in southern California; swimming is popular on the Atlantic, Pacific, and Gulf coasts **Parasailing** and **windsurfing** attract enthusiasts wherever there are prevailing strong winds. The Windsurfing Capital of the World is actually inland, though, at Hood River in Oregon's Columbia River Gorge. **Diving** and **snorkeling** are spectacular in Florida's Keys, where your companions are often dolphins. Limestone regions, such as Crystal River in central Florida, offer diving in crystal-clear spring-fed sinkholes frequented by manatees. Santa Rosa on the hot, dusty plains of eastern New Mexico is a unique find: its 80ft (25-meter) -deep, spring-fed Blue Hole is popular with desert divers.

Boating is virtually an art form in coastal regions, and along the US-Canada border regions of the Great Lakes in the Midwest and Finger Lakes of upstate New York. Boats are more than recreation on the calm Intracoastal Waterways and offshore islands of the Gulf Coast, New England, and Washington State: they are often residences and transportation. Above major dams, western mountain rivers – such as the Colorado through the Grand Canyon, and the Rio Grande in Big Bend National Park – have spectacular **whitewater** and **flatwater rafting**. Below the dams, flatwater sports are popular at Amistad Reservoir on the Rio Grande and Lake Powell on the Colorado, a good place to rent a houseboat or kayak.

Wherever there are bodies of water, people like to fish. Non-resident licenses are available at town offices and sporting goods shops. **Fishing** next to highways, along canal banks or in small boats, is common in the South, particularly in the Everglades and in the bayous of the Mississippi Delta where fishing for crawfish has deep cultural roots. Fishing in high mountain streams and lakes requires a little more effort, with fly fishermen often hiking (or, these days, riding all-terrain vehicles) to catch rainbow trout and salmon. Resorts offering log cabins near stocked lakes and streams are popular in mountain regions of the US as summer vacation spots.

Hiking

Hiking is popular in every region. Many of the best-known trails follow historic Native American and frontier trails through mountains, valleys, and open deserts. National parks, and other federally managed lands, usually offer the greatest diversity of trails for hikers, from short paved accessible trails to scenic overlooks for disabled users to short day hikes for families and longer cross-country trails.

Walkers and **joggers** in cities will increasingly find designated urban trail networks linking the city and adjoining countryside in places such as Austin, Texas, and Flagstaff, Arizona.

Most challenging are **long-distance trails** like the Appalachian Trail in the East and the John Muir Trail in California's Sierra Nevada in the West. **Backcountry hiking** requires preparation, stamina, and time: many hikers split trails into segments hiked over years. Come well prepared and know your limits when you set out.

Desert cities

Cities such as Phoenix, Tucson, and Albuquerque, and Florida locations (Tampa and Fort Myers for example), with their mild winter temperatures, are major destinations for **off-season outdoor activities** such as hiking, marathon training, bicycling, golf, tennis, and spring training for professional footballers and baseball players.

Mountains and "Sky Islands"

The Rockies, Cascades, Sierra Nevada, Appalachians, Smokies, and isolated desert "sky island" chains of southern deserts offer an escape from 90–100°F (32–38°C) summer temperatures at lower elevations. These same mountainous locales are even busier when winter snows hit, attracting downhill and cross-country skiers and snowboarders to **ski resorts** as far south as Ski Apache in southern New Mexico's Sacramento Mountains. Most ski areas, though, are in the Rockies, Sierra Nevada, and northern New England.

The steady 58°F (14°C) temperature of subterranean limestone **cavern systems** such as Carlsbad Caverns in New Mexico makes them excellent for caving year round; Carlsbad offers wild-cave tours as well as main-cavern touring.

The Western States

The western states – particularly Arizona, Colorado, New Mexico, and Utah, where the mile-high Colorado Plateau has been carved into sinuous canyons by the Colorado River and its tributaries – have the country's most enchanting combination of outdoor activities and tourism on the largest federally managed acreage in the Lower 48. Professional tour companies in gateway communities next to parks are usually the best way of experiencing **remote wilderness areas** where vehicles aren't allowed, particularly if it's your first time in an area. They take care of all the planning, permits, transportation, and meals, and some use low-impact horses and llamas to carry equipment so you don't have to, freeing you up to enjoy the experience.

Extreme sports, such as backcountry canyoneering in Zion National Park, free- and roped climbing on cliffs in Yosemite National Park, and mountain climbing in North Cascades National Park in Washington are also available through adventure companies. These are aimed at very experienced and fit outdoorspeople, familiar with the local environments, and should never be attempted by beginners.

Bicycle tours of regions such as the Texas Hill Country, California's Wine Country, and New England in autumn are both cultural as well as challenging, often incorporating upscale amenities such as bed-and-breakfasts, wine tastings, gourmet meals, and guided tours with pedal time. In urban areas, you can usually rent a bicycle (or rollerblades) to get around. Some cities offer designated bicycle trails through historic communities, such as the Pinellas Trail between St Petersburg and Tarpon Springs on Florida's Gulf and the Venice Boardwalk in southern California – the quintessential LA experience.

National Park System

America currently has 390 units in its vast National Park System. The seed of the national parks came when Yosemite Valley was set aside as a small land grant by Abraham Lincoln in 1864. The first federally mandated national park was Yellowstone, which was set aside in 1872 to protect its unique scenery, followed rapidly by Yosemite, Mt Rainier, Glacier, and Mesa Verde national parks. In 1916 the **National Park Service** was founded with the challenging mission to both protect parks and make them accessible for the public to enjoy.

National parks are few in number and the crown jewels of the system. They preserve large, relatively intact ecosystems and the natural and cultural history associated with them; many also have pristine areas managed as wilderness that allow no mechanized transport within them. **National historic sites** and historical parks are more numerous and found in cities as well as the countryside. They focus on telling America's unique history through diverse stories. **Recreation areas** are reservoirs next to dams managed by the Army Corps of Engineers and operated by the Bureau of Reclamation.

National monuments are a special case: the US president may, at their discretion, unilaterally set aside areas of important scientific and archeological interest for preservation and research if they are in danger of being lost through destruction and overdevelopment.

Outdoor activities vary from park to park but most offer excellent opportunities for hiking, fishing, wildlife watching, horseback riding, and scenic drives. All of the National Parks listed in this book are open daily, year-round. For further information or camping reservations for all of the national parks (except those that don't accept reservations) below, log on to www.nps.gov or call 877-444-6777 (international: 518-885-3639). For general information, telephone on the numbers listed below or visit the individual parks' websites.

Atlantic Route

Everglades National Park
Contact Tel: 305-242-7700
www.nps.gov/ever.
Permits and Licenses Backcountry camping permits required.
General Information Few parks conjure up more mystery or romance than the Everglades. This vast expanse of marshland, grasses, swamp, and cypress forest is the largest subtropical wilderness area in the US. Recently, the Everglades and nearby Big Cypress preserves have been a release point for jaguar, an endangered species that is teetering on the brink of survival here. Alligators are numerous, and drivers should be wary of reptiles crossing the road at all times. Note: June to November is the "wet season" and camping may be uncomfortable at this time.

Northern Route

Badlands National Park
Contact Tel: 605-433-5361, www.nps.gov/badl.
Permits and Licenses No.
Camping First-come, first-served.
General Information Be prepared for sudden changes in weather, high winds and sudden hail, rain or snowstorms. Hikers should carry adequate water – 1 gallon (4 liters) per day per person.

Grand Teton National Park
Contact Tel: 307-739-3300, www.nps.gov/grte.
Permits and Licenses Backcountry camping permits required.
Camping First-come, first-served.
General Information Park concessioners offer horseback rides at Colter Bay and Jackson Lake Lodge. The Teton Range offers many opportunities for climbers and mountaineers. The Jenny Lake Ranger Station is the center for climbing information, routes, conditions, and so on. Contact Grand Teton Lodge Co. (tel: 307-543-2811) for Jackson Lake cruises, float trips on the Snake River, boat rentals, and horseback riding.

Yellowstone National Park
Contact Tel: 307-344-7381, www.nps.gov/yell.
Permits and Licenses Backcountry camping permits required.
Camping Some sites can be reserved in advance by contacting Yellowstone National Park Lodges, PO Box 165, Yellowstone National Park, WY 82190, tel: 307-344-7311. For same day reservations tel: 307-344-7901.
General Information Do not try to approach or feed wildlife. Bison appear placid and slow-moving but can charge quickly and suddenly if irritated. Never approach bears closer than 100 yards (90 meters).

Glacier National Park
Contact Tel: 406-888-7800, www.nps.gov/glac.
Permits and Licenses Backcountry camping permits required.
Camping Fish Creek (tenting only) and St Mary campgrounds can be reserved in advance (tel: 800-365-CAMP); remaining campgrounds first-come, first-served.
General Information Never try to feed or approach wildlife. Glacier Park, Inc. (tel: 406-892-2525) offers a variety of guided bus tours. Glacier Park Boat Co. (tel: 406-257-2426) offers cruises

on McDonald, Many Glaciers, Two Medicine, and St Mary lakes.

Olympic National Park
Contact Tel. 300-565 3130 www.nps.gov/olym.
Permits and Licenses Backcountry camping permits required (fee charged). In summer, some wilderness areas require reservations, tel: 360-565-3100. Washington fishing license.
Camping First-come, first-served except at Kalaloch (mid-June–early Sept.).
General Information Crossing snowfields may require special skills and equipment. Hiking in high elevations can be extremely difficult, causing dizziness, nausea, and shortness of breath. Give yourself a few days to adjust. Obtain a tide table before hiking on the beach; incoming tides can trap hikers between headlands. Look for floating logs, too. An unexpected wave can send them hurtling toward the beach, crushing anything that gets in the way. The ocean is cold and currents are fierce; swim in the lakes instead of the ocean.

Central Route

Shenandoah National Park
Contact Tel: 540-999-3500, www.nps.gov/shen.
Permits and Licenses Visitors may obtain a five-day nonresident fishing license at Big Meadows or sporting goods stores. Camping in the backcountry requires a free permit, available online, at trailheads, and visitor centers.
Camping Most of the campsites in the park's four campgrounds are first-served basis and are very popular so get there early in the day to secure a site. Some 20 percent of sites may be reserved up to 180 days in advance through www.recreation.gov or by calling 1-877-444-6777.
General Information Shenandoah is known for its historic architecture as well as its scenic beauty. It has 340 structures on the National Register of Historic Places, many built in the 1930s by the Roosevelt-era Civilian Conservation Corps (CCC). Shenandoah's 105-mile (169km) -long Skyline Drive, linking the Front Royal with the Waynesboro-Charlottesville area, is a major through road for locals as well as visitors. The park strongly discourages biking, as there is no shoulder on the very winding road and drivers cannot always see bikers in time to maneuver away from them.

Grand Canyon National Park
Contact Tel: 928-638-7888, www.nps.gov/grca.
Seasons The South Rim is open year-round. The North Rim is open mid-May through mid-October.
Campsites can be reserved in advance at the Mather Campground on the South Rim and at the North Rim Campground. All others are on a first-come, first-served basis, and usually fill up by noon. RV sites are available on South Rim year-round at Grand Canyon Village (no hook-ups), tel: 877-444-6777, and Trailer Village (full hook-ups), tel: 888-297-2757; for same day reservation, 928-638-2631.
Permits and Licenses Arizona fishing license. Inexpensive backcountry permits (for overnight hiking; not required for day hikes) can be obtained by mail from Backcountry Information Center, PO Box 129, Grand Canyon, AZ 86023, fax: 928-638-2125. Reserve well in advance; popular trails tend to fill up early.
General Information Most of the five million people who visit this park each year see the canyon from the South Rim, which is more easily accessed than the North Rim. The canyon itself can be seen by hikers, mule riders, and river runners. Several shuttle buses go to the park from the Visitor Center, hotels, campgrounds and the airport. The inner canyon is subject to extreme heat in summer. Hikers should carry adequate food and water, at least 1 gallon (4 liters) per person per day.

Southern Route

Big Bend National Park
Contact Tel: 432-477-2251, www.nps.gov/bibe
Permits and Licenses Backcountry camping permits required ($10).
Camping First-come, first-served in three campgrounds; limited sites may be reserved at Rio Grande Village and Chisos Basin campgrounds November to April. Contact 877-444-6777, www.recreation.gov.
General Information Big Bend is over 800,000 acres (323,000 hectares) in size and extremely rugged and remote; you will need at least two days to see most of the park on main roads. Hikers and four-wheel-drive explorers should allow a week. The sun is intense all year: wear a high SPF sunscreen, sunglasses, and broad-brimmed hat. Carry high-energy food and water in the car, and on every hike, no matter how short, taking care to eat and sip water in equal measures to avoid salt imbalances in the body. Allow 1

gallon (4 liters) per person per day. Don't overexert yourself: the nearest hospital is 100 miles (160km) away. This is wild country. Be alert for rattlesnakes, mountain lions, bears, and javelinas.

Pacific Route

Redwood National and State Parks
Contact Tel: 707-464-6101, www.nps.gov/redw
Permits and Licenses California fishing license and backcountry camping permits required.
Camping Four developed campgrounds run by California State Parks require a fee. Campsites in all but Gold Bluffs Beach Campground may be reserved May through August (strongly suggested); first-come, first-served other times. Contact Reserve America (tel: 800-444-7275; www.reserveamerica.com).
General Information Access to the Tall Trees Grove is limited; a summer shuttle bus transports visitors down the rugged 7-mile (11km) road to the trailhead. Otherwise, a limited number of free private-vehicle permits are distributed on a first-come, first-served basis. Backpackers must secure a free permit at any information center. Animal-proof food canisters are available to borrow free of charge at Thomas H. Kuchel Visitor Center. Swimming can be extremely dangerous. Ocean water is cold, currents are strong, and no lifeguards are on duty. National park entrance is free; state parks require a day-use fee.

SHOPPING

Shopping is a lot of fun in America! For lovers of kitsch, **Florida** and the **American West** won't disappoint, with their doctored postcards, fossil rocks, saltwater taffy, cactus jelly, snowglobes, and other Americana. **Cities** such as New York, Los Angeles, San Francisco, and Houston are good places to buy contemporary art. Cowboy and pioneer art is easily found in towns adjoining **ranch country** in Arizona, New Mexico, Wyoming, and Colorado. Indian Market in Santa Fe offers Native American-made jewelry, pottery, carvings, sandpaintings, and other items. Mexican souvenirs are best purchased in main **cities near the southern border** such as Tucson, Phoenix, San Antonio, and San Diego. Most American cities feature at least one large shopping mall, with chain stores, restaurants, cafés, and movie theaters on the outskirts of town.

More and more are also revitalizing their historic Downtowns with unique shopping areas featuring boutiques, restaurants, museums, and art galleries. **Small towns** in rural locations and roadside stands are often the most interesting places to find unique souvenirs of the region, from preserved foods to handmade clothing and crafts.

Atlantic Route

New York City

Shopping is a major pastime in New York City: there isn't much to be found anywhere that can't be found here, and usually more of it. **Art**, of course, is a good bet; apart from the major auctioneers, **Sotheby's** and **Christies**, there are hundreds of art galleries in which to browse and buy. **Antiques** can be found in Greenwich Village along Bleecker Street and on side streets off University Place; along Upper Madison Avenue, on 60th Street near Third Avenue. The city's famous **department stores** offer something for almost everyone: the most famous are the bustling **Bloomingdale's** (1000 Third Avenue at 59th Street) and **Macy's** (151 W. 34th Street), **Lord & Taylor** (424 Fifth Avenue at 39th Street); and **Saks Fifth Avenue** (611 Fifth Avenue). Savvy New York shoppers also flock to Manhattan's **flea markets**, the current favorite is the Hell's Kitchen Flea Market (the area was once a notorious tenement district for European immigrants). Vendors, collectors, and hagglers; fashion elite, celebrities, and bargain hunters swarm to W. 39th between Ninth and 10th every Saturday and Sunday.

New Jersey

At a time when downloaded music dominates, the **Princeton Record Exchange** (20 South Tulane Street) soldiers on, buying and selling CDs, DVDs and LPs, with more than 140,000 new, used and obscure titles. The **Princeton Corkscrew Wine Shop** (49 Hulfish Street) offers an outstanding selection of handcrafted, family-produced wines. Lambertville overflows with antique stores. In Morristown, Century 21 Department Store sells deeply discounted, high-end designer clothing and accessories. Enjou Chocolat on Dehart Street declares its confectionaries are

the best in New Jersey.

Pennsylvania

In Philadelphia, numerous haute couture boutiques line the streets around Liberty Place and Rittenhouse Square. The largest shopping district in the city is on Market Street east of Broad Street. Here you'll find **Lord & Taylor** (13th and Market), the grandad of Philadelphia department stores housed in a landmark building across from City Hall. Farther east on **Market Street**, past discount shops, sporting goods, electronics, shoes, and clothing stores, is **The Gallery**, a modern shopping mall, which occupies three square blocks and four levels between 11th and Eighth streets. There are over 200 shops and restaurants around the airy, sky-lit atrium including three department stores and a surprisingly interesting food court that's convenient for quick and inexpensive meals or snacks. **Market Place East** is next to **The Gallery** at Eighth and Market streets. Housed in a magnificent cast-iron structure once occupied by **Lit Brothers Department Store**, this block-long mixed-use complex is now divided between offices and about 25 stores and restaurants. For more adventurous tastes, **South Street** is the place to go. The shops and eateries on or near South Street from Ninth to Front streets include everything from punk shops and art galleries to rock bars and fine restaurants. This is the hip, edgy part of town, popular with, but certainly not limited to, young people. At one time, South Street ran through a large Jewish neighborhood. A remnant of those days can still be found on **Fabric Row**, which runs along Fourth Street south of South Street. Mammoth **King of Prussia Mall** is beaten in size only by Minnesota's Mall of America.

Maryland

There are some fun shops along Baltimore's 36th Street, a neighborhood that prides itself on its display of quirky humor and eccentricities. Fells Point at the eastern end of the harbor is another haven for unique shops with personality. North Howard Street is known as Antiques Row. **Harborplace and The Gallery** is a sensational atrium mall at 200 East Pratt Street with over 100 shops, restaurants, and cafés, most of them national retailers. In Annapolis, Main Street from Church Circle to the City Dock and Maryland Avenue off State

Circle both support dozens of locally owned shops.

Virginia

Outlet malls are a big attraction in Virginia. **Potomac Mills Mall** (2700 Potomac Mills Circle, Woodbridge), at Exit 156 of I-95, has more than 200 stores featuring most of the big names, from Ralph Lauren to L.L. Bean. Williamsburg has a swarm of outlets, including the massive Pottery Factory Outlets – which does make and sell pottery – as well as stocking anything else you can imagine, including imported items from 20 countries. Staunton is noted for its Downtown amenities. Roanoke's daily market is not to be missed. Crafts and local artists have galleries and co-ops in many of the smaller towns. Look for posters announcing craft and art shows.

North Carolina

Traditionally this state is known for the quality and range of its furniture, and you could easily furnish a house from one of the showrooms lining many highways. Fashion retailing is also strong in the main cities. One of the biggest shopping centers is **Hanes Mall** in Winston-Salem, with more than 200 stores and 7,861 parking spaces. Durham has converted several tobacco warehouses into artist studios and co-ops. In the mountains, look for local crafters.

South Carolina

An unusual South Carolina craft is the handwoven Gullah sweetgrass basket, an art form of African origin that comes in many intricate designs. For traditional shopping, the **Market Common**, built on the former Myrtle Beach Air Force Base, creates the feel of an urban village community by including restaurants and residential properties in its mix. Wilmington's mile-long boardwalk is lined with shops. While in Georgetown, many stores have rear entrances accessed by the boardwalk along the river.

Georgia

Savannah's cobblestoned River Street has many art galleries, Broughton and Bull streets are known for their antique shops, and the Ellis Square area surrounding the old City market is a center for artists' studios and specialty shops. Malls include **Oglethorpe Mall** (7804 Abercorn Street), **Savannah Festival Factory Stores** (11 Gateway Boulevard, South), and **Savannah Mall** (Rio Road and Abercorn Extension).

Florida

Shopping in Florida will either grab you or leave you shaking your head. Some people really do, apparently, need a collection of plastic flamingoes for their front lawn. And the state's many flea markets are the perfect place to find them. More tasteful (literally) is the variety of fruits such as oranges, tangerines, limes, kumquats, and grapefruits that can be shipped home for a fee. But if you look a little harder, Florida also has an array of quality goods to take home from a trip. There are shops worth seeking out that sell designer clothing at factory prices, primitive Haitian art, Art Deco, and old Florida antiques, Native American crafts, and shells that forever remind one of the sea.

The **Gold Coast** has the biggest choice of malls, particularly Miami, Fort Lauderdale, and Boca Raton. Just ask the staff in your hotel for details of the best malls in your area.

Miccosukee Indian Village, west of the Shark Valley entrance of Everglades National Park, sells Native American crafts at premium prices. Worth Avenue in elegant Palm Beach is home to some of the country's most upscale boutiques. **Gingerbread Square Gallery** at 1207 Duval Street, Key West, sells works by local artists. **Aventura Mall**, 19501 Biscayne Boulevard, is one of Miami's many malls. Over 200 shops with a half dozen of the major nationals including **Macy's**, **Abercrombie & Fitch**, and many other chains.

Northern Route

Massachusetts

Three major shopping areas in Boston attract strollers as well as serious shoppers. The Back Bay's **Newbury Street**, which stretches for eight blocks from the Public Garden to Massachusetts Avenue, is lined with boutiques, salons, and galleries. The Public Garden end attracts the big spenders, while toward Massachusetts Avenue the atmosphere is more funky and shoppers are students, not international travelers. Also in Back Bay: **Copley Place** and the **Prudential Center, with high-end retailers, specialty shops, and other outlets along glass-enclosed malls. Downtown Crossing**, an outdoor pedestrian mall, is anchored by Macy's. The 150-plus shops and restaurants of **Faneuil Hall Marketplace** attract over 1 million visitors a month. Food stalls fill the Quincy Market Buildings, flanked by colorful pushcarts selling handmade crafts and souvenirs. In Cambridge, independently owned shops line **Massachusetts Avenue** and the squares; the **Harvard Square** area, however, with numerous chain and independent stores, is the city's predominant shopping district. It is claimed that here is the greatest concentration of bookshops in the nation. Most are in and around the Square, and some open until midnight.

New Hampshire

In Portsmouth, **New Hampshire Art Association-Robert Lincoln Levy Gallery** exhibits paintings, photographs and prints for sale. The non-profit, state-wide **League of NH Craftsmen** represents some of the state's finest artists. Their show each August at Mount Sunapee is recommended. The **Dorr Mill Store** in Newport is a national craft center for hook hooking, braiding, and wool quilting. Shops fill Portsmouth's revitalized **waterfront area** near Market, Bow, and Ceres streets. Route 16 in North Conway, with more than 200 outlet stores, is one of the region's premier shopping destinations. No sales tax of 5 to 6 percent commonly charged in other states makes the deals even sweeter.

Maine

Portland's **Bayview Gallery** represents pre-eminent New England artists. There are free samples at Stonewall Kitchens in York, makers of sauces, preserves, and condiments, with stores in Portland and Camden, too. Freeport is home base for legendary L.L.Bean, open 24 hours every day. Kittery and Freeport's many outlet stores are major destinations for bargain hunters. Several potters make Blue Hill their home.

Vermont

Woodstock's **F.H. Gillingham and Sons has been the town's general store for more than 125 years**, and its **Sugarbrush Farm** is one of the state's many sugarhouses open for tours. **Danforth Pewter** in Middlebury, Quechee, Waterbury, and Burlington is also worth a visit. The huge **Orvis** store in Manchester has everything necessary to take to the great outdoors, and the town itself is home to a multitude of factory outlet stores. **Ben & Jerry's Ice Cream Factory** in Waterbury is a big tourist attraction. To see ice cream being made, come on a weekday. Stock up on java at **Green Mountain Coffee at Waterbury Station in** Waterbury Village. Also in Waterbury is one of the state's premier co-operative cheese companies, the **Cabot Annex Store**, which lets visitors sample their wares. Cider and donuts are made all year at **Cold Hollow Cider Mill** where there's a huge retail store. Vermont's Frog Hollow Craft Center in Burlington exhibits works by some of the state's finest crafts people.

New York State

Lyrical Ballad Bookstore in Saratoga Springs specializes in out-of-print books, first editions, and antique prints. For crafts, Saratoga Springs' Crafters Gallery has been showcasing the works of local artisans since 1993. For speciality produce, visit **Eagle Mills Cider Mill**, who have a waterwheel-powered mill and nature walks, or **Steininger's** in Salem for their chocolates. For antiques, visit **Ballston Spa** about 15 minutes south of Saratoga Springs; it is chock full of them!

In the Leatherstocking District antique shops lie along every highway and in major cities. Among them is **Wood Bull Antiques** in Cooperstown. One-off shops in Cooperstown include **Brewery Ommegang**, which brews authentic Belgian beer on the banks of the Susquehanna River.

Premium Outlets at Waterloo houses more than 100 stores. **Windmill Farm and Craft Market** sells Mennonite and Amish items and is open Saturday from April through early Dec.

In the Greater Niagara region, antiques can be bought at **Canal Country Artisans** in Medina. **Fashion Outlets** at Niagara Falls has 150 brand-name outlets. In Buffalo, visit **Broadway Market** in the historic Broadway-Fillmore neighborhood where more than 40 vendors sell ethnic foods.

Pennsylvania

Saturday's market in Middletown sells everything from food to antiques. The outdoor market is open weekends until 3 or 4pm , while the indoor market is open only on Saturday. The landmark store and the "world's oldest continuously-operating bookseller," the **Moravian Book Shop**, is located in the historic area of Bethlehem.

Ohio

The **Hall China Company**, based in East Liverpool, has a factory outlet store, the most famous of their ceramics being the nautical teapot and donut jug. The **North Union Farmer's Market** at historic

Shaker Square on Cleveland's East side is recognized by the American Farmland Trust as one of the top 20 farmers' markets in the country while **Malley's Chocolates** have 17 locations throughout the state – the hand-dipped strawberries are recommended. **Libbey Glass** has an outlet store in Toledo and is now the world's second-largest producer of glassware. Family-run **Longaberger** handcrafted maple wood baskets can be bought at fairs and markets.

Indiana
Family-run **Clay City Pottery** produces traditional stoneware in Clay City, while **DeBrand Fine Chocolates**, a small, artisan chocolatier, has three locations in Fort Wayne. Baseball fans should stop by the **Hoosier Bat Company** in Valparaiso, whose bats are used by major and minor league players. The Aladdin's cave that is **Mundt's Candies** in Madison is unmissable. Founded in 1893 and known for its fish-shaped candy and soda fountain.

Illinois
Chicago has a number of vertical shopping malls, in particular along N. Michigan Avenue. It also has several of America's best department stores and a myriad of boutiques. The **Magnificent Mile** (Michigan Avenue from Chicago River to Oak Street) is the glamorous shopping area including **Tiffany** and **Cartier**. **Chicago Place Mall** (700 N. Michigan Avenue) houses fifty specialty shops including **Saks Fifth Avenue** and **Williams-Sonoma**. Oak Street's outstanding shops emphasize diversity and quality. The antique district is on the North Side in Lakeview and there are a number of stores and malls on W. Kinzie Street including **Chicago Antique Center**. One of Chicago's most famous shops is **Ikram**, affectionately titled "the Red Box." The three-story red store and café is located at 15 East Huron Street in downtown Chicago and carries some of the most unique women's apparel you'll ever lay eyes on. The owner, Ikram Goldman, is a frequent wardrobe advisor to first lady Michele Obama, among other fashionable femmes.

Wisconsin
Known as the "dairy state" and the "cheese capital of the nation," Wisconsin is the leading dairy farming state, so cheese and other dairy products are the obvious purchases. Also known for beer production, with the large producer **MillerCoors**

Brewing Company based in Milwaukee. Two of the most popular beers are Coors Light and Miller Lite.

Minnesota
In Minneapolis, **Ingebretsen's** is situated in a quiet marketplace on East Lake Street, and sells Scandinavian foods and crafts. **Nicollet Mall** is on a Downtown pedestrian avenue, lined with boutiques and department stores – links to further shops by means of the city skyway system. The **World Trade Center** in St Paul, at 30 East Seventh Street, contains specialty shops and restaurants. And, the Mall of America (nicknamed the "Megamall") has over 500 stores and an aquarium, movie theatre, and amusement park.

South Dakota
The **South Dakota Store** at The Empire Mall at 41st and Louise Avenue in Sioux Falls only carries items made in or in some way linked to the state. These range from literature, Black Hills gold, Native American crafts and music to Missouri River sapphires and prints of South Dakota landscapes. The Prairie Star Gallery on 207 South Phillips Avenue in Sioux Falls also carries beautiful Native American art and jewelry; owner Linda Boyd can tell you a story about everything in her gallery.

Handmade crafts, such as jewelry, furniture, rugs and hand-rolled beeswax candles can be found in most towns and cities, not just in the larger Sioux Falls and Rapid City.

Wyoming
Wyoming is the place to shop for snap-buttoned shirts, Western hats and boots, and all things cowboy. Sheridan's main street is lined with Western wear stores. Try **Dan's Western Wear** at 504 South Tschirgi Street, a few blocks from Main Street, for Stetson and Resistol hats, Tony Lama boots, and other top brands. Down the block at **King's Saddlery**, 184 North Main Street, you can buy a Western tack ranging from an authentic rancher's rope to a hand-tooled leather saddle; there is also a selection of lovely jewelry, wallets, and gifts. Jackson Hole has an interesting mix of stores ranging from Western wear, ski and outdoor gear to designer fashions, art and jewelry Jackson Hole's historic town square and nearby Teton Village are the best areas for shopping.

Montana
Montana is a good place to shop for outdoor gear such as skis, hiking

boots, backpacks, sleeping bags, fishing tackle, tents, camping, and mountaineering gear, as well as the latest in outer wear. Most towns have outdoor and sporting goods retailers with a good selection.

In Missoula The Trail Head offers one-stop shopping for the whole family. Schnee's of Bozeman, with three locations in the city, is renowned for its pac boots and hunting and outdoor gear Also in Bozeman is **Country Mall Antiques**, 8350 Huffine Lane, with around two dozen stalls selling antiques and collectables.

In Helena, **Reeder's Alley**, 100 South Park Avenue, has a shop selling restored antiques in a district that developed during the Gold Rush.

Idaho
The **Cedar Street Bridge Public Market** in downtown Sandpoint is set within a historic covered bridge spanning Sand Creek. It has arts and crafts gift shops, home decor, a jewelry boutique and apparel made from natural Alpaca wool at **Pedro's Pride Fashions**. Coeur d'Alene offers everything from large shopping malls to specialty shops in Downtown's quaint, cobbled **Sherman Avenue**.

Washington
The best shopping in Washington state is found in Seattle. In addition to its mind-boggling array of produce stalls, the popular **Pike's Peak Market** has shops selling gourmet goodies, cooking supplies, T-shirts, and souvenirs. **Westlake Center** and **Pacific Place** shopping malls, as well as **Macy's** and **Nordstrom's** department stores, cluster round the intersection of Fifth Avenue and Pine Street. Upscale boutiques such as **Louis Vuitton** and **Gucci** are found at Rainier Square, also part of the downtown shopping hub. The **Pioneer Square Antique Mall** has more than 60 dealers selling vintage jewelry, toys, and collectibles. Pioneer Square is also the heart of Seattle's art scene, with many galleries and artists' workshops to explore.

Central Route

Washington, DC
Two of Washington's best shopping districts are on opposite sides of the Potomac, in **Georgetown** on the DC side and **Old Town** in Alexandria on the Virginia side. Both were busy ports well into the 19th century. The surviving weathered red-brick buildings have been converted into trendy shops, with

lots of art galleries, antique shops, cafés, and more. Downtown stores include old reliables such as **Brooks Brothers** (1201 Connecticut Avenue), and **J. Press** (1801 L Street, NW). One of the best malls is **Georgetown Park** at M Street and Wisconsin Avenue; it is quaintly Victorian.

Virginia

The **Made in Virginia Store** on Caroline Street in Fredericksburg brings the best of locally made products together. Choose from hams, wines, crafts, and cookbooks full of southern cooking recipes, amongst a host of Virginia-branded clothing. A similar style shop, the **Virginia Made Shop**, is located in Staunton.

North Carolina

The leading producer of tobacco in the US and known for its production of cotton, hogs, broiler chickens, and turkey, The best place for souvenirs, or a taste of this state, is the **Western North Carolina Farmers' Markets**, one of which is in downtown Asheville, with views of the Biltmore Estate. One of the five open-air sheds is reserved for farmers who sell directly to the consumer. A garden and plant nursery center and café are also present; open daily.

Tennessee

Good buys include musical instruments (acoustic stringed instruments and amplified guitars) and studio recording equipment, and, of course, Tennessee whiskey, which must be produced within the state to make this claim. The two distilleries are **Jack Daniels** in Lynchburg, producing the famous Old No. 7 Brand, and George Dickel whiskey, whose distillery lies in Normandy in between Nashville and Chattanooga.

Arkansas

Try Arkansas Black apples from **roadside stands** in the Ozark Mountains area, and mineral water from Hot Springs. **Whetstones** can also be bought from Hot Springs, while iron art from Mountain View and quartzite crystals from Mt Ida make good local buys. Rock Town Distillery on Sixth Street in Little Rock produces "white lightening," vodka, gin, whiskey, and rum. Tours of the distillery are every Saturday at 1.30 and 3.30pm, with tastings for those over 21 (charge).

Oklahoma

The quintessential **John Deere** Tractor (farm machinery manufacturer) cap

forms part of almost every farmer or agricultural worker's outfit, so if you find one of these at a flea market, buy it! Vases, dishes, and pitchers from the Frankoma Pottery in Sapulpa, which closed in 2010, are now collector's items, which you will find in antique shops as well as major western museum stores. Wine from vineyards in Bristow, Geary, Stroud, and Vinita; root beer from **Weber's Superior Root Beer** stand in Tulsa; and ice cream from Braum's are all good local buys.

Texas

Route 66 throughout Texas offers perilously little to buy, apart from kitsch souvenirs, such as dinner plates with western motifs, cowboy hats, and other western goods at the gift shop in Big Texan Steak Ranch in Amarillo.

New Mexico

Santa Fe is one of the largest art markets in the United States. Galleries selling all kinds of contemporary and fine art paintings and sculpture line **Canyon Road,** and more can be found in Downtown in and around the **Plaza** and the Railyard district. Santa Fe is a good place to buy Native American arts and crafts, particularly silver and turquoise jewelry; Pueblo pottery based on traditional designs; Navajo rugs, pottery, and folk art; and Hopi kachina dolls. Some of the best Native American artisans sell their work by permit from the Museum of New Mexico under the portal at the **Palace of the Governors**. Indeed, Museum of New Mexico gift stores at museums Downtown and on Museum Hill are reliably good places to buy authentic arts and crafts, as is Case Trading Post in the Wheelwright Museum on Museum Hill. **Indian Market is held on the Plaza every August and** draws Native American artists and buyers from around the world in the largest adjudicated art show its kind. You can also visit some of the pueblos around Santa Fe and Albuquerque and buy art directly from artists in their home workshops. Also held on the Plaza are the adjudicated **Traditional Spanish Market and Contemporary Spanish Market,** both held in July. Earlier that month is the immensely popular International Folk Art Market on Museum Hill, where you can buy arts and crafts from around the world and meet the artisans.

In Albuquerque, the **Old Town plaza** is the place to find a charming array of galleries and gift shops selling Native American jewelry and Southwestern arts and crafts.

Arizona

Sedona is one of the most popular New Age destinations in the US, which is reflected in the number of shops scattered throughout the town selling crystals, dreamcatchers, and so on. It is also a leading art market, with numerous galleries selling painting, sculpture, and other works by nationally known artists. With Hopi and Navajo Nation tribal lands covering much of northern Arizona, this is a prime place to buy Native American arts and crafts, baskets, jewelry, rugs, and textiles. There are trading posts and gift shops in Flagstaff and throughout the region. Some good outlets to try are the historic **Cameron Trading Post**, Highway 89N, approximately 53 miles (85km) north of Flagstaff, and **Navajo Arts and Crafts Enterprises**, off route 264 adjacent to Navajo Nation Inn in Window Rock.

California

For intrepid shoppers, Los Angeles, though a sprawling city, has shopping neighborhoods that are up there with major destinations like New York, Paris, London, and Hong Kong. Some of the biggest names in high-end fashion have exclusive shops along glitzy Rodeo Drive in Beverly Hills, including **Chanel**, **Armani**, and **Ungaro**. A trip down **Melrose Avenue in West Hollywood** will net edgier fashions. The **Pacific Design Center** – The Blue Whale – has 200 designers' showrooms at the corner of San Vicente, and you'll find several blocks of raffish shops between **Croft** and **La Brea**. Downtown LA's Garment District is *the* place to go for designer fashions on a budget. Over 1,000 stores sell to the public at wholesale discount prices of up to 70 percent off retail.

Lively **Chinatown**, redolent with the aromas of herbs, dried fish, ginseng, and ginger, is the primary source of Asian imports. For mall lovers, Southern California is a shopper's Valhalla. Favorites include the **Beverly Center**, with more than 200 stores, bordering Beverly Hills and West Hollywood, and **Westfield Century City Shopping Center**.

Nearby San Fernando Valley ("the Valley") is renowned for its malls, most famous and biggest of which are **Glendale Galleria**, **Northridge Fashion Center**, and **Sherman Oaks Fashion Square**. Farther afield, in Orange County, you'll find **South Coast Plaza, Del Amo Fashion Square** in Torrance, and the breezy Mediterranean-village type atmosphere of Newport Beach's **Fashion Island**.

Southern Route

Georgia

Georgia is known for its peaches, tomatoes, and other fruits, best purchased roadside in the Chattahoochee Hill Country or Atlanta's **Saturday Green Market**. Most of the good shopping in rural Georgia is in and around Atlanta. In Downtown, the **Mall at Peachtree Plaza** has 250 stores on four levels. Little **Five Points** is a good place to go for funkier offerings, such as vintage clothing and crystals and hip dining. Midtown's **Atlantic Station**, a 140-acre (56.5-hectare) live-work-play community, has more than 200 hotels, stores, and restaurants. Lenox Square, in residential Buckhead on the woodsy north end of town, is a pleasant place to stroll and shop. It has the city's toniest restaurants and a **Whole Foods Market**. **North Georgia Premium Outlets**, in Dawsonville 45 minutes north of Atlanta, offers an upscale village-style outlet center with 140 stores, including Ann Taylor and Michael Kors.

Alabama

A mainly rural farm state like Georgia, Alabama is known for its pecans and strawberries, grown in small towns like Castleberry, which proclaims itself Home of the Alabama Strawberry. Muscadine grapes grown at Perdido Vineyards in Perdido produce mostly sweet wines for sale.

Montgomery's historic Downtown is a good place to find antiques; books, posters, cards, and other items promoting civil rights education at the **Southern Poverty Law Center**; and fresh produce, flowers, and home-prepared foods at the **Montgomery Curb Market** on Madison.

The state's most modern and affluent city is Mobile on the Gulf Coast, which has a number of big outlying shopping malls. The smaller residential communities on the other side of Mobile Bay, such as Fairhope, are known for their flowers, particularly azaleas, and small unique shops and restaurants. Downtown's historic district has interesting antiques and a candle factory.

Mississippi

Gulf Coast Mississippi was hard hit by Hurricane Katrina. The **Hard Rock Hotel/Casino** in Biloxi has reopened and is selling its famous T-shirts and other souvenirs, but much of what you'll find are bland chainstore items.

The most interesting place to shop is Ocean Springs. The walkable Downtown has a number of charming art galleries, food purveyors, clothing boutiques, and gift shops. Art lovers will find reproductions of Walter Anderson's gorgeous paintings and ceramics in the terrific little store inside the **Walter Anderson Museum of Art**. **Shearwater Pottery**, begun in 1928 by Anderson's brother Peter, sells glazed ceramics by his son Jim. And award-winning **Miner's Doll and Toy Store** has classic toys and fine dolls.

Louisiana

Cajun Country offers many intriguing shopping possibilities. New Orleans is the best one-stop shop, with its compact **French Quarter** a beehive of commerce. **Royal Street**, parallel to Bourbon Street, is a great place to find gorgeous antiques. Touristy **Decatur Street**, along the waterfront, has a number of souvenir shops selling Mardi Gras souvenirs, gumbo spices, jambalaya mixes, hot sauces, and its famous pralines. The ritzy **Canal Place Shops** has a movie theater and high-end clothing stores.

In Lafayette and the surrounding heartland of Arcadiana, you'll find tiny towns like Breaux Bridge selling wonderful antiques and fresh crawfish.

Texas

Houston's most visited destination is **The Galleria**, which has more than 375 department and specialty stores and restaurants. Historic Houston Heights, along Heights Boulevard and Yale Street, has Victorian buildings containing boutiques selling antiques, vintage clothing, and art galleries.

In the heart of Austin, you'll find many unique local boutiques in the Second Street District, including favorites like **Heritage Boot**, where owner Jerry Ryan designs each pair of his artsy footwear. The **23rd Street Renaissance Market**, across from UT, is a good place to pick up unique handicrafts. **Waterloo Records** is renowned for its knowledgeable staff and extensive selection of recordings by Texas musicians.

San Antonio is home to **Luchese Boots**, maker of fine hand-tooled cowboy boots. You'll find unique gifts and souvenirs at the **San Antonio Museum of Art**, and in other museum shops. At **North Star** mall (Loop 410 between San Pedro and MacCullough) there are over 200 stores, including many big names. **El Mercado** mall (514 W. Commerce) offers 32 specialty shops with Mexican arts

and crafts. Several well-known artists make their home in Marathon. **Baxter Gallery** specializes in landscapes of Big Bend by local artists.

Marfa sells lots of contemporary art in the chicest galleries you'll ever see in a ranch town. One-of-a-kind offerings include minimalist furniture carved from juniper at **Benton/Garza**. **Marfa Book Company** has a great selection of books, including tomes on Marfa art guru Donald Judd. Several interesting artisans in Fort Davis sell handcrafted western items along State Street. Check out the beaver felt western hats at **Limpia Creek Custom Hats**. A number of art galleries and bookstores in Alpine focus on the rugged beauty of the Big Bend, and many artists and writers call this area home. One great way to view the work of local artists and writers is to visit during the annual Alpine Art Walk every November. A number of art galleries take part, as well as the excellent little independent **Front Street Books**. El Paso is the home of the cowboy boot manufacturer, **Tony Lama**. There are three factory outlets in the city.

New Mexico

Options for shopping in southern New Mexico are more limited than the famous north. Alamogordo is famous for its pistachio orchards. At family-run **Eagle Ranch** north of town, you can tour the orchards, sample the produce, and take some home.

The small alpine village of Cloudcroft sells unique western art, such as antler furniture and large-scale chainsaw carvings of bears. Mescalero and the **Inn of the Mountain Gods** on the Apache reservation are good places to find authentic Apache crafts, such as paintings and carvings of mountain *gaan* spirits, jewelry, beadwork, and tooled leather. There are numerous **art galleries** in or near Ruidoso. Dave McGary, known for his lifesize bronzes of Native Americans, has a gallery in Downtown, while artist Michael Hurd, son of the famed early 20th-century artists Peter Hurd and Henriette Wyeth, operates **Hurd/La Rinconada Gallery** and several guesthouses on the old family ranch in nearby San Patricio.

If you want to try your hand at authentic Southwestern cooking, don't miss a detour to tiny Hatch, the **chile capital of the world**, a few miles north of Las Cruces. There's nothing better than fresh-roasted green chili **(note New Mexican Spanish spelling is "chile")**, and one of the joys of the fresh harvest season in August is the smell of roasting chili at small stands throughout New Mexico; locals freezer bags of roasted green chili for use throughout the year. After harvest, chili is strung into hanging bunches called *ristras* and hung from portals, where it turns from green to red as it dries and looks very decorative. The dried pods take on a complex taste and can be either rehydrated and blended into a sauce or ground into a powder. Dried chili can be easily transported and makes a perfect New Mexico gift. **La Mesilla Plaza** is an atmospheric place to shop for gifts.

Arizona

Phoenix has several large malls ,as well as the upscale **Biltmore Fashion Park**, 2502 East Camelback Road, and **Arizona Center**, Van Buren Street, in Downtown. Some of the city's best restaurants are located in and around historic **Heritage Square**, also in Downtown Phoenix.

Scottsdale is known for its Western and contemporary art galleries, many of which are concentrated in the downtown Arts District. It adjoins Old Town, where you can buy everything from cowboy boots to Native American jewelry, rugs, and crafts. Scottsdale also has two of the metro area's finest shopping centers: Fashion Square at 7014 East Camelback Road, and the Borgata, with 42 galleries, restaurants, and specialty stores set amid a Tuscan-style village with fountains and courtyard.

Tucson is a good center for Southwestern crafts. Downtown on North Court Avenue, behind the Tucson Art Museum, Old Town Artisans is a warren of small shops selling high-quality ceramics, painting, sculpture, photography and other arts in a block of adobe buildings from the mid-19th century, set around a shady courtyard. Nearby is the historic Fourth Avenue shopping district, with more galleries and one-of-a-kind shops. A Tucson favorite is De Grazia's Gallery in the Sun, 6300 North Swan, where you can buy reproductions of the artist's distinctive Southwest paintings in the gallery gift shop.

About 30 miles (48km) south of Tucson, the artists' colony at historic **Tubac** is another popular shopping destination for everything from fine art to Southwestern crafts and imported Mexican decorative arts. Tubac Festival of the Arts takes place every February. Downtown **Yuma** is a pleasant shopping district, with a number of interesting specialty shops.

Pacific Route

California

San Diego's historic 16-block **Gaslamp Quarter** is the place to browse for arts and crafts downtown. Here too is the multilevel Westfield **Horton Plaza** shopping center. **Seaport Village** has more than 70 cute touristy shops on the harbor, while **Old Town Esplanade** is lined with specialty shops, many selling Mexican crafts, blankets, embroidered shirts, dresses, and other items.

San Diego is also just a short hop away from the Mexican border town of Tijuana, where you can bargain for souvenirs (look for leather) at lower prices. Also at the border in San Ysidro is **Las Americas Premium Outlets**, the area's largest outlet center. Upscale art galleries and shops line the central village and main streets of Laguna Beach. **Wyland Galleries**, 509 South Coast Highway, exhibits works by Wyland, a leading environmental marine-life artist. Newport Beach is another shopping highlight with luxury shopping at **Fashion Island**, set around bougainvillea-lined courtyards and fountains, and charming boutiques along Balboa Island's **Marine Avenue**.

Santa Monica's **Third Street Promenade** is a pedestrian mall originally designed by architect Frank Gehry and lined with whimsical topiaries between its popular chain stores and one-off outlets. It intersects with Arizona Avenue, where a fabulous **Farmers' Market** is held on Wednesdays and Saturdays, with the colorful bounty of Southern California on display. Along Main Street you'll find everything from thrift shops to chic boutiques, while pricy Montana Avenue has designer apparel and furnishings. **State Street** runs through the heart of downtown Santa Barbara, lined with trees, bright flags, and brick-paved sidewalks. Here you will find an eclectic mix of boutiques selling shoes, fashions, art, and homewares. Look for the delightful **Retroville**, 521 State Street, with vintage clothes, accessories, art, and home furnishings. On either side of State Street are charming shopping enclaves such as **La Arcada Court**, a cheerful Spanish-style courtyard adorned with tile and ornamental ironwork and home to luxury jewelers and antiques shops, and **Paseo Nuevo**, an attractive open-air mall of specialty shops and movie theaters set between adobe arches and palms.

There are 20 distinct shopping districts in San Francisco. You might want to start by exploring some or all of the following: **Union Square** includes the charming **Maiden Lane** with boutiques and galleries; **Chinatown**, between Stockton, Kearny, and Bush streets, and Broadway, is good for fresh produce, fish, poultry, traditional herbs, antiques, and jewelry; **North Beach** offers a mix of book shops, Italian restaurants and delicatessens, cafés, vintage clothing, and designer boutiques; **Fisherman's Wharf** shopping extends from **Pier 39** to **Ghirardelli Square** in **The Cannery**.

Oregon

Shopping in Oregon is particularly good value, as the state has no sales tax. Resorts all along the coast feature shops selling art, crafts, and souvenirs. Lincoln City is a larger shopping city, with its **Tanger Outlet Center** in the business district along Highway 101, and many antiques stores also located here. Portland's **Farmers' Market** offers locally grown foods and arts and crafts booths amid a bustling, lively atmosphere. The main market is held on Saturdays from late spring to early autumn, in the South Park Blocks of Portland State University; other markets operate elsewhere in the city on other days. The **Old Town** district features specialty shops in a lovely setting. Note: all gas stations are full service in Oregon, as state law prohibits you from pumping your own gas.

Washington

The popular Long Beach peninsula on the southwest Washington coast offers small villages with a few farms and u-pick berry locations, boutiques, art galleries, souvenir shops, and even a couple of bookstores. In Ocean Park, check out Adelaide's Books in the 1887 Taylor Hotel building for books and coffee, Thursday to Monday, and Weir Studio, a working studio making fused-glass art jewelry. Willapa Bay Tile in Willapa has beautiful handmade tiles with a marine motif by Renee O'Connor. In Ilwaco, Painted Lady Lavender Farm makes for a very relaxing stop for the whole family, with homemade lavender products and a petting zoo. At the farmer's market in Ilwaco on Saturdays, look for blueberries from Cranguyma Farms, July to September, or stop by the farm to pick them yourself. The state's best shopping is, of course, in Seattle.

A – Z

A HANDY SUMMARY OF PRACTICAL INFORMATION

A

Admission Charges

Admission is usually charged at both private and public museums and attractions, and national and state parks. As a rule, entrance fees are under $10 per person, although very popular sites, such as Grand Canyon and special traveling exhibits at nationally known museums may charge as much as $20. Museums often offer free or reduced entrance fees certain days or evenings.

Consider buying **multi-site passes** for attractions in the larger cities, if available. Local visitor centers can assist you with planning and many also offer discount coupons, with excellent deals on local attractions, hotels, and dining.

Anyone planning to visit several national parks is strongly advised to buy an **annual pass** ($80 in 2012) that allows unlimited entry into federally managed public lands across the US. Passes are available at the entrance gate to national parks or at www.nps.gov/findapark/passes.htm.

Age Restrictions

Few age restrictions are imposed at attractions. Theme parks, such as Disney World, may state age, weight, and height restrictions for safety reasons. To enter premises serving alcohol, you must be 21 or over in most states.

B

Budgeting for Your Trip

Although the days of extremely favourable exchange rates for the Euro and Pound against the dollar are over for the time being, both currencies continue to hold an advantage despite the European financial crises of 2011–2012.The US remains a good buy for travelers, especially those on a road trip, where the main cost will be car rental, gas, lodging, and food, and you can search out bargains en route.

You can save considerably if you camp, stay in budget motels, eat in hometown cafés like the locals or bring your own food for picnics, and keep to a budget for visiting attractions. Allow $80–100/day for good-quality lodgings for two people, although really memorable hotels and bed-and-breakfasts tend to run you closer to $150/night (more in big cities). At the other end of the spectrum, you'll find an array of hostels and attractive campgrounds with full facilities for $16–18/night; bare-bones motel lodgings can be found for less than $50; and reliable chains are in the $60–80 range (look for AAA discounts and online deals at chains like Best Western and La Quinta). You can probably get away with $30/day per person for basic meals if you stick to diners, cafés, markets, and inexpensive restaurants and don't drink alcohol.

Meals in better restaurants cost a lot more but if you're determined to visit that famous high-end establishment and don't have the cash, one insider trick is to eat lunch there: you'll find many of the items on the dinner menu at much lower prices and still get to say you've eaten at a hip eatery.

Budget at least $3.50 per gallon for gas costs for your rental car; most economy vehicles get over 30 miles per gallon. Trams, light rail, buses, and other public transportation in cities like Tampa, Miami, San Francisco, and Atlanta are just a few dollars per ride, allowing you to get around for much less.

C

Children

Two words of advice about traveling with children: first, be prepared and, second, don't expect to cover too much ground. Take everything you need, along with a general first-aid kit: Western towns may be small and remote with supplies limited. If you need baby formula, special foods, diapers or medication, carry them with you along with those wonderful all-purpose traveler's aids: wet wipes and Ziplock bags. Games, books, and crayons help kids pass time in the car. Carrying snacks and drinks in a daypack will come in handy when kids (or adults) get hungry on the road. Give yourself plenty of time, as kids do not travel at the same pace as adults.

Be sure wilderness areas and other backcountry places are suitable for children. Are there abandoned mine shafts, steep stairways, cliffs or other hazards?

Is a lot of walking necessary? Are food, water, shelter, bathrooms, and other essentials available at the site? Avoid dehydration by having children drink plenty of water before and during outdoor activities. And particularly in summer, be sure they wear sunscreen with an SPF of at least 30, a hat, sunglasses, sturdy sandals or hiking boots, and layered clothing. Don't push children beyond their limits. Rest often and allow for extra napping.

Climate

The US climate is mostly temperate, but tropical in Hawaii and semi-tropical in Florida and the Deep South in summer; arctic in Alaska; semi-arid in the great plains west of the Mississippi River – and arid in the Great Basin of the Desert Southwest.

Low winter temperatures in the Northwest are ameliorated occasionally in January and February by warm Chinook winds from the eastern slopes of the Rocky Mountains, but ice storms are common in the Columbia River Gorge, on the Washington-Oregon boundary, the only sea-level thoroughfare through the Cascade Mountains.

Hurricane season, which affects Florida and the Gulf Coast and runs from June 1 to November 30, has produced devastating hurricanes, storm surges, and torrential rain. Tornadoes, the bane of the Midwest, can strike very suddenly and specifically in the spring, and even late winter, if the right conditions arise. Between July and September in the Southwest, "monsoon" rainstorms can be dangerous, creating flashfloods that sweep away everything in their path.

Out west, the shift in jetstream in winter blows northwesterly winds onshore over mountain ranges that, along with frigid temperatures, bring heavy snows. Snowfall can be heavy in the Great Lakes region and Northeast, paralyzing some of the country's busiest areas in winter.

When to visit

With school out, long lazy summer days ahead, and vacation days piling up, summer is the traditional time for a US family road trip. Consider this only if you don't mind soaring temperatures, hot and humid conditions near water, desiccatingly hot, dry, dusty conditions in the desert, and crowded freeways, hotels, campgrounds, and attractions across the US. Far better is to time your road

trip to enjoy the singular glories of spring and fall across the magical US landscape.

After Labor Day, the kids are back in school; roads, parks, and campgrounds are quieter; and weather conditions – usually warm days and cool nights – are perfect for outdoor activities. Winter has its own particular charm, but with frigid temperatures, heavy snows and winds, and road closures across the country, it's not the best time for a road trip.

Only the Southern, Atlantic, and Pacific routes are suitable for winter travel, and even then come prepared for bad weather that occasionally brings snow to low-desert areas like Tucson. Think twice before driving the Central, Northern, and Atlantic routes in this book in winter. If skiing is the main attraction, you'd do better to fly to a resort. Most winter travelers head for the Southern US, particularly Florida, where the sun shines 300 days of the year and winters are mild; the high season is January through April, rates plummet in summer. Many locals time their trips for the quieter, still-pleasant "shoulder" seasons of May and June and October to December.

What to wear

The US climate is varied and quite intense, often changing rapidly from one extreme to another. Your best bet is to bring layers of lightweight clothing, which can cover exposed skin or be rolled up; a hat; polarized sunglasses; sturdy walking shoes or sandals; and a packable waterproof shell in summer. In winter, long underwear made of silk or breathable technical fabrics can be slipped under fleece or wool for warmth. Don't forget wool gloves, scarf, and hat, and possibly a lightweight packable down jacket in high-elevation areas and those in the northern US. A sunscreen with an SPF of 30 or above is a good idea at any time of year.

Crime and Safety

If you are driving, never pick up anyone you don't know. Always be wary of who is around you. If you have trouble on the road, stay in the car and lock the doors, turn on your hazard lights and/or leave the hood up to increase your visibility and alert passing police. It's well worth carrying a sign requesting help. Do not accept a rental car that is obviously labeled as such. Company decals and special license plates

may attract thieves on the lookout for tourist valuables.

Hitchhiking

Hitchhiking is illegal in many places and ill-advised everywhere. It is an inefficient and dangerous method of travel. Don't do it!

In the city

Most big cities have their share of crime. Common sense is your most effective weapon. Try to avoid walking alone at night – at the very least stick to livelier, more brightly lit thoroughfares and move about as if you know where you are going. Don't carry large sums of money or expensive video/camera equipment.

Keep an eye on your belongings. Never leave your car unlocked, or small children by themselves. Hotels usually warn that they do not guarantee the safety of belongings left in their rooms. If you have any valuables, you may want to lock them in the hotel safe. Many better hotels now have room safes with changeable codes.

Take particular care when using bank ATMs at night. If you are in doubt about which areas are safe, seek advice from hotel staff or police.

Customs Regulations

You may bring in **duty-free gifts** worth **up to $800** (American citizens) or $100 (foreign travelers). Visitors over 18 may bring in **200 cigarettes** and **50 cigars** (not Cuban) or 4.4lbs (**2kg of tobacco**). Those over 21 may bring in **34 fl. oz (1 liter) of alcohol**. Travelers with more than **$10,000 in US or foreign currency**, travelers' checks, or money orders must declare these upon entry. Among the prohibited goods are meat or meat products, illegal drugs, firearms, seeds, plants, and fruits. For a breakdown of customs allowances write to: **United States Customs and Border Protection, 1300 Pennsylvania Avenue NW**, Washington, DC 20229; tel. 877-227-5511; 703-526-4200 from abroad; www.cbp.gov.

D

Disabled Travelers

The 1995 Americans with Disabilities Act (ADA) brought sweeping changes to facilities across America.

Accommodations with five or more rooms must be useable by persons with disabilities. Older and smaller inns and lodges are often wheelchair-accessible.

For the sight-impaired, many hotels provide special alarm clocks, captioned TV services, and security measures. To comply with ADA hearing-impaired requirements, many hotels have begun to follow special procedures; local agencies may provide TTY and interpretation services.

Check with the front desk when you make reservations to ascertain the degree to which the hotel complies with ADA guidelines. Ask specific questions regarding bathroom facilities, bed height, wheelchair space, and availability of services.

Many major attractions have wheelchairs for loan or rent; most national parks today also offer paved "barrier-free" or "accessible" trails. Some provide visitor guides and interpreters for hearing- and sight-impaired guests. The **Society for Accessible Travel and Hospitality** (tel: 212-447-7284; www.sath.org) publishes a quarterly magazine on travel for the disabled.

Electricity

Standard electricity in North America is 110–115 volts, 60 cycles AC. An adapter is necessary for most appliances from overseas, with the exception of Japan.

Embassies and Consulates

Australia: 1601 Massachusetts Avenue NW, Washington, DC 20036 Tel: 202-797-3000
Canada: 501 Pennsylvania Avenue

Emergencies

Dial 911 (the operator will put you through to the police, ambulance or fire services). The call is toll free anywhere in the US, including on cellphones. If you can't get through, **dial 0** for an operator. In national parks, it's best to **contact a ranger**. For free emergency roadside assistance in Mexico, contact the **Green Angels** at 800-903-9200.

NW, Washington, DC 20001 Tel: 202-682-1740
Great Britain: 3100 Massachusetts Avenue NW, Washington, DC 20008 Tel: 202-588-6500
Ireland: 2234 Massachusetts Avenue NW, Washington, DC 20008 Tel: 202-462-3939
Mexico: 1911 Pennsylvania Avenue NW, Washington, DC 20006 Tel: 202-728-1600
New Zealand: 37 Observatory Circle NW, Washington, DC 20008 Tel: 202-328-4800

Etiquette

Visitors often associate the US with relaxed manners. While that may be true up to a point, particularly in dress and table manners, you should also be prepared for many Americans, particularly those who live in conservative areas of the Midwest and the South, to be surprisingly polite and formal, in speech, dress, and the intricate dance of social interaction.

Americans, as a rule, are positive, curious about others, generally accepting of differences, warm, effusive, and tactile. This being a nation of immigrants, care is generally taken in polite society not to give offence to any one group, and chauvinism and racism, though evident, are not tolerated in most

Gay bar in San Francisco.

social situations, so be careful about making off-color jokes or making assumptions about different regions of the country.

Visiting Native American reservations, which are sovereign lands within the US with their own laws and moral code, calls for unique sensitivity and cultural awareness. Make an effort to blend in, dress conservatively, behave modestly – particularly at Native American dances, which are religious rituals – and never enter a home without being invited (nor refuse a meal if invited on a feast day, as that is considered rude). Many tribes rely on tourism for their income and have developed luxury resorts on their scenic lands to rival any in Las Vegas. In remote areas, you will usually be asked to pay a small fee to take photos of family members.

Gay and Lesbian Travelers

On the whole, urban areas in the US are safer places to visit for gay and lesbian travelers than rural destinations away from the cities. Keep a low profile in such areas, particularly in the conservative Bible

Belt in the South, to avoid problems. Having said that, the lucrative GLBT market is one of the hottest targeted markets in the US, and most states now offer information on gay-friendly travel within their communities. Cities like New York, South Beach (Miami), Seattle, San Francisco, Los Angeles, Phoenix, and Tucson roll out the red carpet. Smaller arts and university cities, such as Santa Fe, Austin, and Flagstaff, also have surprisingly large gay communities.

For more information, check out the **Gay and Lesbian Yellow Pages** (tel: 713-942-0084; 800-697-2812 in the US; www.glyp.com). **Damron Company** (tel: 415-255-0404; 800-462-6654; www.damron.com) publishes guides aimed at gay travelers and lists gay-owned and gay-friendly accommodations nationwide.

Health and Medical Care

Medical services are extremely expensive. Always arrange comprehensive travel insurance to cover treatment and emergencies. Check the small print – most policies exclude treatment for water, winter or mountain sports accidents unless excess cover has been included.

If you need medical assistance, consult the *Yellow Pages* for the physician or pharmacist nearest to you. The bigger hotels may have a resident doctor. In large cities, there is usually a physician referral service number listed.

If you need immediate attention, go directly to a hospital emergency room (ER); most are open 24 hours a day. You may be asked to produce proof of insurance cover before being treated. Walk-in medical clinics are much cheaper than hospital emergency rooms for minor ailments.

Care should be taken to avoid dehydration and overexposure to the sun. In the desert, or at high altitude, this can happen rapidly even on cloudy days. A cover-up, high-factor sun lotion, hat, and one-liter water bottle are essential accessories. Avoid excess alcohol, caffeine, and sugar to cut down on dehydration, and pace yourself at high elevation. Allow a day or two to acclimatize to elevation that changes gradually.

Internet and Websites

Many public libraries, copy centers, hotels, and airports offer high-speed (DSL) or wireless internet (Wi-fi) email and internet access. Some (usually not libraries) charge a fee for access, either on their computer or your laptop. Surprisingly, lower-priced chain hotels are less likely to charge than expensive places. At all company-owned Starbucks coffeehouses Wi-fi is free, as it is at many other coffeehouses and restaurants. At some airports, you must first purchase a T-Mobile Hot Spot pass or Boingo Pass (currently about $9.95/day), before being able to log on. The modems of many foreign laptops and handheld computers won't work in the US. You may need to purchase a global modem before leaving home or a local PC-card modem once you arrive in the US. For more information, log on to www.teleadapt. com.

Luggage Storage

For security reasons, most airports and train stations in the US no longer operate luggage storage facilities for travelers, although some private companies do offer luggage lockers. Check with the individual location. Most hotels will allow you to check out and leave your luggage in a safe storage area. You will be taking a calculated risk if you leave your luggage in the car. In practice, though, if you lock all valuables (especially laptops and other electronic items) out of sight, you will probably be okay.

Lost Property

If you lose property, your best bet is to immediately report it to management of the attraction or hotel where the loss occurred, then file a report in person at the local police station; some police stations allow you to file an electronic report via email. All airlines have lost luggage desks and will usually forward any delayed bags to your destination.

Maps

A detailed road map is essential for any road trip. They are widely available from state welcome and city visitor centers, large bookstores such as Barnes & Noble, outdoor stores, filling stations, supermarkets, and convenience stores. Cross-country travelers may find it useful to purchase a road-map book with maps of all 50 states, such as the one published by Rand McNally. The American Automobile Association (AAA) provides excellent maps free of charge to members . Free maps of national parks, forests, and other public lands are usually offered by the managing government agency at entrance stations. Extremely detailed topographical maps of states are available from the US Geological Survey (www.usgs.gov/pubprod). Topo maps are usually available in higher-end bookstores and shops that sell outdoor gear.

Media

Newspapers

In this rapidly expanding era of electronic publishing and free information on the World Wide Web, print media has undergone a major contraction. Yet most communities across the US still publish print editions of newspapers, as well as electronic editions, and the opinions and endorsements of columnists and editorial boards continue to play an important role in American public life. The **top 10 newspapers** by circulation in the US are: *USA Today*, the *Wall Street Journal*, the *New York Times*, the *Los Angeles Times*, the *San Jose Mercury News*, the *Washington Post*, the *New York Daily News*, the *New York Post*, the *Chicago Tribune*, and the *Chicago Sun-Times*. The top three are available throughout the US.

Television

Unlike many countries, the US does not have national broadcasting. Instead, three major TV networks – ABC, CBS, and NBC – are carried in local markets by affiliates who also produce local programming and news that can usually be watched for free. In addition to the Big Three, the conservative network Fox Broadcasting Corporation is gaining an increasing market share. Univision, a network of Spanish-language channels, is the fifth-largest TV channel.

Non-commercial broadcasting plays a much smaller role in American TV than in other countries, but what there is is excellent, led by the stations of the Public Broadcasting System (PBS).

Among the most popular public interest channels on cable or satellite are CNN, ESPN, MSNBC, Discovery Channel, the Food Network, USA Network, TNT, TLC, BRAVO, Disney, National Geographic, and BBC America. Movie channels include HBO, Showtime, Stars, TMC, TCM, and pay-per-view movies through satellite providers such as DirecTV and Dish.

Radio

A good way to learn about American culture is to turn on the radio. Cities have a vast array of stations, from talk radio by right-wing host Rush Limbaugh to hip-hop, contemporary, and classic rock music. On long, lonely highways, country music and religion predominate along with Spanish-language shows and AM talk radio. You'll find more cultural programming at the lower and upper ends of the dial. National Public Radio (NPR), syndicated through local community radio stations, broadcasts the country's most listened-to public programs as well as opera, classical music, jazz, and often indigenous programming.

In the Southwest, Hopi Radio (KUYI FM at 88.1) and Navajo Radio (660 KTNN AM) broadcast locally in their native languages. Cajun Radio (1470 AM) in Lake Charles, Louisiana belts out zydeco and Cajun music

Public Holidays

Holidays celebrated no matter on what day they fall in the year are:
January 1 New Year's Day
July 4 Independence Day
November 11 Veteran's Day
December 25 Christmas Day
Other holidays are:
Third Monday in January
Martin Luther King Jr Day
Third Monday in February
Presidents' Day
March/April
Good Friday, Easter Monday
Last Monday in May
Memorial Day
First Monday in September
Labor Day
Second Monday in October
Columbus Day
Fourth Thursday in November
Thanksgiving

throughout Cajun Country. You can tune in to Radio Sonora (96.9 FM) to enjoy lively polka-influenced Norteño music as you travel southern Arizona near the US-Mexico border.

A radio show dedicated to Route 66 is broadcast on St Louis station KMOX (1120 AM) every Saturday from 8pm to 1am. Information about local road conditions and attractions can often be tuned in at 95 AM. Truckers with CB equipment talk to each other on dedicated channels, usually Line 19 in most of the country (Line 17 on the West Coast). There is also a truckers' channel among the large lineup on satellite radio SiriusXM Radio, available in many rental cars. SiriusXM carries channels dedicated to just about every kind of music, including oldies' channels keyed to different decades.

Money

American dollars come in bills of $1, $5, $10, $20, $50, and $100, all the same size. The dollar is divided into 100 cents. Coins come in 1 cent (penny), 5 cents (nickel), 10 cents (dime), 25 cents (quarter), 50 cents (half-dollar), and $1 denominations (these last two are uncommon). Credit cards are accepted almost everywhere, although not all cards at all places. Most hotels, restaurants, and shops take the major ones such as American Express, MasterCard, and Visa; Diners Club less commonly. Along with out-of-state or overseas bank cards, they can also be used to withdraw money at ATMs.

Travelers' checks are widely accepted, although you may have to provide proof of identification when cashing them at banks (this is not required at most stores). Travelers' checks in US dollars are much more widely accepted than those in other currencies. The best rates of exchange for them are in banks. Take along your passport.

Tipping

Although rarely obligatory, many service personnel in the US rely on tips for a large part of their income. Going rates are: **waiters and bartenders** 15–20 percent; **taxi drivers** 15 percent; **airport/hotel baggage handlers** around $1 per bag; **chambermaids** $1–2 per day; **doormen** $1 for helping unload a car or other services; more if you have a lot of luggage, and $4-5 if luggage is brought to your room. **Hairdressers, manicurists, and massage therapists** 15 percent.

Opening Hours

Banks 9am–5pm, weekdays. Most close on Saturdays, or are open morning only.
Post Offices 8am–4 or 5.30pm, weekdays, Saturdays, usually mornings only, especially in small towns.
Shops 9am–5pm daily, later in tourist areas; shopping malls typically open 10am–9pm Mon–Sat, noon–5pm Sun.
All-hours services Most cities have 24-hour restaurants, convenience stores, and supermarkets.
Museums Usually open Tue–Sun, closed Mon.

Photography

Even in this era of instant-view digital cameras, film is still widely available throughout the US. Business centers and discount chains often offer rapid development or conversion of digital to paper prints. The US is spectacularly photogenic. Some of the most rewarding photography is of cultural events such as costume parades, Native American dances, and wildlife.

If you plan on photographing in the desert, avoid the flat, washed-out light in the middle of the day and shoot in the early morning or evening instead; cloudy days will offer better contrast than bright sunny days.

Observe appropriate etiquette when photographing Native Americans. Pueblos in New Mexico usually require you to pay a fee to photograph within the pueblos and during dances. Native American people will usually be happy to pose for you for a small fee. Always ask permission and get a photo release, if it's for commercial purposes, before taking a photo of anyone.

Postal Services

Post offices

Even the most remote towns are served by the US Postal Service. Stamps are sold at all post offices, plus at some convenience stores, filling stations, hotels, and transportation terminals, usually from vending machines. Postage rates in 2012 were 45 cents for a first-class domestic stamp up to 1oz (28 grams) with 20 cents for each additional ounce. Postcards are 32 cents each. Postage for overseas letters is $1.05 for 1oz (28 grams); 85 cents to Mexico and Canada. Postage for overseas postcards is currently 98 cents; 79 cents to Mexico and 75 cents to Canada.

Public Toilets

Public toilets are rarely available in the US, unless you are visiting an attraction. Most businesses allow you to use their "bathroom." At special outdoor events, you will often find temporary Port-a-Potties brought in to serve large crowds.

Religious Services

The majority of Americans believe in God and many attend religious or spiritual services regularly in their communities. Roman Catholicism, mainstream Protestantism, and evangelical Christianity are the most visible religious expression across the US, but you'll also find Jewish synagogues (mostly in larger cities and their suburbs), Mormon tabernacles and temples, Quaker meeting houses, Buddhist zendos, pagan Wicca ceremonies, evangelical tent revivals on Native American reservations, and other religious gathering places in the unlikeliest places, even remote national parks.

Visitors are welcome at most church services; however, whites attending Sunday services at black-majority gospel churches in the South should be prepared for a certain amount of suspicion of outsiders.

Smoking

There are no federal bans on smoking, but many states and individual cities and towns in the US now ban smoking in workplaces, on public transportation, in bars, hotels, restaurants, airports, and

in and around public buildings and public parks, so always check before lighting up.

Student Travelers

The **International Student Identity Card** (ISIC) is recognized throughout the world. Major cities across the US, such as New York and Atlanta, accept the card and offer substantial discounts on everything from entertainment and restaurants to lodging and airport parking. The **International Youth Travel Card** (IYTC) offers travelers under 26 low-cost fares on buses, trains, flights, and hotels. Both cards cost $25 a year. The ISIC includes a comprehensive travel insurance policy and ISIConnect, a complete communication tool with both calling card and cellphone options. For more information, tel. 800-223-7986 in the US or log on to www. isic.com.

STA Travel (tel: 800-781-4040; www.statravel.com) also offers students discounts on airfares. Admission charges to attractions across the US are usually a couple of dollars less than full adult price for students, and children under 12 are often admitted free. Check at your destination.

Tax

Most states levy a sales tax. The amount varies from state to state (up to around 8 percent in some) and is invariably excluded from the marked price. You may also have to pay a local sales tax on top of this. When looking at prices, beware of other costs that may or may not be included in the stated price such as taxes on lodgings, restaurant meals, drinks and car rental. These are especially hefty in tourist towns like Miami. If in doubt – ask.

Telephones

In this era of cellphones, you'll find fewer **public telephones** in hotel lobbies, restaurants, drugstores, garages, roadside kiosks, convenience stores, and other locations. The cost of making a local call from a payphone for three minutes is 50–75 cents, and charges for long distance or extra minutes can be astronomical. To make a

long-distance call from a payphone, use either a **pre-paid calling card**, available in airports, post offices, and a few other outlets, or your credit card, which you can use at any phone: dial 800-CALLATT, key in your credit-card number, and wait to be connected. In many areas, local calls have now changed to a 10-digit calling system, using the area code. Watch out for in-room connection charges in the more upmarket hotels; it's cheaper to use the payphone in the lobby. Ditto: wireless and broadband internet connections in your room: many hotel lobbies and "business centers" offer free wireless but charge for it in guest rooms. Inquire ahead of time.

Toll-free calls

When in the US, make use of toll-free (no-charge) numbers. They start with 800, 888, 866, or 877. You need to dial 1 before these numbers.

Cheaper rates

Long-distance rates are cheaper after 5pm on weekdays and throughout weekends. Many wireless plans offer unlimited free cellphone minutes on weekends and between 9pm and 6am.

Useful Numbers

Operator 0 (dial if you are having any problems with a line from any phone) Local: 411 Long-distance: 1+area code+555-1212 Toll-free directory: 800-555-1212

Phone Codes

More than perhaps any other country, the United States has embraced the telephone. But now, with the proliferation of fax lines, modems, and cellphones, the system is seriously overloaded. To cope with these demands, the country has been forced to divide, then sub-divide, its existing telephone area codes, in some cases every six months. Although every effort has been made to keep the telephone prefixes listed here up to date, it's always a good idea to check with the operator if you're in any doubt about a number.

Tour Operators and Travel Agents

The US has a huge variety of travel agents and tour operators to assist with both general and specialty travel packages. Even if you are planning on doing the driving yourself, you may want to hook up with a local tour operator to let someone else show you around for a few days. You can locate a US tour operator by checking listings on the websites of the **US Tour Operator Association** – USTOA (www.ustoa.com) and the **National Tour Association** (www.ntaonline.com) or contacting the Visitor Center at your destination for official listings.

Top tour operators serving all of the US include top-rated **Tauck Tours** (tel: 800-788-7885; www. tauck.com), a family-run company that has been in business since 1924, and **Abercrombie and Kent** (tel: 888-785-5379; www. abercrombiekent.com), both of which specialize in small-group luxury tours. **The Smithsonian Institution** (tel: 855-330-1542; www.smithsonianjourneys.com) offers educational study tours to sites of archeological, historic, and scientific interest in the US, such as the ancient Native American ruins of the Southwest, guided by authorities in the field. National park concessionaires, such as **Fred Harvey** at Grand Canyon National Park, offer bus tours, mule rides, and other guided tours; park staff have listings of individual outfitters. Check individual parks for more information. Gray Line (tel: 303-394-6920; www.grayline.com) runs guided bus tours in most large US cities.

Specialty tour operators offer guided trips tailored to your interests, from tours of ghost towns in Arizona to historic walking tours in cities like Santa Fe, Seattle, and Boston. Outfitters offer guided trips of the outdoors. You can enjoy hunting, fishing, river rafting, horseback riding, and skiing with outdoor outfitters in the Mountain West; rock climbing and bicycle and Jeep touring in the Southwest; wildlife watching in Florida; ballooning and wine tours in California; heritage tours on private ranches, Native American reservations, and archeological sites in the West; tours of Civil War battlefields and communities in the South; and tours aimed at those with special needs, health issues, disabilities, singles, women only, and the gay and lesbian community, among others.

Tourist Information

Check the website www.usa.gov and click on "Visitors to the United States" then "Travel, Study, and Work" for links to government-run tourist offices, including tribal government offices, for all 50 states. **Welcome**

Centers are usually located at the state line. They are staffed by volunteers who can give you maps and general advice on your stay and have restrooms, water, and often hot coffee. Most communities have visitor centers that offer information and trip planning. When visiting national parks, be sure to stop at the Visitor Center first. Rangers there can help you get the most out of your time in the park.

The website **www.usa.gov** displays travel warnings and information on road conditions and highways, gas prices, and public transport, and offers tips on driving. The website www.byways.org has information on America's designated **scenic byways** – a little-known resource of great interest to road trippers meandering America's inspiring Blue Highways.

Route 66
National Historic Route 66 Federation
Tel: 909-336-6131
www.national66.com

State Tourism Offices
Alabama Tourism Department
Tel: 334-242-4169
www.alabama.travel
Arizona Office of Tourism
Tel: 866-275-5816
www.arizonaguide.com
Arkansas Department of Parks and Tourism
Tel: 501-682-7777
www.arkansas.com
California Tourism

Toll free: 877-225-4367
www.visitcalifornia.com
Connecticut Commission on Culture and Tourism
Toll free: 888-288-4748
www.ctvisit.com
Visit Florida
Toll free: 888-735-2872
www.visitflorida.com
Georgia Department of Economic Development
Toll free: 800-847-4842
www.exploregeorgia.org
Idaho Division of Tourism Development
Toll free: 800-VISITID
www.visitidaho.org
Illinois Bureau of Tourism – Chicago Office
Toll free: 800-226-6632
www.enjoyillinois.com
Indiana Office of Tourism Development
Toll free: 800-677-9800
www.in.gov/visitindiana
Louisiana Office of Tourism
Tel: 225-342-8119
www.louisianatravel.com
Maine Office of Tourism
Toll free: 888-624-6345
www.visitmaine.com
Maryland Office of Tourism Development
Toll free: 866-639-3526
www.mdisfun.org
Massachusetts Office of Travel and Tourism
Toll-free: 800-227-MASS
www.massvacation.com
Explore Minnesota Tourism
Toll free: 888-868-7476

Gift shop on Route 66, Seligman, Arizona.

Time Zones

The continental US spans four time zones. These are divided as follows:
Eastern (Greenwich Mean Time minus five hours)
Central (Greenwich Mean Time minus six hours)
Mountain (Greenwich Mean Time minus seven hours)
Pacific (Greenwich Mean Time minus eight hours)

www.exploreminnesota.com
Mississippi: Division of Tourist Development
Toll free: 866-733-6477
www.visitmississippi.org
Travel Montana
Toll free: 800-847-4868
www.visitmt.com
New Hampshire Department of Resources and Economic Development
Tel: 603-271-2665
www.visitnh.gov
New Jersey Division of Tourism and Travel Information
Toll free: 800-VISIT NJ
www.visitnj.org
New Mexico Department of Tourism
Tel: 505-827-7400
www.newmexico.org
New York State Tourist Information
Toll free: 800-225-5697
www.iloveny.com
North Carolina Division of Tourism
Toll free: 800-847-4862
www.visitnc.com
Ohio Division of Travel and Tourism
Toll free: 800-BUCKEYE
www.discoverohio.com
Oklahoma Tourism And Recreation Department
Toll free: 800-652-6552
www.travelok.com
Oregon Tourism Commission
Toll free: 800-547-7842
www.traveloregon.com
Pennsylvania Tourism Office
Toll Free: 800-847-4872
www.visitpa.com
South Carolina Department of Tourism
Toll free: 866-224-9339
www.discoversouthcarolina.com
South Dakota Office of Tourism
Toll free: 800-732-5682
www.travelsd.com
State of Tennessee Department of Tourist Development
Toll free: 800-462-8366
www.tnvacation.com
Texas Tourism
Toll free: 800-8888-TEX
www.traveltex.com

Vermont Department of Tourism and Marketing
Toll free: 800-vermont
www.800-vermont.com
Virginia Tourism Corporation
Toll free: 800-847-4882
www.virginia.org
Washington State Tourism Division
Toll free: 800-544-1800
www.experienceWA.com

Washington, DC: Destination DC
Tel: 202-789-7000
www.washington.org
Wisconsin Department of Tourism
Toll free: 800-432-8747
www.travelwisconsin.com
Wyoming Travel and Tourism
Tel: 302-777-7777
www.wyomingtourism.org

Visas and Entry

Immigration and visitation procedures can change rapidly depending on real and perceived threats to security. Check the relevant websites listed here for up-to-date information.

To enter the United States, foreign visitors need a passport and many also need a visa. You may be asked to provide evidence that you intend to leave the United States after your visit is over (usually in the form of a return or onward ticket).

You may not need a visa if you are a resident of one of 27 countries that participate in the Visa Waiver Program (VWP) and are planning to stay in the US for less than 90 days. You must, however, log onto the Electronic System for Travel Authorization's unmemorably named website, esta.cbp.dhs.gov, at least 48 hours before traveling and provide personal information and travel details; either your application will be accepted (and will be valid for multiple visits over two years) or you will be told to apply for a visa. If you don't have Internet access, you'll need to find someone who does.

Anyone wishing to stay longer than 90 days must apply for a visa in any case. This can be done by mail to the nearest US Embassy or Consulate. Visa extensions can be obtained in the US from the United States Immigration and Naturalization Service offices. Applications can be downloaded at [wwn1]travel.state.gov.

Canadian citizens traveling to the US by air or across the land border

need a passport to enter the country.

The US Department of Homeland Security maintains a website at: dhs.gov/xtrvlsec.

HIV: Travelers who are HIV-positive may not enter the US under the Visa Waiver Program. They must file for a visa. For information, log onto: travel.state.gov.

Immunization Requirements
Log onto travel.state.gov for a complete list of immunization requirements by country.

Weights and Measures

The US operates on the imperial system of weights and measures.

Women Travelers

Driving is a wonderful, generally safe way for a woman to travel across the US. You are unlikely to have any trouble, and, from the safety of your vehicle, you will enjoy an unaccustomed, and possibly addictive, feeling of true adventure and freedom.

Although it's fun to meet new people on the road, if you are a lone female, be a little cautious to avoid unwarranted attention. Be conservative in dress and avoid engaging with anyone partying hard, especially groups of men in bars, where things can rapidly get out of control. Don't go home with strangers or pick up hitchhikers if you're a female traveling alone.

Plan on staying in slightly more expensive motels and public campgrounds, and get in the habit of keeping your car doors locked at all times. Avoid walking around at night in poorly lit areas, whether in the city or the country, and keep to public places. Try to let someone know your planned itinerary.

Daylight Saving Time

This begins each year at 2am on a Sunday in March when clocks are advanced one hour ("spring forward"), and ends on the first Sunday in October ("fall back."). Arizona and Indiana do not observe Daylight Saving Time; however, confusingly for travelers, the huge Navajo reservation, spanning Arizona and New Mexico, does.

FURTHER READING

General

Basin and Range, In Suspect Terrain, Rising from the Plains, Annals of the Former World, and Assembling California by John McPhee. The definitive layman's account of the geology of the U.S, and of the time the author spent with the people who study it.

The Great Deluge: Hurricane Katrina, New Orleans, and the Mississippi Gulf Coast by Douglas Brinkley. Historian Brinkley, a New Orleans resident and survivor of the hurricane, captures the experience and politics of the deadly storm.

Great Plains and On the Rez by Ian Frazier. The first is a thoughtful travelogue by the *New Yorker* writer on his 25,000-mile odyssey through the historic American heartland; the second is an account of life on the modern West's Native American reservations.

This House of Sky: Landscapes of a Western Mind by Ivan Doig. The western novelist's recollection of growing up in the vastness of 1940s and 1950s Montana.

Writing New York and Writing LA, Library of America. Two superb anthologies of fiction and non-fiction reveal the personalities of these huge, complex, and quintessentially American places.

Fiction

The Border Trilogy by Cormac McCarthy. McCarthy captures the feeling of Border Country, *macho* cowboys, and their love of horses.

Brokeback Mountain by Annie Proulx. This poignant short story of enduring love between two cowboys evokes the real American West of the 1960s with its spare prose, haunting characters, and authentic sense of place.

Death Comes to the Archbishop by Willa Cather. Based on the life of Santa Fe's 19th-century Archbishop Lamy who worked to "civilize" the city.

The Friends of Eddie Coyle by George Higgins. Set among Boston's criminal fraternity, this novel is celebrated for its dialogue and authenticity.

The Grapes of Wrath by John Steinbeck. This classic novel follows an Oklahoma family's experiences as migrant field workers in California during the Dust Bowl years of the Great Depression. It still resonates today.

Ernest Hemingway: Many of Hemingway's novels and short stories were written in the 10 years he lived in Key West, but *To Have and Have Not* is the only one set in the town (published in 1937). The Nick Adams Stories brings readers to a different Hemingway haunt, the woods and lakes of northern Michigan, where he spent boyhood summers.

Carl Hiassen: *Miami Herald* journalist Hiassen writes bestselling comic thrillers set in Florida, including *Native Tongue* (1992), which makes fun of theme parks.

Tony Hillerman: The former journalist's novels about Navajo policemen Sgt Joe Leaphorn and detective Jim Chee offer insights into the Navajo people and their vast reservation.

Lake Wobegon Days by Garrison Keillor. Charming stories about daily life in a mythical Minnesota burg based on the popular radio show *Prairie Home Companion*.

Send Us Your Thoughts

We do our best to ensure the information in our books is as accurate and up-to-date as possible. The books are updated on a regular basis using local contacts, but some details are liable to change, and we are grateful for your feedback.

Maybe we recommended a hotel that you liked (or another that you didn't), or you came across a new attraction we missed.

We will acknowledge all contributions, and we'll offer an Insight Guide to the best letters received.

Please write to us at:
Insight Guides
PO Box 7910
London SE1 1WE
Or email us at:
insight@apaguide.co.uk

Lonesome Dove by Larry McMurtry. The classic evocation of life on a Texas cattle drive.

Tales of the City by Armistead Maupin. A series of stories set among San Francisco's gay community.

On the Road

Blue Highways: A Journey into America by William Least Heat Moon. This exploration of life along the blue-lined highways on the map is still essential road-trip reading.

The Lost Continent: Travels in Small Town America by Bill Bryson. Hysterical look at growing up in the Midwest by an expat American living in the UK.

North Country by Howard Frank Mosher. The Vermont author travels the borderland between the US and Canada, chronicling the people and places he encounters.

On the Road by Jack Kerouac. A syncopated-jazz wild ride of a tale capturing the romance of the road and crazy, amped-up lifestyles of 1950s Beat poets.

Roadfood by Jane and Michael Stern. The ultimate guide to authentic American "eats" gives details on hundreds of diners, barbecue joints, ice-cream stands, and other places that stand apart from the chains.

Route 66 Adventure Handbook: Expanded Third Edition by Drew Knowles. An exhaustive tome with lots of personal charm.

Route 66 Magazine quarterly from PO Box 1129, Port Richey FL 34673-1129, tel: 928-853-8148, www.route66magazine.com.

Travels with Charley: In Search of America by John Steinbeck. A classic road-trip book featuring a standard poodle and a vast continent.

Other Insight Guides

Companion titles include Insight Guides to **Arizona and the Grand Canyon, California, Florida**, and **New England**; City Guides to **Boston, Las Vegas, New York City, San Francisco**, and **Seattle**. Durable and practical Insight Fleximaps include **Los Angeles, New York City**, and **Washington, DC**.

CREDITS

Insight Guide Credits

Project Editor
Siân Lezard

Series Manager
Carine Tracanelli

Art Editor
Tom Smyth

Map Production
Original cartography Colourmap
Scanning Ltd and Phoenix
Mapping, updated by
Apa Cartography Department

Production
Tynan Dean, Linton Donaldson and
Rebeka Ellam

Distribution
UK
Dorling Kindersley Ltd
A Penguin Group company
80 Strand, London, WC2R 0RL
customerservice@dk.com

United States
Ingram Publisher Services
1 Ingram Boulevard, PO Box 3006,
La Vergne, TN 37086-1986
customer.service@ingram
publisherservices.com

Australia
Universal Publishers
PO Box 307
St Leonards NSW 1590
sales@universalpublishers.com.au

New Zealand
Brown Knows Publications
11 Artesia Close, Shamrock Park
Auckland, New Zealand 2016
sales@brownknows.co.nz

Worldwide
Apa Publications GmbH & Co.
Verlag KG (Singapore branch)
7030 Ang Mo Kio Avenue 5
08-65 Northstar @ AMK
Singapore 569880
apasin@singnet.com.sg

Printing
CTPS-China

INDEX

Atlantic Route

	New York, NY	Baltimore, MD	Roanoke, VA	Savannah, GA	Orlando, FL	Miami, FL	Key West, FL
New York, NY		202	543	811	1170	1597	1761
Baltimore, MD			341	609	968	1395	1559
Roanoke, VA				268	627	1054	1218
Savannah, GA					359	786	960
Orlando, FL						427	591
Miami, FL							164
Key West, FL							

Northern Route

	Boston, MA	Buffalo, NY	Chicago, IL	Pierre, SD	Cody, WY	Seattle, WA	Cape Flattery, WA
Boston, MA		872	1419	2309	2891	3961	4095
Buffalo, NY			547	1437	2019	3089	3223
Chicago, IL				890	1472	2542	2676
Pierre, SD					582	1652	1786
Cody, WY						1070	1204
Seattle, WA							134
Cape Flattery, WA							

Central Route

	Washington, DC	Memphis, TN	Joplin, MO	Amarillo, TX	Gallup, NM	Flagstaff, AZ	Los Angeles, CA
Washington, DC		940	1371	1850	2270	2452	2922
Memphis, TN			431	910	1330	1512	1982
Joplin, MO				479	899	1081	1551
Amarillo, TX					420	602	1072
Gallup, NM						182	652
Flagstaff, AZ							470
Los Angeles, CA							

Southern Route

	Atlanta, GA	New Orleans, LA	Houston, TX	San Antonio, TX	Lordsburg, NM	Phoenix, AZ	San Diego, CA
Atlanta, GA		473	825	1070	1989	2213	2572
New Orleans, LA			352	597	1516	1740	2099
Houston, TX				245	1164	1388	1747
San Antonio, TX					919	1143	1502
Lordsburg, NM						224	583
Phoenix, AZ							359
San Diego, CA							

Pacific Route

	San Diego, CA	Los Angeles, CA	San Francisco, CA	Eureka, CA	Crescent, OR	Newport, OR	Seattle, WA
San Diego, CA		124	504	785	867	1108	1399
Los Angeles, CA	124		380	661	743	984	1275
San Francisco, CA	504	380		281	363	604	895
Eureka, CA	785	661	281		82	323	614
Crescent, OR	867	743	363	82		241	532
Newport, OR	1108	984	604	323	241		291
Seattle, WA	1399	1275	895	614	532	291	

Atlantic Route
New York (NY) - Key West (FL)

Northern Route
Boston (MA) - Cape Flattery (WA)

Central Route
Washington, DC - Los Angeles (CA)

Southern Route
Atlanta (GA) - San Diego (CA)

Pacific Route
San Diego (CA) - Seattle (WA)

All distances shown are in miles.

Interstate Route Marker

Even numbers indicate east-west routes: odd show north-south routes.

US Highway Marker

Four-way Stop Sign

Traffic from all four directions must stop. The first vehicle to reach the intersection should move first.

Yield Ahead

Reduce speed and allow vehicles crossing your path right-of-way.

One-w
trave

Traffic Merges (from right)

Traffic flows merge from indicated direction.

2-Way Traffic

Traffic flows in both directions.

Traffic Lane Joins

Traffic enters carriageway with new lane.

Yield Ahead

A yield sign is ahead.

Divi

Divid
to adj

Dead End

Not a through road, no access to other streets.

Crossing Traffic

Highway is crossed by road. Look to left and right for cars.

Stop sign ahead

Stop sign ahead, prepare to stop.

Slippery Surface

Road surface is slippery when wet. First half-hour of rain is most hazardous.

Be pr
cros

Construction Ahead

Distance given until construction begins. Watch for further signs.

Railroad Crossing Ahead

Slow and prepare to stop at crossing ahead.

Left Turn

All traffic must turn left.

Keep Right

Traffic is required to keep to the right of medians or obstructions.

R

Re

The la
certain p
Requi
usual

One Way

One-way traffic in direction of arrow.

School Zone

Follow speed limit displayed when lights above sign flash.

Camping

Direction to camping site.

School

Children crossing road.

Rest Area

Roadside park and rest area.

Lane Control

Travel in lane.

Hospital

Watch for pedestrians and emergency vehicles.

Lane Control

Clear the lane. If flashing, left turn is permitted.

Lane Contro

Don't use lane, t
approaching